T0240599

Lecture Notes in Computer Science 14573

Founding Editors

Gerhard Goos, Germany
Juris Hartmanis, USA

Editorial Board Members

Elisa Bertino, USA
Wen Gao, China

Bernhard Steffen ⓘ, Germany
Moti Yung ⓘ, USA

Advanced Research in Computing and Software Science
Subline of Lecture Notes in Computer Science

Subline Series Editors

Giorgio Ausiello, *University of Rome 'La Sapienza', Italy*
Vladimiro Sassone, *University of Southampton, UK*

Subline Advisory Board

Susanne Albers, *TU Munich, Germany*
Benjamin C. Pierce, *University of Pennsylvania, USA*
Bernhard Steffen ⓘ, *University of Dortmund, Germany*
Deng Xiaotie, *Peking University, Beijing, China*
Jeannette M. Wing, *Microsoft Research, Redmond, WA, USA*

Lecture Notes in Computer Science　14573

More information about this series at https://link.springer.com/bookseries/558

Dirk Beyer · Ana Cavalcanti
Editors

Fundamental Approaches to Software Engineering

27th International Conference, FASE 2024
Held as Part of the European Joint Conferences
on Theory and Practice of Software, ETAPS 2024
Luxembourg City, Luxembourg, April 6–11, 2024
Proceedings

 Springer

Editors
Dirk Beyer
LMU Munich
Munich, Germany

Ana Cavalcanti
University of York
York, UK

ISSN 0302-9743   ISSN 1611-3349 (electronic)
Lecture Notes in Computer Science
ISBN 978-3-031-57258-6   ISBN 978-3-031-57259-3 (eBook)
https://doi.org/10.1007/978-3-031-57259-3

This Springer imprint is published by the registered company Springer Nature Switzerland AG
The registered company address is: Gewerbestrasse 11, 6330 Cham, Switzerland

Paper in this product is recyclable.

ETAPS Foreword

Welcome to the 27th ETAPS! ETAPS 2024 took place in Luxembourg City, the beautiful capital of Luxembourg.

ETAPS 2024 is the 27th instance of the European Joint Conferences on Theory and Practice of Software. ETAPS is an annual federated conference established in 1998, and consists of four conferences: ESOP, FASE, FoSSaCS, and TACAS. Each conference has its own Program Committee (PC) and its own Steering Committee (SC). The conferences cover various aspects of software systems, ranging from theoretical computer science to foundations of programming languages, analysis tools, and formal approaches to software engineering. Organising these conferences in a coherent, highly synchronized conference programme enables researchers to participate in an exciting event, having the possibility to meet many colleagues working in different directions in the field, and to easily attend talks of different conferences. On the weekend before the main conference, numerous satellite workshops took place that attracted many researchers from all over the globe.

ETAPS 2024 received 352 submissions in total, 117 of which were accepted, yielding an overall acceptance rate of 33%. I thank all the authors for their interest in ETAPS, all the reviewers for their reviewing efforts, the PC members for their contributions, and in particular the PC (co-)chairs for their hard work in running this entire intensive process. Last but not least, my congratulations to all authors of the accepted papers!

ETAPS 2024 featured the unifying invited speakers Sandrine Blazy (University of Rennes, France) and Lars Birkedal (Aarhus University, Denmark), and the invited speakers Ruzica Piskac (Yale University, USA) for TACAS and Jérôme Leroux (Laboratoire Bordelais de Recherche en Informatique, France) for FoSSaCS. Invited tutorials were provided by Tamar Sharon (Radboud University, the Netherlands) on computer ethics and David Monniaux (Verimag, France) on abstract interpretation.

As part of the programme we had the first ETAPS industry day. The goal of this day was to bring industrial practitioners into the heart of the research community and to catalyze the interaction between industry and academia. The day was organized by Nikolai Kosmatov (Thales Research and Technology, France) and Andrzej Wąsowski (IT University of Copenhagen, Denmark).

ETAPS 2024 was organized by the SnT - Interdisciplinary Centre for Security, Reliability and Trust, University of Luxembourg. The University of Luxembourg was founded in 2003. The university is one of the best and most international young universities with 6,000 students from 130 countries and 1,500 academics from all over the globe. The local organisation team consisted of Peter Y.A. Ryan (general chair), Peter B. Roenne (organisation chair), Maxime Cordy and Renzo Gaston Degiovanni (workshop chairs), Magali Martin and Isana Nascimento (event manager), Marjan Skrobot (publicity chair), and Afonso Arriaga (local proceedings chair). This team also organised the online edition of ETAPS 2021, and now we are happy that they agreed to also organise a physical edition of ETAPS.

ETAPS 2024 is further supported by the following associations and societies: ETAPS e.V., EATCS (European Association for Theoretical Computer Science), EAPLS (European Association for Programming Languages and Systems), and EASST (European Association of Software Science and Technology).

The ETAPS Steering Committee consists of an Executive Board, and representatives of the individual ETAPS conferences, as well as representatives of EATCS, EAPLS, and EASST. The Executive Board consists of Marieke Huisman (Twente, chair), Andrzej Wąsowski (Copenhagen), Thomas Noll (Aachen), Jan Kofroň (Prague), Barbara König (Duisburg), Arnd Hartmanns (Twente), Caterina Urban (Inria), Jan Křetínský (Munich), Elizabeth Polgreen (Edinburgh), and Lenore Zuck (Chicago).

Other members of the steering committee are: Maurice ter Beek (Pisa), Dirk Beyer (Munich), Artur Boronat (Leicester), Luís Caires (Lisboa), Ana Cavalcanti (York), Ferruccio Damiani (Torino), Bernd Finkbeiner (Saarland), Gordon Fraser (Passau), Arie Gurfinkel (Waterloo), Reiner Hähnle (Darmstadt), Reiko Heckel (Leicester), Marijn Heule (Pittsburgh), Joost-Pieter Katoen (Aachen and Twente), Delia Kesner (Paris), Naoki Kobayashi (Tokyo), Fabrice Kordon (Paris), Laura Kovács (Vienna), Mark Lawford (Hamilton), Tiziana Margaria (Limerick), Claudio Menghi (Hamilton and Bergamo), Andrzej Murawski (Oxford), Laure Petrucci (Paris), Peter Y.A. Ryan (Luxembourg), Don Sannella (Edinburgh), Viktor Vafeiadis (Kaiserslautern), Stephanie Weirich (Pennsylvania), Anton Wijs (Eindhoven), and James Worrell (Oxford).

I would like to take this opportunity to thank all authors, keynote speakers, attendees, organizers of the satellite workshops, and Springer Nature for their support. ETAPS 2024 was also generously supported by a RESCOM grant from the Luxembourg National Research Foundation (project 18015543). I hope you all enjoyed ETAPS 2024.

Finally, a big thanks to both Peters, Magali and Isana and their local organization team for all their enormous efforts to make ETAPS a fantastic event.

April 2024

Marieke Huisman
ETAPS SC Chair
ETAPS e.V. President

Preface

FASE 2024 is the 27th edition of the International Conference on Fundamental Approaches to Software Engineering conference series. It is a forum for researchers, developers, and users interested in the broad field of software engineering. The topics of interest include requirements, design, architecture, modeling, applications of AI to software engineering and software engineering for AI-based systems, quality, model-driven engineering, processes, and software evolution. FASE 2024 was part of the 27th federation of European Joint Conferences on Theory and Practice of Software (ETAPS 2024), held on April 6–11 in Luxembourg.

There were four submission categories for FASE:

1. *Research papers* clearly identify and justify a principled advance to the fundamentals of software engineering.
2. *Empirical-evaluation papers* evaluate existing software challenges or critically validate current proposed solutions with scientific means, that is, by empirical studies, controlled experiments, rigorous case studies, and simulations.
3. *New Ideas and Emerging Results (NIER) papers* seek to disrupt the status quo with forward-looking, thought-provoking, innovative research on the foundations of software engineering, as well as lessons learned from the past.
4. *Tool demonstration papers* present a new tool, a new tool component, or novel extensions to an existing tool.

This year, 41 papers were submitted to FASE in categories 1–4, consisting of 29 research papers, 2 empirical-evaluation papers, 8 NIER papers, and 2 tool-demonstration papers. Each paper was reviewed by three program-committee members, who could make use of subreviewers. It was possible to submit an artifact for evaluation alongside a paper, if made long-term available and declared in the Data-Availability Statement. The program committee extensively discussed the papers and ultimately decided to accept 14 papers included here. This is an acceptance rate of 34%.

Artifacts comprise tools, models, proofs, or other data for validating the results of a paper. The artifact-evaluation committee (AEC) reviewed the artifacts based on their documentation, ease of use, and, most importantly, whether the results presented in the corresponding paper could be accurately reproduced.

In an endeavor to unify artifact evaluation (AE) processes across ETAPS conferences, the FASE 2024 AEC joined forces with the ESOP and FoSSaCS AECs. Across all three conferences, AEC members were recruited by direct nominations from PC members or the AEC chairs.

The joint call for artifacts imposed few requirements on the artifact packaging; in particular, there was no predefined environment in which submitted artifacts were supposed to be executable. Instead, author-defined container and VM submissions were strongly encouraged and this advice was followed by most authors. We also chose to adopt a documentation standard. This greatly facilitated artifact reviews, and we believe that it will equally facilitate future use of the artifacts.

AEC members from all three committees bid to review artifacts submitted by all the conferences. This gave the AEC flexibility to accommodate varying submission numbers or topic of artifacts from the conferences. The evaluation was conducted in three phases, an initial "kick-the-tires" phase and author response, a main review phase, and a discussion phase. FASE 2024 received 6 artifact submissions. All of them met the requirements for the "Artifacts Available" badge. In addition, 4 submissions were awarded the "Artifacts Evaluated – Functional" badge and 2 submissions the "Artifacts Evaluated – Reusable" badge.

FASE 2024 hosted the ETAPS unifying keynote by Sandrine Blazy from the University of Rennes, France. These proceedings contain the invited paper supporting the keynote. In *From Mechanized Semantics to Verified Compilation: The Clight Semantics of CompCert*, Blazy reports on the use of operational semantics in the very successful CompCert project based on the Coq theorem prover.

FASE 2024 also hosted Test-Comp 2024, the 6th International Competition on Software Testing. This event evaluated 20 software systems for automatic test-case generation for C programs. From the 14 actively participating teams, the jury selected 5 short papers that describe their test systems. These papers are also published in these proceedings. They were reviewed by a separate program committee (jury). Each of the Test-Comp papers was assessed by at least four jury members. Two sessions in the FASE program were reserved for the presentation of the results: (1) a presentation session with a report by the competition chair and summaries by the developer teams, and (2) an open community meeting.

Finally, we would like to thank all the people who helped to make FASE 2024 successful. First, we thank the authors for submitting their papers. The PC members and additional reviewers did a great job: they contributed informed and detailed reports and engaged in the PC discussions. We thank Jan Kofron and Sebastian Junges for their support in our use of HotCRP for artifact evaluation. We thank Reiner Hähnle, chair of the FASE steering committee, and Marieke Huisman, chair of the ETAPS steering committee, for their valuable advice. Lastly, we would like to thank the overall organization team of ETAPS 2024.

February 2024

Dirk Beyer
PC Chair, Competition Chair

Ana Cavalcanti
PC Chair

Stefan Winter
AEC Chair

Organization

Program Committee

Dirk Beyer (Chair)	LMU Munich, Germany
Ana Cavalcanti (Chair)	University of York, UK
Erika Abraham	RWTH Aachen, Germany
Maurice ter Beek	Italian National Research Council, Italy
Ipek Caliskanelli	RACE/UKAE, UK
Lucas Cordeiro	University of Manchester, UK
Priyanka Darke	Tata Consulting, India
Bernd Fischer	Stellenbosch University, South Africa
Stijn de Gouw	Open Universiteit, Netherlands
Reiner Haehnle	TU Darmstadt, Germany
Einar Broch Johnsen	University of Oslo, Norway
Leen Lambers	BTU Cottbus-Senftenberg, Germany
Thierry Lecomte	CLEARSY, France
Mercedes G. Merayo	Universidad Complutense de Madrid, Spain
Marjan Mernik	University of Maribor, Slovenia
Vince Molnár	Budapest TU, Hungary
Jose Nuno Oliveira	University of Minho, Portugal
Patrizio Pelliccione	Gran Sasso Science Institute, Sweden
Luigia Petre	Åbo Akademi University, Finland
Matteo Rossi	University of Milan, Italy
Augusto Sampaio	Universidade Federal de Pernambuco, Brazil
Marielle Stoelinga	University of Twente, Netherlands
Jun Sun	Singapore Management University, Singapore
Sebastian Uchitel	University of Buenos Aires, Argentina
Daniel Varro	McGill University, Canada
Vesal Vojdani	University of Tartu, Estonia
Andrzej Wasowski	IT University Copenhagen, Denmark
Manuel Wimmer	University of Linz, Austria
Naijun Zhan	Chinese Academy of Sciences, China

ESOP/FASE/FoSSaCS Joint Artifact Evaluation Committee

AEC Co-chairs

Tobias Kappé	Open Universiteit and ILLC, University of Amsterdam, The Netherlands
Ryosuke Sato	University of Tokyo, Japan
Stefan Winter	LMU Munich, Germany

AEC Members

Arwa Hameed Alsubhi	University of Glasgow, UK
Levente Bajczi	Budapest University of Technology and Economics, Hungary
James Baxter	University of York, UK
Matthew Alan Le Brun	University of Glasgow, UK
Laura Bussi	University of Pisa, Italy
Gustavo Carvalho	Universidade Federal de Pernambuco, Brazil
Chanhee Cho	Carnegie Mellon University, USA
Ryan Doenges	Northeastern University, USA
Zainab Fatmi	University of Oxford, UK
Luke Geeson	University College London, UK
Hans-Dieter Hiep	Leiden University, Belgium
Philipp Joram	Tallinn University of Technology, Estonia
Ulf Kargén	Linköping University, Sweden
Hiroyuki Katsura	University of Tokyo, Japan
Calvin Santiago Lee	Reykjavík University, Iceland
Livia Lestingi	Politecnico di Milano, Italy
Nuno Macedo	University of Porto and INESC TEC, Portugal
Kristóf Marussy	Budapest University of Technology and Economics, Hungary
Ivan Nikitin	University of Glasgow, UK
Hugo Pacheco	University of Porto, Portugal
Lucas Sakizloglou	Brandenburgische Technische Universität Cottbus-Senftenberg, Germany
Michael Schröder	TU Wien, Austria
Michael Schwarz	TU Munich, Germany
Wenjia Ye	University of Hong Kong, China

Test-Comp 2024 Program Committee and Jury

Dirk Beyer (Chair)	LMU Munich, Germany
Sumesh Divakaran	College of Engineering Trivandrum, India
Marie-Christine Jakobs	LMU Munich, Germany
Zhenbang Chen	National University of Defense Technology, China
Marek Trtík	Masaryk University, Brno, Czechia
Mohannad Aldughaim	University of Manchester, UK/King Saud University, Saudi Arabia
Kaled Alshmrany	University of Manchester, UK/Institute of Public Administration, Saudi Arabia
Yurii Kostyukov	RnD Toolchain Labs, Huawei, China
Léo Andrès	OCamlPro/LMF, France
Thomas Lemberger	LMU Munich, Germany
Adam Štafa	Masaryk University, Brno, Czechia
Martin Jonáš	Masaryk University, Brno, Czechia

Matthias Kettl   LMU Munich, Germany
Joxan Jaffar   National University of Singapore, Singapore
Max Barth   LMU Munich, Germany

FASE 2024 Steering Committee

Reiner Hähnle (Chair)   TU Darmstadt, Germany
Dirk Beyer   Ludwig-Maximilians-Universität München, Germany
Ana Cavalcanti   University of York, UK
Reiko Heckel   University of Leicester, UK
Marie-Christine Jakobs   Ludwig-Maximilians-Universität München, Germany
Einar Broch Johnsen   University of Oslo, Norway
Leen Lambers   BTU Cottbus-Senftenberg, Germany
Tiziana Margaria   University of Limerick, Ireland
Mariëlle Stoelinga   University of Twente, The Netherlands
Gabriele Taentzer   Philipps-Universität Marburg, Germany
Sebastian Uchitel   Universidad de Buenos Aires, Argentina/Imperial
                           College London, UK
Andrzej Wąsowski   IT University of Copenhagen, Denmark
Heike Wehrheim   University of Oldenburg, Germany
Manuel Wimmer   Johannes Kepler University Linz, Austria

Additional Reviewers

Supriya Agrawal   Violet Ka I Pun
Jie An   Eduard Kamburjan
Pedro Antonino   Kristóf Marussy
Aren Babikian   Milán Mondok
Carlos Baquero   Simon Nagy
Davide Basile   Michel Reniers
Richard Bubel   Arend Rensink
Yan Cai   Maya R. Ayu Setyautami
Michele Chiari   Marco Scaletta
Bharti Chimdyalwar   Jorge Sousa Pinto
Frank de Boer   Martin Steffen
Pieter-Tjerk de Boer   R. Venkatesh
Daniel Drodt   Adele Veschetti
João Faria   Erik Voogd
Luca Favalli   Shuling Wang
Máté Földiák   Bohua Zhan
Hans-Dieter Hiep   Bertalan Zoltán Péter
Karoliine Holter

Contents

From Mechanized Semantics to Verified Compilation: the Clight Semantics of CompCert

Sandrine Blazy$^{(\boxtimes)}$ (ID)

Inria, Univ Rennes, CNRS, IRISA, Rennes, France
`sandrine.blazy@irisa.fr`

Abstract. CompCert is a formally verified compiler for C that is specified, programmed and proved correct with the Coq proof assistant. CompCert was used in industry to compile critical embedded software. Its correctness proof states that the compiler does not introduce bugs. This semantic preservation property involves the formal semantics of the source and target languages of the compiler.

Reasoning on C semantics to prove compiler correctness is challenging, as C is a real language that was not designed with semantics in mind. This paper presents the operational style that was designed for the C semantics of CompCert in order to facilitate the mechanized reasoning on terminating and diverging programs, and details the semantics of the Clight source language of CompCert.

Keywords: operational semantics of programming languages · verified compilation · machine-checked proofs

1 Introduction

Deductive verification provides very strong mathematical guarantees that a piece of software is correct with respect to its specification, written in a logical language to avoid ambiguities. A proof is conducted to provide these guarantees. The outcome of deductive verification is a verified software, consisting of an implementation and a proof that can be replayed or given to a certification authority for scrutiny. This proof requires reasoning on properties related to the involved programming language; they become mathematically precise as soon as this language has formal semantics. Defining and reasoning on realistic languages requires mechanized semantics and machine-checked proofs, ensuring that the proof is complete and that no semantic rule has been forgotten.

There are mainly two families of deductive proof tools (also known as program provers), each with its pros and cons: automatic tools (such as Dafny [22], F* [30] or Why3 [15]) where formulas (expressing pre- and post-conditions and invariants) are discharged to logic solvers, and interactive proof assistants (*e.g.*, Coq [17], Isabelle [2] or Agda [1]) where the user decides how to reason and conducts the proof interactively with the tool, that automates part of the reasoning, ensures that the proof is complete and follows the laws of mathematical logic. Automatic program provers are easier to use when the discharged formulas are proved without requiring extra work (namely adding assertions to help the logic solvers).

D. Beyer and A. Cavalcanti (Eds.): FASE 2024, LNCS 14573, pp. 1–21, 2024.
https://doi.org/10.1007/978-3-031-57259-3_1

However, when program provers fail to prove some formulas, interactive proof assistants are better adapted to conduct more advanced proofs. A prototypical example is a proof requiring reasoning on a data structure that is not used by the software under scrutiny, but only defined for the sole purpose of the proof (see for instance the proof of correctness of the famous majority algorithm [12]).

One of the first programs whose proof was mechanized in LCF is a rudimentary compiler for arithmetic expressions [31]. In 1972, when this paper was published, a compiler was a representative example of a particularly complex program. The specification of a compiler is rather simple: the generated code must behave as prescribed by the semantics of the source program. This correctness property is a semantic preservation property from the source language to the target language of the compiler. It becomes mathematically precise as soon as these languages are defined by formal semantics.

Nowadays, the compiler remains a particularly complex piece of software (due to the numerous optimizations it performs to generate efficient code). Moreover, it is the mandatory point of passage in the software production chain. Verifying the compiler provides a means of ensuring that no errors are introduced during compilation, and of preserving at target level the guarantees obtained at source level. The idea of having a single theorem demonstrated once and for all, along with a readable proof, was already present in 1972, but it took several decades for verified compilation to develop and scale up.

CompCert is the first optimizing compiler for the C language targeting different assembly languages and used in safety-critical industries (to compile mission-critical embedded software used in avionics and nuclear power), with a mechanized proof of correctness [23, 27, 19]. In industry, the interest for CompCert arose from a need to improve the performances of the generated code, while guaranteeing the traceability requirements required by the certification authorities in force in these critical fields, which CompCert has indeed provided.

Developing a verified compiler requires both programming the compiler using the programming language of the proof assistant (so that it runs efficiently on real programs), and defining a semantic model and abstractions to reason about, in order to conduct the correctness proof. Mechanized reasoning on C-like languages is tricky; it requires a semantic style that is adapted to inductive reasoning and some associated reasoning principles. In CompCert, the chosen proof technique is the use of simulation diagrams between program executions, which required to define a new semantic model that is detailed in this paper. The semantic model and proof technique scale to realistic languages like C. They are general enough to be applied to all the intermediate languages of the compiler. The proof technique was extended and successfully reused in order to ensure other properties than CompCert correctness [5–7].

This paper is about mechanized operational semantics for compiler verification and their application to the CompCert compiler, with a focus on the Clight semantics, that significantly evolved since its first published version [9]. The Clight language is the preferred language to get guarantees from C programs and then compile them with CompCert (*e.g.*, [18, 13, 11, 8, 21, 16, 33]).

This paper aims at providing the prerequisites needed to design new program transformations or analyses operating over Clight.

All results presented in this paper have been mechanically verified using the Coq proof assistant [25, 32, 3]. This paper is organized as follows. First, Section 2 recalls the early days of compiler verification. Then, Section 3 introduces a small-step semantics for terminating programs written using a toy imperative language, together with the associated proof technique based on simulation diagrams. Section 4 extends this language and its semantics to observe diverging program executions; it defines an alternate semantics that facilitates the mechanized proofs. Section 5 defines the semantics of Clight. Related work is discussed in Section 6, followed by conclusions.

Notations. For functions returning "option" types, $\lfloor x \rfloor$ (read: "some x") corresponds to success with return value x, and ϵ (read: "none") corresponds to failure. In grammars and rules, a^* denotes 0, 1 or several occurrences of syntactic category a, and $a^?$ denotes an optional occurrence of syntactic category a. ϵ denotes the empty list, $[x]$ denotes a list made of a single element x and $h :: t$ denotes the list with head h and tail t. The list $l + + l'$ denotes the concatenation of two lists l and l'. Given a binary relation R, R^* denotes its reflexive transitive closure and R^+ its transitive closure.

2 Historical Example: a First Verified Compiler

The idea of verifying a compiler and stating a theorem for compiler correctness dates back to 1967 [29]. The proof of this theorem was mechanized in 1972 using LCF [31]. This compiler translates in a single pass any simple arithmetic expression a to a code p, namely a list of instructions of a simple stack machine (see Fig. 1); this is the familiar translation to reverse Polish notation used by old HP pocket calculators.

For instance, the expression 1+2 is compiled to the code iconst 1 :: iconst 2 :: iplus :: ϵ. The stack contains numbers and the machine instructions pop their arguments off the stack and push their results back. This machine is close to a subset of the Java virtual machine. The machine code for an expression a executes in sequence, and deposits the value of a at the top of the stack π. An instruction either pushes an integer, or pushes the current value of a variable, or pops two integers then pushes their sum.

The source and target languages are defined in Fig. 1 by their semantics. In [29], these are functions interpreting expressions or instructions. In this paper, we rather use inference rules to abstract away the definitions of all our semantics. The semantic judgments for evaluating expression a and executing code p are respectively $\sigma \vdash a \Rightarrow v$ and $\sigma, \pi \vdash p \to \pi'$, where a semantic element, the store σ is injected to assign integer values to variables, and the evaluation stack π contains temporary integer values.

The correctness theorem of the compiler is Theorem 2: it states that for any expression a, its value v computed by the semantics of the source language

Arithmetic expressions:

$$a ::= x \mid c \mid a + a \quad \text{source language (variable, integer constant, addition)}$$

CONSTANT

$$\sigma \vdash c \Rightarrow c$$

VARIABLE

$$\sigma \vdash x \Rightarrow \sigma(x)$$

ADDITION

$$\frac{\sigma \vdash a_1 \Rightarrow v_1 \quad \sigma \vdash a_2 \Rightarrow v_2}{\sigma \vdash a_1 + a_2 \Rightarrow v_1 + v_2}$$

VM instructions:

$$i ::= \mathsf{ivar}\, x \mid \mathsf{iconst}\, c \mid \mathsf{iplus} \quad \text{target language}$$

EMPTY STACK

$$\sigma, \epsilon \vdash c \to c$$

CONSTANT

$$\frac{\sigma, c :: \pi \vdash \mathsf{p} \to \pi'}{\sigma, \pi \vdash \mathsf{iconst}\, c :: \mathsf{p} \to \pi'}$$

VARIABLE

$$\frac{\sigma, \sigma(x) :: \pi \vdash \mathsf{p} \to \pi'}{\sigma, \pi \vdash \mathsf{ivar}\, x :: \mathsf{p} \to \pi'}$$

ADDITION

$$\frac{\sigma, (m + n) :: \pi \vdash \mathsf{p} \to \pi'}{\sigma, n :: m :: \pi \vdash \mathsf{iplus} :: \mathsf{p} \to \pi'}$$

OTHER

$$\frac{\sigma, \pi \vdash \mathsf{p} \to \pi'}{\sigma, \pi \vdash i :: \mathsf{p} \to \pi'}$$

Translation from arithmetic expressions to machine code (compile function):

$$x \mapsto \mathsf{ivar}\, x \qquad c \mapsto \mathsf{iconst}\, c \qquad \frac{a_1 \mapsto i_1 \quad a_2 \mapsto i_2}{a_1 + a_2 \mapsto i_1 + + i_2 + + [\mathsf{iplus}]}$$

Theorem 1 (first correctness). $\forall a\, \sigma\, \pi, \sigma \vdash a \Rightarrow v \;\to\; \sigma, \pi \vdash \mathsf{compile}(a) \to v :: \pi$

Proof. By induction on the structure of arithmetic expressions.

Theorem 2 (compiler correct). $\forall a\, \sigma, \sigma \vdash a \Rightarrow v \;\to\; \sigma, \epsilon \vdash \mathsf{compile}(a) \to [v]$

Proof. By theorem 1.

Fig. 1: Historical example: a first verified compiler.

is exactly the value returned by executing the compiled code compile(a). This theorem is proved only once, for any expression given as input to the compiler. The verification of this tiny compiler is now taught as an exercise in masters courses (*e.g.*, [25, 32]). It is an illustrative example of the need to generalize a theorem, so that it can be proved by induction (here on expressions). This explains why Theorem 1 is proved by induction on expressions and used to prove Theorem 2, the main theorem for compiler correctness.

3   A First Semantics for a Toy Imperative Language

The previous section defines a big-step semantics for a rudimentary language for arithmetic expressions. In this section, we first extend this language (into a toy imperative language called IMP), and then introduce simulation diagrams, a convenient proof technique for reasoning on IMP programs.

Boolean expressions:

$$b ::= true \mid false \mid a = a \mid a \leq a \mid \sim b \mid b \wedge b \quad \text{source language}$$

IMP commands:

$$c ::= \text{skip} \mid x := a \mid c; c \qquad\qquad \text{skip, assignment, sequence}$$
$$\mid \text{if}\,(b)\,c\,\text{else}\,c \mid \text{while}\,(b)\,c \qquad \text{conditional, while loop}$$

EQUALITY TEST
$$\frac{\sigma \vdash a_1 \Rightarrow v_1 \quad \sigma \vdash a_2 \Rightarrow v_2}{\sigma \vdash a_1 + a_2 \Rightarrow v_1 + v_2}$$

NEGATION
$$\frac{\sigma \vdash b \Rightarrow v}{\sigma \vdash\, \sim b \Rightarrow\, \sim v}$$

AND
$$\frac{\sigma \vdash b_1 \Rightarrow v_1 \quad \sigma \vdash b_2 \Rightarrow v_2}{\sigma \vdash b_1 + b_2 \Rightarrow v_1 + v_2}$$

ASSIGN
$$\frac{\sigma \vdash a \Rightarrow v}{(x := a, \sigma) \rightarrow (\text{skip}, \sigma[x \rightarrow v])}$$

IF TRUE
$$\frac{\sigma \vdash b \Rightarrow true}{(\text{if}\,(b)\,c_1\,\text{else}\,c_2, \sigma) \rightarrow (c_1, \sigma)}$$

IF FALSE
$$\frac{\sigma \vdash b \Rightarrow false}{(\text{if}\,(b)\,c_1\,\text{else}\,c_2, \sigma) \rightarrow (c_2, \sigma)}$$

SEQUENCE DONE
$$(\text{skip}; c, \sigma) \rightarrow (c, \sigma)$$

SEQUENCE
$$\frac{(c_1, \sigma_1) \rightarrow (c_2, \sigma_2)}{(c_1; c, \sigma_1) \rightarrow (c_2; c, \sigma_2)}$$

WHILE DONE
$$\frac{\sigma \vdash b \Rightarrow false}{(\text{while}\,(b)\,c, \sigma) \rightarrow (\text{skip}, \sigma)}$$

WHILE LOOP
$$\frac{\sigma \vdash b \Rightarrow true}{(\text{while}\,(b)\,c, \sigma) \rightarrow (c; (\text{while}\,(b)\,c), \sigma)}$$

Fig. 2: IMP operational semantics: big-step semantics for expressions, and small-step semantics for commands.

3.1 Small-step Semantics

IMP is made of arithmetic expressions (reused from Section 2), boolean expressions and commands (skip, assignment, sequence, conditional and loop). Boolean expressions are used in conditionals and loops. IMP is defined in Fig. 2, where the semantics of arithmetic expressions defined in Fig. 1 is reused.

Semantics observe the possible behaviors of programs and are defined using an operational style, that is the preferred style for machine-checked reasoning about semantics. Operational semantics consist of big-step semantics and small-step semantics, and both styles are equivalent. Moreover, proving this equivalence is a valuable way of getting confidence in the semantics and supporting both styles may be interesting, as it offers the possibility of choosing the most appropriate one for different needs.

Choosing a style may be a matter of taste. However, big-step semantics are not adapted to define in a natural way some semantic features such as unstructured control, diverging and concurrent executions, whereas small-step semantics are more suitable. Because of while loops (*e.g.*, while $(true)$ skip), the execution of IMP programs may diverge, contrary to the evaluation of IMP expressions.

So, we rather choose small-step semantics to define IMP commands, and big-step semantics to define IMP expressions.

The small-step semantics is a reduction semantics between semantic states. A semantic state is a pair (c, σ) made of a command and a store. The semantics takes the form of a relation $(c, \sigma) \rightarrow (c', \sigma')$, where a command c is reduced into a command c' in an execution step. The c' command represents all the remaining steps and σ' is the store resulting from this computation step. The execution of a sequence of commands $c_1; c_2$ first iterates the reduction of c_1 until the final reduction to skip. Then, c_2 is reduced. The execution of a while loop unfolds the loop when its body is executed at least once. So, this rule generates a sequence of commands that will be further reduced.

The evaluation of expressions always terminates and the big-step semantics of expressions observe these terminating behaviors. Contrary to big-step semantics, small-step semantics observe in a similar and convenient way terminating executions of commands together with diverging executions. The reflexive transitive closure $\rightarrow^*$ of this step relation is used to chain the finite transition sequences. In a similar way, $\rightarrow^\infty$ is used to chain infinite execution steps. Given initial and final stores σ_i and σ_f, the termination of a command c is defined as $\mathsf{terminates}(\sigma_i, c, \sigma_f) \triangleq (c, \sigma_i) \rightarrow^* (\mathsf{skip}, \sigma_f)$: c terminates when it is reduced to a skip command. Given an initial store σ, the diverging execution of a command c is defined as $\mathsf{diverges}(\sigma_i, c) \triangleq (c, \sigma_i) \rightarrow^\infty$: all transition sequences starting from σ_i are infinite.

Moreover, the semantics observe a third kind of behaviors, going wrong behaviors (or abnormal termination), that happen for instance because of a division by zero. Given a command c and a store σ, this behavior is defined as $\mathsf{goeswrong}(\sigma, c) \triangleq \exists c', \exists \sigma'. (c, \sigma) \rightarrow^* (c', \sigma') \wedge (c', \sigma') \nrightarrow \wedge c' \neq \mathsf{skip}$: after a finite number of execution steps to (c', σ'), this state cannot reduce (written $\nrightarrow$) and it is not a final state as c' differs from the skip command. However, abnormal termination is not preserved by verified compilation, as compiler optimizations may remove instructions leading to going wrong behaviors [24].

3.2   Reasoning on Operational Semantics: Simulation Diagrams

From a proof point of view, with big-step semantics, the proof follows naturally the structure of programs and is conveniently conducted by induction on derivations of big-step executions. With small-step semantics, the standard proof technique is to rely on simulation diagrams between semantic states and involving invariants defining matching states. Proving a simulation requires reasoning by case analysis on each possible step. An interesting property of simulations is that they are compositional: they are chained together to describe complete program executions. Thus, the proof of correctness of a compiler pass mainly amounts to the proof of a simulation, and the tricky part often consists in finding the right invariants to preserve.

The choice between a big-step and a small-step style simply on the basis of the adequacy to describe semantic features sometimes comes at the expense of the choice of the proof technique. As an example, choosing a small-step style to

$$\begin{array}{ccc} \mathcal{S}_1 & \longrightarrow & \mathcal{S}_2 \\ \approx \vdots & & \vdots \approx \\ \mathcal{S}_1' & \longrightarrow & {\mathcal{S}_2'}^+ \end{array} \qquad \begin{array}{ccc} \mathcal{S}_1 & \longrightarrow & \mathcal{S}_2 \\ \approx \vdots & \diagup \approx & \\ \mathcal{S}_1' & & \end{array} \quad \text{with } m(\mathcal{S}_2) < m(\mathcal{S}_1)$$

Fig. 3: Forward-simulation diagram with measure. Black lines are hypotheses, red lines are conclusions.

represent in a convenient way diverging executions of IMP prevents the use of standard simulations. Indeed, these simulations also represent the troublesome situation where infinitely many consecutive steps in the source program are simulated by no step at all in the target program. Such situations denote incorrect program transformations, since some diverging behaviors are simulated by some terminating behaviors. In order to handle diverging execution steps and rule out this infinite stuttering problem, a common solution is to strengthen the invariant of the simulation with the definition of a well-founded measure (over the states of the source language) that for instance strictly decreases in cases where stuttering could occur.

An example of a simulation diagram is the forward simulation diagram shown in Fig. 3 and expressed in the following theorem. Given a program P_1 and its transformed program P_2, each transition step in P_1 (from semantic state $\mathcal{S}_1$ to semantic state $\mathcal{S}_2$) must correspond to transitions in P_2 (from semantic state $\mathcal{S}_1'$ to semantic state $\mathcal{S}_2'$) and preserve as an invariant a relation $\approx$ between semantic states of P_1 and P_2. The measure $m(\cdot)$ is defined over the states of P_1 and strictly decreases in cases where stuttering could occur. The diagram ensures that if the source program diverges, it must perform infinitely many non-stuttering steps, so the compiled code executes infinitely many transitions.

4 Continuation-based Small-step Semantics for IMP

Proving simulation diagrams is a general and convenient technique to reason on small-step semantics. This section explains how the simulation diagram defined in Section 3 can be used to reason on a toy imperative language extended with statements. Semantics describe the dynamic of programs, in contrast to compiler passes, which are statically defined, for any source program. A simulation relates the two, by expressing that target execution steps must correspond to source execution steps. One issue with standard small-step semantics is that they describe intermediate steps involving new commands that are subcommands of the source program (*e.g.*, the last rule of Fig. 2).

A consequence of this spontaneous generation of commands is that the reasoning required to prove a simulation becomes difficult and complicates the definition of the anti-stuttering measure. This section first defines an alternative small-step semantics for IMP that is better adapted to mechanized reasoning. Then, it shows that it is equivalent to the first small-step semantics.

4.1   Semantic Rules

The solution adopted in CompCert is to define an original small-step style based on continuations, where the new semantic states become triples, as the command to be executed is explicitly decomposed into a sub-command c under focus, where computation takes place, and a context k that describes the position of the sub-command in the whole command; or, equivalently, a continuation that describes the parts of the whole command that remain to execute once the sub-command terminates. More precisely, the semantic states become of the shape (c, k, σ), and the semantic judgment becomes $(c, k, \sigma) \rightsquigarrow (c', k', \sigma')$. Continuations k are of three kinds, defined in Fig. 4.

- The continuation stop means that nothing remains to be done once the sub-command terminates. In other words, the sub-command under focus is the whole command. This happens either at the beginning or at the end of a program execution.
- A continuation $c; k$ means that when the sub-command terminates, we will then execute the command c, then continue as described by k.
- A continuation $\circlearrowleft(b, c, k)$ means that when the sub-command c terminates, we will then execute the loop while (b) c. When this loop terminates, we will continue as described by k.

Dealing with continuations requires adding new semantic rules to define the execution of commands. The evaluation of expressions remains unchanged. In the end, there are three kinds of semantic rules (see Fig. 4):

- Computation rules evaluate arithmetic and boolean expressions, and modify the triple accordingly. They are close to the rules of the previous semantics.
- Focusing rules describe how to replace the sub-command by a sub-sub-command that must be executed first, enriching the continuation accordingly.
- Resumption rules describe how to extract a continuation in order to execute the next sub-command. More precisely, when the sub-command under focus is skip, and therefore has terminated, resumption rules examine the head of the continuation to find the next sub-command to focus on.

The semantics if IMP rules defines two focusing rules, one for sequences and one for loops. Focusing on a sequence means executing its left part, while pushing the right part to the current continuation. Focusing on a loop means executing its body, while pushing the loop to the current context. The semantics also defines two resumption rules. The resumption rule for a sequence is triggered when its left part is reduced to the skip command; it then steps to the right part of the sequence. The resumption rule for a loop steps to the next execution of the loop body.

Thanks to continuations, semantic rules become genuine reduction rules. For instance, an if command is now rewritten into a sub-command, namely one of its branches. Moreover, as in the previous small-step semantics, termination and divergence are defined using transition sequences. Initial semantic states are of

Continuations:
$$k ::= \mathsf{stop} \mid c; k \mid \circlearrowleft(b, c, k) \quad \text{stop, sequence, while}$$

ASSIGN (COMPUTATION)
$$\frac{\sigma \vdash a \Rightarrow v}{(x := a, k, \sigma) \rightsquigarrow (\mathsf{skip}, k, \sigma[x \rightarrow v])}$$

SEQUENCE (FOCUSING)
$$((c_1; c_2), k, \sigma) \rightsquigarrow (c_1, c_2; k, \sigma)$$

IF TRUE (COMPUTATION)
$$\frac{\sigma \vdash b \Rightarrow true}{(\mathtt{if}\,(b)\,c_1\,\mathtt{else}\,c_2, k, \sigma) \rightsquigarrow (c_1, k, \sigma)}$$

IF FALSE (COMPUTATION)
$$\frac{\sigma \vdash b \Rightarrow false}{(\mathtt{if}\,(b)\,c_1\,\mathtt{else}\,c_2, k, \sigma) \rightsquigarrow (c_2, k, \sigma)}$$

WHILE DONE (COMPUTATION)
$$\frac{\sigma \vdash b \Rightarrow false}{(\mathtt{while}\,(b)\,c, k, \sigma) \rightsquigarrow (\mathsf{skip}, k, \sigma)}$$

WHILE LOOP (COMPUTATION + FOCUSING)
$$\frac{\sigma \vdash b \Rightarrow true}{(\mathtt{while}\,(b)\,c, k, \sigma) \rightsquigarrow (c, \circlearrowleft(b, c, k), \sigma)}$$

SKIP SEQUENCE (RESUMPTION)
$$(\mathsf{skip}, c; k, \sigma) \rightsquigarrow (c, k, \sigma)$$

SKIP WHILE (RESUMPTION)
$$(\mathsf{skip}, \circlearrowleft(b, c, k), \sigma) \rightsquigarrow (\mathtt{while}\,(b)\,c, k, \sigma)$$

Fig. 4: Continuation-based small-step semantics for IMP

the shape $(c, \mathsf{stop}, \sigma_i)$ and final states are of the shape $(\mathsf{skip}, \mathsf{stop}, \sigma_f)$. Given initial and final stores σ_i and σ_f, the termination of a command c is defined as $\mathsf{kterminates}(\sigma_i, c, \sigma_f) \triangleq (c, \mathsf{stop}, \sigma_i) \rightsquigarrow^* (\mathsf{skip}, \mathsf{stop}, \sigma_f)$. Given an initial store σ_i, the diverging execution of c is defined as $\mathsf{kdiverges}(\sigma_i, c) \triangleq (c, \mathsf{stop}, \sigma_i) \rightsquigarrow^\infty$.

4.2   Equivalence between the Two small-step Semantics

The equivalence between the two small-step semantics states that they agree on which commands terminate and which commands diverge. In other words, it amounts to the two following properties.

Theorem 3 (Equivalence of terminating behaviors).
$\forall c, \sigma_i, \sigma_f. \mathsf{terminates}(c, \sigma_i, \sigma_f) \leftrightarrow \mathsf{kterminates}(c, \sigma_i, \sigma_f)$.

Theorem 4 (Equivalence of diverging behaviors).
$\forall c, \sigma_i. \mathsf{diverges}(c, \sigma_i) \leftrightarrow \mathsf{kdiverges}(c, \sigma_i)$.

We use a simulation diagram to prove each theorem in a direction. More precisely, we only have to define the matching invariant $\approx$ between semantic states, the anti-stuttering measure between source states. Conducting these proofs is yet another opportunity to validate these semantics.

As an example, we show that every transition of the continuation semantics is simulated by zero, one or several reduction steps. Given a semantic state (c, k, σ) the measure is defined by a recursive function that counts the nesting of sequence operators constructs in c. The invariant $(c, k, \sigma) \approx (c', \sigma')$ is defined in Fig. 5.

BUILD STOP
$(\mathsf{stop}, c) \hookrightarrow c$

BUILD SEQ
$$\frac{(k_1, (c; c_1)) \hookrightarrow c'}{((c_1; k_1), c) \hookrightarrow c'}$$

BUILD LOOP
$$\frac{(k_1, (c; \mathtt{while}\,(b)\ c)) \hookrightarrow c'}{(\circlearrowleft(b_1, c_1, k_1), c) \hookrightarrow c'}$$

MATCHING INVARIANT
$$\frac{(k, c) \hookrightarrow c'}{(c, k, \sigma) \approx (c', \sigma)}$$

Fig. 5: Equivalence between the two semantics: matching invariant

The command c' is computed from the command c following the $\hookrightarrow$ function, that takes the sub-command c and the continuation k, and rebuilds the whole command. This is achieved by inserting c to the left of the nested sequence constructors described by k. For instance, the second rule builds a sequence of commands from the left command of a sequence and the sequence continuations related to it. The proof of the simulation proceeds by structural induction on continuations.

5   Clight Semantics

Simulation-based proof techniques scale to realistic languages such as C and continuation-based semantics are the privileged style to facilitate compiler correctness proofs, as shown by their use in the CompCert compiler. There are two C-like languages in CompCert, CompCertC the source language of the compiler and Clight, that is a choice language to reason on C programs. This section introduces some background on CompCert generic semantics. Then, it defines the Clight semantics.

5.1   Form IMP to CompCert

In order to model the execution of programs written in realistic languages such as C, the semantic judgments introduced in Section 4.1 need to be extended in three directions. First, C programs are composed of two kinds of functions, depending whether they are defined in the program (internal) or not (external, that are declared with a name and a signature). So, to ensure some guarantees on external functions, the semantics observe traces of input/output operations performed during execution. These traces belong to program behaviors. Second, because of pointer arithmetic, variables need to be generalized to left values, and the store becomes a memory model storing different kinds of values, with different permissions to prevent memory overflows. Third, because of the presence of global, local and temporary variables and functions, semantic states are more involved. This section gives the background to understand these three extensions that are explained in more detail in [9, 24, 26].

Instrumenting the semantics to collect traces of observables. Traces of input/output operations (*e.g.*, memory accesses to global volatile variables used by hardware devices) are part of the observed behavior. The correctness theorem is strengthened to show preservation of these observable effects (that can not modify memory), and it becomes: if the source program terminates (resp. diverges) and performs observable effects t, then the generated program terminates (resp. diverges) and performs the same effects t, and has no other behavior. Semantic judgments $\mathcal{S} \to \mathcal{S}'$ become $\mathcal{S} \xrightarrow{t} \mathcal{S}'$, where the trace t is a list of (possibly infinite) events. An execution step $\mathcal{S} \xrightarrow{\varepsilon} \mathcal{S}'$ means that no event is triggered during this step.

Memory model. The memory model of CompCert is shared by all the languages of the compiler. It provides an abstract view of memory refined into a concrete memory layout. The memory is a collection of disjoint blocks identified by memory addresses, and with fixed lower and upper bounds. Blocks store values (*i.e.*, byte-sized quantities) that can be either machine integers (stored on 32 and 64 bits), pointers, floating-point numbers, or undef. A pointer (or a memory location) is a pair (ℓ, δ) made of a block identifier and an integer offset within that block. The special undef value is also used to denote arbitrary bit patterns, such as the value of uninitialized variables.

Basic memory operations are load, store, alloc, and free operations. Among the properties of memory operations are good variables properties, that ensure memory safety (*e.g.*, no out-of-bound array access) in terminating and diverging executions of programs. Moreover, memory operations are preserved by generic memory transformations called extensions and injections. They preserve the properties of memory operations. Last, in the C semantics of CompCert, each variable allocation creates a new block, and the number of blocks decreases during compilation.

Semantics states. Three environments are used in the semantic judgments for Clight, in addition to the memory store.

- A global environment G maps global variables to memory blocks, and function pointers to their definitions. It does not change during evaluation and execution.
- A local environment σ maps local variables to pairs made of a memory block and a type.
- A temporary environment σ_l maps local temporaries (namely a special class of local variables that do not reside in memory and whose address cannot be taken) to values.

Semantic states all carry a memory store M, mapping addresses to values, and a continuation k materializing the call stack. These states are of three kinds:

- regular states $\mathcal{S}(f, c, k, \sigma, \sigma_l, M)$, that are execution points within an internal function f at statement c,

Statements

$$c ::= \mathsf{skip}$$

	skip	empty statement
$\mid$	$a_1^{\tau_1} = a_2^{\tau_2}$	assignment to a left value
$\mid$	$id \leftarrow a^\tau$	assignment to a temporary variable
$\mid$	$(a_1^{\tau_1})^? = a_2^{\tau_2}((a^\tau)^*)$	function call
$\mid$	$(a_1^{\tau_1})^? = \mathsf{ef}\ \tau_{ext}^*\ (a^\tau)^*$	builtin invocation
$\mid$	$c_1 ; c_2$	sequence
$\mid$	$\mathsf{if}\ (a^\tau)\ c_1\ \mathsf{else}\ c_2$	conditional
$\mid$	$\mathsf{switch}\ (a^\tau)\ ls$	multi-way test and branch
$\mid$	$\mathsf{loop}\ (c_1)\ c_2$	infinite loop
$\mid$	break	exit from the current loop
$\mid$	$\mathsf{continue}$	next iteration of the current loop
$\mid$	$\mathsf{return}\ a^\tau$	return from current function
$\mid$	$lbl : c$	labeled statement
$\mid$	$\mathsf{goto}\ lbl$	jump to a label

Switch cases:
$$ls ::= \epsilon \mid (lbl^? : c) :: ls$$

Fig. 6: Clight syntax

– call states $\mathcal{C}(\mathsf{Fd}, v^*, k, M)$, that are reached each time a function defined by Fd is called; the state carries the parameters passing v^* from the caller,
– return states $\mathcal{R}(v, k, M)$ from a caller to a callee, with resulting value v.

5.2   Clight Syntax

The syntax of Clight is defined in Fig. 6. Clight is a simplified version of the CompCertC source language of CompCert, where expressions are pure, and assignments and function calls are commands instead of expressions. Clight expressions are annotated with their types and written a^τ; expressions are not detailed in this paper as they are similar to those defined in [9]. A novelty in expressions is the bitfield access mode for members of struct or unions.

Base statements are skip, assignments, function calls (with optional assignment of the return value to a local variable) and builtin invocations, break, continue and function return. Other statements describe the control flow: sequences, conditionals, loops, switch and goto statements.

An infinite loop written $\mathsf{loop}\ (c_1)\ c_2$ executes c_1 then c_2 repeatedly. It is equivalent to the C loop written for (; ; c1) c2. A continue in c_1 branches to c_2. The three C loops are derived forms; a while loop $\mathsf{while}\ (e)\ c$ is defined as $\mathsf{loop}\ (\{\mathsf{if}\ (e)\ \mathsf{skip}\ \mathsf{else}\ \mathsf{break}\}; c)\ \mathsf{skip}$, and a for loop $\mathsf{for}\ (c_1; a_2; c_3)\ c_4$ is defined as the sequence $c_1; \mathsf{loop}\ (\mathsf{if}\ (a_2)\ \mathsf{skip}\ \mathsf{else}\ \mathsf{break}; c_3)\ c_4$. A switch statement consists of an expression and a list of cases. A case is a labeled statement $\lfloor lbl \rfloor : c$ or the default case $\epsilon : c$.

A program is composed of several definitions of functions, global variables and struct and union types. A function definition Fd is either $\mathsf{internal}(f)$ or $\mathsf{external}(\mathsf{ef}, \mathsf{targs}, \mathsf{tres}, \mathsf{cconv})$. The definition of an internal function f is composed of a signature, local variables and a body (namely a statement, called f.body). The definition of an external function ef only declares its signature.

The signature of a function f is composed of a return type called f.return, the types of parameters and information cconv related to calling conventions (e.g., the possibility to return struct for functions, or the use of old-style unprototyped functions). External functions model input/output operations; they include system calls and compiler built-in functions (e.g., volatile reads and stores, memory allocation and deallocation, and copy of memory blocks). Function calls and built-in invocations are annotated with their signature.

5.3   Clight Semantics

The semantics of Clight is defined by the following semantic judgments. The terminating (resp. diverging) execution of a whole program is defined using the relation $\to^*$ (resp. $\to^\infty$), as in Section 3.

- The big-step evaluation $G, \sigma, \sigma_l, M \vdash a_1^{\tau_1} \Leftarrow (\ell, \delta), b$ of an expression $a_1^{\tau_1}$ in left-value position results in a memory location (ℓ, δ) that contains the value of $a_1^{\tau_1}$ and the bitfield designation b, that is the access mode for members of structs or unions (either a plain field or a bitfield).
- The big-step evaluation $G, \sigma, \sigma_l, M \vdash a^\tau \Rightarrow v$ of an expression a^τ computes its value v.
- The big-step evaluation $G, \sigma, \sigma_l, M \vdash (a^\tau)^* \Rightarrow v^*$ of a list of expressions computes a list of values.
- The small-step execution $G \vdash S \xrightarrow{t} S'$ from a semantic state S steps to state S' and emits trace t.

The semantic rules for statements are defined in Fig. 7, Fig. 8 and Fig. 9. The rules of Fig. 7 and Fig. 8 step within the currently-executing function and do not trigger any external event, hence the empty trace ε in the rules. Fig. 7 defines the continuations for these statements and the semantics of assignments, sequences of statements, loops, break and continue statements. The rule for if statements is not shown as it is similar to the rule of Fig. 4.

As in Fig. 4, a continuation k consists of the remainder of a command c and a control stack that describes the context in which k occurs. The stop and sequence (;) continuations are defined as in Fig. 4. Two continuations are defined for loops: $\circlearrowleft(c_1, c_2, k)$ means after c_1 in loop (c_1) c_2, and $\circlearrowleft\circlearrowleft(c_1, c_2, k)$ means after c_2 in this loop. A continuation $\nearrow(k)$ is defined to catch in k a break statement arising out of a switch statement. To handle a call to a function f, we need a new form $\rightsquigarrow(x^?, f, \sigma, \sigma_l, k)$ of continuation representing pending function calls in k, given the local (resp. temporary) environment σ (resp. σ_l) of the calling function and the optional identifier x where the result is stored.

An assignment $a_1^{\tau_1} := a_2^{\tau_2}$ to a left-value $a_1^{\tau_1}$ evaluates $a_2^{\tau_2}$ to a memory location (ℓ, δ), and expression $a_1^{\tau_1}$ to value v_2, then casts v_2 into v in order to take into account the types of both expressions. The value v is stored at this memory location, which may fail. Last, the memory M' is returned after storing

Continuations:
$$k ::= \mathsf{stop} \mid c; k \mid \circlearrowleft(c, c, k) \mid \circlearrowleft\circlearrowleft(c, c, k) \quad \text{stop, sequence, loops}$$
$$\mid \nearrow(k) \mid \rightsquigarrow(x^?, f, \sigma, \sigma_l, k) \quad\quad\quad \text{switch, call}$$

ASSIGN (COMPUTATION)
$$\frac{G, \sigma, \sigma_l, M \vdash a_1^{\tau_1} \Leftarrow (\ell, \delta), b \quad G, \sigma, \sigma_l, M \vdash a_2^{\tau_2} \Rightarrow v_2 \quad \mathsf{semCast}(v_2, a_2^{\tau_2}, a_1^{\tau_1}, m) = \lfloor v \rfloor \quad G \vdash \tau_1, m, (\ell, \delta) : b, v, m'}{G \vdash \mathcal{S}(f, (a_1^{\tau_1} := a_2^{\tau_2}), k, \sigma, \sigma_l, M) \xrightarrow{\varepsilon} \mathcal{S}(f, \mathsf{skip}, k, \sigma, \sigma_l, M')}$$

SET (COMPUTATION)
$$\frac{G, \sigma, \sigma_l, M \vdash a^\tau \Rightarrow v}{G \vdash \mathcal{S}(f, (id \leftarrow a^\tau), k, \sigma, \sigma_l, M) \xrightarrow{\varepsilon} \mathcal{S}(f, \mathsf{skip}, k, \sigma, \sigma_l[id \rightarrow v], M)}$$

SEQUENCE (FOCUSING)
$$G \vdash \mathcal{S}(f, (c_1; c_2), k, \sigma, \sigma_l, M) \xrightarrow{\varepsilon} \mathcal{S}(f, c_1, c_2; k, \sigma, \sigma_l, M)$$

SKIP SEQUENCE (RESUMPTION)
$$G \vdash \mathcal{S}(f, \mathsf{skip}, c; k, \sigma, \sigma_l, M) \xrightarrow{\varepsilon} \mathcal{S}(f, c, k, \sigma, \sigma_l, M)$$

CONTINUE SEQUENCE (RESUMPTION)
$$G \vdash \mathcal{S}(f, \mathsf{continue}, c; k, \sigma, \sigma_l, M) \xrightarrow{\varepsilon} \mathcal{S}(f, \mathsf{continue}, k, \sigma, \sigma_l, M)$$

BREAK SEQUENCE (RESUMPTION)
$$G \vdash \mathcal{S}(f, \mathsf{break}, c; k, \sigma, \sigma_l, M) \xrightarrow{\varepsilon} \mathcal{S}(f, \mathsf{break}, k, \sigma, \sigma_l, M)$$

LOOP (COMPUTATION + FOCUSING)
$$G \vdash \mathcal{S}(f, (\mathsf{loop}\,(c_1)\ c_2), k, \sigma, \sigma_l, M) \xrightarrow{\varepsilon} \mathcal{S}(f, c_1, \circlearrowleft(c_1, c_2, k), \sigma, \sigma_l, M)$$

SKIP OR CONTINUE LOOP (RESUMPTION)
$$\frac{x \in \{\mathsf{skip}; \mathsf{continue}\}}{G \vdash \mathcal{S}(f, x, \circlearrowleft(c_1, c_2, k), \sigma, \sigma_l, M) \xrightarrow{\varepsilon} \mathcal{S}(f, c_2, \circlearrowleft\circlearrowleft(c_1, c_2, k), \sigma, \sigma_l, M)}$$

BREAK LOOP1 (RESUMPTION)
$$G \vdash \mathcal{S}(f, \mathsf{break}, \circlearrowleft(c_1, c_2, k), \sigma, \sigma_l, M) \xrightarrow{\varepsilon} \mathcal{S}(f, \mathsf{skip}, k, \sigma, \sigma_l, M)$$

BREAK LOOP2 (RESUMPTION)
$$G \vdash \mathcal{S}(f, \mathsf{break}, \circlearrowleft\circlearrowleft(c_1, c_2, k), \sigma, \sigma_l, M) \xrightarrow{\varepsilon} \mathcal{S}(f, \mathsf{skip}, k, \sigma, \sigma_l, M)$$

SKIP LOOP (RESUMPTION)
$$G \vdash \mathcal{S}(f, \mathsf{skip}, \circlearrowleft\circlearrowleft(c_1, c_2, k), \sigma, \sigma_l, M) \xrightarrow{\varepsilon} \mathcal{S}(f, \mathsf{loop}\,(c_1)\ c_2, k, \sigma, \sigma_l, M)$$

Fig. 7: Clight semantics for statements (first rules)

the value v in the datum of type τ stored at memory location (ℓ, δ), and the

LABEL (COMPUTATION)
$$G \vdash \mathcal{S}(f, (lbl : c), k, \sigma, \sigma_l, M) \xrightarrow{\varepsilon} \mathcal{S}(f, c, k, \sigma, \sigma_l, M)$$

GOTO (COMPUTATION + FOCUSING)
$$\frac{\mathsf{findLabel}(lbl, f.\mathsf{body}, \mathsf{callCont}(k)) = \lfloor (c', k') \rfloor}{G \vdash \mathcal{S}(f, (\mathsf{goto}\, lbl), k, \sigma, \sigma_l, M) \xrightarrow{\varepsilon} \mathcal{S}(f, c', k', \sigma, \sigma_l, M)}$$

SWITCH (COMPUTATION + FOCUSING)
$$\frac{G, \sigma, \sigma_l, M \vdash a^\tau \Rightarrow v \quad \mathsf{semSwitchArg}(v, \tau) = \lfloor lbl \rfloor}{G \vdash \mathcal{S}(f, (\mathsf{switch}\, (a^\tau)\, \mathsf{sl}), k, \sigma, \sigma_l, M) \xrightarrow{\varepsilon} \mathcal{S}(f, \mathsf{seq}(\mathsf{selectSwitch}(lbl) = \mathsf{sl}), \nearrow(k), \sigma, \sigma_l, M)}$$

SKIP BREAK SWITCH (RESUMPTION)
$$\frac{x \in \{\mathsf{skip}; \mathsf{break}\}}{G \vdash \mathcal{S}(f, x, \nearrow(k), \sigma, \sigma_l, M) \xrightarrow{\varepsilon} \mathcal{S}(f, \mathsf{skip}, k, \sigma, \sigma_l, M)}$$

CONTINUE SWITCH (RESUMPTION)
$$G \vdash \mathcal{S}(f, \mathsf{continue}, \nearrow(k), \sigma, \sigma_l, M) \xrightarrow{\varepsilon} \mathcal{S}(f, \mathsf{continue}, k, \sigma, \sigma_l, M)$$

Fig. 8: Clight semantics for goto and switch statements

statement is reduced to skip. An assignment $id \leftarrow a^\tau$ to a temporary variable id evaluates a^τ to a value v and updates the local environment accordingly.

The two rules for sequences are similar to the rules given in Fig. 4. The execution of a continue statement in a loop body interrupts the current execution of this loop body and triggers its next iteration. So, when a continue statement is after c_1 in a loop $\mathsf{loop}(c_1)\, c_2$, then c_2 is the next statement to execute and the continuation is updated accordingly.

The execution of a break statement in a loop body terminates the execution of the current loop body. So, the statements c_1 and c_2 of the loop body are popped from the continuation stack. Moreover, when a continue or a break statement is followed by a statement c, then c is not executed, hence it is popped from the continuation stack. The resumption rule for loops steps to the execution of the next execution of the loop body, when the continuation is a $\circlearrowright$ continuation.

Fig. 8 defines the semantics of labeled, goto and switch statements. The execution of a labeled statement $lbl : c$ steps to the execution of c. The execution of a goto lbl statement in a function f first pops the continuation stack k until a call or a stop, in order to remove from k its local context part. Then, from this continuation $\mathsf{callCont}(k)$ representing the control flow from the last caller of f, findLabel computes recursively (if any) the control flow in f from its entry point until the statement labeled lbl. A new continuation k' that extends k and represents this control flow is then manufactured, and findLabel returns (if any) the pair (c', k'), where c' is the leftmost sub-statement of c labeled lbl. The rule thus steps to statement c' and continuation k', with no change in environments.

The execution of a statement $\mathsf{switch}\,(a^\tau)$ sl first evaluates a^τ into value v, which is then casted into an unsigned integer when τ is an integer type (and fails otherwise). The rule steps to the appropriate case of the switch, given the value of the selector expression, and the corresponding statements are executed (after being converted into a sequence of statements from a labeled statement). In other words, the rules focus on a case switch and the continuation remembers this control flow. This rule is general enough to model executions of unstructured switch statements such as Duff's device [14].

The execution of a break statement in a switch case terminates the execution of this case. In other words, the execution of break (or a skip) statement in a switch case steps to skip and updates the continuation into k. The execution of a continue statement in a switch case updates the continuation into k as well, while keeping the continue statement as the current statement.

The semantic rules involving call and return states are defined in Fig. 9. First, the rule for a call to an internal function identified by $a_f^{\tau_f}$ evaluates $a_f^{\tau_f}$ into v and each argument a^τ of the function. The value v identifies the block where the function definition Fd is stored in the global environment G, and $\mathsf{funct}(G, v)$ returns this definition if any. The rule requires that the signature of the called function matches the signature τ_f annotating the call, namely $\tau_f\#\mathsf{sigOf}(\mathsf{Fd})$.

The rule for a builtin invocation also evaluates the list of its arguments. A builtin is an external function ef and the rule applies ef to arguments v^*: it mainly checks that the builtin is known, that ef cannot modify the memory state M, that v^* are integers or floats and that they agree in number and types with the function signature (see [24]).

The execution of a return statement frees in memory M all the blocks of the current environment σ, and steps to a return state with the retuned value in any (or undef otherwise), and updated continuation and memory state.

A step from a callstate with an internal function f steps to a regular state to further execute the statements f.body of f. The semantics for allocation of variables (hence the modified memory M') and binding of parameters is given by $\mathsf{functionEntry}(f, v^*, M, \sigma, \sigma_l, M')$. Two semantics are supported, one where parameters are local variables, reside in memory, and can have their address taken, and the other where parameters are temporary variables and do not reside in memory.

A step from a callstate with an external function ef steps directly to a return state (to further return to its caller) after generating the appropriate event in the trace t. Moreover, the rule applies ef to arguments v^*, to perform similar checks to those performed by the rule for builtin invocation. Last, a step from a return state either ends the program execution (when the call stack becomes empty) or reaches the regular state of the caller that carries a skip statement and the returned value v stored in the local environment.

FUNCTION CALL
$$\frac{G, \sigma, \sigma_l, M \vdash a_f^{\tau_f} \Rightarrow v \quad G, \sigma, \sigma_l, M \vdash (a^\tau)^* \Rightarrow v^*}{\text{funct}(G, v) = \lfloor \text{Fd} \rfloor \quad \tau_f \#\text{sigOf}(\text{Fd})}$$
$$G \vdash \mathcal{S}(f, id^? = a_f^{\tau_f}((a^\tau)^*), k, \sigma, \sigma_l, M) \xrightarrow{\varepsilon} \mathcal{C}(\text{Fd}, v^*, \leadsto(id^?, f, \sigma, \sigma_l, k), M)$$

BUILTIN INVOCATION
$$\frac{G, \sigma, \sigma_l, M \vdash (a^\tau)^* \Rightarrow v^* \quad G \vdash \text{ef}(v^*), M \xrightarrow{t} v, M'}{G \vdash \mathcal{S}(f, id^? = \text{ef } \tau_{ext}^* \ (a^\tau)^*, k, \sigma, \sigma_l, M) \xrightarrow{t} \mathcal{S}(f, \text{skip}, k, \sigma, \sigma_l\{id^? \leftarrow v\}, M)}$$

RETURN 1
$$\frac{\text{semCast}(v, \tau, f.\text{return}, m) = \lfloor v' \rfloor \quad \text{freeAll}(M, \sigma) = \lfloor M' \rfloor}{G \vdash \mathcal{S}(f, \text{return } \lfloor a^\tau \rfloor, k, \sigma, \sigma_l, M) \xrightarrow{\varepsilon} \mathcal{R}(v', \text{callCont}(k), M')}$$

RETURN 0
$$\frac{\text{freeAll}(M, \sigma) = \lfloor M' \rfloor}{G \vdash \mathcal{S}(f, \text{return } \epsilon, k, \sigma, \sigma_l, M) \xrightarrow{\varepsilon} \mathcal{R}(\text{undef}, \text{callCont}(k), M')}$$

SKIP CALL
$$\frac{\text{freeAll}(M, \sigma) = \lfloor M' \rfloor}{G \vdash \mathcal{S}(f, \text{skip}, k, \sigma, \sigma_l, M) \xrightarrow{\varepsilon} \mathcal{R}(\text{undef}, k, M')}$$

INTERNAL FUNCTION
$$\frac{\text{functionEntry}(f, v^*, M, \sigma, \sigma_l, M')}{G \vdash \mathcal{C}(\text{internal}(f), v^*, k, M) \xrightarrow{\varepsilon} \mathcal{S}(f, f.\text{body}, k, \sigma, \sigma_l, M')}$$

EXTERNAL FUNCTION
$$\frac{G \vdash \text{ef}(v^*), M \xrightarrow{t} v, M'}{G \vdash \mathcal{C}(\text{external}(\text{ef}, \text{targs}, \text{tres}, \text{cconv}), v^*, k, M) \xrightarrow{t} \mathcal{R}(v, k, m')}$$

RETURNSTATE
$$G \vdash \mathcal{R}(v, \leadsto(id^?, f, \sigma, \sigma_l, k), M) \xrightarrow{\varepsilon} \mathcal{S}(f, \text{skip}, k, \sigma, \sigma_l\{id^? \leftarrow v\}, M)$$

Fig. 9: Clight semantics for functions

6 Related Work

The semantics of the Clight language were first mechanized using big-step semantics [9] that were targeting a smaller language and only observing terminating behaviors. Then, a co-inductive interpretation of big-step semantics for diverging behaviors was defined [28]. However, this approach did not scale to conduct compiler correctness proofs of CompCert, contrary to the current continuation-based small-step semantics. Indeed, the cost for extending the correctness proof to diverging behaviors was relatively high (and Coq support for coinductive proofs is temperamental). Compared to [9], the Clight language was extended to model assignments of temporary variables, single infinite loops (instead of C lops), labeled and general goto statements and switch statements.

Other mechanized semantics were defined for realistic languages such as Java, the JVM [20] and JavaScript [10]. In [20], the authors define a big-step semantics and a small-step semantics, which are proved equivalent. A correctness proof of a two-stage compiler from Java to a virtual machine is proved correct using the simulation proof technique. These semantics target a simpler compiler than CompCert and only observe terminating behaviors and do not use continuations.

The idea of using continuations to facilitate some mechanized semantic reasoning first appeared in [4], where an axiomatic semantics (a.k.a. program logics) was defined from an operational semantics. The considered language was Cminor, a lower-level language than Clight, that is the target language of the CompCert front-end. Thanks to continuations, the soundness proof of the axiomatic semantics reuses the induction principles generated by Coq, thus avoiding to craft error-prone induction principles. Continuation-based small-step semantics were then used in the backend of the CompCert compiler [24].

7 Conclusion

This paper presented some operational styles for defining mechanized semantics of programming languages, starting from a toy imperative language to the C language. Exploration on toy languages is essential, but the results do not directly scale to big languages. This paper details the Clight semantics of CompCert, a reasonable proposal that works well in the context of compiler verification and a choice language to reason on C programs.

The continuation-based small-step semantics style detailed in this paper is the style chosen for all the languages of the CompCert compiler. It models terminating and diverging executions of programs and facilitates the semantic reasoning using simulation proof techniques.

Mechanized semantics is a need shared by many verification efforts, not just verified compilation. It is still a difficult task, especially for realistic programming languages. Better tooling for defining and maintaining mechanized semantics for realistic languages is needed.

References

1. Agda version 2.6.4 (2023), https://wiki.portal.chalmers.se/agda/Main/HomePage
2. Isabelle2023 (2023), https://isabelle.in.tum.de/
3. Online Coq development for CompCert version 3.13 (2023), https://compcert.org/doc/index.html
4. Appel, A.W., Blazy, S.: Separation logic for small-step cminor. In: Schneider, K., Brandt, J. (eds.) Theorem Proving in Higher Order Logics, 20th International Conference, TPHOLs 2007, Kaiserslautern, Germany, September 10-13, 2007, Proceedings. Lecture Notes in Computer Science, vol. 4732, pp. 5–21. Springer (2007), https://doi.org/10.1007/978-3-540-74591-4_3
5. Barrière, A., Blazy, S., Flückiger, O., Pichardie, D., Vitek, J.: Formally verified speculation and deoptimization in a JIT compiler. Proc. ACM Program. Lang. (POPL) (2021), https://doi.org/10.1145/3434327

6. Barrière, A., Blazy, S., Pichardie, D.: Formally verified native code generation in an effectful JIT: turning the CompCert backend into a formally verified JIT compiler. Proc. ACM Program. Lang. **7**(POPL), 249–277 (2023), https://doi.org/10.1145/3571202

7. Barthe, G., Blazy, S., Grégoire, B., Hutin, R., Laporte, V., Pichardie, D., Trieu, A.: Formal verification of a constant-time preserving C compiler. Proc. ACM Program. Lang. **4**(POPL), 7:1–7:30 (2020). https://doi.org/10.1145/3371075, https://doi.org/10.1145/3371075

8. Blazy, S., Hutin, R.: Formal verification of a program obfuscation based on mixed boolean-arithmetic expressions. In: Mahboubi, A., Myreen, M.O. (eds.) Proceedings of the 8th ACM SIGPLAN International Conference on Certified Programs and Proofs, CPP 2019, Cascais, Portugal, January 14-15, 2019. pp. 196–208. ACM (2019). https://doi.org/10.1145/3293880.3294103, https://doi.org/10.1145/3293880.3294103

9. Blazy, S., Leroy, X.: Mechanized semantics for the Clight subset of the C language. Journal of Automated Reasoning **43**(3), 263–288 (2009). https://doi.org/10.1007/s10817-009-9148-3, https://hal.inria.fr/inria-00352524

10. Bodin, M., Charguéraud, A., Filaretti, D., Gardner, P., Maffeis, S., Naudziuniene, D., Schmitt, A., Smith, G.: A trusted mechanised javascript specification. In: Jagannathan, S., Sewell, P. (eds.) The 41st Annual ACM SIGPLAN-SIGACT Symposium on Principles of Programming Languages, POPL '14, San Diego, CA, USA, January 20-21, 2014. pp. 87–100. ACM (2014). https://doi.org/10.1145/2535838.2535876, https://doi.org/10.1145/2535838.2535876

11. Bourke, T., Brun, L., Dagand, P., Leroy, X., Pouzet, M., Rieg, L.: A formally verified compiler for lustre. In: Cohen, A., Vechev, M.T. (eds.) Proceedings of the 38th ACM SIGPLAN Conference on Programming Language Design and Implementation, PLDI 2017, Barcelona, Spain, June 18-23, 2017. pp. 586–601. ACM (2017). https://doi.org/10.1145/3062341.3062358, https://doi.org/10.1145/3062341.3062358

12. Boyer, R.S., Moore, J.S.: MJRTY: A fast majority vote algorithm. In: Boyer, R.S. (ed.) Automated Reasoning: Essays in Honor of Woody Bledsoe. pp. 105–118. Kluwer Academic Publishers (1991)

13. Cao, Q., Beringer, L., Gruetter, S., Dodds, J., Appel, A.W.: VST-Floyd: A separation logic tool to verify correctness of C programs. J. Autom. Reason. **61**(1-4), 367–422 (2018). https://doi.org/10.1007/S10817-018-9457-5, https://doi.org/10.1007/s10817-018-9457-5

14. Duff, T.: (1983), www.lysator.liu.se/c/duffs-device.html

15. Filliâtre, J.C., Paskevich, A.: Why3 — where programs meet provers. In: Proceedings of the 22nd European Symposium on Programming. LNCS, vol. 7792, pp. 125–128. Springer (Mar 2013). https://doi.org/10.1007/978-3-642-37036-6_8, https://doi.org/10.1007/978-3-642-37036-6_8

16. Herklotz, Y., Pollard, J.D., Ramanathan, N., Wickerson, J.: Formal verification of high-level synthesis. Proc. ACM Program. Lang. **5**(OOPSLA) (oct 2021). https://doi.org/10.1145/3485494, https://doi.org/10.1145/3485494

17. Inria: The Coq proof assistant reference manual (2022), http://coq.inria.fr, version 8.12.1

18. Jourdan, J., Laporte, V., Blazy, S., Leroy, X., Pichardie, D.: A formally-verified C static analyzer. In: Rajamani, S.K., Walker, D. (eds.) Proceedings of the 42nd Annual ACM SIGPLAN-SIGACT Symposium on Princi-

ples of Programming Languages, POPL 2015, Mumbai, India, January 15-17, 2015. pp. 247–259. ACM (2015). https://doi.org/10.1145/2676726.2676966, https://doi.org/10.1145/2676726.2676966

19. Kästner, D., Barrho, J., Wünsche, U., Schlickling, M., Schommer, B., Schmidt, M., Ferdinand, C., Leroy, X., Blazy, S.: CompCert: Practical Experience on Integrating and Qualifying a Formally Verified Optimizing Compiler. In: ERTS2 2018 - 9th European Congress Embedded Real-Time Software and Systems. pp. 1–9. 3AF, SEE, SIE (Jan 2018)

20. Klein, G., Nipkow, T.: A machine-checked model for a java-like language, virtual machine, and compiler. ACM Trans. Program. Lang. Syst. **28**(4), 619–695 (jul 2006). https://doi.org/10.1145/1146809.1146811, https://doi.org/10.1145/1146809.1146811

21. Koenig, J., Shao, Z.: CompCertO: Compiling certified open c components. In: Proceedings of the 42nd ACM SIGPLAN International Conference on Programming Language Design and Implementation. p. 1095–1109. PLDI 2021, Association for Computing Machinery, New York, NY, USA (2021). https://doi.org/10.1145/3453483.3454097, https://doi.org/10.1145/3453483.3454097

22. Leino, R.M.: Program Proofs. The MIT Press (2023), https://mitpress.mit.edu/9780262546232/program-proofs/

23. Leroy, X.: Formal verification of a realistic compiler. Communications of the ACM (2009). https://doi.org/10.1145/1538788.1538814

24. Leroy, X.: A formally verified compiler back-end. Journal of Automated Reasoning **43**(4), 363–446 (2009). https://doi.org/10.1007/s10817-009-9155-4

25. Leroy, X.: Coq development for the course "mechanized semantics" (2019), https://github.com/xavierleroy/cdf-mech-sem/tree/master

26. Leroy, X., Blazy, S.: Formal verification of a c-like memory model and its uses for verifying program transformations. J. Autom. Reason. **41**(1), 1–31 (2008). https://doi.org/10.1007/S10817-008-9099-0, https://doi.org/10.1007/s10817-008-9099-0

27. Leroy, X., Blazy, S., Kästner, D., Schommer, B., Pister, M., Ferdinand, C.: CompCert - A Formally Verified Optimizing Compiler. In: ERTS 2016: Embedded Real Time Software and Systems, 8th European Congress. SEE (Jan 2016)

28. Leroy, X., Grall, H.: Coinductive big-step operational semantics. Information and Computation **207**(2), 284–304 (2009). https://doi.org/10.1016/j.ic.2007.12.004

29. Mac Carthy, J., Painter, J.: Correctness of a compiler for arithmetic expressions. Mathematical Aspects of Computer Science (1967)

30. Martínez, G., Ahman, D., Dumitrescu, V., Giannarakis, N., Hawblitzel, C., Hriţcu, C., Narasimhamurthy, M., Paraskevopoulou, Z., Pit-Claudel, C., Protzenko, J., Ramananandro, T., Rastogi, A., Swamy, N.: Meta-F*: Proof automation with SMT, tactics, and metaprograms. In: Caires, L. (ed.) Programming Languages and Systems. pp. 30–59. Springer International Publishing, Cham (2019). https://doi.org/10.1007/978-3-030-17184-1_2, https://doi.org/10.1007/978-3-030-17184-1_2

31. Milner, R.J., Weyrauch, R.: Proving compiler correctness in a mechanized logic. Machine Intelligence **7**, 51–73 (1972)

32. Pierce, Benjamin, e.a.: Software foundations - volume 1: logical foundations (2023), https://softwarefoundations.cis.upenn.edu/lf-current/Imp.html, version 6.6

33. Tassarotti, J., Tristan, J.B.: Verified density compilation for a probabilistic programming language. Proc. ACM Program. Lang. **7**(PLDI) (jun 2023). https://doi.org/10.1145/3591245, https://doi.org/10.1145/3591245

Foundations for Query-based Runtime Monitoring of Temporal Properties over Runtime Models

Lucas Sakizloglou[1]([✉]) [iD], Holger Giese[2] [iD], and Leen Lambers[1] [iD]

[1] Brandenburg University of Technology, Cottbus, Germany
lucas.sakizloglou@b-tu.de
[2] Hasso Plattner Institute at the University of Potsdam, Potsdam, Germany

Abstract. In model-driven engineering, runtime monitoring of systems with complex dynamic structures is typically performed via a runtime model capturing a snapshot of the system state: the model is represented as a graph and properties of interest as graph queries which are evaluated over the model online. For temporal properties, history-aware runtime models encode a trace of timestamped snapshots, which is monitored via temporal graph queries. In this case, the query evaluation needs to consider that a trace may be incomplete, thus future changes to the model may affect current answers. So far there is no formal foundation for query-based monitoring over runtime models encoding incomplete traces. In this paper, we present a systematic and formal treatment of incomplete traces. First, we introduce a new definite semantics for a first-order temporal graph logic which only returns answers if no future change to the model will affect them. Then, we adjust the query evaluation semantics of a querying approach we previously presented, which is based on this logic, to the definite semantics of the logic. Lastly, we enable the approach to keep to its efficient query evaluation technique, while returning (the more costly) definite answers.

1 Introduction

Modern safety-critical systems, *e.g.*, smart healthcare and autonomous transportation, consist of numerous interconnected technologies such as sensors, smart devices, and information systems [15]. These systems are human-in-the-loop and operate in highly dynamic environments [16]. Moreover, they are real-time, *i.e.*, their safe operation depends on the timing of their actions, and missed deadlines for these actions may lead to hazardous situations [46]. These characteristics hinder complete quality assurance during the design of such systems and increase the uncertainty about their behavior at runtime. Consequently, their safe operation relies on formally precise *Runtime Monitoring* (RM) techniques [34], which are capable of handling the complex underlying structure and its dynamic [13] as well as timing constraints when monitoring the system behavior [4].

As shown by recent surveys [9, 52], in model-driven engineering, RM of systems with complex dynamic structures is typically performed via a (structural) *Runtime Model* (RTM) [12] capturing a snapshot of the system state: the model is represented as a graph of interacting components and properties of interest

© The Author(s) 2024
D. Beyer and A. Cavalcanti (Eds.): FASE 2024, LNCS 14573, pp. 22–55, 2024.
https://doi.org/10.1007/978-3-031-57259-3_2

as graph queries which are evaluated over the model online; query matches constitute monitoring issues. For efficiency, the evaluation of graph queries is based on methods which afford incremental and *change-driven* evaluation [54], *i.e.*, triggered only when changes to the RTM are relevant to a query.

For temporal properties, *history-aware* RTMs capture past changes to the model and their timing [11], thereby encoding a trace of timestamped snapshots. These RTMs are then monitored via the evaluation of *temporal graph queries* which specify the ordering and timing constraints that matches should satisfy. In this case, the query evaluation needs to consider that the trace encoded by the history-aware RTM may be *incomplete*, *i.e.*, the execution may be ongoing, and hence future changes to the RTM may affect current query answers. So far there is no formal foundation for temporal-query-based RM over incomplete RTMs.

In our previous work, we presented a querying approach for the evaluation of temporal graph queries over history-aware RTMs named INTEMPO [49]—see Section 2.3 for an overview and Fig. 1 for an illustration. INTEMPO advances the state-of-the-art by: enabling a *formally precise answer set* which pairs matches with their *temporal validity*, *i.e.*, the set of all time points for which a match exists and satisfies a temporal property according to a first-order temporal graph logic; featuring sound methods for *incremental and change-driven evaluation* as well as the optional *pruning* of the RTM, *i.e.*, the removal of temporally irrelevant history. Extensive experimental evaluation showed that our implementation of INTEMPO efficiently evaluated complex queries over considerably large models (approx. from 10K to 48M elements) [49]. The experimental evaluation included an RM application scenario, in which INTEMPO evaluated queries faster than an RTM-based tool and a tool from the related RM approach known as *Runtime Verification* (RV).

However, the formal foundation of INTEMPO assumes that the RTM encodes a complete trace. For the RM scenario, we equipped INTEMPO with a check that was applied to the answer set and, based on the timing constraint of the property, filtered matches that could be affected by future changes to the RTM. In this paper, we present a formal foundation for temporal-query-based RM over incomplete RTMs. The foundation entails the introduction of an answer set which formalizes the intuition behind the check and allows approaches like INTEMPO to maintain their efficiency while returning formally precise answers.

Specifically, our contributions are the following. First, we introduce a *definite* semantics for a temporal graph logic (Section 3), which only returns answers if they are definite, *i.e.*, no future change to the RTM will affect them; we show that the definite semantics is sound. Then, we introduce a new *definite answer set* (Section 4) for the query language of INTEMPO which pairs matches with their definite temporal validity and invalidity. Compared to the original (non-definite) answer set, the definite answer relies on the time point on which a query is evaluated and thus requires the re-computation of the definite temporal validity and invalidity in each evaluation. The definite answer set is thus inefficient, *i.e.*, not amenable to change-driven evaluation. However, we use this theoretical result to show that our last contribution, the *effective answer set* (Section 5), which

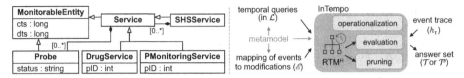

Fig. 1: An excerpt of the SHS metamodel from [49] (left) and an operational overview of the INTEMPO implementation where arrows denote input and output.

essentially incorporates the check mentioned above, can return definite answers while relying on the original, and thus efficient, answer set.

The presented contributions are based on unpublished material from the doctoral thesis of the first author [47]. Section 2 reiterates preliminaries and INTEMPO, Section 6 discusses related work, and Section 7 concludes the paper.

Running Example As a running example we will use the *Smart Healthcare System* (SHS) introduced in [49]. Fig. 1 shows an excerpt of the SHS metamodel. An SHS is an envisioned smart medical environment [45], based on the service-based exemplar in [55], which supports clinicians in medical treatments by automating tasks via smart devices. In the context of an SHS, RM may be used to verify whether treatments comply with the requirements in a guideline, which typically contain timing constraints [17]. In the SHS, services are invoked by a main service called SHSService to collect measurements from patient sensors, *i.e.*, PMonitoringService, or take medical actions via smart medical devices such as a smart pump, *i.e.*, DrugService. The results of service invocations are tracked via monitoring probes (Probe) that are attached to Services. Probes are generated periodically or upon events in the real world. Each Probe has a *status* attribute whose value depends on the type of Service. Each Service has a *pID* attribute which identifies the patient for whom the Service is invoked. The MonitorableEntity is explained in Section 2.1.

We focus on a property P that tracks time between triage and admission, as often done in medical guidelines [39]; in the context of an SHS, these activities are represented by the invocation of a sensor service and a drug service, respectively: *"When a sensor service is invoked for a patient, there should be a drug service invoked for the same patient within one minute and, until then, there should be no other sensor service invoked for the same patient."* The specific timing constraint is adjusted for the purpose of presentation. Assume an RTM that captures that a sensor service has just been invoked for a patient, but contains no drug invocation yet; for monitoring P, it is important to consider that a future state which contains the drug service invocation may follow in time; therefore, the present state does not yet violate P.

2 Preliminaries

In this section, we summarize preliminaries and the INTEMPO query language. An overview of the notation used in the paper is shown in Table 2 in Section A.

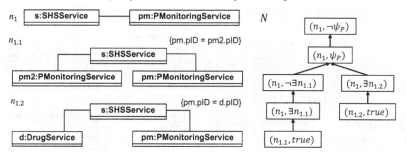

Fig. 2: Patterns for the SHS (left) and the GDN N for the query $(n, \neg\psi_P)$.

2.1   Formal Representation of Models and Queries

An RTM is typically represented as a graph, where system entities are captured by vertices, information about the entities by attributes, and relationships between entities by edges [25, 14, 24]. In this paper, for the formal representation of RTMs, we rely on the well-known *typed graphs* [20], *i.e.*, graphs *typed* over a *type graph* which defines types of vertices, edges, and valid structures for typed graphs.

Definition 1 ((typed) graph, (typed) graph morphism, type graph). *A graph $G = (G^V, G^E, s^G, t^G)$ consists of a set of vertices G^V, a set of edges G^E, a source function $s^G : G^E \to G^V$, and a target function $t^G : G^E \to G^V$. Given two graphs $G = (G^V, G^E, s^G, t^G)$ and $K = (K^V, K^E, s^K, t^K)$, a graph morphism $f : G \to K$ is a pair of mappings $f^V : G^V \to K^V, f^E : G^E \to K^E$ such that $f^V \circ s^G = s^K \circ f^E$ and $f^V \circ t^G = t^K \circ f^E$. A graph morphism $f : G \to K$ is a monomorphism, denoted by $\hookrightarrow$, if f^V and f^E are injective. A type graph is a distinguished graph $TG = (TG^V, TG^E, s^{TG}, t^{TG})$. A tuple $(G, type)$ consisting of a graph G and a graph morphism $type : G \to TG$ is called a typed graph. Given two typed graphs $G^T = (G, type)$ and $K^T = (K, type')$, a typed graph morphism $f : G^T \to K^T$ is a graph morphism $f' : G \to K$ such that $type' \circ f' = type$.*

Type graphs can be extended to support the well-known concepts of *inheritance* and *multiplicities* from the object-oriented paradigm [53]. Moreover, typed graphs can be extended by vertex and edge *attributes*, each associated with a data type, *i.e.*, a character string, an integer, a real number, or a boolean, to obtain *typed attributed graphs* [20]. Attribute *assignments* assign data-type-compatible values to attributes, and attribute *constraints*, *i.e.*, a boolean expression over attribute values, restrict the possible assignments. Our contributions rely on such graphs, defined in detail in our prior work [50]; to avoid the complication of presentation, here we omit these extensions from our definitions.

The metamodel in Fig. 1 may be seen as an informal representation of the type graph of the SHS, where only vertices have attributes. Correspondingly, the RTM G_7 in Fig. 3 is an informal representation of a typed attributed graph. We henceforth refer to typed attributed graphs simply as graphs or *patterns*. The RTM G_7 contains assignments, which assign values to attributes, *e.g.*, $pm_1.pID$

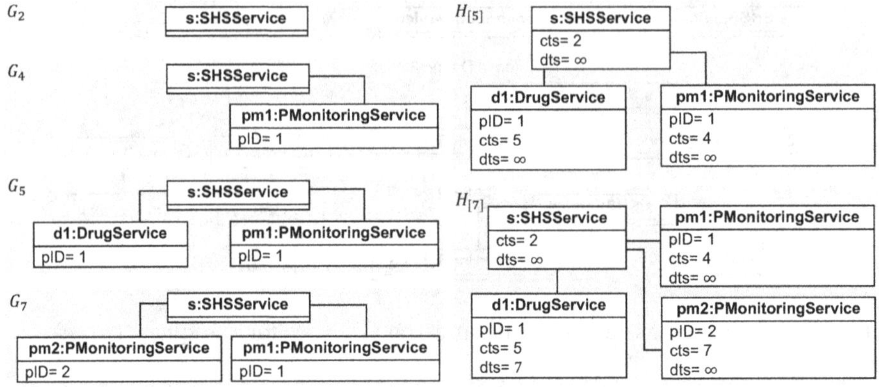

Fig. 3: Snapshots as RTMs (G_*) and traces as RTM^H instances $(H_{[*]})$.

$= 1$. The representation of the textual statements in property P of the running example by patterns is illustrated in Fig. 2: The invocation of a sensor service is captured in patterns n_1 and $n_{1.1}$, and the invocation of a drug service is captured in $n_{1.2}$; constraints are illustrated between braces, e.g., $n_{1.1}$ requires that the values for pID of pm and pm2 are equal; vertices with the same label refer to the same vertex in the queried RTM.

We assume that the system is instrumented to generate (instantaneous) events upon changes to its state, and identify the system execution with a possibly infinite sequence of such events. The system has a clock whose time domain is the set of non-negative real numbers $\mathbb{R}_0^+$, and uses the clock to timestamp events. We refer to an element of the time domain as a *time point*. Intuitively, an (execution) *trace* h_τ of a system with respect to an event at time point τ is the sequence of all observed events in the execution from its beginning, i.e., time point 0, up to and including τ. For brevity, we group all changes with the same time point in one event. However, we require that no event groups an infinite amount of changes, thereby ruling out Zeno behaviors—in the use-cases of interest, all traces will eventually terminate and differences between measurements cannot become infinitely small. We denote the time point at position i of h_τ by τ_i, with $i \in \mathbb{N}^+$.

For a model-based representation of a trace h_τ, we rely on a *Runtime Model with History* (RTM^H) [49]. An RTM^H H is a distinguished RTM where the following conditions hold. All vertices in H have a distinguished *creation timestamp* cts and a *deletion timestamp* dts to which a value is assigned—therefore in Fig. 1, all vertices inherit from the MonitorableEntity.[3] When a vertex is created, the time point of creation is assigned to cts and the value ∞ is assigned to the dts; the dts value changes when the vertex is deleted in the modeled system. As a vertex cannot have been deleted prior to its creation or deleted simultaneously to its creation, the value of dts, if not ∞, has to be larger than the value of cts.

---

[3] If tracking changes to attribute values or edges in an RTM is of importance, those can be modeled as vertices, which is a customary modeling technique, e.g., [36].

An h_τ can be transformed to an RTM^H H based on a mapping $\mathscr{E}$ from the set of all possible events to corresponding graph modifications [48]; to capture the period covered by H in this case, we denote it by $H_{[\tau]}$. Each trace *continuation* $h_{\tau'}$ that is yielded by an event at time point τ' with $\tau' > \tau$ can be similarly transformed to a $H_{[\tau']}$ by applying the changes in the event at τ' to $H_{[\tau]}$; we refer to $H_{[\tau']}$ as a new *version* of $H_{[\tau]}$. This process generates a trace of RTMs $h_{\tau'}^H$, called an *RTM^H-trace*, which mirrors h_τ'; we refer to members of $h_{\tau'}^H$ as *instances* of the RTM^H. Formally, an $H_{[\tau]}$ is a compact representation of a *timed graph sequence* [26], *i.e.*, a sequence of timestamped graphs where additions and deletions between two consecutive graphs are represented by morphisms. As an example of an RTM^H, see $H_{[5]}$ in Fig. 3 which contains all changes in events up to time point 5; $H_{[5]}$ represents the timed graph sequence $G_2 G_4 G_5$ (left in Fig. 3; morphisms are omitted). A new event at time point 7 which contains the deletion of d1, and the addition of pm2 is transformed into $H_{[7]}$; this RTM represents the sequence $G_2 G_4 G_5 G_7$. If τ in h_τ, h_τ^H, or $H_{[\tau]}$ is irrelevant, we omit it.

2.2   Metric Temporal Graph Logic

For the specification and analysis of temporal properties in temporal queries, INTEMPO relies on the *Metric Temporal Graph Logic* (MTGL) [50, 26]. MTGL builds on *Nested Graph Conditions* (NGCs) [27] and *Metric Temporal Logic* (MTL) [35] to enable the formulation of *Metric Temporal Graph Conditions* (MT-GCs). The language of NGCs can formulate requirements that are as expressive as first-order logic on graphs [18], as shown in [27, 44], and constitutes as such a natural formal foundation for pattern-based queries. As NGCs, MTGCs support *bindings*, *i.e.*, morphisms between patterns which bind elements in outer conditions to inner (nested) conditions, and are therefore able to track the evolution of a given binding in a sequence of graphs separately to other bindings.

In the following definition of MTGL, we focus on a subset of MTGL operators which contains the *metric*, *i.e.*, interval-based, temporal operators *until* (U_I, with I an interval in $\mathbb{R}_0^+$) and its dual *since* (S_I) from MTL. The existential quantifier features a binding between the patterns n and $\hat{n}$.

Definition 2 (metric temporal graph conditions). *Let $n, \hat{n}$ be patterns and $f : n \hookrightarrow \hat{n}$ a binding. Moreover, let I be an interval in $\mathbb{R}_0^+$. Then ψ is a* Metric Temporal Graph Condition *(MTGC) over n defined as follows.*

$$\psi_n ::= \text{true} \mid \neg\psi_n \mid \psi_n \wedge \psi_n \mid \exists(f : n \hookrightarrow \hat{n}, \psi_{\hat{n}}) \mid \psi_n \, U_I \psi_n \mid \psi_n \, S_I \psi_n$$

In the remainder, we abbreviate $\exists(f, true)$ by $\exists f$ and, when the domain of f is clear from the context, $\exists(f : n \hookrightarrow \hat{n}, \phi_{\hat{n}})$ by $\exists(\hat{n}, \phi)$. Other abbreviations, *e.g.*, disjunction ($\vee$), *eventually* ($\Diamond_I$) can be defined as usual.

Based on the patterns in Fig. 2, property P from the running example can be reformulated into "given a binding for n_1 at a time point τ, at least one binding for $n_{1.2}$ is found at some time point $\tau' \in [\tau, \tau + 60]$, *i.e.*, at most 60 seconds later; in addition, at each time point $\tau'' \in [\tau, \tau')$ in between, no binding for $n_{1.1}$ is present." In MTGL, this property is captured by the MTGC $\psi_P := \neg\exists(n_1 \hookrightarrow$

$n_{1.1}, true)\, U_{[0,60]}\, \exists\, (n_1 \hookrightarrow n_{1.2}, true)$, or, abbreviated, $\neg \exists n_{1.1}\, U_{[0,60]}\, \exists n_{1.2}$. The system is assumed to track time in seconds; vertices s and pm from n_1 are bound in the patterns $n_{1.1}$ and $n_{1.2}$, *i.e.*, all patterns refer to the same s and pm.

MTGL reasons over (finite) timed graph sequences. However, MTGCs can also be equivalently checked over a graph with history [26], which here corresponds to an RTM^H. In the following, we define the semantics of the satisfaction relation of MTGL based on an RTM^H.

Definition 3 (satisfaction of metric temporal graph conditions over an RTM). *Let H be an RTM^H, n a pattern, and $m : n \hookrightarrow H$ a binding. Moreover, let τ be a time point in $\mathbb{R}_0^+$ and ψ be an MTGC over n. Then m in H satisfies ψ at τ, written $(H, m, \tau) \models \psi$, if $max_{e \in E} e.\text{cts} \leq \tau < min_{e \in E} e.\text{dts}$, with E the vertices of m, and one of the following cases applies.*

- $\psi = true.$
- $\psi = \neg\chi$ *and* $(H, m, \tau) \not\models \chi.$
- $\psi = \chi \wedge \omega,\ (H, m, \tau) \models \chi,$ *and* $(H, m, \tau) \models \omega.$
- $\psi = \exists(f : n \hookrightarrow \hat{n}, \chi)$ *and there exists* $\hat{m} : \hat{n} \hookrightarrow H$ *such that* $\hat{m} \circ f = m$ *and* $(H, \hat{m}, \tau) \models \chi.$
- $\psi = \chi\, U_I\, \omega$ *and there exists* τ' *with* $\tau' - \tau \in I$ *such that* $(H, m, \tau') \models \omega$ *and for all* $\tau'' \in [\tau, \tau')\ (H, m, \tau'') \models \chi.$
- $\psi = \chi\, S_I\, \omega$ *and there exists* τ' *with* $\tau - \tau' \in I$ *such that* $(H, m, \tau') \models \omega$ *and for all* $\tau'' \in (\tau', \tau]\ (H, m, \tau'') \models \chi.$

Intuitively, a binding m for n in the RTM H satisfies the MTGC $\exists(f : n \hookrightarrow \hat{n}, \chi)$ at time point τ if (i) all elements of m are already created but not yet deleted at τ, and (ii) there exists a binding $\hat{m}$ for $\hat{n}$ in H such that $\hat{m}$ is *compatible* with m, *i.e.*, respects the binding between the two patterns captured in $n \hookrightarrow \hat{n}$, and $\hat{m}$ satisfies the MTGC χ at τ. The intuition behind *true*, negation, conjunction, *until*, and *since* is the usual.

2.3   INTEMPO: Query Language and Overview of Operation

INTEMPO introduces a query language, henceforth referred to as $\mathcal{L}$, which has two distinguishing features: it enables the formulation of ordering and temporal constraints in MTGL, *i.e.*, as an MTGC, thereby enabling formal precision in checking whether matches satisfy those constraints; it computes the period for which a match satisfies an MTGC, thereby enabling practical query evaluations, as the query does not have to be evaluated for each time point of interest. We summarize core concepts of graph queries and $\mathcal{L}$ below.

In its plainest form, a *graph query* is characterized by a pattern n. A *match* for this query is a binding from n to a queried graph which preserves structure and type. $\mathcal{L}$ allows for the specification of *temporal graph queries*, *i.e.*, queries of the form (n, ψ) with ψ an MTGC over n, whereby matches for n in an RTM^H H need to satisfy the temporal requirement captured in ψ. Based on the running example, the query $(n_1, \neg\psi_P)$, searches H for matches for n_1, *i.e.*, sensor services, which falsify ψ_P.

Vertices in H have lifespans, defined by their cts and dts. Similarly, a match m in H is valid only if there is a non-empty interval $\lambda^m = \cap_{e \in E}[e.cts, e.dts)$, with E the vertices of m, called the *lifespan of a match*. According to its definition, the values of regular attributes in H cannot change and, hence, cannot affect λ^m. In the special case where the pattern of a query is the empty graph $\varnothing$, an (empty) match m is always found with $\lambda^m = \mathbb{R}$. Temporal logics that reason over intervals, such as MTGL, are capable of deciding the truth value of a property for the entire time domain; in INTEMPO, the set of time points satisfying a property is called the *satisfaction span* and defined as $\mathcal{Y}(m, \psi) = \{\tau \mid \tau \in \mathbb{R} \wedge (H, m, \tau) \models \psi\}$ with ψ an MTGC. The *temporal validity* $\mathcal{V}(m, \psi)$ is equal to $\lambda^m \cap \mathcal{Y}(m, \psi)$ and defined as the period for which m exists in H *and* satisfies ψ.

The following computation, called the *satisfaction computation* $\mathcal{Z}$ of m for ψ, soundly computes $\mathcal{Y}$, as shown in [49]. The computation relies on interval operations defined as usual [see 41]: Let k, z be intervals; then $k \oplus z = [\ell(k) + \ell(z), r(k) + r(z)]$, $k \ominus z = [\ell(k) - r(z), r(k) - \ell(z)]$ with $\ell(k)$ and $r(k)$ the left and right end-point of k, respectively. We denote the unions $\ell(k) \cup k$ by ^+k, and $k \cup r(k)$ by k^+; when $r(k) = \infty$, $k^+ = k$. The interval k is *overlapping* z when $k \cap z \neq \emptyset$ and *adjacent* to z when $k \cap z = \emptyset$ but $k \cup z$ is an interval.

Definition 4 (satisfaction computation $\mathcal{Z}$). *Let $n, \hat{n}$ be patterns and ψ, χ, ω be MTGCs. Moreover, let m be a match for n in an RTM H, and $\hat{M}$ a set of matches for $\hat{n}$ that are compatible with the (enclosing) match m. The* satisfaction computation $\mathcal{Z}(m, \psi)$ *is recursively defined as follows.*

$$\mathcal{Z}(m, \text{true}) = \mathbb{R} \tag{1}$$

$$\mathcal{Z}(m, \neg\chi) = \mathbb{R} \setminus \mathcal{Z}(m, \chi) \tag{2}$$

$$\mathcal{Z}(m, \chi \wedge \omega) = \mathcal{Z}(m, \chi) \cap \mathcal{Z}(m, \omega) \tag{3}$$

$$\mathcal{Z}(m, \exists(\hat{n}, \chi)) = \bigcup_{\hat{m} \in \hat{M}} \lambda^{\hat{m}} \cap \mathcal{Z}(\hat{m}, \chi) \tag{4}$$

$$\mathcal{Z}(m, \chi \mathsf{U}_I \omega) = \begin{cases} \displaystyle\bigcup_{i \in \mathcal{Z}(m,\omega), j \in J_i} j \cap ((j^+ \cap i) \ominus I) & \text{if } 0 \notin I \\ \displaystyle\bigcup_{i \in \mathcal{Z}(m,\omega)} i \cup \bigcup_{j \in J_i} j \cap ((j^+ \cap i) \ominus I) & \text{if } 0 \in I \end{cases} \tag{5}$$

$$\mathcal{Z}(m, \chi \mathsf{S}_I \omega) = \begin{cases} \displaystyle\bigcup_{i \in \mathcal{Z}(m,\omega), j \in J_i} j \cap ((^+j \cap i) \oplus I) & \text{if } 0 \notin I \\ \displaystyle\bigcup_{i \in \mathcal{Z}(m,\omega)} i \cup \bigcup_{j \in J_i} j \cap ((^+j \cap i) \oplus I) & \text{if } 0 \in I \end{cases} \tag{6}$$

with J_i the set of all intervals in $\mathcal{Z}(m, \chi)$ that are either overlapping or adjacent to some $i \in \mathcal{Z}(m, \omega)$.

The intuition behind the equations for *true*, negation, and conjunction is clear. Regarding *exists*, the satisfaction span is the union of the temporal validity of all matches $\hat{m}$ for $\hat{n}$ which are compatible with m. Regarding *until*, if $0 \notin I$, the satisfaction includes every time point τ in the intersection of some $i' \in Z(m, \omega)$ with a $j' \in \mathcal{Z}(m, \chi)$ for which a time point $\tau' \in i'$ occurs within I. Furthermore, j'

needs to overlap i', *e.g.*, $j' = [1,3]$, $i' = [2,4]$ or be adjacent to i', *e.g.*, $j' = [1,2)$, $i' = [2,4]$. If j' and i' are adjacent, during the computation j becomes right-closed to ensure that their intersection produces a non-empty set. If $0 \in I$, then, according to Definition 3, it may be that j' is empty, *i.e.*, does not exist, and *until* is satisfied by every $i' \in \mathcal{Z}(m, \omega)$. Therefore, the computation includes every i' and remains unchanged otherwise. The intuition behind *since* is analogous.

The intersection of two intervals is always an interval, whereas the union of two intervals may result in disjoint sets. Hence, technically $\mathcal{Z}$ and $\mathcal{V}$ are *interval sets* which may contain disjoint or empty intervals.

We define below the answer set $\mathcal{T}$ for a query in $\mathcal{L}$.

Definition 5 (query answer set $\mathcal{T}$). *Given a pattern n, an MTGC ψ, and an RTM^H H, the* answer set $\mathcal{T}$ *of a query in $\mathcal{L}$ over H is given by:*

$$\mathcal{T}(H) = \{(m, \mathcal{V}(m, \psi)) | m \text{ is a match for } n \wedge \mathcal{V}(m, \psi) \neq \emptyset\}$$

Regarding the operation of INTEMPO (see Fig. 1), the approach expects a metamodel, a set of queries in $\mathcal{L}$, a mapping $\mathcal{E}$ from events to modifications, and an event trace h_τ as input—see definitions earlier. INTEMPO operationalizes queries (see Section 5). For each event events in h_τ, INTEMPO performs the corresponding changes to an RTM^H and, after each change, evaluates the queries. Pruning may follow, which triggers another query evaluation to update stored matches. Finally, INTEMPO returns the answer set $\mathcal{T}$ or, for RM, performs the check described in Section 1 and essentially returns matches in the effective answer set $\mathcal{T}^e$ (see Section 5). In our implementation of INTEMPO, the metamodel, the queries, and the mapping are defined based on model-based technologies [48].

We present an example that demonstrates that $\mathcal{T}$ may contain imprecise answers in the context of an incomplete trace.

Example 1 (imprecision over incomplete trace). Evaluated over $H_{[7]}$ in Fig. 3, the query $(n_1, \neg \psi_P)$ returns an answer set $\mathcal{T}(H_{[7]})$ which contains a pair $(m_2, [7, \infty))$; m_2 is a match for n_1 involving the vertex pm2, and $[7, \infty)$ is the temporal validity $\mathcal{V}$ which states that m_2 falsifies ψ_P from time point 7 onward. $\mathcal{V}$ is the result of the intersection of $\lambda^{m_2} = [7, \infty)$ with $\mathcal{Z}(m_2, \neg \psi_P) = \mathbb{R}$. The satisfaction span $\mathcal{Z}$ is computed according to Definition 4—see Table 1 for details.

This computation is definite only if $H_{[7]}$ is the last instance in an RTM^H-trace; if the trace is incomplete, and it is to be continued by a new $H_{[\tau]}$ with $\tau \leq 67$, the match m_2 may still satisfy ψ_P, as there is still time for a DrugService to be created timely, *i.e.*, a match for the pattern $n_{1.2}$, which is compatible with m_2, to be found—assuming that until then there would be no match for $n_{1.1}$.

3   Definite Semantics for Metric Temporal Graph Logic

This section presents our contribution to MTGL. Specifically, we introduce a new semantics, called *definite*, which only returns answers if they are definite, *i.e.*, no future change to the RTM^H will affect them. Similarly to temporal logics which account for RM over incomplete traces [8, 21], the definite semantics is *three-valued*, as they return the value *unknown* when the result of the satisfaction check is not definite. We show the soundness of the definite semantics in Theorem 1 based on the regular semantics in Definition 3. Moreover, we show that for a certain period the definite and the regular semantics are equivalent (Theorem 2); this equivalence enables our contribution in Section 5, *i.e.*, it allows INTEMPO to return definite answers efficiently. Finally, we demonstrate an intrinsic limitation of the definite semantics: we show that for unsatisfiable properties, the semantics may return decisions with a delay, compared to the earliest time point on which the decisions could have been returned. We compute the maximum possible magnitude of the delay (Corollary 2).

We begin with the definition of the definite semantics. In the context of an RTM^H $H_{[c]}$, a satisfaction decision for time point $\tau \in [0, c]$ is *definite* if the decision for τ remains the same in all possible future versions of $H_{[c]}$. We obtain the definite satisfaction span by adjusting the satisfaction relation of MTGL from Definition 3 to this notion of definiteness. Moreover, we obtain the definite falsification by negating the statements in the cases of the definite satisfaction. We present the adjusted satisfaction relation, called *definite satisfaction relation*, and the *definite falsification relation* over an RTM^H below.

Definition 6 (definite satisfaction and definite falsification of metric temporal graph conditions over an RTM^H). *Let $H_{[c]}$ be a RTM^H, n a pattern, and $m : n \hookrightarrow H_{[c]}$ a match. Moreover, let $\tau \in \mathbb{R}$ be a time point and ψ be an MTGC over n. Then the definite satisfaction relation $\models^d$ and definite falsification relation $\models^d_F$ are defined via mutual recursion as follows. The match m definitely satisfies ψ at τ, written $(H_{[c]}, m, \tau) \models^d \psi$, iff $\tau \in \lambda^m \cap [0, c]$, or m is the empty match, and one of the following cases applies.*

- $\psi = \text{true}$.
- $\psi = \neg\chi$ and $(H_{[c]}, m, \tau) \models^d_F \chi$.
- $\psi = \chi \wedge \omega$, $(H_{[c]}, m, \tau) \models^d \chi$, and $(H_{[c]}, m, \tau) \models^d \omega$.
- $\psi = \exists(f : n \hookrightarrow \hat{n}, \chi)$ and there exists $\hat{m} : \hat{n} \hookrightarrow H_{[c]}$ such that $\hat{m} \circ f = m$ and $(H_{[c]}, \hat{m}, \tau) \models^d \chi$.
- $\psi = \chi \, U_I \omega$ and there exists τ' with $\tau' - \tau \in I$ such that $(H_{[c]}, m, \tau') \models^d \omega$ and for all $\tau'' \in [\tau, \tau')$ $(H_{[c]}, m, \tau'') \models^d \chi$.
- $\psi = \chi \, S_I \omega$ and there exists τ' with $\tau - \tau' \in I$ such that $(H_{[c]}, m, \tau') \models^d \omega$ and for all $\tau'' \in (\tau', \tau]$ $(H_{[c]}, m, \tau'') \models^d \chi$.

The definite falsification relation is based on a logical negation of the statements in the cases of the definite satisfaction relation. The match m definitely falsifies ψ at τ, written $(H_{[c]}, m, \tau) \models^d_F \psi$, iff $\tau \in \lambda^m \cap [0, c]$, or m is the empty match, and one of the following cases applies.

- $\psi = \neg\chi$ and $(H_{[c]}, m, \tau) \models^d \chi$.
- $\psi = \chi \wedge \omega$ and $(H_{[c]}, m, \tau) \models^d_F \chi$ or $(H_{[c]}, m, \tau) \models^d_F \omega$.
- $\psi = \exists(f : n \hookrightarrow \hat{n}, \chi)$ and either there does not exist an $\hat{m} : \hat{n} \hookrightarrow H_{[c]}$ such that $\hat{m} \circ f = m$, or there exists $\hat{m}$ and $(H_{[c]}, \hat{m}, \tau) \models^d_F \chi$.

- $\psi = \chi \, U_I \omega$ and for all τ' with $\tau' - \tau \in I$ $(H_{[c]}, m, \tau') \models^d_F \omega$ or there exists $\tau'' \in [\tau, \tau')$ such that $(H_{[c]}, m, \tau'') \models^d_F \chi$.
- $\psi = \chi \, S_I \omega$ and for all τ' with $\tau - \tau' \in I$ $(H_{[c]}, m, \tau') \models^d_F \omega$ or there exists $\tau'' \in (\tau', \tau]$, $(H_{[c]}, m, \tau'') \models^d_F \chi$.

In comparison to $\models$, $\models^d$ confines the lifespans of matches and the satisfaction of *exists* to the period that has been observed, *i.e.*, $[0, c]$. Moreover, $\models^d$ relies on $\models^d_F$ for the satisfaction of a negation. Similarly to $\models^d$, $\models^d_F$ confines the decisions for matches to $[0, c]$, and relies on $\models^d$ for the falsification of negation. The match m never falsifies *true*. We note that $\models^d_F$ and $\not\models^d$ are not equivalent; $\not\models^d$ returns true for time points that do not definitely satisfy the operator, *i.e.*, points that falsify it but also points for which a definite decision cannot yet be made.

The following theorem shows the soundness of the *definite relations* $\models^d$ and $\models^d_F$ by relating them to the regular satisfaction relation $\models$ from Definition 3 and its negation $\not\models$. The theorem refers to observed prefixes of a possibly infinite RTM^H-trace h^H and their possible continuations; an RTM^H $H_{[\tau_i]}$ in h^H is associated with the τ of the event with index $i \in \mathbb{N}^+$ in the execution h—see Section 2.1. The theorem states that a *definite decision*, *i.e.*, a decision made by either $\models^d$ or $\models^d_F$, for a certain time point τ over an $H_{[\tau_i]}$ in h^H implies that the same decision is made by $\models$ (or $\not\models$) for τ over $H_{[\tau_i]}$; moreover, $\models$ makes the same decision for τ over all possible future versions of $H_{[\tau_i]}$ in h^H.

Theorem 1 (definite relations imply satisfaction relation over trace).
Let ψ be an MTGC over a pattern n. Moreover, let $h^H_{\tau_\mathcal{D}}$ be RTM^H-trace, with $\mathcal{D} \in \mathbb{N}^+$. For all $i \in [1, \mathcal{D}] \cap \mathbb{N}^+$, if m is a match for n in $H_{[\tau_i]}$ and $\tau \in [0, \tau_i]$, then for all $k \in [i, \mathcal{D}] \cap \mathbb{N}^+$, (i) if $(H_{[\tau_i]}, m, \tau) \models^d \psi$, then $(H_{[\tau_k]}, m, \tau) \models \psi$, and (ii) if $(H_{[\tau_i]}, m, \tau) \models^d_F \psi$, then $(H_{[\tau_k]}, m, \tau) \not\models \psi$.

Proof (idea). By mutual structural induction over ψ. The implication is shown to hold for each MTGL operator. See Section B.1 for the complete proof. □

In the following, we discuss the second important result of this section, *i.e.*, the equivalence of the definite and regular semantics.

The satisfaction decision for future temporal operators at time point τ may depend on a $\tau' > \tau$. The upper bound of the distance between τ' and τ is given by the *non-definiteness window*, defined below.

Definition 7 (non-definiteness window w). *Given an MTGC ψ, the non-definiteness window w, i.e., the period for which a satisfaction decision for ψ at a time point τ may be non-definite, is defined as follows.*

$$w(\psi) = \begin{cases} r(I) + \max\left(w(\chi), w(\omega)\right) & \text{if } \psi = \chi \, U_I \, \omega \\ \max\left(w(\chi), w(\omega)\right) & \text{if } \psi = \chi \, S_I \, \omega \\ \max\left(w(\chi), w(\omega)\right) & \text{if } \psi = \chi \wedge \omega \\ w(\chi) & \text{if } \psi = \neg \chi \\ w(\chi) & \text{if } \psi = \exists(n, \chi) \\ 0 & \text{if } \psi = \text{true} \end{cases} \tag{7}$$

As usual in (online) RM, we assume that $w \neq \infty$, *i.e.*, MTGCs contain no unbounded future operators which may render a property non-monitorable [42].

Based on w, we present a variation of Theorem 1 which states that, given an $H_{[\tau_i]}$, if $\tau \in [0, \tau_i - w]$, with i an index in a RTM^H-trace, then definite decisions made by either the definite satisfaction relation $\models^d$ or definite falsification relation $\models^d_F$ are equivalent to the decisions of the satisfaction relation $\models$. If $w \neq 0$, in order for $[0, \tau_i - w]$ to be a valid interval, it is implicitly required that $\tau_i \geq w$, *i.e.*, $H_{[\tau_i]}$ covers a period that is larger than the non-definiteness window.

Theorem 2 (definite relations are equivalent to satisfaction relation over certain period of trace). *Let ψ be an MTGC over a pattern n and w the non-definiteness window of ψ. Moreover, let $h_{\tau_D}^H$ be an RTM^H-trace, with $\mathcal{D} \in \mathbb{N}^+$. For all $i \in [1, \mathcal{D}] \cap \mathbb{N}^+$, if m is a match for n in $H_{[\tau_i]}$ and $\tau \in [0, \tau_i - w]$, then for all $k \in [i, \mathcal{D}] \cap \mathbb{N}^+$, (i) $(H_{[\tau_i]}, m, \tau) \models^d \psi$ iff $(H_{[\tau_k]}, m, \tau) \models \psi$, and (ii) $(H_{[\tau_i]}, m, \tau) \models^d_F \psi$ iff $(H_{[\tau_k]}, m, \tau) \not\models \psi$.*

Proof (idea). By mutual structural induction over ψ. The equivalence is shown to hold for each MTGL operator. See Section B.2 for the complete proof. □

Theorem 2 enables our contribution to change-driven evaluation in Section 5.

Finally, we present the third important result of the section, *i.e.*, the limitation of the semantics. The following corollary states that all time points for which a definite decision cannot be made belong to a certain period in the observed trace.

Corollary 1 (period in trace with non-definite decisions). *Let ψ be an MTGC, w be the non-definiteness window of ψ, $H_{[\tau_i]}$ be an RTM^H instance associated with the time point τ_i, m be a match for a pattern n, and τ a time point in $[0, \tau_i]$. If $(H_{[\tau_i]}, m, \tau) \not\models^d \psi$ and $(H_{[\tau_i]}, m, \tau) \not\models^d_F \psi$, then $\tau \in (\tau_i - w, \tau_i]$.*

Proof (idea). Follows from Theorem 2—see Section B.3 for the complete proof. □

We demonstrate below that, in case an MTGC is unsatisfiable (or unfalsifiable), the definite relations may return an answer with a delay. The maximum possible delay depends on the non-definiteness window w from Definition 7.

Let $\models_{\mathbb{T}}$ and $\models_{F,\mathbb{T}}$ be respectively a satisfaction and falsification relation for MTGL that reflect the *timeliest knowledge*: Given a match m, an MTGC ψ, an RTM^H instance $H_{[\tau_i]}$ from a sequence of instances, and a time point $\tau \in [0, \tau_i]$, $(H_{[\tau_i]}, m, \tau) \models_{\mathbb{T}} \psi$ if $(H_{[\tau_i]}, m, \tau) \models \psi$ and there exists no possible successor of $H_{[\tau_i]}$ in the sequence that could falsify ψ at τ; analogously, $(H_{[\tau_i]}, m, \tau) \models_{F,\mathbb{T}} \psi$ if $(H_{[\tau_i]}, m, \tau) \not\models \psi$ and there exists no possible successor of $H_{[\tau_i]}$ that could satisfy ψ at τ. These timeliest relations can only make decisions for m over the observed trace, as m may not exist in the parts covered by successors of $H_{[\tau_i]}$, *i.e.*, in time points larger than τ_i.

Given a sequence of RTM^H instances h^H with $H_{[\tau_i]}$ an instance in h^H, let $H_{[\tau_k]}$ be the first successor of $H_{[\tau_i]}$ in h^H for which $\tau_k \geq \tau_i + w$. The following corollary states that, contrary to $\models_{\mathbb{T}}$ and $\models_{F,\mathbb{T}}$, the definite relations may have to wait for $H_{[\tau_k]}$ to be able to make a definite decision for $\tau \in (\tau_i - w, \tau_i]$.

Corollary 2 (maximum possible delay before definite decision). *Let ψ be an MTGC, w be the non-definiteness window of ψ, m be a match for a pattern n, and $H_{[\tau_i]}$ be an RTM^H instance from a sequence of RTM^H instances $h_{\tau_{\mathcal{D}}}^H$ with $i \in [1, \mathcal{D}] \cap \mathbb{N}^+$. Moreover, let $\tau \in (\tau_i - w, \tau_i]$ and k be the smallest index in $[i, \mathcal{D}] \cap \mathbb{N}^+$ such that $\tau_k \geq \tau_i + w$. If $(H_{[\tau_i]}, m, \tau) \not\models^d \psi$ and $(H_{[\tau_i]}, m, \tau) \not\models_F^d \psi$, then a definite decision for τ can be made over $H_{[\tau_k]}$.*

Proof. Follows from Corollary 1.   □

Thus, compared to $\models_\mathbb{T}$ and $\models_{F,\mathbb{T}}$, the definite relations may make a decision for $\tau \in (\tau_i - w, \tau_i]$ with a delay of at most $(\tau_k - \tau_i)$ time points.

Example 2. (delay in definite decision) Let $\psi_c := \Diamond_{[0,1]}(\neg \exists n_1 \wedge \exists n_1)$. Consider an RTM^H-trace comprising two RTM^H instances: $H_{[7]}$ in Fig. 3 and a hypothetical $H_{[9]}$ which is yielded by an unrelated change and all elements from $H_{[7]}$ are unchanged. Therefore, a match m_1 exists in both instances. The check $(H_{[7]}, m_1, 7) \models_{F,\mathbb{T}} \psi_c$ returns true, as $(H_{[7]}, m_1, 7) \not\models \psi_c$ and there is no possible successor of $H_{[7]}$ that could satisfy ψ_c; on the other hand, $(H_{[7]}, m_1, 7) \models_F^d \psi_c$ makes no decision, as according to its definition, the relation waits first for a duration of history that covers the timing constraint of *until* to be observed. The check $(H_{[9]}, m_1, 7) \models_F^d \psi_c$ returns true, as enough time has elapsed. Thus, compared to $\models_{F,\mathbb{T}}$, this decision has been made with a delay of two time points.

Avoiding this delay would require that the definite relations recognize whether an MTGC is satisfiable which is undecidable for NGCs and thus MTGCs. The delay is not observed with the running example, *i.e.*, $\psi_P := \neg \exists n_{1.1} \, \mathrm{U}_{[0,60]} \exists n_{1.2}$ or similar MTGCs, *e.g.*, $(\Diamond_{[0,2]} \exists n_{1.1}) \wedge (\Diamond_{[0,3]} \exists n_{1.2})$.

4   Computations and Answer Set for Definite Semantics

This section presents our contribution to the semantics of $\mathcal{L}$, the query language of INTEMPO. Specifically, we adjust the satisfaction computation presented in Definition 4 to the definite satisfaction relation ($\models^d$) from Definition 6. Moreover, we introduce the analogous concepts for the definite falsification relation ($\models_F^d$). Theorem 3 shows the soundness of the introduced computations. Based on these computations, we introduce a definite answer set for $\mathcal{L}$.

In the context of a temporal query (n, ψ) the *definite satisfaction span* related to a match m for n in $H_{[c]}$ is defined similarly to the satisfaction span $\mathcal{Y}$ in Section 2.3, *i.e.*, $\mathcal{Y}^d = \{\tau | \tau \in \mathbb{R} \wedge (H_{[c]}, m, \tau) \models^d \psi\}$. The *definite falsification span* is defined as $\mathcal{F}^d = \{\tau | \tau \in \mathbb{R} \wedge (H_{[c]}, m, \tau) \models_F^d \psi\}$. Any time point in the time domain not in $\mathcal{Y}^d$ or $\mathcal{F}$ belongs to the *unknown span* X. The sets $\mathcal{Y}^d, \mathcal{F}^d$, and X are disjoint. It also holds that $\mathbb{R} = \mathcal{Y}^d \uplus \mathcal{F}^d \uplus X$. The *definite satisfaction computation* $\mathcal{Z}^d$ and the *definite falsification computation* F^d for an MTGC are defined below.

Definition 8 (definite satisfaction computation $\mathcal{Z}^d$ and definite falsification computation F^d). *Let $n, \hat{n}$ be patterns and ψ, χ, ω be MTGCs. Moreover, let m be a match for n in an RTM^H H, and $\hat{M}$ a set of matches for $\hat{n}$ that are compatible with the (enclosing) match m. The* definite satisfaction computation $\mathcal{Z}^d(m, \psi)$ *and* definite falsification computation $F^d(m, \psi)$ *are defined via mutual recursion as follows.*

$$\mathcal{Z}^d(m, \text{true}) = \mathbb{R} \tag{8}$$

$$\mathcal{Z}^d(m, \neg\chi) = F^d(m, \chi) \tag{9}$$

$$\mathcal{Z}^d(m, \chi \wedge \omega) = \mathcal{Z}^d(m, \chi) \cap \mathcal{Z}^d(m, \omega) \tag{10}$$

$$\mathcal{Z}^d(m, \exists(\hat{n}, \chi)) = (-\infty, \tau] \cap \bigcup_{\hat{m} \in \hat{M}} \lambda^{\hat{m}} \cap \mathcal{Z}^d(\hat{m}, \chi) \tag{11}$$

$$\mathcal{Z}^d(m, \chi \mathrm{U}_I \omega) = \begin{cases} \bigcup_{i \in \mathcal{Z}^d(m,\omega), j \in J_i^d} j \cap \left((j^+ \cap i) \ominus I\right) & \text{if } 0 \notin I \\ \bigcup_{i \in \mathcal{Z}^d(m,\omega)} i \cup \bigcup_{j \in J_i^d} j \cap \left((j^+ \cap i) \ominus I\right) & \text{if } 0 \in I \end{cases} \tag{12}$$

$$\mathcal{Z}^d(m, \chi \mathrm{S}_I \omega) = \begin{cases} \bigcup_{i \in \mathcal{Z}^d(m,\omega), j \in J_i^d} j \cap \left((^+j \cap i) \oplus I\right) & \text{if } 0 \notin I \\ \bigcup_{i \in \mathcal{Z}^d(m,\omega)} i \cup \bigcup_{j \in J_i^d} j \cap \left((^+j \cap i) \oplus I\right) & \text{if } 0 \in I \end{cases} \tag{13}$$

with J_i^d the set of all intervals in $\mathcal{Z}^d(m, \chi)$ that are either overlapping or adjacent to some $i \in \mathcal{Z}^d(m, \omega)$.

Based on $\mathbb{R} = \mathcal{Y}^d \uplus \mathcal{F}^d \uplus X$, the definite falsification computation $F^d(m, \psi)$ can be generally defined as $F^d = \mathbb{R} \setminus (\mathcal{Z}^d \uplus X)$, which leads to the following equations.

$$F^d(m, \text{true}) = \emptyset \tag{14}$$

$$F^d(m, \neg\chi) = \mathcal{Z}^d(m, \chi) \tag{15}$$

$$F^d(m, \chi \wedge \omega) = F^d(m, \chi) \cup F^d(m, \omega) \tag{16}$$

$$F^d(m, \exists(\hat{n}, \chi)) = (-\infty, \tau] \cap \left(\mathbb{R} \setminus \mathcal{Z}^d(m, \exists(\hat{n}, \chi))\right) \tag{17}$$

$$F^d(m, \chi \mathrm{U}_I \omega) = \begin{cases} \mathbb{R} \setminus \left(\bigcup_{i \in \mathcal{Z}^d(m,\omega) \uplus X(m,\omega), j \in J_i^d} j \cap \left((j^+ \cap i) \ominus I\right)\right) & \text{if } 0 \notin I \\ \mathbb{R} \setminus \left(\bigcup_{i \in \mathcal{Z}^d(m,\omega) \uplus X(m,\omega)} i \cup \bigcup_{j \in J_i^d} j \cap \left((j^+ \cap i) \ominus I\right)\right) & \text{if } 0 \in I \end{cases} \tag{18}$$

$$F^d(m, \chi \mathrm{S}_I \omega) = \begin{cases} \mathbb{R} \setminus \left(\bigcup_{i \in \mathcal{Z}^d(m,\omega) \uplus X(m,\omega), j \in J_i^d} j \cap \left((^+j \cap i) \oplus I\right)\right) & \text{if } 0 \notin I \\ \mathbb{R} \setminus \left(\bigcup_{i \in \mathcal{Z}^d(m,\omega) \uplus X(m,\omega)} i \cup \bigcup_{j \in J_i^d} j \cap \left((^+j \cap i) \oplus I\right)\right) & \text{if } 0 \in I \end{cases} \tag{19}$$

where J_i^d is the set of all intervals in $Z^d(m, \chi) \uplus X(m, \chi)$ that are either overlapping or adjacent to some $i \in Z^d(m, \omega) \uplus X(m, \omega)$.

Regarding Z^d, the equations for conjunction, *until*, and *since* have the same structure with their corresponding equations in Definition 4, but rely on Z^d instead of Z. Analogously to $\models^d$, the computation for negation relies on F^d. The computation for *exists* confines its decisions to the period that has been observed.

Regarding F^d, a match m never falsifies *true*; analogously to $\models_F^d$, F^d relies on Z^d for the falsification of negation; the operator *exists* confines its computation to the observed period; the equations for *until* and *since* complement their respective definite satisfaction computations, whereby the definite satisfaction computation for their operands χ and ω instead of considering only time points that definitely satisfy χ and ω, *i.e.*, their satisfaction spans $Z^d(m, \chi)$ and $Z^d(m, \omega)$, considers time points *that do not definitely falsify* χ and ω, *i.e.*, $Z^d(m, \chi) \uplus X(m, \chi)$ and $Z^d(m, \omega) \uplus X(m, \omega)$.

The following theorem states that the set of time points in the definite satisfaction span $\mathcal{Y}^d$ and definite falsification span $\mathcal{F}^d$ are equal to the sets of time points obtained by the definite satisfaction computation Z^d and definite falsification computation F^d, respectively.

Theorem 3 (equality of definite spans and definite computations for satisfaction and falsification). *Given a match m in an RTM^H $H_{\lceil \tau \rceil}$ and an MTGC ψ, it holds that $\mathcal{Y}^d(m, \psi) = Z^d(m, \psi)$ and $\mathcal{F}^d(m, \psi) = F^d(m, \psi)$.*

Proof (idea). The proof for Z^d proceeds by structural induction over ψ. The proof for F^d is based on the application of $F^d = \mathbb{R} \setminus (Z^d \uplus X)$ for each MTGL operator. See Section B.4 for the complete proof.   □

Based on the definite computations, we now extend $\mathcal{L}$ with a notion of definite answers by adjusting the answer set $\mathcal{T}$ in Definition 5. To this end, we define the notion of *temporal invalidity* $\mathcal{IV}$ as the dual notion of temporal validity $\mathcal{V}$ from Section 2.3, *i.e.*, the intersection of the lifespan λ^m of a match m with the falsification span. Moreover, we define the *definite temporal validity* $\mathcal{V}^d$ as $\lambda^m \cap Z^d$, and the *definite temporal invalidity* $\mathcal{IV}^d$ as $\lambda^m \cap F^d$.

Definition 9 (definite answer set $\mathcal{T}^d$). *Given a pattern n, an MTGC ψ, and an RTM^H H, the definite answer set $\mathcal{T}^d$ of a query in $\mathcal{L}$ over H is given by:*

$$\mathcal{T}^d(H) = \{(m, \mathcal{V}^d(m, \psi), \mathcal{IV}^d(m, \psi)) | m \text{ is a match for } n \wedge (\mathcal{V}^d \neq \emptyset \vee \mathcal{IV}^d \neq \emptyset\}$$

Example 3 (precision of definite computations over incomplete trace). As in Example 1, the query $(n_1, \neg\psi_P)$ is evaluated over $H_{[7]}$. This time however, we obtain the definite answer set $\mathcal{T}^d(H_{[7]})$. The match m_2 for n_1, that involves the object pm2, is not contained in $\mathcal{T}^d$; m_2 is matched and its lifespan is computed to be $\lambda^{m_2} = [7, \infty)$ but no compatible match for $n_{1.2}$ is found; As shown in Table 1, $Z^d(m_2, \psi_P) = (-\infty, -53]$ and $F^d(m_2, \psi_P) = \emptyset$. Therefore, both $\mathcal{V}^d$ and $\mathcal{IV}^d$ are empty, and the match is excluded from $\mathcal{T}^d$. Note that $\mathcal{T}^d(H_{[7]})$ contains

Table 1: Computations $\mathcal{Z}$, $\mathcal{Z}^d$, and F^d for two matches for $(n_1, \neg\psi_P)$ over $H_{[7]}$.

MTGC	m_1			m_2		
	$\mathcal{Z}$	$\mathcal{Z}^d$	F^d	$\mathcal{Z}$	$\mathcal{Z}^d$	F^d
true	$\mathbb{R}$	$\mathbb{R}$	$\emptyset$	$\mathbb{R}$	$\mathbb{R}$	$\emptyset$
$\exists n_{1.1}$	$\emptyset$	$\emptyset$	$(-\infty, 7]$	$\emptyset$	$\emptyset$	$(-\infty, 7]$
$\neg\exists n_{1.1}$	$\mathbb{R}$	$(-\infty, 7]$	$\emptyset$	$\mathbb{R}$	$(-\infty, 7]$	$\emptyset$
true	$\mathbb{R}$	$\mathbb{R}$	$\emptyset$	$\mathbb{R}$	$\mathbb{R}$	$\emptyset$
$\exists n_{1.2}$	$[5, 7)$	$[5, 7)$	$\{(-\infty, 5), [7, 7]\}$	$\emptyset$	$\emptyset$	$(-\infty, 7]$
ψ_P	$[-55, 7)$	$[-55, 7)$	$\{(-\infty, -55), [7, 7]\}$	$\emptyset$	$\emptyset$	$(-\infty, -53]$
$\neg\psi_P$	$\{(-\infty, -55), [7, \infty)\}$	$\{(-\infty, -55), [7, 7]\}$	$[-55, 7)$	$\mathbb{R}$	$(-\infty, -53]$	$\emptyset$

a match m_1 for n_1 that involves pm1, as its $\mathcal{V}^d$ is non-empty (see Table 1), *i.e.*, there are time points for which m_1 definitely falsifies $\neg\psi_P$, or definitely satisfies ψ_P. All computations in Table 1 are interval sets (see Section 2.3), however, for presentation purposes, singletons are displayed as intervals.

Let $H_{[67]}$ be an RTM^H that is yielded by an event at time point 67; the changes by this event do not affect vertices or nodes in $H_{[7]}$; m_2 would be returned by $\mathcal{T}^d$, paired with $\mathcal{V}^d = [7, 7]$, as there would be no future version of the RTM^H which could satisfy ψ_P at time point 7.

5   Keeping to Change-driven Evaluation

The operationalization of queries in INTEMPO (see also Fig. 1) is based on *Generalized Discrimination Networks* (GDNs) [28, 10]. Specifically, a query in $\mathcal{L}$ is decomposed into a suitable ordering, *i.e.*, a *network*, N of simple sub-queries. N is a tree where each node represents a query and each edge a dependency between queries—see Fig. 2 (right) for the GDN for ψ_P. N is executed bottom-up, *i.e.*, the execution starts with leaves and proceeds upward. The root of N computes the answer set $\mathcal{T}(H)$ of q. Each node in N stores intermediate matches paired with their $\mathcal{Z}$; therefore N is amenable to *change-driven* and incremental execution: changes to H are propagated through N, whose nodes only recompute their stored matches if the change is relevant to them or one of their dependencies. Moreover, INTEMPO offers a method to remove temporally irrelevant history from the RTM^H, thereby rendering the query evaluation memory-efficient.

Based on these features, an extensive experimental evaluation of our implementation of INTEMPO showed efficient performance in the evaluation of temporal graph queries over considerably large models (approximately from 10K to 48M elements) [49]. INTEMPO also evaluated queries faster than the established RV tool MONPOLY [6] as well as the RTM-based tool HAWK [24] in an RM application scenario. In the scenario, incomplete traces were handled by performing a check for each match which, based on the timing constraints of the property, postponed returning the match if future changes could affect it.

The definite answer set $\mathcal{T}^d$ from Definition 9 handles incomplete traces comprehensively, as it only includes matches and time points which no future change can affect. However, $\mathcal{T}^d$ relies on the definite MTGL semantics from Definition 6 which, contrary to the regular semantics from Definition 3, considers the time point on which a query is evaluated; consequently, adjusting N to compute the definite computations $\mathcal{Z}^d$ and F^d, and thus to return $\mathcal{T}^d$, would imply that every new version of $H_{[\tau]}$ would trigger a re-computation of all spans stored in N. Therefore, $\mathcal{T}^d$ is not amenable to change-driven evaluation.

Based on the intuition behind the check from above, we lastly present a new answer set, called *effective*, that contains definite results while relying on $\mathcal{T}$, which *is* amenable to change-driven evaluation. Specifically, based on the equivalence in Theorem 2, we show that $\mathcal{T}$ is equivalent to a subset of $\mathcal{T}^d$ if the $\mathcal{V}$ of matches in $\mathcal{T}$ is restricted to a period with definite decisions (see Corollary 1). This last contribution formalizes the intuition behind the check from above, and allows approaches like INTEMPO to maintain their efficiency while returning sound results. We define the effective answer set $\mathcal{T}^e$ for $\mathcal{L}$ based on $\mathcal{T}$ below.

Definition 10 (effective answer set $\mathcal{T}^e$). *Given a pattern n, an MTGC ψ with w the non-definiteness window of ψ, an RTM^H $H_{[\tau]}$, and an answer set $\mathcal{T}(H_{[\tau]})$ of a query in $\mathcal{L}$, the effective answer set $\mathcal{T}^e(H_{[\tau]})$ of the query is the set of all tuples $(m, \mathcal{V} \cap [0, \tau - w])$ such that (i) $(m, \mathcal{V}(m, \psi)) \in \mathcal{T}(H_{[\tau]})$ and (ii) $\mathcal{V}(m, \psi) \cap [0, \tau - w] \neq \emptyset$.*

The following theorem states that $\mathcal{T}^e$ is equal to a restricted version of $\mathcal{T}^d$ whose $\mathcal{V}^d$ excludes a period equal to w. We assume that the trace duration is larger than w and that the trace has more than one member.

Theorem 4 (equality of effective answer set and restricted definite temporal validity answer set over trace). *Let (n, ψ) be a query with ψ an MTGC, w be the non-definiteness window of ψ, and $h_{\tau_{\mathcal{D}}}^H$ be a RTM^H-trace with $\mathcal{D} \in [2, \infty] \cap \mathbb{N}^+$, and i be an index in $[k, \mathcal{D} - 1] \cap \mathbb{N}^+$ such that $\tau_k \geq w$. Moreover, let $\mathcal{T}_{\mathcal{V},r}^d(H_{[\tau_i]})$ be the restricted definite temporal validity answer set over $H_{[\tau_i]}$ which has been obtained from the definite answer set $\mathcal{T}^d$ but contains (i) only pairs of matches with their temporal validity $\mathcal{V}^d$, with $\mathcal{V}^d \neq \emptyset$ and (ii) $\mathcal{V}^d$ is intersected with $[0, \tau_i - w]$. Then, $\mathcal{T}^e(H_{[\tau_i]}) = \mathcal{T}_{\mathcal{V},r}^d(H_{[\tau_i]})$.*

Proof (idea). Based on the more general Theorem 2. See Section B.5 for the complete proof.   □

Theorem 4 shows how INTEMPO returns definite results while using the change-driven evaluation for $\mathcal{T}$ described above. On the other hand, as $\mathcal{T}_{\mathcal{V},r}^d$ excludes F^d, obtaining F^d with $\mathcal{T}^e$ requires the evaluation of a separate query $(n, \neg\psi)$ in parallel to (n, ψ). Moreover, due to postponing returning answers that may be non-definite, $\mathcal{T}^e$ may return answers with a delay; although this is not observed in ψ_P from the running example, it may affect other properties, as demonstrated in Example 4. Hence, $\mathcal{T}^e$ is intended for application scenarios where this impact is either absent or acceptable.

Example 4 (Delay in detection). Let $\psi_D := (\neg\exists n_{1.1})\wedge(\neg\Diamond_{[0,2]}\exists n_{1.2})$ be an MTGC and $(n_1, \neg\psi_D)$ a query in $\mathcal{L}$. Let $H_{[5]}$ be a hypothetical RTM^H that contains a match for n_1 and a match for $n_{1.1}$, whose lifespans are $[5, \infty)$. The time point 5 is contained in $\mathcal{V}^d(m_1, \neg\psi_D)$, *i.e.*, the decision for 5 is definite; however, this time point is not admitted to $\mathcal{T}^e(H_{[5]})$ due to the intersection with $[0, 5 - w]$, where, for ψ_D, $w = 2$. The time point will be admitted to $\mathcal{T}^e$ when w has elapsed.

6   Related Work

In our previous work, we presented an analysis procedure with preliminary support for RM of MTGL, as the procedure can be adjusted so that it returns true either as soon as a falsification is detected or only when it has become definite [51]. When a falsification is detected, the procedure returns the time point on which the procedure was last executed. The result abstracts the interval-based semantics of MTGL into a point-based interpretation which lacks precision. The definite semantics from Section 3 supports RM of MTGL directly, *i.e.*, at the level of semantics. Moreover, it enables the computations of the definite falsification and satisfaction spans, which in turn enable practical query evaluations.

Compared to INTEMPO and its advancement we presented, other query-based approaches for RM over structural RTMs either lack a formal treatment of monitoring, *e.g.*, [24, 1], or do not support other key features, *e.g.*, first-order quantification [19], temporal operators [14, 13], or timing constraints [40]. On the other hand, these approaches have their own advantages over the foundations we presented, *e.g.*, support for distributed query evaluation [14] and more temporal primitives [24].

Runtime Verification (RV) is also concerned with formally precise online RM over incrementally processed, and thus possibly incomplete, traces of events. Despite the similarity of their aim, RV and RTMs are different in their applications and characteristics: for instance, state representations in RV focus on a low level of abstraction and are typically inaccessible during monitoring. Conversely, an RTM aims at a richer knowledge representation [14] and has to be accessible to end-users or other technologies during monitoring, as it acts as an interface to manage the system [23]—see [47, 49] for a more elaborate comparison. In RV, properties may be specified using various formalisms, *e.g.*, temporal logics and regular expressions [3], comparisons among which are non-trivial [33, 43]. In the following, we focus on approaches based on temporal logics. According to a recent classification, no approach simultaneously supports key features of INTEMPO such as first-order quantification, metric temporal constraints, interval-based interpretations, and native support for graph queries and bindings [22].

The RV approach most relevant to our work is MONPOLY [6]. MONPOLY, an established tool that has been among the top-performers in an RV competition [2], is an implementation of an incremental monitoring algorithm based on *Metric First-Order Temporal Logic* (MFOTL) [7]. The semantics of MFOTL is point-based, *i.e.*, the logic assesses the truth of a formula only for the time points of events in a trace, which means the logic cannot support the computation of a temporal validity or represent the lifespan of a match straightforwardly. MONPOLY cannot always encode complex graph queries: for instance, expressing the MTGC from the running example, which prohibits the existence of a pattern, is not possible as MONPOLY restricts the use of negation in this place at the formula for reasons of monitorability. Even when possible, this encoding may become overly technical and, as indicated by the performance comparison of INTEMPO to MONPOLY [49] as well as another similar comparison [19], may affect performance: for instance, emulating graph pattern matching requires that partial orderings of match candidates are explicitly formulated in MFOTL which may bloat the size of the formula.

The RV tool DEJAVU [31, 30] monitors properties specified in a first-order metric past-only logic with point-based semantics. Translating MTGCs in this logic would require emulating graph-based encodings and bindings (similar to MONPOLY) and, moreover, reformulating MTGCs such that they feature only past operators. Such reformulations are not always possible and could be significantly less compact [37, 32]. Monitoring algorithms for interval-based propositional or signal logics with metric timing constraints [5, 38] are capable of interval-based interpretations; although inapplicable to a graph-based first-order setting, they are therefore based on interval computations which are similar to ours. Havelund et al. present a monitoring approach for a logic defined over intervals; properties in the logic refer to interval relations, *e.g.*, requiring that two intervals overlap, where the intervals my contain data [29]. The logic supports quantification over intervals but does not support quantification over the data.

7   Conclusion and Future Work

We present a formal and systematic treatment of incomplete traces in query-based runtime monitoring of temporal properties over structural runtime models. First, we introduce a new semantics for a first-order temporal graph logic, called definite, which only returns decisions if no future change to the model will affect them. Then, based on the definite semantics, we introduce a new definite answer set for the query language of INTEMPO, a querying scheme we previously presented. Lastly, we present the effective answer set which, contrary to the definite answer set, is amenable to change-driven evaluation. This answer set allows approaches like INTEMPO to maintain their efficiency while returning definite answers.

Our plans for future work include a consideration of a rewriting procedure for properties in MTGL, such that the rewritten properties avoid or minimize possible delays in returning results, while allowing for a comparable performance to the property before rewriting. We plan to extend the API of the INTEMPO implementation with the option to return the effective answer set directly. Moreover, we plan to implement the definite answer set and investigate its impact on performance. Although not as efficient as the effective answer set, we also plan to use the definite answer set for testing the answers in the effective answer set. Finally, we plan to extend INTEMPO with a decision procedure that, depending on the property, switches to the answer set that is more appropriate.

A Overview of Notation

The overview is shown in Table 2.

B Proofs

Following are the proofs for the theorems in the paper, as presented in the doctoral thesis of the first author [47].

B.1 Theorem 1: definite relations imply satisfaction relation over trace

Following is the proof for Theorem 1 (see [47, Section A.3.2]), *i.e.*, given an MTGC ψ over a pattern n and an RTM^H-trace $h_{\tau_D}^H$ with $D \in \mathbb{N}^+$ the last index, for all $i \in [1, D] \cap \mathbb{N}^+$, if m a match for n in $H_{[\tau_i]}$ and $\tau \in [0, \tau_i]$, then for all $k \in [i, D] \cap \mathbb{N}^+$, (i) if $(H_{[\tau_i]}, m, \tau) \models^d \psi$, then $(H_{[\tau_k]}, m, \tau) \models \psi$, and (ii) if $(H_{[\tau_i]}, m, \tau) \models^d_F \psi$, then $(H_{[\tau_k]}, m, \tau) \not\models \psi$.

Proof. By definition of the RTM^H, a match m in $H_{[\tau_i]}$ will be structurally present in all $H_{[\tau_k]}$ with $k \in [i, D] \cap \mathbb{N}^+$—what may change (once) in future versions of $H_{[\tau_i]}$ is the lifespan of m, *i.e.*, if the *dts* of all matched elements is ∞ and one of these elements is updated to a value less than ∞; even then, this change will not affect the lifespan of m in the period $[0, \tau_i]$, that is, in $H_{[\tau_i]}$, the observation on whether m is present in $\lambda^m \cap [0, \tau_i]$ will never be refuted.

The proof proceeds by mutual structural induction over ψ. In the base case, we show the theorem to be true for the MTGL operator *true*. We omit the straightforward step for conjunction.

– *Base case: true.*
  We begin with the definite satisfaction. We assume $(H_{[\tau_i]}, m, \tau) \models^d$ *true* and show that $(H_{[\tau_k]}, m, \tau) \models$ *true* for an arbitrary $k \in [i, D] \cap \mathbb{N}^+$. By the semantics of MTGL, *true* is always satisfied. Therefore, m in $H_{[\tau_k]}$ also satisfies *true* at τ. We have shown that the implication is true.
  We proceed with the definite falsification. Based on the semantics of the definite falsification relation, a match m never falsifies *true*. Therefore, the antecedent $(H_{[\tau_i]}, m, \tau) \models^d_F$ *true* is false, making the consequent $(H_{[\tau_k]}, m, \tau) \not\models$ *true* true.
– *Induction step: $\psi = \neg\chi$.*
  We begin with the definite satisfaction. Assume that $(H_{[\tau_i]}, m, \tau) \models^d_F \chi \Rightarrow (H_{[\tau_k]}, m, \tau) \not\models \chi$ for an arbitrary $k \in [i, D] \cap \mathbb{N}^+$. By the semantics of negation and the definite relations, $(H_{[\tau_i]}, m, \tau) \models^d_F \chi \Leftrightarrow (H_{[\tau_i]}, m, \tau) \models^d \neg\chi$. Similarly, $(H_{[\tau_k]}, m, \tau) \not\models \chi \Leftrightarrow (H_{[\tau_k]}, m, \tau) \models \neg\chi$. Therefore, it also holds that $(H_{[\tau_i]}, m, \tau) \models^d \neg\chi \Rightarrow (H_{[\tau_k]}, m, \tau) \models \neg\chi$.
  We proceed with the definite falsification. Assume that $(H_{[\tau_i]}, m, \tau) \models^d \chi \Rightarrow (H_{[\tau_k]}, m, \tau) \models \chi$. Analogously to the definite satisfaction, $(H_{[\tau_i]}, m, \tau) \models^d \chi \Leftrightarrow (H_{[\tau_i]}, m, \tau) \models^d_F \neg\chi$ and $(H_{[\tau_k]}, m, \tau) \models \chi \Leftrightarrow (H_{[\tau_k]}, m, \tau) \not\models \neg\chi$. Therefore, $(H_{[\tau_i]}, m, \tau) \models^d_F \neg\chi \Rightarrow (H_{[\tau_k]}, m, \tau) \not\models \neg\chi$.

Symbol	Concept	Formal Representation	Def.
P	temporal property from running example	–	p. 3
G_τ	runtime model, at time point τ	typed attributed graph	p. 4
τ	time point	real number	p. 5
h_τ	event trace, spanning the interval $[0, \tau]$	sequence of events	p. 5
i	index of sequence member	natural number	p. 5
τ_i	time point at i-th member of sequence	real number	p. 5
$\mathcal{E}$	mapping from events to graph modifications	function	p. 6
$H_{[\tau]}$	runtime model with history, spanning the interval $[0, \tau]$	typed attributed graph	p. 6
h_τ^H	RTM^H-trace, spanning the interval $[0, \tau]$	sequence of runtime models with history	p. 6
ψ, χ, ω	temporal property	metric temporal graph condition	p. 6
$n, \hat{n}$	(graph) pattern	typed attributed graph	p. 6
$\models$	(regular) satisfaction relation of metric temporal graph logic	relation	p. 7
$m, \hat{m}$	match	morphism	p. 7
$\mathcal{L}$	query language of INTEMPO	set of queries	p. 7
E	set of matched vertices	set of vertices in given match	p. 7
e	matched vertex	vertex in E	p. 7
λ^m	lifespan of a match m	interval	p. 8
$\mathcal{Y}$	satisfaction span	interval set	p. 8
$\mathcal{Z}$	satisfaction computation	interval set	p. 8
$\mathcal{V}$	temporal validity	interval set	p. 8
$\hat{M}$	set of matches of $\hat{m}$ compatible to m	set of matches	p. 8
$\mathcal{T}$	(regular) answer set of $\mathcal{L}$	set of $(m, \mathcal{V})$ pairs	p. 9
$\models^d$	definite satisfaction relation	relation	p. 10
$\models_F^d$	definite falsification relation	relation	p. 10
c	current time point	real number	p. 10
$\mathcal{D}$	last member of sequence	natural number	p. 11
w	non-definiteness window	interval	p. 11
$\models_T$	timeliest satisfaction relation	relation	p. 12
$\models_{F,T}$	timeliest falsification relation	relation	p. 12
$\mathcal{Y}^d$	definite satisfaction span	interval set	p. 13
$\mathcal{Z}^d$	definite satisfaction computation	interval set	p. 13
$\mathcal{F}^d$	definite falsification span	interval set	p. 13
F^d	definite falsification computation	interval set	p. 13
X	unknown span	interval set	p. 13
$\mathcal{V}^d$	definite temporal validity	interval set	p. 15
$\mathcal{IV}$	temporal invalidity	interval set	p. 15
$\mathcal{IV}^d$	definite temporal invalidity	interval set	p. 15
$\mathcal{T}^d$	definite answer set of $\mathcal{L}$	set of $(m, \mathcal{V}^d, \mathcal{IV}^d)$ triples	p. 15
N	network	generalized discrimination network	p. 16
$\mathcal{T}_{\mathcal{V},r}^d$	restricted temporal validity answer set of $\mathcal{L}$	subset of $\mathcal{T}^d$ only with $\mathcal{V}^d$	p. 17
$\mathcal{T}^e$	effective answer set of $\mathcal{L}$	subset of $\mathcal{T}$ with $\mathcal{V}$ capped based on w	p. 17

Table 2: Main symbols, their denoted concept, and formal representation; the rightmost column shows the page on which the symbol was first defined.

- *Induction step*: $\psi = \exists(\hat{n}, \chi)$.

  Let the induction hypothesis be $(H_{[\tau_i]}, \hat{m}, \tau) \models^d \chi \Rightarrow (H_{[\tau_k]}, \hat{m}, \tau) \models \chi$ and $(H_{[\tau_i]}, \hat{m}, \tau) \models^d_F \chi \Rightarrow (H_{[\tau_k]}, \hat{m}, \tau) \not\models \chi$, where $\hat{m}$ is a match for the pattern $\hat{n}$ and k an arbitrary index in $[i, \mathcal{D}] \cap \mathbb{N}^+$.

  We begin with the definite satisfaction. We assume $(H_{[\tau_i]}, m, \tau) \models^d \exists(\hat{n}, \chi)$ and show this implies $(H_{[\tau_k]}, m, \tau) \models \exists(\hat{n}, \chi)$. Since $(H_{[\tau_i]}, m, \tau) \models^d \exists(\hat{n}, \chi)$, there exists matches m and $\hat{m}$ such that $\hat{m}$ is compatible with m and $\tau \in \lambda^m \cap \lambda^{\hat{m}}$. The matches $m, \hat{m}$ will be structurally present and $\hat{m}$ will be compatible with m in all future versions of $H_{[\tau_i]}$. Moreover, there will be no changes in $\lambda^m, \lambda^{\hat{m}}$ for the period $[0, \tau]$. Also, by the induction hypothesis, $\hat{m}$ satisfies χ at τ. Therefore, by the semantics of the satisfaction relation for *exists*, $(H_{[\tau_k]}, m, \tau) \models \exists(\hat{n}, \chi)$. We have shown that the implication is true.

  We proceed with the definite falsification. We assume that $(H_{[\tau_i]}, m, \tau) \models^d_F \exists(\hat{n}, \chi)$ and show that this implies $(H_{[\tau_k]}, m, \tau) \not\models \exists(\hat{n}, \chi)$. Since $(H_{[\tau_i]}, m, \tau) \models^d_F \exists(\hat{n}, \chi)$, (i) either there exists no $\hat{m}$ in $H_{[\tau_i]}$ such that $\hat{m}$ is compatible with m, or (ii) there exists $\hat{m}$ compatible with m, but $\tau \notin \lambda^m \cap \lambda^{\hat{m}}$, or (iii) there exists $\hat{m}$ compatible with m with $\tau \in \lambda^m \cap \lambda^{\hat{m}}$ but $\hat{m}$ definitely falsifies χ at τ. If (i) is true, it will be true in all future versions of $H_{[\tau_i]}$, as matches cannot be found retrospectively. If (ii) is true, the lifespan of $\lambda^{\hat{m}}$ in the period $[0, \tau_i]$ will not change in all future versions of $H_{[\tau_i]}$. Finally, if (iii) is true, we know from the induction hypothesis that $(\hat{m}, \tau) \not\models \chi$ also over $H_{[\tau_k]}$. Therefore, in any case, $(H_{[\tau_k]}, m, \tau) \not\models \exists(\hat{n}, \chi)$. We have shown that the implication is true.

- *Induction step*: $\psi = \chi \mathrm{U}_I \omega$.

  We begin with the definite satisfaction. Induction hypothesis: $(H_{[\tau_i]}, m, \tau) \models^d \chi \Rightarrow (H_{[\tau_k]}, m, \tau) \models \chi$ and $(H_{[\tau_i]}, m, \tau) \models^d \omega \Rightarrow (H_{[\tau_k]}, m, \tau) \models \omega$ with k an arbitrary index in $[i, \mathcal{D}] \cap \mathbb{N}^+$.

  We assume $(H_{[\tau_i]}, m, \tau) \models^d \chi \mathrm{U}_I \omega$ and show this implies $(H_{[\tau_k]}, m, \tau) \models \chi \mathrm{U}_I \omega$. Since $(H_{[\tau_i]}, m, \tau) \models^d \chi \mathrm{U}_I \omega$, there exists τ' such that $\tau' - \tau \in I$ and $(H_{[\tau_i]}, m, \tau') \models^d \omega$, and for all $\tau'' \in [\tau, \tau')$ $(H_{[\tau_i]}, m, \tau'') \models^d \chi$. The decisions for the time point τ' and for all time points τ'' either concern a match or not: if they do concern a match, then they are confined to $[0, \tau_i]$ and remain unaltered throughout the trace; if they do not concern a match, *e.g.*, they concern *true* or $\neg true$, then they again remain unaltered. Therefore, also over $H_{[\tau_k]}$ it will hold that at τ' $(H_{[\tau_k]}, m, \tau') \models \omega$, and for every τ'' $(H_{[\tau_k]}, m, \tau'') \models \chi$. Thus, by the semantics of the satisfaction relation for *until*, $(H_{[\tau_k]}, m, \tau) \models \chi \mathrm{U}_I \omega$. We have shown that the implication is true.

  We proceed with the definite falsification. Let the induction hypothesis be $(H_{[\tau_i]}, m, \tau) \models^d_F \chi \Rightarrow (H_{[\tau_k]}, m, \tau) \not\models \chi$ and $(H_{[\tau_i]}, m, \tau) \models^d_F \omega \Rightarrow (H_{[\tau_k]}, m, \tau) \not\models \omega$.

  We assume $(H_{[\tau_i]}, m, \tau) \models^d_F \chi \mathrm{U}_I \omega$ and show that this implies $(H_{[\tau_k]}, m, \tau) \not\models \chi \mathrm{U}_I \omega$. Since $(H_{[\tau_i]}, m, \tau) \models^d_F \chi \mathrm{U}_I \omega$, for all τ' such that $\tau' - \tau \in I$, either (i) $(H_{[\tau_i]}, m, \tau') \models^d_F \omega$ or (ii) there exists $\tau'' \in [\tau, \tau')$ such that $(H_{[\tau_i]}, m, \tau'') \models^d \chi$. Regardless of which is the case, *i.e.*, (i) or (ii) or both, analogously to the definite satisfaction, if the decisions for all τ' and at τ'' concern a match, they will remain unaltered, and so will they if they do not concern a match. Therefore, the case will also hold over $H_{[\tau_k]}$. Therefore, $(H_{[\tau_k]}, m, \tau) \not\models \chi U_I \omega$. We have shown that the implication is true.

– *Induction step*: $\psi = \chi S_I \omega$.

The proof proceeds analogously to *until*. We begin with the definite satisfaction. Let the induction hypothesis be $(H_{[\tau_i]}, m, \tau) \models^d \chi \Rightarrow (H_{[\tau_k]}, m, \tau) \models \chi$ and $(H_{[\tau_i]}, m, \tau) \models^d \omega \Rightarrow (H_{[\tau_k]}, m, \tau) \models \omega$ with k an arbitrary index in $[i, \mathcal{D}] \cap \mathbb{N}^+$. We assume $(H_{[\tau_i]}, m, \tau) \models^d \chi S_I \omega$ and show this implies $(H_{[\tau_k]}, m, \tau) \models \chi S_I \omega$. Since $(H_{[\tau_i]}, m, \tau) \models^d \chi S_I \omega$, there exists τ' such that $\tau - \tau' \in I$ and $(H_{[\tau_i]}, m, \tau') \models^d \omega$, and for all $\tau'' \in (\tau', \tau]$ $(H_{[\tau_i]}, m, \tau'') \models^d \chi$. The decisions for the time point τ' and all time points τ'' either concern a match or not: if they do concern a match, then they are confined to $[0, \tau_i]$ and remain unaltered throughout the trace; if they do not concern a match, then they will again remain unaltered. Therefore, also over $H_{[\tau_k]}$ it will hold that at τ' $(H_{[\tau_k]}, m, \tau') \models \omega$, and for all τ'' $(H_{[\tau_k]}, m, \tau'') \models \chi$. Thus by the semantics of the satisfaction relation for *since*, $(H_{[\tau_k]}, m, \tau) \models \chi S_I \omega$. We have shown that the implication is true.

We proceed with the definite falsification. Let the induction hypothesis be $(H_{[\tau_i]}, m, \tau) \models^d_F \chi \Rightarrow (H_{[\tau_k]}, m, \tau) \not\models \chi$ and $(H_{[\tau_i]}, m, \tau) \models^d_F \omega \Rightarrow (H_{[\tau_k]}, m, \tau) \not\models \omega$.

We assume $(H_{[\tau_i]}, m, \tau) \models^d_F \chi S_I \omega$ and show that this implies $(H_{[\tau_k]}, m, \tau) \not\models \chi S_I \omega$. Since $(H_{[\tau_i]}, m, \tau) \models^d_F \chi S_I \omega$, for all τ' such that $\tau - \tau' \in I$, either (i) $(H_{[\tau_i]}, m, \tau') \models^d_F \omega$ or (ii) there exists $\tau'' \in (\tau', \tau]$ such that $(H_{[\tau_i]}, m, \tau'') \models^d \chi$. Regardless of which is the case, *i.e.*, (i) or (ii) or both, analogously to the definite satisfaction, if the decisions for all τ' and at τ'' concern a match, they will remain unaltered, and so will they if they do not concern a match. Therefore, the case will also hold over $H_{[\tau_k]}$. Therefore, $(H_{[\tau_k]}, m, \tau) \not\models \chi S_I \omega$. We have shown that the implication is true.

From the base case and induction steps, it follows that Theorem 1 holds. □

B.2 Theorem 2: definite relations are equivalent to satisfaction relation over certain period of trace

Following is the proof for Theorem 2 (see [47, Section A.3.3]), that is, given an MTGC ψ over a pattern n, the non-definiteness w window of ψ, and a sequence of RTM^H instances $h^H_{\tau_{\mathcal{D}}}$ with $\mathcal{D} \in \mathbb{N}^+$ the last index, for all $i \in [1, \mathcal{D}] \cap \mathbb{N}^+$, if m a match for n in $H_{[\tau_i]}$ and $\tau \in [0, \tau_i - w]$, then for all $k \in [i, \mathcal{D}] \cap \mathbb{N}^+$, (i) $(H_{[\tau_i]}, m, \tau) \models^d \psi$ iff $(H_{[\tau_k]}, m, \tau) \models \psi$, and (ii) $(H_{[\tau_i]}, m, \tau) \models^d_F \psi$ iff $(H_{[\tau_k]}, m, \tau) \not\models \psi$.

By definition of the RTM^H, a match m in $H_{[\tau_i]}$ will be structurally present in all $H_{[\tau_k]}$ with $k \in [i, \mathcal{D}] \cap \mathbb{N}^+$—what may change (once) in future versions of $H_{[\tau_i]}$ is the lifespan of m, *i.e.*, if the *dts* of all matched elements is ∞ and one of these elements is updated to a value less than ∞; even then, this change will not affect the lifespan of m in the period $[0, \tau_i]$, that is, in $H_{[\tau_i]}$, the observation on whether m is present in $\lambda^m \cap [0, \tau_i]$ will never be refuted.

Proof. The direction $\Rightarrow$ of the equivalence has been shown by the more general Theorem 1, which concerned an arbitrary τ. We therefore focus on direction $\Leftarrow$ of the equivalence. As m is present in $H_{[\tau_i]}$, its lifespan λ^m in the period $[0, \tau_i]$ will remain unchanged in subsequent versions of $H_{[\tau_i]}$. In the following, the non-definiteness window w is computed according to Definition 7.

The proof proceeds by mutual structural induction over ψ. In the base case, we show the theorem to be true for the MTGL operator *true*. We omit the straightforward step for conjunction.

– *Base case: true.*

We begin with the satisfaction. We assume $(H_{[\tau_k]}, m, \tau) \models$ *true* for an arbitrary $k \in [i, \mathcal{D}] \cap \mathbb{N}^+$ and $\tau \in [0, \tau_i - w]$ with $w^{nd} = 0$, and show that this implies $(H_{[\tau_i]}, m, \tau) \models^d$ *true*. As *true* is always satisfied, m in $H_{[\tau_i]}$ definitely satisfies *true* at τ. Hence, the implication to be true.

We proceed with the falsification. Based on the semantics of satisfaction, a match m never satisfies $\not\models$ *true*. Therefore, the antecedent $(H_{[\tau_k]}, m, \tau) \not\models$ *true* is false, making the consequent $(H_{[\tau_i]}, m, \tau) \models^d_F$ *true* true.

– *Induction step:* $\psi = \neg\chi$.

We begin with the satisfaction. Let $(H_{[\tau_k]}, m, \tau) \not\models \chi \Rightarrow (H_{[\tau_i]}, m, \tau) \models^d_F \chi$ for an arbitrary $k \in [i, \mathcal{D}] \cap \mathbb{N}^+$ and $\tau \in [0, \tau_i - w]$ with $w(\neg\chi) = w(\chi)$. By the semantics of negation and the satisfaction relation, $(H_{[\tau_k]}, m, \tau) \not\models \chi \Leftrightarrow (H_{[\tau_k]} m, \tau) \models \neg\chi$. Similarly, $(H_{[\tau_i]}, m, \tau) \models^d_F \chi \Leftrightarrow (H_{[\tau_i]}, m, \tau) \models^d \neg\chi$. Therefore, it also holds that $(H_{[\tau_k]}, m, \tau) \models \neg\chi \Rightarrow (H_{[\tau_i]}, m, \tau) \models^d \neg\chi$.

We proceed with the falsification. Assume $(H_{[\tau_k]}, m, \tau) \models \chi \Rightarrow (H_{[\tau_i]}, m, \tau) \models^d \chi$. Analogously to the satisfaction, $(H_{[\tau_k]}, m, \tau) \models \chi \Leftrightarrow (H_{[\tau_i]}, m, \tau) \not\models \neg\chi$ and $(H_{[\tau_k]}, m, \tau) \models^d \chi \Leftrightarrow (H_{[\tau_i]}, m, \tau) \models^d_F \neg\chi$. Therefore, $(H_{[\tau_k]}, m, \tau) \not\models \neg\chi \Rightarrow (H_{[\tau_i]}, m, \tau) \models^d_F \neg\chi$.

– *Induction step:* $\psi = \exists(\hat{n}, \chi)$.

Let the induction hypothesis be $(H_{[\tau_k]}, \hat{m}, \tau) \models \chi \Rightarrow (H_{[\tau_i]}, \hat{m}, \tau) \models^d \chi$ and $(H_{[\tau_k]}, \hat{m}, \tau) \not\models \chi \Rightarrow (H_{[\tau_i]}, \hat{m}, \tau) \models^d_F \chi$, where $\hat{m}$ is a match for the pattern $\hat{n}$, k an arbitrary index in $[i, \mathcal{D}] \cap \mathbb{N}^+$, and $\tau \in [0, \tau_i - w]$. The non-definiteness window w is given by $w(\exists(\hat{n}, \chi)) = w(\chi)$.

We begin with the satisfaction. We assume that $(H_{[\tau_k]}, m, \tau) \models \exists(\hat{n}, \chi)$ and show that this implies $(H_{[\tau_i]}, m, \tau) \models^d \exists(\hat{n}, \chi)$. Since $(H_{[\tau_k]}, m, \tau) \models \exists(\hat{n}, \chi)$, there exists matches m and $\hat{m}$ in $H_{[\tau_k]}$ such that $\hat{m}$ is compatible with m and $\tau \in \lambda^m \cap \lambda^{\hat{m}}$. The match m is present in $H_{[\tau_i]}$ and, according to the induction hypothesis, the match $\hat{m}$ is also present in $H_{[\tau_i]}$. As the matches are structurally the same, $\hat{m}$ is also compatible with m in $H_{[\tau_i]}$. Moreover, as there are no changes in $\lambda^m, \lambda^{\hat{m}}$ for the period $[0, \tau_i]$, $\tau \in \lambda^m \cap \lambda^{\hat{m}}$ over $H_{[\tau_i]}$. We also know that $\tau \leq \tau_i$ and, by the induction hypothesis, that $\hat{m}$ satisfies χ at τ. Therefore, by the semantics of the definite satisfaction relation for *exists*, $(H_{[\tau_i]}, m, \tau) \models^d \exists(\hat{n}, \chi)$. We have shown that the implication is true.

We proceed with the falsification. We assume that $(H_{[\tau_k]}, m, \tau) \not\models \exists(\hat{n}, \chi)$ and show that this implies $(H_{[\tau_i]}, m, \tau) \models^d_F \exists(\hat{n}, \chi)$. Since $(H_{[\tau_k]}, m, \tau) \not\models \exists(\hat{n}, \chi)$, (i) either there exists no $\hat{m}$ in $H_{[\tau_k]}$ such that $\hat{m}$ is compatible with m, or (ii) there exists $\hat{m}$ compatible with m, but $\tau \notin \lambda^m \cap \lambda^{\hat{m}}$, or (iii) there exists $\hat{m}$ compatible with m with $\tau \in \lambda^m \cap \lambda^{\hat{m}}$ but $\hat{m}$ falsifies χ at τ. If (i) is true, it will be true in all future versions of $H_{[\tau_i]}$, as matches cannot be found retrospectively. If (ii) is true, the lifespan of $\lambda^{\hat{m}}$ in the period $[0, \tau_i]$ will not change in all future versions of $H_{[\tau_i]}$. Finally, if (iii) is true, we know from the induction hypothesis that $(\hat{m}, \tau) \models_F^d \chi$ also over $H_{[\tau_i]}$ and that $\tau \leq \tau_i$. Therefore, in any case, $(H_{[\tau_i]}, m, \tau) \models_F^d \exists(\hat{n}, \chi)$. We have shown that the implication is true.

– *Induction step*: $\psi = \chi \mathrm{U}_I \omega$.

   We begin with the satisfaction. Let the induction hypothesis be $(H_{[\tau_k]}, m, \tau) \models \chi \Rightarrow (H_{[\tau_i]}, m, \tau) \models^d \chi$ and $(H_{[\tau_k]}, m, \tau) \models \omega \Rightarrow (H_{[\tau_i]}, m, \tau) \models^d \omega$ with k an arbitrary index in $[i, \mathcal{D}] \cap \mathbb{N}^+$ and $\tau \in [0, \tau_i - w]$. The non-definiteness window w is given by $max(w(\chi), w(\omega)) + r(I)$.

   We assume $(H_{[\tau_k]}, m, \tau) \models \chi \mathrm{U}_I \omega$ and show $(H_{[\tau_i]}, m, \tau) \models^d \chi \mathrm{U}_I \omega$. Since $(H_{[\tau_k]}, m, \tau) \models \chi \mathrm{U}_I \omega$, there exists τ' such that $\tau' - \tau \in I$ and $(H_{[\tau_k]}, m, \tau') \models \omega$, and for all $\tau'' \in [\tau, \tau')$ $(H_{[\tau_k]}, m, \tau'') \models \chi$. From $\tau \in [0, \tau_i - w]$ and $\tau' \in [\tau + \ell(I), \tau + r(I)]$, it follows that $\tau' \leq \tau_i - max(w(\chi), w(\omega))$. Based on this and the induction hypothesis, $(H_{[\tau_i]}, m, \tau') \models^d \omega$. Moreover, as τ' stems from a period outside the non-definiteness window of ω, the decision at τ', whether it concerns a match or not, will remain unaltered once made. The decision at τ' as well as the preceding period $[\tau, \tau')$ are also outside the non-definiteness window of χ. Thus, all $\tau'' \in [\tau, \tau')$ stem from a period covered by $H_{[\tau_i]}$, and decisions for χ made in this period are definite. Therefore, for all $[\tau + \ell(I), \tau + \tau')$ $(H_{[\tau_i]}, m, \tau'') \models^d \chi$, and, by the definite semantics, $(H_{[\tau_i]}, m, \tau) \models^d \chi \mathrm{U}_I \omega$. We have shown that the implication is true.

   We proceed with the falsification. Let the induction hypothesis be that $(H_{[\tau_k]}, m, \tau) \not\models \chi \Rightarrow (H_{[\tau_i]}, m, \tau) \models_F^d \chi$ and $(H_{[\tau_k]}, m, \tau) \not\models \omega \Rightarrow (H_{[\tau_i]}, m, \tau) \models_F^d \omega$.

   We assume $(H_{[\tau_k]}, m, \tau) \not\models \chi \mathrm{U}_I \omega$ and show $(H_{[\tau_i]}, m, \tau) \models_F^d \chi \mathrm{U}_I \omega$. Since $(H_{[\tau_k]}, m, \tau) \not\models \chi \mathrm{U}_I \omega$, it holds that for all τ' such that $\tau' - \tau \in I$ either (i) $(H_{[\tau_k]}, m, \tau') \not\models \omega$ or (ii) there exists $\tau'' \in [\tau, \tau')$ such that $(H_{[\tau_k]}, m, \tau'') \models \chi$. Regardless of which is the case, *i.e.*, (i) or (ii) or both, analogously to the satisfaction, the decisions for all τ' and at τ'' stem from a period that is covered by $H_{[\tau_i]}$, and decisions made in this period regarding χ and ω are definite. Therefore, the case will also hold over $H_{[\tau_i]}$. Therefore, $(H_{[\tau_i]}, m, \tau) \models_F^d \chi \mathrm{U}_I \omega$. We have shown that the implication is true.

– *Induction step*: $\psi = \chi \mathrm{S}_I \omega$.

   We begin with the satisfaction. Let the induction hypothesis be $(H_{[\tau_k]}, m, \tau) \models \chi \Rightarrow (H_{[\tau_i]}, m, \tau) \models^d \chi$ and $(H_{[\tau_k]}, m, \tau) \models \omega \Rightarrow (H_{[\tau_i]}, m, \tau) \models^d \omega$ with k an arbitrary index in $[i, \mathcal{D}] \cap \mathbb{N}^+$ and $\tau \in [0, \tau_i - w]$. The non-definiteness window w is given by $max(w(\chi), w(\omega))$.

   We assume $(H_{[\tau_k]}, m, \tau) \models \chi \mathrm{S}_I \omega$ and show $(H_{[\tau_i]}, m, \tau) \models^d \chi \mathrm{S}_I \omega$. Since $(H_{[\tau_k]}, m, \tau) \models \chi \mathrm{S}_I \omega$, there exists τ' such that $\tau - \tau' \in I$ and $(H_{[\tau_k]}, m, \tau') \models \omega$, and for all $\tau'' \in (\tau', \tau]$ $(H_{[\tau_k]}, m, \tau'') \models \chi$. From $\tau \in [0, \tau_i - w]$ and $\tau' \in [\tau - r(I), \tau - \ell(I)]$, it follows that $\tau' \leq \tau_i - max(w(\chi), w(\omega))$. Hence, the decision at τ' can already be made over $H_{[\tau_i]}$, and, moreover, as τ' stems from a period outside the non-definiteness window of ω, the decision at τ', whether it concerns a match or not, will remain unaltered once made. Therefore, $(H_{[\tau_i]}, m, \tau') \models^d \omega$. The decision at τ' as well as the succeeding period $(\tau', \tau]$ is also outside the non-definiteness window of χ. Thus, all $\tau'' \in (\tau', \tau]$ stem from a period covered by $H_{[\tau_i]}$, and decisions for χ made in this period are definite. Therefore, for all $\tau'' \in (\tau', \tau]$ $(H_{[\tau_i]}, m, \tau'') \models^d \chi$, and, by the definite semantics, $(H_{[\tau_i]}, m, \tau) \models^d \chi S_I \omega$. We have shown that the implication is true. We proceed with the falsification. Let the induction hypothesis be that $(H_{[\tau_k]}, m, \tau) \not\models \chi \Rightarrow (H_{[\tau_i]}, m, \tau) \models_F^d \chi$ and $(H_{[\tau_k]}, m, \tau) \not\models \omega \Rightarrow (H_{[\tau_i]}, m, \tau) \models_F^d \omega$.

We assume $(H_{[\tau_k]}, m, \tau) \not\models \chi S_I \omega$ and show $(H_{[\tau_i]}, m, \tau) \models_F^d \chi S_I \omega$. Since $(H_{[\tau_k]}, m, \tau) \not\models \chi S_I \omega$, it holds that for all τ' such that $\tau - \tau' \in I$ either (i) $(H_{[\tau_k]}, m, \tau') \not\models \omega$ or (ii) there exists $\tau'' \in (\tau', \tau]$ such that $(H_{[\tau_k]}, m, \tau'') \models \chi$. Regardless of which is the case, $i.e.$, (i) or (ii) or both, analogously to the satisfaction, the decisions for all τ' and at τ'' stem from a period that is covered by $H_{[\tau_i]}$, and decisions made in this period regarding χ and ω are definite. Therefore, the case will also hold over $H_{[\tau_i]}$. Therefore, $(H_{[\tau_i]}, m, \tau) \models_F^d \chi S_I \omega$. We have shown that the implication is true.

From the base case and induction steps, it follows that Theorem 2 holds.   □

B.3   Corollary 1: Period in trace with non-definite decisions

Following is the proof for Corollary 1 (see [47, p. 32]), that is, if ψ is an MTGC, w is the non-definiteness window of ψ, $H_{[\tau_i]}$ is a RTM^H instance associated with the time point τ_i, m is a match for a pattern n, and τ a time point in $[0, \tau_i]$, then if $(H_{[\tau_i]}, m, \tau) \not\models^d \psi$ and $(H_{[\tau_i]}, m, \tau) \not\models_F^d \psi$, then $\tau \in (\tau_i - w, \tau_i]$.

Proof. The proof follows from Theorem 2. The satisfaction relation and its negation make a decision for every time point in $[0, \tau_i - w]$, $i.e.$, the relation does not support the value *unknown*; Theorem 2 shows that the decisions made by the satisfaction relation and its negation for $[0, \tau_i - w]$ are equivalent to the decisions made by the definite relations. Consequently, if no definite decision is made for $\tau \in [0, \tau_i]$, then $\tau \notin [0, \tau_i - w]$.   □

B.4   Theorem 3: Equality of definite spans and definite computations for satisfaction and falsification

Following is the proof for Theorem 3 (see [47, Section A.3.4]), $i.e.$, given a match m over a RTM^H $H_{[\tau]}$ and an MTGC ψ, the definite satisfaction span $\mathcal{Y}^d$ of m for ψ over $H_{[\tau]}$ is given by the definite satisfaction computation $\mathcal{Z}^d$ of m for ψ over $H_{[\tau]}$ in Definition 8, that is, $\mathcal{Y}^d(m, \psi) = \mathcal{Z}^d(m, \psi)$. Moreover, the definite falsification span $\mathcal{F}$ of m for ψ over $H_{[\tau]}$ is given by the definite falsification computation F of m for ψ over $H_{[\tau]}$ in Definition 8, that is, $\mathcal{F}(m, \psi) = F(m, \psi)$.

Proof. The proof for the definite satisfaction span $\mathcal{Z}^d$ proceeds almost identically to the proof for Theorem 1 for $\mathcal{Z}$ in [47, Section A.3.1], *i.e.*, by structural induction over ψ, and therefore omitted. For *true*, conjunction, *exists*, *until*, and *since* in Definition 8, inclusion can be shown in both directions—the proof for the negation relies on a reasoning analogous to the one presented below for negation for the definite falsification span.

The proof for the definite falsification F is based on the application of $F = \mathbb{R} \setminus (\mathcal{Z}^d \uplus X)$ for each MTGL operator—which follows from $\mathbb{R} = \mathcal{Y}^d \uplus \mathcal{F} \uplus X$. The unknown span X for *true* is $X = \emptyset$, whereas for *exists*, by definition of the RTM^H $H_{[\tau]}$, it is $X = (\tau, \infty)$. If F is known, it can be used to compute $\mathcal{Z}^d \uplus X$.

- $\psi = \text{true}$: From Equation 8 in Definition 8, we have $\mathcal{Z}^d(m, \text{true}) = \mathbb{R}$, therefore $F(m, \text{true}) = \emptyset$.
- $\psi = \neg\chi$: It holds that

$$\overline{F}(m, \neg\chi) = \mathcal{Z}^d(m, \neg\chi) \uplus X(m, \neg\chi)$$

and

$$\overline{\mathcal{Z}^d}(m, \chi) = \mathcal{Z}^d(m, \neg\chi) \uplus X(m, \neg\chi)$$

Therefore,

$$F(m, \neg\chi) = \overline{\overline{\mathcal{Z}^d}}(m, \chi) = \mathcal{Z}^d(m, \chi)$$

- $\psi = \chi \wedge \omega$: Let each time point that does not definitely falsify the MTGC a that χ encloses to be assumed to satisfy the a. In practice, this includes all time points in $\mathcal{Z}^d(m, \chi) \uplus X(m, \chi)$ for a. Subtracting this maximal satisfaction span from the time domain $\mathbb{R}$ yields the set of time points that definitely falsify χ. Let the satisfaction span of ω be defined analogously. If the satisfaction span of conjunction is computed based on these maximal satisfaction spans of χ and ω, *i.e.*, by $(\mathcal{Z}^d(m, \chi) \uplus X(m, \chi)) \cap (\mathcal{Z}^d(m, \omega) \uplus X(m, \omega))$, the definite falsification span of conjunction can be computed analogously.

$$\begin{aligned} F(m, \chi \wedge \omega) &= \mathbb{R} \setminus \left((\mathcal{Z}^d(m, \chi) \uplus X(m, \chi)) \cap (\mathcal{Z}^d(m, \omega) \uplus X(m, \omega)) \right) \\ &= \mathbb{R} \setminus \left((\mathbb{R} \setminus F(m, \chi)) \cap (\mathbb{R} \setminus F(m, \omega)) \right) \\ &= F(m, \chi) \cup F(m, \omega) \end{aligned}$$

- $\psi = \exists(\hat{n}, \chi)$: Let τ be the time point of the RTM^H $H_{[\tau]}$. As $\mathcal{Z}(m, \exists(\hat{n}, \chi))$ is known and $X(m, \exists(\hat{n}, \chi)) = (\tau, \infty)$, to obtain the falsification computation, we can directly solve $\mathbb{R} \setminus (\mathcal{Z}^d \uplus X)$.

$$\begin{aligned} F(m, \exists(\hat{n}, \chi)) &= \mathbb{R} \setminus \left(\mathcal{Z}^d(m, \exists(\hat{n}, \chi)) \cup (\tau, \infty) \right) \\ &= \left(\mathbb{R} \setminus (\tau, \infty) \right) \cap \left(\mathbb{R} \setminus \mathcal{Z}^d(m, \exists(\hat{n}, \chi)) \right) \\ &= (-\infty, \tau] \cap \left(\mathbb{R} \setminus \mathcal{Z}^d(m, \exists(\hat{n}, \chi)) \right) \end{aligned}$$

- $\psi = \chi \mathsf{U}_I \omega$ and $0 \notin I$: The computation for *until* relies on the reasoning explained in the case of conjunction. The satisfaction span of *until* is computed based on the maximal satisfaction spans of ω, *i.e.*, $\mathcal{Z}^d(m, \omega) \uplus X(m, \omega)$, and χ, that is, J_i^X is obtained by $\mathcal{Z}^d(m, \omega) \uplus X(m, \omega)$ and $\mathcal{Z}^d(m, \chi) \uplus X(m, \chi)$, thus the *until* satisfaction span is similarly maximal. Therefore, complementing this maximal satisfaction span yields all time points that definitely falsify *until*. Therefore, we have:

$$F(m, \chi \mathsf{U}_I \omega) = \mathbb{R} \setminus \left(\bigcup_{i \in \mathcal{Z}^d(m, \omega) \cup X(m, \omega), \, j \in J_i^X} j \cap \left((j^+ \cap i) \ominus I \right) \right)$$

- $\psi = \chi \mathsf{U}_I \omega$ and $0 \in I$: The reasoning is similar to the case where $0 \notin I$.
- $\psi = \chi \mathsf{S}_I \omega$ and $0 \notin I$: The case proceeds analogously to the corresponding case of *until*.
- $\psi = \chi \mathsf{S}_I \omega$ and $0 \in I$: The case proceeds analogously to the corresponding case of *until*.

By showing that $\mathcal{Y}^d(m, \psi) = \mathcal{Z}^d(m, \psi)$ and the equations for $F(m, \psi)$, we have shown that theorem holds.

B.5 Theorem 4: Equality of effective answer set and restricted definite temporal validity answer set over trace

Following is the proof for Theorem 4 (see [47, p. 57]), which states that, if $\zeta := (n, \psi)$ is a temporal query with ψ an MTGC, w is the non-definiteness window of ψ, $h_{\tau_{\mathcal{D}}}^H$ is a RTM^H-trace with $\mathcal{D} \in [2, \infty] \cap \mathbb{N}^+$, i is an index in $[k, \mathcal{D} - 1] \cap \mathbb{N}^+$ such that $\tau_k \geq w$. $\mathcal{J}_{\mathcal{V},r}^d(H_{[\tau_i]})$ is the restricted definite temporal validity answer set over $H_{[\tau_i]}$ which has been obtained from the definite answer set $\mathcal{J}^d$ but contains (i) only pairs of matches with their temporal validity $\mathcal{V}^d$ with $\mathcal{V}^d \neq \emptyset$ and (ii) $\mathcal{V}^d$ is intersected with $[0, \tau_i - w]$, then the effective answer set $\mathcal{J}^e(H_{[\tau_i]})$ is equal to $\mathcal{J}_{\mathcal{V},r}^d(H_{[\tau_i]})$.

Proof. Based on the more general Theorem 2 which shows that, for $\tau \in [0, \tau_i - w]$, the satisfaction decision for τ in $H_{[\tau_i]}$ is equivalent to definite satisfaction decision for τ in $H_{[\tau_i]}$. The computations of $\mathcal{V}$ and $\mathcal{V}^d$ over $H_{[\tau_i]}$ rely on the computations of $\mathcal{Z}$ and $\mathcal{Z}^d$ over $H_{[\tau_i]}$, respectively. Theorem 1 in [47, Section A.3.1] and Theorem 3 show that satisfaction relation and definite satisfaction relation over $H_{[\tau_i]}$ are soundly reflected in $\mathcal{Z}$ and $\mathcal{Z}^d$ over $H_{[\tau_i]}$, respectively. □

References

[1] Gala Barquero, Javier Troya, and Antonio Vallecillo. "Improving Query Performance on Dynamic Graphs". In: *Softw Syst Model* 20.4 (Aug. 1, 2021), pp. 1011–1041. ISSN: 1619-1374. DOI: 10.1007/s10270-020-00832-3.
[2] Ezio Bartocci et al. "First International Competition on Runtime Verification: Rules, Benchmarks, Tools, and Final Results of CRV 2014". In: *Int J Softw Tools Technol Transfer* 21.1 (Feb. 1, 2019), pp. 31–70. ISSN: 1433-2787. DOI: 10.1007/s10009-017-0454-5.

[3]   Ezio Bartocci et al. "Introduction to Runtime Verification". In: *Lectures on Runtime Verification: Introductory and Advanced Topics*. Ed. by Ezio Bartocci and Yliès Falcone. Lecture Notes in Computer Science. Cham: Springer International Publishing, 2018, pp. 1–33. ISBN: 978-3-319-75632-5. DOI: 10.1007/978-3-319-75632-5_1.

[4]   Ezio Bartocci et al. "Specification-Based Monitoring of Cyber-Physical Systems: A Survey on Theory, Tools and Applications". In: *Lectures on Runtime Verification*. Ed. by Ezio Bartocci and Yliès Falcone. Vol. 10457. Cham: Springer International Publishing, 2018, pp. 135–175. ISBN: 978-3-319-75631-8. URL: http://link.springer.com/10.1007/978-3-319-75632-5_5.

[5]   David Basin, Felix Klaedtke, and Eugen Zălinescu. "Algorithms for Monitoring Real-Time Properties". In: *Acta Informatica* 55.4 (June 1, 2018), pp. 309–338. ISSN: 1432-0525. DOI: 10.1007/s00236-017-0295-4.

[6]   David Basin, Felix Klaedtke, and Eugen Zălinescu. "The MonPoly Monitoring Tool". In: *Kalpa Publications in Computing*. RV-CuBES 2017. An International Workshop on Competitions, Usability, Benchmarks, Evaluation, and Standardisation for Runtime Verification Tools. Vol. 3. EasyChair, Dec. 14, 2017, pp. 19–28. DOI: 10.29007/89hs.

[7]   David Basin et al. "Monitoring Metric First-Order Temporal Properties". In: *J. ACM* 62.2 (May 6, 2015), 15:1–15:45. ISSN: 0004-5411. DOI: 10.1145/2699444.

[8]   Andreas Bauer, Martin Leucker, and Christian Schallhart. "The Good, the Bad, and the Ugly, But How Ugly Is Ugly?" In: *Runtime Verification*. Ed. by Oleg Sokolsky and Serdar Taşıran. Lecture Notes in Computer Science. Berlin, Heidelberg: Springer, 2007, pp. 126–138. ISBN: 978-3-540-77395-5. DOI: 10.1007/978-3-540-77395-5_11.

[9]   Nelly Bencomo, Sebastian Götz, and Hui Song. "Models@run.Time: A Guided Tour of the State of the Art and Research Challenges". In: *Softw Syst Model* 18.5 (Oct. 1, 2019), pp. 3049–3082. ISSN: 1619-1374. DOI: 10.1007/s10270-018-00712-x.

[10]   Thomas Beyhl et al. "On the Operationalization of Graph Queries with Generalized Discrimination Networks". In: *Graph Transformation*. Ed. by Rachid Echahed and Mark Minas. Lecture Notes in Computer Science. Cham: Springer International Publishing, 2016, pp. 170–186. ISBN: 978-3-319-40530-8. DOI: 10.1007/978-3-319-40530-8_11.

[11]   Robert Bill et al. "On the Need for Temporal Model Repositories". In: *Software Technologies: Applications and Foundations*. Ed. by Martina Seidl and Steffen Zschaler. Lecture Notes in Computer Science. Cham: Springer International Publishing, 2018, pp. 136–145. ISBN: 978-3-319-74730-9. DOI: 10.1007/978-3-319-74730-9_11.

[12]   Gordon Blair, Nelly Bencomo, and Robert B. France. "Models@ Run.Time". In: *Computer* 42.10 (Oct. 2009), pp. 22–27. ISSN: 1558-0814. DOI: 10.1109/MC.2009.326.

[13] Márton Búr. "Query-Based Runtime Monitoring in Real-Time and Distributed Systems". PhD thesis. Canada: McGill University, 2021. URL: https://escholarship.mcgill.ca/concern/theses/w95055572.

[14] Márton Búr et al. "Distributed Graph Queries Over Models@run.Time for Runtime Monitoring of Cyber-Physical Systems". In: *Int J Softw Tools Technol Transfer* 22.1 (Feb. 1, 2020), pp. 79–102. ISSN: 1433-2787. DOI: 10.1007/s10009-019-00531-5.

[15] L. Catarinucci et al. "An IoT-Aware Architecture for Smart Healthcare Systems". In: *IEEE Internet of Things Journal* 2.6 (Dec. 2015), pp. 515–526. ISSN: 2327-4662. DOI: 10.1109/JIOT.2015.2417684.

[16] Federico Ciccozzi et al. "Model-Driven Engineering for Mission-Critical IoT Systems". In: *IEEE Software* 34.1 (Jan. 2017), pp. 46–53. ISSN: 1937-4194. DOI: 10.1109/MS.2017.1.

[17] Carlo Combi et al. "Modelling Temporal, Data-Centric Medical Processes". In: *Proceedings of the 2nd ACM SIGHIT International Health Informatics Symposium*. IHI '12. New York, NY, USA: Association for Computing Machinery, Jan. 28, 2012, pp. 141–150. ISBN: 978-1-4503-0781-9. DOI: 10.1145/2110363.2110382.

[18] Bruno Courcelle. "The Expression of Graph Properties and Graph Transformations in Monadic Second-Order Logic". In: *Handbook of Graph Grammars and Computing by Graph Transformation: Volume I. Foundations*. USA: World Scientific Publishing Co., Inc., Feb. 1, 1997, pp. 313–400. ISBN: 978-981-02-2884-2. DOI: 10.1142/9789812384720_0005.

[19] Wei Dou, Domenico Bianculli, and Lionel Briand. "A Model-Driven Approach to Trace Checking of Pattern-Based Temporal Properties". In: *Proceedings of the ACM/IEEE 20th International Conference on Model Driven Engineering Languages and Systems*. MODELS '17. Austin, Texas: IEEE Press, Sept. 17, 2017, pp. 323–333. ISBN: 978-1-5386-3492-9. DOI: 10.1109/MODELS.2017.9.

[20] Hartmut Ehrig, Ulrike Prange, and Gabriele Taentzer. "Fundamental Theory for Typed Attributed Graph Transformation". In: *Graph Transformations*. Ed. by Hartmut Ehrig et al. Lecture Notes in Computer Science. Berlin, Heidelberg: Springer, 2004, pp. 161–177. ISBN: 978-3-540-30203-2. DOI: 10.1007/978-3-540-30203-2_13.

[21] Cindy Eisner et al. "Reasoning with Temporal Logic on Truncated Paths". In: *Computer Aided Verification*. Ed. by Warren A. Hunt and Fabio Somenzi. Berlin, Heidelberg: Springer, 2003, pp. 27–39. ISBN: 978-3-540-45069-6. DOI: 10.1007/978-3-540-45069-6_3.

[22] Yliès Falcone et al. "A Taxonomy for Classifying Runtime Verification Tools". In: *Int J Softw Tools Technol Transfer* 23.2 (Apr. 1, 2021), pp. 255–284. ISSN: 1433-2787. DOI: 10.1007/s10009-021-00609-z.

[23] Robert France and Bernhard Rumpe. "Model-Driven Development of Complex Software: A Research Roadmap". In: *Future of Software Engineering (FOSE '07)*. May 2007, pp. 37–54. DOI: 10.1109/FOSE.2007.14.

[24]   Antonio García-Domínguez et al. "Querying and Annotating Model Histories with Time-Aware Patterns". In: *2019 ACM/IEEE 22nd International Conference on Model Driven Engineering Languages and Systems (MODELS)*. Sept. 2019, pp. 194–204. DOI: 10.1109/MODELS.2019.000-2.

[25]   Sona Ghahremani, Holger Giese, and Thomas Vogel. "Improving Scalability and Reward of Utility-Driven Self-Healing for Large Dynamic Architectures". In: *ACM Trans. Auton. Adapt. Syst.* 14.3 (Feb. 25, 2020), 12:1–12:41. ISSN: 1556-4665. DOI: 10.1145/3380965.

[26]   Holger Giese et al. "Metric Temporal Graph Logic over Typed Attributed Graphs". In: *Fundamental Approaches to Software Engineering*. Ed. by Reiner Hähnle and Wil van der Aalst. Lecture Notes in Computer Science. Cham: Springer International Publishing, 2019, pp. 282–298. ISBN: 978-3-030-16722-6. DOI: 10.1007/978-3-030-16722-6_16.

[27]   Annegret Habel and Karl-Heinz Pennemann. "Correctness of High-Level Transformation Systems Relative to Nested Conditions". In: *Mathematical Structures in Computer Science* 19.2 (Apr. 2009), pp. 245–296. ISSN: 1469-8072, 0960-1295. DOI: 10.1017/S0960129508007202.

[28]   E. N. Hanson, S. Bodagala, and U. Chadaga. "Trigger Condition Testing and View Maintenance Using Optimized Discrimination Networks". In: *IEEE Transactions on Knowledge and Data Engineering* 14.2 (Mar. 2002), pp. 261–280. ISSN: 1558-2191. DOI: 10.1109/69.991716.

[29]   Klaus Havelund, Moran Omer, and Doron Peled. "Monitoring First-Order Interval Logic". In: *Software Engineering and Formal Methods*. Ed. by Radu Calinescu and Corina S. Păsăreanu. Cham: Springer International Publishing, 2021, pp. 66–83. ISBN: 978-3-030-92124-8. DOI: 10.1007/978-3-030-92124-8_4.

[30]   Klaus Havelund and Doron Peled. "BDDs for Representing Data in Runtime Verification". In: *Runtime Verification*. Ed. by Jyotirmoy Deshmukh and Dejan Ničković. Vol. 12399. Cham: Springer International Publishing, 2020, pp. 107–128. ISBN: 978-3-030-60508-7. DOI: 10.1007/978-3-030-60508-7_6.

[31]   Klaus Havelund and Doron Peled. "First-Order Timed Runtime Verification Using BDDs". In: *Automated Technology for Verification and Analysis*. Ed. by Dang Van Hung and Oleg Sokolsky. Lecture Notes in Computer Science. Cham: Springer International Publishing, 2020, pp. 3–24. ISBN: 978-3-030-59152-6. DOI: 10.1007/978-3-030-59152-6_1.

[32]   Klaus Havelund and Doron Peled. "Runtime Verification: From Propositional to First-Order Temporal Logic". In: *Runtime Verification*. Ed. by Christian Colombo and Martin Leucker. Lecture Notes in Computer Science. Cham: Springer International Publishing, 2018, pp. 90–112. ISBN: 978-3-030-03769-7. DOI: 10.1007/978-3-030-03769-7_7.

[33]   Klaus Havelund et al. "Monitoring Events That Carry Data". In: *Lectures on Runtime Verification: Introductory and Advanced Topics*. Ed. by Ezio Bartocci and Ylès Falcone. Lecture Notes in Computer Science. Cham: Springer International Publishing, 2018, pp. 61–102. ISBN: 978-3-319-75632-5. DOI: 10.1007/978-3-319-75632-5_3.

[34]   Kerianne L. Hobbs et al. "Runtime Assurance for Safety-Critical Systems: An Introduction to Safety Filtering Approaches for Complex Control Systems". In: *IEEE Control Syst.* 43.2 (Apr. 2023), pp. 28–65. ISSN: 1066-033X, 1941-000X. DOI: 10.1109/MCS.2023.3234380.

[35]   Ron Koymans. "Specifying Real-Time Properties with Metric Temporal Logic". In: *Real-Time Syst* 2.4 (Nov. 1, 1990), pp. 255–299. ISSN: 1573-1383. DOI: 10.1007/BF01995674.

[36]   Christian Krause et al. "An SQL-Based Query Language and Engine for Graph Pattern Matching". In: *Graph Transformation*. Ed. by Rachid Echahed and Mark Minas. Vol. 9761. Cham: Springer International Publishing, 2016, pp. 153–169. ISBN: 978-3-319-40530-8. DOI: 10.1007/978-3-319-40530-8_10.

[37]   F. Laroussinie, N. Markey, and P. Schnoebelen. "Temporal Logic with Forgettable Past". In: *Proceedings 17th Annual IEEE Symposium on Logic in Computer Science*. July 2002, pp. 383–392. DOI: 10.1109/LICS.2002.1029846.

[38]   Oded Maler and Dejan Ničković. "Monitoring Properties of Analog and Mixed-Signal Circuits". In: *Int J Softw Tools Technol Transfer* 15.3 (June 1, 2013), pp. 247–268. ISSN: 1433-2787. DOI: 10.1007/s10009-012-0247-9.

[39]   Felix Mannhardt and Daan Blinde. "Analyzing the Trajectories of Patients with Sepsis Using Process Mining". In: *RADAR+EMISA@CAiSE, Essen, Germany, June 12-13, 2017*. Ed. by Jens Gulden et al. Vol. 1859. CEUR Workshop Proceedings. CEUR-WS.org, 2017, pp. 72–80. URL: http://ceur-ws.org/Vol-1859/bpmds-08-paper.pdf.

[40]   Diego Marmsoler and Ana Petrovska. "Runtime Verification for Dynamic Architectures". In: *Journal of Logical and Algebraic Methods in Programming* 118 (Jan. 1, 2021), p. 100618. ISSN: 2352-2208. DOI: 10.1016/j.jlamp.2020.100618.

[41]   Ramon E. Moore, R. Baker Kearfott, and Michael J. Cloud. *Introduction to Interval Analysis*. Society for Industrial and Applied Mathematics, Jan. 2009. ISBN: 978-0-89871-771-6. DOI: 10.1137/1.9780898717716.

[42]   Doron Peled and Klaus Havelund. "Refining the Safety–Liveness Classification of Temporal Properties According to Monitorability". In: *Models, Mindsets, Meta: The What, the How, and the Why Not? Essays Dedicated to Bernhard Steffen on the Occasion of His 60th Birthday*. Ed. by Tiziana Margaria, Susanne Graf, and Kim G. Larsen. Lecture Notes in Computer Science. Cham: Springer International Publishing, 2019, pp. 218–234. ISBN: 978-3-030-22348-9. URL: https://doi.org/10.1007/978-3-030-22348-9_14.

[43]   Giles Reger and David Rydeheard. "From First-order Temporal Logic to Parametric Trace Slicing". In: *Runtime Verification*. Ed. by Ezio Bartocci and Rupak Majumdar. Lecture Notes in Computer Science. Cham: Springer International Publishing, 2015, pp. 216–232. ISBN: 978-3-319-23820-3. DOI: 10.1007/978-3-319-23820-3_14.

[44]   Arend Rensink. "Representing First-Order Logic Using Graphs". In: *Graph Transformations*. Ed. by Hartmut Ehrig et al. Lecture Notes in Computer

Science. Berlin, Heidelberg: Springer, 2004, pp. 319–335. ISBN: 978-3-540-30203-2. DOI: 10.1007/978-3-540-30203-2_23.

[45]   Patrice C Roy, Samina Raza Abidi, and Syed Sibte Raza Abidi. "Monitoring Medication Adherence in Smart Environments in the Context of Patient Self-Management: A Knowledge-Driven Approach". In: *Smart Technologies in Healthcare*. CRC Press, 2017, pp. 195–223. ISBN: 978-1-315-14568-6. DOI: 10.1201/9781315145686-8.

[46]   John Rushby. "Critical System Properties: Survey and Taxonomy". In: *Reliability Engineering & System Safety*. Special Issue on Software Safety 43.2 (Jan. 1, 1994), pp. 189–219. ISSN: 0951-8320. DOI: 10.1016/0951-8320(94)90065-5.

[47]   Lucas Sakizloglou. "Evaluating Temporal Queries over History-Aware Architectural Runtime Models". PhD thesis. Universität Potsdam, 2023. DOI: 10.25932/publishup-60439.

[48]   Lucas Sakizloglou, Matthias Barkowsky, and Holger Giese. "Keeping Pace with the History of Evolving Runtime Models". In: *Fundamental Approaches to Software Engineering*. Ed. by Esther Guerra and Mariëlle Stoelinga. Lecture Notes in Computer Science. Cham: Springer International Publishing, 2021, pp. 262–268. ISBN: 978-3-030-71500-7. DOI: 10.1007/978-3-030-71500-7_13.

[49]   Lucas Sakizloglou et al. "Incremental Execution of Temporal Graph Queries over Runtime Models with History and Its Applications". In: *Softw Syst Model* 21.5 (Oct. 1, 2022), pp. 1789–1829. ISSN: 1619-1374. DOI: 10.1007/s10270-021-00950-6.

[50]   Sven Schneider et al. "Formal Testing of Timed Graph Transformation Systems Using Metric Temporal Graph Logic". In: *Int J Softw Tools Technol Transfer* 23.3 (June 2021), pp. 411–488. ISSN: 1433-2779, 1433-2787. DOI: 10.1007/s10009-020-00585-w.

[51]   Sven Schneider et al. "Optimistic and Pessimistic On-the-fly Analysis for Metric Temporal Graph Logic". In: *Graph Transformation*. Ed. by Fabio Gadducci and Timo Kehrer. Lecture Notes in Computer Science. Cham: Springer International Publishing, 2020, pp. 276–294. ISBN: 978-3-030-51372-6. DOI: 10.1007/978-3-030-51372-6_16.

[52]   Michael Szvetits and Uwe Zdun. "Systematic Literature Review of the Objectives, Techniques, Kinds, and Architectures of Models at Runtime". In: *Softw Syst Model* 15.1 (Feb. 1, 2016), pp. 31–69. ISSN: 1619-1374. DOI: 10.1007/s10270-013-0394-9.

[53]   Gabriele Taentzer and Arend Rensink. "Ensuring Structural Constraints in Graph-Based Models with Type Inheritance". In: *Fundamental Approaches to Software Engineering*. Ed. by Maura Cerioli. Lecture Notes in Computer Science. Berlin, Heidelberg: Springer, 2005, pp. 64–79. ISBN: 978-3-540-31984-9. DOI: 10.1007/978-3-540-31984-9_6.

[54]   Dániel Varró et al. "Road to a Reactive and Incremental Model Transformation Platform: Three Generations of the Viatra Framework". In:

Softw Syst Model 15.3 (July 1, 2016), pp. 609–629. ISSN: 1619-1374. DOI: 10.1007/s10270-016-0530-4.

[55]   Danny Weyns and Radu Calinescu. "Tele Assistance: A Self-Adaptive Service-Based System Exemplar". In: *2015 IEEE/ACM 10th International Symposium on Software Engineering for Adaptive and Self-Managing Systems*. May 2015, pp. 88–92. DOI: 10.1109/SEAMS.2015.27.

Probabilistic Runtime Enforcement of Executable BPMN Processes

Yliès Falcone[ID], Gwen Salaün[ID], and Ahang Zuo[(✉)][ID]

Univ. Grenoble Alpes, CNRS, Grenoble INP, Inria, LIG, 38000 Grenoble, France
ahang.zuo@inria.fr

Abstract. A business process is a collection of structured tasks corresponding to a service or a product. Business processes do not execute once and for all, but are executed multiple times resulting in multiple instances. In this context, it is particularly difficult to ensure correctness and efficiency of the multiple executions of a process. In this paper, we propose to rely on Probabilistic Model Checking (PMC) to automatically verify that multiple executions of a process respect some specific probabilistic property. This approach applies at runtime, thus the evaluation of the property is periodically verified and the corresponding results updated. However, we go beyond runtime PMC for BPMN, since we propose runtime enforcement techniques to keep executing the process while avoiding the violation of the property. To do so, our approach combines monitoring techniques, computation of probabilistic models, PMC, and runtime enforcement techniques. The approach has been implemented as a toolchain and has been validated on several realistic BPMN processes.

1 Introduction

Business processes are structured tasks that model a specific service or product. Such processes are present in any company or institution worldwide, and there is a need for better controlling these processes to reduce costs and improve throughput. Many companies model their services and processes, thereby increasing their level of automation. One of the challenges in this context is to ensure the quality, correctness, and efficiency of these processes. In this paper, we assume that processes are described using Business Process Model and Notation (BPMN) [20], the standard business process modelling language. BPMN processes are not executed once but multiple times, resulting in multiple instances.

In this study, we focus on quantitative analysis of processes, which is particularly useful for computing probabilistic properties or other metrics related to time, costs or resource usage. More precisely, we use probabilistic model checking (PMC) to automatically verify that multiple executions of a process respect probabilistic properties [15]. In the context of BPMN processes, probabilistic properties help verifying that some task usage does not go above a certain threshold or for computing how many resources have to be associated with specific tasks to execute the process smoothly. Evaluating a probabilistic property is strongly related to the number of process instances being executed. Therefore, PMC should

© The Author(s) 2024
D. Beyer and A. Cavalcanti (Eds.): FASE 2024, LNCS 14573, pp. 56–76, 2024.
https://doi.org/10.1007/978-3-031-57259-3_3

be applied at runtime to analyse the current execution of running instances. The property is periodically verified, and the corresponding results are updated.

In this paper, we not only verify probabilistic properties on BPMN processes using PMC at runtime, but also enforce the process executions to not violate the property. To do so, we rely on runtime verification and enforcement techniques. Runtime verification [3,10] is a technique to verify whether system's executions satisfy a given correctness property at runtime. Runtime Enforcement (RE) [12,13] is complementary to runtime verification and provides techniques that can intervene in the system at runtime to ensure that the behaviour of the system respects the expected properties. In this paper, the system consists in the multiple executions of a process and we want these executions to always satisfy a given property. This is possible by catching the flow of executions of these process instances and by changing it (when the property is violated) using correcting actions (such as buffering or reordering specific tasks).

More precisely, we introduce probabilistic runtime enforcement, allowing BPMN processes to satisfy a given probabilistic property at runtime. To achieve this, we first convert the BPMN process into a formal model represented by a Labelled Transition System (LTS). We then monitor the multiple executions of the process and extract the corresponding traces (one trace per process instance). Based on these execution traces, we can annotate the LTS model of the process by adding execution probabilities to transitions of the LTS, thus obtaining a Probabilistic Transition System (PTS) model. It is worth noting that recent actions are taken into account to compute this PTS but are not effectively released and considered executed. Probabilistic model checking is then used to verify whether the PTS model satisfies the given property. If the property is satisfied, all recent actions are released. If the property is violated, the enforcement mechanism is triggered and the aforementioned recent actions are retained, removed or re-ordered to avoid the property violation. This approach was fully implemented and its effectiveness was validated on several examples of processes and properties.

The contributions of this work can be summarised as follows:

- A novel algorithm, which analyses (possibly incomplete) execution traces and builds a Probabilistic Transition System.
- A probabilistic enforcement mechanism, which avoids probabilistic property violation when executing multiple process instances.
- An entire toolchain supporting the whole approach and its validation on realistic processes.

The organisation of this paper is as follows. Section 2 introduces the background notions required to this work. Section 3 presents the probabilistic enforcement approach for BPMN. Section 4 describes the toolchain automating all the approach steps, illustrates the approach with a case study, and presents experimental results. Section 5 surveys related work, and Section 6 concludes.

2 Background

This section outlines the fundamental concepts, such as BPMN, Labelled Transition System (LTS), Probabilistic Transition System (PTS), execution traces, and probabilistic properties.

2.1 Business Process Model and Notation

Business Process Model and Notation (BPMN) is a widely used workflow-based notation for describing and modelling business processes [20]. The syntax of a BPMN process is defined as a graph-based structure, where vertices or nodes represent various elements such as events, tasks, and gateways, and edges or flows connect these nodes. Figure 1 introduces the key elements of the BPMN notation.

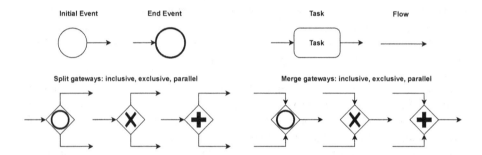

Fig. 1: Excerpt from the BPMN notation.

The diagram includes the *initial event* and the *end event*, which serve to initialise and terminate processes, respectively. It is assumed that there is only one initial event, which corresponds to the initiation of a process and at least one end event, which corresponds to the completion of a process. *Task* represents an atomic activity and typically has only one incoming flow and one outgoing flow, denoting the sequence of activities within the process. *Gateways* are used to describe the control flow of the process. There are two patterns for each gateway type: the split pattern and the merge pattern. The split pattern consists of a single incoming flow and multiple outgoing flows. The merge pattern consists of multiple incoming flows and a single outgoing flow. Several types of gateways are available, such as exclusive, parallel, and inclusive gateways. An exclusive gateway corresponds to a choice among several flows. A parallel gateway executes all possible flows at the same time. An inclusive gateway executes one or several flows. The choice of flows to execute in exclusive and inclusive gateways depends on the evaluation of data-based conditions.

This paper focuses on the multiple executions of a single process, known as process instances. Each instance is characterised by an identifier and by the list of tasks executed by this instance. It is assumed that each instance eventually completes, thus resulting in a finite list of tasks.

2.2 LTS & PTS

Labelled and Probabilistic Transition Systems are used in this paper as semantic models for BPMN. Moreover, they allow the automated analysis of the corresponding BPMN processes.

Definition 1 (LTS). *A Labelled Transition System (LTS) is a tuple $\langle Q, \Sigma, q_{init}, \Delta \rangle$, where: Q is a finite set of states, Σ is a finite set of labels/actions, q_{init} is the initial state, $\Delta \subseteq Q \times \Sigma \times Q$ is a transition relation, where $(q, a, q') \in \Delta$ represents a possible transition from state q to state q' with label a, also written $q \xrightarrow{a} q'$.*

Probabilities are useful for making explicit the likelihood of executing specific tasks in a process. Therefore, we also use Probabilistic Transition Systems [23], an extension of the LTS model that incorporates probabilities for transitions.

Definition 2 (PTS). *A Probabilistic Transition System (PTS) is a tuple $\langle S, A, s_{init}, \delta, P \rangle$ such that $\langle S, A, s_{init}, \delta \rangle$ is a labelled transition system as per Definition 1 and $P : \delta \rightarrow [0, 1]$ is the probability labelling function.*

$P(s \xrightarrow{a} s') \in [0, 1]$ is the probability for the system to move from state s to state s', performing action a. For each state s, the sum of the probabilities associated with its outgoing transitions is equal to 1, that is $\forall s \in S$: $\sum_{s' \in S} P(s, a, s') = 1$. When using LTS or PTS as a semantic model of a BPMN process, the set of labels or alphabet refers to the set of tasks appearing in the BPMN process.

2.3 Execution Traces

A process can be executed multiple times, resulting in multiple instances. Each process instance being executed can be in one of the following three states: waiting state, running/ongoing state, and completed state. Any (ongoing or completed) instance consists of a sequence of tasks within the process. Every time an instance executes, it results in an execution trace of tasks.

Definition 3 (Execution Trace). *An execution trace (σ_T) refers to a sequence of tasks that are executed in a specific order by a specific process instance.*

It is worth noting that in the rest of this work, an execution trace can be completed or not. In the latter case, this is due to the fact that the process instance is still running and has not completed yet.

Several operations can be performed on execution traces. Assuming an execution trace σ of length n and an execution trace σ' of length m, we define the following primitive operations:

- **Size:** $Size(\sigma) = |\sigma|$.
- **Index:** $\sigma[i]$ is the ith element in σ, $i < n$
- **Slice:** $\sigma[0...i] = \sigma[0].\sigma[1]. \cdots .\sigma[i-1]$, $i \leq n$.
- **Concatenation:** $Concat(\sigma, \sigma') = \sigma[0...n].\sigma'[0...m]$.
- **Reorder:** $Reorder(\sigma, \sigma') = \sigma'[0...m].\sigma[0...n]$.

2.4 Probabilistic Properties

The Model Checking Language (MCL) [26] is a branching-time temporal logic that is suitable for expressing properties of concurrent systems using actions. It extends the alternation-free μ-calculus [9] with regular expressions, data-based constructs, and fairness operators. A probabilistic property is a specification or requirement that expresses a probabilistic behaviour of a system or model being analysed. In this paper, probabilistic properties are used to describe the requirements for the probability of execution of a task or a set of combined tasks in a BPMN process. We use MCL to describe probabilistic properties using the prob R is op [?] E end prob construct [24], where R is a regular formula that describes transition sequences, op is a comparison operator such as "$<$", "$\leq$", "$>$", "$\geq$", "$=$", "$<>$", and E is a real number that represents a probability. Given an MCL probabilistic property and a PTS model, we use the CADP Probabilistic Model Checker [24] in order to evaluate the property on the PTS model.

3   Probabilistic Runtime Enforcement

Our approach takes two inputs, a BPMN model and a probabilistic property, and produces as output a list of safe-to-execute tasks, in the sense that they do not violate the given property. This approach consists of three parts: the *monitoring* part, the *transformation* part, and the *probabilistic runtime enforcement* mechanism (Figure 2). First, monitoring is used to observe the multiple executions of the given process, in particular to retrieve the tasks executed by each process instance (resulting in execution traces). Second, the input BPMN model is transformed into its corresponding semantic model, namely an LTS. This step is performed only once. Finally, the probabilistic runtime enforcement mechanism consists of two modules. The first module corresponds to Probabilistic Model Checking (PMC), which determines whether a new version of the PTS violates the given probabilistic property. The second module corresponds to the enforcer, which is activated only when the probabilistic model checking returns false. In such a case, the enforcer applies appropriate techniques to modify the input trace (e.g., by retaining some tasks and not executing them immediately), and thus avoid property violation.

3.1   Monitoring

Monitoring techniques are useful to observe and monitor the current status of the BPMN process executions. More precisely, we monitor process executions

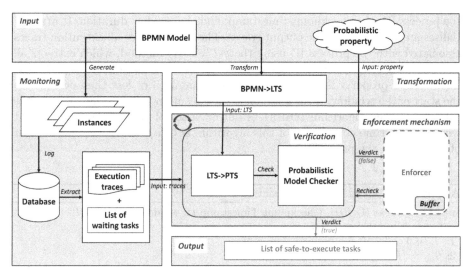

Fig. 2: Approach Overview.

from an instance perspective since the main goal is to extract all traces executed by ongoing process instances on a given period.

Figure 3 illustrates the monitoring process of a BPMN process at runtime, which involves observing every generated instance for that process. Multiple instances can execute concurrently, and all information related to the execution of one process instance is stored in a database. To retrieve execution traces for all process instances, we rely on extraction techniques at varying levels of granularity. As shown in the figure, each instance execution trace is composed of a process ID, an instance ID, a set of tasks, a start time, and an end time.

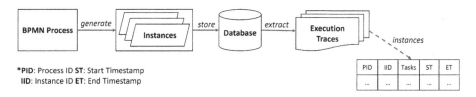

Fig. 3: Runtime monitoring of multiple executions of a BPMN process.

Since we focus here on long-running process executions, it does not make sense to retrieve all execution traces from the beginning. Therefore, the extraction is triggered for a specific time window. This operation is repeated periodically, thus resulting in a *sliding window* algorithm. Algorithm 1 aims at extracting the execution traces for all instances that are either in progress or have already finished during a specified time window. The algorithm takes as input the process ID, the checkpoint timestamp, and the window duration. It first initialises an empty list for the output traces. Then, it retrieves all execution traces associated with the process ID using the *getTraces()* method, which extracts all execution traces as illustrated in Figure 3. For each instance, it checks whether its *endTime* property is None (instance still running), or less than or equal to the start of the window. If so, it appends the execution trace to the output trace list. Finally, the algorithm returns as output a set of traces executed on that window. The time complexity of this algorithm is $\mathcal{O}(n)$, where n is the number of instances in the process.

Algorithm 1 Get traces in the sliding window

Inputs: Process ID *PID*, Checkpoint Timestamp *ts*, window duration *td*
Output: Execution traces $\mathcal{T}$
1: $\mathcal{T} := []$
2: $\mathcal{T}_{all} := PID.getTraces()$
3: **for** each $Tr \in \mathcal{T}_{all}$ **do**
4:     **if** $Tr.endTime$ is None or $Tr.endTime \leq ts - td$ **then** $\mathcal{T}.append(Tr)$
    return $\mathcal{T}$

3.2   Transforming BPMN into LTS

LTS is a semantic model that shows all possible execution paths for a process. To transform BPMN into LTS, we rely on an existing approach that first translates BPMN into the LNT process algebraic specification language, and then transforms it into an LTS by using CADP compilers [17]. For more information on the transformation process from BPMN to LTS, please refer to [22, 27].

3.3   Transforming LTS into PTS

The transformation process from an LTS to a PTS consists of two steps. The initial step aims at traversing all provided instances and identifying all the possible execution paths for each instance (Algorithm 2). In a second step, a counter is added to each transition of the LTS, thus allowing us to track the number of times each transition is executed. This facilitates the calculation of the probability value associated with executing each transition. Finally, the output model is represented as a PTS (Algorithm 3).

An execution path is a sequence of transitions in the LTS that matches with the execution trace of an instance. When an instance has been successfully completed, there exists only one corresponding execution path. The LTS may exhibit non-deterministic behaviour due to the presence of inclusive gateways in the BPMN model. Therefore, when considering unfinished instances, we calculate the execution probabilities of all relevant paths and normalize these probabilities.

Algorithm 2 takes as input an LTS and an execution trace of an instance $\mathcal{T}_{tasks}$ (i.e. a list of tasks), and finds all feasible execution paths in the LTS that satisfy the given execution trace. The algorithm uses a depth-first search (DFS) approach to traverse the LTS, starting from the initial state. It compares the tasks in the transitions of the LTS with the tasks in the ordered sequence of tasks to determine feasible paths. The algorithm maintains a stack to keep track of the current state and partial paths, and recursively explores all possible transitions from the current state until it reaches a state that fully matches the ordered sequence of tasks. Given that it is a non-deterministic model, it then backtracks to explore other possible transitions and continues the exploration process until all paths have been exhaustively explored. The time complexity of the algorithm is $\mathcal{O}(|Q| \times |\Delta|)$, where $|Q|$ represents the number of states in the LTS and $|\Delta|$ represents the number of transitions in the LTS.

Algorithm 2 Get all execution paths of an instance in LTS (FINDPATHS)

Inputs: LTS $= \langle Q, \Sigma, q_{init}, \Delta \rangle$, an execution trace $\mathcal{T}_{tasks} = [t_1, t_2, \ldots, t_n]$
Output: A list of paths (resultPaths)
1: resultPaths $:= []$
    return DFS(LTS, $\mathcal{T}_{tasks}, q_{init}, []$, resultPaths)

2: **function** DFS(LTS, tasks, $q_{current}$, currentPath, resultPaths)
3:    **if** $Size$(tasks) $== 0$ **then**
4:        **return** resultPaths.$append$(currentPath)
5:    **else**
6:        task $:=$ tasks[0]; restTasks $:=$ tasks[1:]
7:        $\mathcal{Q}_{next} := \{q' \in Q \mid (q_{current}, task, q') \in \Delta\}$
8:        **for all** $q_{next} \in \mathcal{Q}_{next}$ **do**
9:            nextPath $:=$ currentPath
10:       nextPath.$append((q_{current}, task, q_{next}))$
11:       DFS(LTS, restTasks, q_{next}, nextPath, resultPaths)

Algorithm 3 takes as input an LTS and a list of execution traces $\mathcal{I}$, and computes a PTS representing the probability distribution of transitions between states of the LTS based on the occurrence of tasks in the set of execution traces. The algorithm first initialises a counter for each transition in the LTS, which records the number of times the transition is taken in the execution trace (line 1). Then, for each execution trace in the list, the algorithm computes the set of possible execution paths in the LTS that correspond to the execution trace (line 5). If there is only one path, the algorithm increments the counter for each transition in the path by 1 (lines 6 to 7). If there are multiple paths, the algorithm increments the counter for each transition in each path by 1, but also keeps track of the number of execution traces that have multiple paths to avoid double-counting (lines 10 to 11). Finally, the algorithm computes the probability of each transition by dividing its counter by the sum of counters for all transitions with the same source state and event (line 12). The resulting probabilities are normalised so that they sum to 1 (line 13). The algorithm returns the PTS, which consists of the set of states, tasks, and transitions of the LTS, along with the computed probabilities for each transition. The time complexity of this algorithm is $\mathcal{O}(|\mathcal{I}| \times |Q| \times |\Delta|)$, where $|\mathcal{I}|$ is the number of execution traces, $|Q|$ represents the number of states in the LTS, and $|\Delta|$ represents the number of transitions in the LTS.

Algorithm 3 Computation of PTS (COMPUTEPTS)

Inputs: LTS $= \langle Q, \Sigma, q_{init}, \Delta \rangle$, a list of execution traces $\mathcal{I} = [I_1, I_2, \ldots, I_n]$
Output: PTS $= \langle S, A, s_{init}, \delta, P \rangle$
 1: **for** each $(q, a, q') \in \Delta$ **do** $cnt((q, a, q')) := 0$
 2: $Paths := []$, $counter := 0$ ▷ $counter$ records the number of unfinished traces
 3: **for all** $I_i \in \mathcal{I}$ **do**
 4:     $\mathcal{T}_{tasks} := I_i.getTasks()$
 5:     $Paths := $ FINDPATHS(LTS, $\mathcal{T}_{tasks}$)   ▷ FINDPATHS (Algorithm 2)
 6:     **if** $Size$(Paths) $== 1$ **then**
 7:         **for** each $(s, a, s') \in Paths[0]$ **do** $cnt((s, a, s')) := cnt((q, a, q')) + 1$
 8:     **else**
 9:         $counter := counter + 1$
10:         **for** each $Path \in Paths$ **do**
11:             **for** each $(s, a, s') \in Path$ **do** $cnt((s, a, s')) := cnt((q, a, q')) + 1$

12: $P := \{(s, a, s') \mapsto cnt((s, a, s'))/$ ▷ calculate probabilities
    $(\sum_{q \in S, a' \in A, (s, a', q) \in \delta} cnt((s, a', q)) - counter) \mid (s, a, s') \in \delta\}$
13: $P := Normalisation(P)$
    return $\langle S, A, s_{init}, \delta, P \rangle$

3.4   Critical Tasks

In this subsection, we describe how to define and compute *critical actions/tasks* given an LTS model of a BPMN process and a probabilistic property. Critical tasks refer to specific tasks that play a crucial role in determining whether a system's behaviour violates or satisfies a given property. This notion is at the heart of the enforcement techniques presented in the next subsection.

The notion of critical task used here is inspired by the notion of *last action of the property* introduced in [16]. This paper states that the violation of a property by a given model is somehow triggered when the last action of the property is executed by the model. In other words, if the last action is not executed, the model does not violate the property. Depending on the actions used in the probabilistic property (including the last action), we can identify one or more execution paths in the LTS, including the actions of the property, where each path consists of an ordered list of transitions. We then traverse this set of paths and for each path we search for the last state (the closest to the end of the path) corresponding to a choice between several transitions. This state

s is particularly important because it is the last opportunity to avoid reaching the last action (of the property) and thus violating the property. The actions or tasks for all transitions outgoing from state s are *candidates* to critical tasks. At this point, the operator of the property needs to be considered. If the operator is less than ("<" or "≤"), there is one critical task, corresponding to the transition outgoing from s and leading to the last action. If the operator is greater than (">" or "≥"), the critical tasks correspond to all transitions outgoing from s and leading to actions other than the last one. If the operator is "=" or "<>", the critical tasks correspond to all tasks appearing on transitions outgoing from s.

Algorithm 4 Computation of critical tasks in LTS (COMPUTECRITICALTASKS)

Inputs: LTS = $\langle Q, \Sigma, q_{init}, \Delta \rangle$, Probabilistic property (pp)
Output: A set of Critical Tasks $(CTasks)$
1: $CTasks := \{\}$, $\mathcal{T}_{tasks} := pp.getTasks()$
2: $Paths := \text{FINDPATHS}(\text{LTS}, \mathcal{T}_{tasks})$ ▷ FINDPATHS (Algorithm 2)
3: **for** each $path \in paths$ **do**
4:     reversedPath := REVERSE$(path)$
5:     **for** each transition $(s, task, s')$ in reversedPath **do**
6:         $\Delta_s \subseteq \{(s, a, q) \in \Delta \mid q \in Q\}$
7:         **if** $Size(\Delta_s) > 1$ **then**
8:             **if** pp.operator() is " > " or " ≥ " **then**
9:                 $CTasks := CTasks \cup \{a \in \Sigma \setminus task \mid \exists q \in Q, (s, a, q) \in \Delta_s\}$
10:        **else if** pp.operator() is " < " or " ≤ " **then**
11:             $CTasks := CTasks \cup \{task\}$
12:        **else**
13:             $CTasks := CTasks \cup \{a \in \Sigma \mid \exists q \in Q, (s, a, q) \in \Delta_s\}$
14:        **break**
    return $CTasks$

Algorithm 4 presents a method for computing the critical tasks $(CTasks)$ given an LTS and a probabilistic property (pp). The algorithm starts by initialising $CTasks$ as an empty set and extracts the set of all tasks $\mathcal{T}_{tasks}$ included in the probabilistic property. Next, it calls FINDPATHS (Algorithm 2) to find all paths in the LTS that include the tasks in $\mathcal{T}_{tasks}$ (line 2). For each path found, the algorithm reverses it and iterates over the transitions in reverse order. For each transition t represented as $(s, task, s')$, the algorithm selects the set of outgoing transitions from state s in the LTS, denoted by Δ_s (line 6). If the size of Δ_s is greater than 1, the algorithm checks the operator specified in pp (lines 7 to 13). If the operator is either $>$ or $\geq$, the algorithm adds to $CTasks$ the set of all actions a in Σ that have outgoing transitions from state s and do not correspond to the task in $task$ (lines 8 to 9). If the operator is $<$ or $\leq$, the algorithm adds the task $task$ to $CTasks$ (lines 10 to 11). Otherwise, the algorithm adds to $CTasks$ the set of all actions a in Σ that have outgoing transitions from state s (line 13). Finally, the algorithm breaks out from the loop for the current path. The algorithm returns the set of critical tasks *CTasks* as output. The time complexity of this algorithm is $\mathcal{O}(f(n) \times |\Delta|)$, where $f(n)$ is the time complexity of the FINDPATHS algorithm and $|\Delta|$ is the number of transitions in the LTS.

3.5   Probabilistic Runtime Enforcement (PRE)

The enforcement mechanism (EM) requires as input a probabilistic property φ and an LTS (Fig. 4). It is triggered right after the monitoring component. At runtime, it periodically receives a list of execution traces and a list of waiting tasks (waiting to be executed) from the monitoring component, and produces as output a list of tasks (to be executed) whose execution does not cause the violation of the probabilistic property, as verified using PMC techniques.

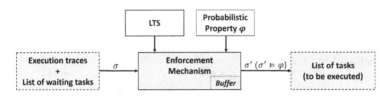

Fig. 4: Overview of PRE.

    The enforcement techniques used in this paper rely on two operations: *reordering* and *buffering*. Reordering techniques correspond to a change in the order of application of some of the tasks received as input. Buffering techniques rely on a FIFO buffer $\mathcal{B}$, which stores critical tasks when necessary. Buffering techniques aim at delaying the execution of specific tasks by adding them temporarily to the buffer $\mathcal{B}$ and taking them out of the buffer when their execution does not induce the violation of the property.

    Algorithm 5 presents the enforcement mechanism in detail. The algorithm takes as input a list of (waiting) tasks, a probabilistic property φ, and an LTS. It returns a list of tasks to be executed (in the best case, the same sequence of tasks given as input) that satisfies φ. The idea is to update the PTS by merging the execution traces and the tasks to be executed (waiting tasks and tasks in the buffer), and to use PMC techniques to determine whether these new tasks would still preserve the satisfaction of the property. If the executions of these tasks would violate the property, buffering or reordering techniques are triggered.

    The algorithm is initialised when the EM is called for the first time. Initialisation consists of (i) computing the critical tasks using the COMPUTECRITICAL-TASKS algorithm (Algorithm 4) and storing them in the global variable *ct*, and (ii) initialising the buffer $\mathcal{B}$ to empty. The COMPUTECRITICALTASKS algorithm computes the tasks of the process that can avoid the property violation and thus will be stored in the buffer $\mathcal{B}$ by the enforcer when necessary. When the enforcement mechanism is used for the first time, the list of tasks to be processed only consists of the waiting tasks. Later on, each time enforcement is used, the list

---

Algorithm 5 Enforcement Mechanism

Inputs: a list of execution traces $\mathcal{T}$, a list of waiting tasks $\sigma_{\mathcal{T}}$, a probabilistic property φ, an LTS.

Output: a list of tasks to be executed $\sigma'_{\mathcal{T}}$

1: **if** EM is not initialised **then**   ▷ ct and $\mathcal{B}$ are **Global** variables.
2:     $ct := \text{COMPUTECRITICALTASKS}(LTS, \varphi)$ ▷ Algorithm 4
3:     $\mathcal{B} := [], \sigma := \sigma_{\mathcal{T}}$ ▷ Initialise Buffer $\mathcal{B}$
4: **else**
5:     $\sigma_{buffer} := \langle task \mid task \in \mathcal{B}.getTasks() \rangle$ ▷ All tasks in Buffer
6:     $\sigma := Concat(\sigma_{buffer}, \sigma_{\mathcal{T}})$ ▷ Concatenation
   return $\sigma'_{\mathcal{T}} := \text{EM}(LTS, \mathcal{T}, \sigma, \varphi, ct)$

7: **function** EM($LTS, \mathcal{T}, \sigma, \varphi, ct$)
8:     **if** CHECK($LTS, \mathcal{T}, \sigma, \varphi$) **then**
9:         $\sigma_s := \langle task \mid task \in \sigma \wedge task \in \mathcal{B}.getTasks() \rangle$
10:        RemovefromBuffer(σ_s)   ▷ Buffering: (Remove)
11:        **return** σ
12:    **else**
13:        $\sigma_1 := \langle task \mid task \in \sigma \wedge task \in ct \rangle, \sigma_2 := \langle task \mid task \in \sigma \wedge task \notin \sigma_1 \rangle$
14:        $\sigma_r := Reorder(\sigma_1, \sigma_2)$ ▷ Reordering
15:        **if** CHECK($LTS, \mathcal{T}, \sigma_r, \varphi$) **then**
16:            $\sigma_s := \langle task \mid task \in \sigma_r \wedge task \in \mathcal{B}.getTasks() \rangle$
17:            RemovefromBuffer(σ_s)   ▷ Buffering: (Remove)
18:            **return** σ_r
19:        **else**
20:            $\sigma', \sigma'' := \text{BISECTION}(\sigma_1)$ ▷ Binary-Search
21:            $\sigma_a := \langle task \mid task \in \sigma'' \wedge task \notin \mathcal{B}.getTasks() \rangle$
22:            AddtoBuffer(σ_a)   ▷ Buffering: (Add)
23:            $\sigma_b := Concat(\sigma_2, \sigma')$ ▷ Concatenation
24:            EM($LTS, \mathcal{T}, \sigma_b, \varphi, ct$)

25: **function** CHECK($LTS, \mathcal{T}, \sigma, \varphi$)   ▷ Probabilistic model checking
26:    **return** UPDATEPTS($LTS, \mathcal{T}, \sigma$) $\models \varphi$? **true** : **false**

27: **function** UPDATEPTS($LTS, \mathcal{T}, \sigma$)   ▷ Transforming LTS into PTS
28:    $\mathcal{I} := []$
29:    **for** each $task \in \sigma$, in order **do** $I := task.getInstance()$ ▷ I: Execution trace
30:        $I.append(task), \mathcal{I}.append(I)$
31:    **for** each $\tau \in \mathcal{T}$ **do** $I := \tau.getInstance()$
32:        **if** $I \notin \mathcal{I}$ **then** $\mathcal{I}.append(I)$
33:    **return** COMPUTEPTS($LTS, \mathcal{I}$)   ▷ COMPUTEPTS (Algorithm 3)

34: **function** BISECTION(σ)   ▷ Binary-Search
35:    $n := Size(\sigma); m := \lfloor n/2 \rfloor$
36:    **return** $\sigma[0...m], \sigma[m...n]$

---

of tasks to be processed is obtained by concatenating all the tasks in the buffer with the tasks in the waiting list (line 6). Function EM then starts processing this list of tasks. The CHECK function first verifies whether the given execution traces and the given list of tasks satisfy the property by using PMC. If this function returns true, all the tasks are removed from the buffer and the algorithm returns the tasks in the buffer and the waiting tasks (lines 8 to 11). Otherwise, the enforcement techniques are triggered. First, reordering techniques are applied as follows. The list of tasks is reordered by favouring (and thus executing first) the non-critical tasks, which are placed at the beginning of the list. Then, the PTS is built again, and PMC called to check whether ordering differently the tasks to be executed avoid the property violation (line 15). If the result is true, the buffer is emptied, and the list of tasks is returned. If the result is false, reordering techniques are not enough, and in such a case, the mechanism then executes some of the tasks only partially. To identify the subset of tasks that can be executed without violating the property, we use the BISECTION function (lines 34 to 36). This function helps to avoid an exhaustive exploration of all possible combinations of tasks (and calling PMC for each solution), which would be too costly and time-consuming. This function divides the list of critical tasks into two parts. The algorithm then puts the second part into the buffer and recursively calls the EM function for this new list of tasks, which is the list of non-critical tasks (computed on line 13) concatenated with the first part returned by the BISECTION function (lines 20 to 24). The algorithm ends when the verdict of PMC is true and returns a list of safe-to-execute tasks.

The time complexity of this algorithm is $\mathcal{O}(\log |\sigma_{\mathcal{T}}| \times f(|\sigma_{\mathcal{T}}|))$, where $|\sigma_{\mathcal{T}}|$ is the size of the given list of tasks, and $f(|\sigma_{\mathcal{T}}|)$ represents the time complexity of using PMC.

3.6   Characteristics

This paper proposes enforcement mechanism that is online, untimed, and operational, meaning it utilises real-time system traces, disregards physical time intervals, and offers a practical implementation guide. This mechanism has three main characteristics: *soundness*, *monotonicity*, and *transparency*. PRE refers to the probabilistic enforcement mechanism, PRE.buff is the buffer $\mathcal{B}$, $\neg E(\text{PRE.buff})$ means that the buffer was not triggered, PRE.out refers to the output of the mechanism, and CHECK refers to the probabilistic model checking function.

Proposition 1 states that the tasks in each trace generated by the mechanism do not violate the properties of the system by their execution.

Proposition 1 (Soundness)
$\forall \sigma : \text{PRE}(\text{LTS}, \mathcal{T}, \sigma, \varphi).\text{out} = \sigma'_{\mathcal{T}} \implies \text{CHECK}(\text{LTS}, \mathcal{T}, \sigma'_{\mathcal{T}}, \varphi) == \textbf{\textit{true}}$

Proof (Sketch). If the PMC's verdict is false, the execution monitor does not produce any tasks as output to maintain soundness.

Proposition 2 states that the enforcer's output sequence consistently grows with respect to the number of non-critical tasks in the input sequence.

Proposition 2 (Monotonicity)
$\forall t \in \sigma, t' \in \sigma', t, t' \notin ct : size(\sigma) \leq size(\sigma') \implies size(\text{PRE}(\text{LTS}, \mathcal{T}, \sigma, \varphi).\text{out}) \leq size(\text{PRE}(\text{LTS}, \mathcal{T}, \sigma', \varphi).\text{out})$

Proof (Sketch). The buffer exclusively stores critical tasks. Therefore, as the number of non-critical tasks in the input increases, the length of the output of the mechanism also increases.

The execution monitor is transparent, which means that it only intervenes if the input tasks to be executed violate the property.

Proposition 3 (Transparency)
$\text{PRE}(\text{LTS}, \mathcal{T}, \sigma, \varphi).\text{out} = \sigma'_{\mathcal{T}}, \neg E(\text{PRE.buff}) \implies \text{PRE}(\text{LTS}, \mathcal{T}, \sigma'_{\mathcal{T}}, \varphi).\text{out} = \sigma$

Proof (Sketch). Since there is no suppression operation in the enforcement mechanism, all tasks in the input σ are the same as in the output $\sigma'_{\mathcal{T}}$ when the buffer is not triggered.

4   Tool Support & Evaluation

This section first presents the toolchain that automates the different steps of our approach. We then provide a practical illustration of the approach and tools using a case study. Finally, additional experiments are presented to evaluate the tools' performance on a series of realistic examples.

4.1   Tool

Figure 5 gives an overview of the toolchain. As far as the inputs are concerned, we rely on the open-source tool Activiti [2] to specify and execute BPMN processes. Probabilistic properties are described using MCL. The monitoring techniques are implemented in Java and aim at extracting the required information about execution traces from a MySQL database. The transformation from BPMN processes to LTS models is performed using an open-source tool called VBPMN [21]. The annotation of the LTS model with probabilities, thus resulting in a PTS model, is implemented in Java. PMC is computed using the CADP probabilistic model checker, which takes as input an MCL probabilistic property and a PTS, and returns a Boolean value. Finally, the enforcer is also implemented in Java and applies the correction when necessary on the input flow of tasks using the techniques (reordering and buffering) presented in Section 3.

4.2   Case Study

The approach is illustrated using the shipment process of a hardware retailer [25]. Figure 6 shows the BPMN process of this example, whose final goal is to deliver goods. More precisely, this process starts when there are goods ready for shipment. Two tasks are then executed concurrently: one involves packaging the

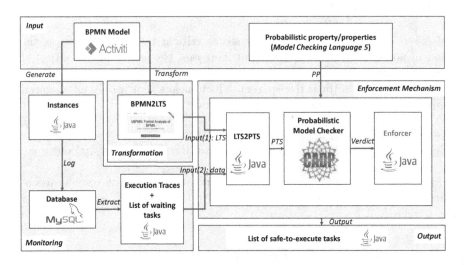

Fig. 5: Toolchain overview.

goods (T7) while the other determines whether a normal or special shipment is required (T1). Based on that decision, the first option verifies the need for additional insurance (T2), followed by the opportunity to purchase additional insurance (T4) and/or complete a post-label (T5). Another option is to request quotes from carriers (T3), followed by assigning a carrier and preparing the paperwork (T6). Finally, the package is transferred to a designated pick-up area (T8).

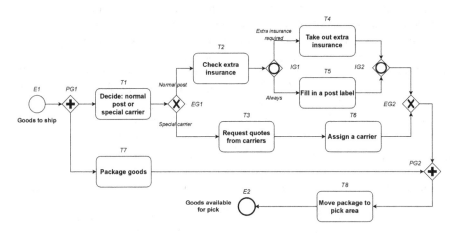

Fig. 6: BPMN shipment process of a hardware retailer.

For illustration purposes, we choose a property checking that the probability of executing task T4 after task T2 is less than 0.5. This is important because the choice of taking extra insurance (T4) comes with a cost, and if this decision is taken too often (more than half of the time here), this could result in high expenses on a short period of time. This property is expressed in MCL as follows: prob true*. T2. true*. T4 is < 0.5 end prob. As the question mark symbol is used, the model checker returns a Boolean value indicating the property's truthfulness and a numerical value representing the probability of executing T4 after T2.

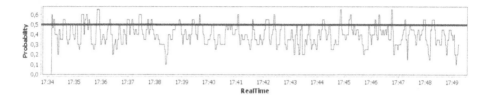

Fig. 7: Experiments on the case study *without* enforcement.

We have conducted two series of experiments with this running example, one without the enforcement mechanism (results are shown in Figure 7) and the other with enforcement (Figure 8). The same randomized workload of 2000 instances was used for each experiment. These experiments show that, without enforcement techniques, there is a 7% risk of violating the property, resulting in a satisfaction rate of 93%. In other words, the property is violated 7% of the time, which corresponds to the situations where the curve goes above the probability threshold represented as an horizontal line in Figure 7. On the other hand, Figure 8 shows that with enforcement, the instance executions keep satisfying the given probabilistic property, resulting in a 100% satisfaction rate and no violation of the property. In practice, this allows one to delay payment of extra insurance over time and thus avoids peaks of extra expenses.

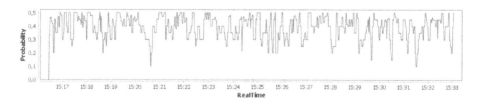

Fig. 8: Experiments on the case study *with* enforcement.

4.3 Experiments

The goal of this section is to evaluate the correctness and performance of the enforcement approach. The correctness is calculated as the percentage of probabilistic properties violated during the running process, while the performance is measured by the average execution time (AET) of an instance. AET is computed by summing the execution time of each instance and by dividing this value by the number of instances. To conduct these experiments, we relied on a set of BPMN processes taken from the literature. Each process was executed 1000 times, resulting in 1000 instances. The time taken between the startup of two new process instances was computed using an exponential distribution with a lambda value of 5 ($\lambda = 5$). These experiments were performed on an Ubuntu OS laptop with a 1.7 GHz Intel Core i5 processor and 8 GB of RAM.

The results of these experiments are presented in Table 1. Each row gives the results for a given process by providing a description, its size in terms of number of tasks and gateways, the size of the corresponding LTS in terms of number of states and transitions, the correctness results without (a) and with (b) enforcement, and the AET without/with enforcement. The correctness value corresponds to the satisfaction rate as a percentage (%). The second is described as the unit of time for AET.

Table 1: Experimental results for some case studies.

No.	BPMN Process	Characteristics		PTS		Correctness	AET (s)
		Tasks	Gateways	States	Transitions		
1	Shipment [25]	8	2 ⬦ + 2 ◆ + 2 ◈	18	38	(a) 93%	0.65
						(b) 100%	1.38
2	Shipment [25]	8	2 ⬦ + 2 ◆ + 2 ◈	18	38	(a) 47%	0.68
						(b) 100%	2.23
3	Shopping [22]	22	8 ⬦ + 2 ◆ + 2 ◈	59	127	(a) 93%	0.94
						(b) 100%	1.98
4	Shopping [22]	22	8 ⬦ + 2 ◆ + 2 ◈	59	127	(a) 54%	0.97
						(b) 100%	3.76
5	AccoutOpening [22]	15	3 ⬦ + 2 ◆ + 2 ◈	20	33	(a) 89%	0.56
						(b) 100%	1.58
6	Online-Shop [22]	19	7 ⬦ + 2 ◆	36	74	(a) 96%	1.98
						(b) 100%	4.52
7	Multi-Inclusives [22]	8	6 ◆	141	1201	(a) 85%	3.42
						(b) 100%	11.44
8	Booking [22]	11	2 ⬦ + 4 ◆	53	252	(a) 88%	2.42
						(b) 100%	6.17

Table 1 first shows that without enforcement techniques, the resulting correctness results present a satisfaction rate below 100%, whereas this rate is systematically of 100% when enforcement is used. As for AET, the execution time is longer when using enforcement techniques. The time increases when the percentage of satisfaction of the property decreases. For instance, examples 1 and 2 use the same process but different properties. The percentage of property violations of example 1 is lower than example 2; therefore, the latter takes more time when using enforcement because it takes more time for the process instances to complete. Similar results can be observed for examples 3 and 4. Although the enforcement mechanism increases the execution time of the process, it systematically ensures that the process executes while preserving the given property.

5   Related Work

In this section, we first compare with existing works on probabilistic verification of business processes, and then we focus on enforcement techniques.

The approaches proposed in [5,6] deal with Bayesian networks to infer the relationship between different events. As an example, the authors in [6] introduce a BPMN normal form based on Activity Theory that can be used for representing the dynamics of a collective human activity from the perspective of a subject. This workflow is then transformed into a Causal Bayesian Network that can be used for modelling human behaviours and assessing human decisions. In [18,19], the authors present a framework for modelling and analysing business workflows. These workflows are described with a subset of BPMN extended with probabilistic nondeterministic branching and general-purpose reward annotations. An algorithm translates such models into Markov Decision Processes (MDP) written in the syntax of the PRISM model checker. This enables quantitative analysis of business processes for properties such as transient/steady-state probabilities, reward-based properties, and best- and worst-case scenarios. These properties are verified using the PRISM model checker. This work supports design time analysis but does not focus on the dynamic execution and runtime verification of processes. The approach in [8] extends BPMN with time and probabilities. Specifically, the authors expect that a probability value is provided for each flow involved in an inclusive or exclusive split gateway. These BPMN processes are then transformed to rewriting logic and analysed using the Maude statistical model checker PVeStA. The authors in [15] propose to compute probabilities from execution traces of executable BPMN and apply probabilistic model checking techniques at runtime to analyse a given property. In this work, we also rely on PMC, but we go beyond the analysis of BPMN processes, because when the property is not satisfied, we apply techniques for enforcing the satisfaction of the property.

As far as runtime enforcement is concerned, existing techniques usually rely on common techniques including buffering, reordering, healing and discarding actions or events [1,4,12,14]. Buffering rely on storing events that violate certain property in a buffer, which helps delaying their execution. Reordering was used in several works for favouring or delaying the execution of some actions. Healing is a technique that enforces properties by repairing or inserting new events to ensure compliance. Suppression of events ensures property enforcement by discarding specific events. In the context of BPMN processes, removing specific tasks or artificially adding other tasks is meaningless due to the overall goal of the running processes, explaining why we made use of reordering and buffering techniques only. The authors of [11, 13] focus on developing runtime enforcement techniques for timed properties, without targetting any specific application area. In [7], the authors study runtime monitoring and enforcement of first-order LTL properties over data evolution using an automata-based technique. Their approach is based on the construction of a first-order automaton that is able to perform the monitoring incrementally and by using exponential space in the size of the property. This theoretical work does not focus on BPMN probabilistic processes, nor on probabilistic properties.

6   Conclusion

In this paper, we have proposed a probabilistic execution enforcement mechanism for BPMN processes at runtime. The BPMN process is first transformed into an LTS model. This model is periodically annotated with the execution probability of each transition in the LTS, resulting in a PTS model. This step is achieved by supervising the multiple executions of the BPMN process and extracting the corresponding execution traces. When new instances are triggered, new tasks are waiting to be executed. We check whether the execution of these tasks will not violate the given probabilistic property. If it is the case, the enforcement techniques are activated by either buffering or reordering tasks in order to avoid the violation of the property. All the steps of the approach are automated by a toolchain consisting of tools we implemented or reused. Experiments show the correctness of the approach, which preserves the truthfulness of the property, and a slight overhead in terms of performance, which comes from the time needed to apply enforcement techniques.

The two main perspectives of this work are as follows. The first one is to extend the PRE mechanism in order to minimise the frequency of verifications by considering the PMC results. The second future work focuses on applying PMC results to dynamically adjust the resource allocation necessary for efficient process execution.

Acknowledgements. This work was supported by the Région Auvergne-Rhône-Alpes within the "*Pack Ambition Recherche*" programme.

References

1. Aceto, L., Cassar, I., Francalanza, A., Ingólfsdóttir, A.: On Runtime Enforcement via Suppressions. In: 29th International Conference on Concurrency Theory (CONCUR 2018). pp. 34:1–34:17. https://doi.org/10.4230/LIPIcs.CONCUR.2018.34

2. Activiti: Open source business automation (accessed December 2021), `https://www.activiti.org/`

3. Bartocci, E., Falcone, Y., Francalanza, A., Reger, G.: Introduction to runtime verification. Lectures on Runtime Verification: Introductory and Advanced Topics pp. 1–33 (2018). `https://doi.org/10.1007/978-3-319-75632-5_1`

4. Basin, D., Klaedtke, F., Zălinescu, E.: Runtime Verification over Out-of-Order Streams. ACM Trans. Comput. Logic **21**(1) (oct 2019). `https://doi.org/10.1145/3355609`

5. Ceballos, H.G., Cantu, F.J.: Discovering causal relations in semantically-annotated probabilistic business process diagrams. In: Global Conference on Artificial Intelligence, GCAI. pp. 29–40 (2018). `https://doi.org/10.29007/nd7r`

6. Ceballos, H.G., Flores-Solorio, V., Garcia, J.P.: A probabilistic BPMN normal form to model and advise human activities. In: International Workshop on Engineering Multi-Agent Systems. pp. 51–69. Springer (2015). `https://doi.org/10.1007/978-3-319-26184-3_4`

7. De Masellis, R., Su, J.: Runtime enforcement of first-order LTL properties on data-aware business processes. In: Service-Oriented Computing: 11th International Conference, ICSOC 2013, Berlin, Germany, December 2-5, 2013, Proceedings 11. pp. 54–68. Springer (2013). `https://doi.org/10.1007/978-3-642-45005-1_5`

8. Durán, F., Rocha, C., Salaün, G.: Stochastic analysis of BPMN with time in rewriting logic. Science of Computer Programming **168**, 1–17 (2018). `https://doi.org/10.1016/j.scico.2018.08.007`

9. Emerson, E., Jutla, C.S., Sistla, A.: On model checking for the mu-calculus and its fragments. Theoretical Computer Science **258**(1), 491–522 (2001). `https://doi.org/10.1016/S0304-3975(00)00034-7`

10. Falcone, Y., Havelund, K., Reger, G.: A tutorial on runtime verification. Engineering dependable software systems pp. 141–175 (2013). `https://doi.org/10.3233/978-1-61499-207-3-141`

11. Falcone, Y., Jéron, T., Marchand, H., Pinisetty, S.: Runtime enforcement of regular timed properties by suppressing and delaying events. Sci. Comput. Program. **123**, 2–41 (2016). `https://doi.org/10.1016/j.scico.2016.02.008`

12. Falcone, Y., Mounier, L., Fernandez, J.C., Richier, J.L.: Runtime enforcement monitors: composition, synthesis, and enforcement abilities. Formal Methods in System Design **38**, 223–262 (2011). `https://doi.org/10.1007/s10703-011-0114-4`

13. Falcone, Y., Pinisetty, S.: On the Runtime Enforcement of Timed Properties. In: Proceedings of the Runtime Verification 2019 conference, pp. 48–69. Springer (Oct 2019). `https://doi.org/10.1007/978-3-030-32079-9_4`

14. Falcone, Y., Salaün, G.: Runtime Enforcement with Reordering, Healing, and Suppression. In: SEFM 2021 - 19th IEEE International Conference on Software Engineering and Formal Methods. pp. 1–20. IEEE, Virtual, United Kingdom (Dec 2021). `https://doi.org/10.1007/978-3-030-92124-8_3`

15. Falcone, Y., Salaün, G., Zuo, A.: Probabilistic Model Checking of BPMN Processes at Runtime. In: iFM 2022 - International Conference on integrated Formal Methods. pp. 1–17. Lugano, Switzerland (Jun 2022). `https://doi.org/10.1007/978-3-031-07727-2_11`

16. Faqrizal, I., Salaün, G.: Counting Bugs in Behavioural Models using Counterexample Analysis. In: FormaliSE 2022 - International Conference on Formal Methods in Software Engineering. pp. 1–11. Pittsburgh, United States (May 2022). `https://doi.org/10.1145/3524482.3527647`

17. Garavel, H., Lang, F., Mateescu, R., Serwe, W.: CADP 2011: a toolbox for the construction and analysis of distributed processes. Int. J. Softw. Tools Technol. Transf. **15**(2), 89–107 (2013). https://doi.org/10.1007/s10009-012-0244-z

18. Herbert, L., Sharp, R.: Precise quantitative analysis of probabilistic business process model and notation workflows. Journal of Computing and Information Science in Engineering **13**(1), 011007 (2013). https://doi.org/10.1115/1.4023362

19. Herbert, L.T., Sharp, R.: Quantitative analysis of probabilistic BPMN workflows. In: International Design Engineering Technical Conferences and Computers and Information in Engineering Conference. vol. 45011, pp. 509–518. American Society of Mechanical Engineers (2012). https://doi.org/10.1115/DETC2012-70653

20. ISO/IEC: International standard 19510, information technology – business process model and notation. (2013)

21. Krishna, A., Poizat, P., Salaün, G.: VBPMN: Automated Verification of BPMN Processes. In: 13th International Conference on integrated Formal Methods (iFM 2017). Turin, Italy (Sep 2017). https://doi.org/10.1007/978-3-319-66845-1_21

22. Krishna, A., Poizat, P., Salaün, G.: Checking Business Process Evolution. Science of Computer Programming **170**, 1–26 (Jan 2019). https://doi.org/10.1016/j.scico.2018.09.007

23. Larsen, K.G., Skou, A.: Bisimulation through probabilistic testing. Information and Computation **94**(1), 1–28 (1991). https://doi.org/10.1016/0890-5401(91)90030-6

24. Mateescu, R., Requeno, J.I.: On-the-Fly Model Checking for Extended Action-Based Probabilistic Operators. International Journal on Software Tools for Technology Transfer **20**(5), 563–587 (Oct 2018). https://doi.org/10.1007/s10009-018-0499-0

25. Mateescu, R., Salaün, G., Ye, L.: Quantifying the Parallelism in BPMN Processes using Model Checking. In: The 17th International ACM Sigsoft Symposium on Component-Based Software Engineering (CBSE 2014). Lille, France (Jun 2014). https://doi.org/10.1145/2602458.2602473

26. Mateescu, R., Thivolle, D.: A Model Checking Language for Concurrent Value-Passing Systems. In: Cuellar, J., Maibaum, T. (eds.) FM 2008. Lecture Notes in Computer Science, vol. 5014, pp. 148–164. Springer Verlag, Turku, Finland (May 2008). https://doi.org/10.1007/978-3-540-68237-0_12

27. Poizat, P., Salaün, G., Krishna, A.: Checking Business Process Evolution. In: 13th International Conference on Formal Aspects of Component Software (FACS). Besançon, France (Oct 2016). https://doi.org/10.1007/978-3-319-57666-4_4

Combining Look-ahead Design-time and Run-time Control-synthesis for Graph Transformation Systems

He Xu⬤, Sven Schneider^(✉)⬤, and Holger Giese⬤

Hasso Plattner Institute, University of Potsdam, Potsdam, Germany
{he.xu,sven.schneider,holger.giese}@hpi.de

Abstract. The correct operation of safety-critical cyber-physical systems is crucial. However, such systems often feature a large variability of start configurations, an intractably large state space, a high degree of uncertainty, or inherently unsafe behavior. A model of the expected system behavior starting in the current state can be used by look-ahead controllers to derive control decisions to avoid paths to safety violations when possible. However, the computational effort for deriving and analyzing the future system behavior is exponential in the look-ahead.

In this paper, we employ Graph Transformation Systems (GTSs) for the modeling of expected system behavior. We then combine design-time and run-time control synthesis based on Supervisory Control Theory (SCT) achieving an exponential cost-reduction for a given controller look-ahead. For a fixed required reaction time of controllers, much longer look-aheads may therefore be employed. To illustrate and evaluate our approach, we consider a system where shuttles must avoid collisions with ambulances at level crossings.

Keywords: cyber-physical systems, self-adaptive systems, supervisory control, model-predictive control, runtime verification, bounded model checking

1 Introduction

Cyber-physical systems in which software components operate in a physical environment often encompass complex concurrent behavior. The development or synthesis of such control software achieving a given set of goals while also ensuring the satisfaction of a given safety-specification is crucial. In model-predictive control, a model of the expected system behavior is employed to obtain look-ahead controllers. Such controllers derive control decisions based on the set of all behavior sequences of a chosen look-ahead length starting in the current state. However, the set of such behavior sequences is exponential in the look-ahead length limiting the look-ahead to values allowing admissible reaction times.

As a running example, we consider a variation of the *RailCab* system from [38, 30]. In this system, shuttles navigate on a large-scale track topology, which intersects with a road topology at level crossings. Ambulances, which can be

ⓒ The Author(s) 2024
D. Beyer and A. Cavalcanti (Eds.): FASE 2024, LNCS 14573, pp. 77–100, 2024.
https://doi.org/10.1007/978-3-031-57259-3_4

monitored by shuttles with a certain degree of uncertainty, navigate on the road topology and may traverse level crossings. The shuttle control to be derived, must avoid collisions with ambulances when possible by adjusting the speed of the shuttle taking potential ambulance behavior into account. To focus on our approach and to simplify our presentation, we reduce the possible number of steps of actors in the system model by employing a small topology fragment with one level crossing, a single shuttle, and one ambulance.

Besides run-time efficiency, controller synthesis approaches for cyber-physical systems must solve an array of further problems. *P1 (Sets of Start States):* The start state of the system is often not precisely known requiring the consideration of a large or even infinite set of start states. These start states may differ in rigid components but also in the number, the state, and the interconnection of active components. For our running example, the underlying rigid topology and the location of shuttles and ambulances on this topology may vary greatly. *P2 (State space explosion):* Even when selecting a single start state, the state space of the system is often intractably large or even infinite because all steps of all components must be captured in the system model. *P3 (Uncertainty):* The uncontrolled part of the system can often not be modeled faithfully at design time due to uncertainty. For example, uncertainty arises due to behavioral or configuration adaptation as well as from unknown, unreliable, or unpredictable components/actors (such as humans) performing additional steps that cannot be foreseen at design time or fail to perform such steps [45]. *P4 (Unsafe Systems):* Avoidance of unsafe states is not always feasible due to uncertainty or in contexts where unsafe states cannot be avoided by control at all.

For the modeling of the expected future system behavior, we employ Graph Transformation Systems (GTSs), which can be used when system states can be captured by graphs and when the steps of the involved components can be captured using local graph modifications. In the past, various GTS-variants have been developed and employed for the modeling, design, and analysis of such systems in an abundance of publications such as [19, 20, 21, 18, 29, 22, 30, 49, 48, 33] focusing on different system aspects and requirements.

To accommodate for these problems (discussed in more detail in the subsequent section), we propose a model-driven approach based on GTSs and the MAPE-K control framework where we employ a sliding window technique considering actor-specific state fragments to reduce the computational effort (problems P1 and P2) and combine design-time control synthesis with run-time control synthesis as a look-ahead extension technique to efficiently obtain best-effort control (to tackle problems P3 and P4). Both, at design-time and run-time, we employ an extension of Supervisory Control Theory (SCT) with priorities for the synthesis of controllers where the uncontrolled system is modeled using an extension of GTSs with controllability notions.

This paper is structured as follows. In section 2, we discuss our conceptual approach in the context of the MAPE-K framework including the sliding window technique. In section 3, we consider related work. In section 4, we present our extension of SCT with priorities. In section 5, we integrate controllability

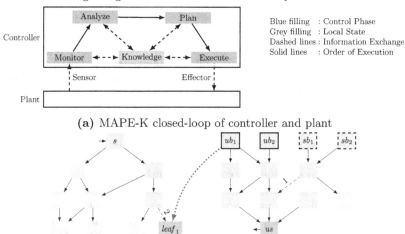

(a) MAPE-K closed-loop of controller and plant

(b) Runtime Model. A Bounded Forward State Space from the current system state s (left). A Bounded Backward State Space leading to the unsafe state us (right). The safe boundary $\{sb_1, sb_2\}$ from which us can be avoided by preventing step 1. The unsafe boundary $\{ub_1, ub_2\}$ from which us cannot be avoided. The state $leaf_1$ contains ub_1 (indicated by the dotted arrow) leading to the prevention of step 2.

Fig. 1. Overview of MAPE-K-based approach

notions into the GTS framework and present our running example. In section 6, we discuss control synthesis at design-time. In section 7, we discuss control synthesis at run-time based on the design-time results. In section 8, we evaluate our approach for a larger case study. Finally, in section 9, we conclude the paper and provide an outlook on future work.

2   MAPE-K Closed-Loop Approach

Software being executed in a cyber-physical system on a device often follows (at least implicitly) the MAPE-K closed-loop design [53, 1] depicted in Figure 1a developed for systems with a high degree of complexity, uncertainty, and dynamicity. Such software interacts with its context in that system via sensors and effectors and keeps a Runtime Model (RTM) to store its local state across its looped executions. It executes (a) the monitoring phase to react to sensor information by updating the RTM accordingly, (b) the analysis phase to determine the impact of the most recent events on its options to achieve its control goals, (c) the planning phase to derive a control plan satisfying suitable quality standards, and (d) the execution phase to send events to the effectors to implement the steps of the derived control plan. Ideally, such a MAPE-K control architecture adapts to unexpected situations at run-time in an ad-hoc manner.

In our approach, the RTM (see Figure 1b) contains (a) a Bounded Forward State Space (BFSS) from the current system state s (derived and maintained at run-time) and (b) a Bounded Backward State Space (BBSS) from unsafe states us (derived at design-time). Both of theses state spaces are (similarly to bounded model checking [50]) derived from the GTS capturing the expected system behavior. Moreover, the RTM contains the controllers derived from these two state spaces, which capture for each depicted state the exiting steps that the shuttle may perform. At run-time the controller obtained from the BFSS and the BBSS are combined by attempting to identify boundary graphs of the BBSS in the leaf states of the BFSS. For a BFSS and BBSS of depth n and k, this combination grants an effective look-ahead of $n+k$ to the controller. Clearly, the look-ahead should be maximized (taking other aspects such as required response time into account) to provide the controller synthesis procedure with as much information as possible to avoid the execution of overly conservative behavior (such as unnecessarily slowing down the shuttle). Not employing a BBSS only constructing a BFSS of depth $n+k$ to achieve the same look-ahead $n+k$ would be exponentially more expensive and, moreover, this additional cost would be incurred at run-time whereas at least the BBSS is obtained in our approach at design-time rendering its cost of construction negligible.

In our approach, the four MAPE phases are as follows.

- *Monitor phase:* when the controller is informed via its sensors about a state change from the BFSS root s to state s', it selects s' as the new root of the BFSS. Unless the step to s' was not expected due to uncertainty, s' is already one of the successors of s contained in the BFSS.
- *Analysis phase:* States of the BFSS unreachable from s' are removed and the GTS model is used to re-extend the BFSS to the chosen depth n. To identify states to be avoided, all leaf states of the BFSS are checked for occurrences of unsafe boundary states of the BBSS. Finally, the run-time controller is then adjusted to the modified BFSS by selecting steps to be prevented that would lead to the states to be avoided.
- *Planning phase:* The controller can then plan the execution of any controllable step exiting the new root state s' of the BFSS (in the running example, these steps are the steps of the shuttle) or let the plant perform the next step.[1]
- *Execute phase:* If a step has been selected in the planning phase, this step is send for execution to the corresponding effector (in the running example, a hardware controller of the shuttle will receive and implement such a signal).

The worst-case controller response time depends on the time required for (a) the full reconstruction of the BFSS and the corresponding controller synthesis thereon (upon an occurrence of an unexpected step) and (b) the identification of leaf states of the BFSS containing unsafe boundary states of the BBSS. The

---

[1] The absence of such controllable steps does not indicate a problem as the controller may just not need to change the behavior of the agent (e.g., the shuttle may already be driving at the desired speed) but, in the considered time-abstract setting, the absence of any step implies that no control strategy guaranteeing the avoidance of unsafe states could be obtained. In this case, fallback behavior such as not modeled emergency maneuvers or decisions by the environment on uncontrollable events may still result in the avoidance of unsafe states.

usage of the BBSS exponentially reduces the computational effort for (a) as discussed but, regarding (b), it also requires that the leaf states of the BFSS need to be checked against a potentially large number of unsafe boundary states instead of only the unsafe states. In our evaluation in section 8, we measure and further discuss these effects for a considered case study.

As mentioned in the introduction already, we employ a sliding window approach reducing the size of the BFSS and BBSS to be constructed. Instead of assuming that each agent maintains a perspective on the entire system state, we adopt the technique from [30] where, in a compositional approach, agent-specific scopes are used. On the one hand, this greatly reduces the number of steps (and thereby the size of the BFSS and BBSS) as only a small number of agents will be typically in the view range of an agent. On the other hand, a smaller view range may result (closely related to the look-ahead) in an overly conservative controller behavior. Besides mitigating the effect of state space explosion, this sliding window approach has the additional advantage that start states must only be determined for each actor individually and not globally. Intuitively, each system step must be followed by suitable postprocessing to update the reached state to the view range of the actor. These postprocessing steps are part of the system model and therefore define changes in the context of the agent to which the controller must suitably respond. In our evaluation in section 8, we further discuss this sliding window technique as we abstract from it in our running example to focus on controller synthesis via BFSS and BBSS.

3 Related Work

Model checking [2] is often inadequate for complex systems due to the state space explosion problem and uncertainty. Bounded Model Checking (BMC) [50, 24, 25] has been devised to reduce analysis costs providing, however, weaker guarantees and no support for uncertainty.

When formal fully-automatic verification is infeasible, Runtime Verification also called Runtime Monitoring [28] is an approach for monitoring the system's states and steps at run-time for notable behavior such as violations of invariants that require a manual or automatic response. However, without look-ahead capabilities, potential near-future unsafe states cannot be detected. Therefore, some RV approaches such as [45, 23, 15, 32, 52, 16] integrate a behavioral model describing expected future evolutions of the system. In [45], the expected future evolutions of a Timed Automata (TA) are analyzed at run-time using BMC. In [15], Deterministic Timed Markov Chains modeling the system are analyzed at design-time to obtain expressions on step-probabilities that will become available at run-time to make probability-maximizing decisions at run-time by evaluating the expressions at run-time instead of performing computationally expensive analysis. In [23], a run-time statistical model checking component has been integrated into a self-adaptive system. However, these approaches also rely on BMC and thereby suffer from state space explosion and in some cases such as [45, 15] also from being unable to react to uncertain events.

The approach of k-induction [26, 11] that has been adopted for variants of GTSs in [47, 48, 3] establishes state invariants by symbolically applying GT rules backwards from unsafe states to accumulate context capturing why and how the symbolic violation could be reached. This approach is thereby a symbolic version of backward BMC. We use a similar approach in this paper tackling the problem of a large number of undesirable backward steps constructed by k-induction.

A combination of forward and backward BMC similar to our approach for the analysis of Hybrid Automata in [54] applies depth first search forward and backward in parallel to find paths to unsafe states for Hybrid Automata with complex state space structure.

SCT as established in [40, 41, 39] for capturing, analyzing, and synthesizing supervisory control when the controllers, the plants, and their closed loops are given by regular languages over events (see also [27, 46] for an in-depth introduction and a discussion of derived approaches) has to our knowledge not been combined with event-priorities. However, priorities have been used to combine supervised modules preventing blocking situations in [6, 7]. Also, approaches in the Model Predictive Control domain (see [51] for a survey) employ models to predict the future system behavior as in our approach but focus usually on continuous time systems minimizing costs as in [4, 5] and have not been combined with SCT to the best of our knowledge. Besides the approach to distinguish between controllable and uncontrollable events as customary in SCT, other approaches of identifying actions of different actors and capturing interactions among such actors in the GT domain include [9] but also SCT for TA (related to [45] above) has been considered in [43, 42]. [35, 36, 34, 33] where a safety constraint has already been violated due to uncertainty or adversarial effects requiring the derivation and execution of recovery mechanisms.

4   Priority-aware Supervisory Control Theory

We recall SCT as introduced in the seminal work of Ramadge and Wonham [40, 41, 39] in which the closed loop is given by the event-synchronizing composition of controller and plant. To provide the essentials of this approach in our notation and to extend this approach with the concept of event priorities, we introduce a variant of Labeled Transition Systems (LTSs) extending finite automata thereby capturing regular languages over an event alphabet as considered in standard SCT. In such an LTS, events are grouped into controllable and uncontrollable events (cf. the MAPE-K closed-loop in Figure 1a), which are executed by the controller (e.g., signals to effectors) and the plant (e.g., signals from sensors). The controller may restrict the execution of controllable events in the closed-loop.

We aim at controller synthesis such that event-prevention ensures that the closed-loop avoids undesirable states (this notion is formalized below as non-blockingness) and no steps executing uncontrollable events have been prevented at the model level (this notion is formalized below as controllability) while not preventing event executions unnecessarily to retain the highest possible degree of freedom for further control steps.[2] We equip events with a priority as motivated in the next section by our running example: steps executing (un)controllable events are then only enabled when no steps executing higher-priority (un)controllable events are enabled (i.e., priorities are checked within the two groups of controllable and uncontrollable events separately).

Definition 1 (Labeled Transition System (LTS)). *A Labeled Transition System (LTS) Γ contains the following components.*

- states(Γ) *contains all states and its subsets* start(Γ), safe(Γ), *and* unsafe(Γ) *contain the start, safe, and unsafe states.*
- events(Γ) *contains the controllable and uncontrollable events* eventsC(Γ) *and* eventsUC(Γ).
- prio(Γ) : events(Γ) $\rightarrow$ **N** *assigns a priority to each event.*
- steps(Γ) $\subseteq$ states(Γ) $\times$ events(Γ) $\times$ states(Γ) *is a set of event-labelled steps.*

Moreover, Γ_1 is a sub-LTS of Γ_2, written $\Gamma_1 \leq \Gamma_2$, when the components of Γ_1 are contained in the corresponding components of Γ_2 and the reversed LTS rev(Γ) *is obtained by reversing* steps(Γ) *and swapping* start(Γ) *and* unsafe(Γ).

The priority-resolved LTS is obtained by omitting all controllable/uncontrollable steps disabled by higher-priority controllable/uncontrollable steps. Only the paths through this priority-resolved LTS can actually be observed.

Definition 2 (Priority-resolved LTS). *For an LTS Γ and a set of events E, $\Gamma' =$ resPrio(Γ, E) is the largest sub-LTS of Γ such that for all $(s, e_1, s_1) \in$* steps(Γ') *with $e_1 \in E$ there is no $(s, e_2, s_2) \in$ steps(Γ') with $e_2 \in E$ and* prio(Γ')(e_2) $>$ prio(Γ')(e_1). *Then, the priority-resolved LTS of Γ is given by* resPrio(Γ) = resPrio(resPrio(Γ, eventsUC(Γ)), eventsC(Γ)).[3]

A controller Γ_C to be synthesized for a given plant Γ_P is a sub-LTS of Γ_P and, hence, the event-synchronizing closed loop of Γ_C and Γ_P is just Γ_C.

The notion of controllability requires that the controller cannot prevent uncontrollable events that the plant can execute.

Definition 3 (Controllability). *A plant Γ_P and a controller $\Gamma_C \leq \Gamma_P$ satisfy controllability, if every path π of* resPrio(Γ_C) *that can be extended by* resPrio(Γ_P) *with a step executing an uncontrollable event $u \in$ eventsUC(Γ_P) can be extended by* resPrio(Γ_C) *with a step executing u as well.*

The notion of non-blockingness requires the liveness property that the closed loop may eventually reach a safe state from any of its states. In our approach, we define unsafe states as those violating a state invariant and safe states as those not having paths to any unsafe states.

Definition 4 (Non-blockingness). *A plant Γ_P and a controller $\Gamma_C \leq \Gamma_P$ satisfy non-blockingness, if every path π of* resPrio(Γ_C) *can be extended to a state in* safe(Γ_P).

---

[2] Note that controllers can only force certain events in a given state in this framework when all events executable from that state are controllable (differing from, e.g., [55]).

[3] Note that, in general, resPrio(Γ) $\neq$ resPrio(Γ, events(Γ)).

For the case of controllers and plants generating regular languages considered here, admissible controllers satisfying controllability and non-blockingness are closed under arbitrary unions [40, 41, 39, 27, 46]. Desired controllers are therefore defined as those admissible controllers that result in the largest closed loops in terms of sets of executable event sequences. Admissible controllers are also closed under arbitrary union in the presence of event priorities because the union of controllers will result in a controller that favors the highest priority steps from any of the controllers and, moreover, LTSs are memoryless (beyond their current state) implying that choosing higher priority steps from different controllers can not lead to states not traversable using any of the controllers. However, only the priority resolved versions of synthesized controllers for which the classic results from [40, 41, 39, 27, 46] readily apply are to be used anyway.

Following SCT, the first controller candidate is the plant LTS Γ. This candidate is then incrementally refined by preventing events enforcing controllability and non-blockingness least-restrictively until an admissible controller control(Γ) is obtained (closedness under arbitrary union also implies that the order in which violations of controllability and non-blockingness are resolved is insignificant). Note that this fixed-point procedure supports also cyclic LTSs in general (in which, as usual, loops may delay the visiting of safe states indefinitely as opposed to [55]). To handle the case with priorities, we resolve priorities among uncontrollable events before applying the fixed-point procedure and resolving priorities of remaining controllable steps afterwards to obtain the priority-aware controller pControl(Γ).

Definition 5 (Priority-Aware Controller). *An LTS Γ induces the LTS $\Gamma' =$* control(Γ) *by adapting Γ as follows:*[4]
- steps(Γ') *is the largest subset of* steps(Γ) *such that for each* $(s, e_1, s_1) \in$ steps(Γ') *(non-blockingness) there is some path from s_1 to a state in* safe(Γ') *using steps in* steps(Γ') *and (controllability) when* $(s_1, u_2, s_2) \in$ steps(Γ) *is a step using an uncontrollable event u_2 from* eventsUC(Γ) *then* (s_1, u_2, s_2) *is also a step in* steps(Γ').

Moreover, pControl(Γ) $=$ resPrio(control(resPrio(Γ, eventsUC(Γ))), eventsC(Γ)) *is the priority-aware controller for Γ.*

As an example for controller synthesis, consider the LTS in Figure 2 representing an uncontrolled plant and the priority-aware controller synthesized for it.[5] First, to resolve blocking at s_4, the controllable priority 2 event c_2 from s_0 is prevented enabling the priority 1 event c_1 from s_0. Second, to resolve blocking at s_3, the uncontrollable event uc_3 from s_1 is prevented. Third, to resolve non-controllability at s_1, the controllable priority 1 event c_1 from s_0 is prevented enabling the priority 0 event uc_1 from s_0. The resulting controller will only contain the path from s_0 to s_2 executing the event uc_1. Note that maintaining the steps of all priorities in the LTS simplifies controller synthesis since the effect of preventing controllable events (such as c_2 and c_1) becomes apparent immediately without

---

[4] For brevity, we omit here the removal of unreachable states from Γ'.

[5] When resolving priorities among uncontrollable events and later among controllable events no steps are removed in this example.

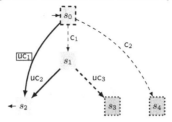

Fig. 2. Example of controllability and non-blockingness. The unsafe states $\{s_3, s_4\}$ are given in red with dotted border, the safe state s_2 is given in green with exiting arrow symbol, the remaining orange states have paths to unsafe states, the start state s_0 has an entering arrow symbol, the bold steps execute the uncontrollable events uc_i, the non-bold steps execute the controllable events c_i, the dashed steps have been prevented, the event c_2 has priority 2, the event c_1 has priority 1, the other events have priority 0, and only the boxed event uc_1 can be executed since the steps executing $\{c_1, c_2\}$ have been prevented.

the need to derive such steps intermittently for then enabled steps (e.g., only the step executing c_2 was enabled initially due to its priority) decoupling LTS generation and control synthesis.

Note that $\mathsf{control}(\mathsf{resPrio}(\Gamma)) \neq \mathsf{resPrio}(\mathsf{control}(\Gamma))$ in general because first resolving the priorities restricts the possible controllers to be synthesized. For example, first resolving priorities in Figure 2 would remove the step with the event uc_1, which would otherwise be the only remaining step.

5   Control-oriented Graph Transformation

We first introduce control-oriented GTSs before discussing the modeling of our running example using this formalism.

To ease presentation, we employ the simple class of typed directed graphs (short graphs) (see [12, 13, 14] for details). In our running example, we employ the type graph TG from Figure 3a, which can be understood to be a simple UML class diagram, and graphs, which can be understood to be simple UML object diagrams. In visualizations of graphs such as Figure 3b, types of nodes are indicated by their names (i.e., S_i and T_i are nodes of type Shuttle and Track), names of edges are omitted, types of edges are only given when required to avoid ambiguity (the only edge types with equal source and target node types are *fast*, *slow*, and *halt*). We denote monomorphisms (monos) from graph H to graph H' mapping nodes and edges injectively by $f : H \hookrightarrow H'$.

To introduce control-oriented GTSs, we first introduce GT rules used to derive GT steps between graphs. A Graph Transformation (GT) rule ρ consists of two monos $\ell : K \hookrightarrow L$ and $r : K \hookrightarrow R$ describing the removal and addition of elements and a set N of monos $n_i : L \hookrightarrow N_i$ of Negative Application Conditions

(NACs) describing forbidden extensions of L.[6] We use the abbreviation $\mathsf{lhs}(\rho) = L$ later on. In visualizations of GT rules (see Figure 3), we use an integrated notation in which L, K, and R are given in a single graph where graph elements marked with $\ominus$ are from $L - K$ and will be deleted, graph elements marked with $\oplus$ are from $R - K$ and will be created, and where all other graph elements are in K and will be preserved. When NACs are present, they are given on the left side of the $\triangleright$ symbol. For example, consider the GT rule in Figure 3c which preserves the ambulance and shuttle nodes A_1 and S_1, removes the edge from S_1 to A_1, creates an edge from A_1 to S_1, and is only applicable when A_1 has no edge to some road node R_1.

We now introduce our novel notion of control-oriented GTSs. Such a GTS S contains a set $\mathsf{start}(S)$ of start graphs, a set $\mathsf{unsafe}(S)$ of unsafe graphs representing violations of invariants, a set $\mathsf{rules}(S)$ of GT rules with the subsets of controllable and uncontrollable GT rules $\mathsf{rulesC}(S)$ and $\mathsf{rulesUC}(S)$, and a mapping $\mathsf{prio}(S)$ assigning a natural number as a priority to each GT rule. Note that, similarly as in our presentation of SCT in section 4, we assign priorities to GT rules and group them into controllable/uncontrollable GT rules capturing which steps can/cannot be prevented by the controller to be synthesized.

GT steps $G \Rightarrow_\sigma G'$ from a graph G to a graph G' are labeled with a pair $\sigma = (\rho, m)$ consisting of a GT rule ρ and a match $m : \mathsf{lhs}(\rho) \hookrightarrow G$ identifying an occurrence of $\mathsf{lhs}(\rho)$ in G. The match m must satisfy the requirement that there is no NAC $n_i : \mathsf{lhs}(\rho) \hookrightarrow N_i$ contained in ρ for which some $m_i' : N_i \hookrightarrow G$ satisfying $m_i' \circ n_i = m$ exists. The graph G' is then constructed from G via the usual Double Pushout (DPO) diagram (see [12, 13, 14] for a details).

A GTS induces a forward LTS by deriving GT steps from already included graphs and adds these steps as well as their target states in the resulting LTS. Note that we merely propagate the priorities of the GT rules into the constructed LTS instead of enforcing them by excluding lower-priority steps when higher-priority steps are present.

Definition 6 (Forward LTS of a GTS, BFSS). *A GTS S induces the unique LTS $\Gamma = [\![S]\!]$ as follows:*

- *states(Γ) contains start(Γ) and the target states of all steps in steps(Γ).*
- *start(Γ) contains the graphs from start(S).*
- *safe(Γ) $\subseteq$ states(Γ) contains the graphs from which unsafe(Γ) can't be reached.*
- *unsafe(Γ) $\subseteq$ states(Γ) contains the graphs G into which a mono $t : H \hookrightarrow G$ from some graph $H \in$ unsafe(S) exists.*
- *eventsC(Γ) and eventsUC(Γ) contain the step labels $\sigma = (\rho, m)$ of the steps in steps(Γ) where $\rho \in$ rulesC(S) and $\rho \in$ rulesUC(S).*
- *prio(Γ)(ρ, m) = prio(S)(ρ) assigns the priority of the used GT rule ρ.*
- *steps(Γ) is the least relation containing all GT steps from states in states(Γ).*

Moreover, the BFSS of depth n, denoted $[\![S]\!]_n$, is the largest sub-LTS of $[\![S]\!]$ in which all paths starting in start(Γ) through distinct states have length $\leq n$.

---

[6] Our approach is orthogonal to the use of more expressive notions of application conditions such as nested graph conditions [18, 14, 10].

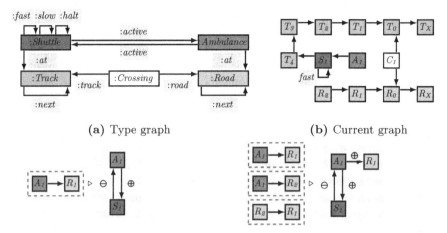

(a) Type graph   (b) Current graph

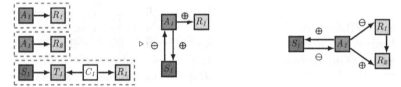

(c) GT rule ρ_{acp} for postponing ambulance creation.

(d) GT rule ρ_{ace} for expected ambulance creation at the farthest road segment from the crossing.

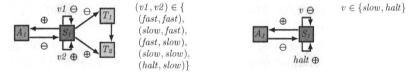

(e) GT rule ρ_{acu} for unexpected ambulance creation at some road segment (not on the crossing when there is a shuttle already).

(f) GT rule ρ_a moving the ambulance to the next road.

$v1 \ominus$ $(v1, v2) \in \{$
$(fast, fast),$
$(slow, fast),$
$(fast, slow),$
$(slow, slow),$
$(halt, slow)\}$

$v \ominus$ $v \in \{slow, halt\}$

$v2 \oplus$

$halt \oplus$

(g) GT rules ρ_{ff}, ρ_{sf}, ρ_{fs}, ρ_{ss}, and ρ_{hs} resulting in a fast or slow shutle on the next track.

(h) GT rules ρ_{sh} and ρ_{hh} resulting in a halted shuttle on the same track.

GT rules	controllable?	priority	S_{FE}	S_{FU}	Figure
ρ_{acp}	no	0	yes	yes	Figure 3c
ρ_{ace}	no	0	yes	no	Figure 3d
ρ_{acu}	no	0	no	yes	Figure 3e
ρ_a	no	0	yes	yes	Figure 3f
ρ_{fs}, ρ_{ss}, ρ_{hs}	yes	1	yes	yes	Figure 3g
ρ_{ff}, ρ_{sf}	yes	2	yes	yes	Figure 3g
ρ_{sh} ρ_{hh}	yes	0	yes	yes	Figure 3h

(i) Overview of the GT rules used in the GTSs S_{FE} and S_{FU}.

Fig. 3. Details on the running example.

We now discuss the modeling of our running example, which is a simplification of the case study considered in our evaluation in section 8. We model shuttles driving on a track topology where subsequent tracks are connected using *next* edges as in Figure 3b. The driving speed of each shuttle is either fast, slow, or halt (as marked using *fast*, *slow*, or *halt* loops). Level crossings (where track and road topology intersect) are indicated by the node type *Crossing* and are connected to the corresponding track and road segments. Ambulances may appear and drive on the road topology including the level crossings.

The graph in Figure 3b represents the current view of the shuttle on the system state. The ambulance A_1 is not yet connected to a road meaning that it can be ignored by the shuttle at this point. Ambulance and shuttle perform steps alternatingly by switching the directed edge between them in each step to ensure a certain level of fairness since the system would otherwise be fundamentally unsafe as the shuttle could not rule out collisions anymore. The edge from the ambulance to the shuttle indicates that the shuttle will perform the next step.

Shuttles may maintain their speed (events ff, ss, and hh) or switch between fast and slow (events fs and sf) as well as between slow and halt (events sh and hs), modeling the stopping and acceleration distance. These seven driving speed transitions are controllable for the shuttle controller but all steps of ambulances are uncontrollable. To allow the shuttle to make timely control decisions, an ambulance detection mechanism informs the shuttle when ambulances are two roads ahead of an upcoming level crossing (i.e., an ambulance would be detected in Figure 3b when it enters the road R_2). We derive shuttle control assuming that this detection mechanism is reliable but analysis will reveal partial robustness against unreliability in situations where ambulances are detected first on the closer road segments R_1 or even R_0. Note that shuttle and ambulance performing steps alternatingly will result in violations of non-blockingness when the controller prevents all controllable steps of the shuttle in a given state, which is thereby implicitly excluded as well.

We use GT rule priorities to model that the shuttle prefers faster driving speeds over slower driving speeds. Therefore, without preventing any steps, the shuttle will maintain its fast speed.

We now discuss the GT rules used in these GTSs in more detail. Again, shuttle and ambulance steps alternate as implemented by switching the direction of the edge between them in every GT rule. When its the ambulances turn, the GT rules ρ_{ace}, ρ_{acu}, and ρ_{acp} are applicable when the ambulance has no edge to some road segment yet and the GT rule ρ_a is used otherwise. The GT rule ρ_{ace} models the expected creation of the ambulance by creating an edge from the ambulance to the road R_2 in Figure 3b (the three NACs check that A_1 is not yet on R_1, that A_1 is not yet on some other road, and that the matched road R_1 has no predecessor). The GT rule ρ_{acu} models the unexpected creation of the ambulance by creating an edge from the ambulance to an arbitrary road unless this road is at the level crossing with a shuttle being already located there as well (the three NACs check that A_1 is not yet on R_1, that A_1 is not yet on some other road, and that S_1 is not on a track connected by a crossing to R_1). The

GT rule ρ_{acp} models the case that the ambulance is not yet created meaning that ambulance detection is postponed (the NAC checks that the ambulance is not yet on a road). Lastly, the GT rule ρ_a models the moving of a detected ambulance to the next road segment (by removing the edge from A_1 to the current road segment R_1 and creating such an edge to the road segment R_2 reached). When its the shuttles turn, the GT rules ρ_{ff}, ρ_{fs}, ρ_{sf}, ρ_{ss}, ρ_{sh}, ρ_{hs}, and ρ_{hh} are used. The GT rules ρ_{sh} and ρ_{hh} do not move the shuttle to the next track while the other GT rules do so. Here, the movement of the shuttle is implemented as for the GT rule ρ_a by deleting and creating an edge and the driving speed transitions are encoded by deleting and creating the driving speed loop at the shuttle.

In our running example, we first consider the GTS S_{FE} with expected ambulance detection: for this GTS, we employ the graph from Figure 3b as start graph, use 10 of the 11 GT rules from Figure 3, split GT rules into controllable and uncontrollable GT rules, and employ priorities as listed in Figure 3i. In particular, when its the ambulances turn, each enabled GT rule has the same priority 0 making all steps derivable using the GT rules ρ_{ace} and ρ_{acp} viable. When its the shuttles turn, GT rules setting the speed to halt, slow, and fast have priorities 0, 1, and 2 favoring a faster driving speed. Also, the GT rules for slowing down or remaining halted (ρ_{fs}, ρ_{sh}, and ρ_{hh}) cannot be prevented as this would lead to a violation of non-blockingness as discussed. Additionally, we consider a second GTS S_{FU} in which ambulances are possibly detected closer or on the level crossing: this GTS differs from S_{FE} by replacing the GT rule ρ_{ace} with ρ_{acu} for detecting an ambulance, which may result in up to four steps detecting the ambulance on any of the four road segments.

In the considered GTSs, only a finite number of graphs can be reached and, in the remainder, we represent each graph using an element of $\{✗, 0, 1, 2, ✔\} \times \{0, 1, 2, 3, 4, ✔\} \times \{f, s, h\} \times \{s, a\}$ where (a) ✗ means that the ambulance has not been detected yet, 0–2 is the distance of the ambulance to the crossing, and ✔ means that the ambulance has advanced beyond the crossing, (b) 0–4 is the distance of the shuttle to the crossing and ✔ means that the shuttle has advanced beyond the crossing, (c) f, s, and h is the driving speed of the shuttle, and (d) s or a means that the shuttle or the ambulance performs the next step. The start graph from Figure 3b is therefore represented by ✗4fs as the ambulance has not yet been detected, the shuttle is four tracks away from the level crossing, the shuttle is in fast driving speed, and the shuttle will perform the next step.

The 6 unsafe graphs in $\{0\} \times \{0\} \times \{f, s, h\} \times \{s, a\}$ of the considered GTSs S_{FE} and S_{FU} all contain a shuttle and an ambulance on the level crossing but differ in the three possible driving speeds of the shuttle and the two cases of which entity performs the next step. While we specify the set of all unsafe states in our GTS by providing it explicitly, unsafe states could also be identified using advanced approaches such as nested graph conditions, Linear Temporal Logic [37], Computation Tree Logic [8, 2], or Metric Temporal Graph Logic [49].

The controller to be synthesized should force the shuttle to drive fast unless an ambulance is present, in which case the controller should ensure that the shuttle reaches the track T_1 with slow speed and then halts there until the ambulance has passed the level crossing. The controller synthesized by our integrated approach results in this controller as discussed subsequently.

6   Design-time Control-synthesis

We now discuss design-time control synthesis based on *(a)* BBSS generation from unsafe states and *(b)* control synthesis based on SCT together resulting in an LTS with unsafe boundary to be avoided at run-time to avoid unsafe states and a safe boundary for which the LTS is a controller avoiding unsafe states.

For our running example, we start the BBSS generation using only two unsafe states $X_0 = \{00\text{sa}, 00\text{fa}\}$ for presentation purposes. We depict the obtained BBSS in Figure 4, which is constructed by adding up to k steps backwards from X_0. From all additional states X_1, unsafe states in X_0 can be reached by construction; to derive viable alternative steps avoiding unsafe states, we include all missing forward steps from states in X_1 to additional states X_2. The states X_2 are by construction safe states (indicated by the exiting arrow symbol) of the resulting LTS from which unsafe states in X_0 cannot be reached (within k steps). The start states of the constructed backward LTS are the last states traversed on each backward path (indicated by the entering arrow symbol). These start states will be grouped into the safe and unsafe boundary in the next step.

We construct a controller from the BBSS given in Figure 4 by applying SCT. First, the two unsafe states 00sa and 00fa violate non-blockingness. To make these states unreachable, all five steps with one of them as a target are prevented resulting in a violation of non-blockingness at 01fs. To make this state unreachable, the step $(11\text{fa}, a, 01\text{fs})$ is prevented resulting in a violation of controllability at 11fa. To make this state unreachable, all three steps with 11fa as target are prevented. Due to event-priorities, only the boxed events can be actually executed. Intuitively, the depicted controller ensures that, in the presence of an ambulance approaching the upcoming level crossing, the shuttle will avoid collisions, e.g., by halting in state 01ha. When the ambulance is created unexpectedly closer to the crossing using ρ_{acu} in S_{FU}, the controller obtained here will fail since it would enter track T_1 with fast speed when no ambulance is detected reaching state ✗1fa and then not be able to halt in front of the level crossing when the ambulance is then unexpectedly detected on the level crossing in the next step reaching state 01fs.

Technically, we construct the BBSS for a given GTS relying on a secondary GTS called the *backward GTS*: We generate the BFSS for the backward GTS (according to Definition 6), reverse the obtained LTS (according to Definition 1), and then add the missing forward steps to safe states as explained above. For our running example, we employ the backward GTSs S_{BE} and S_{BU}, which can be obtained from their forward counterpart GTSs S_{FE} and S_{FU} by reversing their GT rules (see, e.g., [14, Lemma 3.14] for rule reversal based on the L operation) and switching the sets of unsafe and start graphs. The reason for using a backward GTS is a reduced size of the BBSS, since (not simply using rule reversal) modeling the backward GTS separately (while still ensuring that it agrees with

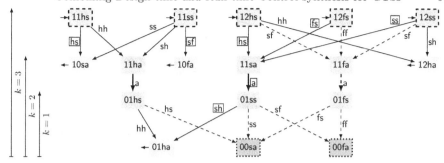

Fig. 4. Design-time controller synthesis based on BBSSs. We reuse the notation from Figure 2 for start states, unsafe states, safe states, potentially unsafe states, steps executing controllable/uncontrollable events, and prevented steps. The depicted BBSS of depth 3 and the resulting synthesized controller for the GTS S_{BE} (or the GTS S_{BU}) based for brevity on only two of the six unsafe states. The two unsafe states can be avoided resulting in an empty unsafe boundary.

the forward GTS as discussed in the next section) as in the case study considered in section 8 allows to enforce known system invariants (such as a minimum distance between level crossings or upper bounds of shuttles in certain areas) to reduce the number of derived steps.

Definition 7 (Backward LTS of a GTS, BBSS). *A (backward) GTS S induces the LTS* $\Gamma = [\![S]\!]^{\text{back}}$ *by adapting* $\Gamma' = \text{rev}([\![S]\!])$ *as follows:*
* states(Γ) *contains* states(Γ') *and the safe states* safe(Γ).
* safe(Γ) *contains the target graphs of all steps in* steps(Γ) $-$ steps(Γ').
* steps(Γ) *contains* steps(Γ') *and all GT steps from states in* states(Γ').
Moreover, the BBSS of depth k, *denoted* $[\![S]\!]^{\text{back}}_k$, *is the largest sub-LTS of* $[\![S]\!]^{\text{back}}$ *in which all paths through distinct states ending in* unsafe(Γ) *have length* $\leq k$.

We now apply the procedure pControl to the BBSS to derive the design-time controller. The unsafe boundary for which no suitable control could be derived is then given by all start states without an outgoing step and the safe boundary is given by the remaining start states (for which a controllable path to a safe state could be established).

Definition 8 (Design-time Controller). *If S is a (backward) GTS and* $k \in \mathbb{N}$, *then* $\Gamma = \text{pControl}([\![S]\!]^{\text{back}}_k)$ *is the design-time controller with unsafe boundary* uBoundary$(S, k) = \{s \in \text{start}(\Gamma) \mid \nexists(s, e, s') \in \text{steps}(\Gamma)\}$.

The design-time controller for the BBSS in Figure 4 is constructed for $k = 3$ and has an empty unsafe boundary. However, when using $k = 2$ (removing the states in the first row and the safe states in the second row), we obtain a design-time controller with safe boundary $\{11\text{ha}, 11\text{sa}\}$ and unsafe boundary $\{11\text{fa}\}$.

As a further example, consider Figure 5 in which the uncontrollable event acu is used by the GTS S_{FU} for an unexpected shuttle detection leading to a nonempty unsafe boundary $\{\text{✗1fa}\}$. In comparison, the controller obtained for S_{FE}

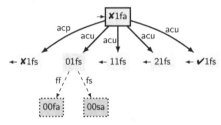

Fig. 5. Design-time controller synthesis with unexpected shuttle detection

not assuming unreliable ambulances detection as in the step (✘1fa, acu, 01fs) is robust by also avoiding (according to Figure 4) the state 01fs preceding a collision in Figure 5. Moreover, this controller is robust against ambulances appearing unexpectedly directly on the crossing using the step (✘2fa, acu, 02fs) unless the shuttle is already closer via step (✘1fa, acu, 01fs). Also, when an ambulance appears one track ahead of the crossing, either no collision occurs (after step (✘2fa, acu, 12fs)) or the ambulance crashes into the shuttle (after step (✘1fa, acu, 11fs)).

7   Run-time Control-synthesis

At run-time, we employ a given (forward) GTS S_{FS} to derive the run-time controller as follows. First, we adapt S_{FS} into S'_{FS} by using the current state of the system as the unique start state and add uBoundary(S_{BS}, k) to the set of unsafe states. Second, we construct the BFSS of depth n (which is assumed to be maintained throughout system execution as described in section 2) for S'_{FS}. Third, we apply SCT to obtain the least-restrictive controller.

Definition 9 (Run-time Controller). *If S is the GTS obtained from the forward GTS as the adjustment to the current system state and the unsafe boundary of the design-time controller and $n \in \mathbf{N}$, then $\Gamma = \mathsf{pControl}(\llbracket S \rrbracket_n)$ is the run-time controller with leaf set $\mathsf{leafs}(S, n) = \{s \in \mathsf{states}(\Gamma) \mid \nexists(s, e, s') \in \mathsf{steps}(\Gamma)\}$.*

We now discuss in more detail how our run-time control synthesis obtains an effective look-ahead of $n + k$ steps towards unsafe states given by the n steps of Γ and the k steps of the design-time BBSS.[7] To this end, we first define a simulation relation to capture when a backward GTS such as S_{BE} and S_{BU} for our running example is correct w.r.t. a forward GTS such as S_{FE} and S_{FU} for our running example. Since we do not consider the step labels (containing the GT rules or matches applied in these steps), we can understand this simulation

---

[7] Our presentation also covers the special case where the backward GTS used at design-time is obtained by reversing the rules of the run-time GTS but also applies to backward GTSs that are designed for improved design-time efficiency and applicability (as mentioned before Definition 7, in relation to k-induction discussed in section 3, and as elaborated in section 8).

to be a weak simulation in which one step of the forward GTS is simulated (backwards) by the backward GTS using any number of GT steps.

Definition 10 (Simulation Relation for GTS-based LTSs). *Given two LTSs Γ and Γ' induced from GTSs according to Definition 6 and Definition 7. A set R of morphisms $f_1 : G_1' \hookrightarrow G_1$ from states $G_1' \in$ states(Γ') to states $G_1 \in$ states(Γ) is a simulation relation from Γ to Γ', if for every $(G_2, \sigma, G_1) \in$ steps(Γ) capturing the forward GT span $(g_2 : D_1 \hookrightarrow G_2, g_1 : D_1 \hookrightarrow G_1)$ there is a sequence of GT steps $(G_2', \sigma_n', G_{2,n-1}'), \ldots (G_{2,1}', \sigma_1', G_1') \in$ steps(Γ') that can be combined (using an iterated E-concurrent GT rule, [12, Theorem 3.26]) into the backward GT span $(g_2' : D_1' \hookrightarrow G_2', g_1 : D_1' \hookrightarrow G_1')$ such that $d_1 : D_1' \hookrightarrow D_1$ and $f_2 : G_2' \hookrightarrow G_2$ exist satisfying $f_2 \in R$, $f_2 \circ g_2' = g_2 \circ d_1$, and $f_1 \circ g_1' = g_1 \circ d_1$.*

$$
\begin{array}{ccccc}
G_2 & \xleftarrow{\hspace{0.5cm}} & D_1 & \xhookrightarrow{\hspace{0.5cm}} & G_1 \\
& g_2 & & g_1 & \\
f_2 \Big\uparrow & & = \Big\uparrow d_1 & = & \Big\uparrow f_1 \\
G_2' & \xleftarrow{\hspace{0.5cm}} & D_1' & \xhookrightarrow{\hspace{0.5cm}} & G_1' \\
& g_2' & & g_1' &
\end{array}
$$

The following theorem then states that the existence of such a simulation relation R from the forward GTS to the backward GTS containing at least all embeddings of unsafe states V into the graphs reachable in the forward GTS within k steps is sufficient to ensure that any safety violation of the forward GTS within n to $n + k$ steps is detected by checking the states reachable by n steps in $[\![S_{\mathsf{FS}}]\!]_n$ against the start states of $[\![S_{\mathsf{BS}}]\!]_k^{\mathsf{back}}$. Note that Theorem 1 does not exclude spurious violation paths in terms of path pairs (π_1, π_2) that are not composable to a path π of S_{FS} due to application conditions in GT rules used in π_1 or π_2. Moreover, note that paths to unsafe states of length at most n steps are detected by constructing $[\![S_{\mathsf{FS}}]\!]_n$ already.

Theorem 1 (Violation Detection). *Given a forward GTS S_{FS}, a backward GTS S_{BS}, and an unsafe graph V contained in unsafe(S_{FS}) and unsafe(S_{BS}), every violation detected in $[\![S_{\mathsf{FS}}]\!]_{n+k}$ in terms of some path π of length $> n$ from start(S_{FS}) to a graph containing V is correspondingly detected by the combined technique using $[\![S_{\mathsf{FS}}]\!]_n$ and $[\![S_{\mathsf{BS}}]\!]_k^{\mathsf{back}}$ by two paths π_1 of length n from start(S_{FS}) to a graph containing B and π_2 of length $\leq k$ from some B' (for which some $b : B' \hookrightarrow B$ exists) to the graph V whenever there is a simulation relation R from $[\![S_{\mathsf{FS}}]\!]_k$ to $[\![S_{\mathsf{BS}}]\!]_k^{\mathsf{back}}$ containing every mono $f : V \hookrightarrow G$ into states G of $[\![S_{\mathsf{FS}}]\!]_k$.*

Proof (sketch). By induction on k, we derive the existence of an embedding of the last graph B of π_2 into the last graph of π_1 ensuring that steps in π reaching a violating graph can be mimicked backwards via the simulation relation.

This theorem thereby ensures that the system has an effective look-ahead of $n+k$ steps at run-time towards unsafe states allowing it to derive suitable control decisions to avoid such unsafe states (if possible for that effective look-ahead).

8 Evaluation

As a case study, we now consider a more complex variation of the running example, including additional track features such as junctions, explicit modeling

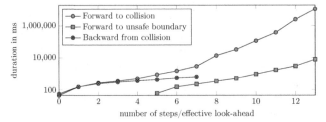

Fig. 6. Evaluation results. Look-ahead for "forward to collision", effective look-ahead for "forward to unsafe boundary", and depth of BBSS for "backward from collision".

of monitoring and signals (traffic lights for shuttles and ambulances). The used GTSs modeling this case study ensure that the sliding window perspective of the controlled shuttle is enforced by removing track and road segments behind the shuttle and enlarging the track/road topology forwards, potentially also including junctions, level crossing, and further components in a way to be expected by the shuttle. While we simply used the reversed rules for the backward GTSs in the running example, this would generate here for our case study, as for typical applications of the related approach of k-induction, a large number of unrealistic track topologies that would need to be singled out using other techniques such as structural constraints reducing the applicability and performance of our approach at design-time. Applying Theorem 1, we constructed a backward GTS with 31 GT rules by hand such that all steps of the forward GTS with 34 GT rules can be mimicked by at most two backward steps while minimizing the overapproximation of additional track topologies that are never reachable in the forward GTS. We used the tool Groove [17, 44] and provide the documented model files an explanation of our evaluation steps online.[8]

We evaluated the efficiency of our integrated approach in terms of consumed time by comparing it to the case where only a BFSS is constructed at runtime.[9] First, we use Groove to construct BFSSs of the forward GTS (for different bounds) thereby simulating the case where our approach is not used. Second, we use Groove to construct BBSSs of the backward GTS (for different bounds) also acquiring the unsafe boundary graphs thereby simulating the design-time aspect of our approach. Finally, we use Groove to construct the BFSS of the forward GTS (for different bounds) using the unsafe boundary graphs as target graphs (which means that the overhead of attempting to match the unsafe boundary graphs is included in our measurement) thereby simulating the run-time aspect of our approach. Generating the entire BFSS (for a given bound) instead of only adjusting it to the last observed step means that we consider the worst-case situation in which the entire BFSS is to be reconstructed due to, e.g., an unexpected step of the system. According to Figure 6 (forward to collision), the BFSS construction requires exponential run-time. In particular, collisions

---

[8] https://github.com/OpenAcademicProject/Running-Example-of-Railway-Transportation-System

[9] System: 64-bit Win10, Intel Core i7-6700HQ, 40GB RAM, Groove 5.8.1

are detected at depth 13 requiring 188 min, indicating that only using a BFSS may incur inacceptable costs at run-time. According to Figure 6 (backward to collision), the BBSS grows much slower compared to the BFSS because of *(a)* our usage of a separate backward GTS and *(b)* the restriction of considering paths that definitely lead to unsafe states. Hence, increasing the bound k for this BBSS is more advantageous compared to increasing the bound n for the BFSS in this scenario. Lastly, according to Figure 6 (forward to unsafe boundary), the first member of the unsafe boundary is found at run-time in the BFSS at depth 8 requiring 8 s with an effective look-ahead of 13 (as the depth 7 BBSS captures 5 forward steps of the forward GTS), which is 1423 times faster. We conclude from our evaluation that the goal of shifting computation time (and memory costs) from run-time to design-time is achieved by a factor of 1423 for the case study.

We note that applying our approach using a value $k > 0$ can increase the run-time cost. This would be the case when the forward/backward GTSs are constructed and the values of n and k are selected such that the time required for checking the leaf states of the run-time controller against the unsafe boundary of the design-time controller exceeds the time saved by generating at run-time a BFSS of depth n instead of $n + k$. This may be the case when, e.g., the BBSS contains a large number of infeasible paths (in the sense that the forward GTS cannot exhibit (instantiations of) them for the considered start states) resulting in an unsafe boundary containing a large number of states that can never be matched. While this issue did not arise for the case study considered here where run-time cost was decreased by a factor of 1423, this issue can be mitigated when it arises by employing assumed state invariants (capturing infeasibility of paths) to exclude states from the BBSS following the approaches in [47, 48, 3].

9   Conclusion and Future Work

In this paper, we presented a novel control-theoretic approach to run-time control for Graph Transformation Systems (GTSs) with priorities modeling large-scale systems with the threat of unexpected events. For the actor to be controller, we combine controllers synthesized at design-time and run-time with look-aheads n and k to obtain combined controllers with look-ahead $n + k$. An evaluation based on a shuttle transportation system shows a decrease of run-time computation cost by a factor of 1423 compared to using only run-time controllers with the same look-ahead suggesting that our approach successfully shifts a large amount of run-time computation cost to design-time. Moreover, we exemplified the robustness of the devised controlled system against unexpected events.

In the future, we will extend our approach to Interval Probabilistic Timed Graph Transformation Systems [31] to model cyber-physical systems and the steps of the contained actors more precisely, incorporate techniques to minimize checking time against unsafe boundary nodes, and combine k-induction with hand-coded backward GTSs to obtain small Bounded Backward State Spaces (BBSSs) that are correct w.r.t. the forward GTS by design.

References

[1] P. Arcaini, E. Riccobene, and P. Scandurra. "Modeling and Analyzing MAPE-K Feedback Loops for Self-Adaptation". In: *10th IEEE/ACM International Symposium on Software Engineering for Adaptive and Self-Managing Systems, SEAMS 2015, Florence, Italy, May 18-19, 2015*. Ed. by P. Inverardi and B. R. Schmerl. IEEE Computer Society, 2015, pp. 13–23. DOI: 10.1109/SEAMS.2015.10.

[2] C. Baier and J. Katoen. *Principles of model checking*. MIT Press, 2008. ISBN: 978-0-262-02649-9.

[3] B. Becker and H. Giese. *Cyber-Physical Systems with Dynamic Structure: Towards Modeling and Verification of Inductive Invariants*. Tech. rep. 64. Hasso Plattner Institute, University of Potsdam, 2012. URL: https://nbn-resolving.org/urn:nbn:de:kobv:517-opus-62437.

[4] T. Brüdigam, V. Gaßmann, D. Wollherr, and M. Leibold. "Minimization of constraint violation probability in model predictive control". In: *International Journal of Robust and Nonlinear Control* 31.14 (2021), pp. 6740–6772. DOI: https://doi.org/10.1002/rnc.5636. eprint: https://onlinelibrary.wiley.com/doi/pdf/10.1002/rnc.5636.

[5] T. Brüdigam, J. Teutsch, D. Wollherr, M. Leibold, and M. Buss. "Probabilistic model predictive control for extended prediction horizons". In: *at - Automatisierungstechnik* 69.9 (2021), pp. 759–770. DOI: doi:10.1515/auto-2021-0025.

[6] Y.-L. Chen, S. Lafortune, and F. Lin. "Modular Supervisory Control with Priorities for Discrete Event Systems". In: *Proceedings of 1995 34th IEEE Conference on Decision and Control*. Vol. 1. 1995, pp. 409–415. DOI: 10.1109/CDC.1995.478832.

[7] Y. Chen, S. Lafortune, and F. Lin. "Resolving Feature Interactions Using Modular Supervisory Control with Priorities". In: *Feature Interactions in Telecommunications Networks IV, June 17-19, 1997, Montréal, Canada*. Ed. by P. Dini, R. Boutaba, and L. Logrippo. IOS Press, 1997, pp. 108–122.

[8] E. M. Clarke, E. A. Emerson, and A. P. Sistla. "Automatic Verification of Finite-State Concurrent Systems Using Temporal Logic Specifications". In: *ACM Trans. Program. Lang. Syst.* 8.2 (1986), pp. 244–263. DOI: 10.1145/5397.5399.

[9] A. Corradini, L. Foss, and L. Ribeiro. "Graph Transformation with Dependencies for the Specification of Interactive Systems". In: *Recent Trends in Algebraic Development Techniques, 19th International Workshop, WADT 2008, Pisa, Italy, June 13-16, 2008, Revised Selected Papers*. Ed. by A. Corradini and U. Montanari. Vol. 5486. Lecture Notes in Computer Science. Springer, 2008, pp. 102–118. DOI: 10.1007/978-3-642-03429-9_8.

[10] B. Courcelle. "The Expression of Graph Properties and Graph Transformations in Monadic Second-Order Logic". In: *Handbook of Graph Grammars and Computing by Graph Transformations, Volume 1: Foundations*. Ed. by G. Rozenberg. World Scientific, 1997, pp. 313–400. ISBN: 9810228848.

[11] A. F. Donaldson, L. Haller, D. Kroening, and P. Rümmer. "Software Verification Using k-Induction". In: *Static Analysis - 18th International Symposium, SAS 2011, Venice, Italy, September 14-16, 2011. Proceedings*. Ed. by E. Yahav. Vol. 6887. Lecture Notes in Computer Science. Springer, 2011, pp. 351–368. ISBN: 978-3-642-23701-0. DOI: 10.1007/978-3-642-23702-7_26.

[12] H. Ehrig, K. Ehrig, U. Prange, and G. Taentzer. *Fundamentals of Algebraic Graph Transformation*. Monographs in Theoretical Computer Science. An EATCS Series. Springer, 2006. ISBN: 978-3-540-31187-4. DOI: 10.1007/3-540-31188-2.

[13] H. Ehrig, C. Ermel, U. Golas, and F. Hermann. *Graph and Model Transformation - General Framework and Applications*. Monographs in Theoretical Computer Science. An EATCS Series. Springer, 2015. ISBN: 978-3-662-47979-7. DOI: 10. 1007/978-3-662-47980-3.

[14] H. Ehrig, U. Golas, A. Habel, L. Lambers, and F. Orejas. "$\mathcal{M}$-adhesive transformation systems with nested application conditions. Part 1: parallelism, concurrency and amalgamation". In: *Mathematical Structures in Computer Science* 24.4 (2014). DOI: 10.1017/S0960129512000357.

[15] A. Filieri, C. Ghezzi, and G. Tamburrelli. "Run-time efficient probabilistic model checking". In: *Proceedings of the 33rd International Conference on Software Engineering, ICSE 2011, Waikiki, Honolulu , HI, USA, May 21-28, 2011*. Ed. by R. N. Taylor, H. C. Gall, and N. Medvidovic. ACM, 2011, pp. 341–350. DOI: 10.1145/1985793.1985840.

[16] S. Gerasimou, R. Calinescu, and A. Banks. "Efficient runtime quantitative verification using caching, lookahead, and nearly-optimal reconfiguration". In: *9th International Symposium on Software Engineering for Adaptive and Self-Managing Systems, SEAMS 2014, Proceedings, Hyderabad, India, June 2-3, 2014*. Ed. by G. Engels and N. Bencomo. ACM, 2014, pp. 115–124. DOI: 10.1145/2593929. 2593932.

[17] GROOVE Team. *Graphs for Object-Oriented Verification (GROOVE)*. https://groove.cs.utwente.nl. University of Twente, 2011.

[18] A. Habel and K. Pennemann. "Correctness of high-level transformation systems relative to nested conditions". In: *Mathematical Structures in Computer Science* 19.2 (2009), pp. 245–296. DOI: 10.1017/S0960129508007202.

[19] R. Heckel. "Open graph transformation systems: a new approach to the compositional modelling of concurrent and reactive systems". PhD thesis. Technical University of Berlin, Germany, 1998. URL: https://d-nb.info/95713598X.

[20] R. Heckel, G. Engels, H. Ehrig, and G. Taentzer. "A View-based Approach to System Modeling Based on Open Graph Transformation Systems". In: *Handbook of Graph Grammars and Computing by Graph Transformation Volume 2: Applications, Languages and Tools*. Ed. by H. Ehrig, G. Engels, H.-J. Kreowski, and G. Rozenberg. World Scientific, 1999, pp. 639–668. ISBN: 978-981-02-4020-2. DOI: 10.1142/9789812815149_0016.

[21] R. Heckel, G. Lajios, and S. Menge. "Stochastic Graph Transformation Systems". In: *Fundam. Inform.* 74.1 (2006), pp. 63–84. URL: https://content.iospress.com/articles/fundamenta-informaticae/fi74-1-04.

[22] R. Heckel and G. Taentzer. *Graph Transformation for Software Engineers - With Applications to Model-Based Development and Domain-Specific Language Engineering*. Springer, 2020. ISBN: 978-3-030-43915-6. DOI: 10.1007/978-3-030-43916-3.

[23] M. U. Iftikhar and D. Weyns. *Towards runtime statistical model checking for self-adaptive systems*. CW Reports CW693. Department of Computer Science, KU Leuven; Leuven, Belgium, Aug. 2016. URL: https://lirias.kuleuven.be/1656638.

[24] N. Jansen, C. Dehnert, B. L. Kaminski, J. Katoen, and L. Westhofen. "Bounded Model Checking for Probabilistic Programs". In: *Automated Technology for Verification and Analysis - 14th International Symposium, ATVA 2016, Chiba, Japan, October 17-20, 2016, Proceedings*. Ed. by C. Artho, A. Legay, and D. Peled. Vol. 9938. Lecture Notes in Computer Science. 2016, pp. 68–85. DOI: 10.1007/978-3-319-46520-3_5.

[25]   J. Katoen. "The Probabilistic Model Checking Landscape". In: *Proceedings of the 31st Annual ACM/IEEE Symposium on Logic in Computer Science, LICS '16, New York, NY, USA, July 5-8, 2016*. Ed. by M. Grohe, E. Koskinen, and N. Shankar. ACM, 2016, pp. 31–45. DOI: 10.1145/2933575.2934574.

[26]   Z. Khasidashvili, K. Korovin, and D. Tsarkov. "EPR-based k-induction with Counterexample Guided Abstraction Refinement". In: *Global Conference on Artificial Intelligence, GCAI 2015, Tbilisi, Georgia, October 16-19, 2015*. Ed. by G. Gottlob, G. Sutcliffe, and A. Voronkov. Vol. 36. EPiC Series in Computing. EasyChair, 2015, pp. 137–150. DOI: 10.29007/scv7.

[27]   R. Kumar and V. K. Garg. *Modeling and Control of Logical Discrete Event Systems*. 1st ed. Springer New York, NY, 1995. DOI: 10.1007/978-1-4615-2217-1.

[28]   M. Leucker and C. Schallhart. "A brief account of runtime verification". In: *J. Log. Algebr. Program.* 78.5 (2009), pp. 293–303. DOI: 10.1016/j.jlap.2008.08.004.

[29]   M. Maximova, H. Giese, and C. Krause. "Probabilistic timed graph transformation systems". In: *J. Log. Algebr. Meth. Program.* 101 (2018), pp. 110–131. DOI: 10.1016/j.jlamp.2018.09.003.

[30]   M. Maximova, S. Schneider, and H. Giese. "Compositional Analysis of Probabilistic Timed Graph Transformation Systems". In: *Fundamental Approaches to Software Engineering - 24th International Conference, FASE 2021, Held as Part of the European Joint Conferences on Theory and Practice of Software, ETAPS 2021, Luxembourg City, Luxembourg, March 27 - April 1, 2021, Proceedings*. Ed. by E. Guerra and M. Stoelinga. Vol. 12649. Lecture Notes in Computer Science. Springer, 2021, pp. 196–217. DOI: 10.1007/978-3-030-71500-7_10.

[31]   M. Maximova, S. Schneider, and H. Giese. "Interval Probabilistic Timed Graph Transformation Systems". In: *Graph Transformation - 14th International Conference, ICGT 2021, Held as Part of STAF 2021, Virtual Event, June 24-25, 2021, Proceedings*. Ed. by F. Gadducci and T. Kehrer. Vol. 12741. Lecture Notes in Computer Science. Springer, 2021, pp. 221–239. DOI: 10.1007/978-3-030-78946-6_12.

[32]   G. A. Moreno, J. Cámara, D. Garlan, and B. R. Schmerl. "Proactive self-adaptation under uncertainty: a probabilistic model checking approach". In: *Proceedings of the 2015 10th Joint Meeting on Foundations of Software Engineering, ESEC/FSE 2015, Bergamo, Italy, August 30 - September 4, 2015*. Ed. by E. D. Nitto, M. Harman, and P. Heymans. ACM, 2015, pp. 1–12. DOI: 10.1145/2786805.2786853.

[33]   O. Özkan. "Decidability of Resilience for Well-Structured Graph Transformation Systems". In: *Graph Transformation - 15th International Conference, ICGT 2022, Held as Part of STAF 2022, Nantes, France, July 7-8, 2022, Proceedings*. Ed. by N. Behr and D. Strüber. Vol. 13349. Lecture Notes in Computer Science. Springer, 2022, pp. 38–57. DOI: 10.1007/978-3-031-09843-7_3.

[34]   O. Özkan. "Infinite-state graph transformation systems under adverse conditions". In: *it Inf. Technol.* 63.5-6 (2021), pp. 311–320. DOI: 10.1515/itit-2021-0011.

[35]   O. Özkan. "Modeling Adverse Conditions in the Framework of Graph Transformation Systems". In: *Proceedings of the Eleventh International Workshop on Graph Computation Models, GCM@STAF 2020, Online-Workshop, 24th June 2020*. Ed. by B. Hoffmann and M. Minas. Vol. 330. EPTCS. 2020, pp. 35–54. DOI: 10.4204/EPTCS.330.3.

[36]   O. Özkan and N. Würdemann. "Resilience of Well-structured Graph Transformation Systems". In: *Proceedings Twelfth International Workshop on Graph Com-

putational Models, GCM@STAF 2021, Online, 22nd June 2021. Ed. by B. Hoffmann and M. Minas. Vol. 350. EPTCS. 2021, pp. 69–88. DOI: 10.4204/EPTCS. 350.5.

[37] A. Pnueli. "The Temporal Logic of Programs". In: *18th Annual Symposium on Foundations of Computer Science, Providence, Rhode Island, USA, 31 October - 1 November 1977.* IEEE Computer Society, 1977, pp. 46–57. DOI: 10.1109/SFCS. 1977.32. URL: https://ieeexplore.ieee.org/xpl/mostRecentIssue.jsp?punumber= 4567914.

[38] RailCab Team. *RailCab Project.* https://www.hni.uni-paderborn.de/cim/ projekte/railcab.

[39] P. J. G. Ramadge and W. M. Wonham. "On the Supremal Controllable Sublanguage of a Given Language". In: *SIAM Journal on Control and Optimization (SICON)* 25.3 (1987), pp. 637–659.

[40] P. J. G. Ramadge and W. M. Wonham. "On the Supremal Controllable Sublanguage of a given Language". In: *Decision and Control, 1984. The 23rd IEEE Conference on.* Vol. 23. 1984, pp. 1073–1080. DOI: 10.1109/CDC.1984.272178.

[41] P. J. G. Ramadge and W. M. Wonham. "Supervisory Control of a Class of Discrete Event Processes". English. In: *Analysis and Optimization of Systems.* Ed. by A. Bensoussan and J. Lions. Vol. 63. Lecture Notes in Control and Information Sciences. Springer Berlin Heidelberg, 1984, pp. 475–498. DOI: 10.1007/ BFb0006306.

[42] A. Rashidinejad, P. van der Graaf, and M. A. Reniers. "Nonblocking Supervisory Control Synthesis of Timed Automata using Abstractions and Forcible Events". In: *16th International Conference on Control, Automation, Robotics and Vision, ICARCV 2020, Shenzhen, China, December 13-15, 2020.* IEEE, 2020, pp. 1033–1040. DOI: 10.1109/ICARCV50220.2020.9305312.

[43] A. Rashidinejad, M. A. Reniers, and M. Fabian. "Supervisory Control Synthesis of Timed Automata Using Forcible Events". In: *CoRR* abs/2102.09338 (2021). arXiv: 2102.09338. URL: https://arxiv.org/abs/2102.09338.

[44] A. Rensink. "The GROOVE simulator: A tool for state space generation". In: *Applications of Graph Transformations with Industrial Relevance: Second International Workshop, AGTIVE 2003, Charlottesville, VA, USA, September 27-October 1, 2003, Revised Selected and Invited Papers 2.* Springer. 2004, pp. 479–485.

[45] J. Rinast. "An online model-checking framework for timed automata". PhD thesis. Hamburg University of Technology, 2015. URL: http://tubdok.tub.tuhh.de/ handle/11420/1256.

[46] S. Schneider. "Deterministic pushdown automata as specifications for discrete event supervisory control in Isabelle". PhD thesis. Straße des 17. Juni 135, 10623 Berlin, Germany: Technische Universität Berlin, Dec. 2019. 286 pp. DOI: 10. 14279/depositonce-9332. In press.

[47] S. Schneider, J. Dyck, and H. Giese. "Formal Verification of Invariants for Attributed Graph Transformation Systems Based on Nested Attributed Graph Conditions". In: *Graph Transformation - 13th International Conference, ICGT 2020, Held as Part of STAF 2020, Bergen, Norway, June 25-26, 2020, Proceedings.* Ed. by F. Gadducci and T. Kehrer. Vol. 12150. Lecture Notes in Computer Science. Springer, 2020, pp. 257–275. DOI: 10.1007/978-3-030-51372-6_15.

[48] S. Schneider, M. Maximova, and H. Giese. "Invariant Analysis for Multi-agent Graph Transformation Systems Using k-Induction". In: *Graph Transformation - 15th International Conference, ICGT 2022, Held as Part of STAF 2022, Nantes,*

France, July 7-8, 2022, Proceedings. Ed. by N. Behr and D. Strüber. Vol. 13349. Lecture Notes in Computer Science. Springer, 2022, pp. 173–192. DOI: 10.1007/978-3-031-09843-7_10.

[49]   S. Schneider, M. Maximova, L. Sakizloglou, and H. Giese. "Formal testing of timed graph transformation systems using metric temporal graph logic". In: *Int. J. Softw. Tools Technol. Transf.* 23.3 (2021), pp. 411–488. DOI: 10.1007/s10009-020-00585-w.

[50]   T. Schüle and K. Schneider. "Bounded model checking of infinite state systems". In: *Formal Methods Syst. Des.* 30.1 (2007), pp. 51–81. DOI: 10.1007/s10703-006-0019-9.

[51]   M. Schwenzer, M. Ay, T. Bergs, and D. Abel. "Review on model predictive control: an engineering perspective". In: *The International Journal of Advanced Manufacturing Technology* 117.5 (Nov. 2021), pp. 1327–1349. ISSN: 1433-3015. DOI: 10.1007/s00170-021-07682-3.

[52]   A. M. Sharifloo and A. Metzger. "Mcaas: Model checking in the cloud for assurances of adaptive systems". In: *Software Engineering for Self-Adaptive Systems III. Assurances.* Springer, 2017, pp. 137–153. DOI: 10.1007/978-3-319-74183-3_5.

[53]   D. Weyns, B. R. Schmerl, V. Grassi, S. Malek, R. Mirandola, C. Prehofer, J. Wuttke, J. Andersson, H. Giese, and K. M. Göschka. "On Patterns for Decentralized Control in Self-Adaptive Systems". In: *Software Engineering for Self-Adaptive Systems II - International Seminar, Dagstuhl Castle, Germany, October 24-29, 2010 Revised Selected and Invited Papers.* Ed. by R. de Lemos, H. Giese, H. A. Müller, and M. Shaw. Vol. 7475. Lecture Notes in Computer Science. Springer, 2010, pp. 76–107. DOI: 10.1007/978-3-642-35813-5_4.

[54]   Y. Yang, L. Bu, and X. Li. "Forward and backward: Bounded model checking of linear hybrid automata from two directions". In: *Formal Methods in Computer-Aided Design, FMCAD 2012, Cambridge, UK, October 22-25, 2012.* Ed. by G. Cabodi and S. Singh. IEEE, 2012, pp. 204–208. URL: https://ieeexplore.ieee.org/document/6462575/.

[55]   R. Zhang, Z. Wang, and K. Cai. "N-Step Nonblocking Supervisory Control of Discrete-Event Systems". In: *2021 60th IEEE Conference on Decision and Control (CDC), Austin, TX, USA, December 14-17, 2021.* IEEE, 2021, pp. 339–344. DOI: 10.1109/CDC45484.2021.9683593.

Formal Specification of Trusted Execution Environment APIs

Geunyeol Yu[1], Seunghyun Chae[1], Kyungmin Bae[1(✉)],
and Sungkun Moon[2]

[1] Pohang University of Science and Technology, Pohang, South Korea
kmbae@postech.ac.kr
[2] Samsung Electronics, Hwasung, South Korea

Abstract. Trusted execution environments (TEEs) have emerged as a key technology in the cybersecurity domain. A TEE provides an isolated environment in which sensitive computations can be executed securely. Trusted applications running in TEEs are developed using standardized APIs that many hardware platforms for TEE adhere to. However, formal models tailored to standard TEE APIs are not well developed. In this paper, we present a formal specification of TEE APIs using Maude. We focus on Trusted Storage API and Cryptographic Operations API, which are foundational to mobile and IoT applications. The effectiveness of our approach is demonstrated through formal analysis of MQT-TZ, an open-source TEE application for IoT. Our formal analysis has revealed security vulnerabilities in the implementation of MQT-TZ, and we patch and confirm its integrity using model checking.

Keywords: Trusted execution environments · formal specification · formal methods · model checking · rewriting logic · Maude

1 Introduction

Trusted execution environments (TEEs) have emerged as a key technology in the cybersecurity of a wide range of software [17]. They provide an isolated program execution environment where sensitive computations can be executed securely, shielding data from both software and hardware attacks. It guarantees the integrity, authenticity, and confidentiality of executed programs and their data. TEE is widely used in security-critical systems such as industrial control systems [5,7], servers [10], mobile security [11], IoT [1,15], etc.

However, the effectiveness of TEEs depends on their proper implementation and use. Inaccuracies or vulnerabilities can compromise the very integrity they seek to maintain; for example, user applications can access an unauthorized region of memory [12], or a kernel can be compromised using a stack-overflow attack [2]. This emphasizes the importance of the formal verification of TEEs. Through rigorous examination and validation, we can ensure the robustness of TEEs, ensuring they operate as intended and providing an additional layer of confidence in their ability to protect critical data.

© The Author(s) 2024
D. Beyer and A. Cavalcanti (Eds.): FASE 2024, LNCS 14573, pp. 101–121, 2024.
https://doi.org/10.1007/978-3-031-57259-3_5

The standardization of TEE is overseen by Global Platform [8]. Many systems that implement TEE, such as Samsung TEEgris, Trustonic Kinibi, Qualcomm QTEE, etc., adhere to this standard. The standard defines the API for trusted applications (TAs) to handle secure resources, such as memory and storage. These APIs are essential because they provide TEE services to applications running in a TEE. The uniformity of this API specification ensures compatibility across a wide range of applications, even when running on different CPUs.

However, there is an evident deficiency in formal models tailored for TEE specification and its associated APIs. This gap is concerning because without rigorous verification and modeling, the integrity of TEEs could be compromised, potentially exposing vulnerabilities. In this paper, we address this concern by providing a comprehensive formal model of TEE APIs that is explicitly designed for the formal analysis of TEE applications. In this approach, we aim to provide a foundational tool that can serve the diverse spectrum of TEE applications and improve the overall security landscape of software.

The architecture and behavior of Trusted Storage API, precisely defined in the standard [8], is quite complicated. Primarily, it arises from the stringent security requirement that each TA is assigned a dedicated storage, isolated and shielded from other TAs. For example, the function responsible for creating a file in TEE involves multifaceted processes, which is briefly illustrated in Section 3. Such intricacies amplify the difficulty in developing a faithful formal model for TEEs, because of a huge *representation gap* between the informal (standard) specification [8] and a formal model to be developed.

In this paper, we address challenge of the representation gap by leveraging a very expressive modeling language, called Maude [4], which supports powerful object-oriented specification. Since TEE API is mainly specified using objects and their interactions [8], it is appropriate to use such object-oriented modeling approaches to formally specify TEE APIs, making it much easier to develop a comprehensive formal model. We formalize important parts of TEE APIs, namely, Trusted Storage API and Cryptographic Operations API, which are central for trusted applications in mobile and IoT domains.

We demonstrate the effectiveness of our approach for formally analyzing MQT-TZ [20,21], an open-source TEE application that secures the IoT protocol MQTT. We have analyzed several security requirements of the implementation of MQT-TZ and found security vulnerabilities using model checking. We are able to fix a code-level bug and verify through model checking that the fixed program satisfies the previously violated requirements.

This paper is organized as follows. Section 2 provides necessary background on trusted execution environments and Maude. Section 3 presents the formal object-oriented specification of Trusted Storage API in Maude. Section 4 presents the Maude specification of Cryptographic Operations API. Section 5 explains how TEE infrastructures, including trusted applications, can be specified in Maude. Section 6 presents a case study on analyzing various requirements of MQT-TZ and improving the implementation of MQT-TZ using our framework. Section 7 discusses related work. Section 8 presents some concluding remarks.

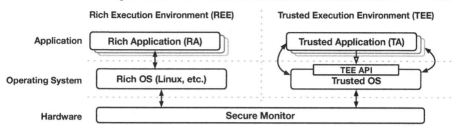

Fig. 1: Overview of the TEE Architecture.

2 Preliminary

Trusted Execution Environments. A trusted execution environment (TEE) uses a physically isolated storage and memory space to protect the security of program codes, executions, sensitive data, and so on. TEE is standardized by Global Platform [8], and many operating systems for TEE (e.g., Samsung TEEgris, Trustonic Kinibi, and Qualcomm QTEE) follow the standard. In particular, the standard defines the API for trusted applications to manage secure resources including memory and trusted storage.

Figure 1 shows the overall architecture of TEE. Trusted applications (TAs) are secure applications running in TEE. In contrast, rich applications (RAs) are normal applications in REE. A trusted OS provides a collection of API functions, specified in the standard document [8], for TAs to perform secure operations. RAs perform secure services by invoking TAs, and the results of such requests are returned to RAs, through a dedicated hardware called a secure monitor.

Maude. Maude [4] is a language and tool for formally specifying and analyzing concurrent systems. A Maude specification consists of: (i) an equational theory (Σ, E) specifying system states as algebraic data types, where Σ is a signature (i.e., declaring sorts, subsorts, and function symbols) and E is a set of equations; and (ii) a set of rewrite rules R of the form $l : t \rightarrow t'$ if *condition*, specifying the system behavior, where l is a label, and t and t' are terms [14].

In Maude, operators are declared with the syntax op $f : s_1 \ldots s_n$ -> s, where $s_1, \ldots, s_n$ denote domain sorts and s denotes a range sort. Rewrite rules are declared with the syntax crl [l]: t => t' if *cond* (or, for unconditional rules, rl [l]: t => t'), where *cond* is a conjunction of equations. Similarly, equations are declared with the syntax ceq $t = t'$ if *cond* (or eq $t = t'$).

A class declaration class C | $att_1 : s_1, \ldots, att_n : s_n$ declares a class C with attributes att_1 to att_n of sorts s_1 to s_n. An instance of a class C is represented as a term < $O : C$ | $att_1 : v_1, \ldots, att_n : v_n$ > of sort Object, where O is the object's identifier, and v_i is the value of each attribute att_i. A subclass inherits the attributes and rewrite rules of its superclasses. A message is represented as a term of sort Msg. A global system state is a term of sort Configuration that has the structure of a multiset composed of objects and messages, where multiset union is denoted by juxtaposition (empty syntax).

Maude provides a number of formal analysis methods, including LTL model checking. Maude's LTL model checker checks whether each behavior from an initial state satisfies a linear temporal logic (LTL) formula. A temporal logic formula is constructed by state propositions and temporal logic operators such as ~ (negation), /\, \/, [] ("always"), <> ("eventually"), and U ("until").

K Framework. K [16] is a rewriting-based framework for defining the semantics of programming languages, in which many languages, including C [6], Java [3], and EVM [9], have been successfully formalized. In K, program states are specified as multisets of cells, called *K configurations*. Each cell represents a component of a program state, such as computations, environments, and stores. Transitions between K configurations are defined by rewrite rules.

A computation in K is defined as a $\curvearrowright$-separated sequence of computational tasks. For example, $t_1 \curvearrowright t_2 \curvearrowright \ldots \curvearrowright t_n$ represents the computation consisting of t_1 followed by t_2 followed by t_3, and so on. A task can be decomposed into simpler tasks, and the result of a task is forwarded to the subsequent tasks. E.g., $(5+x)*2$ is decomposed into $x \curvearrowright 5 + \square \curvearrowright \square * 2$, where $\square$ is a placeholder for the result of a previous task. If x evaluates to some value, say 4, then $4 \curvearrowright 5 + \square \curvearrowright \square * 2$ becomes $5 + 4 \curvearrowright \square * 2$, which eventually becomes 18.

The following shows a typical example of K rules for variable lookup, where the k cell contains a computation, *env* contains a map from variables to locations, and *store* contains a map from locations to values:

$$\text{lookup} : \frac{\langle x \curvearrowright \ldots \rangle_k}{v} \langle \ldots x \mapsto l \ldots \rangle_{env} \langle \ldots l \mapsto v \ldots \rangle_{store}$$

A horizontal line represents a state change, and "..." indicates irrelevant parts. A cell without horizontal lines is not changed by the rule. By the lookup rule, if the first task in k is x, then x is replaced by the value v of x in its location l.

K rules can be translated into ordinary rewrite rules [16]. For example, the lookup rule can be written in Maude as follows, where environments and stores are declared as semicolon-separated multisets of assignments, and and K, ENV, and STORE are Maude variables that match the irrelevant parts:

```
rl [lookup]: k(X ~> K) env(X |-> L ; ENV) store(L |-> V ; STORE)
          => k(V ~> K) env(X |-> L ; ENV) store(L |-> V ; STORE) .
```

3　Formal Specification of Trusted Storage API

Trusted Storage API manages files and cryptographic keys in trusted storage. The architecture and behavior of Trusted Storage API [8] is summarized in Section 3.1. Trusted Storage API is complex due to the security requirement that each TA's storage is isolated and inaccessible to other TAs. We use Maude's object-oriented specification to naturally specify the architecture as a collection of objects (Section 3.2) and the behavior as rewrite rules (Section 3.3).

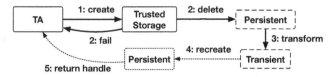

Fig. 2: The flow of TEE_CreatePersistentObject for the case of transformation.

3.1 Overview of Trusted Storage API

In the TEE API standard [8], resources such as files and keys are expressed as objects in an abstract way. A *cryptographic object* contains *attributes*, which are data used to store key material in a structured way. A *persistent object* represents a file associated with a *data stream* in its storage, and may also be a cryptographic object with attributes. A *transient object* represents an object with attributes in memory, but no data streams. *Object handles* are references that identify a particular object and contain access rights information.

There are a total of 26 functions in Trusted Storage API. The persistent API functions can create, rename, and delete persistent objects and their data streams. The data stream API functions can read, write, truncate, or seek data from persistent objects. The transient API functions can allocate and deallocate transient objects, set, reset, or copy cryptographic keys to the objects, or generate random keys. In addition, these functions can open object handles for persistent and transient objects, respectively.

To illustrate the complexity of Trusted Storage API, consider the function TEE_CreatePersistentObject, which creates a persistent object and returns the object handle. It first checks if a persistent object with the same name exists. Then, depending on the overwrite access flag, the operation either fails, or the object is deleted and recreated. A new persistent object can be created either as a cryptographic object or as a pure data object (without attributes). In the former case, attributes can be taken from another cryptographic object, or a transient object can be transformed to the persistent object. We describe the execution flow of transformation when a persistent object already exists, in Figure 2. The dashed box denotes deletion, and the dotted box represents creation.

3.2 Representing Trusted Storage Objects in Maude

Trusted Storage API can naturally be formalized in an object-oriented style. A cryptographic object is modeled as an instance of the class CryptoObj, where the attributes type, max-size, and usages denote the type, maximum size, and usages of a cryptographic key to be created, respectively; and attributes denotes cryptographic attributes.

```
class CryptoObj | type : Type,        max-size : Nat,     usages : Set{Usage},
                  attributes : Set{CryptoAttribute} .
```

A persistent object is modeled as an instance of the class `PersistObj`, where the attribute `file-name` denotes the name of its file, and `data-stream` denotes the associated data stream. Similarly, a transient object is modeled as an instance of the class `TransObj`, where `initialized` indicates whether the object is initialized. Both classes are declared as subclasses of `CryptoObj`, because they are both cryptographic objects according to the standard [8].

```
class PersistObj | file-name : FileName,   data-stream : List{Data} .
class TransObj   | initialized : Bool .
subclass TransObj PersistObj < CryptoObj .
```

A handle is represented as an instance of a subclass of the class `Handle`, where `oid` is the object that it points to. In particular, an object handle is represented as instances of the subclass `ObjHandle`, where `flags` contains data access flags.

```
class Handle | oid : Oid .          class ObjHandle | flags : Set{DataAccessFlag} .
subclass ObjHandle < Handle .
```

The storage of each TA is modeled as an instance of the class `Storage`, where `status` denotes its status, `files` denotes the file names in the storage, and `counter` denotes a counter for creating a new identifier.

```
class Storage | status : StorageStatus,   files : Set{FileName},   counter : Nat .
```

The kernel of each TA is modeled as an instance of the class `TAKernel`, where `status` denotes its status, `storage` denotes its storage, `counter` denotes a counter for creating a new identifier, and `api-call` denotes the status of an API call. The status of a TA can be `normal`, `outOfMemory`, or `panic`.

```
class TAKernel | status : AppStatus,   storage : Oid,
                 counter : Nat,         api-call : CallStatus .
```

We represent an API function call as $f(vl)$ `#` n of sort `CallStatus`, where f is a function identifier, vl is the call parameters, and (optional) n denotes the step of the call. The return of the call is represented as `return(`f`,`rl`)`, where rl denotes the return values. We use `return(`f`)` if there are no return values.

The interactions between the objects are represented as the messages of the form `msg` r`[`vl`] from` *Sender* `to` *Receiver*, where r is the name of a request and vl is a list of arguments for the request. We use `msg` r `from` *Sender* `to` *Receiver* for the request with no arguments. For example, `msg getStatus from TK to SI` represents a request message from the TA kernel TK to its associated storage SI for returning the status with no arguments.

The following example shows a TA and its associated storage, a transient object and its object handle, and a persistent object named `file1`.

```
< tk : TAKernel | status : normal, id-counter : 1, storage : so, ... >
< oh : ObjHandle | oid : to, flags : empty >
< so : Storage | status : normal, files : fileName('file1), counter : 1 >
< to: TransObj | type : rsaKeyPair, max-size : 15, usages : decrypt >
< po : PersistObj | file-name : fileName('file1), type : rsaKeyPair, ... >
```

3.3   Specifying Trusted Storage API Behaviors

Specification of TEE_ReadObjectData. This function takes a single parameter, a handle to a persistent object for data reading. A TA first checks the storage status by sending a message getStatus to an associated storage. When the storage receives getStatus, it returns its status using a message retStatus.

```
rl [read-object-data-get-storage-status]:
   < TK : TAKernel | api-call : readObjData(HI), storage : SI >
=> < TK : TAKernel | api-call : readObjData(HI) # 1 > (msg getStatus from TK to SI)
.

rl [return-storage-status]:
   < SI : Storage | status : STATUS > (msg getStatus from TK to SI)
=> < SI : Storage | > (msg retStatus[STATUS] from SI to TK) .
```

If the storage status is normal, the TA sends a message read to the handle to request data reading. Otherwise, it returns the storage status.

```
rl [read-object-data-storage-status-check]:
   (msg retStatus[STATUS] from SI to TK)
   < TK : TAKernel | api-call : readObjData(HI) # 1 >
=> if STATUS == normal then
     < TK : TAKernel | api-call : readObjData(HI) # 2 > (msg read from TK to HI)
   else < TK : TAKernel | api-call : return(readObjData, STATUS) > fi .
```

When the handle receives read and has the flag accessRead, it reads the first data from the data stream of the persistent object. The data is returned to the TA using a message retData and the TA returns the received data.

```
rl [read-object-data-from-persist]:
   < HI : ObjHandle | oid : PI, flags : (accessRead, FLAGS) >
   < PI : PersistObj | data-stream : DATA :: STREAM > (msg read from TK to HI)
=> < PI : PersistObj | data-stream : STREAM > (msg retData[DATA] from HI to TK)
   < HI : ObjHandle | > .

rl [read-object-data-success]:
   (msg retData[DATA] from HI to TK)
   < TK : TAKernel | api-call : readObjData(HI) # 2 >
=> < TK : TAKernel | api-call : return(readObjData, DATA) > .
```

Specification of TEE_CreatePersistentObject. Due to the page limit, we explain the rules used to specify the behavior in Figure 2. This function takes five parameters: file name, access flags, a handle to another transient or persistent object, initial data, and an optional handle. A TA determines the method for creating a persistent object and sends a creation request to an associated storage.

```
rl [create-persistent-determine-case]:
   < TK : TAKernel | api-call : createPersistent(FILE, FLAGS, HI, DATA, OPT),
                     storage : SI >
=> < TK : TAKernel | api-call : createPersistent(FILE, FLAGS, HI, DATA, OPT) # 1 >
   mkCreationMsg(FILE, FLAGS, HI, DATA, OPT, SI, TK) .
```

The mkCreationMsg function determines the creation method and constructs a create message, where the first argument denotes the method id. If the handle is null, the message is for creating a pure persistent object. If both the handle and optional handle are not null, the message is for creating a persistent object. Otherwise, it's for transforming a transient object into a new persistent object.

```
op mkCreationMsg : FileName Set{DataAccessFlag} HandleId Data HandleId
                   Oid Oid -> Configuration .
eq mkCreationMsg(FILE, FLAGS, null, DATA, OPT, SI, TK)
 = (msg create[pure FILE FLAGS null DATA] from TK to SI) .

ceq mkCreationMsg(FILE, FLAGS, HI, DATA, OPT, SI, TK)
  = if OPT == null
    then (msg create[transform FILE FLAGS HI DATA] from TK to SI)
    else (msg create[persist FILE FLAGS HI DATA] from TK to SI) fi if HI =/= null .
```

When the storage receives the create message, it checks the existence of a persistent object with the same name from the storage. If the object exists and the access flags contain the overwrite flag, it proceeds by sending the create message to the persistent object. Otherwise, it informs TA with createFail.

```
crl [create-persist-overwrite-check]:
   (msg create[METHOD FILE FLAGS HI DATA] from TK to SI)
   < PI : PersistObj | file-name : FILE >
   < SI : Storage | status : normal, files : FILES, counter : N >
=> < PI : PersistObj | >
   if overwrite in FLAGS
   then < SI : Storage | counter : N + 2 >
        (msg create[METHOD FILE FLAGS HI DATA N TK] from SI to PI)
   else (msg createFail from SI to TK) < SI : Storage | > fi if FILE in FILES .
```

When the persistent object receives the create message with the transform method, it transforms the transient object into a persistent object, opens a new object handle, and deletes itself. Then, the handle is sent to the TA through the message createSuccess. The function newOid is used to create a fresh identifier.

```
crl [create-persist-transform]:
   (msg create[transform FILE FLAGS HI DATA N TK] from SI to PI)
   < HI : ObjHandle | oid : OI >
   < OI : TransObj | type : TYPE, usages : USAGES, max-size : M,
                    attributes : ATTRS >
   < PI : PersistObj | file-name : FILE >
=> < NEW-HI : ObjHandle | oid : NEW-PI, flags : FLAGS >
   < NEW-PI : PersistObj | type : TYPE, usages : USAGES, max-size : M,
                           attributes : ATTRS, data-stream : DATA,
                           file-name : FILE >
   (msg createSuccess[NEW-HI] from NEW-PI to TK)
if NEW-HI := newOid(N, SI) /\ NEW-PI := newOid(N + 1, SI) .
```

When the TA receives a createSuccess message with an object handle, it returns the handle. If receiving createFail or detecting insufficient memory, it returns a corresponding error.

```
rl [create-persist-success]: (msg createSuccess[HI] from PI to TK)
   < TK : TAKernel | status : normal, api-call : createPersistent(VL) >
=> < TK : TAKernel | api-call : return(createPersistent, HI) > .

rl [create-persist-fail]: (msg createFail from SI to TK)
   < TK : TAKernel | status : normal, api-call : createPersistent(VL) >
=> < TK : TAKernel | api-call : return(createPersistent, errorAccessConflict) > .

rl [create-persist-mem-err]:
   < TK : TAKernel | app-status : outOfMemory, api-call : createPersistent(VL) >
=> < TK : TAKernel | api-call : return(createPersistent, errorOutOfMemory) > .
```

4   Formal Specification of Cryptographic Operations API

Cryptographic Operations API handles cryptographic algorithms by managing operation states. Cryptographic Operations API is also quite complex due to the internal operation states. This section shows that these difficulties can be effectively dealt with using Maude's object-oriented specification.

4.1   Overview of Cryptographic Operations API

A *cryptographic operation* abstracts a cryptographic process. It has an operation state such as *initial*, *active*, or *extract*. An *operation handle* is a reference to a cryptographic operation. Each handle has a handle state, which is defined by whether a key is set, an operation is initialized, and data can be extracted.

The API provides a total of 30 functions for various types of cryptographic primitives and schemes, including symmetric ciphers, authenticated encryptions, and key derivations. In addition, the generic operation API functions support the operations common to all types. These functions can allocate, free, reset cryptographic operations, and set cryptographic key.

To illustrate the complexity of Cryptographic Operations API, consider the state diagram of symmetric ciphers, described in Figure 3. The operation can be started either with or without key (KEY_SET or **not** KEY_SET). If it has no key, TEE_SetOperationKey is used to set a key. Otherwise, it is initialized (INIT) by TEE_CipherInit. The operation can run the algorithm with TEE_CipherUpdate. After performing the operation, TEE_FreeOperation can be used to deallocate the operation or TEE_CipherDoFinal is used to finish and reset the operation. Figure 4 shows the state diagram of message digest, which is also complex.

4.2   Representing Cryptographic Operations in Maude

Cryptographic operations can naturally be modeled in an object-oriented style. We model cryptographic operations as instances of class CryptoOp. The attribute **attributes** denotes a set of CryptoAttribute, max-size is the maximum size of a key to use, and algorithm is the identifier of an algorithm to operate. The attributes mode, state, and opclass denote the mode, state, and class of the operation, respectively, and acc-data is a list of Data it holds.

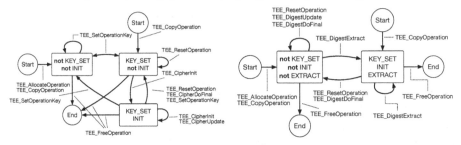

Fig. 3: Symmetric cipher operation.   Fig. 4: Message digest operation.

```
class CryptoOp | attributes : Set{CryptoAttribute},  max-size : Nat,
                 algorithm : Algorithm, mode : Mode, state : State,
                 opclass : OpClass,      acc-data : List{Data} .
```

Operation handles are represented as instances of the class `OpHandle`, which extends `Handle`. The attribute `state` is a handle state and `key-material-set` denotes whether cryptographic key materials are set to the operation.

```
class OpHandle | state : HandleState, key-material-set : Bool .
subclass OpHandle < Handle .
```

Specification of TEE_AllocateOperation. This function takes three parameters: an algorithm identifier, a mode, and the maximum key size. A TA first checks whether the algorithm and mode are compatible using the `compatible` function. If valid, it creates a new cryptographic operation, and opens and returns an operation handle. The function `getClass` is used to retrieve the algorithm class.

```
crl [allocate-operation-success]:
   < TK : TAKernel | api-call : allocOperation(ALGO, MODE, MAXSIZE),
                     status : normal, id-counter : N >
=> < TK : TAKernel | api-call : return(allocOperation, HI), id-counter : N + 2 >
   < HI : OpHandle | oid : OI, state : noKeyNotInit, key-material-set : false >
   < OI : CryptoOp | attributes : empty, max-size : MAXSIZE, handle : HI,
                     algorithm : ALGO, mode : MODE, opclass : getClass(ALGO),
                     acc-data : nil, state : initial >
if compatible(ALGO, MODE) /\ OI := newOid(N, TK) /\ HI := newOid(N + 1, TK) .
```

If the algorithm and mode are not compatible or insufficient memory is detected, the TA returns a corresponding error, specified by the following rules:

```
crl [allocate-operation-params-err]:
   < TK : TAKernel | api-call : allocOperation(ALGO, MODE, MAXSIZE) >
=> < TK : TAKernel | api-call : return(allocOperation, errorNotSupported) >
if not compatible(ALGO, MODE) .

rl [allocate-operation-memory-err]:
   < TK : TAKernel | status : outOfMemory, api-call : allocOperation(VL) >
=> < TK : TAKernel | api-call : return(allocOperation, errorOutOfMemory) > .
```

Specification of TEE_ResetOperation. A TA creates a `resetOp` message to reset a cryptographic operation. If the cryptographic operation receives a request and its key materials are set, it resets the operation state using the `resetState` function, clears the data, and notifies the TA using a message `finishResetOp`. The function `resetState` updates the state to initial if the state is active.

```
rl [reset-operation-request-reset]:
   < TK : TAKernel | api-call : resetOperation(HI) > < HI : OpHandle | oid : CI >
=> < TK : TAKernel | >  < HI : OpHandle | > (msg resetOp[HI] from TK to CI) .

rl [reset-operation-finish-reset]:
   < CI : CryptoOp | state : STATE > (msg resetOp[HI] from TK to CI)
   < HI : OpHandle | oid : CI, key-material-set : true >
=> < CI : CryptoOp | acc-data : nil, state : resetState(STATE) >
   < HI : OpHandle | > (msg finishResetOp from CI to TK) .

rl [reset-operation-success]:    (msg finishResetOp from CI to TK)
                < TK : TAKernel | api-call : resetOperation(VL) >
=> < TK : TAKernel | api-call : return(resetOperation) > .
```

Specification of TEE_CipherUpdate. This function takes two parameters: an operation handle and input data. A TA creates a message `reqCipher` to request data encryption or decryption. When a cryptographic operation receives the message and key materials are set, it checks whether the operation can succeed using the `cipherSuccess` function. If successful, the operation runs the algorithm with `runAlgo` and returns a result to the TA using the `finishCipher` message. Otherwise, it reports failure using the `failCipher` message.

```
rl [cipher-update-request-cipher]:     < HI : OpHandle | oid : CI >
            < TK : TAKernel | api-call : cipherUpdate(HI, DATA) >
=> < TK : TAKernel | > < HI : OpHandle | > (msg reqCipher[HI DATA] from TK to CI) .

rl [cipher-update-try-cipher]:
   (msg reqCipher[HI DATA] from TK to CI)
   < HI : OpHandle | key-material-set : true >
   < CI : CryptoOp | attributes : ATTRS, algorithm : ALGO, mode : MODE,
                     opclass : CLASS, state : STATE >
=> < CI : CryptoOp | > < HI : OpHandle | >
   if cipherSuccess(ALGO, MODE, ATTRS, CLASS, STATE, DATA) then
     (msg finishCipher[runOp(ALGO, MODE, ATTRS, DATA)] from CI to TK)
   else (msg failCipher from CI to TK) fi .
```

When the TA receives the encrypted or decrypted data from `cipherSuccess`, it returns the data. If receiving `failCipher`, it goes to `panic`.

```
rl [cipher-update-success]:      (msg cipherSuccess[VALUE] from CI to TK)
   < TK : TAKernel | api-call : cipherUpdate(VL) >
=> < TK : TAKernel | api-call : return(cipherUpdate, VALUE) > .

rl [cipher-update-panic]:
   < TK : TAKernel | api-call : cipherUpdate(VL) > (msg failCipher from CI to TK)
=> < TK : TAKernel | status : panic > .
```

5 Formal Specification of a TEE Infrastructure

5.1 Representing Rich and Trusted Applications in Maude

Thanks to the K semantics, we can model RA and TA to run programs, written in any programming language. Applications are represented as instances of the following class App, where prog denotes a program and proc is a K configuration for the program execution. RAs and TAs are modeled as instances of the classes RA and TA, respectively. Both classes inherit App but TA also inherits TAKernel.

```
class App | prog : Program, proc : KConfig .

class RA .                    class TA .
subclass RA < App .           subclass TA < App TAKernel .
```

In this paper, we define K rewrite rules for a subset of the C language, including function calls, variables, assignments, loops, and conditional statements. As mentioned in Section 2, the K semantics can be written in Maude.

For TEE API function calls, we use TAKernel to handle them. When a TEE API function FUNC is called with parameters VL, a TA pushes the call to api-call and adds a task $wait(f)$, representing the task waiting for the function f. Then, a TAKernel handles the call as explained in Sections 3 and 4. The isTeeApi function is used to check whether a function is a TEE API.

```
crl [tee-api-call]:
    < TI : TA | proc : (k(FUNC(VL)    ~> K) KS) >
 => < TI : TA | proc : (k($wait(FUNC) ~> K) KS), api-call : FUNC(VL) >
if isTeeApi(FUNC) .
```

After the TAKernel handles the call, the TA assigns the return values to the function's output variables. We use $out(xl)$ to denote output variables xl. The makeRetStmt function is used to create statements for assigning variables.

```
crl [tee-api-call-return]:
    < TI : TA | proc : (k($wait(FUNC) ~> $out(XL) ~> K) KS),
                api-call : return(FUNC, VL) >
 => < TI : TA | proc : (k(STMT ~> K) KS), api-call : noCall >
if isTeeApi(FUNC) /\ STMT := makeRetStmt(VL, XL) .
```

5.2 Representing Execution Environments

We represent the two separated execution environments as a pair $\{S_R\}$ | $[S_T]$, where S_R contains RAs and S_T contains TAs, together with objects and messages introduced in Sections 3 and 4. Trusted OS is represented as an instance of the class TrustedOS, where sess is a map from SessionId to Oid. Sessions are communication channels between RA and TA.

```
class TrustedOS | sess : Map{SessionId,Oid} .
```

We specify the communications between an RA and a TA using Maude rules. The RA calls the TA using a secure monitor call (SMC). We define its semantic using the following rule. A message smcReq represents an SMC and the function makeSmcArgs makes SMC arguments.

```
crl [invoke-ta]:
    < RI : RA | proc : (k(FUNC(VL) ~> K) KS) >
 => < RI : RA | proc : (k($wait(FUNC) ~> K) KS) > smcReq(ARGS)
if isInvokeFunc(FUNC) /\ ARGS := makeSmcArgs(RI, FUNC, VL) .
```

The secure monitor accepts the SMC request by transferring the message smcReq from REE to TEE. Later, it gets a result from TEE through a message smcRet and finishes the request by transferring the message to REE.

```
rl [accept-smc-request]: {REE smcReq(ARGS)} | {TEE} => {REE} | {TEE smcReq(ARGS)} .
rl [return-smc-request]: {REE} | {TEE smcRet(ARGS)} => {REE smcRet(ARGS)} | {TEE} .
```

We define the behavior of a trusted OS when receiving smcReq. The OS invokes a target TA using an invkTa message. The function getTargetTa is used to extract the target TA from SMC arguments and getRequestor is used to get the RA's identifier.

```
crl [accept-smc-request]:
    < OS : TrustedOS | sess : SM > smcReq(ARGS)
 => < OS : TrustedOS | > invkTa(TI, RI, ARGS)
if RI := getRequestor(ARGS) /\ TI := getTargetTa(ARGS, SM) .
```

When the target TA receives invkTa and is not running, it executes a program using the function run. For example, run(p, f, vl) executes the function f of a program p with arguments vl. The functions getFunc and getParams are used to get a function identifier and call parameters from SMC arguments.

```
crl [handle-invoke-ta]:
    < TI : TA | proc : none, prog : P > invkTa(TI, RI, ARGS)
 => < TI : TA | proc : run(P, F, VL) > invkTa(TI, RI, ARGS)
if F := getFunc(ARGS) /\ VL := getParams(ARGS) .
```

After the execution, the TA gets a result from proc using the function getRes and creates an invkTaRet message. Then, the trusted OS creates an smcRet message for sending the result to the secure monitor, which is transferred to REE. The function finished checks whether the process is finished.

```
crl [handle-invoke-ta-finish]:
    < TI : TA | proc : KS > invkTa(TI, RI, ARGS)
 => < TI : TA | proc : none > invkTaRet(RI, RV)
if finished(KS) /\ RV := getRes(KS) /\ RI := getRequestor(ARGS) .

crl [return-smc-request]:
    < OS : TrustedOS | > invkTaRet(RI, RES) => < OS : TrustedOS | > smcRet(ARGS)
if ARGS := makeSmcArgs(RI, RES) .
```

When the RA receives the message smcReq with the result, it finishes the secure monitor call using the function makeRetStmt. The function retVal is used to get return values from smcRet.

```
crl [invoke-ta-finish]:
    < RI : RA | proc : (k($wait(F) ~> $out(XL) ~> K) KS) > smcRet(ARGS)
 => < RI : RA | proc : (k(STMT ~> K) KS) >
if RI == getRequestor(ARGS) /\ VL := retVal(ARGS) /\ STMT := makeRetStmt(VL, XL) .
```

6   A Case study on Formal Analysis of MQT-TZ

This section shows the effectiveness and feasibility of our formal model using MQT-TZ [21], a TEE-based implementation of the message transport protocol. We defined LTL properties for MQT-TZ (Section 6.1), formally analyzed them with threat models, and proposed a patch (Sections 6.2 and 6.3). Our formal specification, case study model, and experimental results are available in [25].

6.1   Overview of MQT-TZ

MQT-TZ [21] is a secure topic-based publish-subscribe protocol utilizing TEE. Figure 5 illustrates the overall architecture, presenting three entities: publisher, subscriber, and broker. Publishers collect, encrypt, and send data as messages to a broker's topic. A subscriber can receive these messages by subscribing to a topic. Brokers manage topics, subscriptions, and message delivery from publishers to subscribers. Each broker is implemented using TEE, consisting of a single RA and TA. The RA retrieves publisher messages and calls the TA for re-encryption or forward re-encrypted messages to subscribers.

The re-encryption is a key mechanism for protecting messages from potential threats. It ensures that messages cannot be exploited, allowing only the intended subscribers to read. This can be accomplished as follows: (i) Clients (publishers and subscribers) generate symmetric keys and securely share them with brokers using TLS, (ii) The publishers encrypt messages with their keys, and (iii) The brokers decrypt the messages using the publisher's keys and re-encrypt them with the subscriber's keys in TEE.

To analyze MQT-TZ, we define various requirements and express them as LTL properties. These properties are summarized in Table 1. The properties P1 to P5 represent requirements for correctness of message reception (P1, P2, and P3), system integrity (P4), and robustness of message sending (P5). P6 is for checking whether the MQT-TZ scenarios satisfy the basic invariant.

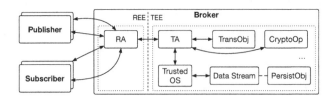

Fig. 5: Overview of MQT-TZ.

Table 1: The LTL properties for MQT-TZ.

Prop.	Description	LTL Formula
P1	If no memory error occurs in the broker, subscribers eventually receive messages.	$\Box \neg memErr.B \rightarrow$ $\Box\ (send.P \rightarrow \Diamond recv.S)$
P2	If the TA panics, subscribers should not receive any messages.	$\Box\ (panic.TA \rightarrow \Box\ \neg recv.S)$
P3	If any memory error occurs in the broker, subscribers should not receive any messages.	$\Box\ (memErr.B \rightarrow \Box\ \neg recv.S)$
P4	When the TA starts running, it should eventually terminate.	$\Box\ (start.TA \rightarrow term.TA)$
P5	If subscribers receive messages from publishers, messages sent from each publisher are in order.	$\Box\ (inQueue.P(a :: b :: c) \rightarrow$ $\Diamond inQueue.S(a :: b :: c))$
P6	The number of tasks handled by the TA cannot exceed five.	$\Box\ (\neg numTaskExceed(5))$

For formal analysis, we represent MQT-TZ's entities (brokers, publishers, and subscribers) as Maude objects. We model brokers as instances of the Broker class, which is a nested object with the execution environments of Section 5 for running RA and TA, along with a buffer for storing publisher messages and a subscriber list. Publishers are modeled as instances of the Publisher class, which has a list of collected data to be sent to brokers. Subscribers are represented as instances of Subscriber, which has a list of received messages from brokers.

We specify the behavior of clients and brokers, depicted in Figure 5. For publishers, we define their behavior with two rules: collecting data, and sending it to brokers with encryption. The behavior of subscribers is represented by a single rule for message reception. We specify the behavior of a broker RA using the following rules: (1) capturing publisher messages and storing them in a message buffer, (2) running the MQT-TZ RA program, which calls a TA (explained in Section 5), and (3) receiving re-encrypted messages from the TA and sending them to subscribers.

For a broker RA and TA, we obtained their C programs from the MQT-TZ Github repository. To run them in our model, we translated a total of 1200 lines of C codes to our C-subset language using a simple translation script. Figure 6 shows the TA's re-encryption function before the conversion.

6.2 LTL Model Checking

We have performed LTL model checking for the properties in Table 1, considering two threat models. We use the following scenario for the analysis:

- Two subscribers (sub_1, sub_2), two publishers (pub_1, pub_2), and one broker participate, where the broker has two topics.
- sub_1 subscribes to a single topic, while sub_2 subscribes to all topics.
- pub_1 sends a single message, while pub_2 sends two.

```
static TEE_Result
  payload_reencryption(void *session,
                       uint32_t param_types,
                       TEE_Param params[4]){
  TEE_Result res;
  uint32_t exp_param_types =
    TEE_PARAM_TYPES(
      TEE_PARAM_TYPE_MEMREF_INPUT,
      TEE_PARAM_TYPE_MEMREF_INOUT,
      TEE_PARAM_TYPE_MEMREF_INOUT,
      TEE_PARAM_TYPE_VALUE_INPUT);

  if (param_types != exp_param_types)
    return TEE_ERROR_BAD_PARAMETERS;
  ...

  if (alloc_resources(session,
                      TA_AES_MODE_DECODE)
      != TEE_SUCCESS){
    res = TEE_ERROR_GENERIC;
    goto exit;
  }
```

```
  if (set_aes_key(session, ori_cli_key)
      != TEE_SUCCESS){
    res = TEE_ERROR_GENERIC;
    TEE_Free((void *) ori_cli_key);
    goto exit;
  }
  ...

  if (cipher_buffer(session,
  (char *) params[0].memref.buffer
  + TA_MQTTZ_CLI_ID_SZ + TA_AES_IV_SIZE,
  data_size, dec_data, &dec_data_size)
  != TEE_SUCCESS){
    res = TEE_ERROR_GENERIC;
    goto exit;
  }
  ...

  TEE_Free((void *) dec_data);
exit:
  return res;
}
```

Fig. 6: The C code of the TA's re-encryption function.

Threat models. We consider two threat models: an out-of-memory threat and a message modification threat. The out-of-memory threat nondeterministically changes the status of a TA to outOfMemory. The message modification threat represents a compromised broker [21] that calls a TA with incorrect arguments. We specify the threats using Maude. For the out-of-memory threat, we model the threat as a single rewrite rule as follows.

```
rl [out-of-memory-threat]: < TK : TAKernel | status : normal >
                    => < TK : TAKernel | status : outOfMemory > .
```

For the message modification threat, we model an intruder as an instance of the Intruder class with a single attribute subs-list, denoting a broker's subscription list. Prior to the attack, the intruder learns the subscription list of a target broker from the messages in the broker's REE and records this in subs-list. After learning, the intruder uses this information and modifies any incoming messages of the broker by replacing the sender with any one of its subscribers. We can model this attack behavior as follows. The modify function replaces the SENDER in a publisher message mqttzMsg to another subscriber using the learned subscription list SUBS-LIST.

```
rl [message-modification-threat]: (mqttzMsg [DATA|TOPIC] from SENDER)
   < INT : Intruder | subs-list : SUBS-LIST >
=> < INT : Intruder | > modify(DATA, TOPIC, SENDER, SUBS-LIST) .
```

Model checking experiment. We consider the following threat scenarios: without any threats (NON), with the message modification threat (MSG), and with the out-of-memory threat (OOM). We measure the size of the state space ($|S|$) in

Table 2: The results of LTL model checking.

Prop.	Type	Safe?	|S|	Time	Prop.	Type	Safe?	|S|	Time	Prop.	Type	Safe?	|S|	Time
	NON	⊤	62	35.7		NON	⊤	62	35		NON	⊤	62	33.8
P1	MSG	⊤	148	90.1	P3	MSG	⊤	148	88.8	P5	MSG	⊤	148	86.9
	OOM	⊤	202	144.2		OOM	⊥	0.1	0.1		OOM	⊤	532	546.7
	NON	⊤	62	34.9		NON	⊤	62	34.9		NON	⊤	62	34.3
P2	MSG	⊥	17	9.1	P4	MSG	⊤	148	88.6	P6	MSG	⊤	148	87.9
	OOM	⊤	532	547.9		OOM	⊤	532	539.3		OOM	⊤	532	542.4

thousands, the model checking result (Safe?), and time in seconds. The ⊤ and ⊥ denote the property is safe and violated, respectively. We use the Maude model checking command for the analysis, which provides counterexamples for violations. We run the experiment on Intel Xeon 2.8GHz with 256 GB memory.

As summarized in Table 2, the two properties P2 and P3 are violated under the threats, indicating the possible vulnerabilities. By analyzing the counterexample of the P2 violation, we have discovered that the TA can panic during the message re-encryption. This occurs because the sender of a message can be modified, leading the TA to decrypt the message with an incorrect sender's key. For the P3 violation, we have found that when insufficient memory is detected, the TA finalizes the re-encryption with an error and returns a re-encrypted message containing (dummy) data. In this case, the RA does not verify whether the TA returns a correct re-encrypted message and continues to transmit the message to subscribers, which results in obtaining the message containing dummy data.

6.3   Patching the MQT-TZ Vulnerabilities

To fix the identified vulnerabilities, we have implemented code-level patches for both the MQT-TZ RA and TA, as illustrated in Figure 7. Newly added patches are highlighted in red, while the original codes are depicted in black. The left side shows the patch for RA, and the right side is for TA. For the TA, we modify it to inform the RA of a memory error or panic. In the case of the

```
TEEC_Result
void main(struct test_ctx *ctx,
  mqttz_client *origin, mqttz_client *dest,
  mqttz_times *times) { ...
  res = TEEC_InvokeCommand(&ctx->sess,
                           TA_REENCRYPT,
                           &op, &ori);
  if (res == TEE_ERROR_OUT_OF_MEMORY ||
      res == TEE_ERROR_TA_DEAD) {
    discardMsg(ctx, origin, dest);
  }
  ... }
```

```
static TEE_Result
  payload_reencryption(void *session,
                       uint32_t param_types,
                       TEE_Param params[4]){
  ...
  if (alloc_resources(session,
                      TA_AES_MODE_DECODE)
      != TEE_SUCCESS){
    res = TEE_ERROR_OUT_OF_MEMORY;
    goto exit;
  }
  ... }
```

Fig. 7: The patch codes for the MQT-TZ RA (left) and TA (right).

Table 3: The results of LTL model checking after applying the patches.

Prop.	Type	Safe?	|S|	Time	Prop.	Type	Safe?	|S|	Time	Prop.	Type	Safe?	|S|	Time
	NON	⊤	62	35.3		NON	⊤	62	34.8		NON	⊤	62	34.1
P1	MSG	⊤	149	89.9	P3	MSG	⊤	149	89.7	P5	MSG	⊤	149	87.4
	OOM	⊤	203	146.2		OOM	⊤	347	285.2		OOM	⊤	347	288.6
	NON	⊤	62	35.1		NON	⊤	62	34.7		NON	⊤	62	34.4
P2	MSG	⊤	149	89.9	P4	MSG	⊤	149	89.4	P6	MSG	⊤	149	87.9
	OOM	⊤	347	294.8		OOM	⊤	347	278.5		OOM	⊤	347	286.1

RA, modifications are made to ignore the re-encrypted message when a memory error or panic notification is received. Additionally, we have implemented the discardMsg function to handle the cleanup of the re-encrypted message.

To validate the patches, we have performed the LTL model checking from the previous section again. As shown in Table 3, P2 and P3 become safe (marked as red), while all other results remain the same. In addition, we observe that the state space is reduced up to approximately 185 thousand states compared to the original experiment. This is because the patches discarded the states related to memory error or panic.

In addition, we have identified redundant functions in the TA program using formal analysis. For example, TEE_ResetOperation is called right after allocating a cryptographic operation. Since the operation has not started, it remains in its initial state and thus the reset operation has no effect. These redundancies can be safely removed. To show this, we have collected all final states of the program with and without redundancies and compared them. We confirm the reachable states of the programs (with and without redundancies) are the same.

7   Related Work

Many studies have investigated the formal analysis of protocols leveraging TEE. The work [13] introduces a protocol for Wasm applications, and verifies the correctness of its authentication, such as aliveness and non-injective agreement. Another work [22] presents a protocol for secure remote credential management using TEE, which is verified against the Dolev-Yao model. Both papers have proven the correctness of their protocols by model checking. On the other hand, the paper [24] formally analyzes direct anonymous attestation schemes running on secure hardware through theorem proving. The papers [18,19] employ a similar approach, but aim at verifying remote attestation services of TEEs provided by Intel. However, unlike our work, they focus on specific protocols and do not propose a formal analysis framework for general TEE-based applications.

A formal analysis technique for an IoT framework using TEE is presented in [23]. It provides a hierarchical colored Petri net for Trusted IoT Architecture (TIoTA), which aims to protect data in IoT networks. This approach has been used to verify security properties in CTL by model checking. However, it is specifically tailored to TIoTA and cannot be applied to general TEE-based applications. In contrast, our work aims to provide a formal analysis framework for general TEE-based applications, written in any programming language whose operational semantics is specified in K.

8   Concluding Remarks

We have presented a formal specification for TEE APIs using Maude. We have specified two important TEE APIs (Trusted Storage API and Cryptographic Operations API) that are fundamental to mobile and IoT applications. We have leveraged Maude's object-oriented specification to reduce a representation gap between the standard document and the formal model, allowing us to effectively specify the complex architectures and behaviors of the TEE APIs.

The effectiveness and feasibility of our approach have been demonstrated through formal analysis of MQT-TZ [21,20], an open-source TEE application for IoT. We have analyzed security requirements of MQT-TZ under given threat models. Our formal analysis has revealed security vulnerabilities in the MQT-TZ implementation. We have patched a code-level bug and verified the previously violated requirements.

The future work includes providing comprehensive formal specifications for TEE APIs, covering the time API, TEE arithmetical API, and peripheral and event APIs. Additionally, we should verify the TEE API itself or generate test cases for real-world validations using our formal specification. Another important direction involves developing state space reduction techniques to enhance the efficiency of TEE application analysis.

Acknowledgments. This work was partially supported by SAMSUNG Electronics Co., Ltd., and the National Research Foundation of Korea (NRF) grant (No. 2021R1A5A1021944) and Institute of Information & communications Technology Planning & Evaluation (IITP) grant (No. 2022-0-00103), both funded by the Korea government (MSIT).

Data Availability Statement. The TEE formal specification, the MQT-TZ case study, and experimental results are available in [25,26].

References

1. Ayoade, G., Karande, V., Khan, L., Hamlen, K.: Decentralized IoT data management using blockchain and trusted execution environment. In: IEEE International Conference on Information Reuse and Integration (IRI). pp. 15–22. IEEE (2018). https://doi.org/10.1109/IRI.2018.00011
2. Beniamini, G.: Trust issues: Exploiting TrustZone TEEs. Accessed: Aug 03, 2022 (online) (2017), https://googleprojectzero.blogspot.com/2017/07/trust-issues-exploiting-trustzone-tees.html

3. Bogdanas, D., Roşu, G.: K-Java: A complete semantics of Java. In: ACM SIGPLAN-SIGACT Symposium on Principles of Programming Languages (POPL). pp. 445–456. ACM (2015). https://doi.org/10.1145/2676726.2676982

4. Clavel, M., Durán, F., Eker, S., Lincoln, P., Martí-Oliet, N., Meseguer, J., Talcott, C.: All about Maude - A high-performance logical framework, Lecture Notes in Computer Science, vol. 4350. Springer (2007). https://doi.org/10.1007/978-3-540-71999-1

5. Coppolino, L., D'Antonio, S., Formicola, V., Mazzeo, G., Romano, L.: VISE: Combining Intel SGX and homomorphic encryption for cloud industrial control systems. IEEE Transactions on Computers **70**(5), 711–724 (2021). https://doi.org/10.1109/TC.2020.2995638

6. Ellison, C., Rosu, G.: An executable formal semantics of C with applications. In: ACM SIGPLAN-SIGACT Symposium on Principles of Programming Languages (POPL). pp. 533–544. ACM (2012). https://doi.org/10.1145/2103656.2103719

7. Fitzek, A., Achleitner, F., Winter, J., Hein, D.: The ANDIX research OS — ARM TrustZone meets industrial control systems security. In: IEEE International Conference on Industrial Informatics (INDIN). pp. 88–93. IEEE (2015). https://doi.org/10.1109/INDIN.2015.7281715

8. GlobalPlatform: TEE Internal Core API Specification v1.3.1 (2021), https://globalplatform.org/specs-library/tee-internal-core-api-specification/

9. Hildenbrandt, E., Saxena, M., Rodrigues, N., Zhu, X., Daian, P., Guth, D., Moore, B., Park, D., Zhang, Y., Stefanescu, A., Rosu, G.: KEVM: A complete formal semantics of the Ethereum virtual machine. In: IEEE Computer Security Foundations Symposium (CSF). pp. 204–217. IEEE (2018). https://doi.org/10.1109/CSF.2018.00022

10. Hua, Z., Gu, J., Xia, Y., Chen, H., Zang, B., Guan, H.: vTZ: virtualizing ARM TrustZone. In: USENIX Conference on Security Symposium (SEC). pp. 541–556. USENIX Association (2017), https://dl.acm.org/doi/10.5555/3241189.3241232

11. Li, W., Xia, Y., Lu, L., Chen, H., Zang, B.: TEEv: Virtualizing trusted execution environments on mobile platforms. In: ACM SIGPLAN/SIGOPS International Conference on Virtual Execution Environments (VEE). pp. 2–16. ACM (2019). https://doi.org/10.1145/3313808.3313810

12. Machiry, A., Gustafson, E., Spensky, C., Salls, C., Stephens, N., Wang, R., Bianchi, A., Choe, Y.R., Kruegel, C., Vigna, G.: BOOMERANG: Exploiting the semantic gap in trusted execution environments. In: Network and Distributed System Security Symposium (NDSS) (2017). https://dx.doi.org/10.14722/ndss.2017.23227

13. Ménétrey, J., Pasin, M., Felber, P., Schiavoni, V.: WaTZ: A trusted WebAssembly runtime environment with remote attestation for TrustZone. In: IEEE International Conference on Distributed Computing Systems (ICDCS). pp. 1177–1189. IEEE (2022), https://doi.ieeecomputersociety.org/10.1109/ICDCS54860.2022.00116

14. Meseguer, J.: Conditional rewriting logic as a unified model of concurrency. Theoretical Computer Science **96**(1), 73–155 (1992). https://doi.org/10.1016/0304-3975(92)90182-F

15. Nguyen, H., Ivanov, R., Phan, L.T., Sokolsky, O., Weimer, J., Lee, I.: LogSafe: Secure and scalable data logger for IoT devices. In: IEEE/ACM International Conference on Internet-of-Things Design and Implementation (IoTDI). pp. 141–152. IEEE (2018). https://doi.org/10.1109/IoTDI.2018.00023

16. Roşu, G., Şerbănută, T.F.: An overview of the K semantic framework. The Journal of Logic and Algebraic Programming **79**(6), 397–434 (2010). https://doi.org/10.1016/j.jlap.2010.03.012

17. Sabt, M., Achemlal, M., Bouabdallah, A.: Trusted execution environment: what it is, and what it is not. In: IEEE International Conference on Trust, Security and Privacy in Computing and Communications (TrustCom). pp. 57–64. IEEE (2015). https://doi.org/10.1109/Trustcom.2015.357

18. Sardar, M.U., Faqeh, R., Fetzer, C.: Formal foundations for Intel SGX data center attestation primitives. In: International Conference on Formal Engineering Methods (ICFEM). Lecture Notes in Computer Science, vol. 12531, pp. 268–283. Springer (2020). https://doi.org/10.1007/978-3-030-63406-3_16

19. Sardar, M.U., Musaev, S., Fetzer, C.: Demystifying attestation in Intel Trust Domain Extensions via formal verification. IEEE Access 9, 83067–83079 (2021). https://doi.org/10.1109/ACCESS.2021.3087421

20. Segarra, C., Delgado-Gonzalo, R., Schiavoni, V.: MQT-TZ fork of the open source Mosquitto MQTT broker leveraging ARM TrustZone, https://github.com/mqttz/mqttz

21. Segarra, C., Delgado-Gonzalo, R., Schiavoni, V.: MQT-TZ: hardening IoT brokers using ARM TrustZone. In: International Symposium on Reliable Distributed Systems (SRDS). pp. 256–265. IEEE (2020). https://doi.org/10.1109/SRDS51746.2020.00033

22. Shepherd, C., Akram, R.N., Markantonakis, K.: Remote credential management with mutual attestation for trusted execution environments. In: IFIP International Conference on Information Security Theory and Practice (WISTP). Lecture Notes in Computer Science, vol. 11469, pp. 157–173. Springer (2019). https://doi.org/10.1007/978-3-030-20074-9_12

23. Valadares, D.C.G., Sobrinho, Á.A.d.C.C., Perkusich, A., Gorgonio, K.C.: Formal verification of a trusted execution environment-based architecture for IoT applications. IEEE Internet of Things Journal 8(23), 17199–17210 (2021). https://doi.org/10.1109/JIOT.2021.3077850

24. Wesemeyer, S., Newton, C.J., Treharne, H., Chen, L., Sasse, R., Whitefield, J.: Formal analysis and implementation of a TPM 2.0-based direct anonymous attestation scheme. In: ACM Asia Conference on Computer and Communications Security (ASIACCS). pp. 784–798. ACM (2020). https://doi.org/10.1145/3320269.3372197

25. Yu, G., Chae, S., Bae, K., Moon, S.: The artifact of TEE formal specification (2023). https://doi.org/10.5281/zenodo.10462106

26. Yu, G., Chae, S., Bae, K., Moon, S.: Supplementary material. (2023), https://github.com/postechsv/tee-formal-spec

Monitoring the Future of Smart Contracts*

Margarita Capretto[1,2]([✉]) [iD], Martin Ceresa[1] [iD], and César Sánchez[1] [iD]

[1] IMDEA Software Institute, Madrid, Spain
{margarita.capretto,martin.ceresa,cesar.sanchez}@imdea.org
[2] Universidad Politécnica de Madrid (UPM), Madrid, Spain

Abstract. Blockchains are decentralized systems that provide trustable
execution guarantees through the use of programs called smart contracts.
Smart contracts are programs written in domain-specific programming
languages running on blockchains that govern how tokens and cryptocurrency are sent and received. Smart contracts can invoke other smart contracts during the execution of transactions initiated by external users.
Once deployed, smart contracts running code cannot be modified, so
techniques like runtime verification are very appealing for improving their
reliability. Moreover, the conventional model of computation of smart
contracts is transactional: once operations commit, their effects are permanent and cannot be undone. Therefore, errors in smart contracts may
lead to millionaire losses of money.
In this paper, we present the concept of *future monitors* which allows
monitors to remain waiting for future transactions to occur before committing or aborting. This is inspired by optimistic rollups, which are
modern blockchain implementations that increase efficiency (and reduce
cost) by delaying transaction effects. We exploit this delay to propose
a model of computation that allows bounded future monitors. We show
our monitors correct respect with legacy transactions, how they implement bounded future monitors and how they guarantee progress. We
illustrate the use of bounded future monitors by implementing correctly
multi-transaction flash loans.

1 Introduction

Blockchains [20] were first introduced as distributed infrastructures that eliminate the need of trustable third parties in electronic payment systems. Modern blockchains incorporate smart contracts [27,28] (contracts hereon), which
are stateful programs stored in the blockchain that govern the functionality of
blockchain transactions. Users interact with blockchains by invoking contracts[3],
whose execution controls the exchange of cryptocurrency. Contracts allow sophisticated functionality, enabling many applications in decentralized finances
(DeFi), decentralized governance, Web3, etc.

---

* This work was funded in part by PRODIGY Project (TED2021-132464B-
I00)—funded by MCIN/AEI/10.13039/501100011033/ and the European Union
NextGenerationEU/PRTR—by DECO Project (PID2022-138072OB-I00)—funded
by MCIN/AEI/10.13039/501100011033 and by the ESF+—and by a research grant
from Nomadic Labs and the Tezos Foundation.
[3] Non-contract addresses can be considered as unit contracts.

D. Beyer and A. Cavalcanti (Eds.): FASE 2024, LNCS 14573, pp. 122–142, 2024.
https://doi.org/10.1007/978-3-031-57259-3_6

Contracts are written in high-level programming languages, like Solidity [2] and Ligo [4], which are then typically compiled into low-level bytecode languages like EVM [28] or Michelson [1]. Even though contracts are typically small compared to conventional software, writing contracts is notoriously difficult. The open nature of the invocation system—where every contract can invoke every other contract—facilitates that malicious users break programmer's assumptions and steal user tokens (e.g. [23]). Once installed, contract code is immutable[4], and the effect of running a contract cannot be reverted (the contract *is* the law).

Two classic reliability approaches can be applied to contracts:

- **static techniques** ranging from static analysis [26] and model checking [22] to deductive software verification techniques [3,21,8,14], theorem proving assistants [7,5,24] or assisted formal construction of programs [25].
- **dynamic verification** [15,6,18,10] dynamically inspecting the execution of contracts against specifications taking corrective measures.

We follow in this paper a dynamic monitoring technique. Monitors are a defensive mechanism to express desired properties that must hold during the execution of the contracts. If the property fails, the monitor fails the whole transaction. Otherwise, the execution finishes normally according to the contract code. In practice, monitors are mixed within the contract code, which limits the properties that can be monitored. In [10], the authors presented a hierarchy of monitors, including operation and transaction monitors. An operation monitor for a contract A runs alongside A and reads and modifies specific monitor variables stored in A [15,6,18]. Operation monitors can only execute when A is invoked and cannot inspect or invoke other contracts. Transaction monitors [10] can inspect information across a full transaction, even after the last invocation of A in the transaction. For example, the return of a loan *within the transaction* is an important property that can be monitored with a transaction monitor and not by an operation monitor, because a transaction must fail if the money lent is not returned by the end of the transaction.

Traditional blockchain systems cannot implement transaction monitors [10], but fortunately, this is easy to achieve by extending the execution model with two simple features: a `first` instruction and a Fail/NoFail hookup mechanism. Instruction `first` returns *true* during the first invocation of the contract in the current transaction. The Fail/NoFail mechanism equips each contract with a new flag, `fail`, that can be assigned (to *true* or *false*) during the execution of the contract (and that is *false* by default). The semantics of `fail` is that transactions fail if at least one contract has its `fail` flag set to *true* at the end of the transaction.

In this paper, we study an even richer notion of monitors that enables to fail or commit depending on *future transactions*. Future monitors can predicate on sequences of transactions during a bounded period of time. This period of time, called the *monitoring window* is fixed a priori.

---

[4] Although there are techniques to upgrade the behaviour of smart contracts, like proxy patterns and diamond proxy [19], the actual code does not change.

Optimistic rollups. Future monitors can be implemented easily in Layer-2 Optimistic Rollups[5], which are an approach to improve blockchain scalability by moving computation and data off-chain. The most popular optimistic rollup implementation is Arbitrum [9], implemented on top of the Ethereum blockchain [28]. Arbitrum offers the same API as Ethereum, allowing to install and invoke Ethereum contracts. Arbitrum transactions are executed off-chain and their effects are submitted as *assertions*. Assertions are *optimistically* assumed to be correct and a fraud-prove arbitration scheme allows to detect invalid assertions. Assertions are pending during a challenging period[6] to allow observers to check their correctness. The arbitration game consists of a bisection protocol, played between the challenger and asserter, which has the property that the honest player can always win the dispute. Assertions that survive until the end of the challenge period become permanent. Future monitors can exploit the delay imposed by the challenging period to fail or commit based on information from the future.

Bounded Future Monitoring. In this article, we enrich transaction monitors with a controlled ability to predicate about the future evolution of blockchains. Contracts are extended to include: `txid`, `failmap`, and `timeout`. The instruction `txid` returns the (unique) current transaction identifier. Each contract is equipped with a map `failmap` indicating—for each transaction involving the contract—whether the future monitor of the transaction is activated or not, and if so, its monitoring status (commit, fail or undecided). By default, future monitoring is deactivated. Contracts can modify their `failmap` (1) to activate the future monitor of the current transaction, or (2) to commit or fail undecided future monitors of previous transactions within the monitoring window. If a contract sets a past transaction `failmap` entry to fail, the corresponding transaction fails. The `timeout` function is invoked at the end of the monitoring window to decide whether to fail or commit if the future monitor of the transaction is still undecided. This guarantees that transactions cannot be pending after a bounded amount of time.

We call our monitors *future monitors* since the decision to commit or fail may depend on transactions that will execute in the future. Future monitors expand the monitor hierarchy presented in [10], which included operation and transaction monitors as well as monitors that involve several contracts (multicontract monitors) or even the whole blockchain (global monitors), but always in the context of a single transaction. When combined with future monitors, we obtain *multicontract future monitors* and *global future monitors*, but we leave these extensions as future work. A particular subclass of *multicontract future monitors* was studied in [16] focusing on long-lived transactions [17], whose lifetime span blockchain transactions and potentially involve different contracts and parties. Fig. 1 shows the updated monitoring hierarchy including future monitors.

---

[5] Optimistic Rollups for short.

[6] Currently a week.

2   Model of Computation

We introduce now our abstract model of computation to reason about blockchains.

Blockchains Execution Overview. Blockchains are incremental permanent records of executed transactions packed in blocks. Transactions are in turn composed of a sequence of operations where the initial operation is an invocation from an external user. Each operation invokes a destination contract, which is identified by its unique address. The execution of an operation follows the instructions of the program (the contract) stored at the destination address. Contracts can modify their local storage and invoke other contracts.

Transaction execution consists of executing operations, computing their effects (which may include the generation of new operations) until either (1) there are no more pending operations, or (2) an operation fails or the available gas is exhausted. In the former case, the transaction commits and all changes are made permanent. In the latter case, the transaction fails and no effect takes place in the storage of contracts, except that some gas is consumed. Therefore, the state of contracts is determined by the effects of committing transactions.

Model of Computation. Our model computation describes blockchain state evolution as the result of sequential transaction executions. Blockchain configurations are records containing all information required to compute transactions, such as: a partial map between addresses and their storage and balance, plus additional information about the blockchain such as block number. We use Σ to denote blockchain configurations and $\mathcal{U}$ to denote balances of external users.

Transactions are the result of executing a sequence of operations starting from an external operation placed by a user. Transactions can either commit, if every operation is successful, or fail, if one of its operations fails or the gas is exhausted. We use function basicTx, which takes a transaction, a blockchain configuration, and balances of external users as inputs, and returns the blockchain configuration and the external user balances that result from executing the transaction in the input configuration. Additionally, predicate succ indicates whether the execution of a transaction commits or fails in a given blockchain configuration and external user balances. Furthermore, function discount deducts the specified amount of tokens from the balance of the indicated user in the provided external user balances. The following relation $\leadsto_{tx}$ defines the evolution of the blockchain

Present	Future
Global monitors	Global future monitors [future work]
Multicontract monitors	Multicontract future monitors [16] [future work]
Transaction monitors [10]	Future monitors [this work]
Operation monitors [6,15,18]	

Fig. 1. Monitor hierarchy. The first column belongs to [10].

using basicTx, succ and discount:

$$\text{commit} \frac{\substack{\text{basicTx}(tx, \Sigma, \mathcal{U}) = (\Sigma', \mathcal{U}') \\ \text{succ}(tx, \Sigma, \mathcal{U}) = \text{commit}}}{\Sigma, \mathcal{U} \rightsquigarrow_{tx} \Sigma', \mathcal{U}'} \qquad \text{fail} \frac{\substack{\mathcal{U}' = \text{discount}(\mathcal{U}, \text{src}(tx), \text{cost}(tx)) \\ \text{succ}(tx, \Sigma, \mathcal{U}) = \text{fail}}}{\Sigma, \mathcal{U} \rightsquigarrow_{tx} \Sigma, \mathcal{U}'}$$

If a transaction fails (rule `fail`), the blockchain configuration is preserved, but the external user originating the transaction pays for the resources consumed. Cost and resource analysis are out of the scope of this paper, so we ignore the computation of $\mathcal{U}$.

Operation and transaction monitors are defined at the operation and transaction level, and thus, they are implemented inside basicTx and abstracted away in this model.

3   Bounded Future Monitored Blockchains

In this section, we present a modified model of computation supporting future monitors. The main addition is the implementation of monitoring transactions predicating on future transactions within a monitoring window k. The monitoring window captures for how long (in the number of transactions) the monitor can predicate on. This additional feature enables us to install a monitor per transaction. Future instances of contracts that activated a future monitor can decide to either fail or commit the past transaction within the monitoring window. If any contract sets to fail the transaction future monitor of a past transaction, the monitored transaction fails. Otherwise, when all contracts that monitor a given transaction commit the transaction becomes permanently committed.

3.1   Future k-bounded Monitors

Transactions can commit or fail depending on their subsequent k transactions, and thus, the post-state after executing a transaction may depend on future transactions. At any given point in time, transaction future monitors may:

 – fail because at least one contract involved set the monitor to fail;
 – commit because all contracts involved set the monitor to commit;
 – stay pending.

Therefore, we identify three transaction monitor states: known to fail, (denoted by Fail), known to commit (denoted by Commit) and undecided (denoted by ?). Finally, we add another value to represent transactions without monitors: None.

Failing Map. A contract C can only interact with the future monitor of transaction t if C was involved in t. To keep track of different monitors for C (for different transactions), every contract C has a map, called *failing map*, from transactions to monitor states.

At the start of a transaction, the monitor is deactivated and can only be activated during the current transaction. Therefore, if at the end of a transaction

t no contract updated the failing map of its monitor for t, then the behavior is like legacy unmonitored transactions (as previously described in Section 2).

A contract C can modify its failing map many times but only the entries of those transactions where C was involved and activated the monitor. Changes to failing maps at the end of transactions can be (1) the activation of the monitor for the current transaction (from None to Fail, Commit, or ?, indicated by dashed arrows in Fig. 2); or (2) decisions reached for undecided monitors (from ? to Fail or Commit, indicated by plain arrows).

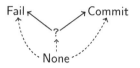

Fig. 2. Monitor transitions.

Timeout. Contracts have a new special function called timeout that can be used to describe the decision of undecided monitors at the monitoring window. Function timeout takes a transaction identifier and returns either Fail or Commit and it is set by contracts. The default timeout function returns Commit.

At the end of the monitor window, the system invokes timeout if the failing map entry for that transaction is marked as ?. If at least one contract involved in the transaction decides to fail, the transaction fails, and otherwise the transaction commits.

3.2   Extending the Model of Computation

We extend blockchain configurations with a *future monitor context* Δ associating contracts with their failing map and timeout function.

Transaction Execution: Transactions can immediately commit or fail, or depend on future transactions that happen within the monitoring window, so the execution of a transaction can return one of the following cases:
- a new configuration as an immediate commit,
- a new configuration as an immediate fail,
- two *possible* new configurations, one for failing and one for committing, which depends on the future.

These behaviors are captured by a new function applyTx that checks if future monitors were activated during the transaction. Future monitors restrict the behavior of the blockchain, because they only modify the blockchain evolution making transactions fail more often.

Non-monitored transactions either immediately commit or fail based on function succ, and their effects are equivalent to the traditional model.

The function applyTx, when applied to a monitored not failing transaction, returns two blockchain configurations, describing the only two possible futures. The first configuration represents the effects if the transaction commits, and the second represents a failing transaction, so in these cases the post-configurations are identical to the previous configurations (modulo resources consumed).

A contract C can only modify its failing map to activate the future monitor of the current transaction or to decide future monitors that C had previously activated but not yet decided. If a contract incorrectly updates its failing map, the current transaction fails. When transactions fail, the system does not modify any failmap map or timeout function.

Blockchain System. There are two types of transactions: *permanent* (committed or failed) and *pending* transactions. *Blockchain runs* are pairs (H, τ) consisting of a sequence H of consolidated blockchain configurations called the *history* and a directed tree τ where each internal node has one or two children. H contains only permanent transaction. Tree τ is called the *monitoring tree* and includes pending transactions. Each node in the monitoring tree is a blockchain configuration. The monitoring tree represents all possible sequences of blockchain states that the list of pending transactions can generate. Exactly one path in the tree will eventually survive and become part of H, which depends on whether the corresponding transactions commit of fail. Each level in the tree corresponds to the execution of transactions up to that level but different configuration at the same level is a different possible reality. To simplify notation, we use n to refer to the blockchain configuration captured by node n in the tree. The root of the monitoring tree is the last blockchain configuration that was consolidated, that is, the last blockchain configuration in the history sequence.

The height of the monitoring tree is at most k. It can be shorter than k at the genesis of the blockchain but once the first k transactions have been executed the monitoring tree reaches and maintains a height k. In the worst case, depending on the contracts deployed in the blockchain, the monitoring tree can have $2^{k+1} - 1$ nodes, but in general not every transaction is going to be monitored which reduces the branching and hence the size of the tree.

Fig. 3 shows a blockchain run (H, τ). The first $j + 1$ transactions are permanent and the last k transactions are pending. The last permanent blockchain configuration is (Σ, Δ) and it is also the root of the monitoring tree τ. When the first pending transaction, t_{j+1}, executes from configuration (Σ, Δ), a contract C that executed in t_{j+1} activated the transaction future monitor generating a branching in τ. However, not all transactions generate a branching in the monitoring tree as not all transactions are necessarily monitored, (for example t_{j+k}). Configuration (Σ', Δ') is a one of the possible outcomes of executing all pending operations.

Notation. We use the following functions:
- nextTx(n): returns the transaction that labels the outgoing edges from n.
- The *successor* of a node $n \xrightarrow{t} n'$ in the monitoring tree.
- successors(n): given a node n that is not a leaf, returns all successors of n, which can be (n_c, n_f), where n_c is the committing successor and n_f the failing successor, or n' if n is not branching.
- the *committing subtree* of n: the maximal subtree rooted at the committing successor of n.
- the *failing subtree* of n: the maximal subtree rooted at the failing successor of n.
- allFutures(n): the set of leaves reachable from node n.

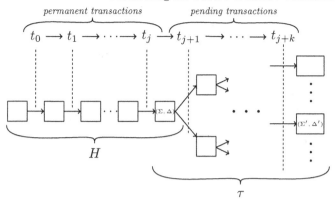

Fig. 3. A blockchain run of $j + 1$ permanent transactions and k pending transactions.

Consider $n \xrightarrow{t} n'$. The configuration at n' is one of the possible results of executing transaction t from the blockchain configuration at n. For simplicity, when referring to a monitoring tree τ with the root node n, we use the terms τ and n interchangeably. Thus, successors(τ) denotes the successors of the root node of τ. The possible futures of the root node of monitoring tree τ, denoted by allFutures(τ), is referred as the futures in τ.

Example 1. The following figure shows an example run after 7 transactions, starting at initial blockchain configuration N_0 and monitoring window $k = 2$.

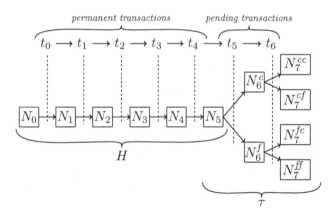

History H corresponds to the first 5 permanent transactions. The remaining transactions are pending forming a directed tree τ whose root is N_5. The transaction at node N_5 is nextTx$(N_5) = t_5$. Node N_5 successors are successors$(N_5) = (N_6^c, N_6^f)$. The committing subtree of N_5 is the subtree with root N_6^c and the failing subtree of N_5 is the subtree with root N_6^f. Finally, the futures in τ are allFutures$(\tau) = \{N_7^{cc}, N_7^{cf}, N_7^{fc}, N_7^{ff}\}$. We annotate with superscript c and f the committing and failing transactions, respectively, and group them in sequences describing paths in monitoring trees.

function step$((H, \tau), t)$	function attach(τ, t) ▷ Extends monitoring trees.

$\tau' \leftarrow$ attach(τ, t)
if height$(\tau') \le k$ then
   return(H, τ')
else
   $\tau'' \leftarrow$ decide(τ')
   tx $\leftarrow$ nextTx(τ)
   H.add$(\tau \xrightarrow{\text{tx}} \tau'')$
   return(H, τ'')
	$\tau' \leftarrow \tau$
	for $l \in$ allFutures(τ) do
	   switch applyTx(t, l) do
	      case **Commit**(l_c) : τ'.add$(l \xrightarrow{t} l_c)$
	      case **Fail**(l_f) : τ'.add$(l \xrightarrow{t} l_f)$
	      case **Pending**(l_c, l_f): τ'.add$(l \xrightarrow{t} (l_c, l_f))$
	return τ'

Fig. 4. Functions step and attach.

3.3 Blockchain evolution

The evolution of the blockchain is defined by function step (see Fig. 4) which takes blockchain runs and transactions, and extends runs. The system has only one rule:

$$\frac{\text{step}((H, \tau), t) = (H', \tau')}{(H, \tau) \twoheadrightarrow_t (H', \tau')}$$

Valid traces are defined by the relation $\twoheadrightarrow$ and consist of chains of related blockchain states $(H_0, \tau_0) \twoheadrightarrow_{t_0} (H_1, \tau_1) \twoheadrightarrow_{t_1} \ldots$ where (H_0, τ_0) is an initial blockchain run with $\tau_0 = H_0 = (\Sigma, \Delta)$.

Let (H, τ) be a blockchain run and t a transaction. We extend the monitoring tree τ by adding a new level attaching t from every possible leaf, which increases by one the height of τ (see Fig. 4). Let τ' be the result of attach(τ, t). If τ' has height $k + 1$, the monitoring window for the first transaction in τ' has expired and its monitor must fail or commit. To take this decision, function step invokes function decide. The resulting monitoring tree τ'' returned by function decide becomes the new monitoring tree. Finally, function step extends H making the first pending transaction permanent.

Function decide (see Fig. 5) determines whether to commit or fail the first pending transaction tx in monitoring tree τ with height $k + 1$ returning either the committing or failing subtree of τ. If τ has only one successor, the decision is trivial, otherwise we analyze tx possible futures. Function decide checks all futures assuming tx commits, (i.e., all leaves in the committing subtree of τ); if the future monitor of transaction tx commits in all of them, then tx commits and the committing subtree of τ becomes the new monitoring tree. Otherwise, tx fails and the failing subtree of τ becomes the new monitoring tree. If decide cannot assert whether the monitored transaction fails or commits, decide invokes timeout to decide (see function knownToCommitWithTimeout in Fig. 5).

In some cases, the decision of future monitors is known before the monitoring windows ends. In such instances, some nodes are unreachable, called *impossible nodes*. For example, when a transaction future monitor is waiting for a transaction in the future and that transaction happens before the monitoring window ends, the future monitor is going to be set to commit, which turns all nodes

function decide(τ)   ▷ Decides commit/fail of the root transaction of τ
    assert height(τ) = $k + 1$
    $\tau' \leftarrow$ prune(τ)
    $t \leftarrow$ nextTx(τ)
    switch successors(τ') **do**
        case τ'': **return** τ''
        case (τ_c, τ_f):
            if $\forall l \in$ allFutures(τ_c) : knownToCommitWithTimeout(l, t) **then return** τ_c
            else return τ_f

---

function prune(τ)
    if τ is a leaf **then return** τ
    $t \leftarrow$ nextTx(τ)
    switch successors(τ) **do**
        case τ': **return** $\tau \overset{t}{\to}$ prune(τ')
        case (τ_c, τ_f):
            $\tau'_c \leftarrow$ prune(τ_c)
            $\tau'_f \leftarrow$ prune(τ_f)
            if $\forall l \in$ allFutures(τ'_c) : knownToCommit(l, t) **then return** $\tau \overset{t}{\to} \tau'_c$
            if $\forall l \in$ allFutures(τ'_c) : knownToFail(l, t) **then return** $\tau \overset{t}{\to} \tau'_f$
            return $\tau \overset{t}{\to} (\tau'_c, \tau'_f)$

---

function failmapCommit(Δ, c, t) **return** $\Delta[c]$.failmap$[t]$ = Commit
function failmapFail(Δ, c, t) **return** $\Delta[c]$.failmap$[t]$ = Fail
function timeoutCommit(Δ, c, t) **return** $\Delta[c]$.timeout$[t]$ = Commit
function undecided(Δ, c, t) **return** $\Delta[c]$.failmap$[t]$ = ?
function monitoringContracts (l, t) **return** $\{c : l.\Delta[c]$.failmap$[t] \neq$ None$\}$
function knownToCommit (l, t)
    return $\forall c \in$ monitoringContracts(l, t) : failmapCommit($l.\Delta, c, t$)
function knownToFail (l, t)
    return $\exists c \in$ monitoringContracts(l, t) : failmapFail($l.\Delta, c, t$)
function commitWithTimeout(Δ, c, t)
    return failmapCommit(Δ, c, t) $\vee$ (undecided(Δ, c, t) $\wedge$ timeoutCommit(Δ, c, t))
function knownToCommitWithTimeout (l, t)
    return $\forall c \in$ monitoringContracts(l, t) : commitWithTimeout($l.\Delta, c, t$)

Fig. 5. Functions decide, prune and auxiliary functions.

in its failing subtree impossible nodes. Concretely, if in all possible futures in the committing subtree of node n its transaction is known to commit, then all nodes in the failing subtree of n are impossible nodes. Similarly, if in all possible futures in the committing subtree of node n its transaction is known to fail, then all nodes in the committing subtree of n are impossible. Impossible nodes are removed before deciding whether a transaction commits or not, since we may incorrectly deduce that a monitor fails because of an impossible future

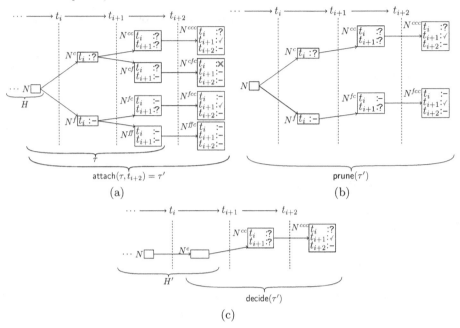

Fig. 6. Application of function step in a blockchain run.

node. Consequently, decide invokes prune to remove all impossible nodes, and only then, decide determines whether the root transaction commits or not as explained above.

Function prune (see Fig. 5) shows how to prune impossible nodes from trees. To guarantee that impossible nodes are pruned before checking if roots of trees are impossible (either commit or fail), we perform a bottom-up recursion.

Example 2. Fig. 6 shows the result of applying function step to blockchain run (H, τ) with a monitoring window $k = 2$ and two pending transactions t_i and t_{i+1}. Each node in the monitoring tree is annotated with the monitor state of all pending transactions up to that node: a question mark means undecided monitors, a tick means known to commit monitors, a cross means known to fail monitors, and a dash denotes no monitored transactions. Initially, no monitors are decided in any node in τ.

Function $\text{step}((H, \tau), t_{i+2})$ first invokes function $\text{attach}(\tau, t_{i+2})$. This function adds a new level to τ by applying transaction t_{i+2} at all leaves in τ, obtaining monitoring tree τ', Fig. 6(a). Transaction t_{i+2} immediately commits at all leaves in τ, generating nodes $N^{ccc}, N^{cfc}, N^{fcc}$ and N^{ffc}. The future monitor for transaction t_i is known to fail at node N^{cfc} while remaining undecided at node N^{ccc} and the future monitor for transaction t_{i+1} is known to commit at nodes N^{ccc} and N^{fcc}. Next, as the height of the new monitoring tree, τ', is $3 > 2$, function step invokes function $\text{decide}(\tau')$ to decide if the first pending transaction, t_i, fails or commits. Function decide invokes function prune to remove all impossible nodes in τ'. When computing prune, the failing subtree of node N^c, rooted at node N^{cf}, is removed because at node N^{ccc} the future monitor for the transaction at node N^c, t_{i+1}, is known to commit and node N^{ccc} is the only future in the committing subtree of node N^c, making the subtree rooted at N^{cf} an impossible subtree. Similarly, the subtree rooted at N^{ff} is an impossible subtree and it is also removed by function prune.

Subtrees with roots N^{cf} and N^{ff} are the only ones removed when applying function prune to monitoring tree τ', as shown in Fig. 6(b).

Finally, to decide whether to commit or not transaction t_i function decide consider node N^{ccc}, as it is the only future in the committing subtree of node N in the monitoring tree returned by function prune. At node N^{ccc} the future monitor for transaction t_i is undecided. However, since its monitoring window has ended, function decide uses the timeout of the contracts that are undecided. Assuming for all undecided contracts their timeout function commit transaction t_i, then function decide commits transaction t_i, returning the subtree rooted at N^c as the new monitoring tree (see Fig. 6(c)), it would fail if at least one contract timeout function fails. Finally, function step extends H by making transaction t_i permanent. If prune had not been applied before function decide evaluated all futures in the committing subtree of N, transaction t_i would have incorrectly failed, as in impossible future N^{cfc}, the future monitor for transaction t_i fails.

An example of contracts that only lend their tokens if they receive them back within 2 transactions in the future can be found in [11].

4   Properties

We discuss now properties of the model of computation defined in Section 3. In particular, we establish how the new model extends the previous one, that the size of monitoring trees is manageable, and the blockchain always progresses. We assume a fixed monitoring window k. All proofs can be found in [11].

After the monitoring window has expired, the root transaction is confirmed and one of two possible successors is consolidated.

Lemma 1. *Let (H, τ) be the system run after k transactions, t a transaction and $(H', \tau') = \mathsf{step}((H, \tau), t)$. The root of τ' is one of the successors of the root of τ and all paths in τ' without leaves are also paths in τ. Moreover, H' is obtained by extending H with the first pending transaction on τ.*

The first k transactions from the genesis are just added to the tree. From the previous lemma, after k transactions and when a new step is taken, the first pending transaction is either committed or failed and a new pending transaction is attached to all leaves. Moreover, the transaction added to the history is the root of the previous monitoring tree and one of its successors is the root of the new monitoring tree. In other words, exactly one of the paths in the monitoring tree eventually becomes permanent, and thus, the blockchain always progresses.

Corollary 1 (Progress). *Function* step *is total and, after the first k invocations, each execution of* step *makes one transaction permanent.*

The height of the monitoring tree is bounded by the monitoring window.

Lemma 2 (Bounded Certainty). *Let τ be a monitoring tree in a blockchain run obtained by applying function step l times. Then, the height of τ is the minimum between l and k. Moreover, all leaves in τ are in its last level.*

Function prune removes all impossible nodes from monitoring trees. Function prune recursively removes impossible nodes in the committing and failing subtrees, and then, determines if it can remove any subtree by inspecting all possible futures in the committing successor.

Lemma 3. *Function* prune(τ) *returns a sub-monitoring tree of τ without impossible nodes and only impossible nodes were removed.*

Function step consistently makes the blockchain progress. After more than k transactions were added, the first pending transaction is made permanent (see Corollary 1). The resulting monitoring tree keeps the order of the rest of the pending transactions and it also preserves the same information of the pending transactions except the last.

Lemma 4. *Let τ be a monitoring tree, η be the result of expanding τ with a new transaction, t be the first pending transaction in τ, and ν be the decided subtree of η.*
- *If η has only one successor then ν is the result of pruning η's successor.*
- *If η has two successors, then let η_c and η_f be the result of pruning the committing and failing subtrees of η respectively.*
  - *Monitoring tree ν is η_c if in all possible futures assuming t commits, transaction t does not fail or if no decision has been reached, all pending* timeout *functions of t commit.*
  - *Monitoring tree ν is η_f if there is a possible future where assuming transactions t commits, leads to the monitor of t fail or some of the pending* timeout *function of t fail.*

The size of monitoring trees can be exponential in the number of monitored transaction rather than in the monitoring window size, as monitored transactions are the only ones branching monitoring trees.

Lemma 5. *Let τ be a monitoring tree and m be the number of monitored transactions in τ (so $m \leq k$). Then, the size of τ is in $\mathcal{O}(2^m \times k)$.*

In practical scenarios, the number of monitored transactions typically is small compared to the monitoring window because most transactions do not require future monitors. This makes the size of the monitoring tree much smaller than the theoretical maximum.

Corollary 2. *If the number of monitored transactions in monitoring trees is constant then the size of monitoring trees is bounded by $\mathcal{O}(k)$.*

Finally, we show that adding future bounded monitors preserves legacy executions, so for blockchain runs where no contracts use future monitors, the monitoring tree is a chain with no branching.

A legacy monitoring tree τ is such that every configuration obtained from applying applyTx coincides with rule $\rightsquigarrow$.

Lemma 6 (Legacy Pending Transactions). *Let τ be a legacy monitoring tree. Then, τ is a chain and the effect of executing all transactions in τ is equivalent to executing them in the traditional model of computation.*

If we add that the permanent history is equivalent (up to now) to the traditional model, then the evolution of the blockchain in both models coincide.

Lemma 7 (Legacy History). *Let τ be a legacy monitoring tree and H be a history such that every permanent transaction coincides with rule $\rightsquigarrow$. Then, the result of concatenating H and τ is equivalent to the traditional model of computation.*

From Corollary 1 and Lemma 7, we conclude that the new model of computation is consistent with the previous model of computation and eventually creates a chain. Additionally, Corollary 2 implies that in practical scenarios, the size of monitoring trees is linear on the monitoring window, making it a feasible and practical blockchain implementation.

5   Atomic Loans

Flash loan contracts allow other contracts to borrow tokens *without any collateral* only if the borrowed tokens are repaid during the same transaction [12] (typically with some interest). Atomic loans are a generalization of flash loans where the borrowing party can repay the lending party in future transactions. It is not possible to implement flash loans unless additional mechanisms are added to the blockchain [10]. Similarly, it is impossible to implement atomic loans in traditional blockchain computational models. As transaction monitors [10] enable flash loans transactions, future monitors allow monitors to check properties across transactions enabling atomic loans. We illustrate now how to implement atomic loans using the monitoring window as the maximum payback time.

We specify lender contracts as contracts respecting the following two properties:

Specification 1 (Atomic Loans) *We say contract A is an atomic lender if:*
AL-safety: *A loan from A is repaid to A within the monitoring window.*
AL-progress: *Contract A grants loans unless* **AL-safety** *is violated.*

The following contract `FlashLoanLender` shows a simple contract implementing a flash loan lender[7] using Fail/NoFail hookup [10], i.e. with no future monitors but transaction monitors. We highlight monitor code with gray background.

---

[7] Flash loan lender are atomic loan lenders with paying back window of one.

```
contract FlashLoanLender {
  uint pending_returns = 0;
  uint fee;
  function lend(address payable dest, uint amount) public
    { require(amount <= this.balance);
      dest.receiveLoan{value: amount}(fee);
      pending_returns += amount + fee;
      this.fail = (pending_returns != 0); }
  function returnLoan() external payable
    { pending_returns -= msg.value;
      this.fail = (pending_returns != 0); } }
```

Function `lend` lends as long as the lender has enough funds, annotates the borrowed tokens in `pending_returns` and sets its `fail` bit so the transaction commits only if the loan is paid back. When the loan is returned, `returnLoan` decreases `pending_returns` and updates its `fail` bit. At the end of each transaction, if there are pending loans the `fail` bit will make the transaction fail.

The above contract implements flash loans that must be returned within a transaction, but does not work properly if future transactions are considered. It is not possible to successfully predict or check whether the loan is returned in some future transactions. We show now how future monitors solve this problem.

The following contract `Lender` is an atomic lender using future monitors. All loans are treated equally and should be paid back on time, and if one loan is not returned, then all loans issued at the same transaction would be rejected. Here we are being too strict compared to practical cases, but it is enough to illustrate the use of future transaction monitors.

```
contract Lender {
  uint fee;
  function lend(address payable dest, uint amount) public
    { require(amount <= this.balance);
      dest.receiveLoan{value: amount}(fee);
      pending_returns[msg.txid] += amount + fee;
      if(pending_returns[msg.txid] != 0)
        this.failmap[msg.txid] = UNDECIDED; }
  function returnLoan(txId id) public
    { pending_returns[id] -= msg.value;
      if(pending_returns[id] == 0) this.failmap[id] = COMMIT; }
} with monitor {
  map<txId, int> pending_returns;
  function timeout(txId id) { return FAIL; } }
```

Contract `Lender` uses a map `pending_returns`, from transactions to the amount borrowed within that transaction, to determine whether a transaction should commit or fail. Function `lend` grants a loan if the lender has enough funds, increases the corresponding entry in map `pending_returns` for the current transaction and sets the `failmap` entry activating the current transaction monitor. Client contracts can repay loans by invoking `returnLoan`, which receives the transaction identifier of the lending transaction to decrease the corresponding

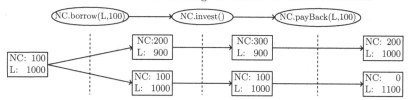

Fig. 7. Balance of contracts NC and L in the monitoring tree after executing the three transactions posted by a client.

entry in **pending_returns** by the amount received. If **pending_returns** reaches 0 for a given transaction, the **failmap** entry of that transaction is set to COMMIT. Finally, **timeout** returns FAIL to fail transactions with unpaid loans at the end of their monitoring window.

Clients can request loans without further collateral, satisfying **AL-progress**, and if loans are not returned within the monitoring window, the lending transaction will retroactively fail, satisfying **AL-safety**.

The following contract **NaiveClient** requests a loan invoking **borrow**.

```
contract NaiveClient {
  map<pair<txId,Lender>, uint> toPay;
  function borrow(Lender l, uint amount) onlyOwner
    { l.lend(amount);
      toPay[(msg.txid(),l)] = amount; }
  function receiveLoan(uint fee)
    { toPay[(msg.txid,msg.sender())] += fee; }
  function invest() onlyOwner { ... }
  function payBack(Lender l, uint amount, txId id) onlyOwner
    { require(toPay[(id,l)] >= amount);
      toPay[(id,l)] -= amount;
      l.returnLoan{value: amount}(id); } }
```

In subsequent transactions, the client can invest the funds, and in a final transaction, return the loan to the lender invoking **payBack**.

Let NC and L be two contracts installed in a blockchain with a monitoring window of length 2, where NC runs **NaiveClient** and L runs **Lender**. Consider (Σ, Δ) to be the current state of the blockchain at which NC has 100 tokens and L has 1000 tokens. From (Σ, Δ), the sequence of transactions is: (1) NC requests a loan, (2) NC invests assuming contract L lends the money, and (3) NC returns the loan. Because L employs future monitors to guarantee clients pay back, the first transaction generates a branching on the blockchain evolution. The next two transactions are not monitored, thus they do not create any branching. Therefore, after these three transactions, there exist two possible futures as shown in Fig.7, one where L grants the loan and another where it does not. We can see that NC pays back in all possible futures. Moreover, contract NC pays back even in the future where contract L fails the past lending operation (for a detailed explanation see [11]).

A malicious lender can take advantage of such behavior, for example using the following contract `MaliciousLender`.

```
contract MaliciousLender {
  uint fee;
  function lend(address payable dest, uint amount) public
    { dest.receiveLoan{value: amount}(fee);
      this.failmap[msg.txid] = UNDECIDED; }
  function returnLoan(txId id) public { return; }
} with monitor {
    function timeout(txId id) { return FAIL; } }
```

The above malicious lender, upon receiving a loan request in function `lend`, if it has enough tokens, it grants the loan and marks the transaction as undecided using its `failmap` map. However, this lender contract does not update its `failmap` map when receiving paybacks. Therefore, at the end of the monitoring window, the monitor remains undecided making the lending transaction fail due to the `timeout` function. In other words, the malicious lender never lends any tokens, as all its loans are reverted, but it looks like it does. When combined with `NaiveClient` and the same three transactions described earlier, the malicious lender will receive the repayment of a loan from client NC without having given the loan. In Fig. 7, the bottom branch is the one that survives when the lender implements a malicious contract.

The problem arises because client NC does not implement any mechanism to check in which branch it is executing when repaying the loan. The naive contract does not distinguish between the scenario where the loan will ultimately be committed and the scenario where it will fail. As a result, client NC ends up providing payments in both cases.

The following contract `Client` presents a correct client implementing two maps, `requested` and `toPay`, to keep track of the amounts requested from lenders and its debts owed to lenders, respectively.

```
contract Client {
  map<pair<txId,Lender>, uint> toPay, requested;
  function borrow(Lender l, uint amount) onlyOwner
    { l.lend(amount);
      requested[(msg.txid,l)] = amount; }
  function receiveLoan (uint fee)
    { require(requested[(msg.txid,msg.sender)] == msg.value);
      requested[(msg.txid,msg.sender)] = 0;
      toPay[(msg.txid,msg.sender)] = msg.value + fee; }
  function invest() onlyOwner { ... }
  function payBack(Lender l, uint amount, txId id)
    { require(toPay[(id,l)] >= amount);
      toPay[(id,l)] -= amount;
      l.returnLoan{value: amount}(id); } }
```

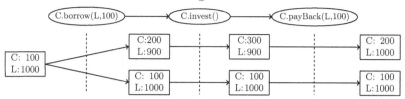

Fig. 8. Balance of contracts C and L in the monitoring tree after executing the three transactions posted by a client.

The above contract allows clients to determine the specific path in which it is executing, and thus, to decide whether to repay. Consequently, clients can successfully get loans from correct lenders while being resistant to attacks from malicious lenders.

Fig. 8 shows an execution following the same transactions as before but with the correct contract Client: clients request a loan, invest the money, and payback the loan. The top branch shows the case where the lender sends the money and the client returns it, while the bottom branch shows the case where the loan is not given. In the former cases, the client returns the money, and in the latter case, the client just fails the transaction.

These examples show how even contracts not monitoring transactions need to be aware that transactions can create potential executions in the blockchain evolution that may be reverted due to future monitors. Since the same transaction is executed in all possible scenarios, but their effects may be different, contracts need to know in which temporal line they are executing and act accordingly. Contract Client accomplishes this by maintaining a record of debts owed to lenders in variable toPay.

6   Related Work

Dynamic verification of smart contracts Runtime monitoring tools like ContractLarva [15,6] and Solythesis [18] take a smart contract code and its properties as input and produce a safe smart contract that fail transactions violating the given properties. They achieve this be injecting the monitor into the smart contract as additional instructions. Therefore, these monitors are restricted to one operation in a single contract. Transaction Monitors [10] extend monitoring beyond a single operation to observe the effect of an entire transaction execution on a given contract.

While these existing works provide strong foundations for smart contract verification, none directly address the ability to react based on future transactions, as proposed in this work.

Branching Computational Models The monitoring tree generated by pending transactions might reassemble the tree-like structure in branching-time logic such as CTL [13]. However, the branching in the monitoring tree represents all possible futures given by the monitors of the pending transaction, and exactly one path eventually consolidates. In particular, future monitors are not aware of the existence of other paths in the monitoring tree and therefore cannot reason about them. CTL, on the other hand, can be used to express properties that reason about different paths in the tree.

7   Conclusion

We presented future monitors for smart contracts. Future monitors are a defense mechanism enabling contracts to state properties across multiple transactions. These kinds of properties are motivated by long-lived transactions, in particular by atomic loans, which are not implementable in their full generality in current blockchains. To implement future monitors, we introduced the notion of monitoring window and two additional new mechanisms to blockchains, namely failing maps and timeout functions.

Future monitors delay the consolidation of transactions, but the system remains consistent and we gain in expressivity. The outcome of transactions remains deterministic and depends solely on the transactions themselves, but now transactions can fail because of future actions. Combining all elements we obtained a deterministic semantics with future monitors in place.

We have also illustrated that contracts need to be aware of the existence of possible executions. Future monitors introduce a branching model to describe the evolution of blockchain systems where transactions may commit or not, caused by the temporary uncertainty regarding the effect of pending transactions. Consequently, when new transactions are added to the blockchain, they are executed in multiple blockchain configurations, representing possible timelines. Therefore, contracts need to be aware of the different contexts in which they are executing, ensuring that the transaction produces the desired effects in all possible realities.

The main contribution of this paper is theoretical and we left the full implementation of future monitors as future work. Optimistic rollup systems, where the effect of transactions is already delayed due to the fraud-prove arbitration scheme, present an ideal environment to incorporate future monitors into practical blockchain systems without further implications. In particular, optimistic rollup systems can allow future transaction monitors with little modifications, and more importantly, without modifying the underlying blockchain.

For simplicity, we have neglected a specific analysis of the additional gas consumption that arises for using future monitors, which might lead to the failure of accepting transactions. Nevertheless, we conjecture that future monitors are simple enough to guarantee that a calculable amount of gas will prevent gas failing situations. However, we leave a detailed study for future work.

References

1. Michelson: the language of smart contracts in Tezos. `https://tezos.gitlab.io/whitedoc/michelson.html`.
2. Ethereum. Solidity documentation — release 0.2.0. `http://solidity.readthedocs.io/`, 2016.
3. W. Ahrendt and R. Bubel. Functional verification of smart contracts via strong data integrity. In *Proc. of ISoLA (3)*, number 12478 in LNCS, pages 9–24. Springer, 2020.
4. G. Alfour. LIGO: a friendly smart-contract language for Tezos. `https://ligolang.org`, 2020. last accessed: 2022-05-03.
5. D. Annenkov, J. B. Nielsen, and B. Spitters. ConCert: a smart contract certification framework in Coq. In *Proc. of the 9th ACM SIGPLAN Int'l Conf. on Certified Programs and Proofs (CPP'20)*, pages 215–218. ACM, 2020.
6. S. Azzopardi, J. Ellul, and G. J. Pace. Monitoring smart contracts: ContractLarva and open challenges beyond. In *Proc. of the 18th International Conference on Runtime Verification (RV'18)*, volume 11237 of *LNCS*, pages 113–137. Springer, 2018.
7. B. Bernardo, R. Cauderlier, Z. Hu, B. Pesin, and J. Tesson. Mi-Cho-Coq, a framework for certifying Tezos smart contracts. In *Proc. of the FM 2019 International Workshops, Part I*, volume 12232 of *LNCS*, pages 368–379. Springer, 2019.
8. K. Bhargavan, A. Delignat-Lavaud, C. Fourneta, A. Gollamudi, G. Gonthier, N. Kobeissi, N. Kulatova, A. Rastogi, T. Sibut-Pinote, N. Swamy, and S. Z. Béguelin. Formal verification of smart contracts: Short paper. In *Proc. of Workshop on Programming Languages and Analysis for Security (PLAS@CCS'16)*, pages 91–96. ACM, 2016.
9. L. Bousfield, R. Bousfield, C. Buckland, B. Burgess, J. Colvin, E. Felten, S. Goldfeder, D. Goldman, B. Huddleston, H. Kalonder, F. Lacs, H. Ng, A. Sanghi, T. Wilson, V. Yermakova, and T. Zidenberg. Arbitrum nitro: A second-generation optimistic rollup. `https://github.com/OffchainLabs/nitro/blob/master/docs/Nitro-whitepaper.pdf`, 2022.
10. M. Capretto, M. Ceresa, and C. Sánchez. Transaction monitoring of smart contracts. In T. Dang and V. Stolz, editors, *Proc. of the 22nd Int'l Conf. on Runtime Verification (RV'22)*, volume 13498 of *LNCS*, pages 162–180. Springer, 2022.
11. M. Capretto, M. Ceresa, and C. Sánchez. Monitoring the future of smart contracts. *arXiv*, abs/2401.12093, 2024.
12. A. C. Cañada, F. Kobayashi, fubuloubu, and A. Williams. Eip-3156: Flash loans. `https://eips.ethereum.org/EIPS/eip-3156`.
13. E. M. Clarke and E. A. Emerson. Design and synthesis of synchronization skeletons using branching time temporal logic. In D. Kozen, editor, *Logics of Programs*, pages 52–71, Berlin, Heidelberg, 1982. Springer Berlin Heidelberg.
14. S. Conchon, A. Korneva, and F. Zaïdi. Verifying smart contracts with Cubicle. In *Proc. of the 1st Workshop on Formal Methods for Blockchains (FMBC'19)*, volume 12232 of *LNCS*, pages 312–324. Springer, 2019.
15. J. Ellul and G. J. Pace. Runtime verification of Ethereum smart contracts. In *Proc. of the 14th European Dependable Computing Conference (EDCC'18)*, pages 158–163. IEEE Computer Society, 2018.
16. J. Ellul and G. J. Pace. Optional monitoring for long-lived transactions. In *Proc. of the 5th ACM Int'l Workshop on Verification and mOnitoring at Runtime EXecution, Virtual Event(VORTEX'21)*, pages 35–39. ACM, 2021.

17. J. Gray. *The Transaction Concept: Virtues and Limitations*, page 140–150. Morgan Kaufmann Publishers Inc., San Francisco, CA, USA, 1988.

18. A. Li, J. A. Choi, and an. Long. Securing smart contract with runtime validation. In *Proc. of ACM PLDI'20*, pages 438–453. ACM, 2020.

19. N. Mudge. Erc-2535: Diamonds, multi-facet proxy. `https://eips.ethereum.org/EIPS/eip-2535`, February 2020. Ethereum Improvement Proposals, no. 2535.

20. S. Nakamoto. Bitcoin: a peer-to-peer electronic cash system, 2009.

21. Z. Nehaï and F. Bobot. Deductive proof of industrial smart contracts using Why3. In *Proc. of the 1st Workshop on Formal Methods for Blockchains (FMBC'19)*, volume 12232 of *LNCS*, pages 299–311. Springer, 2019.

22. A. Permenev, D. Dimitrov, P. Tsankov, D. Drachsler-Cohen, and M. Vechev. VerX: Safety verification of smart contracts. In *Proc of the 41st IEEE Symp. on Security and Privacy (S&P'20)*, pages 1661–1677. IEEE, 2020.

23. D. Phil. Analysis of the DAO exploit. `https://hackingdistributed.com/2016/06/18/analysis-of-the-dao-exploit/`, 2016.

24. J. Schiffl, W. Ahrendt, B. Beckert, and R. Bubel. Formal analysis of smart contracts: Applying the KeY system. In *Deductive Software Verification: Future Perspectives - Reflections on the Occasion of 20 Years of KeY*, volume 12345 of *LNCS*, pages 204–218. 2020.

25. I. Sergey, A. Kumar, and A. Hobor. Scilla: a smart contract intermediate-level LAnguage. *CoRR*, abs/1801.00687, 2018.

26. J. Stephens, K. Ferles, B. Mariano, S. Lahiri, and I. Dillig. SmartPulse: Automated checking of temporal properties in smart contracts. In *Proc. of the 42nd IEEE Symp. on Security and Privacy (S&P'21)*. IEEE, May 2021.

27. N. Szabo. Smart contracts: Building blocks for digital markets. *Extropy*, 16, 1996.

28. G. Wood. Ethereum: A secure decentralised generalised transaction ledger. *Ethereum project yellow paper*, 151:1–32, 2014.

Comprehending Object State
via Dynamic Class Invariant Learning*

Jan H. Boockmann$^{(\boxtimes)}$ and Gerald Lüttgen

Software Technologies Research Group,
University of Bamberg, Bamberg, Germany
{jan.boockmann,gerald.luettgen}@swt-bamberg.de

Abstract. Maintaining software is cumbersome when method argument constraints are undocumented. To reveal them, previous work learned preconditions from exemplary valid and invalid method arguments. In practice, it would be highly beneficial to know class invariants, too, because functionality added during software maintenance must not break them. Even more so than method preconditions, class invariants are rarely documented and often cannot completely be inferred automatically, especially for objects exhibiting complex state such as dynamic data structures.

This paper presents a novel dynamic approach to learning class invariants, thereby complementing related work on learning method preconditions. We automatically synthesize assertions from an adjustable assertion grammar to distinguish valid and invalid objects. While random walks generate valid objects, a combination of bounded-exhaustive testing techniques and behavioral oracles yield invalid objects. The utility of our approach for code comprehension and software maintenance is demonstrated by comparing our learned invariants to documented invariant validation methods found in real-world Java classes and to the invariants detected by the Daikon tool.

1 Introduction

Comprehending the behavior of a complex software component is challenging, but necessary for component reuse and maintenance. The object-oriented programming paradigm has enforced the principle of information hiding, which separates externally observable behavior from internal implementation. To make a component *reusable*, it typically suffices to document its external behavior and the constraints imposed on its method argument values. When following the principles of defensive programming [4], a thorough input validation at the entry of each method checks whether the constraints are satisfied. For components that lack input validation, previous work has shown that appropriate preconditions can be inferred automatically [2,8,27,30,33].

---

* This research is supported by the German Research Foundation (DFG) under project DSI2 (grant no. LU 1748/4-2).

D. Beyer and A. Cavalcanti (Eds.): FASE 2024, LNCS 14573, pp. 143–164, 2024.
https://doi.org/10.1007/978-3-031-57259-3_7

To make a component *maintainable*, however, information on its external behavior alone is insufficient, because maintenance may require modifications of the component's implementation. *Class invariants* [19,20] capturing the constraints on the component's program state exhibited at runtime are essential for maintainers to ensure that their source code modifications, such as bug fixing, refactoring, or implementing new functionalities, match the assumptions implicitly encoded in the existing source code. A failure to do so may result in unpredictable behavior or even system crashes. Despite this, class invariants are rarely documented and checked even more rarely during input validation.

Approaches to dynamic assertion learning generalize from observations, e.g., object states, to synthesize assertions such as preconditions and class invariants. Related tools include *Daikon* [8], *Proviso* [2], *Hanoi* [22], and *EvoSpex* [25]. Daikon observes program states during execution and uses templates to obtain a set of candidate assertions, including class invariants, that hold at certain program locations. Proviso learns preconditions that also consider complex data types and uses a test generator as an oracle to detect invalid method arguments. Hanoi infers representation invariants for data types in a functional programming language. EvoSpex employs an evolutionary algorithm to learn postconditions from (in)valid pre/post state pairs. Overall, the exploration of approaches to dynamic class invariant learning for complex types remains relatively limited, despite the potential benefits for software maintenance.

This paper proposes a dynamic analysis approach that learns a class invariant using iterative refinements from (in)valid objects. We perform random walks in object state spaces to construct valid objects and combine bounded-exhaustive testing techniques [3,6,18] with behavioral oracles to create invalid objects. As oracles, one can either adapt the random walks or provide property-based tests [9]. We refine our candidate invariant by removing existing or introducing new assertions, which are dynamically constructed along an assertion grammar. This process iterates until all obtained (in)valid objects are classified correctly.

We have implemented our class invariant learning approach for Java in a prototype tool, called *Geminus*. Our evaluation shows, for real-world Java classes taken primarily from the the `java.util` package, that our learned class invariants are at least as accurate as, and often surpass, those detected by Daikon or documented in the code. Beyond software maintenance, class invariants also support various software development activities, including software testing [13].

Organization Section 2 introduces the notions of class invariant and bounded-exhaustive/property-based testing alongside a running example. Section 3 explains our class invariant learning approach and Section 4 evaluates it. Section 5 discusses related work, while Section 6 presents our conclusions and future work.

2   Foundations

This section reviews the concepts of class invariant in the context of the object-oriented paradigm by means of a running example. We subsequently outline how property-based and bounded-exhaustive testing relate to class invariants.

```
 1 public class SimpleSquare {
 2   //@ invariant w == h && w > 0;
 3   private int w, h; // width and height
 4
 5   public SimpleSquare() { setLength(1); }
 6   public void setLength(int length) {
 7     if (length <= 0) { throw new IllegalArgumentException(); }
 8     this.w = length;
 9     this.h = length;
10   }
11
12   public int area() { return w*h; }
13   public int perimeter() { return 2*(w+h); }
14   public int aspectRatio() { return w/h; }
15
16   public SimpleRectangle toRect() {
17     return new SimpleRectangle(w, h);
18   }
19 }
```

Fig. 1: Running example Java class SimpleSquare.

Running Example The class SimpleSquare in Figure 1 models a square with a non-zero positive length using the two integer attributes *width* (w) and *height* (h). Other objects can interact with SimpleSquare by invoking its public methods to set the length of the square or to compute its geometric properties, or to obtain an equivalent object of class SimpleRectangle. Note that method setLength performs thorough input validation and throws an IllegalArgumentException if the provided method argument value is not strictly positive.

Class Invariants Objects play a fundamental role in object-oriented programming. They are created via constructors, interact with other objects via method calls, and are disposed by a destructor. Throughout method execution, an object may call methods of other objects, including itself, or alter the accessible attributes of other objects. Often, invoking a method results in a side-effect or modification of the object's state, either through modifying its primitive attributes or by modifying the object state of a referenced object.

The notion of a class invariant in object-oriented programming has first been explored in [19] and since been adapted by specification languages such as JML [16]. Understanding class invariants is crucial during development and maintenance, because they provide guarantees about the object state at the start of a *qualified method call* [20] and the end of such a call. In contrast, the class invariant may not hold for *unqualified method calls*, which the object invokes on itself. For example, calling *setLength* in the constructor is considered unqualified. Accordingly, the class invariant holds for all objects derived via a constructor or via a qualified call invoked on an object that satisfies the invariant.

```
1 @Test public void traditionalTest() {
2   SimpleSquare s = new SimpleSquare();
3   s.setLength(5);
4   assert s.area() == 25;
5 }
6
7 @Test public void propertyBasedTest(SimpleSquare s) {
8   assert s.toRect().area() == s.area();
9   s.toRect().toSquare(); // implicitly checks absence of exception
10 }
```

Fig. 2: A traditional and a property-based tests for class `SimpleSquare`.

In the running example, the assertion that the width and height are equal and strictly positive is a suitable class invariant. Accordingly, method `aspectRatio` does not need to check that attribute `h` is non-zero to avoid a division-by-zero exception, because this is implied by the invariant. Similarly, method `toRect` can assume that constructing a new `SimpleRectangle` object always succeeds.

The set of reachable objects that a class invariant has to satisfy can be constructed incrementally by performing random walks in the object state space. A random walk starts at an object state derived from a constructor and continues by invoking methods on the current object; this kind of state exploration is used in the context of fuzz testing [17] and test suite generation [10,26]. Even for finite object state spaces, an exhaustive exploration is often practically infeasible.

Property-Based Testing While traditional tests first establish a testing scenario, property-based tests [9] are parameterized over inputs supplied by a test engine. Property-based testing is primarily used in functional languages, e.g., in Haskell using *QuickCheck* [5], but can also be applied to object-oriented programs.

Figure 2 depicts a traditional and a property-based test for our running example. Note that the property-based test is parameterized over an object of the class under test and checks that the obtained rectangle has the same area as the former square. It also implicitly tests that the translation from rectangle to square via method `toSquare` does not raise an exception.

Bounded-Exhaustive Testing Deriving a representative set of objects, e.g., for property-based testing, is often a tedious and error-prone task when done manually. Bounded-exhaustive testing [6,11,21] is a testing technique that automatically tests a software for all valid inputs within specified size bounds.

While primitive types like integers are often sampled from a range of values, complex object states usually require a create-and-test approach: a systematic enumeration artificially assigns values to private and public attributes to create all object states within a provided bound, and a manually specified predicate, i.e., a class invariant, tests for validity and retains valid objects only.

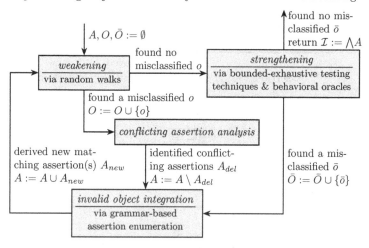

Fig. 3: Overview of our approach to dynamic class invariant learning.

3   Approach

This section introduces our approach to dynamic class invariant learning, which is depicted in Figure 3. Each step either modifies the set of collected valid (O) or invalid ($\bar{O}$) objects, or the set of assertions (A) whose conjunction forms the candidate class invariant ($\mathcal{I}$). If an object is reachable, we consider it valid. If an object is unreachable, we consider it invalid. The class invariant we aim to learn classifies all reachable objects as valid and all unreachable objects as invalid.

The *weakening* step aims to refine the candidate class invariant $\mathcal{I}$ by finding a valid object o that is classified as invalid by $\mathcal{I}$. If successful, we remove the conflicting, overly restrictive assertion(s) that caused the incorrect classification. Previously collected invalid objects that are no longer classified as invalid due to the removed assertions are reintegrated subsequently. If no valid object is misclassified, we perform *strengthening* to find an invalid object $\bar{o}$ that is misclassified. The *invalid object integration* step then derives a matching assertion that correctly classifies an invalid object as invalid but all prior found valid objects still as valid. If no $\bar{o}$ is found, we return the candidate class invariant.

Because our approach learns from a finite set of objects, the learned class invariant is only correct for the collected (in)valid objects, but not in general. However, if no assertion can be generated to distinguish a valid from an invalid object, the learned invariant correctly classifies only all identified valid objects, but mistakenly classifies some invalid objects as valid.

The high-level weakening, strengthening, and invalid object integration steps are generic and can be instantiated by different techniques. Our approach leverages random walks to generate valid objects and combines bounded-exhaustive testing techniques with behavioral oracles to obtain invalid objects. We derive assertions to distinguish valid from invalid objects using a grammar. In contrast to related approaches [25,30], our objects are guaranteed to be (in)valid.

Table 1: Intermediate states of our approach to class invariant learning in each iteration, for the `SimpleSquare` running example.

it.	current assertions A	found new $o/\bar{o}$	removed assertions A_{del}	new assertions A_{new}
1	$\emptyset$	$\bar{o} : \boxed{0\_\_0}$	$\emptyset$	$\{false\}$
2	$\{false\}$	$o : \boxed{1 \quad 1}$	$\{false\}$	$\{w = 1\}$
3	$\{w = 1\}$	$\bar{o} : \boxed{1\_\_0}$	$\emptyset$	$\{w = h\}$
4	$\{w = 1, w = h\}$	$o : \boxed{2 \quad 2}$	$\{w = 1\}$	$\{w > 0\}$
5	$\{w = h, w > 0\}$	$\perp$		

Table 1 shows the execution state of our approach in each iteration when learning class invariant $w = h \wedge w > 0$ for our running example `SimpleSquare`. Valid objects such as $\boxed{1 \quad 1}$ are indicated by a solid box, while invalid objects such as $\boxed{0\_\_0}$ are shown in a dashed box. The remainder of this section uses this example to illustrate the workings of our invariant learning approach.

3.1 A Triangle of Oracles

Our approach exploits the insight that an executable implementation, a testable assumption, and an object form a closed loop of information. Assuming two elements are correct one to allows constructing a test-based oracle to assess the correctness of the third. This leads to the creation of three distinct oracles:

1. *Implementation*: Given a correct assumption and a valid object, any failure upon testing the assumption indicates a faulty implementation.
2. *Assumption*: Given a correct implementation and a valid object, any failure upon testing the assumption indicates an incorrect assumption.
3. *Object*: Given a correct implementation and a correct assumption, any failure upon testing the assumption indicates an invalid object.

The implementation oracle is leveraged in software testing to detect faulty implementations. It either encodes assumptions as traditional tests, which create objects assumed to be valid by construction and checks assertions on them, or as property-based tests, which evaluate properties on valid objects supplied by the test engine. When learning a class invariant for a given implementation, one can ignore the question of implementation correctness, because the invariant is supposed to reflect the implementation. However, a learned invariant that does not match the expectations may indicate a faulty implementation.

The assumption oracle can be employed to identify an incorrect invariant that misclassifies valid objects as invalid when considering the invariant as the assumption. By generating valid objects in our weakening step, we detect an overly restrictive, i.e., unsound, invariant. Analogously, the second oracle can be used to identify invariants that misclassify invalid objects as valid. If an object is invalid, but the candidate invariant holds, the invariant is incomplete, which allows our strengthening step to detect overly permissive invariants. We consider an invariant/oracle *sound* if it classifies all valid objects as valid, and *complete* if it classifies all invalid objects as invalid. The objects revealing an incorrect candidate class invariant are added to the training set during weakening/strengthening, and the invariant is updated accordingly.

The object oracle can detect invalid objects if implementation and assumption are correct. Invalid objects can be used by the assumption oracle to spot overly permissive invariants. Providing assumptions to detect both valid and invalid objects is challenging and equivalent to learning the class invariant.

3.2 Generating Valid Object States via Random Walks

The weakening step leverages the assumption oracle to assess whether the candidate class invariant misclassifies valid objects as invalid. To construct valid objects, we perform random walks in object state spaces: any object derived via a sequence of qualified method calls starting from a freshly constructed object is valid. Because the implementation can be considered correct, a method invocation in a random walk may only throw *expected exceptions*, which are associated with a failed input validation such as the `IllegalArgumentException` thrown by method `setLength`. In contrast, *unexpected exceptions* are prevented by the class invariant. For example, a division-by-zero exception cannot be thrown in method `aspectRatio`, because the invariant guarantees that the height is nonzero. In practice, all checked exceptions in Java are typically expected exceptions and some unchecked exceptions are unexpected exceptions.

We parameterize the random walks using a set of *builders* and *actions*. Builders construct fresh objects using the available constructors, and actions invoke methods. Following the naming convention of [31] for methods, we use the term *observer/modifier* action to denote an action that does not/does alter the considered object's state. In our example, a single builder invoking the zero-argument constructor and a single action invoking method `setLength` with value 2 suffice. To enforce termination, we bound the random walk with respect to the number of walks and the number of method calls per walk. To ensure deterministic behavior, one may either randomly select a builder/action using a fixed seed (like Randoop [26]) or exhaustively explore all builder/action combinations up to a given depth (like EvoSpex [25]). Thus, not finding a valid object that is misclassified as invalid by the candidate class invariant does not guarantee the absence of one. The effectiveness of finding a misclassified object depends on the object state coverage achieved by the random walk.

The candidate invariant before the second iteration (*false*) in Table 1 misclassifies $\boxed{1 \quad 1}$ obtained directly from the constructor. In contrast, the invariant at the start of the fourth iteration ($w = 1 \land w = h$) misclassifies $\boxed{2 \quad 2}$, which is obtained after invoking `setLength(2)` on the freshly constructed object. No valid object is misclassified as invalid for the invariant at the start of the fifth

Table 2: Accuracy of properties for detecting artificially created invalid `SimpleSquare` objects (• detected, ○ undetected)

invoked method/tested property	[0 0]	[1 0]	[-1 -1]	[1 2]	[3 2]
`aspectRatio()`	•	•	○	○	○
`toRect()`	•	•	•	○	○
`area()>0`	•	•	○	○	○
`perimeter()>0`	•	○	•	○	○
`aspectRatio()==1`	•	•	○	•	○
`toRect().toSquare()`	•	•	•	•	•

iteration ($w = h \wedge w > 0$). Hence, this invariant is sound and, as we will see later, it is also complete.

3.3   Detecting Invalid Objects via Behavioral Oracles

An object is considered invalid if it cannot be reached via a random walk. However, exhaustive state space exploration is impossible for infinite state spaces which occur, e.g., when objects use references to establish unbounded structures such as linked lists. Even for finite state spaces as exhibited by the running example, an exhaustive exploration often remains practically infeasible. In general, a partial exploration does not provide a sound oracle to determine if a supplied object is unreachable. To detect invalid objects, we instead consider *behavioral oracles* that exploit the behavior of the object under analysis exposed upon method invocations. We consider two sound but possibly incomplete behavioral oracles for detecting invalid objects: random walks and property-based tests.

Random Walks as Weak Oracles During the random walks used to generate valid objects, any thrown expected exception indicates a failed input validation and is ignored. Conversely, if an unexpected exception occurs during a walk starting from an artificially created object, it implies that all objects along the walk, including the initial object, are invalid. The use of random walks for detecting invalid objects shares similarities with *fuzz testing* [17] for identifying faulty implementations. In fuzz testing, a program is subjected to a range of different input values to cause an observable error [38], indicating a bug in the implementation. For a correct implementation, any unexpected exception indicates an invalid object. While behavioral oracles based on random walk-based are sound by construction for detecting invalid objects, they are rarely complete.

Table 2 shows the detection results of six properties for five invalid objects. The first two properties resemble observer actions during a random walk. Method `aspectRatio` throws a division-by-zero exception if the height is zero, thus detecting the first two invalid objects. Method `toRect` creates a new rectangle with the same width and height as the current square. The constructor of class

SimpleRectangle (not shown) validates the input width and height and throws an exception if argument values are not strictly positive, thus subsuming the aspectRatio method in terms of its detection capabilities. However, it fails to detect objects whose strictly positive width and height differ.

Property-based Tests as Strong Oracles Property-based tests [9] are a stronger behavioral oracle when compared to random walks. Not only can they detect invalid objects that throw unexpected exceptions, but they can also interpret the absence of an exception and method return values as an indication of object invalidity. Because property-based tests operate at a behavioral level, they do not require knowledge about internal implementation details. Information regarding expected behavior can be found in the documentation of the class under analysis and (formal) specifications, e.g., for abstract data types [12]. Because property-based tests are assumed to be sound but incomplete, a passing property-based test suite does not guarantee the validity of the object under analysis. However, a single failed test is sufficient to deem the object invalid.

The last four properties in Table 2 resemble candidate property-based tests. We may assume that the expected behavior of class SimpleSquare is that the area and the perimeter must be greater than zero and that the aspect ratio must be equal to one. In addition, the translation from a square to a rectangle and back to a square should be possible without raising an exception. Observe that the area property detects invalid objects with either the width, height or both equal to zero. The perimeter property detects those invalid objects where the sum of width and height is not strictly positive. Note that the aspect ratio property, in addition to its corresponding observer action, detects some states (due to integer division) where w and h differ. The last property subsumes its associated observer action and detects all invalid objects.

3.4 Generating Invalid Objects via Bounded-Exhaustive Testing Techniques

By considering invalid objects, we can not only check if the invariant is complete, i.e., sufficiently restrictive, but also automatically identify equivalent assertions [1,28]. While misclassified valid objects found during weakening widen the scope, misclassified invalid object found during strengthening narrow it.

Acquiring a representative set of invalid objects is a non-trivial task. Existing assertion learning approaches primarily derive possibly invalid objects by executing a mutated program [15,23,30] or by mutating valid program states [25,29]. Nevertheless, these approaches often assume the derived object state to be invalid without conducting further validation. Consequently, the quality of the learned assertion is compromised if a valid object state is mistakenly labeled as invalid. Using generators for complex test inputs from *bounded-exhaustive testing* (BET), such as *Korat* [3,21], enables the artificial creation of a large number of (in)valid object states. We combine these generators with behavioral oracles, and contrary to the conventional practice in BET of retaining only valid objects, we retain only those objects that are classified as invalid. Behavioral oracles can also be applied to objects constructed using program or state mutation; however, we favor the complex test input generators from BET because they produce a larger and more representative set of invalid objects.

The five invalid object states displayed in Table 2 are included in the output of a bounded-exhaustive object state generator when supplied with a lower/upper bound of -1/3 on integer values. The invalid objects $[0\_\_0]$ and $[1\_\_0]$ are suitable for strengthening the candidate invariant.

3.5   Invalid Object Integration

Our approach generates new assertions on-the-fly in order to integrate so far misclassified invalid objects and classify them correctly. Each assertion is evaluated in the context of an object of the class under study. The following assertion grammar suffices for our running example:

Int	::=	$0 \mid 1$
Bool	::=	$true \mid false \mid \textbf{Int} = \textbf{Int} \mid \textbf{Int} > \textbf{Int}$
Int	::=$^{+}$	$w \mid h$

The first two rule fragments reason about integer and boolean values, while the last fragment provides access to the attributes of a `SimpleSquare` object. Terminals such as "1" or "$>$" denote constants or operators, and non-terminals such as **Int** are types. Symbol ::=$^{+}$ indicates that we supplement a non-terminal with new rules.

The invalid object integration step is performed after strengthening or weakening. In the former case, a single invalid object is provided, while in the latter case there may be multiple or no invalid objects. In case of a single misclassified invalid object, we search for an assertion that classifies the said object as invalid, but does not classify any previously collected valid object as invalid. For multiple invalid objects, we iteratively search for a suitable assertion.

Our invalid object integration step can be substituted with any model learning approach that accepts valid and invalid object states as input. While neural networks [24] and support vector machines [30] generally achieve high accuracy, their black-box nature makes them less ideal for program comprehension. In contrast, decision tree models [2] offer interpretability, but their internal disjunctive encoding is disparate to how developers express class invariants in code, usually as a sequence of assert statements. Hence, we favor conjunctive models for modeling class invariants in the context of comprehending object states, because they are interpretable and align with how invariants are phrased in practice.

Caching Suitable Assertions An unsuitable assertion either incorrectly detects a valid object or does not detect the candidate invalid object. Because our approach only adds objects and never removes existing ones, an assertion that incorrectly detects a valid object is not only unsuitable to integrate the currently misclassified invalid object but also for any future one. In contrast, an

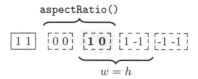

Fig. 4: The behavioral oracle `aspectRatio()` and the assertion $w = h$ both detect the invalid object $\overline{1\_\_0}$, but classify other objects differently.

assertion that satisfies all valid objects and the misclassified invalid object may still be suitable in the future.

Our caching mechanism only stores assertions that satisfy all valid objects. For example, after observing $\boxed{1 \quad 1}$ we store the assertion *true* in the cache, but we do not store *false*.

Preventing Equivalent Assertions Our approach only adds assertions to distinguish invalid from valid objects, which prevents the generation of equivalent assertions. This strategy exploits *observational equivalence* [1,28], which creates equivalence partitions among assertions based on the values to which they evaluate. Because our approach only adds an assertion if the existing assertions cannot distinguish an invalid object from the valid objects, the added assertion is observationally inequivalent to any existing assertion. This property remains true because we only add (in)valid objects, thus refining this notion of equivalence. For example, *false* and *w=1* are considered to be equivalent with respect to $\overline{0\_\_0}$, but are inequivalent when also considering $\boxed{1 \quad 1}$.

Observational equivalence cannot be used for approaches that only consider valid objects [8,27,34], because all suitable assertions are deemed equivalent. Instead, these approaches require static analysis to detect equivalent assertions.

Inexpressive Assertion Grammars If the assertion grammar for the example in Figure 4 would only be capable of generating the assertion $w = h$, then the invalid object $\overline{0\_\_0}$ cannot be integrated. This invalid object is said to be *indistinguishable* from the valid objects such as $\boxed{1 \quad 1}$ with respect to the employed assertion grammar. Because our collected objects are proven (in)valid, indistinguishability can only be resolved by increasing the grammar's expressiveness. Instead, we continue learning but label the class invariant as *approximate*, which ensures that it is overly permissive and, thus, remains sound. Note that once the candidate class invariant becomes approximate, it remains so. However, an overly permissive invariant is still useful for program comprehension, because a subsequent manual invariant refinement only needs to add assertions.

Outperforming the Behavioral Oracle Our approach does not learn an invariant from a single complete oracle, utilizes two sources of sound information: behavioral oracles for invalid objects and random walks for valid objects. This can result in invariants that improve upon the accuracy of the underlying behavioral oracle. For example, the oracle `aspectRatio()` in Figure 4 detects the invalid object ⟦1_ _0⟧, which can be integrated by adding the assertion $w = h$ to the candidate class invariant. Note that this assertion also detects the invalid object ⟦1_ _-1⟧ that is not detected by the oracle.

Qualities of Learned Class Invariants The quality of our learned class invariants depends on the expressiveness of the assertion grammar, the accuracy of the behavioral oracle, and the object state coverage achieved by the random walk for generating valid objects and the bounded-exhaustive object state generator for generating potential invalid objects. While an inexpressive assertion grammar may be detected during learning, an incomplete oracle or an insufficient object state coverage cannot be detected. Accordingly, no soundness/completeness guarantees can be given for a learned non-approximate class invariant except that it correctly classifies all collected (in)valid objects. Approximate class invariants classify some of the collected invalid objects as valid, which still aids comprehension in the presence of an inexpressive assertion grammar.

Learning a complete invariant that also correctly classifies so far unseen objects is only possible if the assertion grammar is sufficiently expressive, the behavioral oracle is complete, and the object state coverage is sufficient, e.g., exhaustive for finite object state spaces.

4 Evaluation

To evaluate our class invariant learning approach, we have implemented the prototype tool *Geminus* for Java. Our bounded-exhaustive object state generator uses the Java Reflection API to modify the internal object state and prevents the generation of symmetric object states in the style of [21]. Our grammar-based assertion generator performs an explicit top-down enumeration and generates strings representing native Java expressions, which allows for a simple grammar definition. We use the Java JShell to dynamically compile these strings into executable lambda expressions at runtime.

Our experiments focus on the following research questions:

RQ1 How do random walks and property-based tests compare to a ground-truth class invariant in terms of detecting invalid objects?

RQ2 What is the disparity between the class invariant learned by Geminus and the employed behavioral oracle?

RQ3 How does the accuracy of the class invariant(s) learned by Geminus, detected by Daikon, and documented as invariant validation methods differ?

4.1 Benchmark Composition

Our benchmark contains several dynamic data structures, whose implementations exhibit complex invariants. In addition, the corresponding classes are one of the few in the Java collections framework that contain state validation methods.

From the evaluation examples of Daikon [8], we pick `StackAr` and `QueueAr`, which were adapted from [37] and provide an array-based implementation of a stack and queue, respectively. The majority of our dynamic data structures originate from the Java collections framework `java.util`. Class `ArrayList` and legacy class `Vector` both provide a linear collection via an array-based implementation. In addition, class `LinkedList` provides `Deque`/`Queue` functionalities via a linkage-based implementation, while class `ArrayDeque` uses an array-based implementation. Class `PriorityQueue` handles comparable elements via an array-based priority heap, and class `BitSet` offers a memory-efficient bit vector.

For verification, a class invariant needs to be strong enough to prove an assertion. In our learning setting, we search for a class invariant that correctly classifies all reachable objects as valid and all unreachable objects as invalid. Depending on the verification task, the class invariant required for this may be weaker than the invariant we aim to learn. Accordingly, the manually specified ground-truth invariants for evaluating each benchmark item must be as strong as possible. Thus, the number of benchmark items is primarily limited by the cost of manually specifying these strong class invariants. Evaluating our approach on further data structures, including *Maps* and *Sets*, is left for future work.

To evaluate our approach, we have instantiated a random walk and bounded-exhaustive generator for each benchmark item and have written property-based tests using the provided documentation. We configure the assertion grammar to include binary operators among integers (+, -, ==, !=, >=, >), object identity, range null checks in arrays, and the ternary operator (`c?b:true`) to encode implications. Extending the grammar with additional operators, such as multiplication or division among integers, is straightforward and may improve the expressiveness of the grammar. However, the increase of assertions expressible in the grammar may lead to timeouts during assertion synthesis. For our experiments, we limit assertion generation to a maximum of 75 000 assertions.

4.2 Evaluation Results

Our results in Table 3 show the number of valid (val.) and invalid (inv.) objects produced by the bounded-exhaustive generator for our ground-truth invariant, which contains A assertions. Because random walks (RW) and property-based tests (PBT) are sound, i.e., all objects classified as invalid are guaranteed to be invalid, we only report false-negatives (FN), i.e., the number of invalid objects that remain undetected. As a behavioral oracle, our random walks have a walk length and a walk count of 50. Increasing the walk length and count may improve detection accuracy, but at the cost of increased computation time.

Our evaluation results in Table 4 report on the accuracy of the class invariant learned by Geminus using random walks or property-based tests as oracle, the class invariant detected by Daikon in its default configuration, and the invariant validation method documented in the source code (Doc). Geminus and Daikon receive the same set of valid objects derived from deterministic random walks with both a walk length and a walk count of 500, respectively. Analogously to using random walks as oracles, increasing the walk length and count may

Table 3: Accuracy comparison in detecting invalid objects using manually written ground-truth class invariants, random walks, and property-based tests; best results are highlighted in bold.

Item	Ground-truth			RW	PBT
	val.	inv.	A	FN	FN
SimpleSquare	10	431	2	90	**0**
StackAr	4097	4095	3	**0**	**0**
QueueAr	322	10 678	13	3 078	**152**
PriorityQueue	1918	154 954	8	63 149	**36 708**
BitSet	2047	40 961	6	19 099	**18 434**
ArrayList	4083	38 925	4	**16 398**	**16 398**
Vector	4083	38 925	4	**16 398**	**16 398**
LinkedList	4	38 335	4	4	**0**
ArrayDeque	385	345 727	12	169 593	**0**

further improve the object state space coverage in terms of valid objects, but at the cost of increased computation time. In addition, Geminus derives invalid objects from the bounded-exhaustive object state generator using its respective oracle. We only report false-positives (FP) for Daikon, because the invariants learned by Geminus classify all valid object as valid in our experiments. We report the computation time (t) in seconds. All experiments were conducted on an Apple MacBook Air M2 with 16 GB RAM.

Regarding threats to validity, we manually examined the source code of the benchmark items to define the ground-truth class invariant. To mitigate the risk of specifying an overly restrictive invariant, we validated it against the objects visited by our random walk. To address threats to internal validity that may arise from random walks, we fixed the random number generator's seed to ensure that the same objects are generated during each walk. Furthermore, we excluded probabilistic data structures like *skip lists* [32] from the benchmark to ensure identical internal object states.

4.3   Oracle Accuracy Comparison

When used as a behavioral oracle, random walks detect numerous invalid object states in our experiments. They exhibit comparable accuracy to property-based tests for benchmark items StackAr, ArrayList, and Vector. Additionally, random walks identify a significant portion of invalid objects for LinkedList. The majority of unexpected exceptions arise from null dereferencing or accessing out-of-bounds indices in arrays. Random walks cannot assess whether the retrieved elements from a PriorityQueue are in the correct order. The documentation states that retrieving the first element from an ArrayDeque throws an exception

Table 4: Comparing the accuracy in detecting invalid objects using the class invariant learned by Geminus, detected by Daikon, and invariant validation methods documented in the code; best results are highlighted in bold.

Item	Geminus+RW					Geminus+PBT					Daikon				Doc	
	FN	t	A	O	$\bar{O}$	FN	t	A	O	$\bar{O}$	FN	FP	t	A	FN	A
SimpleSquare	**0**	3	2	2	2	**0**	4	2	1	2	1	0	7	2	–	–
StackAr	**0**	6	2	3	4	**0**	5	2	3	4	**0**	0	7	4	–	–
QueueAr	2 229	7	4	13	12	**542**	93	15	39	50	2 513	0	9	9	–	–
PriorityQueue	62 545	31	2	4	5	**9 277**	298	3	11	11	112 462	0	32	6	–	–
BitSet	18 434	11	2	3	4	18 434	9	2	3	4	55	2036	45	3	**0**	3
ArrayList	16 398	10	2	3	4	16 398	10	2	3	4	16 398	0	53	3	**7 181**	2
Vector	16 398	21	2	3	4	16 398	21	2	3	4	16 398	0	49	4	**7 181**	2
LinkedList	**0**	15	10	4	29	**0**	15	10	4	29	0	4	26	16	729	1
LinkedList*	**0**	10	2	3	2	**0**	10	2	3	2						
ArrayDeque	98 966	74	5	6	9	**0**	60	8	23	24	169 593	0	23	7	30 079	7

if the structure is empty, but random walks cannot detect cases where the queue is considered empty, yet a retrieval does not throw an exception.

The property-based tests fail to identify some invalid objects for five items. BitSet, ArrayList, and Vector implementations nullify unused array elements to aid garbage collection, which does not affect functional behavior. However, our tests, which focus on functional behavior, cannot detect objects violating this property. Random walks can also only uncover faults related to functional behavior. In the case of StackAr, where the ground-truth class invariant is limited to functional aspects only, both our tests and the random walks detect all invalid objects. For PriorityQueue, polling the first element involves a sift-down operation, partially repairing an invalid object state. In contrast, a QueueAr with a capacity of zero is considered both empty and full simultaneously, leading any method to return immediately, and concealing the remaining state. This is a known debugging scenario [38], where a bug can lead to an invalid object state without necessarily causing an observable error.

Regarding **RQ1**, our benchmark in Table 3 leads to the conclusion that property-based tests outperform random walks in terms of accuracy. Furthermore, we observed that the remaining undetected invalid objects either do not affect functional behavior or are partially repaired during method invocation, rendering their detection challenging.

4.4   Disparity between Learned Invariants and Leveraged Oracles

Using random walks as behavioral oracles, Geminus learns and often surpasses the accuracy of the oracles in our experiments. Although our random walks do not detect all invalid objects for class `SimpleSquare` (see Table 2), Geminus still manages to learn the correct class invariant. The accuracy of the learned class invariant depends on the assertion grammar and the order in which candidate assertions are generated. For `SimpleSquare`, assertions $w = h$ and $w > 0$ are generated before assertions $w \geq 1$ and $h \geq 1$, which would also resolve all misclassified objects found by the random walk oracle.

Using property-based tests as the oracle, Geminus learns an approximate class invariant for class `PriorityQueue` and `ArrayDeque`. The current assertion grammar is not sufficiently expressive to generate a parametrized assertion such as `queue[(i-1)/2].compareTo(queue[i])<=0`, which is required for item `PriorityQueue`. Nevertheless, the learned invariant is more accurate than the underlying oracle. In contrast, Geminus learns a less accurate class invariant for `QueueAr`. While the assertion grammar is expressive enough to generate a suitable assertion with multiple conditions that resolves the indistinguishability, the current assertion limit is insufficient in this case.

Regarding **RQ2**, our benchmarks in Tables 3 and 4 demonstrate Geminus's ability to learn a class invariant that outperforms the oracle, resulting in a lower number of false-negatives. Both cases of approximate invariants are due to the inability of the assertion grammar to generate suitable assertions. To generate parametrized assertions, the assertion grammar needs to be extended with lambda expressions. To better support assertions with multiple conditions, which would pave the way for analyzing more complex Java projects, we plan to replace our conjunctive assertion model with a conjunctive normal form model for model training (cf. Section 6).

4.5   Comparing Geminus, Daikon, and Invariant Validation Methods

Daikon [8] generates assertions using templates and retains only those assertions that hold for valid objects. It performs equally well for simple data structures like `StackAr`, but it generates less accurate class invariants for other benchmark items. For `SimpleSquare`, it identifies the incorrect invariant $w = h \wedge w \geq 0$, which fails to detect $\overline{0}\_\_\overline{0}$. While [20] excludes unqualified calls, Daikon considers them, which may result in learning an overly permissive invariant. In contrast, Geminus considers qualified calls only and learns the correct invariant.

The invariants learned by Geminus may produce false-positives, but never did so in our experiments. The invariants documented in the state validation methods also produce no false-positives, as anticipated. However, Daikon does report false-positives for `BitSet` and `LinkedList`. For `BitSet`, this is due to the random walk configuration inadequately representing the object state space, which leads Daikon to retain the overly restrictive assertion `words[] elements >= 0`, encoding that all array elements are greater than or equal to zero. Because Geminus solely adds assertions to detect previously undetected invalid objects, it learns the correct invariant in this example. While this mechanism proves advantageous when dealing with unrepresentative valid objects, Geminus relies on a representative set of invalid objects.

The `LinkedList` class uses a doubly-linked list structure with `prev` and `next` attributes. Daikon detects assertions aiding program comprehension, but it lacks the necessary guards to avoid false-positives. While Daikon only considers valid objects and thus does not require an additional oracle to detect invalid objects, it may learn overly permissive invariants. For example, Daikon identifies the doubly-linked style through the `first == first.next.prev` assertion. However, it overlooks the need for a guard to prevent null dereferencing. Identifying necessary assertions containing guards is a challenging task when only valid objects are available. Considering invalid objects assists Geminus in finding the necessary assertions, like `first != last ? first == first.next.prev : true`. Despite its recursive structure, Geminus learns an invariant that accurately detects all invalid objects. This is possible because the bounded-exhaustive object state generator only covers object states for `LinkedList`, including up to three list nodes. Note that linkage-based classes exhibit large object state spaces even for a small number of linked elements, which is due to reference aliasing. While the documented validation method accurately characterizes the case of an empty list, it imposes an overly permissive constraint for non-empty lists, namely `first.prev == null && last.next == null`. The crucial constraint that the previous attribute of the next node is the current node is not documented.

The *linearization* [7] technique maps a linkage-based structure to an array representation. We can enrich our grammar with the *closure* abstraction to store the objects that are reachable from a given object, using a specific attribute in an array. While the linearization in [7] is used to reason about the *values* stored in a list, this closure abstraction allows one to characterize the double linkage *structure* by expressing that the closure from the `first` element via the `next` attribute is reverse to the closure from the `last` element via the `prev` attribute. In `LinkedList*`, Geminus uses this grammar to learn an invariant that generalizes to lists of arbitrary length.

The invariant validation methods for `BitSet`, `ArrayList`, and `Vector` require null elements at the *next* free array location, while our ground-truth checks all *remaining* locations. Both constraints do *not* affect the functional behavior and are thus not detectable by our oracles. In practice, invariants ensuring a functionally equivalent behavior typically suffice. Similarly, `ArrayDeque` requires elements in the queue to be different from null. It concludes from a null value when fetching the first/last element that the queue is empty. The documentation mentions that all non-live elements in the array are null, but this is only partially checked in their `checkInvariants` method, leading to numerous undetected invalid objects.

Regarding **RQ3**, our benchmark in Table 4 demonstrates that Geminus learns more accurate invariants when using the more accurate property-based tests as oracle, instead of the random walk oracle. Moreover, it often outperforms Daikon in terms of accuracy. Unlike Daikon, our tool identifies necessary guards for complex object states most of the time, avoiding overly permissive or incorrect invariants. Notably, Geminus achieves greater accuracy than the documented validation methods, especially for the complex object states of `LinkedList` or `ArrayDeque`.

5   Related Work

This section contrasts our dynamic class invariant learning to related dynamic assertion learning approaches.

Daikon [8] exhaustively instantiates its assertion templates and retains only those assertions that hold for all observed states at desired program locations. In contrast, Geminus uses the first assertion that suffices to detect a so far misclassified invalid object. Because Daikon considers valid objects only, it relies on static analysis to prune overly permissive, equivalent, or redundant assertions. In contrast, Geminus employs invalid objects to exclude such assertions, which allows us to consider a much larger set of candidate assertions.

PIE [27] learns preconditions and loop invariants from (in)valid objects and uses a feature grammar to construct assertions in conjunctive normal form on-the-fly; however, Valiant's algorithm [36] limits PIE to small formulas. While PIE requires a postcondition to correctly label the set of predefined program states during learning, Geminus uses behavioral oracles to detect invalid objects.

Alearner [30] derives preconditions and uses a test suite to detect invalid method inputs. While Geminus keeps the object graph of each (in)valid example, Alearner only stores an abstraction, which limits precondition expressiveness and hinders manual inspection of training data. Alearner uses program mutation to obtain potentially invalid object states, but does not validate this assumption.

OASIs [15] assesses soundness and completeness of an assertion located within the program. Similar to our random walks, OASIs generates execution scenarios to identify overly restrictive assertions. It uses mutation testing to deem an assertion overly permissive; however, this technique cannot be applied to class invariants, because they cannot be mapped to a *single* program location. *GAssert* [35] uses OASIs to evaluate the quality of an assertion and enhance it for soundness, completeness, and assertion size using an evolutionary learning algorithm. Its evolutionary technique can be an alternative to our grammar-based assertion enumeration, but necessitates defining evolutionary operators.

Proviso [2] addresses, like Geminus does, complex object states, but learns preconditions from observer methods. In contrast, Geminus learns class invariants from private attributes. While Proviso uses a test generator to obtain (in)valid argument values, invalid object states cannot be derived in this way. If no distinguishable feature can be constructed, Proviso relabels valid objects as invalid. Geminus' objects are guaranteed to be (in)valid.

Hanoi [22] and Geminus both learn invariants from (in)valid objects. While Hanoi's notion of constructible value bears similarity with random walks, their invalid objects are not proven invalid and must be recomputed after finding a new so far misclassified valid object. Hanoi learns representation invariants for types in a functional language and constructs a single definition that captures the recursive structure of the type. In contrast, Geminus iteratively refines a set of assertions to learn the invariant of a class in an object-oriented language.

EvoSpex [25] employs an evolutionary algorithm, but learns postconditions from (in)valid pre/post state pairs. Invalid pairs are obtained via state mutation, which does however not necessarily yield invalid states. Geminus solves this problem for class invariants using behavioral oracles, and only considers thereby proven invalid states. While Geminus utilizes Java expressions, EvoSpex encodes assertions in the Alloy language [14]. The assertion enumeration component in Geminus is language agnostic and can be replaced with, e.g., Alloy.

SpecFuzzer [23] tackles the problem that inferred specifications often contain equivalent assertions. It uses Daikon to remove overly restrictive assertions and then applies program mutation to derive possibly invalid states in order to construct equivalence partitions among the remaining assertions. Geminus prevents the generation of equivalent assertions, similar to SpecFuzzer, via observational equivalence reduction [1,28]. While equivalence partitions can be constructed without knowing whether a state is valid or invalid, guaranteed to be invalid states allow us to assess whether an invariant is sufficient. Geminus generates new assertions until a suitable assertion that detects an invalid state is found.

6 Conclusions

To ensure that modifications to legacy software conform to existing assumptions, it is essential to make implicit guarantees explicit, e.g., in the form of method preconditions and class invariants. However, class invariants encoding object state assumptions are rarely documented and almost never checked automatically.

In this paper, we presented a dynamic analysis for class invariant learning that automatically derives (in)valid objects and distinguishes between them by grammar derived assertions. We leverage random walks in object state spaces to find valid objects and a combination of complex test input generators from bounded-exhaustive testing with behavioral oracles to find invalid objects. In this setting, random walks can even be reused as behavioral oracles. Our prototype tool *Geminus* improves upon related tools such as *Daikon* by learning invariants for complex classes, such as dynamic data structures included in the `java.util` package, resulting in a higher accuracy in detecting invalid objects. Considering invalid objects, too, allows Geminus to prevent the generation of equivalent assertions, thereby leading to concise invariants without the need for static assertion equivalence checks.

The capabilities of dynamic class invariant learning approaches primarily rely on finding so far misclassified (in)valid objects and training a suitable invariant model. While finding execution paths that result in a representative set of valid objects is well understood in the context of software testing, finding representative *invalid* objects is studied less and should be in the focus of future work. Sampling object states while executing a mutated program is likely a source for potentially invalid objects worth to be explored. Our conjunctive assertion model struggles to scale with respect to invariants containing multiple guards per assertion. Future work should focus on crafting heuristics for learning formulas in conjunctive normal form to model complex class invariants with multiple guards.

Data-Availability Statement The source code of Geminus, the benchmark items, the evaluation results and instructions for reproduction are available online via DOI **10.5281/zenodo.10514765**.

References

1. Albarghouthi, A., Gulwani, S., Kincaid, Z.: Recursive program synthesis. In: Sharygina, N., Veith, H. (eds.) Computer Aided Verification (CAV). LNCS, vol. 8044, pp. 934–950. Springer (2013). https://doi.org/10.1007/978-3-642-39799-8_67

2. Astorga, A., Madhusudan, P., Saha, S., Wang, S., Xie, T.: Learning stateful preconditions modulo a test generator. In: McKinley, K.S., Fisher, K. (eds.) Conference on Programming Language Design and Implementation (PLDI). pp. 775–787. ACM (2019). https://doi.org/10.1145/3314221.3314641

3. Boyapati, C., Khurshid, S., Marinov, D.: Korat: Automated testing based on Java predicates. In: Frankl, P.G. (ed.) International Symposium on Software Testing and Analysis (ISSTA). pp. 123–133. ACM (2002). https://doi.org/10.1145/566172.566191

4. Cheng, D.Y., Deutsch, J.T., Dutton, R.W.: "Defensive programming" in the rapid development of a parallel scientific program. IEEE Trans. Comput. Aided Des. Integr. Circuits Syst. $9(6)$, 665–669 (1990), https://doi.org/10.1109/43.55196

5. Claessen, K., Hughes, J.: Quickcheck: A lightweight tool for random testing of haskell programs. In: Odersky, M., Wadler, P. (eds.) International Conference on Functional Programming (ICFP). pp. 268–279. ACM (2000). https://doi.org/10.1145/351240.351266

6. Coppit, D., Yang, J., Khurshid, S., Le, W., Sullivan, K.J.: Software assurance by bounded exhaustive testing. IEEE Trans. Software Eng. $31(4)$, 328–339 (2005). https://doi.org/10.1109/TSE.2005.52

7. Ernst, M.D., Griswold, W.G., Kataoka, Y., Notkin, D.: Dynamically discovering program invariants involving collections. In: University of Washington Department of Computer Science and Engineering technical report UW-CSE-99-11-02, (Seattle, WA), November 16, 1999. Revised March 17, 2000. (2000)

8. Ernst, M.D., Perkins, J.H., Guo, P.J., McCamant, S., Pacheco, C., Tschantz, M.S., Xiao, C.: The Daikon system for dynamic detection of likely invariants. Sci. Comput. Program. $69(1\text{-}3)$, 35–45 (2007). https://doi.org/10.1016/j.scico.2007.01.015

9. Fink, G., Bishop, M.: Property-based testing: A new approach to testing for assurance. ACM SIGSOFT Softw. Eng. Notes $22(4)$, 74–80 (1997). https://doi.org/10.1145/263244.263267

10. Fraser, G., Arcuri, A.: Evosuite: Automatic test suite generation for object-oriented software. In: Gyimóthy, T., Zeller, A. (eds.) Symposium on the Foundations of Software Engineering and European Software Engineering Conference (FSE/ESEC). pp. 416–419. ACM (2011), https://doi.org/10.1145/2025113.2025179

11. Gligoric, M., Gvero, T., Jagannath, V., Khurshid, S., Kuncak, V., Marinov, D.: Test generation through programming in UDITA. In: Kramer, J., Bishop, J., Devanbu, P.T., Uchitel, S. (eds.) International Conference on Software Engineering (ICSE). pp. 225–234. ACM (2010), https://doi.org/10.1145/1806799.1806835

12. Guttag, J.V., Horowitz, E., Musser, D.R.: Abstract data types and software validation. Commun. ACM $21(12)$, 1048–1064 (1978), https://doi.org/10.1145/359657.359666

13. Hierons, R.M., Bogdanov, K., Bowen, J.P., Cleaveland, R., Derrick, J., Dick, J., Gheorghe, M., Harman, M., Kapoor, K., Krause, P.J., Lüttgen, G., Simons, A.J.H., Vilkomir, S.A., Woodward, M.R., Zedan, H.: Using formal specifications to support testing. ACM Comput. Surv. $41(2)$, 9:1–9:76 (2009), https://doi.org/10.1145/1459352.1459354

14. Jackson, D.: Alloy: A language and tool for exploring software designs. Commun. ACM **62**(9), 66–76 (2019), https://doi.org/10.1145/3338843

15. Jahangirova, G., Clark, D., Harman, M., Tonella, P.: Oasis: Oracle assessment and improvement tool. In: Tip, F., Bodden, E. (eds.) International Symposium on Software Testing and Analysis (ISSTA). pp. 368–371. ACM (2018), https://doi.org/10.1145/3213846.3229503

16. Leavens, G.T., Baker, A.L., Ruby, C.: Preliminary design of JML: A behavioral interface specification language for Java. ACM SIGSOFT Softw. Eng. Notes **31**(3), 1–38 (2006). https://doi.org/10.1145/1127878.1127884

17. Manès, V.J.M., Han, H., Han, C., Cha, S.K., Egele, M., Schwartz, E.J., Woo, M.: The art, science, and engineering of fuzzing: A survey. IEEE Trans. Software Eng. **47**(11), 2312–2331 (2021). https://doi.org/10.1109/TSE.2019.2946563

18. Marinov, D., Khurshid, S.: Testera: A novel framework for automated testing of Java programs. In: International Conference on Automated Software Engineering (ASE). p. 22. IEEE Computer Society (2001). https://doi.org/10.1109/ASE.2001.989787

19. Meyer, B.: Eiffel: A language and environment for software engineering. J. Syst. Softw. **8**(3), 199–246 (1988). https://doi.org/10.1016/0164-1212(88)90022-2

20. Meyer, B.: Class invariants: concepts, problems, solutions. CoRR **abs/1608.07637** (2016). https://doi.org/10.48550/arXiv.1608.07637

21. Milicevic, A., Misailovic, S., Marinov, D., Khurshid, S.: Korat: A tool for generating structurally complex test inputs. In: International Conference on Software Engineering (ICSE). pp. 771–774. IEEE Computer Society (2007). https://doi.org/10.1109/ICSE.2007.48

22. Miltner, A., Padhi, S., Millstein, T.D., Walker, D.: Data-driven inference of representation invariants. In: Donaldson, A.F., Torlak, E. (eds.) International Conference on Programming Language Design and Implementation (PLDI). pp. 1–15. ACM (2020). https://doi.org/10.1145/3385412.3385967

23. Molina, F., d'Amorim, M., Aguirre, N.: Fuzzing class specifications. In: International Conference on Software Engineering (ICSE). pp. 1008–1020. ACM (2022), https://doi.org/10.1145/3510003.3510120

24. Molina, F., Degiovanni, R., Ponzio, P., Regis, G., Aguirre, N., Frias, M.F.: Training binary classifiers as data structure invariants. In: Atlee, J.M., Bultan, T., Whittle, J. (eds.) International Conference on Software Engineering (ICSE). pp. 759–770. IEEE / ACM (2019), https://doi.org/10.1109/ICSE.2019.00084

25. Molina, F., Ponzio, P., Aguirre, N., Frias, M.F.: Evospex: An evolutionary algorithm for learning postconditions. In: International Conference on Software Engineering (ICSE). pp. 1223–1235. IEEE Computer Society (2021), https://doi.org/10.1109/ICSE43902.2021.00112

26. Pacheco, C., Lahiri, S.K., Ernst, M.D., Ball, T.: Feedback-directed random test generation. In: International Conference on Software Engineering (ICSE). pp. 75–84. IEEE Computer Society (2007), https://doi.org/10.1109/ICSE.2007.37

27. Padhi, S., Sharma, R., Millstein, T.D.: Data-driven precondition inference with learned features. In: Krintz, C., Berger, E.D. (eds.) Conference on Programming Language Design and Implementation (PLDI). pp. 42–56. ACM (2016). https://doi.org/10.1145/2908080.2908099

28. Peleg, H., Polikarpova, N.: Perfect is the enemy of good: Best-effort program synthesis. In: Hirschfeld, R., Pape, T. (eds.) European Conference on Object-Oriented Programming (ECOOP). LIPIcs, vol. 166, pp. 2:1–2:30. Schloss Dagstuhl - Leibniz-Zentrum für Informatik (2020). https://doi.org/10.4230/LIPIcs.ECOOP.2020.2

29. Pham, L.H., Sun, J., Le, Q.L.: Compositional verification of heap-manipulating programs through property-guided learning. In: Lin, A.W. (ed.) Asian Symposium on Programming Languages and Systems (APLAS). LNCS, vol. 11893, pp. 405–424. Springer (2019), https://doi.org/10.1007/978-3-030-34175-6_21

30. Pham, L.H., Thi, L.T., Sun, J.: Assertion generation through active learning. In: Duan, Z., Ong, L. (eds.) International Conference on Formal Engineering Methods (ICFEM). LNCS, vol. 10610, pp. 174–191. Springer (2017). https://doi.org/10.1007/978-3-319-68690-5_11

31. Ponzio, P., Bengolea, V.S., Brida, S.G., Scilingo, G., Aguirre, N., Frias, M.F.: On the effect of object redundancy elimination in randomly testing collection classes. In: Galeotti, J.P., Gorla, A. (eds.) International Workshop on Search-Based Software Testing (ICSE). pp. 67–70. ACM (2018), https://doi.org/10.1145/3194718.3194724

32. Pugh, W.W.: Skip lists: A probabilistic alternative to balanced trees. In: Dehne, F.K.H.A., Sack, J., Santoro, N. (eds.) Workshop on Algorithms and Data Structures (WADS). LNCS, vol. 382, pp. 437–449. Springer (1989), https://doi.org/10.1007/3-540-51542-9_36

33. Sankaranarayanan, S., Chaudhuri, S., Ivancic, F., Gupta, A.: Dynamic inference of likely data preconditions over predicates by tree learning. In: Ryder, B.G., Zeller, A. (eds.) International Symposium on Software Testing and Analysis (ISSTA). pp. 295–306. ACM (2008), https://doi.org/10.1145/1390630.1390666

34. Smith, C., Albarghouthi, A.: Program synthesis with equivalence reduction. In: Enea, C., Piskac, R. (eds.) International Conference on Verification, Model Checking and Abstract Interpretation (VMCAI). LNCS, vol. 11388, pp. 24–47. Springer (2019), https://doi.org/10.1007/978-3-030-11245-5_2

35. Terragni, V., Jahangirova, G., Tonella, P., Pezzè, M.: Evolutionary improvement of assertion oracles. In: Devanbu, P., Cohen, M.B., Zimmermann, T. (eds.) Joint European Software Engineering Conference and Symposium on the Foundations of Software Engineering (ESEC/FSE). pp. 1178–1189. ACM (2020), https://doi.org/10.1145/3368089.3409758

36. Valiant, L.G.: A theory of the learnable. Commun. ACM **27**(11), 1134–1142 (1984), https://doi.org/10.1145/1968.1972

37. Weiss, M.A.: Data structures and algorithm analysis in Java, vol. 2. Addison-Wesley (2007)

38. Zeller, A.: Why programs fail - A guide to systematic debugging, 2nd ed. Academic Press (2009)

Smart Issue Detection for Large-Scale Online Service Systems Using Multi-Channel Data

Liushan Chen[1]([✉]), Yu Pei[2][ORCID], Mingyang Wan[1], Zhihui Fei[1], Tao Liang[1], and Guojun Ma[1]

[1] ByteDance Inc., Shenzhen, China
chenliushan@bytedance.com
[2] Department of Computing, The Hong Kong Polytechnic University, Hong Kong, Hong Kong S.A.R., China

Abstract. Given the scale and complexity of large online service systems and the diversity of environments in which the services are to be invoked, it is inevitable that those service systems contain bugs that affect the users. As a result, it is essential for service providers to discover issues in their systems based on information gathered from users. iFeedback is a state-of-the-art technique for user-feedback-based issue detection. While it has been deployed to help detect issues in real-world service systems, the accuracy of iFeedback's detection results is relatively low due to limitations in its design. In this paper, we propose the SKYNET technique and tool that analyzes both user feedback gathered via specific channels and public posts collected from social media platforms to more accurately detect issues in service systems. We have applied the tool to detect issues for three real-world, large-scale online service systems based on their historical data gathered over a ten-month period of time. SKYNET reported in total 2790 issues, among which 93.0% were confirmed by developers as reflecting real problems that deserve their close attention. It also detected 58 out of the 62 severe issues reported during the period, achieving a recall of 93.5% for severe issues. Such results suggest SKYNET is both effective and accurate in issue detection.

1 Introduction

Large-scale online service systems are becoming indispensable for people's work and everyday life nowadays. They also get more and more complex so as to support the ever-growing needs of their users for new and more powerful functionalities. The scale and complexity of such services as well as the diversity of environments in which the services are to be invoked, however, have made it more challenging than ever for developers to make sure the services will always behave as expected. Despite the tremendous amount of time and effort developers invest in testing and debugging such online service systems, it is almost inevitable that some bugs escape the developers' attention, get released into the field, and negatively impact users' experience with the services. It is, therefore, extremely important for the service providers to discover issues in their systems based on information gathered from users in a timely manner.

© The Author(s) 2024
D. Beyer and A. Cavalcanti (Eds.): FASE 2024, LNCS 14573, pp. 165–187, 2024.
https://doi.org/10.1007/978-3-031-57259-3_8

In view of that, Zheng et al. [45] recently proposed the iFeedback approach to detecting issues based on user feedback. While the approach has been deployed to help detect issues in large-scale online service systems and has successfully detected severe issues, the overall precision of its results is relatively low, 76.2% to be exact [45]. We conjecture there are three reasons for that. First, iFeedback extracts word combinations from feedback texts as indicators of issues. Since word combinations only capture the lexical, rather than semantical, characteristics of feedback texts, they, as issue indicators, tend to be overly sensitive to the wording of user feedback. Second, iFeedback detects anomalies at the level of time intervals based on all the user feedback gathered during those intervals, which is too coarse-grained. Since a wide range of different types of user feedback, concerning issues or not, may get reported during each time interval, it is more likely for iFeedback's judgment to be influenced or even misled by user feedback that does not report any issues. Third, iFeedback applies an unsupervised algorithm to cluster the feedback during anomalous time intervals based on the word combinations and their contexts. While unsupervised clustering algorithms are less expensive to apply, they tend to produce less precise results than supervised algorithms in general [36].

To address these limitations of iFeedback and improve the quality of issue detection results, we propose in this paper a novel approach, named SKYNET, to automatically detecting issues in online service systems based on multi-channel user input, including both user feedback and messages posted on social media platforms. More concretely, SKYNET first employs a cascading classifier to label the user feedback texts based on an input hierarchical label system for different types of user experiences. Then, it applies time-series data analysis to predict, based on historical data, a threshold for the normal frequencies of user feedback reporting each known type of negative user experience; and it reports an issue when more feedback of the same type than allowed by the threshold is gathered from the users. Meanwhile, for user feedback reporting negative experiences of previously unknown types, SKYNET reports an issue when an abnormous amount of such user feedback concerns similar negative user experiences. The semantic embedding of feedback texts and the customized issue detection process adopted by SKYNET enables it to detect more real issues in service systems and to prune out most false positives. In view that social media platforms have become important and popular venues for users to share their experiences with various services and products, SKYNET also monitors and analyzes messages posted on social media platforms to detect issues before they generate a large number of user feedback or attract considerable unwanted public attention.

We have implemented the SKYNET approach into a tool with the same name. To empirically evaluate SKYNET's effectiveness, we applied it to detect issues for three real-world, large-scale online service systems based on their historical data gathered from a ten-month duration. SKYNET reported in total 2790 issues, 93.0% of which were confirmed by operators and developers as reflecting real problems that deserve their close attention. Besides, SKYNET was able to detect

58 of the 62 severe issues that occurred during that period of time. Such results suggest SKYNET is highly effective and accurate in issue detection.

Contributions. This paper makes the following contributions:

- We propose the SKYNET technique that analyzes both user feedback gathered from specific channels and public posts collected from social media platforms to accurately detect issues in large-scale online service systems.
- We develop SKYNET into a tool with the same name.
- We empirically evaluate SKYNET by applying it to detect issues for three real-world service systems based on historical data. The results produced suggest that SKYNET is highly effective and accurate.

2 Related Work

Our work is closely related to existing work in the following areas.

Anomaly detection based on backend monitoring. In view that many issues in online service systems affect performance attributes like "disk queue length" and "network retransmission rate" of the backend systems, people often monitor the corresponding key performance indicators (KPIs) of the systems and rely on the values to detect anomalies in those services [15,18,21,22,23,25,26,39,44]. For instance, Laptev et al. [21] proposed the EGADS system that combines a collection of anomaly detection and forecasting models to detect anomalies in time-series KPI data. Liu et al. [25] proposed the Opprentice system that trains a random forest with labeled KPI features to select appropriate parameters and thresholds for existing detectors. Xu et al. [44] proposed an unsupervised anomaly detection algorithm, named Donut, to effectively detect anomalies in seasonal KPIs. Given that online service systems automatically generate issue reports and alerts when the monitored indicators exhibit anomalous values, techniques have also been developed to mine attribute collections of issue reports [15,24] to characterize and detect incidents [22].

Issue detection based on user feedback. Many issues, e.g., user interface defects and silent back-end issues, in those systems, however, are not reflected by pre-defined KPIs [45]. In view of that and the fact that user opinions coming in different forms (e.g., user feedback, tweets, and forum posts) contain valuable information to support software development and maintenance [12,13,29,30,41,42], Zheng et al. [45] proposed the iFeedback approach to detecting issues based on user feedback on-the-fly. iFeedback first extracts word combination-based indicators to represent an issue and collects each indicator's historical occurrence trend (HOT), then the long-term and short-term windows of the HOTs are fed to a binary classifier to identify anomalous time intervals, and in the end, user feedback from time intervals containing issues are clustered as reporting different issues. SKYNET improves on iFeedback from three perspectives. First, iFeedback extracts word combinations from feedback texts as indicators of issues, which captures only the lexical characteristics of feedback texts, while SKYNET employs the ALBERT-tiny model to encode user feedback so that the semantics of user feedback can be taken into account during the issue detection process.

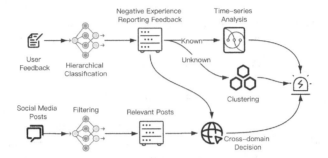

Fig. 1: An overview of the issue detection process with SkyNet.

Second, iFeedback detects anomalies at the level of time intervals based on all the gathered user feedback, which is often too coarse-grained and increases the chance of coincident non-issue-reporting feedback influencing and misleading the issue detection process. In contrast, SkyNet employs a cascading classification algorithm to label user feedback based on a hierarchical label system and only takes feedback that reports negative user experiences into account in the remaining issue detection process. Third, SkyNet also monitors and analyzes messages posted on social media platforms to detect issues in a timely manner, which complements user-feedback-based issue detection.

Learning from user opinions in other forms. User opinions in other forms have also been utilized to support various types of activities in software development. Gao et al. [14] proposed the IDEA framework that detects issues from review texts of apps. Stanik et al. [38] proposed an approach to identify aspects of software systems to improve based on user comments received on Twitter. While those identified aspects may indeed need improvement, they not necessarily are issues in the corresponding software systems. Guzman et al. [16] proposed the ALERTme approach that automatically classifies, groups, and ranks tweets to facilitate the analysis of application-related tweets. Williams and Mahmoud [43] conducted a study on leveraging Twitter as a main source of software user requirements. Johann et al. [19] proposed the SAFE approach that extracts keywords from app feature descriptions written by developers and app reviews on app stores to better characterize the apps. Compared with these works, SkyNet focuses on detecting issues in online service systems based on user feedback and social media posts.

3   The SkyNet Approach

Figure 1 depicts an overview of the issue detection process with SkyNet. SkyNet leverages deep learning algorithms to detect issues based on multi-channel data and it combines two loosely coupled processes: The main process is designed for detecting issues based on user feedback texts gathered through dedicated channels that are embedded in the service systems, while the auxiliary process complements the main process and aims to detect issues using posts collected from social media platforms. Each issue detected by SkyNet is associated with a collection of user feedback, a social media post in case it is the main concern of the post, and a list of ten keywords extracted from the user feedback and post using the TF-IDF method [6]. While the keywords help provide a rough idea about an issue, developers must examine the associated user input to determine whether the reported issues reflect real problems in the service systems. In the rest of this section, we explain in detail the steps in SKYNET's main and auxiliary issue detection processes.

Note that, as in other model-based approaches, we periodically review the input user feedback and social media posts as well as the detected issues, manually rectify the incorrect detection results if any, and use the new data to fine-tune the models that SKYNET utilizes so as to keep the models fit for the updated business situation and to prevent model degradation. Also note that, although sometimes users include images in their feedback and social media posts to help explain the problems they have encountered, SKYNET does not utilize such information in its current implementation. We leave the development of new techniques that exploit the extra image information to facilitate issue detection for future work.

3.1 Hierarchical Classification of User Feedback

The first step in issue detection with SKYNET is to decide the type of user experience that each piece of the gathered user feedback reports. SKYNET makes such decisions on the basis of a hierarchical label system, where the labels characterize with different levels of detail the types of (negative) user experiences that users report in their feedback.

SKYNET differentiates three broad categories of user feedback in issue detection, namely feedback reporting negative user experiences of a known type, feedback reporting negative user experiences of unknown types, and feedback not reporting negative user experiences. User feedback from the first two categories is collectively called *negative experience reporting feedback*. Note that not all negative user experiences are caused by issues in service systems. For example, although a user's access to an online service will be blocked if her device is offline due to a hardware failure, the experience does not indicate anything problematic in the online service system.

Feedback Encoding Since SKYNET is designed to detect issues in large-scale online service systems, and it may need to process a large number of user feedback under tight time constraints, we use ALBERT-Tiny [20] to encode the user feedback. BERT [11] is a pre-trained state-of-the-art language representation neural network model with strong semantic comprehension capability. ALBERT [20] is a lite BERT architecture, and it lowers the memory consumption and increases the training speed of BERT, while without significantly sacrificing BERT's semantic comprehension ability, by sharing parameters across layers and reducing embedding dimensions of words. ALBERT-Tiny [20] is the smallest version of ALBERT that is 10x times faster than BERT for inference.

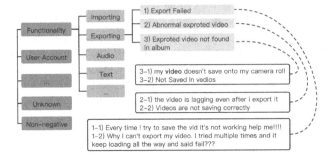

Fig. 2: A sample hierarchical label system (in blue) and some examples of the associated user feedback.

Hierarchical Label System To correctly decide which type of user experience each user feedback reports is crucial since incorrect decisions made here may mislead the downstream steps and cause the whole task of issue detection to fail. SKYNET employs an existing hierarchical label system to facilitate making those decisions. In the system, each label corresponds to a particular type of user experience that users may have with the target online service system.

Designing a label system to properly characterize user experiences is a challenging task. SKYNET adopts a hierarchical, rather than flat, label system mainly because it is extremely difficult, if not impractical, to decide *a priori* on the right granularity level for the labels in a flat system so as to strike a good balance between the accuracy and the value of the classification results based on that label system. On the one hand, a coarse-grained label system often makes it easier for a classifier to correctly label the input data, but the classification results may not be very useful since each label encodes little extra information. On the other hand, a fine-grained label system typically makes it harder for a classifier to correctly label the input data, but a correct label in this case can be highly valuable since it encodes abundant extra information. In the context of user feedback classification for issue detection, coarse-grained labels provide relatively vague information about the user experience, which may not be sufficient to help developers effectively confirm or understand the underlying issues.

Figure 2 displays part of the hierarchical label system that SKYNET uses for classifying the user feedback on an online video editing system. In the hierarchical label system, labels at the top level classify all the user feedback into broad categories concerning aspects like "Functionality" and "User Account" of the online system, labels at the intermediate level partition the broad categories into smaller, finer-grained ones, while labels at the bottom level correspond to specific types of experiences that users may have when using the online system. Two top-level labels in the hierarchical label system, namely "Unknown" and "Non-negative", are special in the sense that they do not have subordinate labels because they are for user feedback texts that report negative user experiences of previously unknown types and that do not report negative user experiences,

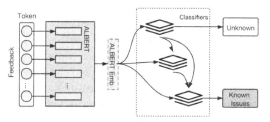

Fig. 3: The process of hierarchical user feedback classification in SKYNET.

respectively. Since some user experiences of previously unknown types may still reveal important issues of the systems, SKYNET conducts extra analysis on the related feedback to determine if they report any issues. Section 3.2 gives more details about the analysis. User feedback classified as "Non-negative" will not be further processed by SKYNET.

Figure 2 also lists some example feedback snippets from users of the online video editing system and associates the snippets to their corresponding labels. Two things from the examples are worth noting. First, users often use different words in describing the same issue. For example, the words "save" and "export" were used in snippets 1-1 and 1-2 to refer to the action of exporting a video, respectively. Second, different words with similar meanings may be used to describe user experiences of distinct types. For example, the word "save" was used in both snippets 2-2 and 3-2, which report different types of negative user experiences. Due to such flexibility in natural language expressions, using word combinations like ("save" and "video") to characterize and group user feedback, as was done in previous work [45], may often produce results of low precision. In view of that, SKYNET extracts the semantics of the experiences reported in user feedback via deep learning and classifies user feedback based on their semantics.

We do not consider the requirement for an input hierarchy of user feedback labels as a major restriction to SKYNET's applicability for two reasons. First, although not every service system readily has a dedicated hierarchy of user feedback labels, hierarchies from similar systems could be used instead to bootstrap the application of SKYNET on a new service system since, according to our experience, systems with similar functionalities often share hierarchies of user feedback labels. Second, a collection of appropriate issue labels is essential for the effective management of issues in large online service systems. Developers need to devise the labels with or without tool support, and the labels can be organized into a hierarchy to drive SKYNET. While the construction of such a hierarchical label system may require some manual effort, such investment is worthwhile in the long term since a high-quality label system can greatly improve the result accuracy of feedback classification and issue detection.

Cascading Classification SKYNET employs cascading classification to associate user feedback to the labels from the hierarchical label system. Cascading is a particular case of ensemble learning based on the concatenation of several sub-classifiers [2]. In SKYNET's cascading classification for hierarchical labels, each sub-classifier targets only the labels at a particular level, and the output of a high-level sub-classifier is used as additional input to drive lower-level sub-classifiers in the cascade. In such a setting, it is relatively easier for high-level sub-classifiers to produce proper classification results since the number of labels they need to consider is small and the differences between instances from different classes are big; It is also relatively easier for low-level sub-classifiers to achieve more precise classification results since they only need to focus on the labels subordinate to those labels output by high-level sub-classifiers [35].

Figure 3 shows the cascade classifier SKYNET employs to categorize the user feedback on the online video editing system described in Section 3.1. The classifier contains three sub-classifiers, each for one level of the label hierarchy. Each sub-classifier is a two-layer network, with the neural cells on each layer being fully connected with each other, and it takes all its parent-level classifiers' output, if any, as input for the current level's classification. For instance, the top-level sub-classifier classifies user feedback based on the highest level labels like "Functionality" and "User Account" according to the input text embedding. While the bottom-level sub-classifier takes both the text embedding and the output of the two sub-classifiers at higher levels as input to conduct the most fine-grained classification. The connections between classifiers help preserve the cascade relationship between multi-level labels and improve classification accuracy.

Particularly, each sub-classifier is a multi-class classifier with a loss function defined as $L = \frac{1}{N} \sum_{i=1}^{N} \sum_{c=1}^{C} loss(y_{ic}, \hat{y}_{ic})$, where N is the number of samples, C is the total number of classes in the classification, $\hat{y}_{ic}$ is the probability of ith training example belonging to the cth class, y_{ic} is a binary indicator function that represents the ground truth label, while $loss(y_{ic}, \hat{y}_{ic})$ is the cross-entropy loss between the classification results and the ground truth. Cross-entropy loss [10] is a common loss function for classification tasks, and its value increases as the predicted probability diverges from the actual labels.

The loss function for the overall cascading classification model is defined as $L_{overall} = \alpha L_1 + \beta L_2 + \gamma L_3$. That is, the overall loss $L_{overall}$ of the model is the weighted sum of the loss L_n at the n-th cascading level ($1 \leq n \leq 3$), with α, β and γ being the weights of corresponding levels. We assign decreasing values 0.8, 0.6, and 0.4, to α, β and γ, respectively, based on the intuition that an incorrect label at any level will lead to incorrect labels for all the underneath levels. With the cascading connections, the weight of the first level sub-classifier will be adjusted with respect to the loss of all classifiers at the three levels during back-propagation, and the weight of the second level sub-classifier will be adjusted with respect to the loss of sub-classifiers at the second and third levels.

3.2   Issue Detection Based on User Feedback

While it is useful to classify feedback texts based on the types of user experiences they report, it is neither necessary nor practical to manually examine all the user feedback that reports negative experiences. On the one hand, not all user feedback reporting negative experiences is caused by issues in online service systems that demand manual inspection by developers. On the other hand, user feedback reporting negative experiences with popular service systems often comes in overwhelming numbers, and therefore it can be prohibitively expensive to manually handle all those user feedback.

To help developers better distribute their time and effort on tasks for issue handling, SKYNET only reports issues for negative experiences shared by a large number of users. Particularly, SKYNET employs a time series forecasting technique to dynamically predict a threshold for the frequency of each known type of negative user experience. An alert indicating the discovery of an issue that needs to be handled will be raised if negative user experiences of the related type get reported more often than allowed by the threshold.

Issues of Known Types When SKYNET classifies a piece of user feedback text to a known type of negative user experience, we say the feedback is an *instance* of the user experience type. By concatenating the instance numbers of a known negative user experience type within each time unit, we form time-series data about the frequency of that type of user experience. Based on the hypothesis that a rising issue of known type will cause outliers in the time-series data of its corresponding label, SKYNET determines that there is an issue when the number of user feedback reporting a particularly known type of negative experience in a time period exceeds a threshold.

Since the normal frequency of each type of negative user experience is closely related to several factors that vary across experience types and over time, adopting a fixed threshold for all negative user experience types would be too rigid. First, different types of negative experiences naturally occur in different frequencies. For example, in our experience, it is normal to have in each day a few hundred users of a large-scale service system reporting that they cannot receive the verification code, and the reasons often include things like typos in their phone numbers, unstable connections of their phones, and the low response speed of their network operators, none of which is indicative of issues in our systems. On the contrary, the daily number of users reporting problems with uploading files is typically much smaller, and when that number increases significantly, it is highly likely that an issue in our system is the cause. Second, the normal frequency of any type of negative user experience fluctuates at different times in a day, a week, or a month. For instance, most negative experiences occur more often during the day when most users are active than at midnight when most users have fallen asleep. Since predicting a dynamic threshold with historical data is a widely accepted way to detect issues [33,21], SKYNET naturally formulates the issue detection problem as a time series forecasting problem that predicts the normal frequency range for each label based on historical data.

More concretely, we apply a sliding window strategy for the segmentation of each label's historical data, and we adopt a classical bidirectional long short-term memory (BiLSTM) [17] network to learn the historical trends of individual labels. The window size is set to 50 time units in the current implementation, and

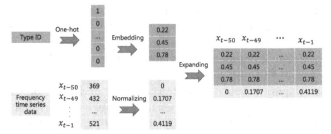

Fig. 4: Expansion of frequency data with feedback type ID, which enables the prediction of multiple thresholds with a unified BiLSTM model.

the window slides with a stride length of one time unit. Note that all outliers—data points outside the interquartile range [4]—in the time series are removed, the Min-Max normalization [31,32] is applied for feature scaling before training.

BiLSTM is a recurrent neural network that takes historical time series data as input to make a prediction based on the trend. To predict a value y'_t for time t, the model takes a series of historical data $[x_{t-50}, ..., x_{t-1}]$ as input, where x_t represents the feature vector for the time unit immediately after t. During training, the model loss is the mean squared error between the actual value y_t and the predicted value y'_t for time t.

Based on the predicted frequency y'_t for a label, SKYNET calculates the threshold th_t for the label as $y'_t * dr$, where dr is a dynamic ratio calculated as $\log(std([x_{t-50}, ..., x_{t-1}])/mean([x_{t-50}, ..., x_{t-1}]))$. The rationale behind the calculation of the threshold is that the magnitude of acceptable frequency fluctuations should be proportional to the absolute value of the frequency prediction for the label. For example, when the occurrence of a label increases by ten, this fluctuation would be relatively smaller if the label's regular frequency y_t is ten thousand instead of a hundred. We apply a log transformation when calculating dr to keep it relatively small.

Predicting Multiple Thresholds with A Unified BiLSTM Model Usually, predicting the normal frequency of a particular type of user feedback requires training a specialized model with the historical frequency data associated with that type. Training one specialized model for each prediction task, however, would cause high costs for the application and maintenance of SKYNET. To reduce those costs, we expand the values in the time series data for each type of user feedback with the identity of that type and use the expanded time series data of all feedback types to train a unified BiLSTM model. The unified model is then able to predict the normal frequencies of different types of user feedback.

Particularly, we expand the feedback frequency data in three steps, as depicted in Figure 4. We first apply one-hot encoding to produce a unique value as the identity of each type of user feedback. Since one-hot type IDs generated in this way are typically sparse, we then transfer them to a dense vector via a fully-connected network $g(\cdot)$. Afterward, the frequency data and the dense vector will

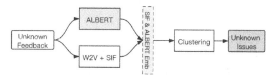

Fig. 5: Detecting issues of unknown types by clustering user feedback.

be combined to form the expanded frequency data. That is, given the one-hot ID δ of a user feedback type and the vectorized frequency $\overline{x_t}$ of this user feedback type at time t, the expanded frequency is constructed as $\overline{x_t} \oplus g(\delta)$, where $\oplus$ indicates vector concatenation. Here, the transfer of one-hot type IDs to dense vectors is necessary because, without it, all but one dimensions of the input data would be for the feedback type ID, and it will be extremely hard for the BiLSTM model to learn meaningful knowledge about the feedback frequency.

Evaluation results of SKYNET on three real-world large-scale online service systems, as detailed in Section 4, show that such unification does help improve the efficiency, while without significantly sacrificing the effectiveness, of threshold prediction in SKYNET.

Issues of Unknown Types Recall that all feedback reporting previously unknown types of negative user experiences will be classified into the "Unknown" category, and such feedback may also reveal issues if many of them concern similar experiences. In view of that, SKYNET clusters user feedback in category "Unknown" periodically (e.g., every half an hour) and raises an issue when the number of feedback in a cluster exceeds a threshold. Figure 5 depicts the main steps SKYNET takes to detect issues of unknown types based on clustering.

To increase the chance that user feedback reporting similar user experiences gets placed into one cluster, it is important that the embedding properly captures the semantic characteristics of the feedback texts. To that end, SKYNET naturally uses the fine-tuned ALBERT-Tiny model to generate the deep semantic embedding of these feedback texts. Feedback clustering solely based on that embedding, however, may suffer from the overfitting problem and miss issues of unknown types because the ALBERT-Tiny model was fine-tuned w.r.t. the input hierarchical label system. Therefore, SKYNET also incorporates the shallow semantics extracted with Word2Vec [27,28] and Smooth Inverse Frequency (SIF) [9] to facilitate the clustering. Word2Vec is a pre-trained model that masters word associations from a large corpus of text, while SIF uses the vector calculated as the weighted average of all word vectors to embed a sentence. Given a piece of feedback text, SKYNET first applies Word2Vec to produce the embedding for each token in the text and then converts the token embeddings to a sentence embedding with SIF. Afterward, the overall embedding of the feedback combining its shallow and deep semantic information is formed by concatenating the embeddings produced by ALBERT-Tiny and SIF, respectively.

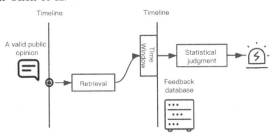

Fig. 6: Cross-domain decision mechanism. The valid public opinion is used to retrieve feedback according to both syntactic and semantic similarity from the database in a time window. The retrieved feedback results then go through a statistical judgment for issue alert.

With the overall semantic embedding as input, SKYNET employs the K-means algorithm to cluster "Unknown" feedback into groups. Note that, since the "Unknown" user feedback usually concerns a wide range of user experiences without concentrating on any specific types, we expect the resultant clusters to be small in size. Correspondingly, when those user feedback texts form large groups, it is highly likely that the feedback in those groups reveals issues in the system. Specifically, SKYNET reports an issue if the size of a cluster exceeds a threshold $H_f = \text{MAX}(N_{total}/m * \alpha, \beta)$, where N_{total} is the total number of feedback being clustered, m is the (predefined) number of clusters to produce, while both α and β are constants. In other words, an alert will be raised if the number of feedback in a cluster is larger than both α times the average cluster size and a fixed value β. We conservatively set α to 5 in SKYNET since, according to our experience, an issue often causes the size of its corresponding feedback cluster to increase by 10 times or even more. β is introduced to avoid reporting issues merely because the value of $N_{total}/m * \alpha$ is very small, e.g., when the total number of user feedback to be clustered is small, and we empirically set it to 10.

3.3   Issue Detection Based on Social Media Data

Due to the potentially high cost and the impact that negative public opinions may cause when they are overlooked, SKYNET dedicates an auxiliary process to detecting issues reflected by posts on social media platforms.

Compared with user feedback collected from dedicated channels that is more informative and has labeled historical data for training, social media posts usually contain noisy data, are less structured, and often cover a wide range of topics, making it more challenging to extract issue-related information from them. In view of that, SKYNET adopts a two-stage denoising process to prune out most posts that are either not directly related to the service system under consideration or not reporting experiences likely associated with issues.

More concretely, during the two-stage denoising process, SKYNET first applies keyword-based search to filter out posts that do not mention the name of the target service system, and then applies a binary classification model constructed with ALBERT-Tiny to further filter out posts not reporting negative user experiences. To train the classification model, we collect product-related posts and manually labeled them to distinguish whether they report negative user experiences. We refer to all the social media posts that are retained after the two-stage denoising process as *relevant* posts.

To identify social media posts that report negative experiences likely associated with issues, SKYNET employs a cross-domain joint-decision-making process based on both user feedback and social media posts. As depicted in Figure 6, for each relevant social media post, SKYNET first retrieves similar user feedback from past time windows. We consider two types of similarities between user feedback and social media posts. The lexical similarity is calculated using the Lucene correlation algorithm that comes with ElasticSearch [3], which is based on the classic BM25 algorithm [8]. We consider a piece of user feedback to be a lexical match of a social media post if the BM25 score between them is higher than a threshold 40. The semantic similarity is calculated as the Euclidean distance between the ALBERT-Tiny embeddings of the user feedback and the social media post. We consider a piece of user feedback to be a semantic match of a social media post if the distance is smaller than a threshold of 0.4. A piece of user feedback is considered a match for a social media post if it is a lexical or semantic match for the post. Obviously, it is possible that a piece of user feedback is both a lexical and a semantic match of a social media post.

Given a relevant social media post p, let N_h and N_d be the total number of matching user feedback for p in the past hour and day, respectively, SKYNET raises an issue if N_h exceeds the threshold $H_h = MAX(\alpha_h * \overline{N_h}, \beta_h)$ or N_d exceeds the threshold $H_d = MAX(\alpha_d * \overline{N_d}, \beta_d)$, where $\overline{N_h}$ and $\overline{N_d}$ are the average number of matching user feedback for p in each hour and day of the past week, respectively, while α_h, α_d, β_h, and β_d are constants. Intuitively, an alert will be generated if (1) the number of similar user feedback in the past hour is larger than both α_h times the hourly average across the past week and a fixed value β_h or (2) the number of similar user feedback in the past day is larger than both α_d times the daily average across the past week and a fixed value β_d. We empirically assign 3, 3, 5, and 10 to α_h, α_d, β_h, and β_d, respectively, in the current implementation of SKYNET, and we leave the development of more sophisticated techniques for predicting the threshold values for future work.

4   Experimental Evaluations

We experimentally evaluated the effectiveness of SKYNET and the usefulness of its components based on its application results produced on real-world online service systems. Our evaluation aims to address the following research questions:

RQ1: How effective is SKYNET in detecting issues in industry-level online service systems? In RQ1, we assess the effectiveness of SKYNET in issue detection in terms of the precision and recall it achieves from a user's perspective.

Table 1: Industry-level online service systems used as the subjects in our experiments.

ID	DESCRIPTION	MAU	#FEEDBACK	#LABEL		
				TOP	INTERM.	BOTTOM
S1	An online video sharing platform	$> 600m$	$> 100,000$	36	140	360
S2	An online video editing system	$> 130m$	$> 1,000$	13	188	442
S3	An online beauty camera platform	$> 27m$	> 200	7	51	84

RQ2: How useful are the individual component mechanisms of SKYNET for the overall issue detection? Recall that SKYNET integrates three components to effectively detect issues in large-scale online service systems, namely a component C_k that applies cascading classification and time series analysis to detect issues of known types based on user feedback, a component C_u that applies the K-means clustering algorithm to detect issues of unknown types based on user feedback, and a component C_p that applies joint decision making to detect issues based on social media posts. In RQ2, we investigate how much each of these components contributes to the overall effectiveness of SKYNET.

We were not able to experimentally compare SKYNET with iFeedback for two reasons. First, the implementation of iFeedback is not publicly available. Second, faithfully re-building the tool is hardly viable because important information regarding its implementation is missing from the related publication. For example, we only know from the publication that iFeedback employs an XGBoost-based model to classify whether a time interval contains an issue, and it applies a hierarchical algorithm to cluster the user feedback as reporting different issues [45], but no information about the settings and parameters of the model and algorithm adopted in their implementation was given in the publication, although those settings and parameters may greatly affect iFeedback's issue detection capabilities.

4.1 Subject Systems

In our experiments, we applied SKYNET to three industry-level online service systems. Table 1 summarizes the basic information about the systems. For each system, the table gives its ID, a brief description, its number of monthly active users (MAUs) in millions, and the average number of user feedback items received per day for the system. System S1 is an online video-sharing social media platform, system S2 is an online video editing system, and system S3 is an online beauty camera platform. The subjects include systems of different types for different users, with different magnitudes of MAUs, and receiving different amounts of user feedback. The diversity in the subject systems helps to ensure that the experiments are representative of SKYNET's behavior in different situations.

4.2 Model Training

Since all three subject systems mainly target Chinese users, we configured SKYNET to utilize a pre-trained ALBERT model [1], the DSG embedding corpora [7], and the Jieba text segmentation library [5] for processing texts in Chinese. Meanwhile, we configured SKYNET to utilize the texts posted on Weibo[3], one of the biggest social media platforms in China, for issue detection in the experiments.

For each system, we utilized historical user feedback with labels manually assigned by the system developers over a one-month period to fine-tune the ALBERT-Tiny model and to train the cascading classification model as a whole. To prepare the hierarchical label system, first, we invited the system developers to decide which labels associated with negative user experience reporting feedback should be retained as the bottom layer labels. Then, following the principles described in Section 3.1, the developers were asked to group and summarize the bottom layer labels to form the intermediate and top layer labels. Finally, all the other labels indicating negative user experiences were converted to "Unknown", and the remaining labels were converted to "Non-negative". In this way, we prepared for each online service a hierarchical label system and a large number of user feedback associated with those labels. For each constructed hierarchical label system, Table 1 gives the numbers of labels at its three different layers.

Afterward, we followed the standard practice [34] to tune the hyperparameters to be used with the classification and BiLSTM models. Particularly, for each service system, we we selected via random search a group of 10 hyperparameters that enables the classification model to correctly label the most historical user feedback texts, and then we looked for values adjacent to these hyperparameters via grid search [34] that produced the highest number of correct labels and used the values for the classification model in our experiments. The BiLSTM model was trained through stochastic gradient descent [37] on the time series data derived from the given historical feedback data. For example, for the experiments on service system S1, the cascading classification model used the following non-default hyperparameters: `batch_size=24`; `dropout=0.1`; `learning_rate=`$2e-5$; `warm_up_proportion=0.1`; `max_epoch=10`, while the BiLSTM model used the following non-default hyperparameters: `dropout=0.1`; `max_epoch=50`; `sequence_len=50`; `learning_rate=0.1`; `batch_size=24`.

4.3 Experimental Setup

We applied SKYNET to detect issues in each subject system based on historical data collected over a ten-month period of time. Each detected issue was checked manually by operators and developers of the systems to confirm whether it indicates a real problem that needs to be handled. Moreover, the operators and developers also assessed the severity of each issue based on the functionalities it may impact, the costs it may incur, and the extent to which users' experience may be jeopardized. An issue is called a *severe* issue if its impact in at least one of those aspects is substantial.

---

[3] https://www.weibo.com

To answer RQ1, we collected all the issues reported by SKYNET for the subject systems as well as the results of manual inspections on the issues. Following the practice in previous work [45], we measure the effectiveness of SKYNET in terms of the *precision* and *recall* of the issue detection results produced by the tool. In particular, the precision is calculated as the percentage of real issues in all the detected issues, i.e., N_c^i/N_d^i, where N_c^i and N_d^i are the numbers of issues confirmed by developers and detected by SKYNET, respectively; The recall is calculated as the ratio of detected severe issues to all the severe issues recorded for the whole experiment period, i.e., N_d^s/N_r^s, where N_d^s and N_r^s are the numbers of severe issues detected by SKYNET and recorded by developers, respectively. Note that metric recall concerns only severe issues in the system because severe issues will be reported eventually due to their high impact even if SKYNET fails to detect them, while there is no practical way for us to find out the exact total number of real issues in those systems.

To answer RQ2, we ran SKYNET two more times on all the user feedback data and the social media posts to detect issues for the systems, the first time with component C_p being disabled and the second time with both components C_p and C_u being disabled. Then, we compared the issue detection results from the three runs in the number of issues detected as well as the precision and recall of the corresponding results.

4.4   Experimental Results

In this section, we report on the results produced in the experiments and answer the research questions.

RQ1: Effectiveness Table 2 lists the basic information about the issue detection results SKYNET produced on the systems. For each system, the table lists its system ID, the numbers of issues detected by SKYNET and confirmed by developers, the numbers of severe issues detected by SKYNET and recorded by developers, and the precision (PREC) and recall (RECA) achieved accordingly.

SKYNET detected 2790 issues in total, 2595 of them were manually confirmed to be true issues, achieving a precision of 93.0%. As for severe issues, developers recorded in total 62 cases for the three systems in ten months, and 58 of them were detected by SKYNET, achieving a recall of 93.5%. In comparison, iFeedback [45] was able to achieve 76.2% and 93.2% for precision and recall, respectively, in its evaluation. SKYNET managed to significantly outperform iFeedback in terms of precision while slightly improving the recall. Such results suggest that SKYNET is both effective and accurate in issue detection.

To understand the reasons for SKYNET's ineffectiveness, we manually inspected all four severe issues that were missed. Three of the four severe issues were missed due to minor fluctuations in the number of associated user feedback. For instance, one severe issue that SKYNET missed occurred during AB-testing [40] of a service system. Since only a small number of users were involved in the AB-test, while the issue seriously damaged the user experience of the system,

Table 2: Issue detection results produced by SKYNET on the subject systems.

SID	ISSUE		SEVERE ISSUE		PREC	RECA
	DETECTED	CONFIRMED	DETECTED	RECORDED		
S1	2003	1895	51	54	94.6%	94.4%
S2	507	452	7	8	89.2%	87.5%
S3	280	248	0	0	88.6%	-
Overall	2790	2595	58	62	93.0%	93.5%

Table 3: Usefulness of SKYNET's individual components for issue detection.

SID	s_{IR}	C_k					$C_k + C_u$					SKYNET ($C_k + C_u + C_p$)				
		N_d^i	N_c^i	N_d^s	P	R	N_d^i	N_c^i	N_d^s	P	R	N_d^i	N_c^i	N_d^s	P	R
S1	54	1975	1870	28	94.7%	51.9%	1997	1889	45	94.6%	83.3%	2003	1895	51	94.6%	94.4%
S2	8	497	444	5	89.3%	62.5%	507	452	7	89.2%	87.5%	507	452	7	89.2%	87.5%
S3	0	277	246	0	88.8%	-	280	248	0	88.6%	-	280	248	0	88.6%	-
Overall	62	2749	2560	33	93.1%	53.2%	2784	2589	52	93.0%	83.9%	2790	2595	58	93.0%	93.5%

the total number of users affected was relatively small, compared with the number of users that routinely access the service provided by the system. Hence, no alert was triggered. The severe issue could have been detected if SKYNET predicts the threshold frequency of issue-reporting feedback texts as a ratio to the total number of users with access to the relevant system feature. SKYNET missed the other severe issue of a previously unknown type due to the imprecise clustering of feedback texts. Since various users' descriptions of the issue were quite different, SKYNET's unsupervised model was not able to group all the user feedback reporting the same issue into a cluster. This is not completely unexpected since, although we have considered both the lexical and semantic characteristics of feedback texts in their embedding, it is not a perfect solution yet. We plan to devise more powerful embedding and clustering techniques to facilitate the detection of issues of unknown types in the future.

> SKYNET was effective and accurate in detecting issues for large-scale online service systems. 93.0% of the issues detected by SKYNET reflect real problems that demand manual inspection. 93.5% of the severe issues recorded for the systems were detected by SKYNET.

RQ2: Usefulness of Component Mechanisms Table 3 shows the results produced by SKYNET with various components being disabled in issue detection. For each system identified by its SID, the table gives the issue detection results from using just component C_k, using both components C_k and C_u, and using all three components of SKYNET. In each setting, the table lists the numbers of issues detected by the tool (N_d^i) and confirmed by developers (N_c^i), the number of severe issues detected by the tool (N_d^s), and the precision (P) and recall (R) achieved accordingly.

When C_k is the only component enabled, SKYNET was able to detect 2749 issues, among which 2560 were manually confirmed, and 33 severe issues for the systems, achieving the overall precision and recall of 93.1% and 53.2%, respectively. To put it in perspective, that is 98.7% (=2560/2595) of the real issues and 56.9% (=33/58) of the severe issues the tool can ever detect with all its components being enabled. Such results clearly show that both cascade feedback classification and dynamic threshold prediction of SKYNET were effective in detecting issues based on user feedback. Although the recall that C_k achieved in detecting severe issues is relatively low, it is understandable since many severe issues are of previously unknown types and hence beyond the detecting capability of C_k.

Component C_u helped capture 29 (=2589-2560) real issues and 19 (=52-33) severe issues that component C_k failed to detect, which caused the precision of the overall result to drop slightly to 93.0% but helped raise the recall of the overall result to 83.9%. The drop in the result precision is understandable since C_u essentially detects issues of previously unknown types via unsupervised learning, and the results of unsupervised learning are relatively low in general. Compared with a few false positives, i.e., reported issues that were manually ruled out as they were not real issues, the 19 severe issues detected by component C_u are significantly more important for the developers. Therefore, we believe component C_u is a valuable complement to component C_k. Note that only feedback items that report negative user experiences of previously unknown types are processed by component C_u.

The issue detection results produced by components C_k and C_u also enable us to directly compare SKYNET and iFeedback's issue detection capability solely based on user feedback. As shown in Table 3, if only having access to user feedback, or when component C_p is disabled, SKYNET was able to detect 2784 issues, among which 2589 were confirmed to be real ones and 52 were considered severe. The precision and recall achieved are therefore 93.0% and 83.9%, respectively. Recall that the precision and recall iFeedback achieved were 76.2% and 93.2%, respectively. The differences suggest that SKYNET and iFeedback make different tradeoffs between issue detection precision and recall. iFeedback is more lenient in reporting issues. On the one hand, many issues it reported turned out to be false positives; On the other hand, it managed to detect more severe issues; SKYNET is stricter in reporting issues. On the one hand, it reported fewer false positives; On the other hand, it missed a few more severe issues.

SKYNET makes up for its relatively low recall in issue detection based on user feedback by taking into account also users' posts on social media platforms. Although component C_p only detected 6 more real issues in our experiments, all of them turned out to be severe, and missing any of these issues may have caused great damage to the company. Therefore, although this component has only slightly improved the overall recall, we consider it to be a crucial and non-dispensable part of SKYNET.

All the three components C_k, C_u, and C_p are important for SKYNET to detect (severe) issues in an effective and accurate manner.

Threat to Validity In this section, we discuss possible threats to the validity of our findings and show how we mitigate them.

Construct validity. In our evaluation, a reported issue could be manually confirmed or rejected as a real or severe issue, but different people may provide different assessments. To mitigate this threat, we directly reused the *independent* issue assessment results from the developers of the service systems.

Internal validity. SKYNET makes use of a list of parameters, including, e.g., the size of the sliding window for BiLSTM and the similarity threshold for matching social-media posts with user feedback texts. We set the parameters based on our experience in the current implementation of SKYNET. Experimental evaluation conducted on three industry-level online service systems produced very promising results, suggesting the chosen parameter values are appropriate. Having said that, we are aware that different values for the parameters may influence SKYNET's effectiveness, and therefore we plan to conduct more experiments in the future to systematically evaluate the possible influence.

We were not able to experimentally compare SKYNET with iFeedback for reasons stated at the beginning of Section 4. As the result, we compared the two tools based on the results they produced on the subject systems in their corresponding evaluations. For the comparison to be as fair as possible, we evaluated SKYNET on service systems of similar scales from various categories of applications. Moreover, the comparison was based on common metrics precision and recall, instead of measurements like the numbers of issues and severe issues detected, which greatly depends on the experimental setup.

External validity. The subject service systems adopted in our experiments were real-world services of different scales and from different application domains. These characteristics help mitigate the risk that our evaluation overfits the subjects. In the future, on the one hand, we will continue monitoring the execution of SKYNET on existing service systems, on the other hand, we will deploy SKYNET on more service systems. We see no intrinsic limitations that would prevent SKYNET from working reliably on different online service systems.

5 Conclusions

This paper presents the SKYNET technique and tool that utilize user data gathered from multiple channels to detect issues for large-scale online service systems. The technique has been applied to detect issues for three real-world online services based on historical data gathered over a ten-month period of time. The produced results suggest that SKYNET is both effective and accurate in detecting issues and severe issues for large-scale online service systems.

6 Data Availability

The SKYNET tool has been integrated into the production issue tracking system in the first author's company. For confidentiality reasons, neither the tool nor the multi-channel user feedback can be available for public download.

References

1. Albert pre-trained model for chinese. `https://github.com/brightmart/albert_zh`. Last accessed 19 May 2022.
2. Cascading classifiers - wikipedia. `https://en.wikipedia.org/wiki/Cascading_classifiers`. Last accessed 19 May 2022.
3. Github elasticsearch. `https://github.com/elastic/elasticsearch`. Last accessed 19 May 2022.
4. Interquartile range. `https://en.wikipedia.org/wiki/Interquartile_range`. Last accessed 19 May 2022.
5. Jieba - chinese text segmentation. `https://github.com/fxsjy/jieba`.
6. Okapi bm25 - wikipedia. `https://en.wikipedia.org/wiki/Okapi_BM25`. Last accessed 19 May 2022.
7. Tencent ai lab embedding corpora for chinese and english words and phrases. `https://ai.tencent.com/ailab/nlp/en/embedding.html`.
8. tf–idf - wikipedia. `https://en.wikipedia.org/wiki/Tf%e2%80%93idf`. Last accessed 19 May 2022.
9. S. Arora, Y. Liang, and T. Ma. A simple but tough-to-beat baseline for sentence embeddings. In *5th International Conference on Learning Representations, ICLR 2017, Toulon, France, April 24-26, 2017, Conference Track Proceedings*. OpenReview.net, 2017.
10. D. R. Cox. The regression analysis of binary sequences. *Journal of the Royal Statistical Society: Series B (Methodological)*, 20(2):215–232, 1958.
11. J. Devlin, M.-W. Chang, K. Lee, and K. Toutanova. Bert: Pre-training of deep bidirectional transformers for language understanding. *arXiv preprint arXiv:1810.04805*, 2018.
12. A. Di Sorbo, S. Panichella, C. V. Alexandru, J. Shimagaki, C. A. Visaggio, G. Canfora, and H. C. Gall. What would users change in my app? summarizing app reviews for recommending software changes. In *Proceedings of the 2016 24th ACM SIGSOFT International Symposium on Foundations of Software Engineering*, pages 499–510, 2016.
13. B. Fu, J. Lin, L. Li, C. Faloutsos, J. Hong, and N. Sadeh. Why people hate your app: Making sense of user feedback in a mobile app store. In *Proceedings of the 19th ACM SIGKDD international conference on Knowledge discovery and data mining*, pages 1276–1284, 2013.
14. C. Gao, J. Zeng, M. R. Lyu, and I. King. Online app review analysis for identifying emerging issues. In M. Chaudron, I. Crnkovic, M. Chechik, and M. Harman, editors, *Proceedings of the 40th International Conference on Software Engineering, ICSE 2018, Gothenburg, Sweden, May 27 - June 03, 2018*, pages 48–58. ACM, 2018.
15. J. Gu, C. Luo, S. Qin, B. Qiao, Q. Lin, H. Zhang, Z. Li, Y. Dang, S. Cai, W. Wu, Y. Zhou, M. Chintalapati, and D. Zhang. Efficient incident identification from multi-dimensional issue reports via meta-heuristic search. In *Proceedings of the 28th ACM Joint Meeting on European Software Engineering Conference and Symposium on the Foundations of Software Engineering*, ESEC/FSE 2020, page 292–303, New York, NY, USA, 2020. Association for Computing Machinery.
16. E. Guzman, M. Ibrahim, and M. Glinz. A little bird told me: Mining tweets for requirements and software evolution. In *2017 IEEE 25th International Requirements Engineering Conference (RE)*, pages 11–20, 2017.

17. S. Hochreiter and J. Schmidhuber. Long short-term memory. *Neural Comput.*, 9(8):1735–1780, 1997.

18. C. Huang, G. Min, Y. Wu, Y. Ying, K. Pei, and Z. Xiang. Time series anomaly detection for trustworthy services in cloud computing systems. *IEEE Transactions on Big Data*, 2017.

19. T. Johann, C. Stanik, W. Maalej, et al. Safe: A simple approach for feature extraction from app descriptions and app reviews. In *2017 IEEE 25th international requirements engineering conference (RE)*, pages 21–30. IEEE, 2017.

20. Z. Lan, M. Chen, S. Goodman, K. Gimpel, P. Sharma, and R. Soricut. ALBERT: A lite BERT for self-supervised learning of language representations. In *8th International Conference on Learning Representations, ICLR 2020, Addis Ababa, Ethiopia, April 26-30, 2020*. OpenReview.net, 2020.

21. N. Laptev, S. Amizadeh, and I. Flint. Generic and scalable framework for automated time-series anomaly detection. In *Proceedings of the 21th ACM SIGKDD international conference on knowledge discovery and data mining*, pages 1939–1947, 2015.

22. L. Li, X. Zhang, X. Zhao, H. Zhang, Y. Kang, P. Zhao, B. Qiao, S. He, P. Lee, J. Sun, F. Gao, L. Yang, Q. Lin, S. Rajmohan, Z. Xu, and D. Zhang. Fighting the fog of war: Automated incident detection for cloud systems. In *2021 USENIX Annual Technical Conference (USENIX ATC 21)*, pages 131–146. USENIX Association, July 2021.

23. Z. Li, Y. Zhao, R. Liu, and D. Pei. Robust and rapid clustering of kpis for large-scale anomaly detection. In *2018 IEEE/ACM 26th International Symposium on Quality of Service (IWQoS)*, pages 1–10. IEEE, 2018.

24. Q. Lin, J.-G. Lou, H. Zhang, and D. Zhang. idice: Problem identification for emerging issues. In *2016 IEEE/ACM 38th International Conference on Software Engineering (ICSE)*, pages 214–224, 2016.

25. D. Liu, Y. Zhao, H. Xu, Y. Sun, D. Pei, J. Luo, X. Jing, and M. Feng. Opprentice: Towards practical and automatic anomaly detection through machine learning. In *Proceedings of the 2015 Internet Measurement Conference*, pages 211–224, 2015.

26. M. Ma, S. Zhang, D. Pei, X. Huang, and H. Dai. Robust and rapid adaption for concept drift in software system anomaly detection. In *2018 IEEE 29th International Symposium on Software Reliability Engineering (ISSRE)*, pages 13–24. IEEE, 2018.

27. T. Mikolov, K. Chen, G. Corrado, and J. Dean. Efficient estimation of word representations in vector space. In Y. Bengio and Y. LeCun, editors, *1st International Conference on Learning Representations, ICLR 2013, Scottsdale, Arizona, USA, May 2-4, 2013, Workshop Track Proceedings*, 2013.

28. T. Mikolov, I. Sutskever, K. Chen, G. Corrado, and J. Dean. Distributed representations of words and phrases and their compositionality. *arXiv preprint arXiv:1310.4546*, 2013.

29. D. Pagano and W. Maalej. User feedback in the appstore: An empirical study. In *2013 21st IEEE international requirements engineering conference (RE)*, pages 125–134. IEEE, 2013.

30. F. Palomba, M. Linares-Vásquez, G. Bavota, R. Oliveto, M. Di Penta, D. Poshyvanyk, and A. De Lucia. User reviews matter! tracking crowdsourced reviews to support evolution of successful apps. In *2015 IEEE international conference on software maintenance and evolution (ICSME)*, pages 291–300. IEEE, 2015.

31. S. K. Panda and P. K. Jana. Efficient task scheduling algorithms for heterogeneous multi-cloud environment. *The Journal of Supercomputing*, 71(4):1505–1533, 2015.

32. S. Patro and K. K. Sahu. Normalization: A preprocessing stage. *arXiv preprint arXiv:1503.06462*, 2015.

33. M. Raginsky, R. M. Willett, C. Horn, J. Silva, and R. F. Marcia. Sequential anomaly detection in the presence of noise and limited feedback. *IEEE Transactions on Information Theory*, 58(8):5544–5562, 2012.

34. K. Ramasubramanian and J. Moolayil. *Applied Supervised Learning with R: Use machine learning libraries of R to build models that solve business problems and predict future trends*. Packt Publishing, 2019.

35. M. Saberian and N. Vasconcelos. Boosting algorithms for detector cascade learning. *Journal of Machine Learning Research*, 15:2569–2605, 2014.

36. R. Sathya, A. Abraham, et al. Comparison of supervised and unsupervised learning algorithms for pattern classification. *International Journal of Advanced Research in Artificial Intelligence*, 2(2):34–38, 2013.

37. S. Sra, S. Nowozin, and S. J. Wright. *Optimization for machine learning*. Mit Press, 2012.

38. C. Stanik, T. Pietz, and W. Maalej. Unsupervised topic discovery in user comments. In *2021 IEEE 29th International Requirements Engineering Conference (RE)*, pages 150–161. IEEE, 2021.

39. Y. Sun, Y. Zhao, Y. Su, D. Liu, X. Nie, Y. Meng, S. Cheng, D. Pei, S. Zhang, X. Qu, et al. Hotspot: Anomaly localization for additive kpis with multi-dimensional attributes. *IEEE Access*, 6:10909–10923, 2018.

40. D. Tang, A. Agarwal, D. O'Brien, and M. Meyer. Overlapping experiment infrastructure: More, better, faster experimentation. In *Proceedings of the 16th ACM SIGKDD international conference on Knowledge discovery and data mining*, pages 17–26, 2010.

41. L. Villarroel, G. Bavota, B. Russo, R. Oliveto, and M. Di Penta. Release planning of mobile apps based on user reviews. In *2016 IEEE/ACM 38th International Conference on Software Engineering (ICSE)*, pages 14–24. IEEE, 2016.

42. P. M. Vu, H. V. Pham, T. T. Nguyen, and T. T. Nguyen. Phrase-based extraction of user opinions in mobile app reviews. In *Proceedings of the 31st IEEE/ACM International Conference on Automated Software Engineering*, pages 726–731, 2016.

43. G. Williams and A. Mahmoud. Mining twitter feeds for software user requirements. In *2017 IEEE 25th International Requirements Engineering Conference (RE)*, pages 1–10. IEEE, 2017.

44. H. Xu, W. Chen, N. Zhao, Z. Li, J. Bu, Z. Li, Y. Liu, Y. Zhao, D. Pei, Y. Feng, et al. Unsupervised anomaly detection via variational auto-encoder for seasonal kpis in web applications. In *Proceedings of the 2018 World Wide Web Conference*, pages 187–196, 2018.

45. W. Zheng, H. Lu, Y. Zhou, J. Liang, H. Zheng, and Y. Deng. ifeedback: exploiting user feedback for real-time issue detection in large-scale online service systems. In *2019 34th IEEE/ACM International Conference on Automated Software Engineering (ASE)*, pages 352–363. IEEE, 2019.

Refinement Verification of OS Services based on a Verified Preemptive Microkernel

Ximeng Li[2], Shanyan Chen[1], Yong Guan[1,3],
Qianying Zhang[2,3], Guohui Wang[2,3], Zhiping Shi[1,2(✉)]

[1] College of Information Engineering,
Capital Normal University, Beijing, China
shizp@cnu.edu.cn
[2] Beijing Key Laboratory of Electronic System Reliability and Prognostics,
Capital Normal University, Beijing, China
[3] Beijing Advanced Innovation Center for Imaging Theory and Technology,
Capital Normal University, Beijing, China

Abstract. An OS microkernel can be extended by implementing services upon it. A service could introduce an object that references a kernel object, and implement a group of functions that invokes the functions for manipulating the kernel object. We consider the scenario where the microkernel has been verified with machine-checkable proofs, while the services remain to be verified. Moreover, the verification of the microkernel is not performed with the verification of subsequent extension in mind. We address the problem of how to build sufficiently on the verification results for the microkernel, in achieving the verification of the services. Our methodology consists of enhancements to the verification framework for the microkernel, and the design of invariants for establishing the connection between the service-level objects and the kernel-level objects. Using the methodology, we have conducted a substantial formal verification of a group of services extending the inter-task communication functionalities of the preemptive microkernel μC/OS-II. Our verification uncovers dormant bugs and provides a level of correctness assurance for the services that is above what is achievable through extensive testing.

1 Introduction

Microkernels provide the most fundamental functionalities of operating systems such as task management, inter-task communication, and interrupt handling. Microkernels are relatively small in size and simple in structure. Compared with monolithic kernels, errors in microkernel-based systems are more likely to occur outside of the kernel. Thus, these errors are less likely to crash the entire system. A *preemptive microkernel* allows a task to be interrupted at any point of execution, as long as interrupts are enabled in the CPU. During interrupt handling, a higher-priority task can be switched to. This mechanism permits the timely processing of urgent workloads, increasing the responsiveness of the system.

© The Author(s) 2024
D. Beyer and A. Cavalcanti (Eds.): FASE 2024, LNCS 14573, pp. 188–209, 2024.
https://doi.org/10.1007/978-3-031-57259-3_9

On the downside, the possibility of preemption results in a great number of inter-dependencies between tasks. This adds to the difficulty in correctly designing and implementing the microkernel. Out of concern for correctness, substantial efforts have been dedicated to achieving the formal verification of preemptive microkernels (e.g., [28]). These verification efforts lay a solid foundation for assuring the correctness of the software systems based on preemptive microkernels.

Since a microkernel only provides the core functionalities in abstracting and managing system resources, the extension of the functionalities for a microkernel is often required in a given application scenario. The functionality of a *kernel object* O_{knl} can be extended in the following way. Firstly, a data structure is introduced — an instance O_{srv} of this data structure contains a reference to O_{knl}, while maintaining some additional attributes. Secondly, the operations that can be performed on O_{srv} are implemented. In these operations, checks and updates are performed on the additional attributes in O_{srv}, and the operations for O_{knl} are invoked to complete the checks and updates on the internal attributes. The extension provides a service to the user. We shall refer to O_{srv} as a *service object*.

For instance, the mutexes in a microkernel might not support modes of operations such as recursive and non-recursive modes. This feature can be introduced in an extension of the microkernel, providing a modes-aware mutex service to the user. Firstly, a service-level mutex object can be introduced. Secondly, the mode of a mutex can be tracked by an attribute of this service object. Thirdly, in an operation that tries to obtain a service-level mutex that the current task already owns, the attribute is checked before deciding whether to invoke the kernel function for obtaining the mutex or not.

In safety-critical scenarios, the correctness of the services that extend the microkernel can be as important as the correctness of the microkernel itself. A reliable way to ensure the correctness of the services is formal verification. If the microkernel itself has been formally verified, the formal specifications and proofs for the functions of the microkernel could be used as a basis for this verification.

The formal verification of the services can still be non-trivial. This is true especially if the tasks executing the service functions (e.g., the function for obtaining a modes-aware mutex) can be preempted. In this case, it can be non-trivial even to ensure that a service object in use always references a corresponding kernel object that has been properly allocated and initialized. For the verification of the services, another problem is how to achieve good reuse of the specifications and proofs for the underlying microkernel. Moreover, if the proofs for the microkernel have been developed using a verification framework, it would be good to sufficiently leverage this verification framework, as opposed to requiring a great amount of modification to the verification framework.

In this article, we address the aforementioned challenges in the formal verification of OS services (in the above sense) that extend a preemptive microkernel. Specifically, we consider the case where *refinement verification* has been performed for the microkernel, using a variant of concurrent separation logic [9] called CSL-R [28, 27]. This is the program logic used in the first formal verification of a practical preemptive microkernel with machine-checkable proofs.

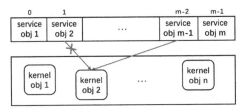

Fig. 1: The connection between service objects and kernel objects

The main contributions of this article include:

1. enhancements to the verification framework of CSL-R to support the compositional specification of the functions implementing the OS services
2. a design of invariants dependent on auxiliary variables for reasoning about the connection between service objects and their underlying kernel objects
3. results obtained by applying the extended verification framework and the invariants design to achieve the formal verification of inter-task synchronization and communication services that extend the corresponding functionalities of the preemptive microkernel μC/OS-II [3]

Specifically, the enhancements to the verification framework of CSL-R enables the integration of the specifications for the kernel functions as components for the specifications of service functions. The connection between the service objects and their underlying kernel objects is shown to satisfy structural properties that are generic to the specific purposes and contents of the services. The verification of the inter-task synchronization and communication services is performed in an industrial verification project in the aerospace domain, while these services also constitute a module of a system to be more widely used in other safety-critical scenarios. We devise the specification of each service function and prove that the specification is refined by the code of the function. The development is performed in the Coq proof assistant [1]. This verification is a substantial effort, in which we have uncovered problems in extensively tested code.

2 Challenges in Verifying an OS Service

We assume a service object (e.g., a service-level task, semaphore, or message queue) is implemented as a struct in C. The service object obj contains a pointer, obj.ptr, to a potential kernel object of the underlying microkernel. The service object contains a number of attributes that are managed outside of the microkernel. Moreover, we assume that all the service objects of the same kind are organized in the array obj_arr. This array is illustrated in the upper part of Fig. 1.

We consider a kernel object to be *active*, if the kernel object has been allocated and initialized. An active kernel object is expected to be in a consistent state. The set of active kernel objects is illustrated in the lower part of Fig. 1.

A desired integrity requirement about the connection between the service objects and the underlying kernel objects is:

Requirement 1 *If a service object is fully created, then the service object references a kernel object that is in a consistent state.*

This requirement is reflected by the arrow without a cross over it in Fig. 1. If the requirement is not met, then an operation on a service object could trigger an operation on an inconsistent kernel object. Hence, the proper completion of the kernel operation with correct results cannot be guaranteed.

Another desired integrity requirement about the connection between the service objects and the underlying kernel objects is:

Requirement 2 *Each kernel object is referenced by at most one service object.*

This requirement is reflected by the arrow with a cross over it in Fig. 1. If a kernel object can be referenced by two or more service objects, then it is difficult to guarantee that all these service objects are consistent with the kernel object. An operation on one of these service objects would update the service object and the kernel object consistently. But this update could break the consistency of another service object with the kernel object.

It can be nontrivial to ascertain the satisfaction of Requirement 1 and Requirement 2 in a preemptive setting. Consider the function service_obj_create in Fig. 2. This function is used to create service objects. The dotted boxes reflect the areas of critical regions, in which the task executing the function cannot be preempted. Line 2 searches for an index idx in obj_arr using the internal function get_free_obj. This index identifies an array element that corresponds to an unused service object. Line 3 checks if the return value of get_free_obj is a valid index for obj_arr. If not, then the entries of obj_arr are used up, and the function service_obj_create returns. Otherwise, obj_arr[idx].ptr gets the special value Dummy at line 4. This value signals that the array entry obj_arr[idx] is reserved — it cannot be used by a different task attempting to create a service object. Then, the critical region is exited. Afterwards, the kernel function kernel_obj_create for creating a kernel object is invoked at line 5. Here, katt is the attribute value used to initialize the kernel object. The function returns the pointer to the kernel object that is allocated and initialized — NULL in case no kernel object can be allocated. This pointer is assigned to the kernel object pointer in the service object obj_arr[idx] at line 6. Then, it is checked whether the pointer is not NULL. The function service_obj_create returns if the kernel object pointer is NULL. Otherwise, the data attributes of the created service object obj_arr[idx] are initialized at line 8. The index idx for this created service object is then returned.

```
service_obj_create(katt, satt):
1   local idx, p
2 | idx <- get_free_obj(obj_arr) |
3 | Check valid(idx)             |
4 | obj_arr[idx].ptr <- Dummy    |

5   p <- kernel_obj_create(katt)
6 | obj_arr[idx].ptr <- p        |
7 | Check p != NULL              |
8 | obj_arr[idx].att <- satt     |
9   return idx
```

Fig. 2: The function service_obj_create

If Requirement 1 is to be satisfied, the following condition related to the function service_obj_create in Fig. 2 should be met.

Condition 1 *After the completion of the assignment* p<-kernel_obj_create(katt), *the pointer* p *points to an active kernel object if* p *is not NULL.*

This condition guarantees that the pointer assigned to obj_arr[idx].ptr points to an active kernel object — thus a kernel object in a consistent state. This helps ensure that the service object obj_arr[idx] references a kernel object that is in a consistent state, once the service object is fully created. However, Condition 1 might not hold, since the data located at the return address of kernel_obj_create could be modified by preemptive tasks. Hence, dedicated reasoning is required to ascertain that the potential modification of data does not break Condition 1.

If Requirement 2 is to be satisfied, the following condition should be met.

Condition 2 *After the completion of the assignment* p<-kernel_obj_create(katt), *no service object already references the kernel object pointed to by* p.

If Condition 2 is not met, then the service object obj_arr[idx] could start to reference the created kernel object, along with some other service object that originally referenced the same kernel object. It appears that the potential kernel object that is allocated in a call to kernel_obj_create must be free before the allocation. Given the code of service_obj_create, it is unlikely that a free kernel object would get referenced from a service object. However, the joint effects of all the functions supporting the creation, deletion, and use of the service object are more complicated than suggested by this observation. Hence, dedicated formal reasoning is required to ascertain the satisfaction of Condition 2.

In the remainder of the article, we will discuss how to ascertain the satisfaction of Condition 1 and Condition 2, thereby ascertaining the satisfaction of Requirement 1 and Requirement 2, in a refinement verification of OS services. A key ingredient of our methodology is the formulation of invariant conditions dependent on auxiliary variables in a separation logic (see Section 5).

Ultimately, the ability to show that Requirement 1 and Requirement 2 are fulfilled supports the formal verification of the service functions against their specifications. We will also discuss how to compose these specifications from the formal specifications of the underlying kernel functions (see Section 4). This enables the reuse of the specifications and proofs for the kernel functions, as previously developed in the formal verification of the microkernel.

3   Refinement Verification of OS Microkernels

To facilitate the understanding of our technical development, we briefly introduce the verification framework for the concurrent separation logic CSL-R [28, 27], as well as the formal verification of an OS microkernel using this framework.

3.1   The Big Picture

Through the refinement verification of an OS microkernel, a simulation is established between the execution of a concrete system and the execution of an abstract system. The concrete system consists of client programs, kernel functions, and interrupt handlers. The abstract system contains the same client programs

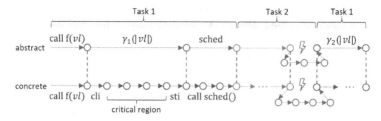

Fig. 3: Execution of a microkernel and simulation by a specification

as the concrete system. In addition, the abstract system contains the specifications for the kernel functions and the interrupt handlers. These specifications are in the form of *abstract programs*, as opposed to concrete C or assembly code.

An example of the simulation between the concrete system and the abstract system is illustrated in Fig. 3. In this figure, the concrete system runs two tasks. Task 1 calls the kernel function f with the list vl of argument values. This function executes a series of steps in a critical region. Then, it needs to wait on an event for a given time period. Hence, it calls the function sched() to trigger rescheduling. Suppose task 2 is scheduled for execution. After several steps taken by task 2, a tick interrupt comes. The arrival of the interrupt is illustrated by ⚡. After the interrupt is handled, the system looks for the highest-priority task that is ready for execution. Suppose task 1 has become ready and it is executed for another time. Task 1 then finishes the kernel function f and returns to user code. In the aforementioned scenario, task 2 is *preempted* by task 1.

The kernel function f is specified using the abstract program ω_f as given by

$$\omega_f \; vl := \gamma_1 (|vl|); \text{sched}; \gamma_2 (|vl|)$$

Here, γ_1 and γ_2 represent two atomic steps of execution. Each step has vl as the list of input values. In addition, sched is a primitive for the scheduling operation. Moreover, γ_1, sched, and γ_2 are sequentially composed. We will give further details about the language in which $\omega_f \; vl$ is expressed in Section 3.2.

Part of the simulation between the concrete system and the abstract system is concerned with the simulation of the execution steps for the function f. The abstract statement $\omega_f \; vl$ is executed in the abstract system after the function f is called with the list vl of arguments. The concrete execution steps in the critical region are simulated by the atomic step γ_1. Furthermore, the concrete execution steps for sched() are simulated by the execution step of sched. In addition, the concrete execution steps taken by task 1 after it is resumed are simulated by the atomic step γ_2. The simulation between the concrete system and the abstract system is required to preserve a global invariant. The global invariant is used to relate the states of the two systems — further details will be given in Section 3.3.

The simulation of the concrete system by the abstract system is established by reasoning about each kernel function separately. This reasoning is performed using the rules of the CSL-R logic. For the kernel function f, the goal of the reasoning is to establish the correspondence between the concrete code of f and the abstract program ω_f. The reasoning goes forward (in the sense of [16]) in the concrete code of f, performing symbolic execution of the abstract statement $\omega_f\ vl$ at appropriate points. Thus, the goal is turned into establishing the correspondence between the remainders of f and the remainders of $\omega_f\ vl$, i.e., the abstract statements $\gamma_1(\!|vl|\!)$; sched; $\gamma_2(\!|vl|\!)$, sched; $\gamma_2(\!|vl|\!)$, and $\gamma_2(\!|vl|\!)$.

3.2 The Specification of Kernel Functions

As illustrated in Section 3.1, a kernel function is specified using a mathematical function ω. This function maps each list vl of argument values to an *abstract statement* s. This abstract statement is expressed using the values in vl. The syntax for abstract statements is given below.

$$s ::= \quad \gamma(\!|vl|\!) \mid \text{sched} \mid \text{end } \hat{v} \mid s_1; s_2 \mid s_1 + s_2$$
$$\hat{v} ::= \quad \text{Some } v \mid \text{None}$$

$$\text{where } v \in Val, vl \in Val^*, \gamma \in Val^* \times AState \times Val^? \times AState$$

Here, Val is the set of values, Val^* is the set of value lists, and $Val^?$ is the set of optional values. An optional value is represented by the meta-variable $\hat{v}$. Furthermore, $AState$ is the set of *abstract states*. In the atomic operation $\gamma(\!|vl|\!)$, γ relates the list vl of input values and an initial abstract state to an optional output value and a resulting abstract state. Furthermore, end $\hat{v}$ signals the completion of execution for an abstract statement. In addition, $s_1; s_2$ is a sequential composition. Lastly, $s_1 + s_2$ is a nondeterministic choice.

An abstract state $\Sigma \in AState$ captures as mathematical objects the memory content that is relevant to the abstract programs of the kernel functions. For example, a C struct s with the members s.a and s.b in the memory can be abstractly represented as a pair (a, b) in the abstract state. Overall, an abstract state could contain the representations of typical kernel objects such as kernel-level tasks, semaphores, mutexes, and message queues. The formal semantics of the abstract statements is defined based on reads and updates of the abstract state. We omit the definition of this semantics here.

3.3 Invariants and Fractional Permission

In a concurrent separation logic, the well-formedness of global resources is expressed using a global invariant. Examples of these global resources include the kernel data structures for tasks, synchronization objects, etc. In a concurrent separation logic that supports refinement verification, the global invariant I is interpreted over a concrete state and an abstract state. Thus, I can be used to assert the well-formedness of the global resources in concrete and abstract representations and the relation between the two. Hence, if the struct s mentioned in Section 3.2 is global, then I can be used to assert the well-formedness of s in the memory, the well-formedness of the tuple (a, b) in the abstract state, and the fact that a and b properly represent the memory values of s.a and s.b.

In reasoning about a kernel function, the global invariant I can be asserted to hold after entering a piece of code that has exclusive access to the global resources (e.g., a critical region in which a task cannot be preempted). The auxiliary information provided by this assertion of I can be used in the subsequent

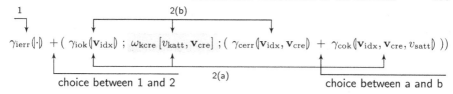

Fig. 4: The abstract statement for service_obj_create

reasoning. The well-formedness of the global resources may be temporarily broken in the code, but it must be re-established at the point where exclusive access to the global resources is given up. At this point (e.g., where a critical region is exited), I must be shown to hold again. Intuitively, a critical region consumes well-formed global resources and gives back well-formed global resources again.

Consider an auxiliary variable that represents the current program location for a task. If the global invariant is formulated to depend on such a variable, then the variable should be treated as a global resource. However, the variable is then modifiable at any point outside of a critical region, by another task that preempts the current one. Nonetheless, the current program location of a task should not be modifiable by a different task. This is where *fractional permission* [8] can be employed to facilitate verification using a concurrent separation logic.

More concretely, an auxiliary variable x can be introduced for a task t, such that t has $\frac{1}{2}$ permission, and the global invariant has $\frac{1}{2}$ permission, over x. A task is allowed (by the program logic) to read a variable, as long as the task has $\frac{1}{2}$ permission over the variable. On the other hand, a task is allowed to modify a variable, only if the task has full permission over the variable. Hence, the task t is allowed to modify the variable x, when the other $\frac{1}{2}$ permission over x is obtained from the global invariant, e.g., in a critical region. The variable x cannot be modified by any preemptive task t'. This is because t' is allowed to obtain at most $\frac{1}{2}$ permission over the variable from the global invariant.

4   Compositional Specification of Service Functions

4.1   Composing Service Specification from Kernel Specification

To enable the refinement verification of the function service_obj_create in Fig. 2, the function should be specified using an abstract statement. This abstract statement should reflect the following cases about the execution of service_obj_create.

1. the execution of service_obj_create could fail, in case there is no usable service object in the system, or
2. service_obj_create could obtain an index $\mathbf{v}_{\mathrm{idx}}$ for a usable service object, attempt at kernel object creation as implemented in kernel_obj_create, obtain the return value $\mathbf{v}_{\mathrm{cre}}$ from kernel_obj_create, and then proceed as follows:
   (a) if $\mathbf{v}_{\mathrm{cre}}$ is the address of a newly allocated and initialized kernel object, then service_obj_create sets the kernel object pointer in the $\mathbf{v}_{\mathrm{idx}}$-th service object to $\mathbf{v}_{\mathrm{cre}}$, sets the data attribute in this service object to the given attribute value v_{satt}, and returns the index value $\mathbf{v}_{\mathrm{idx}}$
   (b) if $\mathbf{v}_{\mathrm{cre}}$ is NULL, then service_obj_create returns an invalid index value

We intend to formulate the abstract statement for service_obj_create using the specification language presented in Section 3.2. A potential formulation is given in Fig. 4. At the top level, this abstract statement is a nondeterministic choice between the part expressing the meaning of item 1 and item 2 above. The meaning of item 1 is expressed using the atomic operation γ_{ierr}. The meaning of item 2 is expressed with two sequential compositions. Here, the atomic operation γ_{iok} is used to express the operation of obtaining $\mathbf{v}_{\text{idx}}$. Furthermore, ω_{kcre} is the abstract program for kernel_obj_create. In addition, the nondeterministic choice between γ_{cerr} and γ_{cok} is used to express a choice between the sub-items 2(b) and 2(a) above. This particular choice is deterministic because of the conditions about $\mathbf{v}_{\text{cre}}$ as expressed in 2(a) and 2(b). The correspondence between the informal expression of the functional requirements for service_obj_create and the formal counterpart is illustrated by the annotations in Fig. 4.

The specification of service_obj_create in Fig. 4 is composed of the abstract program for kernel_obj_create. This compositional aspect enables the reuse of the specification for the functions of the underlying microkernel. This reuse implies that the formal proofs for these kernel functions (as developed in verifying the microkernel) can also be reused. However, a technical problem was encountered with specifications like the one in Fig. 4. The function service_obj_create has two formal parameters (see Fig. 2). According to the CSL-R framework, if the abstract program of the function service_obj_create is ω_{scre}, then the result of calling the function with the arguments v_{katt} and v_{satt} in the abstract system is the abstract statement $\omega_{\text{scre}}[v_{\text{katt}}, v_{\text{satt}}]$. This cannot be the abstract statement in Fig. 4, because the additional parameters $\mathbf{v}_{\text{idx}}$ and $\mathbf{v}_{\text{cre}}$ are not introduced.

To solve the aforementioned problem, we modify the semantics of the specification language such that a call to a function could nondeterministically result in an abstract statement $\omega\,(vl{+}{+}vl')$, where ω is the mathematical function representing the abstract program for the callee, vl is a list that contains exactly the actual arguments for the callee, and vl' is an arbitrary list of values. Intuitively, the list vl' can be used to accommodate the intermediate values generated in the abstract program. For the above example with service_obj_create, we define ω_{scre} such that $\omega_{\text{scre}}\,([v_{\text{katt}}, v_{\text{satt}}]{+}{+}vl')$ yields the abstract statement in Fig. 4. We use the first value of vl' for $\mathbf{v}_{\text{idx}}$, and use the second value of vl' for $\mathbf{v}_{\text{cre}}$.

With this abstract statement, we intend to express that the atomic operation γ_{iok} identifies a specific index $\mathbf{v}_{\text{idx}}$ — the $\mathbf{v}_{\text{idx}}$-th service object is unused in the abstract state from which the operation is performed. Afterwards, the atomic operation γ_{cok} initializes exactly the $\mathbf{v}_{\text{idx}}$-th service object. However, $\mathbf{v}_{\text{idx}}$ is arbitrary if it is the first value of the arbitrary list vl'. How to ensure that $\mathbf{v}_{\text{idx}}$ is the index found by γ_{iok} at the point where the operation γ_{cok} is performed?

We solve this problem by permitting the execution of an abstract statement to reach an *error state*. From the error state no further execution of the abstract statement is permitted. We adjust the refinement condition to express that the concrete system should be simulated by the abstract system *unless the abstract system is in an error state*. In the abstract program for service_obj_create, we define the atomic operation γ_{iok} such that an error state results if the parameter

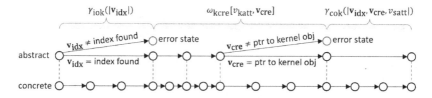

Fig. 5: Simulation for service_obj_create in the extended verification framework
(potential preemption before/after atomic operations omitted)

$\mathbf{v}_{idx}$ is not equal to the found index (see Fig. 5). Hence, if γ_{cok} is executed to simulate the concrete execution of service_obj_create, the previous execution of γ_{iok} could not have ended up in an error state. Thus, $\mathbf{v}_{idx}$ as used in γ_{cok} is equal to the index of the unused service object found by γ_{iok}.

By admitting the error states in the abstract computation, and extending the notion of refinement in CSL-R correspondingly, we permit using the output of operations in the subsequent abstract computation. In particular, this enables the compositional specification of the service functions — where the abstract programs of the kernel functions may produce results that are used in the abstract programs of the service functions. For sound reasoning about the new notion of refinement, we have also introduced new rules into the program logic. Formally, we have re-established the soundness of the verification framework.

Remark 1. In the μC/OS-II microkernel, the computation result of a critical region is rarely passed to another critical region via local variables or return values of functions. Correspondingly, it is unnecessary to capture the output value of an operation and pass this value to another operation in the abstract program of a function. Hence, the CSL-R framework for the verification of μC/OS-II was not originally designed to accommodate additional parameters like $\mathbf{v}_{idx}$ and $\mathbf{v}_{cre}$.

4.2   Expressing Assumptions about the User

A second use of the error states in the abstract computation (as discussed in Section 4.1) is to support the expression of assumptions about user data in the formal specification of the service functions.

For an example of these assumptions, consider a variant of the service function service-obj-create in Fig. 2 that works properly only if the argument satt satisfies a well-formedness condition. More concretely, suppose satt is intended to be a pointer to a struct. This struct contains several attributes for initializing the service object. However, the C language does not provide a feature to check whether satt really points to a well-formed struct that contains these attributes (like instanceof in Java). Hence, this check might not be implemented in the code of this variant of service_obj_create. Then, service_obj_create should be verified under the assumption that satt points to the right type of struct.

The above assumption can be naturally expressed in the pre-condition for a function, if the function is to be verified using an ordinary Hoare-style program logic. However, a service function is specified using an abstract program instead of pre/post-conditions in a refinement verification. Then, the assumption should be expressed in this abstract program. We express such an assumption in the definition of an atomic operation in the abstract program. More concretely, this atomic operation gives the error state if the assumed condition about user data is not satisfied. With our adjusted definition of simulation, the abstract system is required to simulate the concrete system only if the abstract system is not in an error state (see Section 4.1). This corresponds to the meaning of assumptions — the refinement of the abstract programs by the concrete code is only required if the assumptions about user data are satisfied.

5   Reasoning about Service-Kernel Connection

Through refinement verification of an OS service, we establish the simulation between the execution of the service functions and the execution of their abstract programs (see Section 4.1). This simulation preserves the global invariant.

We express Requirement 1 and Requirement 2 (see Section 2) in the global invariant to show that the satisfaction of both requirements is preserved in the simulation. As explained in Section 2, the establishment of Condition 1 and Condition 2 is supportive of showing the fulfillment of Requirement 1 and Requirement 2. The two conditions can be established if they are also formulated in the global invariant, and are shown to be preserved in the simulation. However, these two conditions involve the program location that is local to a task, as well as a task-local pointer to a kernel object. These parameters cannot be directly expressed in the global invariant. In this section, we explain how to capture the program location and the kernel object pointer for each task using auxiliary variables with fractional permission (Section 5.2). We then present a design of invariant conditions that depends on these auxiliary variables (Section 5.3). We are able to show that Condition 1 and Condition 2 are preserved by the execution of each service function, with the help of the invariant conditions.

The satisfaction of Condition 1 and Condition 2 depends on the way each service function affects the connection between a service object and its underlying kernel object. Hence, we will first present a series of code patterns for service functions that capture a proper way to handle this connection (Section 5.1).

5.1   Creation, Deletion, and Use of Service Objects

We assume that the service functions for creating, deleting, and using a service object possess the code patterns in Fig. 6. The scope of critical regions is represented by the dashed boxes. A line with the content Check cond represents a conditional that checks the condition cond. A return from the function is triggered if the check fails. Before each return from inside a critical region, the critical region is exited first. A line in the non-bold face represents an assignment to an auxiliary variable. These assignments will be explained later.

Creation of Service Objects. The function service_obj_create is used to create a service object. The code pattern of this function is shown in Fig. 6a. This code pattern is the same as in Fig. 2, except for containing two extra assignments to auxiliary variables. In addition, the code pattern for the underlying kernel function kernel_obj_create is given in the upper part of Fig. 6b.

```
service_obj_create(katt, satt):
  local idx, p
┌─────────────────────────────────────┐
│ idx <- get_free_obj(obj_arr)        │
│ Check valid(idx)                    │
│ obj_arr[idx].ptr <- Dummy           │
└─────────────────────────────────────┘
  p <- kernel_obj_create(katt)
┌─────────────────────────────────────┐
│ obj_arr[idx].ptr <- p               │
│ Check p != NULL                     │
│ obj_arr[idx].att <- satt            │
│ CurTask->_loc <-_Loc_normal         │
│ CurTask->_ptr <- NULL               │
└─────────────────────────────────────┘
  return idx
```

(a) creation of service objects

```
kernel_obj_create(katt):
  local p
┌─────────────────────────────────────┐
│ // p <- allocate kernel obj.        │
│ // initialize kernel obj.           │
│ CurTask->_loc <-_Loc_cre            │
│ CurTask->_ptr <- p                  │
└─────────────────────────────────────┘
  return p
kernel_obj_delete(p):
┌─────────────────────────────────────┐
│ // delete kernel obj. at p          │
│ CurTask->_loc <-_Loc_normal         │
│ CurTask->_ptr <- NULL               │
└─────────────────────────────────────┘
  return
```

(b) kernel obj. creation/deletion

```
service_obj_oper(idx):
  local p, err
┌─────────────────────────────────────┐
│ Check valid(idx)                    │
│ Check cond(obj_arr[idx].att)        │
│ p <- obj_arr[idx].ptr               │
│ Check p != NULL && p != Dummy       │
│ CurTask->_ptr <- p                  │
└─────────────────────────────────────┘
  err <- kernel_obj_oper(p)
┌─────────────────────────────────────┐
│ CurTask->_ptr <- NULL               │
└─────────────────────────────────────┘
  return err
```

(c) use of service objects

```
service_obj_delete(idx):
  local p
┌─────────────────────────────────────┐
│ Check valid(idx)                    │
│ p <- obj_arr[idx].ptr               │
│ Check p != NULL && p != Dummy       │
│ obj_arr[idx].ptr <- NULL            │
│ CurTask->_loc <-_Loc_del            │
│ CurTask->_ptr <- p                  │
└─────────────────────────────────────┘
  kernel_obj_delete(p)
  return
```

(d) deletion of service objects

Fig. 6: The patterns for creation/deletion/use of service/kernel objects

Deletion of Service Objects. The function service_obj_delete (Fig. 6d) is used to delete a service object. The deleted service object is the one represented by the array element obj_arr[idx]. Here, idx is the argument of the function. The function first checks to ensure that idx is within the array bound for obj_arr. Then, the function remembers the kernel object pointer obj_arr[idx].ptr in the local variable p. Afterwards, the function checks if the pointer p is neither NULL nor Dummy. If so, then obj_arr[idx] should represent a valid service object. The function then sets obj_arr[idx].ptr to NULL. Finally, the function invokes the kernel function kernel_obj_delete (Fig. 6b) to free the kernel object pointed to by p.

Use of Service Objects. The function service_obj_oper (Fig. 6c) outlines the general pattern for an operation on a service object. First, the validity of the index for the target service object is checked. Then, it is checked whether the attribute value of the service object satisfies the conditions for performing the intended operation. Next, it is checked whether the pointer to the kernel object obj_arr[idx].ptr is valid. If so, the kernel function kernel_obj_oper performing the corresponding operation on the underlying kernel object is invoked.

5.2   Auxiliary Variables with Fractional Permission

We introduce an auxiliary variable, _ptr, for each task. This auxiliary variable
reflects the value of the local pointer p at key program locations in the functions of Fig. 6. We employ fractional permission for _ptr. Half of the permission
over _ptr is given to the global invariant. Hence, _ptr can be read in the global
invariant. Half of the permission over _ptr is retained by the task for which _ptr
is introduced. Hence, _ptr can be used to reflect the value of a local pointer.

Via built-in mechanisms of CSL-R, we ensure that whenever a task enters
a service function, the value of _ptr is NULL. This captures that the task is not
working with a kernel object when entering a service function. When the task
running a service function gets hold of a kernel object via p, we set _ptr of the
task to the value of p. For service_obj_create, this is at the end of the critical
region in the underlying kernel function kernel_obj_create — when the kernel
object has just been created. For service_obj_delete and service_obj_oper, this is at
the end of their first critical regions. We reset _ptr to NULL when the task loses
hold of the kernel object. For service_obj_delete, this is at the end of the critical
region in the kernel function kernel_obj_delete — when the kernel object has just
been freed. For service_obj_create and service_obj_oper, this is at their end.

We introduce an auxiliary variable, _loc, for each task. This auxiliary variable
reflects the current program location of the task. We employ fractional permission for _loc. Half of the permission over _loc is given to the global invariant.
Hence, this variable can be read in the global invariant. Half of the permission
over _loc is retained by the task for which _loc is introduced. Hence, the program
location of each task cannot be modified by a different task.

Via built-in mechanisms of CSL-R, we ensure that whenever a task enters a
service function, the value of _loc is _Loc_normal. This reflects that the task is
not at a special program location concerning object creation or deletion when
entering a service function. When a task running a service function starts to
work with a kernel object, we distinguish between the cases for object creation
and object deletion, by setting _loc to different values. We set _loc to _Loc_cre
for object creation (see Fig. 6b). We set _loc to _Loc_del for object deletion (see
Fig. 6d). We reset _loc to _Loc_normal when the task stops working with the
underlying kernel object. If the service function executed is service_obj_oper, then
_loc remains at the value _Loc_normal through the execution of the function.

5.3   Invariant Conditions Dependent on Auxiliary Variables

Via the auxiliary variables, _loc and _ptr, we are able to formalize Condition 1
and Condition 2. The formulation of these conditions is simpler if the abstract
representations of data are used instead of the concrete counterpart. We use
locmp to represent a function from each task identifier to an optional value
of the auxiliary variable _loc for the task. We use *ptrmp* to represent a function
from each task identifier to an optional value of auxiliary variable _ptr for the
task. We also introduce the abstract representations of the service objects and the
kernel objects. We use *sobjmp* to represent a function that maps each index value
i to an optional tuple. The tuple represents the service object obj_arr[idx] if idx

$sobj\_kobj\_aux(locmp, ptrmp, sobjmp, kobjmp, fkobjs) :=$

$\forall t, a : ptrmp(t) = \mathsf{Some} \ (Vptr \ a) \Rightarrow$

$$\left(\begin{array}{l} \left(\begin{array}{l} locmp(t) = \mathsf{Some} \ \_\mathsf{Loc\_cre} \land \\ \boxed{kobjmp(a) \neq \mathsf{None}}^{①} \land \boxed{\neg obj\_ref(sobjmp, a)}^{②} \land \boxed{\neg ptr\_in\_fkobj\_pool(a, fkobjs)}^{③} \end{array} \right) \\ \lor \left(\begin{array}{l} locmp(t) = \mathsf{Some} \ \_\mathsf{Loc\_del} \land \\ \boxed{kobjmp(a) \neq \mathsf{None}}^{④} \land \boxed{\neg obj\_ref(sobjmp, a)}^{⑤} \end{array} \right) \\ \lor \left(\begin{array}{l} locmp(t) = \mathsf{Some} \ \_\mathsf{Loc\_normal} \land \\ (\boxed{kobjmp(a) \neq \mathsf{None}}^{⑥} \lor \boxed{ptr\_in\_fkobj\_pool(a, fkobjs)}^{⑦}) \end{array} \right) \end{array} \right)$$

where $obj\_ref(sobjmp, a) := \exists i, att : sobjmp(i) = \mathsf{Some} \ (KObj \ a, att)$

and $ptr\_in\_fkobj\_pool(a, fkobjs)$ means a is the address of some free kernel object

---

$cre\_del\_mut\_ex(locmp, ptrmp) :=$

$\quad \forall t_1, t_2, a : (locmp(t_1) \in \{\_\mathsf{Loc\_cre}, \_\mathsf{Loc\_del}\} \land ptrmp(t_1) = \mathsf{Some} \ (Vptr \ a)) \Rightarrow$
$\quad\quad (locmp(t_2) \in \{\_\mathsf{Loc\_cre}, \_\mathsf{Loc\_del}\} \land ptrmp(t_2) = \mathsf{Some} \ (Vptr \ a)) \Rightarrow$
$\quad\quad t_1 = t_2$

Fig. 7: The invariant conditions $sobj\_kobj\_aux$ and $cre\_del\_mut\_ex$

has the value i. More concretely, we have $sobjmp(i) = \mathsf{Some} \ (KObj \ a, att)$ if the value of obj_arr[idx].ptr is a, and the value of obj_arr[idx].att is att. Furthermore, we use $kobjmp$ to represent a function that maps the address of each active kernel object to the abstract representation of the kernel object. Hence, the expression $kobjmp(a) \neq \mathsf{None}$ means that there is an active kernel object at the address a.

We devise the condition $sobj\_kobj\_aux(locmp, ptrmp, sobjmp, kobjmp, fkobjs)$ as shown in Fig. 7. We make this condition a part of the global invariant. According to this condition, if a task with the identifier t is working with the kernel object at the address a (i.e., $ptrmp(t) = \mathsf{Some} \ (Vptr \ a)$), then the task could be at a special program location for object creation, at a special program location for object deletion, or not at one of these special program locations. These three cases are reflected by a disjunctive normal form in $sobj\_kobj\_aux$.

The Use of the Invariant Condition sobj_kobj_aux. The invariant condition $sobj\_kobj\_aux$ becomes available to the reasoning task after each critical region is entered. The contents of the parameters $locmp$, $ptrmp$, $sobjmp$, $kobjmp$, and $fkobjs$ correspond to the concrete data they represent. The specific parts ①-⑨ can be exploited depending on the values of the auxiliary variables.

We are able to capture Condition 1 and Condition 2 in Section 2 using $sobj\_kobj\_aux$. If a task t has just completed the assignment p<-kernel_obj_create(katt) in the function service_obj_create, then the task is at a special program location for object creation (i.e., $locmp(t) = \mathsf{Some} \ \_\mathsf{Loc\_cre}$). Hence, Condition 1 in Section 2 is captured by the condition ① in Fig. 7. Furthermore, Condition 2 in Section 2 is captured by the condition ② in Fig. 7. Condition ② is expressed using the predicate *obj_ref*. The definition of this predicate is given below the definition of *sobj_kobj_aux* in the upper part of Fig. 7.

We next explain the use of the condition ④. When a task is in the function kernel_obj_delete (hence at _Loc_del), the task resets the members of the kernel object pointed to by p to their initial values. Condition ④ says that p points to an active kernel object. This helps ensure the safety of the dereferencing operation on p. The condition ⑥∨⑦ serves an analogous purpose. When a task is in the function kernel_obj_oper (hence at _Loc_normal), the task dereferences the pointer p to access the members of the kernel object. The condition ⑥∨⑦ says that p points to a kernel object that is either active or in the pool of the free kernel objects. Thus, the safety of the dereferencing operation is ensured. Here, the disjunction of ⑥ with ⑦ is necessary. This is because before the task enters kernel_obj_oper, the task can be preempted by another task. The latter task could invoke service_obj_delete, obtain the pointer to the kernel object, and free the kernel object in kernel_obj_delete. This deletion does not cause trouble to the execution of kernel_obj_oper — a sensible design of kernel_obj_oper would check whether the kernel object to be used has been freed. This check can be implemented using a data member of kernel objects.

The Proof Obligations for sobj_kobj_aux. Since *sobj_kobj_aux* is specified as a part of the global invariant, a proof obligation in the verification of the service functions is to establish *sobj_kobj_aux* where a critical region is exited. Further invariant conditions are supplied for fulfilling this proof obligation.

Suppose a task with identifier t is about to return to the service function service_obj_create from the kernel function kernel_obj_create. There, we have $locmp(t) =$ Some _Loc_cre. In addition, if the local pointer p has the value a, then we have $ptrmp(t) =$ Some ($Vptr\ a$). Hence, condition ① in *sobj_kobj_aux* requires that there be an active kernel object at the address a. Consider a potential case where the task t is preempted by a different task t', which happens to be entering the function kernel_obj_delete, with the address a as the value for the parameter p. At the point where t' exits from the critical region in kernel_obj_delete, condition ① cannot be established for t. This is because the kernel object at a would have been freed by the task t' — this kernel object is no longer active.

To show that the aforementioned scenario involving the tasks t and t' is impossible, we introduce another condition, $cre\_del\_mut\_ex$, into the global invariant (see bottom part of Fig. 7). The condition says that the actual accesses of the special program locations marked by _Loc_cre and _Loc_del are mutually exclusive, among all the accessing tasks that deal with the same kernel object at some address a. Consider the point where task t' enters the critical region in kernel_obj_delete. The task is then at the program location _Loc_del. If task t is about to return from kernel_obj_create, the task is at the program location _Loc_cre. Hence, the kernel object dealt with by t cannot be the kernel object that is dealt with by t', according to the invariant condition $cre\_del\_mut\_ex$. While task t' is in the critical region of kernel_obj_delete, no other task can execute. Hence, the kernel object dealt with by t cannot be the kernel object dealt with (deleted) by t', when task t' exits the critical region of kernel_obj_delete.

The Proof Obligations for cre_del_mut_ex. Since *cre_del_mut_ex* is specified as a part of the global invariant, a proof obligation in the verification of the
service functions is to establish *cre_del_mut_ex* where a critical region is exited.

For instance, when a task t exits from the critical region in service_obj_delete,
the task gets to the program location _Loc_del. Hence, it should be ascertained
that there is no other task at the program location _Loc_cre, and working with
the kernel object pointed to by the local pointer p in service_obj_delete. Consider
the point where task t has just completed the assignment p<-obj_arr[idx].ptr
in the aforementioned critical region. There, the kernel object O_{knl} pointed
to by p is referenced from a service object. From ② in the invariant condition *sobj_kobj_aux*, if a task t' is at the program location _Loc_cre and working
with a kernel object O'_{knl}, this O'_{knl} is not referenced from any service object.
Hence, O'_{knl} must be different from O_{knl}. Since the other tasks do not execute
while the task t is in a critical region, there is still no task at _Loc_cre and
working with the kernel object O_{knl}, when the task t exits from the critical
region in service_obj_delete. In addition, conditions ③ and ⑤ in the definition
of *sobj_kobj_aux* are also used to establish the condition *cre_del_mut_ex* where
some of the critical regions are exited. We do not expand on the details.

Summary of Invariant Design. The invariant conditions dependent on auxiliary variables enable the establishment of structural integrity properties about
the connection from service objects to kernel objects. This provides a solid foundation for formally verifying the service functions (if they are implemented with
the expected code patterns) based on a microkernel that is already verified in
CSL-R. We provide the formalized code, formal specifications, and correctness
proofs for the functions in Fig. 6 as part of the accompanying artifact.

6 Experimental Evaluation

We apply our methodology in the formal verification of a group of inter-task
synchronization and communication services implemented as an extension to the
preemptive microkernel μC/OS-II. These services are developed by a separate
group of people for safety-critical usage scenarios (e.g., in aerospace vehicles,
self-driving cars, etc). The services provide functions for manipulating mutexes,
semaphores, and message queues. These service objects extend the corresponding
kernel objects of μC/OS-II. For instance, a service-level mutex can be recursive
or non-recursive, a service-level semaphore can be binary or counting, and a
service-level message queue can be blocking or non-blocking. This fine-grained
distinction of object types is not supported by the corresponding kernel objects
of μC/OS-II. We discuss some key aspects of our formal verification below.

Application of the Methodology. Almost all the interface functions for the
inter-task synchronization and communication services invoke the underlying
functions of μC/OS-II to complete operations on kernel objects. This invocation
is usually performed outside of critical regions. For instance, the service function
could be pthread_mutex_lock for obtaining a service-level mutex, and the corresponding kernel function of μC/OS-II would be OSMutexPend. We are able to

compose the specifications of the service functions from the specifications of the corresponding kernel functions in the extended CSL-R verification framework (see Section 4.1). In addition, the service objects are often initialized with pointers to dedicated structs containing attribute values. Our extension to the CSL-R framework also enables us to express the assumption that each of these pointers points to a well-formed struct of the appropriate type.

Almost all the service functions are implemented following the code patterns in Fig. 6. For each kind of service (for mutexes, semaphores, and message queues), we use the method in Section 5 to establish the structural properties about the connection between service objects and kernel objects. A complication arises because μC/OS-II has a common pool for kernel objects of different kinds. On the other hand, each kind of service object is represented using a different struct, and organized in a separate array. In the verification, we establish that each kind of service object in use references a kernel object *of the same kind*, and each kernel object is referenced by at most one service object *of the same kind*.

Verification Efforts. The source code for the interface functions and the newly implemented internal functions totals 1561 lines. Our proof code for these functions totals approximately 49k lines. The statistics about the lines of source code and the lines of proof code for our verification of the interface functions for the mutex service are given in Table 1. The corresponding statistics for the verification of the other two services are omitted for space reasons. The overall ratio between the verified code and the verification code is about 1:31. This ratio is on par with that in the formal verification of μC/OS-II [28, 27]. Owing to the compositional specification of the service functions, we did not need to re-develop the proofs for the microkernel. Hence, we were able to devote more efforts to establishing the structural properties of the connection between the service level and kernel level, which made the verification of the services possible. It took approximately 3 person years to complete the verification. This included 6 person months for extending the CSL-R framework as well as designing and stabilizing all the invariants that connect the service level and the kernel level.

Table 1: The statistics about the formal proofs for the mutex service

Service Function	Source LOC	Proof LOC	Service Function	Source LOC	Proof LOC
pthread_mutex_init	76	1986	pthread_mutexattr_init	60	1150
pthread_mutex_destroy	33	605	pthread_mutexattr_destroy	21	506
pthread_mutex_lock	99	2514	pthread_mutexattr_gettype	36	654
pthread_mutex_trylock	96	2457	pthread_mutexattr_settype	38	705
pthread_mutex_timedlock	106	2765	pthread_mutexattr_getprioceiling	38	726
pthread_mutex_unlock	97	2563	pthread_mutexattr_setprioceiling	39	732

Problems and Fixes. Through formal verification, we uncovered several problems in the code of the inter-task synchronization and communication services. This code had been extensively tested before our verification started. The most common cause for the uncovered problems is the absence of big enough critical regions that ensure the uninterruptible execution of code. The problem with the most complicated cause is: If four tasks create and delete service objects concurrently, service objects that are out-of-sync with their corresponding kernel objects can be brought into existence. For instance, a service-level mutex could start to reference a kernel-level message queue, and a binary service-level semaphore could start to reference a kernel-level semaphore with a value of 10. We uncovered part of the problems after realizing that the services could not be shown to preserve some of the conditions in the global invariant — but these conditions captured the required or intended behaviors of the services.

We reported the uncovered problems to the developers of the OS services. They performed three main types of modifications to the code. The first was enlarging a critical region. The second was adjusting the order of operations. The third was introducing dedicated mechanisms to avoid races over global resources. An example modification to the code was the following. The initial implementation of the service function mq_delete invoked the kernel function OSQDel before it set the pointer from a service queue to the underlying kernel queue to NULL. This order was later reversed such that it agreed with the code pattern of service_obj_delete in Fig. 6d. The reason for this reversion was that the original order was found to cause the existence of service objects that are inconsistent with their underlying kernel objects in a highly concurrent setting.

7   Related Work

Our focus is the formal verification of functional correctness for OS services, building on the verification results for an underlying OS kernel. However, our methodology is also applicable if the service functions are implemented inside the kernel. Hence, one type of related work is the formal verification of OS kernels.

In the literature, there are several developments about the formal verification of OS kernels at the implementation level. The seL4 operating system is formally verified in terms of functional correctness and information security [21, 20]. In the Verisoft project, an operating system kernel encompassing assembly code and device drivers is formally verified [5, 4]. CertikOS [18, 17] is a formally verified concurrent OS. It is carefully organized in layers to facilitate verification. The commercial preemptive microkernel μC/OS-II is formally verified in terms of the functional correctness of the API functions [28, 27]. In [11], queue data structures for inter-process communication are verified using the Iris framework [2].

Like our work, the aforementioned developments verify operating system code using a proof assistant such as Isabelle [23] or Coq [1]. Unlike our work, these developments are not focused on the formal verification of code that builds on an OS kernel, by building on prior verification results for the kernel. Our verification is performed for a group of inter-task synchronization and communication services. On the other hand, the verification performed in the aforementioned related developments either has a comprehensive coverage of the functionalities of an OS, or targets a different component than our verification does.

Apart from the aforementioned related work, several developments (e.g. [25, 12, 13, 24, 22, 6, 7, 29]) formally verify operating systems at a more abstract level than we do, or via an approach that is different from ours – such as through model checking or requiring trust in external solvers (e.g., Z3 [15]). In addition, some of the existing works [20, 14, 30] verify the security properties of operating systems, instead of functional correctness as we verify in the present work.

Our work is about the formal verification of concurrent programs in a broad sense. Notable verification frameworks in this regard include Iris [19] and VST [10]. These frameworks have no builtin support for the type of concurrency in a preemptive OS kernel, where the switch between threads is triggered via interrupt handling. Our use of the auxiliary variables with fractional permission helps express a protocol followed by the concurrent tasks that manipulate the service objects. In the literature, there exist techniques with dedicated abstractions for expressing the protocols followed by concurrent threads. An example abstraction is a state transition system [26]. In the present work, our focus is to achieve the required verification by maximally exploiting the features of the verification framework for the underlying microkernel. Hence, we have not introduced further abstractions for the expression of protocols. Due to space limits, we stop here in our discussion about related work in concurrent program verification.

8   Conclusion

We address the problems in formally verifying a group of OS services that build on a preemptive microkernel, in case the microkernel itself has been formally verified. Specifically, the verification of the microkernel has been a refinement verification performed using a concurrent separation logic that supports fractional permission. Our aim is to build sufficiently on the verification framework and verification code for the microkernel, in verifying the code of the services. Our methodology consists of enhancements to the verification framework that enable the compositional specification of the service functions, as well as a design of invariants for establishing structural integrity properties about the connection between the service level and the kernel level. We use the methodology to accomplish a substantial verification task targeting a group of inter-task synchronization and communication services based on the preemptive microkernel μC/OS-II. The verification uncovers dormant bugs and provides a level of correctness assurance that is above what can be achieved through extensive testing.

A potential direction for future work is the design of deductive systems that facilitate the verification of global properties for a service, based on the abstract programs of all the interface functions of a service. Another direction for future work is the verification of progress properties for the functions of a service.

Data-Availability Statements. The mechanized extension to the CSL-R verification framework and proofs for the OS service in abstract form (as described in Section 4 and Section 5) are published at Zenodo (`10.5281/zenodo.10456998`).

Acknowledgments. This work was partially supported by the National Natural Science Foundation of China (62002246, 62272322, 62272323, 62372311, 62372312). We thank Xinyu Feng for help with the CSL-R verification framework. We thank Qinxiang Cao and Bohua Zhan for advices on some of the technical ingredients facilitating the completion of our work. We thank the anonymous reviewers for providing valuable feedback that helped improve our presentation.

References

1. The Coq proof assistant. `https://coq.inria.fr/`. Accessed: 2023-10-08.
2. Iris – a higher-order concurrent separation logic framework, implemented and verified in the Coq proof assistant. `https://iris-project.org/`. Accessed: 2023-10-12.
3. μC/OS-II. `https://www.osrtos.com/rtos/uc-os-ii/`. Accessed: 2023-10-08.
4. Eyad Alkassar, Mark A. Hillebrand, Dirk Leinenbach, Norbert Schirmer, and Artem Starostin. The Verisoft approach to systems verification. In *Proceedings of Second International Conference on Verified Software: Theories, Tools, Experiments (VSTTE)*, pages 209–224, 2008.
5. Eyad Alkassar, Wolfgang J. Paul, Artem Starostin, and Alexandra Tsyban. Pervasive verification of an OS microkernel - inline assembly, memory consumption, concurrent devices. In *Proceedings of Third International Conference on Verified Software: Theories, Tools, Experiments (VSTTE)*, pages 71–85, 2010.
6. June Andronick, Corey Lewis, and Carroll Morgan. Controlled Owicki-Gries concurrency: Reasoning about the preemptible eChronos embedded operating system. In *Proceedings of Workshop on Models for Formal Analysis of Real Systems, (MARS)*, pages 10–24, 2015.
7. Bernhard Beckert and Michal Moskal. Deductive verification of system software in the Verisoft XT project. *Künstliche Intell.*, 24(1):57–61, 2010.
8. John Boyland. Checking interference with fractional permissions. In *Proceedings of 10th International Symposium on Static Analysis (SAS)*, pages 55–72, 2003.
9. Stephen Brookes and Peter W. O'Hearn. Concurrent separation logic. *ACM SIGLOG News*, 3(3):47–65, 2016.
10. Qinxiang Cao, Lennart Beringer, Samuel Gruetter, Josiah Dodds, and Andrew W. Appel. VST-Floyd: A separation logic tool to verify correctness of C programs. *Journal of Automated Reasoning*, 61(1-4):367–422, 2018.
11. Quentin Carbonneaux, Noam Zilberstein, Christoph Klee, Peter W. O'Hearn, and Francesco Zappa Nardelli. Applying formal verification to microkernel IPC at Meta. In *Proceedings of 11th ACM SIGPLAN International Conference on Certified Programs and Proofs (CPP)*, pages 116–129, 2022.
12. Shu Cheng, Jim Woodcock, and Deepak D'Souza. Using formal reasoning on a model of tasks for FreeRTOS. *Formal Aspects of Computing*, 27(1):167–192, 2015.
13. Nathan Chong and Bart Jacobs. Formally verifying FreeRTOS' interprocess communication mechanism. In *Embedded World Exhibition & Conference*, 2021.
14. David Costanzo, Zhong Shao, and Ronghui Gu. End-to-end verification of information-flow security for C and assembly programs. In *Proceedings of the 37th ACM SIGPLAN Conference on Programming Language Design and Implementation (PLDI)*, pages 648–664, 2016.
15. Leonardo Mendonça de Moura and Nikolaj S. Bjørner. Z3: an efficient SMT solver. In *Proceedings of 14th International Conference on Tools and Algorithms for the Construction and Analysis of Systems (TACAS), Held as Part of ETAPS*, pages 337–340, 2008.
16. Mike Gordon and Hélène Collavizza. Forward with Hoare. In A. W. Roscoe, Clifford B. Jones, and Kenneth R. Wood, editors, *Reflections on the Work of C. A. R. Hoare*, pages 101–121. Springer, 2010.
17. Ronghui Gu, Zhong Shao, Hao Chen, Jieung Kim, Jérémie Koenig, Xiongnan (Newman) Wu, Vilhelm Sjöberg, and David Costanzo. Building certified concurrent OS kernels. *Communications of the ACM*, 62(10):89–99, 2019.

18. Ronghui Gu, Zhong Shao, Hao Chen, Xiongnan (Newman) Wu, Jieung Kim, Vilhelm Sjöberg, and David Costanzo. CertiKOS: An extensible architecture for building certified concurrent OS kernels. In *Proceedings of 12th USENIX Symposium on Operating Systems Design and Implementation (OSDI)*, pages 653–669, 2016.
19. Ralf Jung, Robbert Krebbers, Jacques-Henri Jourdan, Ales Bizjak, Lars Birkedal, and Derek Dreyer. Iris from the ground up: A modular foundation for higher-order concurrent separation logic. *Journal of Functional Programming*, 28:e20, 2018.
20. Gerwin Klein, June Andronick, Kevin Elphinstone, Toby C. Murray, Thomas Sewell, Rafal Kolanski, and Gernot Heiser. Comprehensive formal verification of an OS microkernel. *ACM Transactions on Computer Systems*, 32(1):2:1–2:70, 2014.
21. Gerwin Klein, Kevin Elphinstone, Gernot Heiser, June Andronick, David A. Cock, Philip Derrin, Dhammika Elkaduwe, Kai Engelhardt, Rafal Kolanski, Michael Norrish, Thomas Sewell, Harvey Tuch, and Simon Winwood. seL4: formal verification of an OS kernel. In *Proceedings of 22nd ACM Symposium on Operating Systems Principles (SOSP)*, pages 207–220, 2009.
22. Luke Nelson, Helgi Sigurbjarnarson, Kaiyuan Zhang, Dylan Johnson, James Bornholt, Emina Torlak, and Xi Wang. Hyperkernel: Push-button verification of an OS kernel. In *Proceedings of the 26th Symposium on Operating Systems Principles (SOSP)*, pages 252–269, 2017.
23. Tobias Nipkow, Lawrence C. Paulson, and Markus Wenzel. *Isabelle/HOL - A Proof Assistant for Higher-Order Logic*, volume 2283 of *Lecture Notes in Computer Science*. Springer, 2002.
24. Evgeny Novikov and Ilja S. Zakharov. Verification of operating system monolithic kernels without extensions. In *Proceedings of 8th International Symposium on Leveraging Applications of Formal Methods, Verification and Validation (ISoLA), Part IV*, pages 230–248, 2018.
25. Leandro Batista Ribeiro, Florian Lorber, Ulrik Nyman, Kim Guldstrand Larsen, and Marcel Baunach. A modeling concept for formal verification of OS-based compositional software. In *Proceedings of 26th International Conference on Fundamental Approaches to Software Engineering (FASE), Held as Part of ETAPS*, pages 26–46, 2023.
26. Aaron Joseph Turon, Jacob Thamsborg, Amal Ahmed, Lars Birkedal, and Derek Dreyer. Logical relations for fine-grained concurrency. In *Proceedings of the 40th Annual ACM SIGPLAN-SIGACT Symposium on Principles of Programming Languages (POPL)*, pages 343–356, 2013.
27. Fengwei Xu. *Design and Implementation of A Verification Framework for Preemptive OS Kernels*. PhD thesis, University of Science and Technology of China, 2016.
28. Fengwei Xu, Ming Fu, Xinyu Feng, Xiaoran Zhang, Hui Zhang, and Zhaohui Li. A practical verification framework for preemptive OS kernels. In *Proceedings of 28th International Conference on Computer Aided Verification (CAV)*, pages 59–79, 2016.
29. Jean Yang and Chris Hawblitzel. Safe to the last instruction: automated verification of a type-safe operating system. In *Proceedings of the 2010 ACM SIGPLAN Conference on Programming Language Design and Implementation (PLDI)*, pages 99–110, 2010.
30. Yongwang Zhao, David Sanán, Fuyuan Zhang, and Yang Liu. Refinement-based specification and security analysis of separation kernels. *IEEE Transactions on Dependable and Secure Computing*, 16(1):127–141, 2019.

Fuzzy quantitative attack tree analysis

Thi Kim Nhung Dang[1]([✉])[iD], Milan Lopuhaä-Zwakenberg[1][iD],
and Mariëlle Stoelinga[1,2][iD]

[1] University of Twente, Enschede, The Netherlands
{t.k.n.dang,m.a.lopuhaa,m.i.a.stoelinga}@utwente.nl
[2] Radboud University, Nijmegen, The Netherlands
m.stoelinga@cs.ru.nl

Abstract. Attack trees are important for security, as they help to identify weaknesses and vulnerabilities in a system. Quantitative attack tree
analysis supports a number security metrics, which formulate important
KPIs such as the shortest, most likely and cheapest attacks.

A key bottleneck in quantitative analysis is that the values are usually
not known exactly, due to insufficient data and/or lack of knowledge.
Fuzzy logic is a prominent framework to handle such uncertain values,
with applications in numerous domains. While several studies proposed
fuzzy approaches to attack tree analysis, none of them provided a firm
definition of fuzzy metric values or generic algorithms for computation
of fuzzy metrics.

In this work, we define a generic formulation for fuzzy metric values that
applies to most quantitative metrics. The resulting metric value is a fuzzy
number obtained by following Zadeh's extension principle, obtained when
we equip the basis attack steps, i.e., the leaves of the attack trees, with
fuzzy numbers. In addition, we prove a modular decomposition theorem
that yields a bottom-up algorithm to efficiently calculate the top fuzzy
metric value.

Keywords: Attack trees · quantitative analysis · fuzzy numbers.

1 Introduction

Attack trees. Attack trees (ATs) [32] are a popular tool for modeling and analyzing security risks. They provide a structural way to identify vulnerabilities
in a system, by decomposing the attacker's goal into subgoals, down to basic
attack steps that a malicious actor can take to reach said objective. An attack
tree consists of basic attack steps (BASs) representing atomic adversary actions,
and intermediate AND/OR-gates whose activation depends on the activation of
their children. The attacker's goal is to activate the root (top node), see Fig. 1
for an example. ATs can be trees or directed acyclic graphs (DAGs). ATs have
been supported by commercial tools [1–3] and equipped with semantics [25, 18].

© The Author(s) 2024
D. Beyer and A. Cavalcanti (Eds.): FASE 2024, LNCS 14573, pp. 210–231, 2024.
https://doi.org/10.1007/978-3-031-57259-3_10

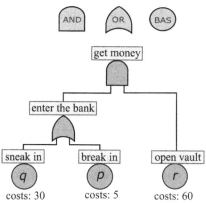

Fig. 1: The AT model visualises the attack steps by which an attacker can illegally take money from a bank. The attacker needs to enter the bank by breaking in or sneaking in, and also needs to open a vault. Sneaking in, breaking in, and opening a vault cost 30, 5 and 60 minutes, respectively. Hence, the quantitative metric minimal cost for the attacks is $\min(30 + 60, 5 + 60) = 65$.

Quantitative analysis. Beyond qualitative analysis, ATs are also used to calculate important security metrics of the system, e.g., the minimal cost (in money, time or resources) the attacker needs to spend for a succesful attack, or the probability of a succesful attack. Such metrics are obtained by assigning an attribute value to each BAS, such as the cost needed to perform that BAS, and using this as input to calculate the security metric. When the AT is treeshaped, the metric is quickly calculated using a bottom-up algorithm, propagating values from the BASs to the top. For DAG-shaped ATs this problem is NP-complete, but good heuristics exist [22]. These algorithms are formulated in the generic algebraic structure of semirings, allowing them to be employed to a vast range of security metrics including cost, time, skill, damage, etc.

Uncertain parameters. The methods described above assume that all BAS parameters are known exactly. However, this is problematic in practice: statistics on attacker capabilities may be hard to obtain, and because of the fast-changing nature of the field historical data are only of limited use. Obtaining accurate and realistic parameter values is a key bottleneck in quantitative security analysis. In its absence, there is a great need for methods that allow us to deal with uncertain and approximately known parameter values.

Fuzzy theory. Fuzzy theory is a prominent framework in which parameter uncertainty and its effect on a calculation's outcome can be expressed mathematically. It has been successfully used in many applications, including machine learning [7], reliability engineering [6], and computational linguistics [24]. Rather than exact ('crisp') values, e.g., $x = 3$, each parameter is assigned a range of values, and to each of these a possibility value in $[0, 1]$ is assigned by means of a *mem-*

bership function. Often, only functions of a specific form are considered, leading to the definition of triangular, trapezoidal, etc. fuzzy numbers [13].

While fuzzy theory has been applied to AT analysis before [17, 35, 19, 11, 36], much of the earlier work lacks mathematical rigor, and none of these apply fuzzy theory to quantitative analysis. As a result, there are no algorithms for calculating AT metrics with fuzzy parameters. In fact, to our knowledge the fuzzy counterpart of quantitative AT analysis has not been defined yet. A key technical hurdle is that the operations typically used in AT analysis do not preserve popular fuzzy number types: for instance, the OR-gate corresponds to the operation min for the minimal cost metric, and applying min to two triangular fuzzy numbers does not yield a triangular fuzzy number.

Contributions. Our first contribution is a clear, mathematically rigorous definition of fuzzy AT metrics. Because these are defined for general fuzzy numbers, rather than specific subtypes such as triangular fuzzy numbers, we sidestep the problem that these subtypes are not preserved under AT metric operations; instead, our definition works for the generic semiring framework defined in [22]. We show that our definition naturally follows from Zadeh's extension principle [38], a general approach for extending functions to fuzzy numbers.

Having defined fuzzy AT metrics, we furthermore develop a linear-time, bottom-up algorithm for calculating them for tree-shaped ATs. We show the validity of this algorithm by showing that fuzzy AT metrics are susceptible to *modular analysis*: when an AT has a module, i.e., a minimally connected subcomponent, a fuzzy metric can be computed by first calculating the metric for the module and then for its complement. When an AT has many modules, this substantially speeds up computation. When an AT is tree-shaped, every node is a module, proving the validity of the algorithm.

Our algorithm generalizes the bottom-up algorithm for crisp AT metrics from [22]. Unfortunately, the algorithm for DAG-shaped metrics from that paper does not transfer to the fuzzy setting. The key reason is that fuzzy numbers do not form a semiring, as we show in this paper. Fuzzy metrics for DAG-shaped ATs require a radically new approach, and we leave this for future work.

Summarized our contributions are:

1. A rigorous, general definition of fuzzy AT metrics;
2. A bottom-up algorithm for computing fuzzy metrics in tree-structured ATs;
3. A proof of modular decomposition for fuzzy AT metrics.

The full version of this paper (including the appendix) is available on Zenodo[9].

2   Related work

Below, we provide a literature review for computation of metrics with fuzzy numbers applied to attack trees and the related formalism of fault trees.

Attack tree analysis with fuzzy numbers. An intuitionistic fuzzy set was used to represent the uncertainty and hesitancy present in data [17], or an attack-defense model was proposed [35, 11], or using a fuzzy analytic hierarchy process to establish a successful probability model of cyber attack [36, 19]. However, there have been several studies on the approach of involving fuzzy attribution in fault tree analysis (FTA) summarized [37, 15, 31, 14, 23] for many years.

Fault tree analysis. Fault trees can be considered as the safety variant of attack trees: whereas attack trees indicate how malicious attacks propagate through a system and lead to damage, fault trees indicate how unintended failures propagate and lead to system level failures. Therefore, leaves of a fault tree model component failures and are called basic events (BEs). Due to their similarities, many approaches to fuzzy fault tree analysis can also be applied to attack trees. Comprehensive literature surveys on fault trees with fuzzy numbers can be found in [37, 23, 31, 14].

Fault tree analysis with fuzzy probabilities. Fuzzy set theory was firstly used in fault tree analysis by Tanaka et al. [34] to address the problem of uncertain BEs failure. In the paper, Zadeh's extension principle was used to estimate the possibility of system failure. The failure possibility of the basic events and top event were represented as trapezoidal fuzzy numbers.

Singer [33] considered the distribution of BEs as fuzzy numbers. The membership function is continuous and is approximated by left and right functions called L-R type fuzzy numbers [10]. Here, L-R type fuzzy numbers are defined by a triplet (m, a, b), where m, a, b are positive real numbers. The author extended algebraic operations on the triplet of L-R type fuzzy numbers and calculated the possibility distribution of the system.

Kim et al. [16] evaluated the possibility of system failure. Similar to [33], L-R type fuzzy numbers are used as the possibilities of BEs. The value m of the triplet (m, a, b) is evaluated by four-expert valuations in the form of triangular fuzzy numbers (TFNs). Each value m is determined to calculate the optimistic and pessimistic possibilities of a system accident. Finally, two cases of possibilities - the pessimistic possibility of system failure with major TFN and the optimistic one with minor TFN - were determined.

Lin et al. [21] estimated failure possibility of ambiguous events. For this purpose, the linguistic variables describing the evaluation data are expressed in triangular or trapezoidal fuzzy numbers denoting failure possibilities. The fuzzy possibility of a top event is calculated using the α-cut fuzzy operators.

Peng et al. [27] presented an approach to fault diagnosis of communication control systems. All probability values of the fault tree were converted to uniform triangle fuzzy numbers. The fuzzy probability of the top event was then calculated using Zadeh's principle. A fault tree (FT) consisting of only OR-gates was shown as an analytical example to determine the confidence interval of probability of top event and achieve fuzzy reasoning diagnosis result.

Fault tree reliability analysis with interval arithmetic. Purba et al.[28] developed a fuzzy probability based fault tree analysis to propagate and quantify epistemic uncertainty raised in basic events. BE reliability characteristics are described in fuzzy probabilities. From the BE fuzzy probabilities, the matrix of fuzzy probabilities of the minimal cut sets is generated and then the top event fuzzy probability is quantified using the Fuzzy multiplication rule in engineering applications.

Purba et al. [29] proposed a fuzzy probability and α-cut based-FTA approach. Each fuzzy probability distribution of BEs is represented uniquely by an α-cut. The top event α-cut is quantified into the best estimate α-cut, the lower bound α-cut, and the upper bound α-cut follow fuzzy arithmetic operations on α-cuts of BEs. The approach was verified by evaluating the reliability of a complex engineering system and the results are compared to the reliability of the same system quantified by conventional FTA.

Fuzzy FTA by conversion of fuzzy number of BEs to crisp probability of BEs. Hu et al. [12] developed an FFTA methodology for analyzing above-ground walled storage system failures. Expert elicitation and fuzzy logic was used to manipulate the ambiguities and vagueness in the linguistic variables of BEs. Fuzzy probability BE was defuzzified to a crisp number. The resultant crisp probability of BEs were used as inputs to generate crisp probability of the top event.

At the time of this writing, fuzzy analysis has not been studied for ATs. The literature has introduced fuzzy analysis of FTs, but it only addresses certain types of fuzzy numbers (trapezoidal, triangular, etc.). This paper thus provides a general mathematical framework for fuzzy analysis of ATs.

3   Fundamentals of fuzzy theory

Fuzzy set theory was introduced by L.A. Zadeh [38] to deal with problems in which vagueness is present. Instead of considering elements x of a set X with a fixed value, we consider fuzzy elements x which can have a range of possible values; the extent to which x can be equal to x is expressed by the *membership degree* of x in x, which is a value $x[x] \in [0, 1]$. The value $x[x]$ is the confidence one has that x has value x. Here $x[x] = 1$ denotes full membership, while $x[x] = 0$ denotes no membership.

For instance, the time needed to perform an attack may be given as a real number, e.g. $x = 3 \in \mathbb{R}$; but often the exact time needed is not known precisely, and can be somewhere around 3. This can be represented by a fuzzy number $x \colon \mathbb{R} \to 1$ which is 0 everywhere except close to 3, and which has a maximum at 3 (see Fig. 2).

Definition 1. *Let X be a set. A* fuzzy element *of X is a function* $x \colon X \to [0, 1]$. *The set of all fuzzy elements of X is denoted* $\mathbf{F}(X) := \{x \mid x \colon X \to [0, 1]\}$.

In the literature, fuzzy elements are usually called *fuzzy sets* [38], on the basis that the membership function $x \colon X \to [0, 1]$ generalizes the indicator function

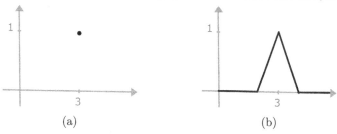

Fig. 2: A non-fuzzy, 'crisp' element x (a) and a fuzzy element x (b).

$1_S \colon X \to \{0,1\}$ of a set $S \subseteq X$; thus a fuzzy set can be thought of as a set of which elements can have partial membership. Instead, we use the term *fuzzy element* to stress that in this paper, fuzzy elements are used to express the uncertainty of individual values, as in Fig. 2b, rather than the uncertainty of set membership. A fuzzy element x behaves similarly to a probability density function in that the uncertainty of an element of X is expressed by a function on X.

Our definition of fuzzy element is very general. Many works in the literature restrict the form of the function $\mathsf{x} \colon X \to [0,1]$ to make computation more convenient, especially for $X = \mathbb{R}$, i.e., for so-called *fuzzy numbers*. Thus there exist triangular, trapezoidal, Gaussian, etc. fuzzy numbers [13, 8].

Example 1. Consider real numbers $a \le b \le c \le d$. The *trapezoidal fuzzy number* $\mathsf{trap}_{a,b,c,d} \in \mathbf{F}(\mathbb{R})$ is defined as (see Fig. 3):

$$\mathsf{trap}_{a,b,c,d}[x] = \begin{cases} \frac{x-a}{b-a}, & \text{if } a < x \le b, \\ 1, & \text{if } b < x < c, \\ \frac{d-x}{d-c}, & \text{if } c \le x < d, \\ 0, & \text{otherwise.} \end{cases} \tag{1}$$

The trapezoidal fuzzy number $\mathsf{trap}_{a,b,c,d}$ has the maximal membership degree of 1, i.e., $\mathsf{trap}_{a,b,c,d}[x] = 1$ for all $x \in [b,c]$. At the same time, a and d are the lower and upper bounds of its support, respectively. In case $b = c$, we have a *triangular fuzzy number* $\mathsf{tri}_{a,b,d}$.

For notational convenience we occasionally abbreviate x via a list of membership values $x \mapsto \mathsf{x}[x]$, omitting x for which $\mathsf{x}[x] = 0$. For example, $\mathsf{x} = \{1 \mapsto 0.7, 2 \mapsto 0.5\} \in \mathbf{F}(\mathbb{Z})$ is defined by

$$\mathsf{x}[x] = \begin{cases} 0.7, & \text{if } x = 1, \\ 0.5, & \text{if } x = 2, \\ 0, & \text{otherwise.} \end{cases}$$

Arithmetic operations on fuzzy elements are performed following Zadeh's extension principle [13, 4, 39, 41, 40, 38]. This principle provides a framework to

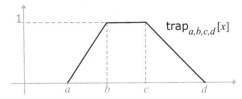

Fig. 3: The trapezoidal fuzzy number $\text{trap}_{a,b,c,d}$.

apply functions and arithmetic operations on sets to their fuzzy elements. Before giving the full definition, we motivate it by an example.

Example 2. Consider $x, y \in \mathbf{F}(\mathbb{N})$ given by

$$x = \{\, 2 \mapsto 0.4, \ 3 \mapsto 1 \},$$
$$y = \{\, 5 \mapsto 1, \ 6 \mapsto 0.6 \}.$$

We wish to calculate the addition of x and y, which we write as $x \tilde{+} y$. This is also an element of $\mathbf{F}(\mathbb{N})$ and so we must specify the confidence $(x \tilde{+} y)[z]$ that the sum values to z, for all $z \in \mathbb{N}$. Consider $z = 8$; the sum values to 8 only in one of these two cases:

- x values to 2 and y values to 6;
- x values to 3 and y values to 5.

Our confidence that x values to 2 is $x[2] = 0.4$, and our confidence that y values to 6 is $y[6] = 0.6$. Our confidence that both of these are true, i.e., that the first case holds, is then $\min\{0.4, 0.6\} = 0.4$. Similarly, our confidence that the second case holds is $\min\{1, 1\} = 1$. Our confidence $(x \tilde{+} y)[8]$ that the sum values to 8 is then the confidence that either of the two cases above holds; this is expressed by the maximum, so

$$(x \tilde{+} y)[8] = \max\{0.4, 1\} = 1.$$

Similarly one can calculate $(x \tilde{+} y)[z]$ for other values of z, by taking all possible outcomes of the sum and calculating their confidence. This yields

$$x \tilde{+} y = \{7 \mapsto 0.4, 8 \mapsto 1, 9 \mapsto 0.6\}.$$

The idea behind Example 2 can be applied to general multivariate functions. The only change that needs to be made is that in general, there may be infinitely many pairs (x, y) such that $f(x, y) = z$; therefore one needs to take the supremum over all $\min\{x[x], y[y]\}$ rather than the maximum.

Definition 2 (Zadeh's Extension Principle). *Let f be a multiargument function $f : X_1 \times X_2 \times \cdots \times X_n \to Y$. The Zadeh extension of f is the function $\tilde{f} \colon \mathbf{F}(X_1) \times \ldots \times \mathbf{F}(X_n) \to \mathbf{F}(Y)$ defined as:*

$$\tilde{f}(x_1, \ldots, x_n)[y] = \begin{cases} \displaystyle\sup_{\substack{(x_1, x_2, \ldots, x_n) \in \prod_i X_i : \\ f(x_1, x_2, \ldots, x_n) = y}} \min_{i=1,\ldots,n} x_i[x_i], & f^{-1}(y) \neq \varnothing, \\ 0 & f^{-1}(y) = \varnothing. \end{cases}$$

Based on the extension principle, different arithmetic operations on fuzzy numbers have been defined [5, 34, 4, 20, 27]. As a result of Definition 2, addition and subtraction operations on fuzzy numbers typically have straightforward formulations. E.g., for two trapezoidal fuzzy numbers we have

$$\text{trap}_{a_1,a_2,a_3,a_4} \widetilde{+} \text{trap}_{b_1,b_2,b_3,b_4} = \text{trap}_{a_1+b_1,a_2+b_2,a_3+b_3,a_4+b_4},$$
$$\text{trap}_{a_1,a_2,a_3,a_4} \widetilde{-} \text{trap}_{b_1,b_2,b_3,b_4} = \text{trap}_{a_1-b_4,a_2-b_3,a_3-b_2,a_4-b_1}.$$

Multiplication and division, however, are nonlinear operations that produce fuzzy numbers of different types than the operands; for example, the quotient of two trapezoidal fuzzy numbers is itself not trapezoidal. For convenience and to simplify the computation, the resulting fuzzy number can be approximated by a fuzzy number of the same type. The computation and visualisation of these estimations can be found in [5].

In section 5, we will apply the general fuzzy element framework to formulate fuzzy attack tree metrics. Unfortunately, the operators considered in AT analysis, such as min, do not preserve triangular, trapezoidal, etc. fuzzy numbers. We therefore need to work with fuzzy numbers and Zadeh extensions in full generality as defined above.

4   Attack trees

In this section, we provide a brief overview of ATs as presented in [22]. Attack trees are hierarchical graphical models that illustrate the attack process. The trees are usually drawn inverted, with the root node located at the top of the tree and branches descending from the root to the lowest levels of the tree – the leaves. The root node represents the attacker's overall objective. The leaves in ATs are called *Basic Attack Steps* (BASs) representing the attacker's activities. Nodes between the leaves and the root node depict transitional states or attacker sub-goals. These intermediate steps are equipped with *logical gates* that indicate whether an intermediate step succeeds, e.g. the AND-gate succeeds if all input children succeed, the OR-gate is successful if at least one child does succeed.

Definition 3. [22] *An* attack tree *is a tuple* $T = (N, E, t)$, *where* (N, E) *is a rooted directed acyclic graph, and* t *is a map* $t: N \to \{\text{BAS}, \text{OR}, \text{AND}\}$ *such that* $t(v) = \text{BAS}$ *if and only if* v *is a leaf for all* $v \in N$.

The root of T is denoted R_T, and the set of children of a node v is denoted $ch(v) = \{w \in N \mid (v, w) \in E\}$. The set of basic attack steps is denoted $\text{BAS}_T = \{v \in N \mid t(v) = \text{BAS}\}$.

4.1   Semantics for attack trees

The semantics of an AT are defined by its successful attacks, i.e., attacks that activate the top node. Formally, an *attack* is a subset $A \subseteq \text{BAS}_T$. For example, in Fig. 1, $\{p, r\}$ is an attack, corresponding to stealing money by breaking in and then opening the vault. An attack's success is most conveniently expressed by the *structure function*, which is defined recursively as follows:

Definition 4. [22] *Let T be an AT. The structure function $f_T \colon N \times 2^{\mathrm{BAS}_T} \to \{0,1\}$ of T is defined, for a node $v \in N$ and an attack $A \subseteq \mathrm{BAS}_T$, by*

$$
f_T(v, A) = \begin{cases}
1 & \textit{if } t(v) = \mathtt{OR} \ \ \textit{and } \exists u \in ch(v) \ s.t \ f_T(u, A) = 1, \\
1 & \textit{if } t(v) = \mathtt{AND} \ \textit{and } \forall u \in ch(v) \ s.t \ f_T(u, A) = 1, \\
1 & \textit{if } t(v) = \mathtt{BAS} \ \textit{and } v \in A, \\
0 & \textit{otherwise.}
\end{cases}
\tag{2}
$$

An attack A is said to *reach* a node v if $f_T(v, A) = 1$, i.e. it makes v succeed. If no proper subset of A reaches v, then A is a *minimal attack on* v. The set of minimal attacks on R_T is denoted $[\![T]\!]$. For example, the AT from Fig. 1, has three successful attacks: $\{r, q\}$, $\{r, p\}$, and $\{r, q, p\}$. The first two are minimal, so we have: $[\![T]\!] = \{\{r, q\}, \{r, p\}\}$.

Discussion regarding attacks and semantics for ATs are presented in [22]. Note that adding BASes to an attack will not make it less successful; hence the successful attacks are determined by $[\![T]\!]$. This leads to the following definition of the semantics.

Definition 5. *The* semantics *of an AT T is its suite of minimal attacks $[\![T]\!]$.*

4.2   Security metrics for attack trees

Quantitative AT analysis may concern various attributes, such as cost, time, damage, etc. To handle all these attributes in a generic way, analysis algorithms work over a so-called *attribute domain* $(V, \triangledown, \triangle)$. Here V is the value domain for the attribute, e.g., $\mathbb{R}_{\geq 0}$ for costs, and $[0, 1]$ for probability. Furthermore, $\triangledown$ and $\triangle$ are binary operators on V, where $\triangledown$ denotes the way values are propagated over an OR-gate: If $T = \mathtt{OR}(a, b)$ and a, b are BASs assigned metric values x_a, x_b, then $x_a \triangledown x_b$ is the security value of T. Similarly $\triangle$ is the operator corresponding to the AND-gate. For technical reasons we assume $\triangledown$ and $\triangle$ satisfy some algebraic properties, which is encoded in the definition of a semiring.

Definition 6. [22] *A semiring is a tuple $(V, \triangledown, \triangle)$ where V is a set, $\triangledown$ and $\triangle$ are commutative associative binary operators on V, and $\triangle$ distributed over $\triangledown$ (i.e. $x \triangle (y \triangledown z) = (x \triangle y) \triangledown (x \triangle z)$).*

To assign a metric value to an AT T, one chooses a semiring V in which the metric takes value, as well as a BAS value $x_a \in V$ for each BAS a; this is encoded as a vector $\vec{x} \in V^{\mathrm{BAS}_T}$. The calculation of T proceeds in two steps: first, we assign values to an attack $A = \{a_1, \ldots, a_n\}$. Since all BASs have to be executed, we set $m_A(\vec{x}) = \triangle_{i=1}^{n} x_{a_i}$. This corresponds to the cost/damage/probability/etc. of the attack A, given the BAS values $\vec{x}$. Next, we calculate the metric value of T as a whole. To do this, we consider the set of all minimal attacks $[\![T]\!] = \{A_1, \ldots, A_m\}$. Since for the top node to be reached one only needs one minimal attack, the metric value for T is calculated via $m_T(\vec{x}) = \triangledown_{i=1}^{m} m_{A_i}(\vec{x})$.

Example 3. We consider the *minimal cost* metric that assigns to an AT the minimal cost the attacker needs to spend to successfully reach the top node. This corresponds to the semiring $(\mathbb{N}, \min, +)$. Indeed, the cost needed to activate the top node in $\text{OR}(a, b)$ is the minimum of the costs x_a and x_b, as only one of the two children needs to be activated; hence $\triangledown = \min$. Similarly, an AND-gate needs to activate all children, so their costs need to be added and $\triangle = +$. Then given a vector $\vec{x} \in \mathbb{R}_{\geq 0}^{\text{BAS}_T}$ assigning a cost value $x_a \in \mathbb{R}_{\geq 0}$ to each BAS a, the metric value of T is defined as $m_T(\vec{x}) = \min_{A \in \llbracket T \rrbracket} \sum_{a \in A} x_a$. Here $\sum_{a \in A} x_a$ is the total cost of performing an attack A, so the metric value corresponds to the cost of the cheapest minimal attack. Consider the AT $T = \text{AND}\big(r, \text{OR}(q, p)\big)$ in Fig. 1. Recall that $\llbracket T \rrbracket = \{\{r, q\}, \{r, p\}\} = \{A_1, A_2\}$, and consider an attribution $\vec{x}$ given by $x_r = 60, x_q = 30, x_p = 5$. Then the metric can be calculated as follows.

$$
m_T(\vec{x}) = \min \left(\sum_{a \in A_1} x_a, \sum_{a \in A_2} x_a \right)
$$
$$
= \min(60 + 30, 60 + 5) = 65.
$$

Formalizing the discussion and example above leads to the following definition.

Definition 7. [22] *Let T be an AT and let $(V, \triangledown, \triangle)$ be a semiring.*

1. *An* attribution *of T in V is an element $\vec{x}$ of V^{BAS_T}.*
2. *Given an attribution $\vec{x}$, the* metric value *of T given V and $\vec{x}$ is defined as*

$$
m_T(\vec{x}) = \bigvee_{A \in \llbracket T \rrbracket} \bigwedge_{a \in A} x_a \in V. \tag{3}
$$

As is implicit from the notation, we consider a metric to be a function $m_T \colon V^{\text{BAS}_T} \to V$ that takes as input the vector $\vec{x}$ of BAS attribute value (e.g. BAS costs), and outputs the AT's security value (e.g. minimal cost needed to succesfully attack the AT). This viewpoint is useful when extending AT metrics to the fuzzy setting in the next section.

5   Fuzzy metrics for attack trees

To define fuzzy AT metrics — as stated, to the best of our knowledge no such definition exist yet — we equip each BAS with a fuzzy element of V, i.e., an element of $\mathbf{F}(V)$. Thus, a fuzzy attribution is an element $\vec{x}$ of $\mathbf{F}(V)^{\text{BAS}_T}$, assigning a fuzzy element x_a to each BAS a. For crisp metrics, the AT's metric value is obtained by applying a function m_T to the crisp attribution vector $\vec{x}$, as outlined in Definition 7. Analogously, we obtain the fuzzy metric value by applying $\tilde{m}_T$ to $\vec{\mathsf{x}}$, where $\tilde{m}_T$ is the Zadeh extension of m_T.

Example 4. Consider the AT $T = \text{AND}(r, \text{OR}(q, p))$ from Fig. 1; recall that $\llbracket T \rrbracket = \{\{r, q\}, \{r, p\}\}$. We consider the *minimal time* metric, corresponding to the semiring $(\mathbb{R}_{\geq 0}, \min, +)$. For this semiring, consider the fuzzy attribution $\vec{x} = (x_r, x_q, x_p)$ given by $x_r = \{50 \mapsto 1, 60 \mapsto 1\}, x_q = \{0 \mapsto 1\}$, and $x_p = \{5 \mapsto 1\}$, respectively; that is, q and p have crisp time values, and r either takes time 50 or 60, with equal possibility.

Since the minimal attacks are $\{r, q\}$ and $\{r, p\}$, the function $m_T \colon V^3 \to V$ is given by $m_T(x_r, x_q, x_p) = \min(x_r + x_q, x_r + x_p)$ for all $x_r, x_q, x_p \in V$. Then the fuzzy metric value is equal to $\tilde{m}_T(x_r, x_q, x_p)$. Using the definition of Zadeh extension from Definition 2, the confidence that this fuzzy metric value is equal to a $y \in \mathbb{R}_{\geq 0}$ is equal to

$$\tilde{m}_T(\vec{x})[y] = \sup_{\substack{x_r, x_q, x_p \in \mathbb{R}_{\geq 0}: \\ \min(x_r + x_q, x_r + x_p) = y}} \min\big(x_r[x_r], x_q[x_q], x_p[x_p]\big).$$

Since $x_q[x_q] \neq 0$ only for $x_q = 0$, where $x_q[x_q] = 1$, we only need to consider $x_q = 0$, and, for the same reason, we only need to consider $x_p = 5$. Thus the expression above is equal to

$$\sup_{\substack{x_r: \\ \min(x_r, x_r + 5) = y}} \min\big(x_r[x_r], 1, 1\big) = \begin{cases} 1, & \text{if } y = 50 \text{ or } y = 60, \\ 0, & \text{otherwise.} \end{cases}$$

so $\tilde{m}_T(\vec{x}) = \{50 \mapsto 1, 60 \mapsto 1\}$.

Formally fuzzy AT metrics are then defined as follows.

Definition 8. *Let T be an AT and let $(V, \triangledown, \triangle)$ be a semiring.*

1. *A fuzzy attribution is an element $\vec{x}$ of $\mathbf{F}(V)^{\mathrm{BAS}_T}$.*
2. *Given a fuzzy attribution $\vec{x}$, the fuzzy metric value of T given V and $\vec{x}$ is defined as $\tilde{m}_T(\vec{x})$, where $\tilde{m}_T \colon \mathbf{F}(V)^{\mathrm{BAS}_T} \to \mathbf{F}(V)$ is the Zadeh extension of the function m_T from Definition 7.*

More concretely, $\tilde{m}_T(\vec{x})$ is the fuzzy element of V defined, for $y \in V$, by

$$
\begin{aligned}
\tilde{m}_T(\vec{x})[y] &= \sup_{\substack{\vec{x} \in V^{\mathrm{BAS}_T}: \\ m_T(\vec{x}) = y}} \min_{v \in \mathrm{BAS}_T} x_v[x_v] \\
&= \sup_{\substack{\vec{x} \in V^{\mathrm{BAS}_T}: \\ \triangledown_{A \in \llbracket T \rrbracket} \triangle_{a \in A} x_a = y}} \min_{v \in \mathrm{BAS}_T} x_v[x_v].
\end{aligned}
\tag{4}
$$

Our choice of using Zadeh's extension to extend crisp AT metrics to fuzzy AT metrics is justified by the fact that Zadeh extension treats the input fuzzy numbers $x_1, \ldots, x_n$ as *independent*, i.e., it assumes that there is no nontrivial joint fuzzy distribution on the product space $\prod_i X_i$ of which the x_i are the marginal distributions [30]. This is a standard assumption on BASes (See [26] for a similar viewpoint on fault trees) which we follow. In theory, one could extend the definition to allow non-independent BASes with more complicated joint fuzzy distributions. However, the prevailing viewpoint is that such relations should be explicitly modeled into the AT itself. For example, if the non-independence is due to a common cause affecting the joint distribution of multiple BAS attribute values, then this common cause should be explicitly modeled into the AT framework by replacing the BAS by sub-ATs with shared nodes [26]. We will follow this philosophy and use the Zadeh extension as the natural way to define fuzzy AT metrics.

An alternative way of defining fuzzy AT metrics would be to replace the crisp operators $\triangledown, \triangle$ in (3) with their fuzzy counterparts $\widetilde{\triangledown}, \widetilde{\triangle}$. However, this does not coincide with our definition, as the following result shows:

Theorem 1. *In general,*

$$\widetilde{m}_T(\widetilde{x}) \neq \widetilde{\bigvee_{A \in \llbracket T \rrbracket}} \widetilde{\bigwedge_{a \in A}} x_a, \tag{5}$$

This result is shown by the following example.

Example 5. We continue Example 4, where $\widetilde{m}_T(x_p, x_q, x_r) = \{50 \mapsto 1, 60 \mapsto 1\}$. On the other hand,

$$\widetilde{\bigvee_{A \in \llbracket T \rrbracket}} \widetilde{\bigwedge_{v \in A}} x_v = \widetilde{\min}\left(x_r \widetilde{+} x_q, x_r \widetilde{+} x_p\right).$$

One could calculate this fuzzy number in a manner analogous to Example 4, but here we show another method that is often more convenient. For a fuzzy number $x \in \mathbf{F}(\mathbb{R}_{\geq 0})$, define $x^{(1)} = \{x \in \mathbb{R}_{\geq 0} \mid x[x] = 1\}$; this is the level 1 $\alpha-cut$ of x [13]. Then from Definition 2 one can deduce that for $x, y \in \mathbf{F}(\mathbb{R}_{\geq 0})$ and $f \colon \mathbb{R}_{\geq 0}^2 \to \mathbb{R}_{\geq 0}$ one has

$$(\widetilde{f}(x, y))^{(1)} = \{f(x, y) \mid x \in x^{(1)}, y \in y^{(1)}\}.$$

For brevity we abbreviate the right hand side of this equation to $f(x^{(1)}, y^{(1)})$. It follows that

$$
\begin{aligned}
\left(\widetilde{\min}\left(x_r \widetilde{+} x_q, x_r \widetilde{+} x_p\right)\right)^{(1)} &= \min((x_r \widetilde{+} x_q)^{(1)}, (x_r \widetilde{+} x_p)^{(1)}) \\
&= \min(x_r^{(1)} + x_q^{(1)}, x_r^{(1)} + x_p^{(1)}) \\
&= \min(\{50, 60\} + \{0\}, \{50, 60\} + \{5\}) \\
&= \min(\{50, 60\}, \{55, 65\}) \\
&= \{50, 55, 60\}.
\end{aligned}
$$

Hence $\left(\widetilde{\bigvee_{A \in \llbracket T \rrbracket}} \widetilde{\bigwedge_{v \in A}} x_v\right)[x] = 1$ if and only if $x \in \{50, 55, 60\}$. Since this fuzzy number only takes possibility values 0 and 1, it follows that

$$\widetilde{\bigvee_{A \in \llbracket T \rrbracket}} \widetilde{\bigwedge_{v \in A}} x_v = \{50 \mapsto 1, 55 \mapsto 1, 60 \mapsto 1\} \neq \{50 \mapsto 1, 60 \mapsto 1\} = \widetilde{m}_T(x_p, x_q, x_r).$$

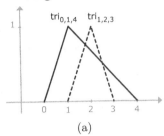

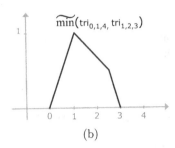

Fig. 4: Two triangular fuzzy numbers and their minimum, as a Zadeh extension of the function min.

The 'extra' possibility $55 \mapsto 1$ on the LHS comes from comparing the attack $\{r, q\}$ with cost $60 + 0$ to the attack $\{r, p\}$ with cost $50 + 5$. In other words, in this comparison r is considered to have costs 50 and 60 simultaneously. By contrast, in the calculation of $\tilde{m}_T(\vec{x})$ the cost x_r can only have one value at a time.

Equation (5) shows that a priori, there are two ways one can define fuzzy AT metrics. We choose to use the definition of $\tilde{m}_T(\vec{x})$ via Zadeh's extension as in Definition 8 for two reasons: first, this accurately captures the independence of the BASes as outlined below Definition 8. Second, we show in Theorem 3 that this definition satisfies modular decomposition, a fundamental property of AT metrics. The RHS of (5) does *not* satisfy modular decomposition, giving another argument why Definition 8 is the preferred definition (see Remark 2 below).

Example 6. Consider the AT $T = OR(a, b)$ with the min cost metric, represented by the semiring $(\mathbb{R}_{\geq 0}, \min, +)$. As fuzzy attributions consider $x_a = tri_{0,1,4}$ and $x_b = tri_{1,2,3}$. Then one can show (see Fig. 4) that $\tilde{m}_T(\vec{x}) = \widetilde{\min}(x_a, x_b)$ is given by

$$\widetilde{\min}(x_a, x_b)[x] = \begin{cases} x, & \text{if } 0 \leq x < 1, \\ 1 - \frac{x-1}{3}, & \text{if } 1 \leq x < 2.5, \\ 3 - x, & \text{if } 2.5 \leq x < 3, \\ 0, & \text{otherwise.} \end{cases}$$

In particular $\widetilde{\min}(x_a, x_b)$ is not a triangular fuzzy number. Hence triangular fuzzy numbers are not preserved by the operations inherent to AT analysis. The same holds for other popular subtypes of fuzzy numbers such as rectangular numbers; for this reason, we define fuzzy quantitative AT analysis for general fuzzy numbers in Definition 8. Finding subtypes of fuzzy numbers that are preserved by AT analysis operations forms an interesting avenue for future research.

Remark 1. Besides AT metrics as defined in this paper, in [22] quantitative analysis for so-called *dynamic ATs* (DATs) is also defined. DATs include a new gate type SAND ("sequential AND") used when attack steps have to be performed in sequential order; the normal AND-gate allows its children to be performed in parallel. This changes both semantics and quantitative analysis: an attack is now a partially ordered set $(A, \prec)$ rather than just a set A of BASes, to denote the relative timing behaviour of the attack steps; and for quantitative analysis a third binary operation $\triangleright$ is introduced to correspond to SAND-gates, and the metric is defined in terms of these operators.

The results of this paper straightforwardly carry over to the DAT setting. That is, fuzzy DAT metrics are defined as the Zadeh extension of crisp DAT metrics akin to Definition 8. Furthermore, this definition satisfies modular decomposition, which follows from the modular decomposition of crisp DAT metrics analogous to Theorem 3. As a result, a bottom-up algorithm analogous to Alg. 1 calculates fuzzy DAT metrics for treelike DATs.

6   Metric computation for ATs

To calculate the fuzzy AT metric $\tilde{m}_T(\mathsf{x})$ directly from Definition 8, one first needs to calculate the function m_T, which in return requires one to find $[\![T]\!]$. In general, this set is of exponential size, making calculation cumbersome for large ATs. Therefore, dedicated algorithms for quantitative AT analysis are needed. For crisp AT metrics these are described in [22]. In this section, we define a bottom-up algorithm for calculating fuzzy AT metrics for tree-shaped ATs, and we show that its validity follows from the fact that fuzzy AT metrics satisfy modular decomposition. We also show that the BDD-based approach for metric calculation for DAG-shaped ATs from [22] does not extend to the fuzzy case, and that a radically new approach is needed.

6.1   Bottom-up algorithm

The bottom-up algorithm presented in Algorithm 1 is adapted from the bottom-up algorithm for crisp AT metrics first presented in [25]. It takes as input an AT T, a node v of T, a semiring $D = (V, \triangledown, \triangle)$, and a fuzzy attribution $\vec{\mathsf{x}}$, and outputs a fuzzy value $\widetilde{\mathsf{BU}}(T, v, D, \vec{\mathsf{x}}) \in \mathbf{F}(V)$ assigned to v; this value corresponds to the metric value associated to reaching v. If $t(v) = \mathsf{BAS}$, this is simply x_v. If $t(v) = \mathsf{OR}$, then $\widetilde{\mathsf{BU}}(T, v, D, \vec{\mathsf{x}})$ is obtained by applying $\widetilde{\triangledown}$ to the values associated to the children of v; for $t(v) = \mathsf{AND}$ we instead use $\widetilde{\triangle}$. The AT's fuzzy metric value is then given by $\widetilde{\mathsf{BU}}(T, R_T, D, \vec{\mathsf{x}})$.

Theorem 2. *Let T be a static AT with tree structure, $D = (V, \triangledown, \triangle)$ a semiring, and $\vec{\mathsf{x}}$ a fuzzy attribution with values in V. Then $\tilde{m}_T(\vec{\mathsf{x}}) = \widetilde{\mathsf{BU}}(T, R_T, D, \vec{\mathsf{x}})$.*

Example 7. We apply the algorithm to Example 4. Then the algorithm calculates the metric as follows

$$\widetilde{\mathsf{BU}}(T, R_T, D, \vec{\mathsf{x}}) = \widetilde{\mathsf{BU}}(T, r, D, \vec{\mathsf{x}}) \; \widetilde{\triangle} \; \widetilde{\mathsf{BU}}(T, \min(q, p), D, \vec{\mathsf{x}})$$
$$= \widetilde{\mathsf{BU}}(T, r, D, \vec{\mathsf{x}}) \; \widetilde{\triangle} \; \left(\widetilde{\mathsf{BU}}(T, q, D, \vec{\mathsf{x}}) \; \widetilde{\triangledown} \; \widetilde{\mathsf{BU}}(T, p, D, \vec{\mathsf{x}}) \right)$$

Input: attack tree $T = (N, E, t)$,
      node $v \in N$,
      semiring attribute domain $D = (V, \triangledown, \triangle)$,
      fuzzy attribution $\vec{x} \in \mathbf{F}(V)^{\mathrm{BAS}_T}$.
Output: Fuzzy element $\widetilde{\mathrm{BU}}(T, v, D, \vec{x}) \in \mathbf{F}(V)$.
if $t(v) = $ OR **then**
    | **return** $\displaystyle\widetilde{\bigtriangledown}_{w \in ch(v)} \widetilde{\mathrm{BU}}(T, w, D, \vec{x})$
else if $t(v) = $ AND **then**
    | **return** $\displaystyle\widetilde{\bigtriangleup}_{w \in ch(v)} \widetilde{\mathrm{BU}}(T, w, D, \vec{x})$
else   `/* `$t(v) = $` BAS */`
    | **return** x_v
end

Algorithm 1: $\widetilde{\mathrm{BU}}$ for tree-structured AT T.

$$= \sup_{\substack{x_r, x_{q \triangledown p} \in \mathbb{R}_{\geq 0}: \\ x_r + x_{q \triangledown p} = y}} \min\left(\mathsf{x}_r[x_r], \sup_{\substack{x_q, x_p \in \mathbb{R}_{\geq 0}: \\ \min(x_q, x_p) = x_{q \triangledown p}}} \min\left(\mathsf{x}_q[x_q], \mathsf{x}_p[x_p]\right)\right)$$

$$= \sup_{\substack{x_r, x_q, x_p \in \mathbb{R}_{\geq 0}: \\ x_r + \min(x_q, x_p) = y}} \min\left(\mathsf{x}_r[x_r], \mathsf{x}_q[x_q], \mathsf{x}_p[x_p]\right)$$

$$= \sup_{\substack{x_r \in \mathbb{R}_{\geq 0}: \\ x_r + \min(0, 5) = y}} \min\left(\mathsf{x}_r[x_r], 1, 1\right)$$

$$= \begin{cases} 1, & \text{if } y = 50 \text{ or } y = 60, \\ 0, & \text{otherwise.} \end{cases}$$

$$= \{50 \mapsto 1, 60 \mapsto 1\}.$$

The algorithm is efficient as we can see that it is linear in $|E|$, making it vastly more efficient than first calculating m_T and then Zadeh-extending it. The algorithm is generic as it is applicable to popular quantitative metrics in ATs such as cost, damage, skill, probability, etc. [22]. We should note, however, that the linearity of the time complexity assumes that the fuzzy operations $\widetilde{\triangledown}$ and $\widetilde{\triangle}$ take constant time.

While the algorithm applies only to tree-structured ATs, this covers a large portion of the ATs found in the literature [25]. As such, the algorithm can be used in many applications.

As we show in the appendix of [9], the proof of Theorem 2 depends on a fundamental property of AT metrics called *modular decomposition*. In the next section, we will explain this and show that fuzzy metrics satisfy this property.

6.2 Modular decomposition

Modular decomposition is a fundamental property of AT metrics as it facilitates the recursive solution of many problems, which typically improves performance.

For a node v in an AT T, let T_v be the AT consisting of all *descendants* of v, i.e., the nodes w for which there exists a path $v \to w$. This is a rooted DAG with root v. A *module* is a node v for which T_v is only minimally connected to the rest of T:

Definition 9. *Let $v \in N \setminus \text{BAS}$. We call node v a module if v is the only node in T_v with connections to $T \setminus T_v$.*

For instance, in Fig. 1, the modules are "enter the bank" and "get money". Finding the modules of an AT aids in calculating metrics as follows. Given a module v, one can split up T into two parts: the sub-AT T_v with root v, and the 'quotient' T^v obtained by replacing the entire sub-AT v with a single new node, which we will still call v (see Fig. 5). Then one can calculate the metric for T_v to find $\widetilde{m}_{T_v}(\vec{x})$, and use this as a BAS attribute value for v in T^v. One then calculates the metric value for T^v with this new BAS value. In [22, Thm. 9.2] it is shown that for crisp metrics this results in the same metric value for T as when one considers the entirety of T at once. As a result, we can split up metric calculations via a divide-and-conquer approach once one has identified the modules. The following theorem shows that this also holds for fuzzy AT metrics.

Theorem 3. *Let $(V, \triangledown, \vartriangle)$ be a semiring. Let v be a module in an AT T, $\vec{x} \in \mathbf{F}(V)^{\text{BAS}_T}$ be a fuzzy attribution for T. Let $\vec{x}_v \in \mathbf{F}(V)^{\text{BAS}_{T_v}}$ be the fuzzy attribution for T_v obtained from restricting x, i.e., $(\vec{x}_v)_w = \mathsf{x}_w$ for all $w \in \text{BAS}_{T_v}$. Let T^v be the AT obtained by replacing T_v in T by a single BAS·still called v. Let $\vec{x}^v \in \mathbf{F}(V)^{\text{BAS}_{T^v}}$ be a fuzzy attribution for T^v given by*

$$\mathsf{x}_{v'}^v = \begin{cases} \mathsf{x}_{v'}, & v' \neq v, \\ \widetilde{m}_{T_v}(\vec{x}), & v' = v. \end{cases}$$

Then $\widetilde{m}_T(\vec{x}) = \widetilde{m}_{T^v}(\vec{x}^v)$.

The theorem is the extension of Theorem 9.2 of [22]. The proof of Theorem 3 is shown in the appendix of [9]. In a treelike AT, every node is a module, and applying modular decomposition then yields Theorem 2.

Remark 2. In the same way that Theorem 3 can be used to prove Theorem 2, it can also be used to show that the alternative definition of fuzzy AT metrics in the RHS of (5) does *not* satisfy modular decomposition. Namely, if the alternative definition would satisfy modular decomposition, Alg. 1 would also calculate the alternative definition for treelike ATs. However, since this does not conform to our Definition 8 even for treelike ATs (see Theorem 1), we conclude that the alternative definition does not satisfy modular decomposition.

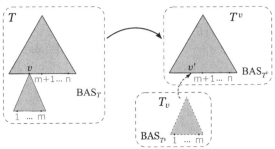

Fig. 5: Calculation of $\widetilde{m}_T(\vec{x})$ can be done by computing $\widetilde{m}_{T^v}(\vec{x}^v)$, where $v' \in$ BAS$_{T^v}$ is assigned with fuzzy attribute $\widetilde{m}_{T_v}(\vec{x}_v)$.

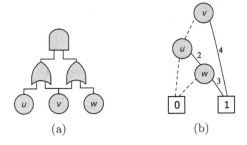

Fig. 6: A DAG AT (a), and its BDD (b).

6.3   Computations for DAG ATs

Directed acyclic graph (DAG) ATs refer to ATs in which a node has more than one parent [22]. Fig. 6a visualizes an AT with DAG structure. Unfortunately, Alg. 1, does not correctly compute the (fuzzy) metric value of DAG-shaped ATs. The reason for this is that the algorithm does not detect whether a node's child is shared with another node or not, which leads to double counting of a child's metric value.

Example 8. Let $x_u = \{1 \mapsto 1\}, x_v = \{0 \mapsto 1, 3 \mapsto 1\}, x_w = \{1 \mapsto 1\}$, and $D = \{\mathbb{N}, \min, +\}$. The min cost computation for the DAG AT shown in Fig. 6a using algorithm 1 gives $\widetilde{\mathsf{BU}}(T, R_T, x, D) = \widetilde{\min}(x_u, x_v) \; \widetilde{+} \; \widetilde{\min}(x_v, x_w) = \{0 \mapsto 1, 1 \mapsto 1\} \; \widetilde{+} \; \{0 \mapsto 1, 1 \mapsto 1\} = \{0 \mapsto 1, 1 \mapsto 1, 2 \mapsto 1\}$, whereas $\widetilde{m}_T(x_u, x_v, x_w) = \{0 \mapsto 1, 2 \mapsto 1\}$.

For crisp metrics, this was solved by the BDD-based approach introduced in [22]. Boolean functions are compactly represented by a binary decision diagram(BDD), a type of directed acyclic graph. One can apply this to the structure function of an AT as in Fig. 6b: as one can see, each nonleaf is labeled with a BAS and has two outgoing edges, while the leafs are labeled 0 and 1. For a given attack A, the BDD evaluates $f_T(R_T, A)$ as follows: at a node with label

v, follow the dashed line if $v \notin A$, and the nondashed line if $v \in A$. The leaf in which one ends up holds the value of $f_T(R_T, A)$. Every Boolean function can be represented as a BDD, and although the corresponding BDD is worst-case of exponential size, BDDs are usually quite compact.

The BDD can also be used to calculate (crisp) AT metrics. We showcase this for the minimal cost metric, but it can be applied to other metrics, so long as the corresponding semiring is *absorbing* (see [22]). Minimal cost is calculated as follows: for each BAS v, the cost x_v is attached to the nondashed edges originating from BDD nodes with label v, while each dashed edge gets label 0 (see Fig. 6b). Then the attack with minimal cost corresponds to the shortest path from R_T to 1 in the BDD; since the BDD is acyclic this computation is linear in the size of the BDD. In total, this means that this is worst-case exponential in the size of the AT, but in practice the calculation is quite fast.

Unfortunately, this approach no longer works for fuzzy AT metrics. The reason is that this approach assumes that the metric arises from a semiring, in particular, that distributivity holds. As the following example shows, if $(V, \triangledown, \triangle)$ is a semiring, then $(\mathbf{F}(V), \widetilde{\triangledown}, \widetilde{\triangle})$ is no longer a semiring, because distributivity no longer holds. It is therefore no surprise that the BDD method no longer works either.

Example 9. Let $(V, \triangledown, \triangle) = (\mathbb{R}_{\geq 0}, \min, +)$, and consider the fuzzy elements $\mathsf{x} = \{0 \mapsto 1, 2 \mapsto 1\}$ and $\mathsf{y} = \mathsf{z} = \{0 \mapsto 1\}$. Then using the methods from Example 5, we find that

$$\widetilde{\min}(\mathsf{x}\widetilde{+}\mathsf{y}, \mathsf{x}\widetilde{+}\mathsf{z}) = \widetilde{\min}(\{0 \mapsto 1, 2 \mapsto 1\}, \{0 \mapsto 1, 2 \mapsto 1\})$$
$$= \{0 \mapsto 1, 1 \mapsto 1, 2 \mapsto 1\},$$
$$\mathsf{x}\widetilde{+}\widetilde{\min}(\mathsf{y}, \mathsf{z}) = \{0 \mapsto 1, 2 \mapsto 1\}\widetilde{+}\{0 \mapsto 1\}$$
$$= \{0 \mapsto 1, 2 \mapsto 1\}.$$

Hence $(\mathbf{F}(\mathbb{R}_{\geq 0}), \widetilde{\min}, \widetilde{+})$ is not distributive, and in particular not a semiring.

The reason that distributivity fails for fuzzy numbers is that, as we discussed in Section 5, a Zadeh-extended operator like $\widetilde{+}$ acts as though its two arguments are independent. However, in an expression like $\widetilde{\min}(\mathsf{x}\widetilde{+}\mathsf{y}, \mathsf{x}\widetilde{+}\mathsf{z})$ the arguments $\mathsf{x}\widetilde{+}\mathsf{y}$ and $\mathsf{x}\widetilde{+}\mathsf{z}$ are typically not independent. This ensures that distributivity is not retained under Zadeh extension.

Since the BDD method used for crisp AT metrics does not work, a new method is needed for calculating fuzzy metrics for DAG-like ATs. This is beyond the scope of this paper. One possible way to approach this problem is to find a way to keep track of the 'double counting' that occurs when applying $\widetilde{\mathrm{BU}}$ to DAG-like ATs, and eliminate it at the end of the algorithm. Such an approach would require a radically new, strategy, and we therefore leave it to future work.

7   Conclusion and future work

In this paper we define a mathematical formulation for deriving AT fuzzy metrics values. In our knowledge, fuzzy theory has been applied in FTs for imprecise data, but fuzzy quantitative metrics remain somewhat implicitly defined. The definition we provide is explicit and generic for commonly used quantitative metrics. Moreover, this definition can be used to better capture uncertainty in quantitative metrics values. In addition, this paper introduces an efficient algorithm to calculate AT metrics with fuzzy attribution. The proposed algorithm is linear in $|E|$, as opposed to the definition of fuzzy metrics which requires calculation of crisp metrics followed by fuzzy operators. The algorithm works for tree-like structure models that satisfy modular decomposition.

In the future, we want to develop an algorithm for fuzzy metrics computation on DAG ATs. For that aim, the algorithm should address the non-semiring property of fuzzy operators and the DAG structure on ATs. Another avenue for future research is the development of subtypes of fuzzy numbers that are preserved by (Zadeh-extended) arithmetic operations inherent to AT analysis, such as min and max. Upon formally defining such subtypes, these can then be used to implement quantitative analysis algorithms efficiently.

Acknowledgement This research has been partially funded by ERC Consolidator grant 864075 CAESAR and the European Union's Horizon 2020 research and innovation programme under the Marie Skłodowska-Curie grant agreement No. 101008233.

Disclosure of Interests The authors have no competing interests to declare that are relevant to the content of this article.

References

1. Isograph. https://www.isograph.com/software/attacktree/
2. Risk Tree. https://risktree.2t-security.co.uk
3. Amenaza's SecurITree. https://www.amenaza.com/AT-tool.php
4. de Barros, L.C., Bassanezi, R.C., Lodwick, W.A.: The Extension Principle of Zadeh and Fuzzy Numbers, pp. 23–41. Springer Berlin Heidelberg, Berlin, Heidelberg (2017). https://doi.org/10.1007/978-3-662-53324-6_2
5. Basiura, B., Duda, J., Gaweł, B., Opiła, J., Pełech-Pilichowski, T., Rębiasz, B., Skalna, I.: Fuzzy Numbers, pp. 1–26. Springer International Publishing, Cham (2015). https://doi.org/10.1007/978-3-319-26494-3_1
6. Bowles, J.B., Pelaez, C.E.: Application of fuzzy logic to reliability engineering. Proceedings of the IEEE **83**(3), 435–449 (1995)
7. Couso, I., Borgelt, C., Hullermeier, E., Kruse, R.: Fuzzy sets in data analysis: From statistical foundations to machine learning. IEEE Computational Intelligence Magazine **14**(1), 31–44 (2019)
8. Czogała, E., Leski, J.: Fuzzy and Neuro-Fuzzy Intelligent Systems, pp. 1–26. Physica Heidelberg (2012). https://doi.org/10.1007/978-3-7908-1853-6
9. Dang, T.K.N., Lopuhaä-Zwakenberg, M., Stoelinga, M.: Fuzzy quantitative attack tree analysis (Jan 2024). https://doi.org/10.5281/zenodo.10554728
10. Dubois, D., Prade, H.: Fuzzy real algebra: Some results. Fuzzy Sets and Systems **2**(4), 327–348 (1979). https://doi.org/10.1016/0165-0114(79)90005-8

11. Garg, S., Aujla, G.S.: An attack tree based comprehensive framework for the risk and security assessment of vanet using the concepts of game theory and fuzzy logic. Journal of Emerging Technologies in Web Intelligence **6**(2), 247 – 252 (2014). https://doi.org/10.4304/jetwi.6.2.247-252

12. Hu, G., Phan, H., Ouache, R., Gandhi, H., Hewage, K., Sadiq, R.: Fuzzy fault tree analysis of hydraulic fracturing flowback water storage failure. Journal of Natural Gas Science and Engineering **72**, 103039 (2019). https://doi.org/10.1016/j.jngse.2019.103039

13. Jezewski, M., Czabanski, R., Leski, J.: Introduction to Fuzzy Sets, pp. 3–22. Springer International Publishing, Cham (2017). https://doi.org/10.1007/978-3-319-59614-3_1

14. Kabir, S.: An overview of fault tree analysis and its application in model based dependability analysis. Expert Systems with Applications **77**, 114–135 (2017). https://doi.org/10.1016/j.eswa.2017.01.058

15. Kabir, S., Papadopoulos, Y.: A review of applications of fuzzy sets to safety and reliability engineering. International Journal of Approximate Reasoning **100**, 29–55 (2018). https://doi.org/10.1016/j.ijar.2018.05.005

16. Kim, C., Ju, Y., Gens, M.: Multilevel fault tree analysis using fuzzy numbers. Computers & Operations Research **23**(7), 695–703 (1996). https://doi.org/10.1016/0305-0548(95)00070-4

17. Komal: Chapter 4 - fuzzy attack tree analysis of security threat assessment in an internet security system using algebraic t-norm and t-conorm. In: Garg, H., Ram, M. (eds.) Engineering Reliability and Risk Assessment, pp. 53–64. Advances in Reliability Science, Elsevier (2023). https://doi.org/10.1016/B978-0-323-91943-2.00003-4

18. Kumar, R., Ruijters, E., Stoelinga, M.: Quantitative attack tree analysis via priced timed automata. In: Sankaranarayanan, S., Vicario, E. (eds.) Formal Modeling and Analysis of Timed Systems. pp. 156–171. Springer International Publishing, Cham (2015)

19. Li, R., Li, F., Zhang, J.: Vehicle network security situation assessment method based on attack tree. In: IOP Conference Series: Earth and Environmental Science. vol. 428. Institute of Physics Publishing (2020). https://doi.org/10.1088/1755-1315/428/1/012021

20. Liang, G.S., Wang, M.J.J.: Fuzzy fault-tree analysis using failure possibility. Microelectronics Reliability **33**(4), 583–597 (1993). https://doi.org/10.1016/0026-2714(93)90326-T

21. Lin, C.T., Wang, M.J.J.: Hybrid fault tree analysis using fuzzy sets. Reliability Engineering & System Safety **58**(3), 205–213 (1997). https://doi.org/10.1016/S0951-8320(97)00072-0

22. Lopuhaä-Zwakenberg, M., Budde, C.E., Stoelinga, M.: Efficient and generic algorithms for quantitative attack tree analysis. IEEE Transactions on Dependable and Secure Computing pp. 1–18 (2022). https://doi.org/10.1109/TDSC.2022.3215752

23. Mahmood, Y.A., Ahmadi, A., Verma, A.K., Srividya, A., Kumar, U.: Fuzzy fault tree analysis: a review of concept and application. International Journal of System Assurance Engineering and Management **4**, 19–32 (2013). https://doi.org/10.1007/s13198-013-0145-x

24. Massanet, S., Riera, J.V., Torrens, J., Herrera-Viedma, E.: A new linguistic computational model based on discrete fuzzy numbers for computing with words. Information Sciences **258**, 277–290 (2014)

25. Mauw, S., Oostdijk, M.: Foundations of attack trees. In: Information Security and Cryptology-ICISC 2005: 8th International Conference, Seoul, Korea, December 1-2, 2005, Revised Selected Papers 8. pp. 186–198. Springer (2006)
26. Pandey, M.: Fault tree analysis. Lecture notes, University of Waterloo, Waterloo (2005)
27. Peng, Z., Xiaodong, M., Zongrun, Y., Zhaoxiang, Y.: An approach of fault diagnosis for system based on fuzzy fault tree. In: Proceedings of the 2008 International Conference on MultiMedia and Information Technology. p. 697–700. MMIT '08, IEEE Computer Society, USA (2009). https://doi.org/10.1109/MMIT.2008.142
28. Purba, J.H., Sony Tjahyani, D., Ekariansyah, A.S., Tjahjono, H.: Fuzzy probability based fault tree analysis to propagate and quantify epistemic uncertainty. Annals of Nuclear Energy **85**, 1189–1199 (2015). https://doi.org/10.1016/j.anucene.2015.08.002
29. Purba, J.H., Tjahyani, D.T.S., Susila, I.P., Widodo, S., Ekariansyah, A.S.: Fuzzy probability and α-cut based-fault tree analysis approach to evaluate the reliability and safety of complex engineering systems. Quality and Reliability Engineering International **38**, 2356 – 2371 (2022). https://doi.org/10.1002/qre.3080
30. Reche, F., Morales, M., Salmerón, A.: Construction of fuzzy measures over product spaces. Mathematics **8**(9), 1605 (2020)
31. Ruijters, E., Stoelinga, M.: Fault tree analysis: A survey of the state-of-the-art in modeling, analysis and tools. Computer Science Review **15-16**, 29–62 (2015). https://doi.org/10.1016/j.cosrev.2015.03.001
32. Schneier, B.: Modeling security threats. Dr. Dobb's journal **24**(12) (1999)
33. Singer, D.: A fuzzy set approach to fault tree and reliability analysis. Fuzzy Sets and Systems **34**(2), 145–155 (1990). https://doi.org/10.1016/0165-0114(90)90154-X
34. Tanaka, H., Fan, L.T., Lai, F.S., Toguchi, K.: Fault-tree analysis by fuzzy probability. IEEE Transactions on Reliability **R-32**(5), 453–457 (1983). https://doi.org/10.1109/TR.1983.5221727
35. Wang, S., Ding, L., Sui, H., Gu, Z.: Cybersecurity risk assessment method of ICS based on attack-defense tree model. J. Intell. Fuzzy Syst. **40**(6), 10475–10488 (jan 2021). https://doi.org/10.3233/JIFS-201126
36. Wen, B., Li, P.: Risk assessment of security and stability control system against cyber attacks. In: 2021 IEEE 2nd China International Youth Conference on Electrical Engineering (CIYCEE). pp. 1–5 (2021). https://doi.org/10.1109/CIYCEE53554.2021.9676799
37. Yazdi, M., Mohammadpour, J., Li, H., Huang, H.Z., Zarei, E., Pirbalouti, R.G., Adumene, S.: Fault tree analysis improvements: A bibliometric analysis and literature review. Quality and Reliability Engineering International **39**(5), 1639–1659 (2023). https://doi.org/10.1002/qre.3271
38. Zadeh, L.: Fuzzy sets. Information and Control **8**(3), 338–353 (1965). https://doi.org/10.1016/S0019-9958(65)90241-X
39. Zadeh, L.: The concept of a linguistic variable and its application to approximate reasoning-iii. Information Sciences **9**(1), 43–80 (1975). https://doi.org/10.1016/0020-0255(75)90017-1
40. Zadeh, L.: The concept of a linguistic variable and its application to approximate reasoning—i. Information Sciences **8**(3), 199–249 (1975). https://doi.org/10.1016/0020-0255(75)90036-5
41. Zadeh, L.: The concept of a linguistic variable and its application to approximate reasoning—ii. Information Sciences **8**(4), 301–357 (1975). https://doi.org/10.1016/0020-0255(75)90046-8

Towards Reliable SQL Synthesis: Fuzzing-Based Evaluation and Disambiguation

Ricardo Brancas[1]([✉]) [iD], Miguel Terra-Neves[2] [iD], Miguel Ventura[2] [iD],
Vasco Manquinho[1] [iD], and Ruben Martins[3] [iD]

[1] INESC-ID / Instituto Superior Técnico, Universidade de Lisboa, Lisbon, Portugal
ricardo.brancas@tecnico.ulisboa.pt
[2] OutSystems, Linda-a-Velha, Portugal
[3] Carnegie Mellon University, Pittsburgh, USA

Abstract In recent years, more people have seen their work depend on data manipulation tasks. However, many of these users do not have the background in programming required to write complex programs, particularly SQL queries. One way of helping these users is automatically synthesizing the SQL query given a small set of examples. Several program synthesizers for SQL have been recently proposed, but they do not leverage multicore architectures.

This paper proposes CUBES, a parallel program synthesizer for the domain of SQL queries using input-output examples. Since input-output examples are an under-specification of the desired SQL query, sometimes, the synthesized query does not match the user's intent. CUBES incorporates a new disambiguation procedure based on fuzzing techniques that interacts with the user and increases the confidence that the returned query matches the user intent. We perform an extensive evaluation on around 4000 SQL queries from different domains. Experimental results show that our parallel approach can scale up to 16 processes with superlinear speedups for many hard instances, and that our disambiguation approach is critical to achieving an accuracy of around 60%, significantly larger than other SQL synthesizers.

1 Introduction

In the age of digital transformation, many people are being reassigned to tasks that require familiarity with programming or database usage. However, many users lack the technical skills to build queries in a language such as Structured Query Language (SQL). Hence, several new systems have been proposed for automatically generating SQL queries for relational databases [32,20,30,33]. The goal of *query synthesis* is to automatically generate an SQL query that corresponds to the user's intent. For instance, the user can specify their intent using natural language [30,33] or examples [28,32,20,27]. Our work targets query synthesis using examples, where an example consists of a database and an output table that results from querying the database. The problem of synthesizing SQL queries from input-output examples is known as Query Reverse Engineering [29].

D. Beyer and A. Cavalcanti (Eds.): FASE 2024, LNCS 14573, pp. 232–254, 2024.
https://doi.org/10.1007/978-3-031-57259-3_11

CourseID	StudentID	Grade
10	36933	A
11	36933	B
12	36933	A
10	37362	A
12	37362	C
11	37453	A
10	37510	B
12	37510	A
10	37955	A

(a) The **Grades** table.

CourseID	CourseName
10	Programming
11	Algorithms
12	Databases

(b) The **Courses** table.

CourseName	GradeCount
Programming	4
Algorithms	2
Databases	3

(c) The output table.

Figure 1: Two input tables: **Courses** and **Grades**. Output table: number of grades per course.

Figure 1 illustrates an input-output example with two input tables (Courses and Grades) and an output table. The output table corresponds to counting the number of grades in each course. In this example, the goal is to synthesize the following SQL query:

```
SELECT CourseName, count(*) AS 'GradeCount'
FROM Grades NATURAL JOIN Courses
GROUP BY CourseName
```

Observe that, for a person with limited database training, it is often easier to define one or more examples than to learn how to write the desired SQL query.

Even though query synthesis tools using examples [28,32,20,27] have seen a remarkable improvement in recent years, they still suffer from scalability problems with respect to the size of the input tables and the complexity of the synthesized queries. Nowadays, multicore processors have become the predominant architecture for common laptops and servers. However, none of the previous query synthesis tools take advantage of the parallelism available in these architectures. In this work, we present CUBES, the *first parallel synthesizer* for SQL queries. CUBES is built on top of an open-source sequential query synthesizer [20], which we further improved by extending the language of queries supported by CUBES and by adding pruning techniques that can prevent incorrect programs from being enumerated. To take advantage of parallel architectures, we extend CUBES by using *divide-and-conquer*. In this approach, each process searches a smaller sub-problem until it either finds a solution or exhausts that subspace and chooses another sub-problem to solve. We present a novel approach to create sub-problems based on considering different subsets of the domain-specific language for each process.

To evaluate our tool, we collected benchmarks from previous works [32,28,27,20]. Also, we created a new dataset by extending existing query synthesis problems using natural language [35] to use examples instead. In the end, we collected around 4000 instances that will be publicly available and can be used by other researchers when evaluating query synthesis tools.

We perform an exhaustive comparison between CUBES and state-of-the-art SQL synthesizers based on examples [32,20,27]. Our evaluation shows that current SQL synthesizers can synthesize many SQL queries that satisfy the examples but do not match the user intent. We observe that *all* state-of-the-art SQL synthesizers return fewer than 50% of queries that match the user intent, i.e., even though they satisfy the example given by the user they do not match the query that the user had in mind. CUBES addresses this challenge by using parallelism to find multiple solutions and interact with the user to *disambiguate* the query that matches the user intent. To disambiguate the queries, we use fuzzing to produce new examples that result in a different output for the possible synthesized queries. We select one of these examples and ask the user if the output is correct for these new input tables. If the user responds affirmatively, we can discard all queries that do not match this new output. Otherwise, if the user responds negatively, we can discard the queries that match the new output. We repeat this process until we are confident that we found the query the user intended.

To summarize, this paper makes the following key contributions:

- a divide-and-conquer procedure for SQL synthesis (section 2).
- a new procedure that uses fuzzing to disambiguate a set of queries that satisfies the initial example (section 3).
- a new large dataset for SQL synthesis using examples with around 4000 instances (section 5).
- a new open-source SQL synthesis tool called CUBES whose parallel version with 16 processes outperforms the sequential version by solving more instances and having a median speedup of around $15\times$ on hard instances (section 5).
- a first study that analyses the accuracy of queries returned by SQL synthesizers showing that more than 55% of the queries do not match the user intent. Our disambiguation procedure improves the accuracy of CUBES to 60% and significantly outperforms other example-based synthesizers (section 5).

2   SQL Synthesis

In this work, we propose CUBES, a divide-and-conquer query synthesizer that builds upon the open-source SQL synthesizer SQUARES [20]. SQUARES is a sequential synthesizer based on enumeration that uses operations from the R programming language as its Domain Specific Language (DSL)[4]. R is more expressive than SQL and allows a more compact representation for database queries. Since SQUARES is modular and open-source, it is easy to modify and extend to a parallel setting. CUBES splits the synthesis problem into disjoint sub-problems to be solved in parallel by each of the available processes. Hence, each process focuses solely on a particular area of the search space.

---

[4] A detailed description of the DSL is available in the extended version of this paper [3].

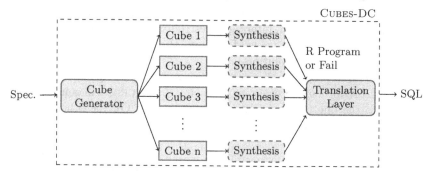

Figure 2: CUBES' architecture for divide-and-conquer.

In our context, each sub-problem is represented by a *cube*: a sequence of operations from CUBES' DSL such that the arguments for the operations are still to be determined. Consider the following cube as an example: [filter, natural_join], which represents the section of the search space composed by programs with two operations, where the first is a filter (equivalent to a WHERE in SQL) and the second is a natural_join.

The overall architecture of CUBES is illustrated in Figure 2. The Cube Generator component is responsible for generating cubes in increasing size (i.e., first the cubes with one operation, then with two operations, and so forth), building a FIFO queue. Observe that since each cube corresponds to a distinct sequence of operations, there is no intersection in the search space of the different cubes. Then, each process receives a specific cube and checks if it is possible to fill in the missing arguments (e.g., columns, tables, filter conditions) to satisfy the input-output examples. Whenever a process finds a solution, the translation layer transforms the R program into SQL. Otherwise, if a cube cannot be extended into a complete program that satisfies the user specification, the process gets a new cube from the Cube Generator queue.

Dynamic Cube Generation. One approach for a cube generation heuristic is to define a static order of operations to be explored. Although a static heuristic can be effective on some specific domains, it is very unlikely that it generalizes to new instances. Therefore, CUBES uses a dynamic cube generator inspired by natural language techniques. Since candidate programs are constructed as a sequence of operations, a bigram prediction model can be used to decide the next operation to be chosen in a given sequence. Therefore, when choosing the next operation, the operation immediately preceding it is used to compute an expectation of which of the possible choices will lead to the desired program.

Program scoring. The initial scores of the bigram can be improved during the search by using information from programs that do not satisfy the examples. For a given program p, we compute the score of the program p as the percentage of elements of the expected output (according to the provided example) that appear in the output of p. A score of 1 indicates that all the expected values occur in the output, and as such, filtering or restructuring might lead to a correct program. On the other hand, a value of 0 means that the candidate program is likely very far from a correct solution.

For each evaluated program, the score, $score(p)$, is used to update the bigram scores. A high score for a given program, p, means that CUBES will generate new cubes similar to the one that originated the program p. On the other hand, a low score means that CUBES will try to diversify the search in the future.

DSL Splitting. Besides the splitting of the search space using cubes, CUBES also splits the DSL operations among the processes. The motivation for this additional split is that some DSL operations have more possible argument completions than others. For instance, there are many more ways to complete an `inner_join` operation than, for example, a `filter` operation. If the program to be synthesized does not require some of the complex operations, then we can solve this program more quickly with a smaller DSL. To ensure that CUBES can always find the correct program, at least one process always runs with the entire DSL while the other processes may contain only subsets of the DSL.

3   Accuracy and Disambiguation

An essential issue in program synthesis is knowing if the returned program corresponds to the user intent. To determine the accuracy of the synthesis tools, we call the query that the user wishes to obtain the *ground truth* query. Observe that SQL synthesis tools that use input-output examples return a query that satisfies the user's examples. However, these examples are an under-specification, and as such, the returned query might not satisfy the true user intent.

CUBES may find multiple queries that satisfy the examples. However, unless these queries are equivalent, only one of them matches the user's intent. To address this challenge, we create new examples with different input-output pairs for the synthesized queries and interact with the user to disambiguate the correct query. Next, we describe how to use fuzzing to create new examples and our disambiguation procedure to improve CUBES's accuracy and meet the user intent.

3.1   Fuzzing

Given a set of synthesized queries, our goal is to determine which one matches the user intent. Since some of them may be equivalent, multiple queries may be correct. One approach is to use query equivalence tools to check the equivalence of these queries and only consider a representative query of each equivalence class. Although recent work in query equivalence tools [6,38,5] has advanced the state-of-the-art, these tools remain incomplete, not supporting many complex queries present in our datasets. To overcome this limitation, we use a fuzzing-based approach to determine the approximate equivalency of different queries.

Consider a synthesis problem with an input-output example (I, O) and let Q_1 and Q_2 be two queries that satisfy this example. Fuzzing consists of taking the input I, slightly modifying it, and producing I'. Next, we apply both Q_1 and Q_2 to I' producing the outputs O_1' and O_2', respectively. If the outputs differ $(O_1' \neq O_2')$, then Q_1 and Q_2 are surely distinct. However, if the outputs are equal $(O_1' = O_2')$, we cannot conclude that the queries are equivalent. Hence, we perform several rounds of fuzzing, generating and testing different inputs, with each round increasing the confidence in our answer.

In order to produce fuzzed input-output examples, we use the Semantic Evaluation suite [37]. Consider a table, $T \in I$. In order to generate a fuzzed version of this table, $T' \in I'$, the suite starts by randomly selecting the number of rows of the new table. Then, to fill the cells of T', three sources are used: (1) values sampled from a uniform distribution for the given type (i.e., for integers a uniform distribution on $[-2^{63}, 2^{63} - 1]$), (2) values taken from the corresponding columns on the original table, T, and closely related values (i.e., if "Alice" is in T then both "Alice" and "Alicegg" might be considered for T'), and (3) values taken from the queries we are comparing, and closely related values. The reason why the suite takes into account values from the queries themselves is to increase code coverage (e.g., making it more likely to find off-by-one errors). Finally, all foreign keys are respected so that the semantics of the database are preserved.

3.2   Disambiguation

CUBES is able to return multiple queries that satisfy the user specification. However, if the example provided is an under-specification of the true user intent, those queries will most likely have slightly different semantics. In order to ease the burden on the user of selecting a correct query, we propose a disambiguation algorithm, shown in Algorithm 1.

CUBES starts by synthesizing all possible solutions under a given time limit. The goal of the disambiguation is then to ask the user questions in order to iteratively discard queries until we find one that satisfies the user intent. Our procedure attempts to minimize the number of questions as much as possible, by trying to discard approximately half of the queries each time we ask a question.

To do this, we start by generating a new input database I' through fuzzing. Next, we execute each of the synthesized queries on this new input I' and group them according to the output they produce. In each disambiguation step, we generate 16 new input databases, by performing fuzzing 16 times, and selecting the input-output example that is closest to splitting the set of queries in half.

Figure 3 shows a real-world disambiguation interaction. Initially, we have 7 queries found by CUBES that satisfy the original input-output example. In this case, we generate a new input I' such that 1 of the 7 queries provides the output table A', 3 queries provide as output table B', and 3 others provide an output C'. Then, we ask the user if the new input-output example (I', B') is correct. If the user answers yes, then the solution is one of the 3 queries. Otherwise, the solution should be one of the 4 remaining queries. Since the user answered yes, then 3 queries remain to disambiguate. The disambiguation procedure terminates

---

Algorithm 1: Disambiguation method

Input: $\mathcal{S}$, the set of synthesized queries, I, input database,
O, output table, R, number of fuzzing rounds

Result: a query considered to be the most likely solution

Disambiguate$(\mathcal{S}, I, O, R)$

1 bestSplit $\leftarrow \emptyset$;

2 **for** $i \leftarrow 1$ **to** R **do**

3 | $I' \leftarrow$ Fuzz$(I, \mathcal{S})$;

4 | split $\leftarrow$ GroupByOutput$(\mathcal{S}, I')$;

5 | **if** BetterSplit(bestSplit, split) **then**

6 | | bestSplit $\leftarrow$ split;

  end

7 **if** bestSplit $= \emptyset$ **then**

8 | **return** First$(\mathcal{S})$;

9 $(I', \mathcal{S}_A, O'_A, \mathcal{S}_B) \leftarrow$ bestSplit;

10 **if** AskUserIfExampleIsCorrect(I', O'_A) **then**

11 | **return** Disambiguate$(\mathcal{S}_A, I, O, R)$;

12 **else**

13 | **return** Disambiguate$(\mathcal{S}_B, I, O, R)$;

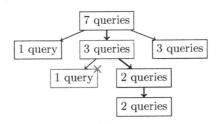

Figure 3: Example disambiguation process from a problem that generated 7 possible queries. Blue boxes represent the input-output example given to the user.

when either there is only one query remaining or the fuzzing procedure is unable to find a new example to distinguish the remaining queries. In the latter case, the remaining queries are deemed equivalent and the first one found by CUBES during the search is returned to the user. Notice that CUBES enumerates queries in increasing order of the number of operators. Hence, the first queries to be found by CUBES have the fewest operations and should be more general.

4   Methods and Data

This section describes the benchmark sets used to evaluate CUBES and compare it to other synthesizers, as well as two distinct methods to perform that comparison: simple evaluation and fuzzy-based evaluation.

Data. We use five different benchmark sets, divided into two groups. The first group, consisting of the benchmarks `recent-posts`, `top-rated-posts`, `textbook`

Algorithm 2: Query checker using fuzzing

Input: q, the synthesized query, Q, the ground truth query,
  I, input database, R, number of fuzzing rounds
Result: a Boolean representing if a distinguishing input was not found
FuzzyCheck(q, Q, I, R)

1 **if** Execute(Q, I) $\neq$ Execute(q, I) **then**
2 | **return** *False*;
3 **for** $i \leftarrow 1$ **to** R **do**
4 | $I' \leftarrow$ Fuzz(I, Q);
5 | **if** Execute(Q, I') $\neq$ Execute(q, I') **then**
6 | | **return** *False*;
  end
7 **return** *True*;

---

and `kaggle` refers to benchmarks that were previously used in other example-based SQL synthesis papers [32,36,20,27]. The second group consists of a single benchmark set: `spider`. We adapted the instances in `spider` from a very large and diverse dataset of queries used for SQL synthesis from Natural Language (NL) descriptions (also known as text-to-SQL) [35]. Overall, we used 176 instances from previously established benchmark sets, and created 3690 new instances.

Simple Evaluation. In this setting, we are simply interested in checking if a synthesizer can produce a query that satisfies the specification given by the user. That is, when executed, the query should produce an output table that is equal to the one specified by the user. Furthermore, we do not take into account the row order of the output table. This method has been extensively used in the past to measure the performance of SQL synthesizers [32,36,20,27]. The problem with simple evaluation is that, in the case of an ambiguous example, it does not address whether the synthesized query actually satisfies the user intent or not.

Fuzzy-based Evaluation. In this setting, we check if the synthesized queries satisfy the true intent of the user and not just the input-output example. The motive for this distinction is that the input-output example might be an under-specification of the query the user wishes to obtain. That is, several queries can satisfy the example, but they do not have the same semantics.

Algorithm 2 shows how we use fuzzing, as introduced in subsection 3.1, to determine if two queries are likely to have the same semantics. We start by sanity checking if the synthesized query, q, and the ground truth query, Q, produce the same output for the provided input database, I (lines 1-2). Then, we perform R rounds of fuzzing (line 3), where for each round, we generate a new input database, I', and check if the two queries still produce the same output table (lines 5-6). If all rounds pass successfully, we consider the queries equivalent (line 7). When comparing two tables, we perform a very lax comparison that: (1) ignores row order – tables are seen as a multiset of rows, (2) ignores column names, and (3) tries to convert the datatypes of columns – if two columns contain the same data but one as a number and the other as a string, they are considered equivalent. Note that several rounds might be needed to find an input that distinguishes the queries. The parameter R controls the maximum number of fuzzing rounds until the algorithm deems the queries equivalent.

5 Evaluation

The evaluation presented next aim to answer the following research questions:

Q1. How does the sequential version of CUBES, CUBES-SEQ, compare with other state-of-the-art SQL synthesizers when using the simple evaluation metric? (subsection 5.2)

Q2. What are the speedups obtained by using the divide-and-conquer approach, CUBES-DC, when using the simple evaluation metric? (subsection 5.3)

Q3. How do CUBES and the other SQL synthesizers perform when using the fuzzy-based evaluation metric? (subsection 5.4)

Q4. What is the impact of program disambiguation in CUBES' fuzzy-based evaluation metric? (subsection 5.4)

All results were obtained on a dual socket Intel® Xeon® Silver 4210R @ 2.40GHz, with a total of 20 cores and 64GB of RAM. Furthermore, a limit of 10 minutes (wall-clock time) and 56GB of RAM was imposed on all synthesizers (sequential or parallel). All limits were strictly imposed using `runsolver` [22].

5.1 Implementation

CUBES is implemented on top of the Trinity [15] framework, using Python 3.8.3. Candidate programs are evaluated by translating the DSL operations into equivalent R instructions. In particular, the `tidyverse`[5] family of packages is used to implement table manipulations. Once a correct R program is found, the `dbplyr`[6] package (version 1.4.4) is used to translate that program to an equivalent SQL query. In the parallel synthesizer, inter-process communication is achieved using a message-passing approach through Python's `multiprocessing` pipes. All source code, instance files, and execution logs are made publicly available.[7]

We use the fuzzing framework developed by Zhong et al. [37] in our disambiguation module to perform accuracy analysis. Furthermore, queries are executed using the SQLAlchemy[8] library (version 1.3.20), and row order is ignored when comparing tables. The original implementation of the fuzzing framework is non-deterministic, so we modified it in two important ways: (1) we added proper seeding for Python's pseudo-random number generator, and (2) we replaced all

---

[5] https://www.tidyverse.org/

[6] https://dbplyr.tidyverse.org/

[7] https://doi.org/10.5281/zenodo.10492998

[8] https://www.sqlalchemy.org/

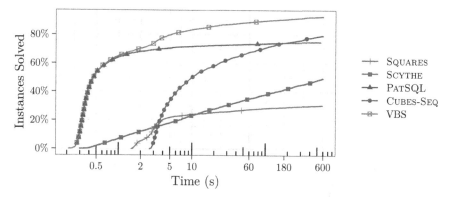

Figure 4: Percentage of instances solved by each tool at each point in time. A mark is placed every 150 solved instances.

usages of the `set` data structure with `OrderedSet` (sets backed with a list so that the iteration order is deterministic). This change was needed so that both the accuracy results presented in the paper and CUBES' disambiguation process are deterministic. The modified framework is also included in CUBES' source files.

5.2   Sequential Performance using Simple Evaluation

We start by evaluating the performance of CUBES-SEQ, the sequential version of CUBES, and perform a comparison with other state-of-the-art SQL Programming by Example (PBE) tools: SQUARES [20], SCYTHE [32] and PATSQL [27]. Figure 4 shows the percentage of instances solved by each synthesizer as a function of time when using the simple evaluation method. Overall, SQUARES was able to solve 30.6% of the instances within the time limit of 10 minutes, while SCYTHE solved 49.5% and PATSQL solved 75.1%. CUBES-SEQ was able to solve 79.4%.

Figure 4 also shows the Virtual Best Solver (VBS) for these four synthesizers. The VBS can be seen as the result of running the four synthesizers in parallel, or, equivalently, having an oracle that predicts which synthesizer is the best for a given instance and using it. The VBS is able to solve more instances than any of the other synthesizers (92.7% vs. the 79.4% for CUBES). This shows two things: (1) not all synthesizers solve the same instances, and (2) it is advantageous to run multiple synthesizers in parallel if the user has the resources for it. Furthermore, if we consider a VBS with only the top-performing synthesizers, PATSQL and CUBES, the percentage of solved instances is 90.5% (vs. 92.7% with the four synthesizers), meaning that using two synthesizers in parallel results in 10%+ extra instances solved compared to just using CUBES.

One interesting difference between these synthesizers is the minimum time in which they can return a solution for any of the instances, with SCYTHE and PATSQL at around 0.3 seconds, while SQUARES and CUBES only solve the first instance at 2 to 3 seconds. The most likely explanation for this difference is the

Table 1: Overall results for 10 seconds and 10 minutes grouped by benchmark. The best tool for each time-limit/benchmark pair is highlighted in **bold**.

Run	kaggle	recent-posts	top-rated-posts	spider	textbook	All	Median Speedup
			10 seconds				
SQUARES	21.2%	3.9%	5.3%	24.7%	28.6%	24.1%	
SCYTHE	0.0%	**49.0%**	**66.7%**	22.5%	28.6%	23.4%	
PATSQL	**57.6%**	41.2%	64.9%	72.5%	**62.9%**	71.7%	
CUBES-SEQ	15.2%	11.8%	33.3%	51.5%	34.3%	50.3%	
CUBES-DC4	24.2%	11.8%	59.6%	70.0%	48.6%	68.5%	
CUBES-DC8	27.3%	15.7%	63.2%	73.2%	54.3%	71.8%	
CUBES-DC16	24.2%	19.6%	63.2%	**75.4%**	51.4%	**73.8%**	
			10 minutes				
SQUARES	21.2%	7.8%	22.8%	31.0%	40.0%	30.6%	
SCYTHE	3.0%	**66.7%**	**80.7%**	49.1%	54.3%	49.5%	
PATSQL	**63.6%**	45.1%	66.7%	75.8%	68.6%	75.1%	
CUBES-SEQ	39.4%	25.5%	66.7%	80.9%	57.1%	79.4%	$(1\times)$
CUBES-DC4	45.5%	31.4%	73.7%	88.4%	71.4%	86.9%	8.4 ×
CUBES-DC8	54.5%	39.2%	73.7%	89.6%	68.6%	88.2%	12.8 ×
CUBES-DC16	51.5%	39.2%	75.4%	**90.4%**	**77.1%**	**89.0%**	15.5 ×

startup time for the programming languages used by the synthesizers. PATSQL and SCYTHE both use Java, while SQUARES and CUBES use Python and also need to initialize the R execution environment. Figure 4 also shows that both SCYTHE and CUBES-SEQ are able to solve more problem instances when we increase the time limit, while PATSQL and SQUARES seem to reach a plateau.

Table 1 shows the results for each benchmark set with virtual time limits of 10 seconds (top half) and 10 minutes (bottom half). We can see that CUBES-SEQ is able to solve more instances than SQUARES in all benchmarks sets while solving more instances than SCYTHE in 3 out of 5 benchmark sets. When comparing with PATSQL, the results shown in Figure 4 are confirmed since although PATSQL solves more instances with a shorter time limit, CUBES-SEQ is able to solve more instances in one benchmark set (spider) with a larger time limit.

5.3 Parallel Performance using Simple Evaluation

Considering the sequential version CUBES-SEQ as our baseline, we now evaluate the performance of the parallel version using divide-and-conquer (CUBES-DC).

Table 1 shows the results for the divide-and-conquer strategy CUBES-DC with 4, 8, and 16 processes. Notice that divide-and-conquer tools improve upon the sequential version, from 79.4% up to 89.0% when using 16 processes. Moreover, within a limit of 10 seconds, the parallel versions are able to solve 68.5%,

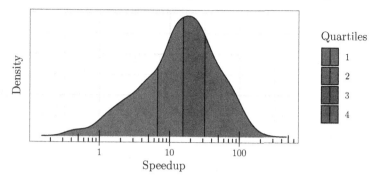

Figure 5: Instance speedup distribution for CUBES-DC16.

71.8%, and 73.8% of the instances when using, respectively, 4, 8, and 16 processes. This contrasts with the sequential version that only solves 50.3% of the instances. Hence, there is a significant speedup when using the divide-and-conquer strategy, especially for shorter time limits. Observe that even within the time limit of 10 seconds, CUBES-DC is the best-performing solver.

Formally, the speedup of method A in relation to method B is defined as the time needed to execute method B divided by the time needed to execute method A, and is a measure of how fast an implementation is compared to another. The last column of Table 1 shows the speedup obtained by each parallel version of CUBES in relation to the sequential version CUBES-SEQ for instances where CUBES-SEQ needed 1 minute (or more) to solve. We focus this analysis on the harder instances for the sequential tool since higher speedups in these instances have a higher impact on the end user's experience.

We can see that most configurations have a median speedup greater than the number of processes used. This is called a super-linear speedup and occurs because programs are enumerated in a different order when using our parallel versions. Figure 5 shows the full speedup distribution for CUBES-DC16 along with the distribution quartiles. We can see that more than 50% of instances have a speedup greater than 10 when using 16 processes, while more than 25% of instances have a speedup greater than 30.

5.4 Results using Fuzzing-based Evaluation

In this section we analyze the number of instances solved by CUBES when using the more thorough fuzzy-based evaluation, as well as comparing it with other program synthesis tools. Furthermore, we also evaluate the program disambiguator introduced in section 3.

Figure 6 shows the results when using the fuzzy-based evaluation method instead of the simple evaluation. For this evaluation, we used 16 fuzzing rounds ($R = 16$). The "FuzzyCheck Timeout" label in the plot represents instances for which the fuzzing evaluation timed out and not a timeout of the synthesizer

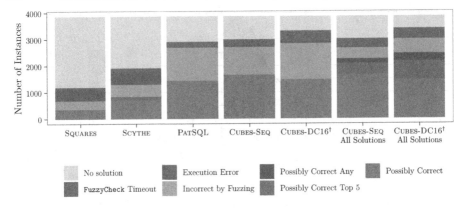

Figure 6: Results of the fuzzy-based evaluation for each synthesizer.

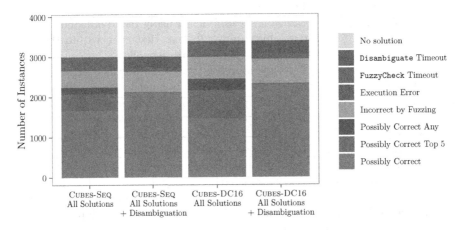

Figure 7: Fuzzy-based evaluation results before and after disambiguation.

used. We used a time limit of 60 seconds per fuzzing round ($16 \times 60s = 960s$). Furthermore, some of the synthesized queries failed to execute (labelled as "Execution Error"). This happens for two reasons: (1) some synthesized queries are incompatible with the SQLite dialect, and (2) some of the synthesized queries contain syntax problems.

We label instances for which we could not find a distinguishing input from the ground truth as "Possibly Correct", while instances for which we did find such input are labelled as "Incorrect by Fuzzing". Furthermore, for synthesizers that return multiple solutions, "Possibly Correct Top 5" means that there was a query in the top-5 returned queries for which we did not find a distinguishing input from the ground truth. Similarly, "Possibly Correct Any" means that the

Table 2: Comparison of the fuzzy-based evaluation with the simple evaluation.

	Scythe	Squares	PatSQL	Cubes-Seq All Solutions	Cubes-DC16 All Solutions
Solved (simple eval.)	49.5%	30.6%	75.1%	79.5%	90.2%
Possibly Correct[a]	21.6%	9.2%	37.1%	58.0%	63.3%
as % of Solved instances	*43.6%*	*30.0%*	*49.4%*	*73.0%*	*70.2%*
Incorrect by Fuzzing	11.6%	8.4%	32.3%	10.7%	14.1%
as % of Solved instances	*23.4%*	*27.5%*	*43.0%*	*13.5%*	*15.6%*
Inconclusive	16.2%	13.1%	5.7%	8.9%	10.2%
as % of Solved instances	*32.7%*	*42.8%*	*7.6%*	*11.2%*	*11.3%*

[a] Includes instances in Possibly Correct Top 5 and Possibly Correct Any.

synthesizer returned a query for which we could not distinguish it from the ground truth.

Previous tools all suffer from fairly low accuracy rates, staying under 45%, as do Cubes-Seq and Cubes-DC16 if we only consider the first solution returned. However, if we consider all solutions returned under 10 minutes, then Cubes generates a correct (using fuzzy-based evaluation) solution on around 63% of the instances, as shown in Table 2.

In order to be able to give that correct solution to the user, as opposed to giving them all the solutions generated, we developed a query disambiguator. Figure 7 shows the results of using that disambiguator on Cubes-Seq and Cubes-DC16. We can see that the disambiguator can almost always identify the correct query if such a query exists in the set of queries synthesized. Note that small differences in the exact number of queries deemed correct using the fuzzy-based evaluation may be due to different fuzzed inputs being generated.

It is also worth noting that a very small number of instances are labeled as "Possibly Correct Top 5". As explained in Section 3, Cubes returns the earliest synthesized query when we reach a set of queries that we cannot distinguish from one another. This means that, for those instances, a correct query was in the final set of queries selected by the disambiguation, but it was not the first one generated by Cubes. This happens because while the accuracy test has access to the ground truth and can thus generate better-fuzzed inputs, the disambiguator is limited to using values from the queries it is trying to disambiguate. Even so, the fact that this only occurs in a very small number of queries indicates that the approach is valid and seems to be able to both correctly disambiguate most queries and catch the cases where the disambiguation fails.

We show that if we only consider the first solution, Cubes' performance is similar to other existing tools. The main improvement comes from (1) synthesizing many possible queries for a given problem and (2) having a program disambiguator to choose the right query. This first point is directly influenced by our parallel approach to program synthesis, which allows us to synthesize more programs that satisfy the examples under the chosen time limit.

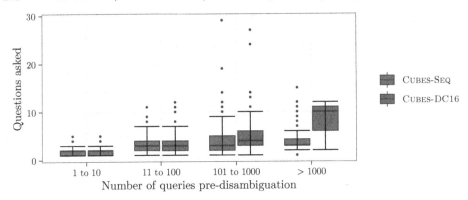

Figure 8: Number of questions that need to be asked to the user in order to perform disambiguation, as a function of the number of queries synthesized.

Finally, we analyze how many questions are asked to the user to disambiguate the queries produced by CUBES. Figure 8 shows this data as a function of the number of queries synthesized. Consider the first bar of the second group, relating to instances where CUBES-SEQ generated 11 to 100 queries. The plot shows that to disambiguate those queries, we need at least 1 question, at most 11 questions, and on average 3 questions.

For CUBES-SEQ the average number of questions needed to disambiguate up to 1000 queries is 2.31, while for CUBES-DC16 it is 2.69. As stated in Section 3, our goal with the disambiguation strategy is to discard half the queries with each question asked. Thus, we would expect that the number of questions needed to disambiguate a given set of queries scales logarithmically with the size of that set. Figure 8 shows that this behavior is, in fact, observed in practice.

6   Discussion

Here we discuss the main threats to validity of this work and some challenges that were raised during the experimental evaluation.

Benchmarks. Our evaluation uses a large set of benchmarks from different domains. However, they may not be representative of tasks commonly performed by users or may have a bias towards a specific synthesis tool. To mitigate this, we included benchmarks from several previous synthesis tools and also extended a large dataset from query synthesis using NLP to use examples instead. In the end, we have around 4000 instances but they are dominated by the spider dataset [35]. Nevertheless, since this dataset has been extensively used in other domains and was not created by us, we believe that it is more general and less prone to bias.

Parallelism. The divide-and-conquer approach already shows scalability for hard instances when using 4 and 8 processes in a multicore architecture with super-linear speedups. However, when increasing the number of processes to 16 the gains are reduced. When the number of processes increases, there is an increase of contention for memory accesses that can slow down the performance of each process. To address this issue, it would be interesting to evaluate CUBES in a distributed setting. Note that the overhead of going from multicore to distributed should be small since the inter-process communication is already done using message-passing techniques, and no shared memory is used. Exchanging information between processes is another source of improvement that would be worth exploring in future work.

Cube generation. One way to further improve the divide-and-conquer approach is to consider other cube generation strategies. For instance, we could learn from data and use machine learning techniques such as pre-trained bigram scores or using neural networks to predict the most likely cubes. We could also explore other techniques similar to the ones used in SAT solvers, such as restarting the search after n programs/cubes have been attempted.

Fuzzy-based Evaluation. Even though query synthesis tools are becoming more efficient and can find a query that satisfies the input-output example given by the user, they may not find the query that the user intended. To the best of our knowledge, this is the first study where fuzzing was used to evaluate if the query returned by the synthesizer matches the user's intent. Even though fuzzing is not a precise measurement of correctness since it may return that some queries are equivalent when they may not be, it is an upper bound on the accuracy of these tools. With the continuous improvement of SQL equivalence tools [6,38,5], it may be possible to have an exact accuracy measurement in the future. However, even with the current results, we already observe that all synthesis tools return many answers that do not match the desired behavior.

Disambiguation. Interacting with the user to perform query disambiguation is essential to increase the accuracy of SQL synthesizers based on examples. However, the questions that we asked the user may be too hard to answer, or the user may answer them incorrectly. To mitigate the difficulty of the questions, we only ask yes or no questions and present examples based on fuzzing that are often similar to the initial example provided by the user. With this approach, we hope that the user can quickly answer these questions. We currently automate the disambiguation procedure and use the ground truth to answer the questions, but a user study could be done in the future to confirm our hypothesis that the questions are easy for users to answer. In this work, we assume that the user never answers the questions incorrectly. However, considering this scenario could open new research directions and is in line with recent work on program synthesis with noisy data [11] where the examples may be incorrect.

7   Related Work

SQL Synthesis. In recent years, several tools for query synthesis have been proposed using input-output examples to specify user intent [28,36,7,32,15,20]. Solving approaches vary from using decision trees with fixed templates [28,36] to abstract representations of queries that can potentially satisfy the input-output examples [32]. Another approach is to use SMT-based representations of the search space [7,19] such that each solution to the SMT formula represents a possible candidate query to be verified. The CUBES framework proposed in this paper is also based on SMT-based representations, but it extends prior work in several dimensions: (i) extends the language in the programs to be synthesized, (ii) proposes pruning techniques that can be directly encoded into SMT, and (iii) it is the first parallel tool for query synthesis.

In this paper, we compare CUBES with three other SQL Synthesis tools that use input-output examples: SCYTHE [32], SQUARES [20] and PATSQL [27]. SCYTHE and PATSQL use sketch-based enumeration, where first a skeleton program with missing parts is generated, and then, if the skeleton satisfies a preliminary evaluation, the synthesizer tries to complete the sketch to obtain a complete program. SQUARES, on the other hand, uses Satisfiability Modulo Theories (SMT)-based enumeration where complete programs are obtained by iterating the possible solutions of an SMT formula. Both SCYTHE and SQUARES have limited DSLs and thus are not as well suited for complex tasks. Furthermore, SCYTHE's ability to solve a given instance is severely limited by the size of its input tables. Although PATSQL has a comparatively more expressive DSL, it is still not able to outperform CUBES.

Another approach for specifying user intent is using natural language [33,30]. However, these approaches often need a large training data set from the query's domain. Recently, several techniques have been proposed that try to better generalize to cross-domain data [34,24]. Although many improvements have been attained in finding the structure of the query through effective semantic table parsing, defining the details (e.g., specific filter conditions) is usually hard, particularly in more complex queries. The use of natural language for query synthesis is complementary to our approach, and a combination of both strategies could improve the accuracy of program synthesizers at the cost of more input from the user, namely examples and a natural language description of the task.

Program Disambiguation. Current synthesizers focus primarily on generating programs that satisfy the user's specifications. However, in many situations, the produced program does not satisfy the true user intent [16,26]. Previous work has shown that this shortcoming can be solved without recurring to complete specifications by introducing a program disambiguator. This component is responsible for interacting with the user and choosing between several possible solutions. Mayer et al. [16] describe two types of user interaction for program disambiguation: in the first approach, users select the correct program among a set of returned solutions, which are presented in a way that allows easy navigation. The second approach is described as *conversational clarification*, where the system iteratively asks questions to the user, further refining the original specification until just one candidate program is left [8,21,14,31,13,17]. In CUBES, we use conversational clarification to improve the confidence in produced solutions while still keeping the complexity for the user low.

Parallel Solving. Solving logic formulas in parallel has been the subject of extensive research work [10,9,1,2], both using memory-shared [25] and distributed approaches [18]. One of the techniques used to explore the search space is called divide-and-conquer [12]. In this approach, the search space is split into disjoint areas such that there is no intersection between the areas explored by each process. In this case, work-stealing techniques [23] are commonly used to avoid starvation since the search space can be unevenly split among the processes. Although we adapt techniques from parallel automated reasoning, the parallelization in the CUBES framework is not done at solving logic formulas but at a more abstract level. In our case, logic formulas continue to be solved sequentially. Moreover, starvation is avoided by producing additional work, i.e., increasing the number of operations from the DSL in the programs to be enumerated.

8   Conclusions

This work introduces CUBES, a new enumeration-based framework for query synthesis from examples. A new robust tool is proposed that is able to synthesize an extensive range of SQL queries. Additionally, CUBES also takes advantage of the current multicore processor architectures, providing the first parallel query synthesizer from examples using a divide-and-conquer approach. The splitting of the program space is done by providing different sequences of operations to each thread, as well as performing DSL splitting among threads.

An in-depth experimental evaluation is also carried out, comparing CUBES with other state-of-the-art query synthesizers in a wide variety of benchmark sets. Experimental results show the effectiveness and robustness of CUBES, being able to successfully synthesize SQL queries for a larger range of problem instances than other tools. Moreover, the parallel versions of CUBES have superlinear speedups for many hard instances and, when using 16 processes, provide a median speedup of 15× over the sequential version of the tool.

Finally, an accuracy analysis of the produced queries is also performed using fuzzing techniques. Results show that the queries produced by current synthesizers often differ from the user intent, and more than 50% of the queries returned to the user do not match the expected behavior the user had in mind. To increase the trust and reliability of SQL synthesizers, we advocate the need to use a fuzzing-based evaluation that can more precisely measure the accuracy of SQL synthesizers. Using this methodology together with the large dataset that we collected will make it easier for other researchers to evaluate their SQL synthesis tools in the future.

Since examples are imprecise specifications, increasing the trust and reliability of SQL synthesizers is essential. To improve the reliability of CUBES, we propose an interactive procedure with the user that can disambiguate among all queries found by CUBES that satisfy the original input-output example. After the disambiguation procedure, the accuracy of CUBES in providing the user intent query is significantly increased from around 40% to 60%. Other synthesizers can use similar disambiguation approaches, and it is also expected to improve their accuracy with respect to the user intent.

Acknowledgments

This work was partially supported under National Science Foundation (NSF) Grant No. CCF-1762363, an Amazon Research Award, and by OutSystems and by Portuguese national funds through FCT, under projects UIDB/50021/2020 (DOI: 10.54499/UIDB/50021/2020), PTDC/CCI-COM/2156/2021 (DOI:10.544-99/PTDC/CCI-COM/2156/2021) and 2022.03537.PTDC (DOI: 10.54499/202-2.03537.PTDC). Support was also provided by FCT through the Carnegie Mellon Portugal Program under Grant PRT/BD/152086/2021.

Data-Availability Statement

The CUBES SQL synthesizer, our dataset and the experimental results presented in this work are available in our supplemental artifact [4].

References

1. Aigner, M., Biere, A., Kirsch, C.M., Niemetz, A., Preiner, M.: Analysis of portfolio-style parallel SAT solving on current multi-core architectures. In: Berre, D.L. (ed.) POS-13. Fourth Pragmatics of SAT workshop, a workshop of the SAT 2013 conference, July 7, 2013, Helsinki, Finland. EPiC Series in Computing, vol. 29, pp. 28–40. EasyChair (2013). https://doi.org/10.29007/73N4
2. Balyo, T., Sanders, P., Sinz, C.: Hordesat: A massively parallel portfolio SAT solver. In: Heule, M., Weaver, S.A. (eds.) Theory and Applications of Satisfiability Testing - SAT 2015 - 18th International Conference, Austin, TX, USA, September 24-27, 2015, Proceedings. Lecture Notes in Computer Science, vol. 9340, pp. 156–172. Springer (2015). https://doi.org/10.1007/978-3-319-24318-4_12
3. Brancas, R., Terra-Neves, M., Ventura, M., Manquinho, V., Martins, R.: CUBES: A parallel synthesizer for SQL using examples. CoRR abs/2203.04995 (2022). https://doi.org/10.48550/ARXIV.2203.04995
4. Brancas, R., Terra-Neves, M., Ventura, M., Manquinho, V., Martins, R.: Towards reliable SQL synthesis: Fuzzing-based evaluation and disambiguation (2024). https://doi.org/10.5281/zenodo.10492998
5. Chu, S., Murphy, B., Roesch, J., Cheung, A., Suciu, D.: Axiomatic foundations and algorithms for deciding semantic equivalences of SQL queries. Proc. VLDB Endow. 11(11), 1482–1495 (2018). https://doi.org/10.14778/3236187.3236200
6. Chu, S., Wang, C., Weitz, K., Cheung, A.: Cosette: An automated prover for SQL. In: 8th Biennial Conference on Innovative Data Systems Research, CIDR 2017, Chaminade, CA, USA, January 8-11, 2017, Online Proceedings. www.cidrdb.org (2017), http://cidrdb.org/cidr2017/papers/p51-chu-cidr17.pdf

7. Feng, Y., Martins, R., Van Geffen, J., Dillig, I., Chaudhuri, S.: Component-based Synthesis of Table Consolidation and Transformation Tasks from Examples. In: Proceedings of the 38th ACM SIGPLAN Conference on Programming Language Design and Implementation. pp. 422–436. PLDI 2017, ACM, New York, NY, USA (2017). https://doi.org/10.1145/3062341.3062351

8. Ferreira, M., Terra-Neves, M., Ventura, M., Lynce, I., Martins, R.: FOREST: an interactive multi-tree synthesizer for regular expressions. In: Groote, J.F., Larsen, K.G. (eds.) Tools and Algorithms for the Construction and Analysis of Systems - 27th International Conference, TACAS 2021, Held as Part of the European Joint Conferences on Theory and Practice of Software, ETAPS 2021, Luxembourg City, Luxembourg, March 27 - April 1, 2021, Proceedings, Part I. Lecture Notes in Computer Science, vol. 12651, pp. 152–169. Springer (2021). https://doi.org/10.1007/978-3-030-72016-2_9

9. Gent, I.P., Miguel, I., Nightingale, P., McCreesh, C., Prosser, P., Moore, N.C.A., Unsworth, C.: A review of literature on parallel constraint solving. Theory Pract. Log. Program. **18**(5-6), 725–758 (2018). https://doi.org/10.1017/S1471068418000340

10. Hamadi, Y., Sais, L. (eds.): Handbook of Parallel Constraint Reasoning. Springer (2018). https://doi.org/10.1007/978-3-319-63516-3

11. Handa, S., Rinard, M.C.: Inductive program synthesis over noisy data. In: Devanbu, P., Cohen, M.B., Zimmermann, T. (eds.) Proc. ACM Joint European Software Engineering Conference and Symposium on the Foundations of Software Engineering. pp. 87–98. ACM (2020). https://doi.org/10.1145/3368089.3409732

12. Heule, M.J.H., Kullmann, O., Biere, A.: Cube-and-conquer for satisfiability. In: Hamadi, Y., Sais, L. (eds.) Handbook of Parallel Constraint Reasoning, pp. 31–59. Springer (2018). https://doi.org/10.1007/978-3-319-63516-3_2

13. Ji, R., Liang, J., Xiong, Y., Zhang, L., Hu, Z.: Question selection for interactive program synthesis. In: Donaldson, A.F., Torlak, E. (eds.) Proceedings of the 41st ACM SIGPLAN International Conference on Programming Language Design and Implementation, PLDI 2020, London, UK, June 15-20, 2020. pp. 1143–1158. ACM (2020). https://doi.org/10.1145/3385412.3386025

14. Li, H., Chan, C., Maier, D.: Query from examples: An iterative, data-driven approach to query construction. Proc. VLDB Endow. **8**(13), 2158–2169 (2015). https://doi.org/10.14778/2831360.2831369

15. Martins, R., Chen, J., Chen, Y., Feng, Y., Dillig, I.: Trinity: An Extensible Synthesis Framework for Data Science. Proc. VLDB Endow. **12**(12), 1914–1917 (Aug 2019). https://doi.org/10.14778/3352063.3352098

16. Mayer, M., Soares, G., Grechkin, M., Le, V., Marron, M., Polozov, O., Singh, R., Zorn, B.G., Gulwani, S.: User interaction models for disambiguation in programming by example. In: Latulipe, C., Hartmann, B., Grossman, T. (eds.) Proceedings of the 28th Annual ACM Symposium on User Interface Software & Technology, UIST 2015, Charlotte, NC, USA, November 8-11, 2015. pp. 291–301. ACM (2015). https://doi.org/10.1145/2807442.2807459

17. Narita, M., Maudet, N., Lu, Y., Igarashi, T.: Data-centric disambiguation for data transformation with programming-by-example. In: Hammond, T., Verbert, K., Parra, D., Knijnenburg, B.P., O'Donovan, J., Teale, P. (eds.) IUI '21: 26th International Conference on Intelligent User Interfaces, College Station, TX, USA, April 13-17, 2021. pp. 454–463. ACM (2021). https://doi.org/10.1145/3397481.3450680

18. Ngoko, Y., Cérin, C., Trystram, D.: Solving sat in a distributed cloud: A portfolio approach. Int. J. Appl. Math. Comput. Sci. **29**(2), 261–274 (2019). https://doi.org/10.2478/amcs-2019-0019

19. Orvalho, P., Terra-Neves, M., Ventura, M., Martins, R., Manquinho, V.: Encodings for Enumeration-Based Program Synthesis. In: Schiex, T., de Givry, S. (eds.) Principles and Practice of Constraint Programming. pp. 583–599. Lecture Notes in Computer Science, Springer International Publishing, Cham (2019). https://doi.org/10.1007/978-3-030-30048-7_34

20. Orvalho, P., Terra-Neves, M., Ventura, M., Martins, R., Manquinho, V.: SQUARES: A SQL synthesizer using query reverse engineering. Proceedings of the VLDB Endowment **13**(12), 2853–2856 (Aug 2020). https://doi.org/10.14778/3415478.3415492

21. Ramos, D., Pereira, J., Lynce, I., Manquinho, V.M., Martins, R.: UNCHARTIT: an interactive framework for program recovery from charts. In: 35th IEEE/ACM International Conference on Automated Software Engineering, ASE 2020, Melbourne, Australia, September 21-25, 2020. pp. 175–186. IEEE (2020). https://doi.org/10.1145/3324884.3416613

22. Roussel, O.: Controlling a Solver Execution with the runsolver Tool: System description. Journal on Satisfiability, Boolean Modeling and Computation **7**(4), 139–144 (Nov 2011). https://doi.org/10.3233/SAT190083

23. Schubert, T., Lewis, M.D.T., Becker, B.: Pamira - A parallel SAT solver with knowledge sharing. In: Abadir, M.S., Wang, L. (eds.) Sixth International Workshop on Microprocessor Test and Verification (MTV 2005), Common Challenges and Solutions, 3-4 November 2005, Austin, Texas, USA. pp. 29–36. IEEE Computer Society (2005). https://doi.org/10.1109/MTV.2005.17

24. Shi, P., Ng, P., Wang, Z., Zhu, H., Li, A.H., Wang, J., dos Santos, C.N., Xiang, B.: Learning contextual representations for semantic parsing with generation-augmented pre-training. In: Thirty-Fifth AAAI Conference on Artificial Intelligence, AAAI 2021, Thirty-Third Conference on Innovative Applications of Artificial Intelligence, IAAI 2021, The Eleventh Symposium on Educational Advances in Artificial Intelligence, EAAI 2021, Virtual Event, February 2-9, 2021. pp. 13806–13814. AAAI Press (2021). https://doi.org/10.1609/AAAI.V35I15.17627

25. Shinano, Y., Heinz, S., Vigerske, S., Winkler, M.: Fiberscip - A shared memory parallelization of SCIP. INFORMS J. Comput. **30**(1), 11–30 (2018). https://doi.org/10.1287/ijoc.2017.0762

26. Shriver, D., Elbaum, S.G., Stolee, K.T.: At the end of synthesis: Narrowing program candidates. In: 39th IEEE/ACM International Conference on Software Engineering: New Ideas and Emerging Technologies Results Track, ICSE-NIER 2017, Buenos Aires, Argentina, May 20-28, 2017. pp. 19–22. IEEE Computer Society (2017). https://doi.org/10.1109/ICSE-NIER.2017.7

27. Takenouchi, K., Ishio, T., Okada, J., Sakata, Y.: PATSQL: efficient synthesis of SQL queries from example tables with quick inference of projected columns. Proc. VLDB Endow. **14**(11), 1937–1949 (2021). https://doi.org/10.14778/3476249.3476253

28. Tran, Q.T., Chan, C., Parthasarathy, S.: Query by output. In: Çetintemel, U., Zdonik, S.B., Kossmann, D., Tatbul, N. (eds.) Proceedings of the ACM SIGMOD International Conference on Management of Data, SIGMOD 2009, Providence, Rhode Island, USA, June 29 - July 2, 2009. pp. 535–548. ACM (2009). https://doi.org/10.1145/1559845.1559902

29. Tran, Q.T., Chan, C.Y., Parthasarathy, S.: Query reverse engineering. VLDB J. **23**(5), 721–746 (2014). https://doi.org/10.1007/s00778-013-0349-3

30. Wang, B., Shin, R., Liu, X., Polozov, O., Richardson, M.: RAT-SQL: relation-aware schema encoding and linking for text-to-sql parsers. In: Jurafsky, D., Chai,

J., Schluter, N., Tetreault, J.R. (eds.) Proceedings of the 58th Annual Meeting of the Association for Computational Linguistics, ACL 2020, Online, July 5-10, 2020. pp. 7567–7578. Association for Computational Linguistics (2020). https://doi.org/10.18653/v1/2020.acl-main.677

31. Wang, C., Cheung, A., Bodík, R.: Interactive query synthesis from input-output examples. In: Salihoglu, S., Zhou, W., Chirkova, R., Yang, J., Suciu, D. (eds.) Proceedings of the 2017 ACM International Conference on Management of Data, SIGMOD Conference 2017, Chicago, IL, USA, May 14-19, 2017. pp. 1631–1634. ACM (2017). https://doi.org/10.1145/3035918.3058738

32. Wang, C., Cheung, A., Bodik, R.: Synthesizing Highly Expressive SQL Queries from Input-output Examples. In: Proceedings of the 38th ACM SIGPLAN Conference on Programming Language Design and Implementation. pp. 452–466. PLDI 2017, ACM, New York, NY, USA (2017). https://doi.org/10.1145/3062341.3062365

33. Yaghmazadeh, N., Wang, Y., Dillig, I., Dillig, T.: SQLizer: Query Synthesis from Natural Language. Proc. ACM Program. Lang. 1(OOPSLA), 63:1–63:26 (Oct 2017). https://doi.org/10.1145/3133887

34. Yu, T., Wu, C., Lin, X.V., Wang, B., Tan, Y.C., Yang, X., Radev, D.R., Socher, R., Xiong, C.: Grappa: Grammar-augmented pre-training for table semantic parsing. In: 9th International Conference on Learning Representations, ICLR 2021, Virtual Event, Austria, May 3-7, 2021. OpenReview.net (2021), https://openreview.net/forum?id=kyaIeYj4zZ

35. Yu, T., Zhang, R., Yang, K., Yasunaga, M., Wang, D., Li, Z., Ma, J., Li, I., Yao, Q., Roman, S., Zhang, Z., Radev, D.R.: Spider: A large-scale human-labeled dataset for complex and cross-domain semantic parsing and text-to-sql task. In: Riloff, E., Chiang, D., Hockenmaier, J., Tsujii, J. (eds.) Proceedings of the 2018 Conference on Empirical Methods in Natural Language Processing, Brussels, Belgium, October 31 - November 4, 2018. pp. 3911–3921. Association for Computational Linguistics (2018). https://doi.org/10.18653/V1/D18-1425

36. Zhang, S., Sun, Y.: Automatically synthesizing SQL queries from input-output examples. In: Denney, E., Bultan, T., Zeller, A. (eds.) 2013 28th IEEE/ACM International Conference on Automated Software Engineering, ASE 2013, Silicon Valley, CA, USA, November 11-15, 2013. pp. 224–234. IEEE (2013). https://doi.org/10.1109/ASE.2013.6693082

37. Zhong, R., Yu, T., Klein, D.: Semantic evaluation for text-to-sql with distilled test suites. In: Webber, B., Cohn, T., He, Y., Liu, Y. (eds.) Proceedings of the 2020 Conference on Empirical Methods in Natural Language Processing, EMNLP 2020, Online, November 16-20, 2020. pp. 396–411. Association for Computational Linguistics (2020). https://doi.org/10.18653/v1/2020.emnlp-main.29

38. Zhou, Q., Arulraj, J., Navathe, S.B., Harris, W., Xu, D.: Automated verification of query equivalence using satisfiability modulo theories. Proc. VLDB Endow. 12(11), 1276–1288 (2019). https://doi.org/10.14778/3342263.3342267

Invariant-based Program Repair

Omar I. Al-Bataineh[✉]

Simula Research Laboratory, Oslo, Norway
omar@simula.no

Abstract. This paper describes a formal general-purpose automated program repair (APR) framework based on the concept of program invariants. In the presented repair framework, the execution traces of a defected program are dynamically analyzed to infer specifications $\varphi_{correct}$ and $\varphi_{violated}$, where $\varphi_{correct}$ represents the set of likely invariants (good patterns) required for a run to be successful and $\varphi_{violated}$ represents the set of likely suspicious invariants (bad patterns) that result in the bug in the defected program. These specifications are then refined using rigorous program analysis techniques, which are also used to drive the repair process towards feasible patches and assess the correctness of generated patches. We demonstrate the usefulness of leveraging invariants in APR by developing an invariant-based repair system for performance bugs. The initial analysis shows the effectiveness of invariant-based APR in handling performance bugs by producing patches that ensure program's efficiency increase without adversely impacting its functionality.

Keywords: Automated program repair · Invariant learning and refinement · Patch overfitting · Program verifier · CPAChecker · Performance bugs

1 Introduction

Automated program repair (APR) has recently gained great attention because it helps to significantly decrease manual debugging effort by automatically generating patches for defected programs. Modern program repair tools have been shown to be effective at fixing bugs in many real-world programs. The poor quality of automatically generated patches [11], however, continues to be a major obstacle to the adoption of automated program repair by software practitioners.
Problem: The primary reason for the low quality of automatically generated patches by current APR tools is the lack of specifications of the intended behavior. Most program repair systems rely on tests as the correctness criteria, because a formal specification is not explicitly provided by software developers. Therefore, current APR approaches produce plausible patches which must be (manually) inspected before being deployed. As a result, there is no guarantee that the generated patches are generally correct and do not introduce new bugs.
Solution: Program verification technology enables developers to prove the correctness of the program before deploying it. One of the key activities underlying this technology involves inferring a program invariant—a logical formula that

This work is supported by the Research Council of Norway through the secureIT project (IKTPLUSS #288787).

D. Beyer and A. Cavalcanti (Eds.): FASE 2024, LNCS 14573, pp. 255–265, 2024.
https://doi.org/10.1007/978-3-031-57259-3_12

serves as an abstract specification of a program. Developers can significantly benefit from program invariants to identify program properties that must be preserved when modifying code. Unfortunately, these invariants are typically absent from code, leading to the dominance of less rigorous APR approaches (e.g., dynamic APR) and the well-known patch overfitting challenge [11].

We argue that by using test cases and reachability-based analysis techniques, an accurate set of invariants may be obtained and utilized to produce high-quality patches. In other words, program verification tools such as CPAChecker [3] and PathFinder [15] can be used to refine the dynamically generated invariant candidates. This can be done by first using the test cases to analyze the execution traces of the program to infer a set of invariant candidates. These candidates are then refined using a program verifier to obtain more accurate invariants. The goal is to infer two specifications: (i) $\varphi_{correct}$, which represents the set of *good patterns* required for a run to succeed, and (ii) $\varphi_{violated}$, which represents the set of *bad patterns* that lead to the target bug. Invariant-based APR offers two key benefits. First, it directs APR towards potentially feasible patches. Second, it enables the formal validation of plausible patches using program verifiers.

Viability of invariant-based APR: Program invariants have shown effectiveness in many applications, such as program understanding, fault localization, and formal verification. Invariants are effective because functional correctness relates to the final result of a program rather than any specific implementation. They can therefore assist in abstracting many concrete execution steps and thus greatly reduce the effort needed to reason about the patch's correctness.

In fact, developers who aim to repair a defected *undocumented program* (a program written without thought for formal specifications) can find invariant-based APR helpful in their repair tasks. The availability of mature automated invariant detection tools like Daikon [4] and practical software verification tools like CPAChecker and PathFinder makes the invariant-based program repair technique viable. At first glance, refining invariants using program verification tools seems too expensive. However, due to tremendous advances in software verification [2], in practice, invariant-based verification can be made pretty efficient. In particular, the software analysis framework CPAChecker, which supports many different reachability analyses, has been effectively used to validate a wide variety of reachability queries against C programs with up to 50K lines of code. This makes reachability analysis a promising technique that can be used to significantly reduce the patch overfitting problem and produce high-quality patches.

2   Invariant-based Program Repair Framework

In this section we reformulate the APR problem using the concept of program invariants. We then describe how one can analyze the execution traces of fault-free runs to infer likely specifications of the program's intended behaviour and execution traces of faulty runs to infer likely suspicious invariants that lead to the faulty behaviour. Before proceeding further, let us introduce some definitions.

Definition 1. *(fault-free vs. faulty runs).* *Let P be a buggy program, $\mathcal{R}$ be the set of runs of P, and φ_{beh} be a property of program P's intended behavior. We say that a run $r \in \mathcal{R}$ is a successful run (i.e., fault-free run) if $P(r) \models \varphi_{beh}$. On the other hand, we say that a run $r' \in \mathcal{R}$ is a faulty run if $P(r) \not\models \varphi_{beh}$.*

From Definition 1 we note that by analyzing information extracted from fault-free runs, one might be able to infer a specification of the program's intended behavior. Similarly, by analyzing the execution information of faulty runs, one might be able to deduce the violating invariants that cause the bug. This is because fault-free runs represent runs in which program invariants are maintained, while faulty runs represent runs in which some program invariants are violated.

Definition 2. *(Invariant-based APR problem).* *Let P be a program containing bug b and $T = (T_P \cup T_F)$ be a test suite, where T_P represents the set of passing tests and T_F represents the set of failing tests. Let D be a dynamic invariant inference tool like Daikon, and V be a program verification tool like CPAChecker. The invariant-based APR process consists of the following steps:*

1. *[Invariant extraction]. Generate an initial set of invariants $\mathcal{I}$ for P using D.*
2. *[Invariant refinement]. Refine the set $\mathcal{I}$ using V to produce specifications $\varphi_{correct}$ and $\varphi_{violated}$. This can be done by asserting invariants at a program's location of interest and using any generated counter-example to refine them.*
3. *[Fault localization]. Compute a list of suspicious statements whose mutation may lead to a valid patch by analyzing specifications $\varphi_{correct}$ and $\varphi_{violated}$.*
4. *[Patch generation]. Construct code that corrects the invariants that are violated while maintaining other program invariants. This can be performed by employing a patch generation procedure like search- or semantic-based.*
5. *[Patch validation]. Validate the correctness of the generated patches using V.*

Depending on the type of the bug being fixed and the structure of the analyzed program, different program locations may be of relevance for properties $\varphi_{correct}$ and $\varphi_{violated}$. Examples include pre- and post-conditions for different functions, or loop invariants for some program loops. Note that the first two steps of the invariant-based APR process described at Definition 2 are necessary for increasing confidence in the precision of patches that are generated. The actual repair steps of the process, steps 3-5, can be formally stated as follows:

$$pt = FV(PGV(FL(\varphi_{correct}, \varphi_{violated}, P), T), \varphi_{correct}, \varphi_{violated}) \tag{1}$$

where FL is an invariant-based fault localization process, PGV is patch generation and validation process using test suite, and FV is a formal patch validation process using the verification tool V. If no plausible patch is found or a plausible patch is found but incorrect, the repair process returns fail. However, if the plausible patch passes the verification step carried out by the tool V, the process returns a patch. We now turn to discuss how one can generate specifications $\varphi_{correct}$ and $\varphi_{violated}$ by analyzing the execution information obtained by running program P using passing and failing tests. The analysis of fault-free and faulty runs leads to the identification of the following formal patterns.

1. $\varphi_{correct} = \mathcal{I}_{good} = V(D(P, T_P))$, invariants deduced using only successful runs. This set of invariants represents the likely intended behavior of P.
2. $\varphi_{faulty} = \mathcal{I}_{mix} = V(D(P, T_F))$, invariants deduced using the set of faulty runs. Note that the set $\mathcal{I}_{mix}$ may contain both good and bad patterns depending on how the target bug affects different functionalities of P.
3. $\varphi_{violated} = (\mathcal{I}_{mix} \setminus \mathcal{I}_{good})$, the set of violated invariants related to the bug.

It is important to categorize and distinguish inferred patterns (invariants) into good and bad patterns, especially when dealing with programs that have several functional requirements. This helps to identify the set of desired invariants to be maintained and violated invariants to be repaired when modifying code. It also helps to identify the set of invariants that are relevant to the analyzed bug. The soundness of inferred $\varphi_{correct}$ and $\varphi_{violated}$ depends heavily on the soundness of the employed invariant inference tool as well as the invariant refinement process. Increasing the amount of program behavior exercised using reachability analysis increases the likelihood that $\varphi_{correct}$ and $\varphi_{violated}$ are true.

Definition 3. *(Patch validation in invariant-based APR). Let P be a program containing bug b and T be a test suite containing at least one failing test and one passing test. Let also pt be a plausible patch that makes P passes all test cases in T. The validity of patch pt can be formally checked as follows*

$$validity(pt) = V(pt, \varphi_{correct}) \wedge \neg V(pt, \varphi_{violated}) \qquad (2)$$

where $V(pt, \varphi_{correct}) \in \{true, false\}$ and that the tool's response depends on whether the specification is fulfilled or violated in the program being examined.

To boost confidence in the validity of the resulting patch, we opt to check patches against both $\varphi_{correct}$ and $\varphi_{violated}$. However, to lower the cost of calling the verifier V against each candidate patch, we aim to implement a three-step patch validation method that uses the test suite first and the program verifier afterwards. Generating plausible patches is done in the first step using test cases. Second step involves formally checking plausible patches against the set of bad patterns (property $\varphi_{violated}$). Patches that pass the first two steps are checked against the set of good patterns (property $\varphi_{correct}$) in the third step.

3   Fixing Performance Bugs Using Invariant-based APR

Performance bugs are programming errors that cause significant performance degradation - lead to low system throughput. Experience has shown that many commercial software that is widely used suffer from performance problems [13, 6, 10]. Therefore, there is a need to develop a rigorous repair framework for performance bugs that ensures efficiency gain without compromising functionality.

One unique characteristic of performance bugs comparing to functional bugs is that performance bugs do not affect the functionality of the program (i.e., the program is *semantically correct but inefficient*) and thus the intended behavior of the program can be automatically deduced using an invariant inference tool.

This section describes an invariant-based APR system for performance bugs and demonstrates how it may be applied to handle performance bugs by producing patches that ensures efficiency improvement without sacrificing functionality.

3.1   Invariant-based Repair Framework for Performance Bugs

In this section we describe an invariant-based repair framework for handling performance bugs. The framework consists mainly of the following components:

1. a set of passing tests (tests that lead to fast runs),
2. a set of failing tests (tests that lead to slow runs),
3. runtime monitor to keep track of the program's execution time and differentiate between fast and slow runs, and
4. an automated invariant inference tool (Daikon or CPAChecker) and automated invariant verification tool (PVS, Z3 solver, or CPAChecker).

We now turn to discuss how we define the notions of passing and failing tests and the process of generating and validating patches for performance bugs.

Passing and failing tests for performance bugs: Performance bugs do not produce debugging information at runtime: they do not produce crashes, exceptions, or incorrect results. We therefore use a runtime monitor with a predefined timer to redefine the concepts of passing and failing tests. We consider test cases that lead to *fast runs* as passing tests while test cases that lead to *slow runs* as failing tests. A repair that transforms slow runs into fast runs while preserving the desired behavior of the original program is considered as a valid repair.

Patch generation strategy for performance bugs: Since we deal with a semantically correct but inefficient program, an efficient version of the program can often be created by restructuring the original program's basic components. Our preliminary analysis demonstrates the effectiveness of genetic repair tools, such as GenProg, in dealing with performance bugs. This suggests that programs with performance bugs can be fixed by relatively simple changes. For instance, various performance bugs can be fixed by using mutation operators like move, swap, delete, and insert employed by genetic repair programs. Consequently, we aim to combine our repair framework with genetic-based patch generation tools.

Patch validation for performance bugs: It should be noted that invariant inference tools can also be used to derive predicates related to the non-functional attributes of the program. This can be achieved by adding extra non-functional variables to the program being repaired. Suppose we have a program P with a set of variables V and that P containing a performance bug. We need to check whether the generated plausible patch for program P fixes the performance bug without introducing new functional bug. To do so, we first generate and validate predicates related to the efficiency attributes of the program, as described below.

1. Add a fresh variable nfv whose value has no impact on the behavior of P. The type of performance bug that is being handled determines how nfv is used to model the efficiency of the program. However, for the loop programs we consider, nfv acts like a counter that is incremented once for each iteration. In other words, the number of loop iterations serves as a model for efficiency.

2. Use the invariant detection tool D to infer the numerical invariants $\mathcal{I}(P, \text{nfv})$ and $\mathcal{I}(pt, \text{nfv})$ for the original and plausible patched version, where $\mathcal{I}(P, \text{nfv})$ represents the collection of invariants in program P involving variable nfv.
3. Compare the numerical predicates in $\mathcal{I}(P, \text{nfv})$ and $\mathcal{I}(pt, \text{nfv})$ to determine whether the patched version pt is more efficient than original program P.

For simplicity reasons, we assume we deal with a program with a single loop. The number of loops in the analyzed program, however, determines how many more variables are needed. The invariant inference tool D is thus used to infer invariants on $(V \cup \{\text{nfv}\})$. We then distinguish the following types of predicates:

- $\mathcal{I}(P, V)$: predicates related to the program's functionality, and
- $\mathcal{I}(P, \text{nfv})$: predicates related to the program's efficiency.

Using the generated predicates, one can check the validity of patch pt as follows

$$validity(pt) = \text{SEMAEQ}\ (\mathcal{I}(P, V), \mathcal{I}(pt, V))\ \wedge \text{PREDSM}\ (\mathcal{I}(pt, \text{nfv}), \mathcal{I}(P, \text{nfv})) \quad (3)$$

where SEMAEQ is a Boolean operation that checks whether the given sets of invariants are semantically equivalent and PREDSM is a Boolean operation that checks whether the upper bound in the predicate related to the patched version is smaller than the upper bound in the one related to the original program.

We now describe two formal procedures to verify the validity of plausible patches (specification (3)) using the available program verification tools.

1. *Daikon-PVS*: In this patch validation procedure, Daikon is used to generate predicates related to the functional and efficiency attributes of programs P and pt. In the event that $\mathcal{I}(P, V)$ and $\mathcal{I}(pt, V)$ (i.e., predicates related to functional attributes) are not identical, it may be necessary to examine both equivalence and implication relations between the predicates in those sets in order to determine whether P and pt are semantically equivalent. By querying the theorem prover PVS, this task can be accomplished.
2. *CPAChecker-PVS*: One interesting feature in CPAChecker is that it produces correctness witnesses in GraphML format and in those witnesses, one can find the invariants of the analyzed program. This feature can be utilized to generate the set of invariants in both the original program and corresponding plausible one. In case that the invariants generated for both programs are not identical, it may be necessary to examine both equivalence and implication relations between the predicates in the two sets by invoking the prover PVS.

3.2   Fixing real-world performance bugs using invariant-based APR

In this section, we show how invariant-based APR can be used to handle real-world performance bugs. For space reasons, we only consider one interesting example of performance bugs (see Listing 1). The bug is based on a real-world flaw that occurred in Apache and has also been analyzed by other researchers [14].
Analysis of the program in Listing 1: The program aims to determine whether a given (target) string is contained within another (source) string. If

```
1   int found = -1;
2   while (found < 0 ) {
3     // Check if string source[] contains target[]
4     char first = target[0];
5     int max = sourceLen - targetLen;
6     for (int i = 0; i <= max; i++) {
7       // Look for first character.
8       if (source[i] != first) {
9         while (++i <= max && source[i] != first);
10      }
11      // Found first character
12      if (i <= max) {
13        int j = i + 1;
14        int end = j + targetLen - 1;
15        for (int k=1; j<end && source[j]==target[k]; j++, k++);
16        if (j == end) {
17          /* Found whole string target. */
18          found = i;
19          break;
20        }
21      }
22    }
23    // append another character; try again
24    source[sourceLen++] = getchar();
25  }
```

Listing 1. A challenging performance bug found in Apache

the target string is found in the source string, the program sets the variable found to the index of the target string's first character. But there is a significant performance flaw in the program: when the target string is at the start of the source string, the run is fast, and the program stops almost instantaneously. On the other hand, the run is slower and takes longer to finish when the target string is closer to the end of the source string. This is mostly because there will be a significant increase in the number of redundant computations. The fault is that the initialization statement of the control variable i of the for loop at line 6 should be placed outside the scope of the main while loop just after the initialization of the variable found. The longest run that we reported occurs when the source string has a length of 10^7 characters, and the target is a single character that is present at the end of the source string. In this instance, the program runs for 30 hours before terminating and producing the correct results.

3.3 Results and analysis

To handle the performance bug at Listing 1, we select two APR tools: the search-based repair tool GenProg [7] and the semantic-based repair tool FAngelix [16].

These are general-purpose repair tools for C code that can be used to fix a range of program bugs, including loop program bugs. While GenProg successfully generated a plausible patch, FAngelix was unable to produce a plausible one. To avoid doing repetitive calculations in the original program, GenProg moved the initialization statement of the variable i outside of the for loop at line 6. In other words, the program starts with the initialization statement of the variable i in the patched version. In this case, the generated patch passes the test cases since i is no longer being set to 0 every time the loop receives a new character.

To check the validity of the plausible patch generated by GenProg, we run the tool Daikon and compare the functional and efficiency predicates obtained for both the original program and the plausible patch. Daikon generates the same set of invariants w.r.t. functional variables (i.e., both the original and the patched versions have the same invariants w.r.t. program variables.) This demonstrates that the patch maintains the functional behavior of the original program.

Listing 1 contains four loops: the while loop at line 2, for loop at line 6, while loop at line 9, and for loop at line 15. To evaluate the efficiency of the original and patched programs, it is sufficient to calculate the upper bound on the number of iterations, as the patch does not modify the logic of any of the loops by adding or removing an operation. That is, each iteration of the four loops in both programs involves the same number of operations. We therefore add four iteration counters $(cnt_2, cnt_6, cnt_9, cnt_{15})$ to model the efficiency of each loop, where the index of the counter corresponds to the line number of the loop being analyzed. For instance, the counter cnt_2 is initially set to zero and advanced by one whenever the loop at line 2 is run. We make the following observations when analyzing the efficiency predicates for both the buggy and patched versions:

– Invariants generated for the counter variables cnt_2 and cnt_{15} in the buggy and patched versions are the same. This indicates that the patch does not affect the number of times the loops at lines 2 and 15 are iterated.
– The counter variable cnt_9 only advances in the buggy version and results in the invariant $cnt_9 \leq 500499$. The fact that the patched version no longer employs the while loop at line 9 is a sign of a major improvement.
– Daikon generated the invariant $cnt_6 \leq 1001$ in the buggy version and invariant $cnt_6 \leq 501$ in the patched version. This shows that the loop at line 6 is iterated 50% less times in the patched version than it is in the original code.

The aforementioned findings, along with the fact that the derived functional predicates of both the original and patched versions are identical, boost our confidence about the validity of the generated patch by the tool GenProg.

4   Related Work

Patch overfitting in APR: Several solutions have been developed to alleviate the overfitting problem in APR, such as symbolic specification inference [8], machine learning-based prioritization of patches [1], fuzzing-based test-suite augmentation [5], and concolic path exploration [12]. These solutions rely on limited incomplete test cases and do not guarantee the general correctness of the patches. Compared to those approaches that generate test inputs, invariant-based APR automatically generates and refines desired invariants that need to be maintained and violated invariants that need to be repaired when modifying code, which makes the approach more reliable than existing repair approaches.

Modern general-purpose APR tools still rely on symbolic execution or concolic execution [9, 12] to discover counterexamples and generate repairs. However, these repair approaches manually inspect to determine whether the generated patches are correct or identical to developer patches, which could be error-prone. Invariant-based APR makes it possible to apply automated verification techniques to alleviate overfitting problem and formally and systematically check the accuracy of generated patches by comparing them to the developers patches.

Handling performance bugs: Several attempts have been made to detect and repair performance bugs in programs using dynamic, static, and hybrid analysis approaches [13, 6, 10]. [10] carried out an empirical investigation into performance bugs and presented several efficiency rules for identifying them. Using dynamic-static analysis techniques, several fix strategies have been developed in [13] to identify and fix performance problems. However, our method is different from previous studies in that it is a more general and rigorous technique that makes use of program invariant to address loop program performance issues and yield reliable patches. Thanks to program invariants, the original program's efficiency can be systematically compared to the patched version.

5   Conclusion and Future Work

We described a novel general-purpose APR system based on the concept of program invariants. Invariant-based APR holds the promise to handle a wider range of bugs and produce more reliable patches than other APR approaches. This is because invariant-based repair systems depend on stronger correctness criteria rather than test suites. We demonstrate the usefulness of leveraging invariants in APR by developing an invariant repair system for performance defects. The preliminary results showed that invariant-based APR can assist in generating valid patches that ensure efficiency improvement without compromising functionality. **Future work:** To complete the line of research initiated here regarding invariant-based APR, we identify the following key directions for future work.

- First and foremost, we aim to conduct a thorough empirical analysis to determine how well invariant-based APR handles functional and non-functional defects in programs. This also entails assessing the invariant inference and invariant verification tools that are currently accessible.
- Accurate invariant generation is required to ensure the validity of patches produced by invariant-based APR. We conjecture that reachability analyses can aid with this complex computational task and we aim to combine invariant-based APR with program verification tools that support both invariant generation and refinement such as CPAChecker and PathFinder.

References

1. J. Bader, A. Scott, M. Pradel, and S. Chandra. Getafix: learning to fix bugs automatically. *Proc. ACM Program. Lang.*, pages 159:1–159:27, 2019.
2. D. Beyer. Automatic verification of C and java programs: SV-COMP 2019. In *Tools and Algorithms for the Construction and Analysis of Systems TACAS*, volume 11429, pages 133–155, 2019.
3. D. Beyer and M. E. Keremoglu. Cpachecker: A tool for configurable software verification. In *Computer Aided Verification*, pages 184–190, 2011.
4. M. D. Ernst, J. H. Perkins, P. J. Guo, S. McCamant, C. Pacheco, M. S. Tschantz, and C. Xiao. The daikon system for dynamic detection of likely invariants. *Sci. Comput. Program.*, 69(1-3):35–45, 2007.
5. X. Gao, S. Mechtaev, and A. Roychoudhury. Crash-avoiding program repair. In *International Symposium on Software Testing and Analysis (ISSTA)*, pages 8–18, 2019.
6. G. Jin, L. Song, X. Shi, J. Scherpelz, and S. Lu. Understanding and detecting real-world performance bugs. In *ACM SIGPLAN Conference on Programming Language Design and Implementation, PLDI '12, Beijing, China - June 11 - 16, 2012*, pages 77–88. ACM, 2012.
7. C. Le Goues, T. Nguyen, S. Forrest, and W. Weimer. GenProg: A Generic Method for Automatic Software Repair. *IEEE Transactions on Software Engineering*, 38(1):54–72, Jan. 2012.
8. S. Mechtaev, J. Yi, and A. Roychoudhury. Angelix: Scalable multiline program patch synthesis via symbolic analysis. In *International Conference on Software Engineering (ICSE)*, pages 691–701, 2016.
9. S. Mechtaev, J. Yi, and A. Roychoudhury. Angelix: Scalable Multiline Program Patch Synthesis via Symbolic Analysis. In *International Conference on Software Engineering (ICSE)*, pages 691–701, May 2016.
10. A. Nistor, T. Jiang, and L. Tan. Discovering, reporting, and fixing performance bugs. In *10th Working Conference on Mining Software Repositories (MSR)*, pages 237–246, 2013.
11. Z. Qi, F. Long, S. Achour, and M. C. Rinard. An analysis of patch plausibility and correctness for generate-and-validate patch generation systems. In *Proceedings of the 2015 International Symposium on Software Testing and Analysis, ISSTA 2015, Baltimore, MD, USA, July 12-17, 2015*, pages 24–36, 2015.
12. R. Shariffdeen, Y. Noller, L. Grunske, and A. Roychoudhury. Concolic program repair. In *SIGPLAN Conference on Programming Language Design and Implementation (PLDI)*. ACM, 2021.
13. L. Song and S. Lu. Performance diagnosis for inefficient loops. In *Proceedings of the 39th International Conference on Software Engineering, ICSE*, pages 370–380, 2017.
14. L. Song and S. Lu. Performance diagnosis for inefficient loops. In *Proceedings of the 39th International Conference on Software Engineering*, ICSE '17, pages 370–380, Buenos Aires, Argentina, 2017.
15. W. Visser, K. Havelund, G. P. Brat, S. Park, and F. Lerda. Model checking programs. *Autom. Software Engineering*, 10(2):203–232, 2003.
16. J. Yi and E. Ismayilzada. Speeding up constraint-based program repair using a search-based technique. *Information and Software Technology*, page 106865, 2022.

Can ChatGPT support software verification?

Christian Janßen, Cedric Richter$^{(\boxtimes)}$ (ID), and Heike Wehrheim (ID)

Carl-von-Ossietzky Universität Oldenburg, Oldenburg, Germany
{christian.janssen1, cedric.richter, heike.wehrheim}@uol.de

Abstract. Large language models have become increasingly effective in software engineering tasks such as code generation, debugging and repair. Language models like ChatGPT can not only *generate* code, but also *explain* its inner workings and in particular its correctness. This raises the question whether we can utilize ChatGPT to support *formal software verification*.
In this paper, we take some first steps towards answering this question. More specifically, we investigate whether ChatGPT can generate *loop invariants*. Loop invariant generation is a core task in software verification, and the generation of *valid* and *useful* invariants would likely help formal verifiers. To provide some first evidence on this hypothesis, we ask ChatGPT to annotate 106 C programs with loop invariants. We check validity and usefulness of the generated invariants by passing them to two verifiers, FRAMA-C and CPAchecker. Our evaluation shows that Chat-GPT is able to produce valid and useful invariants allowing FRAMA-C to verify tasks that it could not solve before. Based on our initial insights, we propose ways of combining ChatGPT (or large language models in general) and software verifiers, and discuss current limitations and open issues.

Keywords: Large language models · Invariant generation · Formal verification.

1 Introduction

Large language models (LLMs) [11,37,30] are increasingly employed to support software engineers in the generation, testing and repair of code [15,14,27]. Generative AI can, however, not only generate code, but also provide explanations of the inner workings of code and give arguments about its correctness. This raises the question whether LLMs can also support *formal software verification*.

In this paper, we provide a first step towards answering this question. In general, one can imagine various ways of supporting verifiers, depending on the verification approach they employ. Central to all verifiers are, however, techniques for dealing with loops. Specifically, for abstracting the behaviour of loops, verifiers aim at computing *loop invariants*. Our first step in evaluating ChatGPT's usefulness for software verification is thus the generation of loop invariants.

To this end, we ask ChatGPT to annotate C-programs with loop invariants. We have chosen 106 C-programs from the Loops category of the annual competition on software verification [7]. To enable the usage of these invariants by

© The Author(s) 2024
D. Beyer and A. Cavalcanti (Eds.): FASE 2024, LNCS 14573, pp. 266–279, 2024.
https://doi.org/10.1007/978-3-031-57259-3_13

Prompt> Compute a loop invariant for the following program!

```
1  void func(unsigned int n)
2  {
3    unsigned int x=n, y=0;
4    //@ loop invariant [mask];
5    while(x>0) {
6      x--; y++;
7    }
8    assert(y==n);
9  }
```

Infilling provided by ChatGPT: x+y==n

Fig. 1. Example task: `loops/count_up_down-1`.

verifiers, we needed the invariants to be given in some formal language. For this, we have chosen ANSI/ISO C Specification Language (ACSL) [5], a design-by-contract like annotation language for C. Initial experiments confirmed that ChatGPT "knows" ACSL. The main part of our experiments then concerned the evaluation of the invariants with respect to (a) *validity* and (b) *usefulness* for verifiers. The first aspect required checking whether a proposed invariant is actually a proper invariant, i.e., whether the computed predicate holds at the beginning of the loop and after every loop iteration. We employ the state-of-the-art interactive verifier FRAMA-C [4] for this validity checking. For evaluating the usefulness of invariants, we provided two state-of-the-art verifiers (FRAMA-C SV [9] and CPAchecker [8]) with the code annotated by the proposed invariant, and evaluated whether the verifiers can then solve verification tasks which they could not solve without the invariant[1]. Our results confirm that ChatGPT can support software verifiers by providing valid and useful loop invariants, but also show that more work needs to be done – both conceptually and practically – to have LLMs provide a significant support for software verification.

2   Invariant Generation with ChatGPT

Our goal is to provide initial insights into the capabilities of large language models, specifically ChatGPT, to support formal software verification. For this, we propose the task of loop invariant generation.

Loop invariant generation. The goal of loop invariant generation is to generate *valid* and *useful* loop invariants for a given program. A valid loop invariant is an invariant that (1) holds true before the first loop execution and (2) after each loop iteration. A useful loop invariant is a valid loop invariant that is useful for proving the given program correct.

To understand this, let us consider the example task shown in Figure 1. Here, the large language model is tasked to analyze the given program and to propose a loop invariant. For the given program, the invariant x + y == n represents a *valid* loop invariant: as x is initialized to n and y to 0, the invariant holds (1)

---

[1] In case of CPAchecker, we restrict CPAchecker's own invariant generation facilities as to be able to see the plain effect of the generated invariant.

before the first loop execution. The invariant furthermore holds (2) after each loop iteration as y is incremented each time x is decremented.

The provided loop invariant also is a *useful* loop invariant: As x == 0 at the end of the loop execution and x + y == n holds after the loop execution, we can deduce that the assertion y == n is not violated after the loop execution. The invariants x <= n and y >= 0 also represent valid loop invariants but they are not useful for proving the program correct.

The idea is now to let ChatGPT generate such loop invariants. To this end, we need to tell ChatGPT what its task is. As briefly mentioned in the introduction, we expect ChatGPT to give loop invariants in the form of ACSL (ANSI C Specification Language [5]) assertions. ACSL is a specification language for C and offers a number of keywords for specifications in a design-by-contract style. Among others, there is the keyword `loop invariant`. ACSL specifications are written inside comments of the form `//@`. Besides the plain code, Figure 1 also shows the *prompt* used to tell ChatGPT its task (first line), and the code location and form of the invariant we expect to be generated (`//@ loop invariant [mask]`)[2]. We thus phrase the task as an *infilling problem* [21], i.e., we require ChatGPT to fill in some meaningful contents for `[mask]`. In this example, ChatGPT returns the above discussed invariant. We arrived at this form of stating the task after several experiments with different prompts.

Feeding loop invariants into verifiers. For evaluation of the generated invariants, we need to determine their validity and usefulness. To this end, we first of all need to feed them into some verifier. Interactive verifiers natively provide ways of feeding in such inputs. In an interactive verification run, a software engineer provides program annotations (e.g., invariants) and the verifier tries to prove that some given specifications are never violated[3].

In this work, our goal is to evaluate the ability of large language models to support verifiers. Therefore, we replace the software engineer by ChatGPT and let it interact with the interactive verifier. Currently, the language model only interacts by exchanging loop invariants (which is inline with our evaluation goal). However, in future work it could be interesting to let the language model generate other types of annotations.

During our evaluation, we use the interactive verifier FRAMA-C [4] to evaluate the validity and usefulness of the provided invariants. For evaluating the usefulness, we furthermore employ an automatic verifier (CPAchecker [8]). To also allow for interaction in this case, we employ ACSL2Witness [10] to convert the ACSL annotated program to a correctness witness which CPAchecker is then able to use in its verification.

Related work. There are only a few works that address invariant generation via machine learning. The work in [32] uses large language models to predict invariants of Java programs. They specifically trained large language models to predict

---

[2] Prompt and answer from ChatGPT are abbreviated to fit the figure; the full prompt is given in the appendix.

[3] There exists a variety of properties that can be checked via verification; we focus here on checking for violations of assertions.

Daikon [20] generated invariants. Their evaluation does not consider validity or usefulness of the generated invariants but only concerns whether Daikon invariants can be recovered. In contrast, in this work, we rely on instruction-tuned large language models such as ChatGPT *without* any training and we use formal verification approaches to evaluate the validity and usefulness of loop invariants generated for C code.

Many approaches [36,31,22,35,12], which are related to or based on Syntax-Guided Synthesis, have addressed invariant generation via machine learning techniques. However, most of the existing techniques rely on traditional machine learning or graph neural network based techniques instead of large language models. We are interested in the capabilities of large language models in supporting C software verifiers.

Beyond invariants, there also exist other ways to support software verifiers. For example, the work in [3,23] supports verifiers with neural-network based termination analyses. However, these approaches are often deeply integrated. We chose loop invariant generation as many software verifiers already support the exchange of invariants.

3 Evaluation

We evaluate ChatGPT on the task of loop invariant generation in C code. For the evaluation, we use a benchmark of 106 verification tasks taken from the SV-COMP Loops category [7]. We have chosen all tasks which (a) have ACSL annotations (to be able to compare the generated with manually constructed invariants), (b) have one loop only and (c) are correct, i.e., the assertions in the code are valid. During our evaluation, we remove all ACSL invariant annotations and let ChatGPT regenerate them. Now, based on our evaluation setup we aim to answer the following research question:

Can ChatGPT support software verifiers with valid and useful loop invariants?

Experimental setup. For generating loop invariants, we employ the ChatGPT (GPT-3.5) snapshot from June 2023. The model is queried via the OpenAI API[4]. During our evaluation, we set the sampling temperature[5] of ChatGPT to 0.2 and sample up to k ($k = 5$) completions per task. We collect all invariants by parsing the generated completions with the infillings.

For checking the validity of the generated invariants, we use the interactive verifier FRAMA-C [4]. We annotate each task with one of the n generated invariants. In total, we thus generate up to n annotated versions of each task which we use for validation. We count loop invariants as validated only if FRAMA-C WP can validate them within 10s[6].

---

[4] https://platform.openai.com/, accessed in Sept. 2023

[5] The temperature controls the randomness of ChatGPT's outputs; a lower temperature leads to more deterministic outputs. We have chosen a low temperature to obtain invariants in a processable format.

[6] Note that a negative answer of FRAMA-C does not necessarily mean that the candidate invariant is invalid.

Table 1. Results for 106 verification tasks, divided by subcategory of the Loops category (giving total number of tasks, number of successfully validated invariants, number of verified tasks per verifier using either the generated or the human provided invariant of the benchmark, and in gray the number of useful invariants)

Subcategory	Tasks		FRAMA-C		k-induction	
	total	val-invs.	GPT invs.	Human invs.	GPT invs.	Human invs.
loop-accelaration	15	8	1 (1)	2 (2)	6 (3)	6 (3)
loop-crafted	2	2	0 (0)	0 (0)	2 (0)	2 (0)
loop-industry-pat.	1	1	0 (0)	0 (0)	1 (0)	1 (0)
loop-invariants	8	4	3 (3)	3 (3)	0 (0)	1 (1)
loop-invgen	3	3	0 (0)	0 (0)	0 (0)	0 (0)
loop-lit	13	4	1 (1)	4 (4)	3 (2)	4 (3)
loop-new	7	4	1 (1)	1 (1)	0 (0)	0 (0)
loop-simple	1	1	1 (1)	1 (1)	1 (0)	1 (0)
loop-zilu	22	18	10 (10)	11 (11)	11 (6)	10 (5)
loops	13	13	5 (5)	6 (6)	8 (1)	8 (1)
loops-crafted-1	21	17	0 (0)	0 (0)	4 (3)	7 (6)
total	106	75	22 (22)	28 (28)	36 (15)	40 (19)

For evaluating the usefulness of the generated invariants, we now annotate the task with the validated invariants from the previous step. If multiple invariants are validated per task, we conjunct them to a single invariant and annotate the task with the conjuncted invariant[7]. As verifiers, we consider the interactive verifier FRAMA-C SV [9][8] and the automatic verifier CPAchecker [8]. We configure CPAchecker to run k-induction without loop unrolling (similar to [10] to be able to see the effect of the generated invariant). Note that this restricts CPAcheckers facilities for verification. Finally, all verifier and validation runs are executed via BenchExec [6] on a 24-core machine with 128GB RAM running Ubuntu 22.04 with a maximum timelimit of 900s.

Results. Our main results are shown in Table 1. On the left side of the table, we show the total number of tasks per subcategory (total) and the number of tasks where at least one of the generated invariants can be validated (val-invs.). On the right side of the table, we report on the verification results obtained from executing FRAMA-C and CPAchecker (using k-induction without loop unfolding) on the verification tasks with at least one validated invariant. We report the total number of tasks that can be verified with a ChatGPT provided invariant (GPT invs.) and a human provided invariant (Human invs.), i.e., the ACSL invariant given in the benchmark. In addition, we also report the number of useful invariants in gray brackets. Useful here means that the verifier cannot complete the verification task without the invariant.

---

[7] The logical conjunction of two valid invariants is again a valid invariant.

[8] FRAMA-C SV is a version of FRAMA-C specifically configured to work well on SV-COMP task.

```
1 void func () {
2   unsigned int x = 0, y = 1;
3   //@ loop invariant [mask];
4   while (x < 6) { x++; y *= 2; }
5   assert (y % 3 != 0);
6 }
```
Infilling provided by ChatGPT: x <= 6 && y == pow(2, x)
Human: (x==0 && y==1) || (x==1 && y==2) || (x==2 && y==4) || ...

Fig. 2. Example task: `loop-acceleration/underapprox_1-2`

ChatGPT can generate valid loop invariants. We find that ChatGPT can generate valid loop invariants for 75 out of 106 tasks (as validated by FRAMA-C). Note that ChatGPT proposes loop invariant candidates for all 106 tasks and by manual inspection we found that some of the generated loop invariant candidates are still *meaningful*, even though they are not validated by FRAMA-C. An example is shown in Figure 2. ChatGPT produces a meaningful loop invariant candidate, but FRAMA-C rejects the candidate due to technical reasons[9]. The human-annotated invariant avoids this problem by enumerating all variable assignments. In total, we found by manual inspection that 10 out of 31 invariant candidates not validated by FRAMA-C are meaningful.

Interestingly, we found during our manual inspection that ChatGPT in many cases seems to apply a set of useful *heuristics* to determine loop invariant candidates. One of the most successful heuristic applied by ChatGPT on our benchmark is the *copy assertion* heuristic. Here, ChatGPT proposes an invariant that is equivalent to a condition found in a nearby assertion. The heuristic is applied in 30 out of 106 tasks and 23 of the resulting invariants are validated.

ChatGPT can support verifiers with useful loop invariants. We find that Chat-GPT can produce useful invariants that can support software verifiers in their verification tasks. In comparison to the human-provided invariants, ChatGPT produced useful invariants for 22 out of 28 tasks in the case of FRAMA-C and for 15 out of 19 tasks in the case of CPAchecker's k-induction. Interestingly, we find one example in the loop-zilu subcategory where the invariant proposed by ChatGPT is more useful for CPAchecker than the human annotated invariant. The example is shown in Figure 3. Here, ChatGPT proposes the invariants j >= 0 and k >= 0 conjuncted with the human-provided invariant which is obviously useful to prove that k >= 0 holds true at the end of the loop. Note that, while this seems to be a case where the copy assertion heuristics is effective, FRAMA-C does not validate the invariant candidate k >= 0 alone. The conjunction with j<=n && k>=n-j is important to validate the invariant. Still, by manual inspection we find that the copy assertion heuristic of ChatGPT is effective for providing useful invariants in 11 out of 22 cases for FRAMA-C and in 5 out of 15 cases for k-induction.

---

[9] FRAMA-C reports an invalid conversion from integer type to a floating point type due to the **pow** operator and thereby fails.

```
void func(int k, int j, int n) {
    if (!(n>=1 && k>=n && j==0)) return;
    //@ loop invariant [mask];
    while (j<=n-1) { j++; k--; }
    assert(k>=0);
}
```

Infilling provided by ChatGPT: j >= 0 && k >= 0 && j <= n && k >= n - j
Human: j <= n <= k + j

Fig. 3. Example task: `loop-zilu/benchmark04_conjunctive`.

4   Limitations and Open Issues

We discuss limitations and open issues in using large language models for supporting software verifiers.

Cooperation between Language Model and Software Verifier. Our evaluation has shown that large language models such as ChatGPT are already capable of producing valid and useful loop invariants for our benchmark tasks. However, to be useful in practice, there are several challenges we have to master. A key challenge is the communication and cooperation between large language model and software verifier. Currently, we have implemented a top-down approach for invariant generation, i.e., we start by querying the language model for invariant candidates, validate them and then provide them to a verifier. The LLM has no knowledge about the specifics of the underlying validator or the verifier used in the process. This can ultimately hinder the large language model from generating valid (as validated by the validator) or useful (as determined by the verifier) loop invariants. During our evaluation, we already have encountered an example where this knowledge gap leads to meaningful but not validated invariant candidates (see Figure 2). Here, the language model has no knowledge about the specifics of the validator used (FRAMA-C) or at least is not informed that the proposed expression leads to a parsing error. Communicating this information allows the large language model to self-debug [17] its invariant proposals and thereby propose invariant candidates that are validated by the validator and that are useful for the verifier. For example, if we report the implicit conversion error back to ChatGPT, it generates a new invariant candidate (y == 1 « x) for our example in Figure 2 that is validated by our validator.

Overall, we envision a cooperative approach between large language model, invariant validator and software verifier as shown in Figure 4. In an inner loop, the large language model cooperates with the validator to identify valid loop invariants. Here, the language model proposes invariant candidates, obtains feedback from the validator and refines its invariant suggestion.

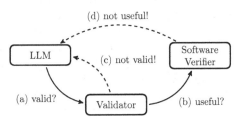

Fig. 4. Conceptual overview.

In the outer loop, the language model cooperates in the same way with the software verifier to find useful loop invariants. This work already implements (a) the validation of invariant candidates and (b) the verification with useful invariants. The key challenge is now to determine which feedback is needed from (c) the validator or (d) the software verifier to effectively guide the language model to valid and useful invariants.

A subsequent study [28] provides first insights in the feasibility of our approach. By providing feedback to the language model (in form of error messages produced by Frama-C), the authors showed that language models can effectively repair its invariant proposals. We believe that providing more detailed feedback (e.g. by providing a more detailed reasoning why the validation process fails) can further boost the performance of language model based invariant generation.

Finally, we can envision that our approach to language model and verifier cooperation may be useful beyond invariant generation. For example, TriCo [2] proposes to check the conformity between implementation and code specification with a verifier. A large language model could react to conformity violations and repair either the implementation or the specification.

Unified assertion language. Our approach for invariant generation requires that large language models, validators and software verifiers communicate invariants with a common specification language (e.g., ACSL in our case). However, in practice, there exists a zoo of interactive verifiers such as DAFNY [29], FRAMA-C [4], KEY [1], KIV [19], and VERIFAST [25] and automated software verifiers such as CBMC [18], CPAchecker [8], Symbiotic [13], and Ultimate Automizer [24]. All of them implement their own custom way to communicate invariants. Therefore, we either have to find a way to unify the communication of invariants between systems or we have to define *transformations* that convert between communication formats. In this work, we have already employed the transformation ACSL2WITNESS [10] to convert ACSL to a format understandable by automated software verifiers. In the future, we plan to explore alternative transformations to support a wider range of validators and verifiers.

Known limitations of LLMs. Large language models have many known limitations such as hallucinations [26], input length limitations [30], and limited reasoning capabilities [34]. All of this can significantly limit the ability of large language models to produce valid and useful loop invariants or to support software verifiers in general. However, active research is underway to overcome these limitations, and a number of proposals have already been made to reduce hallucinations [33], increase input length [16], or improve the reasoning performance [38] of large language models. It would be interesting for future work to evaluate how these solutions impact the loop invariant generation abilities of large language models.

5   Conclusion

In this work, we provided a first step towards answering the question whether large language models can support formal software verification. For this, we have evaluated ChatGPT on the task of loop invariant generation. Our evaluation shows that ChatGPT can support software verifiers by providing valid and useful loop invariants. We plan to further improve the support for software verification in future work by a cooperative approach that enables exchange of information between large language models, invariant validators and software verifiers. In particular, we intend to develop methods for providing feedback to LLMs whenever candidate invariants are found to not be valid.

A   Prompting ChatGPT

The full prompt and the answer of ChatGPT for the example task loops/count_up_down-1 is shown in Figure 5. We use the same prompt for all tasks. The answer of ChatGPT can slightly vary between executions. Therefore, we generate up to k answers and collect invariants from all answers via a regular expression.

Prompt> Compute a loop invariant for the annotated loop including [invariant] in the following C code. Please use the format of ACSL annotations and always end your response with //@ loop invariant X ; where X is the computed invariant.

```
1  [...]
2  unsigned int __VERIFIER_nondet_uint ();
3
4  int main()
5  {
6    unsigned int n = __VERIFIER_nondet_uint ();
7    unsigned int x=n, y=0;
8    //@ loop invariant [invariant];
9    while (x>0)
10   {
11     x--;
12     y++;
13   }
14   __VERIFIER_assert (y==n);
15 }
```

ChatGPT>

The loop invariant for the given code can be stated as follows:

```
'''
//@ loop invariant y + x == n ;
'''
```

[...]

Fig. 5. Full prompt and answer for example task: loops/count_up_down-1.

References

1. Ahrendt, W., Baar, T., Beckert, B., Bubel, R., Giese, M., Hähnle, R., Menzel, W., Mostowski, W., Roth, A., Schlager, S., Schmitt, P.H.: The KeY tool. Softw. Syst. Model. **4**(1), 32–54 (2005). https://doi.org/10.1007/s10270-004-0058-x, https://doi.org/10.1007/s10270-004-0058-x

2. Ahrendt, W., Gurov, D., Johansson, M., Rümmer, P.: Trico - triple co-piloting of implementation, specification and tests. In: Margaria, T., Steffen, B. (eds.) Leveraging Applications of Formal Methods, Verification and Validation. Verification Principles - 11th International Symposium, ISoLA 2022, Rhodes, Greece, October 22-30, 2022, Proceedings, Part I. Lecture Notes in Computer Science, vol. 13701, pp. 174–187. Springer (2022). https://doi.org/10.1007/978-3-031-19849-6_11, https://doi.org/10.1007/978-3-031-19849-6_11

3. Alon, Y., David, C.: Using graph neural networks for program termination. In: Roychoudhury, A., Cadar, C., Kim, M. (eds.) Proceedings of the 30th ACM Joint European Software Engineering Conference and Symposium on the Foundations of Software Engineering, ESEC/FSE 2022, Singapore, Singapore, November 14-18, 2022. pp. 910–921. ACM (2022). https://doi.org/10.1145/3540250.3549095, https://doi.org/10.1145/3540250.3549095

4. Baudin, P., Bobot, F., Bühler, D., Correnson, L., Kirchner, F., Kosmatov, N., Maroneze, A., Perrelle, V., Prevosto, V., Signoles, J., Williams, N.: The dogged pursuit of bug-free C programs: the Frama-C software analysis platform. Commun. ACM **64**(8), 56–68 (2021). https://doi.org/10.1145/3470569, https://doi.org/10.1145/3470569

5. Baudin, P., Filliâtre, J.C., Marché, C., Monate, B., Moy, Y., Prevosto, V.: ACSL: ANSI/ISO C Specification Language, http://frama-c.com/download/acsl.pdf

6. Beyer, D.: Reliable and reproducible competition results with benchexec and witnesses (report on SV-COMP 2016). In: Chechik, M., Raskin, J. (eds.) Tools and Algorithms for the Construction and Analysis of Systems - 22nd International Conference, TACAS 2016. Lecture Notes in Computer Science, vol. 9636, pp. 887–904. Springer (2016). https://doi.org/10.1007/978-3-662-49674-9_55, https://doi.org/10.1007/978-3-662-49674-9_55

7. Beyer, D.: Competition on software verification and witness validation: SV-COMP 2023. In: Sankaranarayanan, S., Sharygina, N. (eds.) TACAS. Lecture Notes in Computer Science, vol. 13994, pp. 495–522. Springer (2023). https://doi.org/10.1007/978-3-031-30820-8_29, https://doi.org/10.1007/978-3-031-30820-8_29

8. Beyer, D., Keremoglu, M.E.: Cpachecker: A tool for configurable software verification. In: Gopalakrishnan, G., Qadeer, S. (eds.) CAV. Lecture Notes in Computer Science, vol. 6806, pp. 184–190. Springer (2011). https://doi.org/10.1007/978-3-642-22110-1_16, https://doi.org/10.1007/978-3-642-22110-1_16

9. Beyer, D., Spiessl, M.: The static analyzer Frama-C in SV-COMP (competition contribution). In: Fisman, D., Rosu, G. (eds.) Tools and Algorithms for the Construction and Analysis of Systems - 28th International Conference, TACAS 2022. Lecture Notes in Computer Science, vol. 13244, pp. 429–434. Springer (2022). https://doi.org/10.1007/978-3-030-99527-0_26, https://doi.org/10.1007/978-3-030-99527-0_26

10. Beyer, D., Spiessl, M., Umbricht, S.: Cooperation between automatic and interactive software verifiers. In: Schlingloff, B., Chai, M. (eds.) Software Engineering and Formal Methods - 20th International Conference, SEFM 2022. Lecture Notes in

Computer Science, vol. 13550, pp. 111–128. Springer (2022). `https://doi.org/10.1007/978-3-031-17108-6_7`, `https://doi.org/10.1007/978-3-031-17108-6_7`

11. Brown, T.B., Mann, B., Ryder, N., Subbiah, M., Kaplan, J., Dhariwal, P., Neelakantan, A., Shyam, P., Sastry, G., Askell, A., Agarwal, S., Herbert-Voss, A., Krueger, G., Henighan, T., Child, R., Ramesh, A., Ziegler, D.M., Wu, J., Winter, C., Hesse, C., Chen, M., Sigler, E., Litwin, M., Gray, S., Chess, B., Clark, J., Berner, C., McCandlish, S., Radford, A., Sutskever, I., Amodei, D.: Language models are few-shot learners. In: Larochelle, H., Ranzato, M., Hadsell, R., Balcan, M., Lin, H. (eds.) Advances in Neural Information Processing Systems 33: Annual Conference on Neural Information Processing Systems 2020, NeurIPS 2020, December 6-12, 2020, virtual (2020), `https://proceedings.neurips.cc/paper/2020/hash/1457c0d6bfcb4967418bfb8ac142f64a-Abstract.html`

12. Chakraborty, S., Lahiri, S.K., Fakhoury, S., Lal, A., Musuvathi, M., Rastogi, A., Senthilnathan, A., Sharma, R., Swamy, N.: Ranking llm-generated loop invariants for program verification. In: Bouamor, H., Pino, J., Bali, K. (eds.) Findings of the Association for Computational Linguistics: EMNLP 2023, Singapore, December 6-10, 2023. pp. 9164–9175. Association for Computational Linguistics (2023), `https://aclanthology.org/2023.findings-emnlp.614`

13. Chalupa, M., Strejcek, J., Vitovská, M.: Joint forces for memory safety checking revisited. Int. J. Softw. Tools Technol. Transf. **22**(2), 115–133 (2020). `https://doi.org/10.1007/s10009-019-00526-2`, `https://doi.org/10.1007/s10009-019-00526-2`

14. Chen, B., Zhang, F., Nguyen, A., Zan, D., Lin, Z., Lou, J., Chen, W.: Codet: Code generation with generated tests. In: The Eleventh International Conference on Learning Representations, ICLR 2023, Kigali, Rwanda, May 1-5, 2023. OpenReview.net (2023), `https://openreview.net/pdf?id=ktrw68Cmu9c`

15. Chen, M., Tworek, J., Jun, H., Yuan, Q., de Oliveira Pinto, H.P., Kaplan, J., Edwards, H., Burda, Y., Joseph, N., Brockman, G., Ray, A., Puri, R., Krueger, G., Petrov, M., Khlaaf, H., Sastry, G., Mishkin, P., Chan, B., Gray, S., Ryder, N., Pavlov, M., Power, A., Kaiser, L., Bavarian, M., Winter, C., Tillet, P., Such, F.P., Cummings, D., Plappert, M., Chantzis, F., Barnes, E., Herbert-Voss, A., Guss, W.H., Nichol, A., Paino, A., Tezak, N., Tang, J., Babuschkin, I., Balaji, S., Jain, S., Saunders, W., Hesse, C., Carr, A.N., Leike, J., Achiam, J., Misra, V., Morikawa, E., Radford, A., Knight, M., Brundage, M., Murati, M., Mayer, K., Welinder, P., McGrew, B., Amodei, D., McCandlish, S., Sutskever, I., Zaremba, W.: Evaluating large language models trained on code. CoRR **abs/2107.03374** (2021), `https://arxiv.org/abs/2107.03374`

16. Chen, S., Wong, S., Chen, L., Tian, Y.: Extending context window of large language models via positional interpolation. CoRR **abs/2306.15595** (2023). `https://doi.org/10.48550/arXiv.2306.15595`, `https://doi.org/10.48550/arXiv.2306.15595`

17. Chen, X., Lin, M., Schärli, N., Zhou, D.: Teaching large language models to self-debug. CoRR **abs/2304.05128** (2023). `https://doi.org/10.48550/arXiv.2304.05128`, `https://doi.org/10.48550/arXiv.2304.05128`

18. Clarke, E.M., Kroening, D., Lerda, F.: A tool for checking ANSI-C programs. In: Jensen, K., Podelski, A. (eds.) Tools and Algorithms for the Construction and Analysis of Systems, 10th International Conference, TACAS 2004. Lecture Notes in Computer Science, vol. 2988, pp. 168–176. Springer (2004). `https://doi.org/10.1007/978-3-540-24730-2_15`, `https://doi.org/10.1007/978-3-540-24730-2_15`

19. Ernst, G., Pfähler, J., Schellhorn, G., Haneberg, D., Reif, W.: KIV: overview and verifythis competition. Int. J. Softw. Tools Technol. Transf. **17**(6), 677–694 (2015). https://doi.org/10.1007/s10009-014-0308-3, https://doi.org/10.1007/s10009-014-0308-3

20. Ernst, M.D., Perkins, J.H., Guo, P.J., McCamant, S., Pacheco, C., Tschantz, M.S., Xiao, C.: The daikon system for dynamic detection of likely invariants. Sci. Comput. Program. **69**(1-3), 35–45 (2007). https://doi.org/10.1016/j.scico.2007.01.015, https://doi.org/10.1016/j.scico.2007.01.015

21. Fried, D., Aghajanyan, A., Lin, J., Wang, S., Wallace, E., Shi, F., Zhong, R., Yih, S., Zettlemoyer, L., Lewis, M.: Incoder: A generative model for code infilling and synthesis. In: The Eleventh International Conference on Learning Representations, ICLR 2023, Kigali, Rwanda, May 1-5, 2023. OpenReview.net (2023), https://openreview.net/pdf?id=hQwb-1bM6EL

22. Garg, P., Neider, D., Madhusudan, P., Roth, D.: Learning invariants using decision trees and implication counterexamples. In: Bodík, R., Majumdar, R. (eds.) Proceedings of the 43rd Annual ACM SIGPLAN-SIGACT Symposium on Principles of Programming Languages, POPL 2016, St. Petersburg, FL, USA, January 20 - 22, 2016. pp. 499–512. ACM (2016). https://doi.org/10.1145/2837614.2837664, https://doi.org/10.1145/2837614.2837664

23. Giacobbe, M., Kroening, D., Parsert, J.: Neural termination analysis. In: Roychoudhury, A., Cadar, C., Kim, M. (eds.) Proceedings of the 30th ACM Joint European Software Engineering Conference and Symposium on the Foundations of Software Engineering, ESEC/FSE 2022, Singapore, Singapore, November 14-18, 2022. pp. 633–645. ACM (2022). https://doi.org/10.1145/3540250.3549120, https://doi.org/10.1145/3540250.3549120

24. Heizmann, M., Hoenicke, J., Podelski, A.: Software model checking for people who love automata. In: Sharygina, N., Veith, H. (eds.) Computer Aided Verification - 25th International Conference, CAV 2013, Saint Petersburg, Russia, July 13-19, 2013. Proceedings. Lecture Notes in Computer Science, vol. 8044, pp. 36–52. Springer (2013). https://doi.org/10.1007/978-3-642-39799-8_2, https://doi.org/10.1007/978-3-642-39799-8_2

25. Jacobs, B., Smans, J., Philippaerts, P., Vogels, F., Penninckx, W., Piessens, F.: Verifast: A powerful, sound, predictable, fast verifier for C and java. In: Bobaru, M.G., Havelund, K., Holzmann, G.J., Joshi, R. (eds.) NASA Formal Methods - Third International Symposium, NFM 2011, Pasadena, CA, USA, April 18-20, 2011. Proceedings. Lecture Notes in Computer Science, vol. 6617, pp. 41–55. Springer (2011). https://doi.org/10.1007/978-3-642-20398-5_4, https://doi.org/10.1007/978-3-642-20398-5_4

26. Ji, Z., Lee, N., Frieske, R., Yu, T., Su, D., Xu, Y., Ishii, E., Bang, Y., Madotto, A., Fung, P.: Survey of hallucination in natural language generation. ACM Comput. Surv. **55**(12), 248:1–248:38 (2023). https://doi.org/10.1145/3571730, https://doi.org/10.1145/3571730

27. Jiang, N., Liu, K., Lutellier, T., Tan, L.: Impact of code language models on automated program repair. In: 45th IEEE/ACM International Conference on Software Engineering, ICSE 2023, Melbourne, Australia, May 14-20, 2023. pp. 1430–1442. IEEE (2023). https://doi.org/10.1109/ICSE48619.2023.00125, https://doi.org/10.1109/ICSE48619.2023.00125

28. Kamath, A., Senthilnathan, A., Chakraborty, S., Deligiannis, P., Lahiri, S.K., Lal, A., Rastogi, A., Roy, S., Sharma, R.: Finding inductive loop invariants using large

language models. CoRR abs/**2311.07948** (2023). https://doi.org/10.48550/ARXIV.2311.07948, https://doi.org/10.48550/arXiv.2311.07948

29. Leino, K.R.M.: Dafny: An automatic program verifier for functional correctness. In: Clarke, E.M., Voronkov, A. (eds.) Logic for Programming, Artificial Intelligence, and Reasoning - 16th International Conference, LPAR-16, Dakar, Senegal, April 25-May 1, 2010, Revised Selected Papers. Lecture Notes in Computer Science, vol. 6355, pp. 348–370. Springer (2010). https://doi.org/10.1007/978-3-642-17511-4_20, https://doi.org/10.1007/978-3-642-17511-4_20

30. Ouyang, L., Wu, J., Jiang, X., Almeida, D., Wainwright, C.L., Mishkin, P., Zhang, C., Agarwal, S., Slama, K., Ray, A., Schulman, J., Hilton, J., Kelton, F., Miller, L., Simens, M., Askell, A., Welinder, P., Christiano, P.F., Leike, J., Lowe, R.: Training language models to follow instructions with human feedback. In: NeurIPS (2022), http://papers.nips.cc/paper_files/paper/2022/hash/b1efde53be364a73914f58805a001731-Abstract-Conference.html

31. Padhi, S., Sharma, R., Millstein, T.D.: Data-driven precondition inference with learned features. In: Krintz, C., Berger, E.D. (eds.) Proceedings of the 37th ACM SIGPLAN Conference on Programming Language Design and Implementation, PLDI 2016, Santa Barbara, CA, USA, June 13-17, 2016. pp. 42–56. ACM (2016). https://doi.org/10.1145/2908080.2908099, https://doi.org/10.1145/2908080.2908099

32. Pei, K., Bieber, D., Shi, K., Sutton, C., Yin, P.: Can large language models reason about program invariants? In: Krause, A., Brunskill, E., Cho, K., Engelhardt, B., Sabato, S., Scarlett, J. (eds.) ICML. Proceedings of Machine Learning Research, vol. 202, pp. 27496–27520. PMLR (2023), https://proceedings.mlr.press/v202/pei23a.html

33. Peng, B., Galley, M., He, P., Cheng, H., Xie, Y., Hu, Y., Huang, Q., Liden, L., Yu, Z., Chen, W., Gao, J.: Check your facts and try again: Improving large language models with external knowledge and automated feedback. CoRR abs/**2302.12813** (2023). https://doi.org/10.48550/arXiv.2302.12813, https://doi.org/10.48550/arXiv.2302.12813

34. Rae, J.W., Borgeaud, S., Cai, T., Millican, K., Hoffmann, J., Song, H.F., Aslanides, J., Henderson, S., Ring, R., Young, S., Rutherford, E., Hennigan, T., Menick, J., Cassirer, A., Powell, R., van den Driessche, G., Hendricks, L.A., Rauh, M., Huang, P., Glaese, A., Welbl, J., Dathathri, S., Huang, S., Uesato, J., Mellor, J., Higgins, I., Creswell, A., McAleese, N., Wu, A., Elsen, E., Jayakumar, S.M., Buchatskaya, E., Budden, D., Sutherland, E., Simonyan, K., Paganini, M., Sifre, L., Martens, L., Li, X.L., Kuncoro, A., Nematzadeh, A., Gribovskaya, E., Donato, D., Lazaridou, A., Mensch, A., Lespiau, J., Tsimpoukelli, M., Grigorev, N., Fritz, D., Sottiaux, T., Pajarskas, M., Pohlen, T., Gong, Z., Toyama, D., de Masson d'Autume, C., Li, Y., Terzi, T., Mikulik, V., Babuschkin, I., Clark, A., de Las Casas, D., Guy, A., Jones, C., Bradbury, J., Johnson, M.J., Hechtman, B.A., Weidinger, L., Gabriel, I., Isaac, W., Lockhart, E., Osindero, S., Rimell, L., Dyer, C., Vinyals, O., Ayoub, K., Stanway, J., Bennett, L., Hassabis, D., Kavukcuoglu, K., Irving, G.: Scaling language models: Methods, analysis & insights from training gopher. CoRR abs/**2112.11446** (2021), https://arxiv.org/abs/2112.11446

35. Si, X., Dai, H., Raghothaman, M., Naik, M., Song, L.: Learning loop invariants for program verification. In: Bengio, S., Wallach, H.M., Larochelle, H., Grauman, K., Cesa-Bianchi, N., Garnett, R. (eds.) Advances in Neural Information Processing Systems 31: Annual Conference on Neural Information Processing Systems 2018, NeurIPS 2018, December 3-8, 2018, Montréal,

Canada. pp. 7762–7773 (2018), `https://proceedings.neurips.cc/paper/2018/hash/65b1e92c585fd4c2159d5f33b5030ff2-Abstract.html`

36. Si, X., Naik, A., Dai, H., Naik, M., Song, L.: Code2inv: A deep learning framework for program verification. In: Lahiri, S.K., Wang, C. (eds.) Computer Aided Verification - 32nd International Conference, CAV 2020, Los Angeles, CA, USA, July 21-24, 2020, Proceedings, Part II. Lecture Notes in Computer Science, vol. 12225, pp. 151–164. Springer (2020). `https://doi.org/10.1007/978-3-030-53291-8_9`, `https://doi.org/10.1007/978-3-030-53291-8_9`

37. Wei, J., Tay, Y., Bommasani, R., Raffel, C., Zoph, B., Borgeaud, S., Yogatama, D., Bosma, M., Zhou, D., Metzler, D., Chi, E.H., Hashimoto, T., Vinyals, O., Liang, P., Dean, J., Fedus, W.: Emergent abilities of large language models. Trans. Mach. Learn. Res. **2022** (2022), `https://openreview.net/forum?id=yzkSU5zdwD`

38. Wei, J., Wang, X., Schuurmans, D., Bosma, M., Ichter, B., Xia, F., Chi, E.H., Le, Q.V., Zhou, D.: Chain-of-thought prompting elicits reasoning in large language models. In: NeurIPS (2022), `http://papers.nips.cc/paper_files/paper/2022/hash/9d5609613524ecf4f15af0f7b31abca4-Abstract-Conference.html`

Combining Deductive Verification with Shape Analysis

Téo Bernier[1], Yani Ziani[1,2], Nikolai Kosmatov[1(✉)],
and Frédéric Loulergue[2]

[1] Thales Research & Technology, Palaiseau, France
{teo.bernier,yani.ziani,nikolai.kosmatov}@thalesgroup.com
[2] Univ. Orléans, INSA Centre Val de Loire, LIFO EA 4022, Orléans, France
frederic.loulergue@univ-orleans.fr

Abstract. Deductive verification tools can prove a large range of program properties, but often face issues on recursive data structures. Abstract interpretation tools based on separation logic and shape analysis can efficiently reason about such structures but cannot deal with so large classes of properties. This short paper presents an ongoing work on combining both techniques. We show how a deductive verifier for C programs, FRAMA-C/WP, can benefit from a shape analysis tool, MEMCAD, where structural and separation properties proved in the latter become assumptions for the former. A case study on selected functions of the tpm2-tss library using linked lists confirms the interest of the approach.

Keywords: deductive verification, shape analysis, abstract interpretation, linked lists, Frama-C, MemCAD

1 Introduction

Context and Motivation. Deductive verification tools were successfully used in many case studies [4] to prove a large range of safety, security and functional properties. Such tools often have issues to conduct automatic proof on code with *recursive data structures* (e.g. linked lists, trees, etc.), in particular, due to complex memory models they need. The user has to guide the proof by interactively proved lemmas, assertions, etc. Abstract interpretation tools based on separation logic and shape analysis [3] can efficiently reason about such structures but typically cannot deal with so large classes of properties. This short paper presents new ideas and emerging results on combining both techniques trying to take the best of both worlds.

Approach and Results. We present a verification approach combining a popular deductive verifier for C programs, FRAMA-C/WP [6], with a shape analysis tool, MEMCAD [10]. The main idea is to prove structural and separation properties in MEMCAD and then to assume them in FRAMA-C/WP in order to increase the level of automation of the latter and overcome some of its limitations. We

D. Beyer and A. Cavalcanti (Eds.): FASE 2024, LNCS 14573, pp. 280–289, 2024.
https://doi.org/10.1007/978-3-031-57259-3_14

apply it on a real-life case study using linked lists: a few (slightly simplified) functions of tpm2-tss[3], a popular library for communication with a Trusted Platform Module (TPM). Recent work [11] demonstrated that deductive verification of the library functions manipulating linked lists was relatively hard, and required many additional lemmas and assertions.

The contributions of this paper include the presentation of a combined verification technique using deductive verification and shape analysis, its illustration with FRAMA-C/WP and MEMCAD on a function manipulating linked lists, as well as a successful case study on a set of functions of the tpm2-tss library.

2   Background

2.1   Deductive Verification with Frama-C/Wp

FRAMA-C [6] is an integrated toolbox built around a kernel offering core services and plugins dedicated to specific analysis or verification tasks for C code, e.g. value analysis, runtime assertion checking and deductive verification. ACSL (ANSI C Specification Language) [6] is the common specification language of the plugins. The WP plugin performs *modular* deductive verification: each function is verified independently. It generates verification conditions (VCs) from the C code with ACSL annotations and requests their proof by the QED simplifier or by external provers.

We illustrate the main ACSL features on the running example[4] of Fig. 1, 3, 4, 5, presented as we go, where ACSL notation (e.g. \forall, integer, ==>, <=, &&) is pretty-printed (resp., as $\forall$, $\mathbb{Z}$, $\Rightarrow$, $\leq$, $\wedge$). Lines 69–85 of Fig. 4 show a *contract* for function list_push (detailed below) that adds a new value into a linked list (cf. Lines 1–2 of Fig. 1), allocating a new cell. The contract includes pre-conditions (requires clauses) and post-conditions (ensures clauses). The assigns clause is a special kind of post-condition that indicates the memory locations the function is allowed to modify. ACSL formulas are mostly multi-sorted first-order logic where types are either C types or logic types (such as $\mathbb{Z}$, the type of mathematical integers). ACSL provides built-in constructs such as \result (the value returned by the function) and predicates such as \valid(p) (stating that pointer p refers to an allocated memory location, so that *p can be safely read and written) and \separated(p1,p2,...) (stating that the memory locations referred to by given pointers do not intersect). Notice that the considered memory locations are here indicated by pointers. Users can define predicates such as those in Fig. 1, adapted here from a previous work [1] on verifying linked lists in WP.

The main predicate is the inductively defined predicate linked_ll (Lines 10–19) stating that a linked list (segment) of int values (defined on Lines 1–2) from pointer bl to pointer el (excluded) is a well-formed list represented by an ACSL logical list ll. In other words, ll contains the pointers to the cells of that list segment (or the whole list if el is NULL). ACSL lists are similar to

---

[3] https://github.com/tpm2-software/tpm2-tss
[4] Available in a companion artifact on http://doi.org/10.5281/zenodo.10497923

```
1  typedef struct cell_s {struct cell_s* next; int data;} cell;
2  typedef cell* list;
3  /*@
4    predicate ptr_sep_from_list{L}(cell* c, \list<cell*> ll) =
5      ∀ ℤ n; 0 ≤ n < \length(ll) ⇒ \separated(c, \nth(ll, n));
6    predicate dptr_sep_from_list{L}(cell** c, \list<cell*> ll) =
7      ∀ ℤ n; 0 ≤ n < \length(ll) ⇒ \separated(c, \nth(ll, n));
8    predicate in_list{L}(cell* c, \list<cell*> ll) =
9      ∃ ℤ n; 0 ≤ n < \length(ll) ∧ \nth(ll, n) == c;
10   inductive linked_ll{L}(cell *bl,cell *el,\list<cell*> ll) {
11     case linked_ll_nil{L}:
12       ∀ cell *el; linked_ll{L}(el, el, \Nil);
13     case linked_ll_cons{L}:
14       ∀ cell *bl, *el, \list<cell*> tail;
15         (\separated(bl, el) ∧ \valid(bl) ∧
16         linked_ll{L}(bl->next, el, tail) ∧
17         ptr_sep_from_list(bl, tail)) ⇒
18           linked_ll{L}(bl, el, \Cons(bl, tail));
19   }
20   predicate unchanged_ll{L1, L2}(\list<cell*> ll) =
21     ∀ ℤ n; 0 ≤ n < \length(ll) ⇒
22       \valid{L1}(\nth(ll,n)) ∧ \valid{L2}(\nth(ll,n)) ∧
23       \at((\nth(ll,n))->next, L1) == \at((\nth(ll,n))->next, L2) ∧
24       \at((\nth(ll,n))->data, L1) == \at((\nth(ll,n))->data, L2);
25   axiomatic cell_to_ll {
26     logic \list<cell*> to_ll{L}(cell* beg, cell* end)
27       reads {node->next | cell* node;
28                \valid(node) ∧ in_list(node, to_ll(beg, end))};
29     axiom to_ll_nil{L}: ∀ cell *node;
30       to_ll{L}(node, node) == \Nil;
31     axiom to_ll_cons{L}: ∀ cell *beg, *end;
32       (\separated(beg, end) ∧ \valid{L}(beg) ∧
33       ptr_sep_from_list{L}(beg, to_ll{L}(beg->next, end))) ⇒
34         to_ll{L}(beg, end) ==
35         \Cons(beg, to_ll{L}(beg->next, end));
36   }
37 */
38 #include "lemmas_min.h"
```

Fig. 1. Types and ACSL predicates for linked lists.

lists in functional programming. In the inductive case (`linked_ll_cons`) overlapping list cells (or cyclic lists) are avoided by requiring that the first cell `bl`
is separated from all the other cells in the list including `el`, so the list is well-
formed. The predicates on Lines 4–9 use predefined functions: `\length` and `\nth`
that returns the nth element of a logic list. Predicates can take one or several
program points (C labels plus some ACSL labels: `Pre` and `Post`). The built-in
`\at(e, L)` specifies the value of an expression `e` at a label `L`. Using these features, `unchanged_ll` states that a logic list does not change between two program
points (Lines 20–24). Finally, Lines 25–36 define an axiomatic function `to_ll`
that constructs a logic list from a C linked list. While it would be possible to
write `requires ∃\list<cell>ll; linked_ll(*pl, NULL, ll);` instead of Line 72
of Figure 4, the scope of the existential quantifier is just this line. Therefore, `ll`
cannot be used in the post-conditions, hence the need for `to_ll`.

Let us now detail the contract of `list_push` (its code is detailed below).
The pre-conditions state that `pl` is a valid pointer to a list (Line 70), separated
from every element in the list (Line 71), and refers to a linked list verifying the

```
a  ll_cell<0,0> :=                        n  cell<0,0> :=
b  | [0]                                   o  | [0]
c    - emp                                 p    - emp
d    - this = 0                            q    - this = 0
e  | [2 addr int]                          r  | [2 addr int]
f    - this->0 |-> $0 * $0.ll_cell() *     s    - this->0 |-> $0 * this->4 |-> $1
g      this->4 |-> $1                       t    - alloc(this, 8) & this ≠ 0.
h    - alloc(this, 8) & this ≠ 0.          u
i                                          v  cell_plist<0,0> :=
j  plist<0, 0> :=                          w  | [2 addr addr]
k  | [1 addr]                              x    - this->0 |-> $0 * $0.cell() *
l    - this->0 |-> $0 * $0.ll_cell()       y      this->4 |-> $1 * $1.plist()
m    - alloc(this, 4) & this ≠ 0.          z    - alloc(this, 8) & this ≠ 0.
```

Fig. 2. Inductive predicates for MEMCAD.

inductive predicate `linked_ll` (Line 72). Line 73 specifies that the only locations the function is allowed to modify are `*pl`, the head pointer of the list, and `\at(**pl, Post)`, the first element of the list at the exit point, i.e. the freshly allocated cell. We cannot reference the new list cell at the entry point because it is not allocated yet. In post-conditions, the returned value indicates whether or not the allocation is successful (Line 76). Regardless of the success, we expect the list invariants to hold (Lines 74–75). In case the allocation fails, we expect the pointer `*pl` and the list contents to be unchanged (Lines 77–79). If it succeeds, we expect the list to be composed of the new cell followed by the old list (Lines 80–81), the old list being unchanged (Lines 82–83), and the fields of the new cell, `next` and `data`, resp., to point to the old list (Line 84) and to contain the expected value (Line 85).

2.2   Shape Analysis with MemCAD

The purpose of MEMCAD [10] is to automatically infer precise invariants about programs manipulating complex data structures. It is based on shape analysis [3], a static code analysis technique that discovers and verifies properties of recursive, dynamically allocated data structures. It relies on separation logic and abstract interpretation. Unlike in WP, the analysis is global.

To use MEMCAD on linked lists defined on Lines 1–2 of Fig. 1, the user first defines an inductive predicate expressing a structural invariant of a well-formed linked list, such as predicate `ll_cell` on Lines a–h of Fig. 2. A list, i.e. a pointer to a list cell, satisfies the predicate in two cases. Each case defines a memory separation formula and additional constraints. In the first case, the pointer is null (Line d) and no specific memory separation is required (Line c). This case has no additional arguments (cf. [0] on Line b). The second case has two (existentially quantified) arguments: an address and an integer (Line e), denoted, resp., by $0 and $1 in the rest of the case. The pointer is non null and refers to a valid memory block of 8 bytes (Line h), assuming a 32-bit system. Lines f–g define the values of the fields `next` and `data` (at offsets 0 and 4) as $0 and $1, and require separation between those fields and the rest of the list. The separation is expressed by the separating conjunction "*" [10]. Notice

```
40 //@ assigns \nothing;
41 void mc_chk_plist(list* pl) {
42   _memcad("check_inductive(pl,plist)");
43 }
44
45 typedef struct {cell* c; list* pl;} cell_plist;
46
47 //@ assigns \nothing;
48 void mc_chk_sep_cell_plist(cell* c, list* pl) {
49   cell_plist tmp;
50   tmp.c = c; tmp.pl = pl;
51   cell_plist* ptmp = &tmp;
52   _memcad("check_inductive(ptmp,cell_plist)");
53 }
```

Fig. 3. Auxiliary MEMCAD checks for linked lists.

that "...*$0.ll_cell()*..." on Line f specifies separation recursively, for all list cells reached by the predicate via the inductive case. The user can insert the instruction _memcad("add_inductive(l,ll_cell)"); to *assume* that list l respects predicate ll_cell, or _memcad("check_inductive(l,ll_cell)"); to *check* the same property in MEMCAD.

Predicate cell on Lines n–t is very close to predicate ll_cell except that it only defines one list cell without recursion. Predicate plist on Lines j–m expresses that a double pointer to a list cell (i.e. of type list*) is valid, refers to a well-formed list and is separated from its cells. Predicate cell_plist is explained below.

3   Combined Approach

3.1   Shape Analysis Assisted Verification

To prove complex memory-related annotations with WP on real-life code [11], the user typically has to manually annotate the code with many additional carefully chosen assertions establishing structural invariants and separation properties at several intermediate program points, and to add numerous lemmas to facilitate reasoning about them (whose proof must usually be done manually in CoQ, an interactive proof assistant). Our approach proposes to let MEMCAD deal with the structural invariants of recursive data structures and separation properties, and to admit them in WP at some key points.

In order to use both tools simultaneously in this way, we first need to show the equivalence between MEMCAD and WP inductive predicates. For MEMCAD, predicate ll_cell (Lines a–h of Fig. 2) specifies that each element of the list is a valid cell, is separated from every other cell of the list and the list is null-terminated. This is equivalent to the linked_ll predicate for WP (Lines 10–19 of Fig. 1) when we consider the whole list. Indeed, when el is NULL, this predicate also means that every list cell is valid and separated from any other list cell, and the list is null-terminated. Explicit separation conditions in the ACSL predicate for WP are expressed by the separating conjunction in the MEMCAD

```
59  /*@
60    assigns \nothing;
61    ensures \result ≠ NULL ⇒ (\valid(\result) ∧
62      \result->next == NULL ∧ \result->data == 0); */
63  cell* calloc_cell() {
64    cell* c = malloc(sizeof(cell));
65    if (c) { c->next = NULL; c->data = 0; }
66    return c;
67  }
68
69  /*@
70    requires \valid(pl);
71    requires dptr_sep_from_list(pl,to_ll(*pl, NULL));
72    requires linked_ll(*pl, NULL, to_ll(*pl, NULL));
73    assigns *pl, \at(**pl, Post);
74    ensures dptr_sep_from_list(pl, to_ll(*pl, NULL));
75    ensures linked_ll(*pl, NULL, to_ll(*pl, NULL));
76    ensures \result \in {0, 1};
77    ensures \result == 0 ⇒
78      unchanged_ll{Pre, Post}(to_ll(*pl, NULL));
79    ensures \result == 0 ⇒ *pl == \old(*pl);
80    ensures \result == 1 ⇒
81      to_ll(*pl, NULL) == ([|*pl|] ^ to_ll(\old(*pl), NULL));
82    ensures \result == 1 ⇒
83      unchanged_ll{Pre, Post}(to_ll(\old(*pl), NULL));
84    ensures \result == 1 ⇒ (*pl)->next == \old(*pl);
85    ensures \result == 1 ⇒ (*pl)->data == data; */
86  int list_push(list* pl, int data) {
87    cell* c = calloc_cell();
88    if (!c) return 0;
89    mc_chk_sep_cell_plist(c, pl);
90    //@ admit ptr_sep_from_list(c,to_ll(*pl,NULL));
91    //@ admit \separated(pl, c);
92    //@ ghost Alloc:;
93    c->next = *pl;
94    //@ assert unchanged_ll{Alloc,Here}(to_ll{Alloc}(*pl,NULL));
95    c->data = data;
96    //@ ghost Link:;
97    *pl = c;
98    /*@ assert unchanged_ll{Link,Here}(
99      to_ll{Link}(\at(*pl,Pre),NULL)); */
100   mc_chk_plist(pl);
101   //@ admit dptr_sep_from_list(pl,to_ll(*pl,NULL));
102   //@ admit linked_ll(*pl,NULL,to_ll(*pl,NULL));
103   return 1;
104 }
```

Fig. 4. Functions `calloc_cell` and `list_push` with contracts.

counterpart. (Notice that separation of `bl` with `NULL` on Line 15 is trivial.) The sequence of list elements, expressed by a logic list in ACSL and used to prove functional properties about the contents of the list (cf. Lines 80–81) in WP, does not need to be specified for MEMCAD, which we only use to reason about structural properties.

To check if invariants hold in MEMCAD, we define check functions shown in Fig. 3. These functions are specified to be side-effect-free (cf. Lines 40, 47) to prevent interference with the proof in WP.

The first function, `mc_chk_plist` (Lines 41–43), checks that `pl` respects the `plist` predicate, i.e. is a valid pointer to a well-formed list from which it is separated (Line 42, see also Lines j–m of Fig. 2).

The goal of the second function, `mc_chk_sep_cell_plist`, is to check that `c` refers to a list cell, `pl` respects the `plist` predicate, and the corresponding pointer and the list cells are separated from the cell referred to by `c`. To do that in MEMCAD, we introduce an ad-hoc structure `cell_plist` with both pointers (Line 45). The function initializes a local structure (Lines 49–50) and takes its address (Line 51) in order to express the required check (Line 52). This check relies on the predicate `cell_plist` (Lines v–z of Fig. 2) stating that the given pointer is non-null and refers to a structure with two pointers at offsets 0 and 4, denoted `$0` and `$1`, referring, resp., to a cell and to a double pointer to a well-formed list, which are separated (between them and from the list cells). Notice that "`...*$1.plist()`" on Line y specifies separation recursively, that is, from all locations considered in separation constraints reached via `plist` (and hence via `ll_cell`).

An important benefit of using MEMCAD is its capacity to automatically handle dynamic memory allocation, which is not yet supported in WP. Thus, we define a custom allocator that simulates the behavior of `calloc` for list cells on Lines 59–67 of Fig. 4. WP uses its contract, which is simple but currently unprovable by WP since dynamic allocation is not supported (it should become provable when this support is added into WP).

3.2 Proof of Function `list_push`

We illustrate our approach on function `list_push` of Fig. 4. It tries to allocate a new cell (Lines 87–88), and, in case of success, puts it on top of the list with the given data (Lines 93, 95, 97, 103). Lines 92, 96 define *ghost* labels (that is, labels used only in annotations).

Lines 89–91 show how we use MEMCAD to verify that the new cell (referred to by `c`) is separated both from the list cells and the pointer referred to by `pl` (Line 89), and introduce these properties as assumptions for WP (`admit` clauses on Lines 90–91). They help WP to prove in an `assert` clause on Line 94 that the list remains unchanged since label `Alloc` (i.e. Line 92) despite writing into the new cell on Line 93, and a similar assertion for the old list on Lines 98–99 despite the assignment on Line 97.

Instead of reasoning about the modified list directly in WP—which often presents another difficulty for deductive verification—we let MEMCAD check the list invariants on Line 100 and admit them on Lines 101–102 for WP to prove the post-conditions. Thanks to those assumptions, WP successfully proves this function. Notice that the check instruction for MEMCAD and the admit instructions for WP are placed (for the moment, manually) at the same program location to ensure the soundness of the global verification.

In order to have a full proof, we also need to run MEMCAD to verify all the checks in `list_push`. For this purpose, we define a wrapper in Fig. 5 to analyze

```
106  int mc_verify_list_push(void) {
107    list* pl; int i; _memcad("add_inductive(pl,plist)");
108    list_push(pl, i);
109  }
```

Fig. 5. Wrapper to verify `list_push` in MEMCAD.

the call to `list_push` on Line 108 with an arbitrary list respecting the given pre-conditions (which correspond in MEMCAD, as we explained above, to assuming predicate `plist` for `pl`, cf. Lines 70–72, 107). MEMCAD also succeeds in its analysis, hence, we can conclude that our function respects its ACSL contract.

While the annotation step is done manually in the current work, it can be better automated in the future. A coordinated generation of checks and assumptions for a given recursive data structure for both tools will facilitate the verification and the justification of soundness of the combined approach. An early idea consists in defining a domain-specific language for the description of the target recursive data structure that is then used for the generation of necessary predicates for MEMCAD and for WP as well as necessary assumptions and checks. The investigation of this research direction is left for future work.

4   Case study on the tpm2-tss library

We tested our approach on a few (slightly simplified) functions of the tpm2-tss library, a widely used open-source implementation of the TPM Software Stack (TSS)[5] designed to access the Trusted Platform Module (TPM). The library uses a linked list to store and use TPM resources, such as objects sent to and received from the TPM. List cells are dynamically allocated. Simplifications were applied to data structures used for list cells (and their treatment).

We consider two functions, to add an object and to look for an object in a list, with one called function, and apply MEMCAD to verify separation properties for a newly allocated cell that WP is currently not able to deduce. A recent study [11] demonstrated that deductive verification with WP of these functions required many additional lemmas and assertions, as well as the replacement of the dynamic memory allocation by a static allocator. Interestingly, the difficulty to verify real-life code was not caused by complex operations on lists—these operations are in reality quite simple in the target code—but by the difficulty to reason about the recursive data structure itself.

The proposed approach combining deductive verification with shape analysis allows us to perform a complete proof with less effort and without replacing dynamic allocator by a static allocator. On the considered functions, the proof with WP alone [11] required 14 lemmas, leading to the generation of 241 proof obligations, one of which required a manually created WP script, and took 4m50s. Thanks to combining WP and MEMCAD in our work, we could remove ∼45

---

[5] https://trustedcomputinggroup.org/work-groups/software-stack/

auxiliary ACSL annotations and 5 lemmas, so the proof required only 9 lemmas, leading to 194 proof obligations using no scripts, and took 1min47s in total for WP and MEMCAD (the latter taking less than 1 sec.).

5   Related Work and Conclusion

Related Work. Various tools based on separation logic were proposed, such as VeriFast [8], Viper [7], VerCors [2]. He et al. [5] extract functional specification from imperative programs using a memory-safe type system and insert dynamic checks into the specification. GRASShopper [9] combines separation logic with an SMT-based verifier. Unlike in our work, GRASShopper does not integrate abstract interpretation based shape analysis (which allows us to infer structural invariants with MEMCAD without having to provide loop invariants for this tool). Issues reported in a recent study [11] motivate such combinations for complex real-life code with recursive data structures. Our work continues previous efforts by proposing a combination of weakest-precondition based deductive verification with abstract interpretation based shape analysis on the source-code level, which, to the best of our knowledge, was not studied and evaluated before.

Conclusion and Future Work. This short paper has presented an approach combining deductive verification with FRAMA-C/WP and shape analysis with MEMCAD. Separation properties and structural invariants for linked data structures can be more easily proved by the latter, and then used as assumptions in the former, thus allowing it to focus on other properties. This work is still ongoing and opens interesting research questions and perspectives: automation of the proposed verification technique including a coordinated generation of checks and assumptions, proof of its soundness, design of a common (higher-level) specification mechanism for recursive data structures with automatic translation into suitable definitions for MEMCAD and FRAMA-C, as well as evaluation on other relevant case studies.

Data-Availability Statement. Code examples used in this paper are available online as a companion artifact on http://doi.org/10.5281/zenodo.10458675. The artifact includes a Virtual Machine containing the installed tools and code examples used, and can be used to reproduce the results of this paper.

Acknowledgment. Part of this work was supported by ANR (grants ANR-22-CE39-0014, ANR-22-CE25-0018) and French Ministry of Defense via a PhD grant of Yani Ziani. We thank Allan Blanchard, Laurent Corbin, Loïc Correnson, Daniel Gracia Pérez and Xavier Rival for fruitful discussions, and the anonymous referees for helpful comments.

References

1. Blanchard, A., Kosmatov, N., Loulergue, F.: Logic against ghosts: Comparison of two proof approaches for a list module. In: 34th Symp. on Applied Comput-

ing, Software Verification and Testing Track (SAC-SVT'19). pp. 2186–2195. ACM (2019)

2. Blom, S., Darabi, S., Huisman, M., Oortwijn, W.: The VerCors tool set: Verification of parallel and concurrent software. In: 13th Int. Conf. on Integrated Formal Methods (iFM'17). LNCS, vol. 10510, pp. 102–110. Springer (2017)

3. Distefano, D., O'Hearn, P.W., Yang, H.: A local shape analysis based on separation logic. In: 12th Int. Conf. on Tools and Algorithms for the Construction and Analysis of Systems (TACAS'06). LNCS, vol. 3920, pp. 287–302. Springer (2006)

4. Hähnle, R., Huisman, M.: Deductive software verification: From pen-and-paper proofs to industrial tools. In: Computing and Software Science - State of the Art and Perspectives, LNCS, vol. 10000, pp. 345–373. Springer (2019)

5. He, P., Westbrook, E., Carmer, B., Phifer, C., Robert, V., Smeltzer, K., Stefanescu, A., Tomb, A., Wick, A., Yacavone, M., Zdancewic, S.: A type system for extracting functional specifications from memory-safe imperative programs. Proc. ACM Program. Lang. **5**, 1–29 (2021)

6. Kirchner, F., Kosmatov, N., Prevosto, V., Signoles, J., Yakobowski, B.: Frama-C: A software analysis perspective. Formal Asp. Comput. **27**(3), 573–609 (2015)

7. Müller, P., Schwerhoff, M., Summers, A.J.: Viper: A verification infrastructure for permission-based reasoning. In: 17th Int. Conf. on Verification, Model Checking, and Abstract Interpretation (VMCAI'16). LNCS, vol. 9583, pp. 41–62. Springer (2016)

8. Philippaerts, P., Mühlberg, J.T., Penninckx, W., Smans, J., Jacobs, B., Piessens, F.: Software verification with VeriFast: Industrial case studies. Science of Computer Programming **82**, 77–97 (2014)

9. Piskac, R., Wies, T., Zufferey, D.: GRASShopper - complete heap verification with mixed specifications. In: 20th International Conference on Tools and Algorithms for the Construction and Analysis of Systems (TACAS'14). LNCS, vol. 8413, pp. 124–139. Springer (2014)

10. Sotin, P., Rival, X.: Hierarchical shape abstraction of dynamic structures in static blocks. In: 10th Asian Symposium on Programming Languages and Systems (APLAS'12). LNCS, vol. 7705, pp. 131–147. Springer (2012)

11. Ziani, Y., Kosmatov, N., Loulergue, F., Gracia Pérez, D., Bernier, T.: Towards formal verification of a TPM software stack (2023), http://arxiv.org/abs/2307.16821

First Steps towards Deductive Verification of LLVM IR *

Dré van Oorschot, Marieke Huisman(✉)(iD), and Ömer Şakar(iD)

Formal Methods and Tools, University of Twente, Enschede, The Netherlands
d.h.m.a.vanoorschot@alumnus.utwente.nl,
{m.huisman,o.f.o.sakar}@utwente.nl

Abstract. Over the last years, deductive program verifiers have substantially improved, and their applicability on non-trivial applications has been demonstrated. However, a major bottleneck is that for every new programming language, a new deductive verifier has to be built.
This paper describes the first steps in a project that aims to address this problem, by language-agnostic support for deductive verification: Rather than building a deductive program verifier for every programming language, we develop deductive program verification technology for a widely-used intermediate representation language (LLVM IR), such that we eventually get verification support for any language that can be compiled into the LLVM IR format.
Concretely, this paper describes the design of VCLLVM, a prototype tool that adds LLVM IR as a supported language to the VerCors verifier. We discuss the challenges that have to be addressed to develop verification support for such a low-level language. Moreover, we also sketch how we envisage to build verification support for any specified source program that can be compiled into LLVM IR on top of VCLLVM.

1 Introduction

As software has become an intrinsic part of our daily lives, we become more and more dependent on software being reliable and dependable, and we need tools that can help us to establish these guarantees. Over the last years, substantial progress has been made in the development of *formal verification techniques* that can be used to ensure that software provides certain guarantees. This covers a wide range of different approaches that can be used to provide guarantees at different levels of abstraction and precision. Here, we focus in particular on *deductive program verification* techniques [11], which are used to provide guarantees directly at code level, by verifying whether a program fragment behaves according to the pre-postcondition-contract that is specified for it. A broad range of deductive verifiers exist, such as VerCors [4], KeY [1], VeriFast [14, 15], Viper [25], Dafny [20], RESOLVE [37], Whiley [31], Frama-C [3], KIV [9] and OpenJML [7], which have been used in several non-trivial case studies, see e.g. [29, 35, 34, 29,

---

* Work on this project is supported by the NWO VICI 639.023.710 Mercedes project and the NWO TTW 17249 ChEOPS project.

D. Beyer and A. Cavalcanti (Eds.): FASE 2024, LNCS 14573, pp. 290–303, 2024.
https://doi.org/10.1007/978-3-031-57259-3_15

13, 10, 17]. A major challenge for deductive verifiers in practice is to enlarge the particular language features that they support. This language-dependency creates a severe limitation on how effective these techniques can be used in current software development, where language standards are regularly updated, new programming languages are frequently used, and applications are often written using multiple programming languages.

In compiler technology, this growth in source level programming languages, as well as the wide range of target architectures has been tackled by the introduction of intermediate representation formats, such as LLVM IR [19]. They require only a compiler into this intermediate representation format for a new programming language, while new architectures are supported by defining a mapping from the intermediate representation format into the new hardware. We propose a similar approach to reduce the language-dependence of deductive program verification technology, by: (1) defining verification technology for LLVM IR, and (2) developing a generic approach to translate contract specifications from a wide range of source languages into contract specifications for LLVM IR.

This paper focuses in particular on the first step in this project: it contributes VCLLVM, a prototype tool that encodes annotated LLVM IR programs into the VerCors verifier [4] to enable deductive verification for LLVM IR. We describe the challenges for the encoding of LLVM IR into VerCors, as LLVM IR is a much lower-level language than the languages that are supported by VerCors already, and how these challenges affect the design and implementation of VCLLVM. We also sketch how we plan to use VCLLVM as a stepping stone in a bigger project to develop language-independent support for deductive verification.

2   Background

This section gives a brief background on the VerCors verifier and LLVM IR.

VerCors VerCors [4] is a deductive verifier for concurrent programs. It can verify programs written in several programming languages (e.g., Java, CUDA, OpenCL, and its internal Prototype Verification Language PVL). To verify programs with VerCors, they are first annotated with pre-postcondition-contract specifications written in *permission-based separation logic* (PBSL) [38], and then the specified programs are encoded into the internal format of VerCors, called COL, which is transformed in several steps into the input language of Viper [25]. The Viper infrastructure is then used for verification. If verification with Viper fails, VerCors translates the error message back to the level of the source program.

PBSL is a concurrent separation logic [27] with support for permissions [5]. Permissions make the language suitable to reason about concurrent programs, as they are used to encode when variables may be read or written. VCLLVM at the moment only supports sequential programs, thus we do not provide further details about PBSL here, and instead refer to the documentation.

LLVM IR LLVM IR (LLVM Intermediate Representation) is the common interface for the *frontend* and *backend* compilers developed as part of the LLVM project [19]. LLVM IR is designed to be *abstract* enough to be compiled to from higher level frontend languages, and *simple* enough to be transformed into assembly or machine code for a specific CPU architecture. It is also the language being operated on by middle-end code optimisation and analysis passes [23]. More details about LLVM IR can be found in its documentation [22].

The LLVM IR language is an assembly language using the single static assignment format. Each LLVM IR file consists of one module. Each module contains multiple functions. Functions are divided into multiple (possibly labelled) blocks, with one dedicated entry block. Every block consists of one or more instructions. We briefly summarise the main features of LLVM IR that are relevant for our work. First of all, LLVM IR features only two basic types, namely integers and floats, with the standard (bitwise) binary operators. Both come with different precisions. These two basic types can be combined into aggregate types, such as vectors, arrays, and structs, and can be referenced via pointers. Further, LLVM IR supports custom-declared constants and several predefined constants, such as **true** and **false**. The constant **undef** is used to present undefined state to the compiler as a range of possible values, which guarantees that the program itself remains well-defined. The constant **poison** indicates erroneous state of a program. LLVM IR offers branch instructions that can conditionally jump to the beginning of any instruction block in the same function. This can be used to encode conditionals and loops, and it offers a basis for error handling instructions. It is important to note that the internals of LLVM IR are not stable, meaning there are no guarantees for compatibility between different LLVM IR versions [21]. However, there are stable LLVM API functions that can analyse and manipulate the internals of LLVM IR.

3   Challenges for Deductive Verification of LLVM IR

In order to encode LLVM IR programs into input for the VerCors verifier, several challenges need to be addressed, as discussed in this section. The next section discusses how these challenges influence our prototype design and implementation. In particular, challenge 1 to 3 have been addressed in our prototype, while providing full solutions to challenges 4 to 7 has been left as future work.

- *Challenge 1: Instability of LLVM IR* As mentioned, LLVM IR is an unstable language [21], without backwards compatibility, and there is no guaranteed interoperability between the syntax of LLVM IR of different LLVM versions.
- *Challenge 2: LLVM IR Specifications* VerCors specifications use expressions from the source language. As expressions in LLVM IR are written as a block of single instructions, this raises the question what a suitable specification language for LLVM IR would be: writing blocks in specifications (or even multiple blocks with branches, e.g. for Boolean expressions) would be impractical and error-prone. However, an upside is that LLVM IR uses the SSA (static single-assignment) format, which makes it hard to write specifications that have side effects, and all instructions in LLVM IR are pure except for memory instructions such as **store** and **alloca**.

- *Challenge 3: Origin of User Errors* Parsing an LLVM IR file with the parser of the LLVM API returns a module object that does not retain any origin information; it is merely a semantically equivalent in-memory representation of the program. This makes it challenging to communicate the origin of a verification problem in the source code to the user. LLVM offers the possibility to construct a string of LLVM IR representing any LLVM value, but calculating line and column numbers or extracting a source string is complex as extraneous white spaces and comments in the source file are ignored.

- *Challenge 4: Control Flow* LLVM IR depends on jumps and branches (i.e. goto statements) in the function body to facilitate any control flow in a program, while VerCors requires structured, reducible programs to be verified. VerCors technically supports goto statements but there are some caveats to be aware of when using them: the inclusion of goto statements obstructs the guarantee that the program is reducible [12], and loop invariants are hard to verify when a loop contains arbitrary goto statements.

With that in mind, the encoding essentially needs to be an LLVM IR decompiler to the high-level COL representation of VerCors. Loops can be especially hard to recover due to their various forms (e.g. for-loops, while-loops, and do-while loops), and the possibility of nesting. The challenge is not so much in detecting cycles in the CFG (control flow graph) of the program (for which trivial graph algorithms exist), but mainly to identify the different parts of the loop (e.g., the loop condition, the loop body, and loop breaks).

- *Challenge 5: Low-level Language Features* LLVM IR introduces new low-level language constructs that have not been handled by VerCors yet, such as loads, stores and other low-level memory instructions, Φ nodes (from the SSA format), and low-level exception handling. All these concepts have to be integrated into COL.

The current VCLLVM prototype simplifies many of these concepts or has not yet implemented them. Some ideas on how other LLVM IR low-level concepts could be translated into COL are discussed in [28].

- *Challenge 6: LLVM Concurrency Model* While LLVM IR does support instructions and control mechanisms that can be useful to ensure thread safety, it does not support constructs for parallel thread creation or signal handling natively. Instead, LLVM IR code depends on being linked against existing concurrency libraries, e.g. the pthread library on POSIX systems for Clang. Thus, in order to support reasoning about these concurrency libraries, their behaviour has to be modeled.

- *Challenge 7:* `undef` *and* `poison` Both constants `undef` and `poison` are semantically complex, and it is challenging to capture their semantics into VerCors. First, `undef` represents a set of possible values, which should be semantically treated as if it is a single value, and this concept does not yet exist in VerCors. Second, `poison` indicates erroneous behaviour, and it will have to be integrated into exception handling support of VerCors.

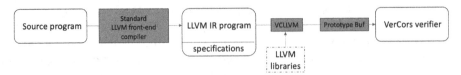

Fig. 1: Workflow of using VCLLVM and VerCors

4   Design and Implementation of VCLLVM

This section discusses the design and implementation of our prototype tool VCLLVM that translates LLVM IR programs into the VerCors internal COL format. Figure 1 gives a general overview how VCLLVM connects to VerCors. We discuss the main decisions in the design of VCLLVM, taking into account the challenges mentioned above. For a more in-depth analysis of the design choices, we refer to the Master thesis accompanying this paper [28].

Embedding versus Externalising The first design choice was whether to embed VCLLVM into the VerCors codebase or to develop it as an extension. Embedding could exacerbate the problems of Challenge 1 (instability of LLVM IR), and it would also restrict the tool implementation language to be JVM-compatible, which makes it hard to interface with existing LLVM IR functionality from the LLVM project. Instead, externalising makes it possible to use C++ to implement VCLLVM and to use all existing LLVM support functionality. We decided to go for this option, as it makes VCLLVM easier to maintain in the future.

VCLLVM Output Format As VCLLVM is developed as an external tool, its output needs to be in a format that is either already interpretable by VerCors or for which an interpreter would be simple to implement. If VCLLVM would generate concrete syntax, this requires that we define a concrete input language that supports all features of LLVM IR. Instead, we opted to use serialisation, which makes it possible to connect to the internal COL AST directly. We use *Protocol Buffers*[1] for this. It offers a largely automatable serialisation method, with language support for Scala (implementation language of VerCors) and C++ (implementation language of VCLLVM). Moreover, it supports code generation both from and to a Protocol Buffer definition, which simplifies the development of the communication layer between VCLLVM and VerCors considerably.

Specification Syntax To specify the properties that need to be verified, we need to embed the specifications into LLVM IR code such that they do not change the behaviour of the program, but are available to VCLLVM after the LLVM IR program has been parsed. Since comments are ignored by the LLVM parser, the only option available is to use LLVM metadata to embed specifications.

---

[1] See: https://developers.google.com/protocol-buffers.

```
!VC.contract !{
  !"ensures",
  !"%var1 = mul i32 %y, %x",
  !"%var2 = add i32 %var1, %z",
  !"%verdict = icmp eq i32 %var2, \result;"
}
```

(a)

```
!VC.contract !{                        !VC.contract !{
  !"ensures %x * %y + %z == \result;"    !"ensures icmp(eq,
}                                          add(mul(%y, %x), %z), \result);"
                                       }
```

(b)   (c)

Fig. 2: Possible Specification Syntax Options

Ideally, the specification syntax stays as close as possible to the LLVM IR syntax, but as explained in Challenge 2, it is not obvious for LLVM IR because of its low-level nature. We considered 3 different options, as illustrated in Figure 2 with contracts that describe the following *add-multiply* LLVM IR function.

```
1  define i32 @addMult(i32 %x, i32 %y, i32 %z)
2  !VC.contract !1 ;, !2 or !3 from Figure 2  {
3    %1 = mul i32 %y, %x
4    %res2 = add i32 %1, %z
5    ret i32 %res2 }
```

This function takes as input parameters x, y and z. First it multiplies x and y, stores the intermediate result in a local variable %1, and then adds z to this, and returns this final result. All specifications in Figure 2 express that the return value is equal to x * y + z. As usual, we use the keyword **ensures** to specify a postcondition of the function, and \result to refer to the output value of the function. Figure 2a uses blocks of instructions to write the specification expressions. This is verbose, error prone and complicates parsing. Figure 2b uses a specification syntax that is independent of LLVM IR syntax. This is readable, but also creates ambiguities, as it makes it harder to connect the specification to the code. Finally, Figure 2c uses the known LLVM IR instruction keywords, but in a more functional manner. This is fairly readable, and avoids the ambiguity. We decided to use this option for VCLLVM. Notice that, as described in Section 7, eventually we hope to use VCLLVM as an intermediate tool to reason about programs in any language that compiles into LLVM IR. In that set up, the specification would be written in the input language of the high-level language, and compiled into a VCLLVM specification.

External library support LLVM IR is often compiled and linked against existing libraries to provide support for external libraries. Support for this is needed in particular to reason about concurrent LLVM IR, which rely on thread libraries. The VCLLVM prototype has been designed with this requirement in mind, but it has not yet been implemented.

5 Evaluation

To use the current version of VCLLVM, one needs to (1) write C code, (2) compile that C code to LLVM IR, (3) optionally run the LLVM opt tool [23] to mitigate program structures VCLLVM cannot yet interpret, (4) annotate the resulting LLVM IR program manually, and (5) let VCLLVM/VerCors verify the LLVM IR program. C is recommended because the C LLVM compiler (Clang) produces concise LLVM IR code (unlike some of the other frontends like clang++ and rustc). Moreover, the regression test suite of VCLLVM currently only supports

The tool is only a prototype, but it has been used on several non-trivial examples, such as functions to compute triangular numbers and Cantor pairs, a function for date comparison (using branching and integer comparison), and recursive functions like Fibonacci and the factorial. In order to specify functional behaviour of these programs, VCLLVM supports the definition of pure specification-only functions, such as for example fib:

```
1  !VC.global = !{!0}
2  !0 = !{
3  !"pure i32 @fib(i32 %n) =
4    br(icmp(sgt, %n, 2),
5      add(call @fib(sub(%n, 1)), call @fib(sub(%n, 2))),1);"}
```

This expresses that for any fib(n) is computed using the following expression: if(n > 2) then fib(n - 1) + fib(n - 2) else 1 (where br denotes a branch and icmp compares two integers).

Using this function, we can write and prove the following contract for a recursive implementation of the Fibonacci function, see [28] for the full program. This contract states that for any n > 1, the correct Fibonacci value is returned.

```
1  define dso_local i32 @fibonacci(i32 noundef %0)
2  !VC.contract !{
3  !"requires icmp(sge, %0, 1);",
4  !"ensures icmp(eq, \result, call @fib(%0));"
5  }
6  { ... }
```

Special attention has been given to give informative feedback when verification fails. For more details about these examples, we refer to [28].

6   Related Work

There exist several projects that develop formal static analysis techniques for bug finding in LLVM IR. SMACK [32] defines a translation of LLVM IR into BoogiePL [20], to reason about C-programs using assertions that are compiled into LLVM IR using Clang. The verification itself is bounded and a potential extension to contract specifications has not yet been explored. The Vellvm project [40, 39]) develops a framework to reason about LLVM IR programs. It provides a mechanised semantics for LLVM IR, which can be used for verification. Reasoning is done directly in Coq, rather than at the code level, which requires Coq expertise. KLEE [6]. is a dynamic symbolic execution engine, which automatically generates suitable unit tests for LLVM IR applications, with a much better coverage than manually created test suites, thus increasing the likelihood of finding bugs. However, KLEE focuses only on bug finding, not on proving correctness. Another recent tool to easily find bugs via a bounded analysis of LLVM IR programs is Alive2 [24], which is tailored to reduce the number of false positives. Other model checkers or bounded verifiers for LLVM IR are LLMC [2], RCMC [16], Serval [26], FauST [33] and SAW [8]. They can only check properties over a bounded state space, in contrast to our approach which uses deductive verification. PhASAR is a static analysis framework for LLVM IR [36]. Users specify arbitrary data-flow properties, and PhASAR then fully automatically tries to analyse these properties. The approach shows promising results, but as it is fully automatic, it also suffers from imprecisions that have to be manually filtered out. Lammich [18] formalises the semantics of LLVM IR, using it as the target language of the Refinement Framework in Isabelle. They do not analyse LLVM IR programs, but rather they derive correct by construction LLVM IR programs. Finally, verifying complex programs in the current VCLLVM/VerCors implementation heavily relies on pure functions. This is similar to approach of Paganoni and Furia [30] using predicates to verify Java bytecode.

7   Next Steps

As mentioned above, the current version of VCLLVM is still a prototype, and it needs to be extended with better support for more language features, control flow reconstruction, concurrency, and library inclusion.

   Ultimately, the idea is not to use VCLLVM as a standalone tool to verify LLVM IR programs directly, but rather to use it as part of a larger infrastructure (called Pallas) that will provide deductive verification support for any programming language that can be compiled into LLVM IR. Figure 3 gives a visual representation of the Pallas infrastructure. It will define a generic specification format for contract specifications. For each source-level programming language supported by Pallas, a concrete contract specification syntax is defined to specify the desired program properties at the level of the source language, and then this should bee embedded into the generic contract specification format. The source to LLVM IR compiler is then used, combined with a compiler

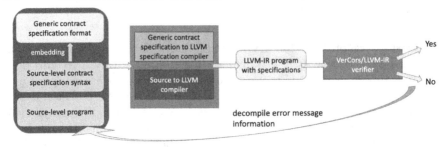

Fig. 3: Pallas Overall Idea

for the contract specifications in the generic contract specification format to the LLVM IR format. VCLLVM then enables VerCors to reason about the program. If verification succeeds, we know that the original source program satisfies the source-code-level contracts; if verification fails, the error message will be translated back into an error message for the source program.

Further research questions that we need to investigate to create the Pallas infrastructure are: (1) How to define a generic contract specification format that can capture program properties for a large class of source-level programming languages? (2) How to define a generic translation from the contract specification format into LLVM IR contract specifications, which can be parametrised by the compiler from a specific source language into LLVM IR? (3) How to provide effective feedback at the level of the source language if verification at the LLVM IR level fails by using decompilation techniques?

8   Conclusions

As a first step to solve the language-dependency problem of deductive verifiers, we propose to use the LLVM IR format as a generic format. This paper sketches the design of VCLLVM, a prototype implementation that enables deductive verification of LLVM IR programs, and we discuss the kind of examples that can already be verified. In future work, we will expand this into a deductive verification framework for any language that can be compiled into LLVM IR.

Data-Availability Statement

The artifact accompanying this paper can be found in [41].

References

[1] W. Ahrendt, B. Beckert, R. Bubel, R. Hähnle, P. H. Schmitt, and M. Ul-
brich. *Deductive Software Verification – The KeY Book*. Vol. 10001. Lecture Notes in Computer Science. Springer International Publishing, 2016.
ISBN: 9783319498126. DOI: 10.1007/978-3-319-49812-6.

[2] F. van der Berg. "LLMC: Verifying High-Performance Software". In: *Computer Aided Verification: 33rd International Conference, CAV 2021, Virtual Event, July 20–23, 2021, Proceedings, Part II 33*. Springer. 2021,
pp. 690–703.

[3] A. Blanchard, F. Loulergue, and N. Kosmatov. "Towards Full Proof Automation in Frama-C Using Auto-active Verification". In: *NASA Formal
Methods - 11th International Symposium, NFM 2019, Houston, TX, USA,
May 7-9, 2019, Proceedings*. Ed. by J. M. Badger and K. Y. Rozier.
Vol. 11460. Lecture Notes in Computer Science. Springer, 2019, pp. 88–
105. DOI: 10.1007/978-3-030-20652-9_6. URL: https://doi.org/
10.1007/978-3-030-20652-9_6.

[4] S. Blom, S. Darabi, M. Huisman, and W. Oortwijn. "The VerCors Tool
Set: Verification of Parallel and Concurrent Software". In: *integrated For-
mal Methods 2017*. Ed. by N. Polikarpova and S. Schneider. LNCS 10510.
Springer, 2017, pp. 102 –110. DOI: 10.1007/978-3-319-66845-1_7.

[5] J. Boyland. "Checking Interference with Fractional Permissions". In: *SAS*.
Vol. 2694. LNCS. Springer, 2003, pp. 55–72.

[6] C. Cadar, D. Dunbar, and D. R. Engler. "KLEE: Unassisted and Automatic Generation of High-Coverage Tests for Complex Systems Programs".
In: *8th USENIX Symposium on Operating Systems Design and Implementation, OSDI 2008, December 8-10, 2008, San Diego, California, USA,
Proceedings*. Ed. by R. Draves and R. van Renesse. USENIX Association,
2008, pp. 209–224. URL: http://www.usenix.org/events/osdi08/
tech/full_papers/cadar/cadar.pdf.

[7] D. R. Cok. "OpenJML: JML for Java 7 by Extending OpenJDK". In: *NASA
Formal Methods*. Ed. by M. Bobaru, K. Havelund, G. J. Holzmann, and R.
Joshi. Berlin, Heidelberg: Springer Berlin Heidelberg, 2011, pp. 472–479.
ISBN: 978-3-642-20398-5.

[8] R. Dockins, A. Foltzer, J. Hendrix, B. Huffman, D. McNamee, and A.
Tomb. "Constructing semantic models of programs with the software analysis workbench". In: *Verified Software. Theories, Tools, and Experiments:
8th International Conference, VSTTE 2016, Toronto, ON, Canada, July
17–18, 2016, Revised Selected Papers 8*. Springer. 2016, pp. 56–72.

[9] G. Ernst, J. Pfähler, G. Schellhorn, D. Haneberg, and W. Reif. "KIV:
overview and VerifyThis competition". In: *STTT* 17.6 (2015), pp. 677–
694. ISSN: 1433-2787. DOI: 10.1007/s10009-014-0308-3. URL: https:
//doi.org/10.1007/s10009-014-0308-3.

[10] S. d. Gouw, F. S. de Boer, R. Bubel, R. Hähnle, J. Rot, and D. Steinhöfel.
"Verifying OpenJDK's Sort Method for Generic Collections". In: *J. Autom.*

Reason. 62.1 (2019), pp. 93–126. DOI: 10.1007/s10817-017-9426-4. URL: https://doi.org/10.1007/s10817-017-9426-4.

[11] R. Hähnle and M. Huisman. "Deductive Software Verification: From Pen-and-Paper Proofs to Industrial Tools". In: *Computing and Software Science - State of the Art and Perspectives.* Ed. by B. Steffen and G. J. Woeginger. Vol. 10000. Lecture Notes in Computer Science. Springer, 2019, pp. 345–373.

[12] M. S. Hecht and J. D. Ullman. "Flow graph reducibility". In: *Proceedings of the fourth annual ACM symposium on Theory of computing.* 1972, pp. 238–250.

[13] H. A. Hiep, O. Maathuis, J. Bian, F. S. de Boer, M. C. J. D. van Eekelen, and S. de Gouw. "Verifying OpenJDK's LinkedList using KeY". In: *Tools and Algorithms for the Construction and Analysis of Systems - 26th International Conference, TACAS 2020, Held as Part of the European Joint Conferences on Theory and Practice of Software, ETAPS 2020, Dublin, Ireland, April 25-30, 2020, Proceedings, Part II.* Ed. by A. Biere and D. Parker. Vol. 12079. Lecture Notes in Computer Science. Springer, 2020, pp. 217–234. DOI: 10.1007/978-3-030-45237-7_13. URL: https://doi.org/10.1007/978-3-030-45237-7_13.

[14] B. Jacobs and F. Piessens. *The VeriFast program verifier.* Tech. rep. CW520. Katholieke Universiteit Leuven, 2008.

[15] B. Jacobs, J. Smans, P. Philippaerts, F. Vogels, W. Penninckx, and F. Piessens. "VeriFast: A powerful, sound, predictable, fast verifier for C and Java". In: *NASA Formal Methods Symposium.* Ed. by M. Bobaru, K. Havelund, G. J. Holzmann, and R. Joshi. Springer. 2011, pp. 41–55. DOI: 10.1007/978-3-642-20398-5_4.

[16] M. Kokologiannakis, O. Lahav, K. Sagonas, and V. Vafeiadis. "Effective stateless model checking for C/C++ concurrency". In: *Proceedings of the ACM on Programming Languages* 2.POPL (2017), pp. 1–32.

[17] N. Kosmatov, D. Longuet, and R. Soulat. "Formal Verification of an Industrial Distributed Algorithm: An Experience Report". In: *Leveraging Applications of Formal Methods, Verification and Validation: Verification Principles - 9th International Symposium on Leveraging Applications of Formal Methods, ISoLA 2020, Rhodes, Greece, October 20-30, 2020, Proceedings, Part I.* Ed. by T. Margaria and B. Steffen. Vol. 12476. Lecture Notes in Computer Science. Springer, 2020, pp. 525–542. DOI: 10.1007/978-3-030-61362-4_30. URL: https://doi.org/10.1007/978-3-030-61362-4_30.

[18] P. Lammich. "Generating Verified LLVM from Isabelle/HOL". In: *10th International Conference on Interactive Theorem Proving (ITP 2019).* Ed. by J. Harrison, J. O'Leary, and A. Tolmach. Vol. 141. Leibniz International Proceedings in Informatics (LIPIcs). Dagstuhl, Germany: Schloss Dagstuhl–Leibniz-Zentrum fuer Informatik, 2019, 22:1–22:19. ISBN: 978-3-95977-122-1. DOI: 10.4230/LIPIcs.ITP.2019.22. URL: http://drops.dagstuhl.de/opus/volltexte/2019/11077.

[19] C. Lattner and V. Adve. "LLVM: A compilation framework for lifelong program analysis & transformation". In: *International Symposium on Code Generation and Optimization, 2004. CGO 2004.* IEEE. 2004, pp. 75–86. DOI: `10.5555/977395.977673`.

[20] K. Leino. "Accessible Software Verification with Dafny". In: *IEEE Software* 34.6 (2017), pp. 94–97. DOI: `10.1109/MS.2017.4121212`.

[21] LLVM Project. *LLVM Developer Policy: IR Backwards Compatibility.* `https://llvm.org/docs/DeveloperPolicy.html{#}ir-backwards-compatibility`. [Accessed 05-Dec-2022]. Dec. 2022.

[22] LLVM Project. *LLVM Language Reference Manual.* `https://releases.llvm.org/15.0.0/docs/LangRef.html`. [Accessed 05-Dec-2022]. Sept. 2022.

[23] LLVM Project. *opt - LLVM optimizer.* `https://releases.llvm.org/15.0.0/docs/CommandGuide/opt.html`. [Accessed 05-Dec-2022]. Sept. 2022.

[24] N. P. Lopes, J. Lee, C. Hur, Z. Liu, and J. Regehr. "Alive2: bounded translation validation for LLVM". In: *PLDI '21: 42nd ACM SIGPLAN International Conference on Programming Language Design and Implementation, Virtual Event, Canada, June 20-25, 2021.* Ed. by S. N. Freund and E. Yahav. ACM, 2021, pp. 65–79. DOI: `10.1145/3453483.3454030`. URL: `https://doi.org/10.1145/3453483.3454030`.

[25] P. Müller, M. Schwerhoff, and A. Summers. "Viper - A Verification Infrastructure for Permission-Based Reasoning". In: *Verification, Model Checking, and Abstract Interpretation. VMCAI.* Ed. by B. Jobstmann and K. R. M. Leino. Springer Berlin Heidelberg, 2016. DOI: `10.1007/978-3-662-49122-5_2`.

[26] L. Nelson, J. Bornholt, R. Gu, A. Baumann, E. Torlak, and X. Wang. "Scaling symbolic evaluation for automated verification of systems code with Serval". In: *Proceedings of the 27th ACM Symposium on Operating Systems Principles.* 2019, pp. 225–242.

[27] P. W. O'Hearn. "Resources, concurrency and local reasoning". In: 375.1–3 (2007), pp. 271–307.

[28] D. van Oorschot. *VCLLVM: A Transformation Tool for LLVM IR programs to aid Deductive Verification.* 2023. URL: `http://essay.utwente.nl/96536/`.

[29] W. Oortwijn, M. Huisman, S. Joosten, and J. van de Pol. "Automated Verification of Parallel Nested DFS". In: *International Conference on Tools and Algorithms for the Construction and Analysis of Systems.* Springer. 2020, pp. 247–265.

[30] M. Paganoni and C. A. Furia. "Verifying Functional Correctness Properties at the Level of Java Bytecode". In: *International Symposium on Formal Methods.* Springer. 2023, pp. 343–363.

[31] D. J. Pearce, M. Utting, and L. Groves. "An Introduction to Software Verification with Whiley". In: *Engineering Trustworthy Software Systems - 4th International School, SETSS 2018, Chongqing, China, April 7-12, 2018,*

Tutorial Lectures. Ed. by J. P. Bowen, Z. Liu, and Z. Zhang. Vol. 11430. Lecture Notes in Computer Science. Springer, 2018, pp. 1–37. DOI: `10.1007/978-3-030-17601-3_1`.

[32]   Z. Rakamaric and M. Emmi. "SMACK: Decoupling Source Language Details from Verifier Implementations". In: *Computer Aided Verification - 26th International Conference, CAV 2014, Held as Part of the Vienna Summer of Logic, VSL 2014, Vienna, Austria, July 18-22, 2014. Proceedings.* Ed. by A. Biere and R. Bloem. Vol. 8559. Lecture Notes in Computer Science. Springer, 2014, pp. 106–113. DOI: `10.1007/978-3-319-08867-9\_7`. URL: `https://doi.org/10.1007/978-3-319-08867-9\_7`.

[33]   H. Riener and G. Fey. "FAuST: A framework for formal verification, automated debugging, and software test generation". In: *Model Checking Software: 19th International Workshop, SPIN 2012, Oxford, UK, July 23-24, 2012. Proceedings 19.* Springer. 2012, pp. 234–240.

[34]   M. Safari and M. Huisman. "Formal Verification of Parallel Stream Compaction and Summed-Area Table Algorithms". In: *Theoretical Aspects of Computing – ICTAC 2020.* Ed. by V. K. I. Pun, V. Stolz, and A. Simao. Springer, 2020, pp. 181–199. DOI: `10.1007/978-3-030-64276-1_10`.

[35]   M. Safari, W. Oortwijn, S. Joosten, and M. Huisman. "Formal verification of parallel prefix sum". In: *NASA Formal Methods Symposium.* Ed. by R. Lee, S. Jha, A. Mavridou, and D. Giannakopoulou. Springer, 2020, pp. 170–186. DOI: `10.1007/978-3-030-55754-6_10`.

[36]   P. D. Schubert, B. Hermann, and E. Bodden. "PhASAR: An Inter-procedural Static Analysis Framework for C/C++". In: *Tools and Algorithms for the Construction and Analysis of Systems.* Ed. by T. Vojnar and L. Zhang. Cham: Springer International Publishing, 2019, pp. 393–410. ISBN: 978-3-030-17465-1.

[37]   M. Sitaraman and B. W. Weide. "A Synopsis of Twenty Five Years of RESOLVE PhD Research Efforts: Software Development Effort Estimation Using Ensemble Techniques". In: *ACM SIGSOFT Softw. Eng. Notes* 43.3 (2018), p. 17. DOI: `10.1145/3229783.3229794`.

[38]   VerCors team. *The VerCors Verifier Tutorial.* URL: `https://vercors.ewi.utwente.nl/wiki/`.

[39]   Y. Zakowski, C. Beck, I. Yoon, I. Zaichuk, V. Zaliva, and S. Zdancewic. "Modular, compositional, and executable formal semantics for LLVM IR". In: *Proc. ACM Program. Lang.* 5.ICFP (2021), pp. 1–30. DOI: `10.1145/3473572`. URL: `https://doi.org/10.1145/3473572`.

[40]   J. Zhao, S. Nagarakatte, M. M. K. Martin, and S. Zdancewic. "Formal verification of SSA-based optimizations for LLVM". In: *ACM SIGPLAN Conference on Programming Language Design and Implementation, PLDI '13, Seattle, WA, USA, June 16-19, 2013.* Ed. by H. Boehm and C. Flanagan. ACM, 2013, pp. 175–186. DOI: `10.1145/2491956.2462164`. URL: `https://doi.org/10.1145/2491956.2462164`.

[41] Ö. Şakar, D. van Oorschot, and M. Huisman. *Artifact for paper (First Steps towards Deductive Verification of LLVM IR)*. en. 2024. DOI: `10.4121/9C8C079E-A941-4A66-89D8-3462BF30FF05.V1`.

FDSE: Enhance Symbolic Execution by Fuzzing-based Pre-Analysis (Competition Contribution)

Guofeng Zhang[1,2,3], Ziqi Shuai[1,2,3], Kelin Ma[1,2], Kunlin Liu[1,2,3],
Zhenbang Chen[1,2(✉)] ⓘ, and Ji Wang[1,2,3]

[1] College of Computer, National University of Defense Technology, Changsha, China
[2] State Key Laboratory of Complex & Critical Software Environment, National University of Defense Technology, Changsha, China
[3] State Key Laboratory of High Performance Computing, National University of Defense Technology, Changsha, China
{zhangguofeng16,szq,kelinma,klliu18,zbchen,wj}@nudt.edu.cn

Abstract. FDSE serves as an automatic test generation tool designed for C programs based on symbolic execution. FDSE employs fuzzing-based pre-analysis and combines static symbolic execution and dynamic symbolic execution to improve the effectiveness of test generation. FDSE achieves 5132 scores and is ranked 4th in the branch coverage track of Test-Comp 2024.

Keywords: Symbolic Execution · Fuzzing · Test-Case Generation.

1 Test Generation Approach

Test case design is one of the most labor-intensive tasks in software engineering. Automatic test case generation helps the test case designers reduce labor and improve testing quality. Existing techniques usually accept more than one type of software artifact (*e.g.*, source code and software models) as input. Then, these techniques utilize existing methods (*e.g.*, optimization [10] or program analysis [11]) to generate test cases. Besides, some approaches combine different methods to achieve better effectiveness and efficiency [1].

Symbolic execution (SE) [5] is one of the underlying techniques that can be used for automatic test case generation. Current SE methods can be categorized into static symbolic execution (SSE) and dynamic symbolic execution (DSE). SSE simulates the execution of the program using symbolic inputs. During analysis, SSE maintains many execution states. When encountering a branch statement, SSE forks states to explore both branches. Many SSE engines have been developed, such as KLEE [4] and SPF [9], to name a few. DSE combines symbolic execution and concrete execution to further improve SE's effectiveness and efficiency. Specifically, DSE executes the program using concrete input and collects path constraint of current execution. Then, based on the path constraints, DSE constructs the new constraint for generating new input that steers the program

---

*Z. Chen—Jury Member.

ⓒ The Author(s) 2024
D. Beyer and A. Cavalcanti (Eds.): FASE 2024, LNCS 14573, pp. 304–308, 2024.
https://doi.org/10.1007/978-3-031-57259-3_16

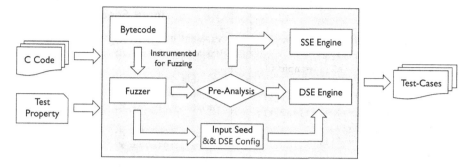

Fig. 1: FDSE's Workflow in Test-Comp.

to different program path. In principle, SSE and DSE provide different means of systematically exploring the program's path space.

FDSE is mainly a SE-based test case generator. In most cases, FDSE uses DSE to generate tests. To mitigate DSE's disadvantage in handling the programs with long-time execution or large symbolic data, e.g., the programs with large symbolic arrays, loops, or many branches, FDSE employs a fuzzing-based pre-analysis and combines SSE to improve DSE's effectiveness and efficiency of generating tests for the benchmarks of Test-Comp.

2   Framework

Figure 1 illustrates the Test-Comp version of FDSE. Firstly, we compile the C program into bytecode and instrument the bytecode to generate a fuzzer for pre-analysis. During fuzzing, we record the runtime features of the program, such as the number of input variables or branches and the size of allocated arrays. Secondly, we selectively employ DSE or SSE according to the number of static branches, which is calculated by a simple static analysis. If the number exceeds a threshold, e.g., 10,000 in the competition, FDSE employs SSE because DSE may face the challenge of long-time execution. Otherwise, FDSE continues to use DSE. Hence, either DSE or SSE is applied to analyze a benchmark program. Finally, when employing the DSE engine, selective symbolization of the variables is performed based on the information generated by fuzzing, aiming to mitigate the problem of large symbolized arrays. Furthermore, the DSE engine limits the number of loop unfolding times to prevent path explosion. This fuzzing-based pre-analysis is based on the following two observations of the Test-Comp benchmarks.

- When the program utilizes large loops to initialize a large-sized symbolic array[4], DSE maintains a huge number of symbolic variables internally, which hinders the analysis's efficiency and frequently exceeds memory limits. To mitigate this, we employ fuzzing for pre-analysis to generate the parameters that restrict the scale for DSE.

---

[4] For example, the benchmark **standard_copy2_ground-1.c**

```
#define N 100000
int main() {
  int a1[N], a2[N], a3[N], i;
  for(i=0; i<N; i++) {
    a1[i]=input(); a2[i]=input();
  }
  for(i=0; i<N; i++) a3[i]=a1[i];
  for(i=0; i<N; i++) a3[i]=a2[i];
  for(i=0; i<N; i++)
    assert(a1[i]==a3[i]);
  return 0;
}
```

Input Seed

Variable_0	= X;	Symbolic
Variable_1	= X;	Variables
......		
Variable_99	= X;	
Variable_100	= X;	
Variable_101	= X;	
......		Concrete
Variable_199998	= X;	Variables
Variable_199999	= X;	

Fig. 2: standard_copy2_ground-1.c   Fig. 3: Selective Symbolization in FDSE

- For programs that contain a large number of static branches [5], executing a terminated path needs much time, which hinders the overall efficiency of DSE. To tackle this problem, we propose using SSE instead of DSE to analyze such programs, as SSE can perform better in this scenario.

Demonstration. We use a benchmark program in Test-Comp to demonstrate the fuzzing-based pre-analysis. Figure 2 shows an example program that contains four loops with a size of 100,000 and requires 200,000 input variables (*i.e.*, symbolic variables). SE is impractical to explore the path space of this program. The key idea is to employ fuzzing first to generate seed inputs and symbolize a part of input variables during SE, which can improve efficiency while ensuring high coverage. Consider the program in Figure 2. The first step is to employ fuzzing to generate input seeds, as shown in Figure 3. These seeds contain 200,000 variables, each with a random value X. Since only eight static branches exist, FDSE uses the DSE engine. During DSE, FDSE limits the boundary of each loop, allowing the loop body to be unrolled up to a configured number of times. This configuration is determined by the information collected by fuzzing. FDSE unrolls the loop only 50 times if the fuzzer detects that the loop body is executed more than 100 times. Then, DSE reads the input seeds obtained from fuzzing. For this example, DSE only symbolizes the first 100 variables due to the 50 times of loop unrolling. The remaining variables only have concrete values. When generating test cases, the generated values of symbolic variables are concatenated with the values of the subsequent concrete variables in the input seed. Thus, DSE can still generate a complete test case.

3   Result and Discussion

FDSE is optimized and achieves 5132 scores (4th place) in the branch coverage track. Our tool performs well in many sub-categories, such as **Arrays, BitVectors**, and **Hardness**. Thanks to Test-Comp's competition, we have identified

---

[5] For example, the program **Problem05_label40+token_ring.01.cil-1.c**

several shortcomings in our DSE engine beyond the common challenges (such as path explosion and constraint solving [2]).

- Our DSE engine does not apply any simplification rule to reduce symbolic expressions, which results in redundant expressions and makes the tool crash on some **Hardware** benchmarks due to exceeding memory limits.
- Our DSE engine is limited in environment modeling, *e.g.*, the common system libraries. When programs call these system libraries, the relevant path constraints are lost, making it difficult to improve coverage, particularly in the tasks in **BusyBox, DeviceDriverLinux64**, and **AWS-C-Common**.
- Our DSE engine is still limited in handling large symbolic arrays. Restricting the number of symbolic variables limits the path exploration ability, which may fail to cover deep branches.
- We do not prioritize or minimize the generated tests, which results in redundant test cases and leads to validator timeout. For example, in the **Combinations** category, over 20% of tests were not executed.
- FDSE is only optimized for branch coverage track. Smarter SE search strategies for branch and error coverage are expected.

4   Software Project and Data Available

The DSE engine's implementation of FDSE is based on SymCC [8]. The SSE engine is KLEE [4]. The fuzzing component is implemented in C++ and based on LLVM[6][6]. The employed constraint solver of DSE is Z3 [7]. The command line interface is implemented in Python.

In Test-Comp 2024, FDSE participated in **coverage-branches** and **coverage-error** categories, where we only optimize FDSE for **coverage-branches**. The benchexec tool information module is **fdse.py**, and the benchmark description is **fdse.xml**. To use our tool script, the parameters of the property file, time budget, and benchmark path must be set as follows:

```
fdse -testcomp -property-file=<..> -max-time=<..> -single-file-name=<..>
```

Our symbolic execution engine treats each benchmark as running on a 64-bit architecture and always tries to maximize code coverage. The test suite generated is written to the directory **fdse_output/test-suite**. According to the definition of Test-Comp rules, the test suite includes a metadata XML file and a test-case XML file that follows the required format.

FDSE, developed by the National University of Defense Technology, can be found at https://github.com/zbchen/fdse-test-comp. FDSE is accessible for download as a binary artifact on Zenodo, and the specific version available for download is **testcomp24** [7], and it is publicly accessible under the Apache-2.0 license terms. Moreover, Test-Comp 2024 [3] [8] provides users with scripts, benchmarks, and FDSE binaries to facilitate the replication of competition results.

---

[6] LLVM's version is 10.0.1.
[7] https://doi.org/10.5281/zenodo.10203198
[8] https://test-comp.sosy-lab.org/2024

Acknowledgement This research was supported by National Key R&D Program of China (No. 2022YFB4501903) and the NSFC Programs (No. 62172429 and 62002107).

References

1. Anand, S., Burke, E.K., Chen, T.Y., Clark, J.A., Cohen, M.B., Grieskamp, W., Harman, M., Harrold, M.J., McMinn, P.: An orchestrated survey of methodologies for automated software test case generation. J. Syst. Softw. **86**, 1978–2001 (2013)
2. Baldoni, R., Coppa, E., D'Elia, D.C., Demetrescu, C., Finocchi, I.: A survey of symbolic execution techniques. ACM Computing Surveys (CSUR) **51**, 1–39 (2016)
3. Beyer, D.: Automatic testing of C programs: Test-Comp 2024. Springer (2024)
4. Cadar, C., Dunbar, D., Engler, D.R.: KLEE: unassisted and automatic generation of high-coverage tests for complex systems programs. In: Draves, R., van Renesse, R. (eds.) 8th USENIX Symposium on Operating Systems Design and Implementation, OSDI 2008, December 8-10, 2008, San Diego, California, USA, Proceedings. pp. 209–224. USENIX Association
5. King, J.C.: Symbolic execution and program testing. Commun. ACM **19**, 385–394 (1976)
6. LLVM: https://llvm.org
7. de Moura, L.M., Bjørner, N.S.: Z3: An efficient smt solver. In: International Conference on Tools and Algorithms for Construction and Analysis of Systems (2008)
8. Poeplau, S., Francillon, A.: Symbolic execution with symcc: Don't interpret, compile! In: USENIX Security Symposium (2020)
9. Păsăreanu, C.S., Rungta, N.: Symbolic pathfinder: symbolic execution of java bytecode. Proceedings of the 25th IEEE/ACM International Conference on Automated Software Engineering (2010)
10. Shahbazi, A., Miller, J.: Black-box string test case generation through a multiobjective optimization. IEEE Transactions on Software Engineering **42**, 361–378 (2016)
11. Tillmann, N., de Halleux, J.: Pex-white box test generation for .net. In: Tests and Proofs. pp. 134–153 (2008)

Fizzer: New Gray-Box Fuzzer*
(Competition Contribution)

Martin Jonáš[ID], Jan Strejček[ID], Marek Trtík[ID][✉], and Lukáš Urban[ID]

Masaryk University, Brno, Czech Republic

trtikm@mail.muni.cz

Abstract. Fizzer is a new gray-box fuzzer. In contrast to common gray-box fuzzers that aim to cover both `true` and `false` branches of branching instructions, Fizzer primarily aims to cover both possible values `true` and `false` of Boolean expressions in the program. When a generated test evaluates a so-called *atomic* Boolean expression to one of these values, our fuzzer computes the distance to the other value, detects bytes that influence this distance, and applies gradient descent on these bytes to flip the value. In Test-Comp 2024, Fizzer placed third in the category *Cover-Branches* after FuSeBMC and FuSeBMC-AI.

Keywords: gray-box fuzzing · dynamic analysis · gradient descent

1 Test-Generation Approach

Fuzzing [5] is an automatic technique that generates test inputs for a given program. *Gray-box fuzzers* first instrument the given program with a code that tracks selected information about a program execution. The instrumented program is then repeatedly executed on various inputs and the tracked information is used to generate new inputs that should execute parts of the program not executed in previous runs.

Successful gray-box fuzzers like AFL [6] collect only very limited information about each program execution and try to quickly perform as many executions as possible. In Fizzer, we use an approach that gathers slightly more information about program executions and uses it to select uncovered parts of the code and make more targeted attempts to cover it.

While typical gray-box fuzzers track only the information about the basic blocks visited during a program execution, our approach tracks also evaluation of each *atomic Boolean expression* (ABE). A Boolean expression is atomic if it is not a variable, not a call of a function whose definition is a part of the program, and not a result of applying a logical operator. Many LLVM instructions yielding `i1` type (i.e., Boolean) from other types are ABEs. An important example is the `icmp` instruction used in translations of C expressions like `(x > 42)` or `(string[i] == 'A')`. Each time an ABE is evaluated to `true` or `false`, the instrumented

---

* This work has been supported by the Czech Science Foundation grant GA23-06506S.
  M. Trtík—Jury member.

D. Beyer and A. Cavalcanti (Eds.): FASE 2024, LNCS 14573, pp. 309–313, 2024.
https://doi.org/10.1007/978-3-031-57259-3_17

code saves the *calling context* (i.e., the sequence of currently evaluated function calls, which loosely corresponds to the call stack), the value of the ABE, and the *distance* to the opposite value. For example, if ABE (x > 42) is evaluated to true, the distance to false is computed as x - 42.

Our fuzzer aims to generate tests that evaluate each ABE in each reached calling context to both true and false. Assume that some input leads to the evaluation of an ABE to true and we want to evaluate it to false in the same calling context. We first repeatedly execute the program on various mutations of the input to detect the bytes of this input that have some influence on the distance of the ABE evaluation. This process is called a *sensitivity analysis* and the detected bytes are called *sensitive*. Then we apply the following two analyses that use the sensitive bytes. One analysis performs a *gradient descent* on the sensitive bytes with the aim to minimize the absolute value of the distance and to evaluate the ABE in the considered calling context to false. Alternatively, if we already know another input evaluating the ABE to false in a different calling context, we can try to use the value of its sensitive bytes instead of the sensitive bytes of the current input. This analysis is called *byteshare analysis*.

The fuzzer maintains the information about ABEs evaluated in all program executions, their calling contexts, values, and distances in a binary tree called *atomic Boolean execution tree*. The tree is used to select the ABE and its value to be covered.

For a more detailed and formal description of our approach, we refer to the corresponding research paper [4].

2 Software Architecture

FIZZER is implemented in C++, consists of around 11,000 lines of code in 125 files and uses the LLVM infrastructure. The compiled tool is dependent only on the CLANG compiler. FIZZER consists of two 64-bit executables, namely SERVER and INSTRUMENTER, and a collection of static LIBRARIES provided in both 32-bit and 64-bit versions. Finally, there is a Python script offering a user friendly interface to the tool.

The input program is first translated to LLVM by CLANG. The INSTRUMENTER then instruments the LLVM program with the code for tracking and collecting data during program execution, as explained in the previous section. The inserted code calls functions from the static LIBRARIES. The instrumented program linked with the corresponding static LIBRARIES is called TARGET.

The SERVER controls the actual test generation process. In particular, SERVER generates inputs using the sensitivity analysis, gradient descent, and byteshare analysis mentioned above and runs the TARGET on these inputs. It also receives and processes the information tracked by the TARGET during its executions and builds the atomic Boolean execution tree. The tree is used to select an ABE value to be covered.

The SERVER is one process and each execution of TARGET runs in another process. The exchange of information between the SERVER's process and the

TARGET's process is done via *shared memory*. This ensures that the SERVER can receive the information about TARGET's execution even if the execution crashes.

3   Strengths and Weaknesses

On the positive side, FIZZER is a relatively simple and very compact tool with minimal external dependencies. As it is a pure fuzzer, it can be applied to programs of an arbitrary size and it can also handle programs that use external functions available only in compiled form. And covering (in)equality constraints, which is often difficult for fuzzers, is boosted by the gradient descent.

Fuzzers in general limit each execution of the program as they need to perform many of these executions. FIZZER sets upper bounds (passed to the tool via command line options) on the number of evaluated ABEs, the size of the input bytes read, the size of the calling context, and other properties. If an execution of the TARGET exceeds some of the bounds, it is terminated. FIZZER thus obtains information about prefixes of real executions and thus it can effectively generate tests only for parts of the program close to the program entry point. This weakness correlates with the well known practical experience with fuzzers in general: they are effective in covering code close to the entry point, but have troubles to get deeper. In FIZZER, we do not attempt to properly deal with this phenomenon. We only use so-called *optimizer* after fuzzing stops (usually due to reaching its timeout). The optimizer simply sets up the upper bounds to large numbers and executes the program on those generated inputs that exceeded some upper bound during fuzzing.

Some weaknesses of FIZZER also come from the fact that it is only a prototype implementation taking advantage of some specific features of the Test-Comp benchmarks. In particular, the only way of reading an input currently supported by FIZZER are the functions `__VERIFIER_nondet_*()`.

Another weakness is related to the use of gradient descent as one of the main techniques to cover a selected ABE. The technique is efficient when flipping Boolean values depending on functions with only few extremes (e.g., quadratic functions), but it can struggle on functions with a complex behavior (e.g., functions used for hashing). To mitigate this issue, we implemented a second version of the gradient descent adjusted for functions with many local extremes and we apply it e.g. on function XOR.

In Test-Comp 2024, FIZZER won the bronze medal in the category *Cover-Branches* where 18 tools were competing. Moreover, it obtained the highest score in 3 out of 23 sub-categories of *Cover-Branches*, namely in *ReachSafety-Floats*, *SoftwareSystems-AWS-C-Common-ReachSafety*, and *SoftwareSystems-BusyBox-MemSafety*. FIZZER also participated in the *Cover-Error* category. It is important to stress that FIZZER cannot currently be instructed to focus on covering one particular location, like the target `reach_error()` of this category. FIZZER thus attempted to cover all ABEs in the program, just like in the other category. Despite of that FIZZER placed seventh out of 19 participants in this category. More details can be found on competition's website [1] and report [2].

4   Tool Setup and Configuration

FIZZER can be downloaded either as a binary or as a source code (links are in Section 6). For the source code, checkout the commit tagged `TESTCOMP24` in order to build the version participating in the competition. The `README.md` file in the root of the repository contains detailed instructions for building the tool. Once the tool is built, all binaries are under `./dist` directory. The content of the directory can be copied "as-is" to a target computer, i.e., no installation is necessary. The tool should be used via `sbt-fizzer.py` script:

```
sbt-fizzer.py [options] --input_file <my-c-program>
                        --output_dir <my-output-dir>
```

All results for the given C program `<my-c-program>` will be stored under the directory `<my-output-dir>` (including generated tests). The list of all available options can be obtained by command `sbt-fizzer.py --help`. Here are the options we used in the competition:

- `max_seconds 865`   The timeout for the fuzzing.
- `optimizer_max_seconds 30`   The timeout for the optimizer.
- `max_exec_milliseconds 500`   The timeout for each TARGET's execution.
- `max_stdin_bytes 65536`   The upper bound for the number of input bytes.
- `stdin_model stdin_replay_bytes_then_repeat_zero`   An input model: Read generated input bytes and then read zeros.
- `test_type testcomp`   The format for the generated tests.

Please note that FIZZER currently does *not* execute the given program in an isolated environment. It is thus *not* advised to run FIZZER directly (outside a container) on any C program accessing disk or other external resources.

5   Software Project and Contributors

FIZZER has been developed at the Faculty of Informatics of Masaryk University by Marek Trtík and Lukáš Urban. Martin Jonáš and Jan Strejček participated in discussions and contributed to the project by some ideas. The tool is open-source and it is available under the ZLIB license.

6   Data-Availability statement

FIZZER is available in a binary form at Zenodo [3] and the source code is available at GitHub:

```
https://github.com/staticafi/sbt-fizzer
```

References

1. Test-Comp 2024, table with results, https://test-comp.sosy-lab.org/2024/results/results-verified/
2. Beyer, D.: Automatic Testing of C Programs: Test-Comp 2024. Springer (2024)
3. Jonáš, M., Strejček, J., Trtík, M., Urban, L.: Fizzer: binary (Nov 2023). https://doi.org/10.5281/zenodo.10183158
4. Jonáš, M., Strejček, J., Trtík, M., Urban, L.: Gray-box fuzzing via gradient descent and Boolean expression coverage. In: Finkbeiner, B., Kovács, L. (eds.) TACAS 2024. LNCS, vol. 14572, pp. 90–109 (2024). https://doi.org/10.1007/978-3-031-57256-2_5
5. Liang, H., Pei, X., Jia, X., Shen, W., Zhang, J.: Fuzzing: State of the art. IEEE Transactions on Reliability **67**(3), 1199–1218 (2018). https://doi.org/10.1109/TR.2018.2834476
6. Zalewski, M.: American fuzzy lop (2013), http://lcamtuf.coredump.cx/afl/.

KLEEF: Symbolic Execution Engine
(Competition Contribution)

Aleksandr Misonizhnik, Sergey Morozov, Yurii Kostyukov(✉),
Vladislav Kalugin, Aleksei Babushkin, Dmitry Mordvinov,
and Dmitry Ivanov

[1]RnD Toolchain Labs, Huawei, Shenzhen, China
kostyukov.yurii@gmail.com

Abstract. KLEEF is a complete overhaul of the KLEE symbolic execution engine for LLVM, fine-tuned for a robust analysis of industrial C/C++ code. KLEEF natively handles complex data structures, such as trees, linked lists, and dynamically allocated arrays, via lazy initialization and symcrete values. KLEEF has fine-tuned modes for both maximal test coverage generation and reproducing error traces, in particular reaching a specific point in the program. In the paper, we describe the above features and a competition configuration of KLEEF.

Keywords: Symbolic Execution · Lazy Initialization · KLEE Fork.

1 Test-Generation Approach

KLEEF is a complete overhaul of the KLEE [11,4] symbolic execution engine. We first describe how KLEE works, then we describe our enhancements over it.

1.1 Symbolic Execution in KLEE

As a *symbolic interpreter* [1], KLEE runs a program on a *symbolic memory*, which maps program locations to symbolic values, representing sets of concrete values. When it meets a branching instruction, it adds target instructions to a queue and after each executed instruction it decides which instruction execute next. Symbolic interpreter collects all conditions from branching instructions in a *path constraint*. It is a formula, which may be either unsatisfiable (if the path is infeasible) or satisfiable, and have multiple solutions. Each solution gives a concrete test, which would visit the corresponding path. A symbolic interpreter usually relies on an *SMT solver* (like Z3 [8]) to get solutions of path constraints.

The KLEE engine is split into two logical parts. The first part is a symbolic interpreter, which takes a symbolic state, executes one instruction, and produces new states. The second part is a *searcher*, which chooses the next symbolic state to execute according to a strategy, specified by input options, e.g., BFS or DFS.

---

*Y. Kostyukov—Jury member.

© The Author(s) 2024
D. Beyer and A. Cavalcanti (Eds.): FASE 2024, LNCS 14573, pp. 314–319, 2024.
https://doi.org/10.1007/978-3-031-57259-3_18

1.2   Our Enhancements over KLEE

We enhanced KLEE with *support for arbitrary data structures* such as trees and linked lists by implementing **lazy initialization** [7]. If KLEE dereferences a symbolic pointer, it forks the symbolic state into many: each one assumes that the pointer refers to one of the existing locations in the memory. In KLEEF we also fork one extra state, where the pointer refers to a fresh, lazy initialized symbolic object, which is distinct from all other object of the current symbolic memory. If there are not enough objects in the memory, KLEEF will create a new one and continue execution while KLEE will not. In the configuration used at the competition we only create lazy initialized symbolic objects for symbolic pointers without forking the state into existing locations beforehand.

We improve KLEE with **symcretes** [10], which help to support dynamically allocated arrays (with symbolic sizes) and external calls. KLEEF thus *supports detecting buffer overflows*. A symcrete is a pair of *sym*bolic value and its con*crete* instance valid in the current context. The concrete part of symcrete values is derived from the model of a path constraint. It stays the same if the solver can find a model for concretized constraints. Having failed, the concretization will be updated by values from the model for the original constraints. When a logical solver receives a query with a symcrete, an equality between the symbolic and concrete parts of the symcrete are added to the query. This helps the solver to solve the query, as a part of the model is already specified in the symcrete. KLEEF thus handles dynamically allocated arrays by making array size and address symcretes. KLEEF uses the solver to minimize possible array size and sparse storage for arrays, so that the entire process does not blow up.

We have implemented **searchers optimized** specifically for maximizing coverage and reaching the error target. That is, KLEEF has *targeted searcher* and *guided searcher* which maximize coverage and error reachability, similar to [3]. The targeted searcher uses the shortest path based algorithm to choose the nearest execution state to the target location. Each execution state carries a set of targets. A guided searcher manages a bunch of targeted searchers with different targets and chooses states from every targeted searcher in interleaved manner.

KLEEF improves over KLEE in **constraint solving** by caching unsatisfiability cores, interning symbolic expressions, tracking constraints during simplification to detect conflicts and using an SMT solver incrementally. In KLEEF we added support for BITWUZLA [9] SMT solver, which performs significantly better on TEST-COMP benchmarks. For example, KLEEF with Z3 achieves 2430 points running for 30 seconds on TEST-COMP 2023 benchmarks, while KLEEF with BITWUZLA achieves 2560 points within the same time limit.

2   Architecture

KLEEF has the same architecture as KLEE [4]. KLEEF is implemented in C/C++ and relies on the LLVM infrastructure. KLEEF supports STP [5], Z3 [8] and BITWUZLA [9] SMT solvers for checking constraint satisfiability.

3 Strengths and Weaknesses of the Approach

KLEEF took 3rd place in TEST-COMP 2024 (Overall) [2], which is impressive as it is a pure symbolic execution engine. That is, it could get even better results if paired with fuzzing or other techniques.

The main reasons for our **advancement in coverage** category are as follows. First, it is a smart searcher which guides the symbolic execution towards uncovered branches. Second, it is fast constraint solving, incorporating a number of caching techniques and solver incrementality. Third, the engine handles allocations with a symbolic size without concretization by using symcrete values.

The main reasons for our **advancement in error reaching** category include a smart searcher guiding the execution towards an error and elimination of syntactically unreachable paths in CFG.

Note that KLEEF took less points than KLEE in error reaching category. KLEEF has more solved benchmarks, yet this number is normalized across subcategories. As KLEEF solves less benchmarks on SoftwareSystems-BusyBox-MemSafety and SoftwareSystems-OpenBSD-MemSafety subcategories than KLEE, we got less points in the error reaching category in total. Poor performance on these two subcategories is due to bugs in KLEEF: it generated a few tests which were not reproduced by the validation system.

4 Tool Setup and Configuration

4.1 How to Use KLEEF

In order to **run the competition version** from the command line, one should get the archive with binaries from Zenodo[1] and follow the `README` inside.

In order to **generate a test coverage** for a project **without configuring** KLEEF manually, one should use a user-friendly wrapper UNITTESTBOT C/C++ [6,12]. It allows KLEEF to be run in VS Code and JetBrains CLion.

In order to **build KLEEF from sources**, one should install LLVM, clone KLEEF from GitHub[2] and run `build.sh` script in the repository root.

4.2 Competition Configuration

KLEEF participates in both Cover-Error and Cover-Branches categories.

Common Parameters. Parameters `--strip-unwanted-calls`, `--delete-dead-loops=false`, `--mock-all-externals` are used to (de)activate necessary LLVM passes to simplify bitcode for a symbolic execution. A parameter `--external-calls=all` allows function calls with symbolic arguments. An option `--libc=klee` makes KLEEF support an extended number of external functions.

Parameters `--cex-cache-validity-cores`, `--use-forked-solver=false`, `--solver-backend=bitwuzla-tree`, `--max-solvers-approx-tree-inc=16` are used to cache unsatisfiability cores and call a BITWUZLA solver incrementally.

---

[1] https://doi.org/10.5281/zenodo.10202734
[2] https://github.com/UnitTestBot/klee

Parameters `--symbolic-allocation-threshold=8192`, `--skip-not-lazy-initialized`, `--use-sym-size-alloc` are used to tune lazy initialization and dynamically allocated arrays.

A parameter `--fp-runtime` adds a floating point support. Parameters starting with `--allocate-determ` activate X86 support. An option `--x86FP-as-x87FP80` adds emulation of X86 floating points as extended 80 bit floating points.

Finally, `--max-memory` and `--max-time` fix memory and time limit.

Parameters for Cover-Error. An option `--optimize=true` simplifies code before execution, e.g., it joins some branches to multiple blocks into selection instructions. Options `--search=dfs --search=bfs` make KLEEF interleave between DFS and BFS. Options `--function-call-reproduce=reach_error`, `--exit-on-error-type=Assert` make KLEEF run towards `reach_error` function and fail only there. An option `--dump-states-on-halt=unreached` permits KLEEF to generate tests for unfinished paths.

Parameters for Cover-Branches. A parameter `--track-coverage=all` makes KLEEF track coverage by both branches and instructions. Options `--optimize=false` and `--optimize-aggressive=false` disable optimizations which decrease coverage. Options `--use-iterative-deepening-search=max-cycles`, `--max-cycles-before-stuck=15` activate an iterative-deepening mode of execution on a number of executed loop cycles. A parameter `--max-solver-time=10s` fixes a time limit for an SMT solver. An option `--only-output-states-covering-new` makes KLEEF only generate tests which increase coverage. Options `--search=dfs`, `--search=random-state` make KLEEF interleave between DFS and taking a random state. A parameter `--dump-states-on-halt=all` makes KLEEF generate tests for the symbolic states remaining in the end. Options `--cover-on-the-fly`, `--delay-cover-on-the-fly`, `--mem-trigger-cof` start on the fly test generation after approaching memory cap.

5   Software Project and Contributors

More information about KLEEF is available on its website[3]. KLEEF is an open-source piece of software which you could contribute to at GitHub[4].

The key developers are the authors of this paper affiliated with RnD Toolchain Labs, Huawei, Shenzhen, China. The authors have decent experience in the implementation of research and industrial symbolic execution engines.

6   Data-Availability Statement

A binary version of KLEEF participating in the competition is publicly available[5]. Also, its source code is available on GitHub[6].

---

[3] https://toolchain-labs.com/projects/kleef.html
[4] https://github.com/UnitTestBot/klee
[5] https://doi.org/10.5281/zenodo.10202734
[6] https://github.com/UnitTestBot/klee/releases/tag/testcomp24

References

1. Baldoni, R., Coppa, E., D'Elia, D.C., Demetrescu, C., Finocchi, I.: A Survey of Symbolic Execution Techniques. ACM Comput. Surv. **51**(3) (2018)
2. Beyer, D.: Automatic testing of C programs: Test-Comp 2024. Springer (2024)
3. Burnim, J., Sen, K.: Heuristics for Scalable Dynamic Test Generation. In: 2008 23rd IEEE/ACM International Conference on Automated Software Engineering. pp. 443–446 (2008). https://doi.org/10.1109/ASE.2008.69
4. Cadar, C., Dunbar, D., Engler, D.R.: KLEE: Unassisted and Automatic Generation of High-Coverage Tests for Complex Systems Programs. In: Draves, R., van Renesse, R. (eds.) 8th USENIX Symposium on Operating Systems Design and Implementation, OSDI 2008, December 8-10, 2008, San Diego, California, USA, Proceedings. pp. 209–224. USENIX Association (2008), http://www.usenix.org/events/osdi08/tech/full_papers/cadar/cadar.pdf
5. Ganesh, V., Dill, D.L.: A Decision Procedure for Bit-Vectors and Arrays. In: Damm, W., Hermanns, H. (eds.) Computer Aided Verification. pp. 519–531. Springer Berlin Heidelberg, Berlin, Heidelberg (2007)
6. Ivanov, D., Babushkin, A., Grigoryev, S., Iatchenii, P., Kalugin, V., Kichin, E., Kulikov, E., Misonizhnik, A., Mordvinov, D., Morozov, S., Naumenko, O., Pleshakov, A., Ponomarev, P., Shmidt, S., Utkin, A., Volodin, V., Volynets, A.: UnitTestBot: Automated Unit Test Generation for C Code in Integrated Development Environments. In: 2023 IEEE/ACM 45th International Conference on Software Engineering: Companion Proceedings (ICSE-Companion). pp. 380–384 (2023). https://doi.org/10.1109/ICSE-Companion58688.2023.00107
7. Khurshid, S., Păsăreanu, C.S., Visser, W.: Generalized Symbolic Execution for Model Checking and Testing. In: Garavel, H., Hatcliff, J. (eds.) Tools and Algorithms for the Construction and Analysis of Systems. pp. 553–568. Springer Berlin Heidelberg, Berlin, Heidelberg (2003)
8. de Moura, L., Bjørner, N.: Z3: An Efficient SMT Solver. In: Ramakrishnan, C.R., Rehof, J. (eds.) Tools and Algorithms for the Construction and Analysis of Systems. pp. 337–340. Springer Berlin Heidelberg, Berlin, Heidelberg (2008)
9. Niemetz, A., Preiner, M.: Bitwuzla. In: Enea, C., Lal, A. (eds.) Computer Aided Verification - 35th International Conference, CAV 2023, Paris, France, July 17-22, 2023, Proceedings, Part II. Lecture Notes in Computer Science, vol. 13965, pp. 3–17. Springer (2023). https://doi.org/10.1007/978-3-031-37703-7_1, https://doi.org/10.1007/978-3-031-37703-7_1
10. Pandey, A., Kotcharlakota, P.R.G., Roy, S.: Deferred Concretization in Symbolic Execution via Fuzzing. In: Proceedings of the 28th ACM SIGSOFT International Symposium on Software Testing and Analysis. p. 228–238. ISSTA 2019, Association for Computing Machinery, New York, NY, USA (2019). https://doi.org/10.1145/3293882.3330554, https://doi.org/10.1145/3293882.3330554
11. The KLEE Team: KLEE Symbolic Execution Engine (2009), http://klee.github.io/
12. The UnitTestBot C/C++ Team: UnitTestBot C/C++ (2021), https://www.utbot.org/cpp

TracerX: Pruning Dynamic Symbolic Execution with Deletion and Weakest Precondition Interpolation (Competition Contribution)

Arpita Dutta[1] , Rasool Maghareh[2] , Joxan Jaffar[3][(✉)] ,
Sangharatna Godboley[4] , and Xiao Liang Yu[5]

National University of Singapore, Singapore, Singapore[1,3,5]
Huawei Canada Research Centre, Toronto, Canada[2],
[3] National Institute of Technology Warangal, Hanamkonda, India
{arpita,joxan,xiaoly}@comp.nus.edu.sg[1,3,5]
rasool.maghareh@huawei.com[2] , sanghu@nitw.ac.in[4]

Abstract. Dynamic Symbolic Execution (DSE) is an important method for the testing of programs. The major advantage of DSE is its path-by-path exploration of the program execution space. However, this often leads to the path explosion problem. To address this issue, a method of abstraction learning has been used. The key step here is the computation of an interpolant to represent the learned abstraction. In Test-Comp 2024, we use two different approaches of interpolant generation viz., Deletion Interpolation and Weakest Precondition Interpolation. The former is our more stable and mature system and briefly discussed in [8]. In this paper, we present the latter approach which is the heart of TracerX. In general, the Weakest Precondition (WP) is the ideal (most general) interpolant. However, WP is intractable to compute and is exponentially disjunctive. A major challenge is to obtain a conjunctive approximation of the WP. Therefore, we generate an approximation of the WP.

Keywords: Dynamic Symbolic Execution, Interpolation, Weakest Precondition

1 Test-Generation Approach

DSE is an important method for program testing. The main challenge in symbolic execution (SE) is path explosion. The method of *abstraction learning* [10] has been used to address this by generating the interpolants to represent the learned abstraction. The core feature in abstraction learning is the subsumption of paths whose traversals are deemed to no longer be necessary due to similarity with already-traversed paths. Despite the overhead of computing interpolants, the *pruning* of the symbolic execution tree (SET) that interpolants provide often brings significant overall benefits. An *interpolant* of a program point (state) is an *abstraction* of it which ensures the safety of the subtree rooted at that state. Thus, upon encountering another state of the same program point, if the context

---

⋆J. Jaffar—Jury Member Test-Comp 2024.

D. Beyer and A. Cavalcanti (Eds.): FASE 2024, LNCS 14573, pp. 320–325, 2024.
https://doi.org/10.1007/978-3-031-57259-3_19

of the state implies the interpolant formula, then continuing the execution from the new state will not lead to any error. Consequently, we can prune the subtree rooted in the new state [6,7].

The heart of TracerX is the use of interpolation to address the path explosion problem in DSE. The use of interpolation to address the path explosion problem in DSE was first implemented in the TRACER system [9]. While TRACER was able to perform bounded verification and testing on many examples, it could not accommodate industrial programs which often dynamically manipulate heap memory. TracerX combines the state-of-the-art DSE technology used in KLEE [5] with the pruning technology in TRACER to address this issue. We presented the software architecture of TracerX in [8]. The default interpolation algorithm used by TracerX is the Deletion Interpolation and it was first developed under TRACER [9].

Since the last Test-Comp, we have designed another interpolation algorithm i.e., *Weakest precondition (WP)* interpolation. The Deletion algorithm generates interpolant as a subset of the incoming context (which is the strongest postcondition on the path to the assume condition), while the WP algorithm generates interpolants from the weakest precondition of a path in the program. Hence, the WP interpolation algorithm provides a more general interpolant which can have a higher chance of subsuming more subtrees in SET.

The ideal (most general) interpolant is the WP of the target, which is the condition that must be satisfied in order to get the target satisfied. For example, consider the following piece of code:

```
assume (not (b1 ∧ ¬ b2 ∧¬ b3))
if (b1) x += 3 else x += 2
if (b2) x += 5 else x += 7
if (b3) x += 9 else x += 14
{x <= 24}
```

The WP before the first if-statement is:

$$b1 \longrightarrow (\neg b2 \wedge b3 \wedge x \leq 7) \vee (b2 \wedge x \leq 4)$$

$$\neg b1 \longrightarrow x < 3$$

Here, WP is expressed as a disjunction of two conditions. This means that either of the two conditions can be satisfied for the target to be reached.

Unfortunately, WP is intractable to compute, which means it is difficult or impossible to find an exact solution for it. One way to approximate WP is to use a conjunctive approximation, which involves expressing the WP as a conjunction of simpler conditions. This can help to make the WP more tractable, but it may also introduce some imprecision to the quality of interpolants (by under approximation). However, this will not effect the soundness of the tool.

1.1 TracerX-WP: Approximation of Weakest Precondition

TracerX-WP implements the algorithm which approximates the ideal WP by defining two components: *path interpolants* and *tree interpolants*. In this section, we briefly explain how these two components are computed and used to generate an approximation of the weakest precondition.

A path interpolant is a formula that represents the WP of a path. It starts from the end of the path (target formula) and works backward to the beginning of the path, using the rules of logic to compute a formula that if satisfiable then target formulas will also be satisfiable. We consider a path to be a sequence of *assignments* and *assume* statements executed in a specific order.

An *assignment* instruction assigns a value to a variable. Interpolant of an assignment instruction is a logical formula that describes the effect of the assignment. For example, having the assignment instruction "$x := z + 2$", and a target "$x \leq 15$", the interpolant is described as $WP(inst, target) : x \leq 13$.

For an *assume* instruction (B), consider the incoming context $\{C\}$ as the precondition and $\{\omega\}$ as the target. An interpolant is a formula that represents the logical relationship between the variables in the context $\{C\}$ and the conditions in B. To find the interpolant, we compute the coarse partition (minimum number of partitions) of $\{C\}$ such that $var(C_i) * var(C_j)$ s.t. $i \neq j$ ($*$ is intuitively the "separating conjunction" from separation logic [12]) as shown in Eq.1:

$$\{C_1 * C_2 * C_3 * ... * C_n\} \text{ assume}(B) \{\omega_1 * \omega_2 * \omega_3 * ... * \omega_m\} \quad (1)$$

We partition C_i into three groups. Constraints are replaced using the rules below:

- **Target independent:** The C_i which are separate from B and ω.
  Action: Replace C_i with *true*, i.e. remove C_i.
- **Guard independent:** Consider $C_{gi} \equiv C_i$ s.t. $C_i * B$; and, $\omega_{gi} \equiv \omega_j$ s.t. $B * \omega_j$.
  Action: Replace C_{gi} by ω_{gi}.
- **Remainder of the C_i:** We do not capture exact WP for this group.
  e.g. $\{z == 5\}$ assume$(x > z - 2)$ $\{x > 0\}$ (Here, $z > 2$ is the WP)
  Action: No change to C_i, i.e. keep C_i.

A tree interpolant is a formula that corresponds to all the branches of a subtree within the SET. It is computed as the *conjunction* of the path interpolants between the root of the tree and each leaf node. Tree interpolants can be used to prove the correctness of subtrees in the SET, by showing that a certain property holds for all possible paths or branches in the subtree.

2   Software Architecture

The software architecture of TracerX-WP is presented in Fig. 1. The core feature of TracerX-WP is its interpolation engine which generalizes the context of a node. TracerX-WP works at

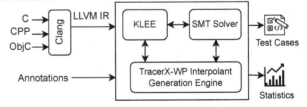

Fig. 1. TracerX-WP Framework

the level of LLVM bitcode, the intermediate language of the widely used LLVM compiler infrastructure [11]. It provides an interpreter that can execute almost arbitrary code represented in LLVM IR, both concretely and symbolically. TracerX-WP has a modular and extensible architecture. It provides a variety of different search heuristics (e.g., Random and DFS) to explore the program state space.

3   Strengths and Weaknesses

In Test-Comp 2024 [4], we participated with two different approaches to prune subtrees viz., Deletion Interpolation and WP Interpolation. We represent the former system as TracerX and the latter as TracerX-WP. TracerX secured a score of 4020 for the 11042 tasks with a CPU time of 694.44 hours and 722.22 hours of wall time. Whereas, TracerX-WP obtained a score of 1480 for 11042 tasks with equal CPU time and wall time of 472.22 hours. The memory used by TracerX and TracerX-WP are 19 TB and 10 TB. The total coverage obtained by TracerX and TracerX-WP are 402000 and 148000 for 11042 tasks respectively.

The major reason for the lower score of TracerX-WP is that the implementation of TracerX-WP is experimental. It crashed due to not supporting some expression types during interpolant computation. Also, in TracerX-WP, test cases with '.ktest' extension are converted into '.xml' format after the symbolic execution engine has finished the exploration while TracerX generates the tests during the exploration. This resulted in the unavailability of test cases for the programs with timeout status in the coverage computation. Moreover, the configuration we used in the 'BenchExec' tool-info for TracerX-WP missed the support for 64-bit architecture. As a result, TracerX-WP was not able to run the tests in some categories like `ReachSafety-Hardware`, and `SoftwareSystems-BusyBox-MemSafety`. The fix for the above mentioned issues is conceptually straight forward but it requires substantial amount of work. Since, we need to modify the data structures used in our system. In subsequent versions, we will come-up more stable system with all fixes and additional features.

In a comparison of TracerX with Symbiotic and Fizzer which won the bronze for the third place in *Cover-Error* and *Cover-Branches* tracks respectively, TracerX has almost equal scores in 13 out of 16 (with at most difference of 3 tasks) and 15 out of 23 categories. TracerX has better results than Fizzer in some categories like `ReachSafety-BitVectors`, `ReachSafety-Hardware`, and `ReachSafety-Combinations`. These observations show the potential of TracerX approach and we hope to get higher scores in the future Test-Comp competitions.

4   Setup and Configuration

The steps to configure and running of TracerX are similar to KLEE [5] with some extra command-line arguments. The argument `-solver-backend=z3` should be provided to run TracerX with Deletion Interpolation. Along with `-wp-interpolant` option is required to invoke WP Interpolation. For detailed information, please see the integrated `--help` option.

5   Software Project and Contributors

Information about TracerX with self-contained binary is publicly available at https://tracer-x.github.io/. Also, the source code can be accessed from GitHub. The authors of this paper and other colleagues have contributed to and developed TracerX at NUS, Singapore. Authors of this paper acknowledge the direct and indirect support of their students, former researchers, and colleagues.

6   Data-Availability Statement

The binary artifact of TracerX with Deletion Interpolation and Weakest Precondition Interpolation used in Test-Comp 2024 are publicly available at Zenodo [2] and [3] respectively. Also, Test-Comp 2024 [1] provides all the necessary scripts, benchmarks, and tool binaries to reproduce the competition's results.

7   Funding Statement

This research project is partially supported by grant MOE-T2EP20220-0012.

References

1. Test-comp 2024, https://test-comp.sosy-lab.org/2024/
2. TracerX with Deletion Interpolation, https://doi.org/10.5281/zenodo.10200610
3. TracerX with WP Interpolation, https://doi.org/10.5281/zenodo.10202605
4. Beyer, D.: Automatic testing of C programs: Test-Comp 2024. Springer (2024)
5. Cadar, C., Dunbar, D., Engler, D.R., et al.: KLEE: unassisted and automatic generation of high-coverage tests for complex systems programs. In: 8th USENIX Symposium on Operating Systems Design and Implementation, OSDI. pp. 209–224 (2008)
6. Godboley, S., Jaffar, J., Maghareh, R., Dutta, A.: Toward optimal MC/DC test case generation. In: Proceedings of the 30th ACM SIGSOFT International Symposium on Software Testing and Analysis. pp. 505–516 (2021)
7. Jaffar, J., Godboley, S., Maghareh, R.: Optimal MC/DC test case generation. In: 2019 IEEE/ACM 41st International Conference on Software Engineering: Companion Proceedings (ICSE-Companion). pp. 288–289. IEEE (2019)
8. Jaffar, J., Maghareh, R., Godboley, S., Ha, X.L.: TracerX: Dynamic symbolic execution with interpolation (competition contribution). In: Fundamental Approaches to Software Engineering (FASE). vol. 12076, p. 530. Springer (2020)
9. Jaffar, J., Murali, V., Navas, J.A., Santosa, A.E.: TRACER: a symbolic execution tool for verification. In: 24th International Conference on Computer Aided Verification (CAV). pp. 758–766. Springer (2012)
10. Jaffar, J., Santosa, A.E., Voicu, R.: An interpolation method for CLP traversal. In: 15th International Conference on Principles and Practice of Constraint Programming (CP). pp. 454–469. Springer (2009)
11. Lattner, C., Adve, V.: LLVM: A compilation framework for lifelong program analysis & transformation. In: International symposium on code generation and optimization, 2004. CGO 2004. pp. 75–86. IEEE (2004)
12. O'Hearn, P., Reynolds, J., Yang, H.: Local reasoning about programs that alter data structures. In: Computer Science Logic: 15th International Workshop, CSL 2001 10th Annual Conference of the EACSL Paris. pp. 1–19. Springer (2001)

ULTIMATE TESTGEN: Test-Case Generation with Automata-based Software Model Checking (Competition Contribution)

Max Barth[1]($\boxtimes$) , Daniel Dietsch[2] , Matthias Heizmann[2] ,
and Marie-Christine Jakobs[1]

[1] LMU Munich, Munich, Germany
[2] University of Freiburg, Freiburg, Germany
Max.Barth@lmu.de

Abstract. We introduce ULTIMATE TESTGEN, a novel tool for automatic test-case generation. Like many other test-case generators, ULTIMATE TESTGEN builds on verification technology, i.e., it checks the (un)reachability of test goals and generates test cases from counterexamples. In contrast to existing tools, it applies trace abstraction, an automata-theoretic approach to software model checking, which is implemented in the successful verifier ULTIMATE AUTOMIZER. To avoid that the same test goal is reached again, ULTIMATE TESTGEN extends the automata-theoretic model checking approach with error automata.

Keywords: ULTIMATE AUTOMIZER· Test-case generation · Software testing · Test Coverage · Software model checking · Automata

1 Test-Generation Approach

Verification technology has been successfully used in the past to automatically generate test cases [12,14,7,1]. Most existing approaches follow a similar principle. Mainly, they perceive reaching an (uncovered) test goal as a property violation and construct test cases from counterexamples [6]. To build a test suite, they repeatedly check the reachability of still uncovered goals and prove their unreachability or generate test cases from counterexamples that testify the reachability of (uncovered) test goals. To improve the performance of the reachability analysis after detecting the reachability of a test goal, many approaches reuse previous information, e.g., continue the reachability analysis but exclude property violations caused by already covered test goals. Also, our new test-case generator ULTIMATE TESTGEN, which is implemented in Java, follows this basic principle.

To analyze the reachability of test goals, ULTIMATE TESTGEN relies on trace abstraction [11], an automata-theoretic approach to software model checking, which performs counterexample-guided abstraction refinement (CEGAR) [9] and

---

* Jury Member: Max Barth

© The Author(s) 2024
D. Beyer and A. Cavalcanti (Eds.): FASE 2024, LNCS 14573, pp. 326–330, 2024.
https://doi.org/10.1007/978-3-031-57259-3_20

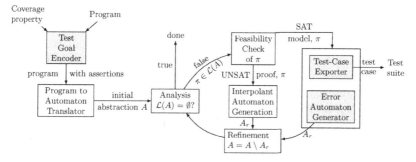

Fig. 1. Overview of the test-case generation approach of Ultimate TestGen

which is implemented in Ultimate Automizer. Figure 1 shows the overview of the test-case generation process performed by Ultimate TestGen. Components highlighted in gray are added to the verification process of Ultimate Automizer and enable test-case generation.

The test-case generation process starts with the encoding of the test goals into the program. To this end, we insert an `assert(false);` statement after each test goal (either a branch or a call to `reach_error()`). Thereafter, we translate the program with the assertions into an automaton A, which becomes the initial abstraction. This initial abstraction represents all possible counterexamples, i.e., the initial automaton accepts a syntactical program path iff it reaches an assert statement (i.e., a violation). Next, we iteratively refine the automaton abstraction until it becomes empty.

If the abstraction still accepts a counterexample path π, we select an arbitrary counterexample path π from the abstraction and check its feasibility. To check the feasibility of π, Ultimate TestGen encodes the path into a formula and checks its satisfiability with an SMT solver. Ultimate TestGen relies on the SMT solvers Z3 [13], CVC4 [3], and MathSAT5 [8]. However, during the check we must ensure that an assert statement introduced to cover an earlier test goal does not prohibit reaching later test goals. Therefore, the feasibility check ignores the assert statements added during test goal encoding.

If the counterexample is spurious, i.e., the formula is unsatisfiable, we use the proof of unsatisfiability to generate an interpolant automaton A_r [10]. The interpolant automaton accepts the counterexample path π and other (counterexample) paths that are infeasible due to a similar reason. We use the interpolant automaton to refine the abstraction and, thus, exclude infeasible paths, which are accepted by the interpolant automaton, from the counterexample search.

If the counterexample is feasible, i.e., the formula is satisfiable, we generate a test case from a model of the formula [6]. To this end, we identify the calls to the `__VERIFIER_nondet` calls and retrieve their values from the model. Then, we export the identified values into a test case in the exchange format[3] used by

---

[3] https://gitlab.com/sosy-lab/test-comp/test-format/blob/testcomp23/doc/Format.md

Test-Comp [5]. The values are exported in the same order as their corresponding calls occur in the counterexample path π. In addition, we generate an error automaton that accepts all counterexample paths that end in the same test goal as the current counterexample π. We use the error automaton to refine the abstraction and exclude paths from the counterexample search that reach test goals that are already covered.

The last step is the refinement of the abstraction A. This step excludes the paths determined irrelevant because they are known to be infeasible or may not reach uncovered test goals. To this end, we substract the interpolant automaton and error automaton, respectively from the existing abstraction. Hence, each step ensures that the abstraction considered in the next step considers fewer counterexample paths and, thus, guarantees progress of the test-case generation.

2   Discussion of Strengths and Weaknesses

For a comparison of ULTIMATE TESTGEN with the other participants of Test-Comp 2024, we refer to the competition report [5].

ULTIMATE TESTGEN checks the reachability of every test goal and generates a test case for every goal that it proved reachable. Due to this goal-oriented procedure, it creates relatively small test suites. In addition, if ULTIMATE TESTGEN completes the test-case generation process (i.e., result done), we can confidently determine that any test goal not addressed by a test case is indeed unreachable.

Nevertheless, proving the reachability of certain test goals can be hard and requires expensive SMT solver calls. When studying the results for the category `cover-error`, we observe that ULTIMATE TESTGEN runs out of resources (time or memory) for many software systems tasks as well as tasks in the categories `XCSP`, `Sequentialized`, `ProductLines`, `ECA`. In addition to the resource issue, we observe that sometimes our tests are not confirmed by the validator, which seems to be a bug of the translation of the counterexamples into the test cases. Still, there also exist categories like `loops`, `heap`, `arrays`, and `fuzzle` in which ULTIMATE TESTGEN performs rather well.

Looking at the `cover-branches` category, we observe that for many software systems tasks as well as for certain float tasks, we already fail to construct the automaton from the program because required C features are yet not supported by the program to automaton translation. In these cases, the test-case generation procedure does not even start. In addition, ULTIMATE TESTGEN has problems in detecting the feasibility of error traces for Linux device driver tasks because large string literals are not precisely encoded. For other task categories like `AWS`, `Sequentialized`, `ProductLines`, `Hardware`, `Fuzzle`, `ECA`, and `Combinations`, we observe that reaching the test goals is expensive and ULTIMATE TESTGEN runs out of resources (time, memory) before covering a significant amount of test goals. While we have seen the resource issue for the `cover-error` category, too, the `Hardness` tasks reveal another issue with our test-case exporter, which makes ULTIMATE TESTGEN crash. The reason for the crash is that our test-case exporter failed to translate values from the SMT-LIB [2] FloatingPoint format back to certain C types such as ulong. Note that the C types float and double were not an issue. Still, there exist task categories like e.g., `loops`, `control-flow`, `bitvectors`, or `XCSP` for which ULTIMATE TESTGEN performs well and achieves high coverage values.

3 Setup and Configuration

ULTIMATE TESTGEN is part of the Ultimate framework[4], which is licensed under LGPLv3. To execute ULTIMATE TESTGEN in the version submitted to Test-Comp 2024 [4], one requires Java 11 and Python 3.6 and must invoke the following command.

```
./Ultimate.py -spec <p> -file <f> -architecture <a> -full-output
```

where `<p>` is a Test-Comp property file, `<f>` is an input C file, and `<a>` is the architecture (`32bit` or `64bit`). During execution of the command, the generated tests are saved as `.xml` files in the exchange format for test cases required by Test-Comp [5]. In Test-Comp 2024, we use the above command to participate with ULTIMATE TESTGEN in both Test-Comp categories: `cover-error` (i.e., bug finding by covering the call to `reach_error`) and `cover-branches` (i.e., code coverage).

Data Availability The Test-Comp 2024 version of ULTIMATE TESTGEN is available online on Zenodo [4] and on GitHub[5]. Its corresponding benchmark definition file is available on GitLab[6].

References

1. Aldughaim, M., Alshmrany, K.M., Gadelha, M.R., de Freitas, R., Cordeiro, L.C.: FuSeBMC_IA: Interval analysis and methods for test-case generation (competition contribution). In: Proc. FASE. pp. 324–329. LNCS 13991, Springer (2023). https://doi.org/10.1007/978-3-031-30826-0_18
2. Barrett, C., Fontaine, P., Tinelli, C.: The Satisfiability Modulo Theories Library (SMT-LIB). www.SMT-LIB.org (2016)
3. Barrett, C.W., Conway, C.L., Deters, M., Hadarean, L., Jovanovic, D., King, T., Reynolds, A., Tinelli, C.: CVC4. In: Proc. CAV. pp. 171–177. LNCS 6806, Springer (2011). https://doi.org/10.1007/978-3-642-22110-1_14
4. Barth, M., Dietsch, D., Heizmann, M., Jakobs, M.C.: Ultimate TestGen. Zenodo (2023), https://doi.org/10.5281/zenodo.10071568
5. Beyer, D.: Automatic testing of C programs: Test-Comp 2024. Springer (2024)

---

[4] https://ultimate.informatik.uni-freiburg.de and github.com/ultimate-pa/ultimate
[5] https://github.com/ultimate-pa/ultimate/tree/ea2a3342b0e9ae9c8710d9bc5a32ec c16b7297dd
[6] https://gitlab.com/sosy-lab/test-comp/bench-defs/-/blob/main/benchmark-defs/ utestgen.xml

6. Beyer, D., Chlipala, A., Henzinger, T.A., Jhala, R., Majumdar, R.: Generating tests from counterexamples. In: Proc. ICSE. pp. 326–335. IEEE (2004). https://doi.org/10.1109/ICSE.2004.1317455

7. Chalupa, M., Novák, J., Strejček, J.: SYMBIOTIC 8: Parallel and targeted test generation (competition contribution). In: Proc. FASE. pp. 368–372. LNCS 12649, Springer (2021). https://doi.org/10.1007/978-3-030-71500-7_20

8. Cimatti, A., Griggio, A., Schaafsma, B.J., Sebastiani, R.: The MathSAT5 SMT solver. In: Proc. TACAS. pp. 93–107. LNCS 7795, Springer (2013). https://doi.org/10.1007/978-3-642-36742-7_7

9. Clarke, E.M., Grumberg, O., Jha, S., Lu, Y., Veith, H.: Counterexample-guided abstraction refinement. In: Proc. CAV. pp. 154–169. LNCS 1855, Springer (2000). https://doi.org/10.1007/10722167_15

10. Heizmann, M., Hoenicke, J., Podelski, A.: Refinement of trace abstraction. In: Proc. SAS. pp. 69–85. LNCS 5673, Springer (2009). https://doi.org/10.1007/978-3-642-03237-0_7

11. Heizmann, M., Hoenicke, J., Podelski, A.: Software model checking for people who love automata. In: Proc. CAV. pp. 36–52. LNCS 8044, Springer (2013). https://doi.org/10.1007/978-3-642-39799-8_2

12. Jakobs, M.C.: COVERITEST with dynamic partitioning of the iteration time limit (competition contribution). In: Proc. FASE. pp. 540–544. LNCS 12076, Springer (2020). https://doi.org/10.1007/978-3-030-45234-6_30

13. de Moura, L.M., Bjørner, N.S.: Z3: An efficient SMT solver. In: Proc. TACAS. pp. 337–340. LNCS 4963, Springer (2008). https://doi.org/10.1007/978-3-540-78800-3_24

14. Ruland, S., Lochau, M., Jakobs, M.C.: HYBRIDTIGER: Hybrid model checking and domination-based partitioning for efficient multi-goal test-suite generation (competition contribution). In: Proc. FASE. pp. 520–524. LNCS 12076, Springer (2020). https://doi.org/10.1007/978-3-030-45234-6_26

Author Index

Printed in the United States
by Baker & Taylor Publisher Services